The
Cyborg
Handbook

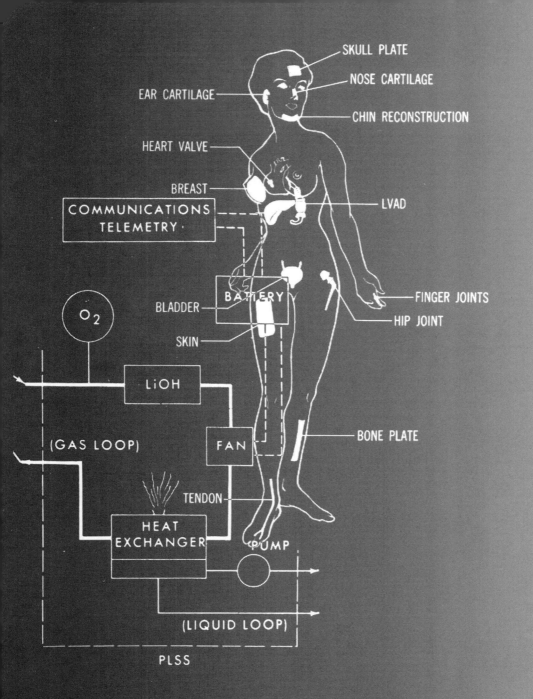

SKULL PLATE

NOSE CARTILAGE

EAR CARTILAGE

CHIN RECONSTRUCTION

HEART VALVE

BREAST

LVAD

COMMUNICATIONS
TELEMETRY·

O₂

BLADDER

BATTERY

FINGER JOINTS

HIP JOINT

SKIN

LiOH

(GAS LOOP)

FAN

BONE PLATE

TENDON

HEAT
EXCHANGER

PUMP

(LIQUID LOOP)

PLSS

The

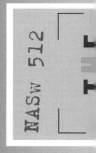

g Cybor

CYBORG
HANDBOOK

Handbook

Edited by **Chris Hables Gray**

**With the Assistance
of Heidi J. Figueroa-Sarriera
& Steven Mentor**

Routledge / New York & London

Published in 1995 by

Routledge
29 West 35th Street
New York, NY 10001

Published in Great Britain by

Routledge
11 New Fetter Lane
London EC4P 4EE

Library of Congress Cataloging-in-Publication Data

The Cyborg Handbook / edited by Chris Hables Gray with Steven
Mentor and Heidi J. Figueroa-Sarriera.
     p.   cm.
     Includes bibliographical references.
     ISBN 0-415-90848-5: ISBN 0-415-90849-3 (pbk.)
     1. Cybernetics.   I. Gray, Chris Hables.   II. Mentor, Steven.
III. Figueroa-Sarriera, Heidi J.
Q360.C93   1995
003'.5—dc20

British Library Cataloguing-in-Publication Data also available

Book and cover design, type, and imaging by Alan Hill

Set in Agfa Rotis Sans Serif; heads in Tardy, Beowolf, and
Keedy Sans

Table of Contents

The Proliferation of Cyborgs

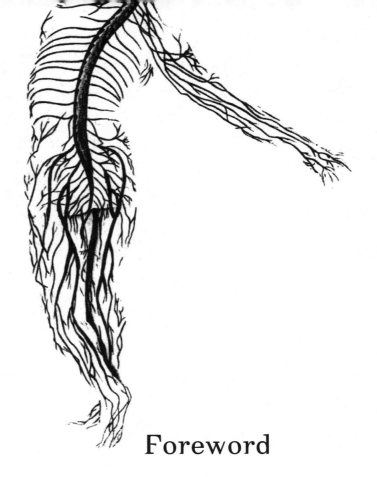

Foreword

Cyborgs and Symbionts

Living Together in the New World Order

Donna J. Haraway

Gaia—the blue- and green-hued, whole, living, self-sustaining, adaptive, auto-poietic earth—and the Terminators—the jelled-metal, shape-shifting, cyber-enhanced warriors fighting in the stripped terrain landscapes and extraterrestrial vacuums of a terrible future—seem at first glance to belong in incompatible universes. Such beings seem to inhabit incommensurable regions of space-time, and to demand different literary and historical chronotopes for their description and narration. These entities do not seem able to share the same evolutionary story. Similarly, the world's first being to be called "cyborg"—a white laboratory rat at New York's Rockland State Hospital in the late 1950s, with a tiny osmotic pump implanted in its body to inject chemicals at a controlled rate to alter its physiological parameters—does not seem to be close kin to the naturally occurring microorganism *Mixotricha paradoxa*—a protist denizen of the hindgut of a South Australian termite. The implanted

rat and the metal-flesh warrior seem to be paradigmatic cyborgs, the perfect postmodern poster-children for the New World Order's ad campaigns. Surely, the whole earth and its natural offspring have a different ontology. But all four of these entities—the cloud-wrapped whole earth named after the Greek goddess who gave birth (incestuously) to the Titans, the machine-enhanced warriors with a cinematic future, the rat cyborg in a psychiatric hospital, and the microorganism with the intriguing Latin name—are members of the same post-World War II clan. This clan is also the human family in a globalized New World Order. That order has emerged from the fusion reactions of the cold war and the space race and from the turbulent planetary flows of capital in the last half-century of the Second Christian Millennium. The practices which bind the global family together in a generative matrix are no mere metaphoric flights of fancy; these practices are the **simultaneously fiercely material and irreducibly imaginary, world-destroying and world-building processes of technoscience.**

Products of promiscuous mixings and fusings, Earth Goddess, Terminator, Enhanced Rat and Termite Guest all demand that we think about three basic questions: What are the terms for living together in the New World Order? Who will find which terms to be livable? and What is to be done? Let us sneak up on these tendentious questions by examining more closely each of the four beings populating my cyborg pretext. This narrative is in the tradition of edifying natural history, or better, natural-technical history; and it prefaces the rich handbook that follows. My imploded story **insists on the inextricable weave of the organic, technical, textual, mythic, economic, and political threads that make up the flesh of the world.**

Gaia is the name that James Lovelock gave in 1969 to his hypothesis that the third planet from the sun, our home, is a "complex entity involving the Earth's biosphere, atmosphere, oceans, and soil; the totality constituting a feedback or cybernetic system which seeks an optimal physical and chemical environment for life on this planet" (Lovelock 1979:11). An independent English specialist in gas chromatography and the inventor of the electron capture detector, in the 1960s Lovelock was working as a consultant for the United States National Aeronautics and Space Administration's (NASA) Voyager program at the Jet Propulsion Laboratory at the California Institute of Technology to devise a means to detect whether there was life on Mars. Fundamental problems for the project turned on defining what constituted life and thinking about how to detect it on Mars gave a fresh perspective on how to think about life on earth. Working with Dian Hitchcock, who was evaluating the logic and information potential of various suggestions for detecting Martian life, Lovelock developed the notion of perceiving life through atmospheric analysis, by looking for persistent entropy-defying disequilibria.

But in 1965 the U.S. Congress abandoned the Martian exploration program, although the venture was later resumed in the Viking expeditions. In the low period for space exploration during the mid-1960s, Lovelock benefited from the free research atmosphere provided by the giant petroleum corporation Shell to study air pollution resulting from burning fossil fuels. The determinations of multinational capital rarely take the shape of restricting the intellectual freedom of the scientific elite. Quite the opposite; no one understands better how critical that kind of free

play is to dynamic accumulation strategies. Lovelock approached the pollution problem from the point of view of the atmosphere as an adaptive mechanism that was an extension of the biosphere. Perturbations had to be studied as part of a self-regulating system, in which compensatory changes in response to toxins could very well produce new dynamic steady states that would change the species composition of earth drastically. Global atmospheric research is at the origin of struggles over livable environments in cyborg worlds.

Going from measurements of gases in the earth's atmosphere, Lovelock reasoned that the observed composition could not be maintained by chemical processes alone. The earth's atmosphere showed a stunning disequilibrium that suggested not only that it was the product of the life-processes of organisms; but more, a disequilibrium of such scale implied that the atmosphere was an extension of a living system designed to maintain an optimal environment for its own support. In short, the whole earth was a dynamic, self-regulating, homeostatic system; the earth, with all its interwoven layers and articulated parts, from the planet's pulsating skin through its fulminating gaseous envelopes, was itself alive. Lovelock's perception was that of a systems engineer gestated in the space program and the multinational energy industry and fed on the heady brew of cybernetics in the 1950s and 1960s, not, say, the intuition of a vegetarian feminist mystic suspicious of the cold war's military-industrial complex and its patriarchal technology. Lovelock's earth—itself a cyborg, a complex auto-poietic system that terminally blurred the boundaries among the geological, the organic, and the technological—was the natural habitat, and the launching pad, of other cyborgs.

And just as the pod people in the classic 1956 film *The Invasion of the Body Snatchers* looked exactly like humans not yet transformed by infectious extrater-

restrial cosmic seeds—vectors of a different life, of species-transforming information—one could not tell by looking that the earth and its inhabitants had become
cyborgs. The transformation implicit in Lovelock's prescient perspective was in the
fleshy tissues of meaning. The whole earth, a cybernetic organism, a cyborg, was
not some freakish contraption of welded flesh and metal, worthy of a bad television program with a short run. As Lovelock realized, the cybernetic Gaia is, rather,
what the earth looks like from the only vantage point from which she could be
seen—from the outside, from above. Gaia is not a figure of the whole earth's
self-knowledge, but of her discovery, indeed, her literal constitution, in a great
travel epic. The signals emanating from an extraterrestrial perspective, such as the
photographic eye of a space ship, are relayed and translated through the information-processing machines built by the members of a voraciously energy-consum-
ing, space-faring hominid culture that called itself Mankind. And Man is, by
self-definition, a globalizing and, therefore, global species. The people who built the
semiotic and physical technology to see Gaia *became* the global species, in which
they recognized themselves, through the concrete practices by which they built
their knowledge. This species depends on an evolutionary narrative technology that
builds dramatically from the first embryonic tool-weapon wielded by the primal
hunter to the transformation of himself into the potent tool-weapon that seeds
other worlds. To see Gaia, Man learns to position himself *physically* as an extraterrestrial observer looking back on his earthly womb and matrix. The cyborg point of
view is literal, material, and technical; it is built, located, and specific—like all
meaning-making apparatuses. Whatever else it is, the cyborg point
of view is always about communication, infection, gender,
genre, species, intercourse, information, and semiology.

The material fictions of Man, his lived primal story, are the imaginative technologies of NASA. On November 9, 1967, Apollo 4 sent back to earth from 9,850 nauti-
cal miles above its surface the first U.S. picture of the whole earth. That family
snapshot—grandmother to the Swedish photographer Leonard Nilsson's 1977
famous, gorgeous, global, gold-gleaming, extraterrestrial, aborted human fetuses
published in *A Child Is Born*—has been disseminated on everything from protesters'
T-shirts at the Nevada nuclear test site, to the cover of the *Whole Earth Catalog*, to
the packaging for the Maxis Corporation's best-selling computer game based on
the Gaia hypothesis, SimEarth. NASA's whole-earth image is like a picture on
a seed catalogue. Seed of the future, concentrating all the potencies of
an infinite series of past acts of generation, the shining,
cloud-wrapped whole earth is like a giant and luscious tomato,
planted around the world with the aid of the marketing apparatus of the petroleum-industry-owned major seed companies
and promising all the lusty tastes of a sun-drenched summer.

Like Gaia, the Terminator is a cyborg. But the clan of enhanced
warriors narrows down the contradictory, weedy, contestable,
wide-band, semiological plenum of Gaia to a laser-focused
line of embodied meanings. Like Gaia, the proliferation in fantasy and in reality of a grotesque menagerie of cyborg
weapons has also occurred in the multi-lobed wombs of bump-
tious multinational capital, ascendant technoscience, and constitutively militarized post—World War II nation states. But the

Terminator is a child-weapon that Man-the-Hunter perhaps did not really anticipate as he struck out on his grand-quest narrative through the fossil volcanic ash
and cosmic moon dust of post—World War II U.S. origin and exploration stories. The
Terminator is much more than the morphed body of a virile film star in the 1990s:
**the Terminator is the sign of the beast on the face of post-
modern culture, the sign of the Sacred Image of the Same.**
The figure of the Terminator appears to take many forms.[1] The Terminator is the
self-sufficient, self-generated Tool in all of its infinite but self-identical variations.
It can be the transfused blood fraternity of information machine and human warrior in the cyber-enhanced airforce cockpit, those pilot projects for the equally—or
maybe more—profitable commercial cyborg theme parks and virtual reality arcades
to follow in the great technology transfer game from military practices to the civilian economy that has characterized cyborg worlds. Or the enhanced weapons can
be the all-information-machine versions called smart bombs, which make such riv-

eting television programming in the New World Order's police
actions. The Terminator, like the decontextualized glowing
fetus, can appear to be our savior; indeed that is its favorite
and most alluring morph. Like Gaia, the mercurial Terminator is
also an image on the seed package of a possible future. We
seem still to be hungry for its enhanced and gleaming fruits.

It is time to move from the all-too-real, ideal cyborg warrior to
the lowly, and decidedly mortal, figure of a laboratory white
rat implanted with a cyber-control device. Like all cyborgs, this
white rat has that something extra, that sign of excess that marks the creature as
somehow "trans" to what once counted as normal and natural. Appropriate to a
world that contains Gaia and the Terminator, the term "cyborg" was coined by
Manfred E. Clynes and Nathan S. Kline (1960) to refer to the enhanced man who
could survive in extra-terrestrial environments.[2] They imagined the cyborgian
man-machine hybrid would be needed in the next great technohumanist
challenge—space flight. Most Western narratives of humanism and technology
require each other constitutively: how else could man make himself? Du Pont had
the right idea: "Better things for better living." A designer of physiological instrumentation and electronic data-processing systems, Clynes was the chief research
scientist in the Dynamic Simulation Laboratory at Rockland State Hospital in New
York. Director of research at Rockland State, Kline was a clinical psychiatrist. Their
article was based on a paper the authors gave at the Psychophysiological Aspects
of Space Flight Symposium sponsored by the U.S. Air Force School of Aviation
Medicine in San Antonio, Texas. Enraptured with cybernetics, they thought of
cyborgs as "self-regulating man-machine systems" (Clynes and Kline 1960:27).
Space-bound cyborgs were like miniaturized, self-contained Gaias. One of Clynes
and Kline's first cyborgs, a kind of pilot project for Gaia-Man, was our standard
white laboratory rat implanted with an osmotic pump designed to inject chemicals
continuously to modify and regulate homeostatic states. The rodent's picture was
featured in the article that named its ontological cyborg condition. The snapshot
belongs in Man's family album.

Beginning with the rats who stowed away on the masted ships of Europe's imperial
age of exploration, rodents have gone first into the unexplored regions in the great
travel narratives of Western technoscience. Odo, the shape-shifter security chief on

the Federation space station *Deep Space Nine*, in one early episode of that television series even morphed himself into the shape of a rat, all the better to get a perspective on the dubious traffic at the entrance to the wormhole, gateway to unexplored regions of space. Anthropologist Deborah Heath, who studies the many-sided cultures of genetic technology, tells me that one of the avidly sought, candidate genes for human breast-cancer has been named Odo by the research team attempting to isolate and sequence it. Meanwhile, *Deep Space Nine*, with all its flexible bodies, is ideal for the reduced expectations of technophilic U.S.-ers in the New World Order of the 1990s (Martin 1994; Harvey 1989). I certainly cannot recall any rats, morphed aliens or not, on the starships *Enterprise* in the earlier generations of the Star Trek myth.

Human mental patients were also part of psychiatric research on neural-chemical implants and telemetric monitoring at Rockland State Hospital in the 1960s, a fact I learned from National Science Foundation and National Institutes of Mental Health grant proposals when I was researching the crafting of non-human primates as model systems for human ills in the U.S. Kline was associated with the Psychiatric Research Foundation in New York, an organization established to promote controversial investigations into psycho-pharmacology. Nancy Campbell's (1994) work on the history of U.S. drug and addiction discourses details the dovetailing of such research in the 1950s and 1960s with Cold War agendas, including CIA-sponsored research on behavior control. The liberal philanthropic foundations, especially the Macy Foundation, which was so important to the configuration of cybernetics as an interdisciplinary field in the late 1940s and early 1950s, were liberally involved. Geof Bowker (1993) analyzes the myriad routes through which technical and popular culture was shooting up with all things cybernetic in the 1950s and 60s in the U.S. Marge Piercy used research at Rockland State Hospital as background for the brain-implant experiments practiced on psychiatric patients in her transformative feminist science-fiction story, *Woman on the Edge of Time* (1976). Influenced by Piercy, in my "Manifesto for Cyborgs," I used the cyborg as a blasphemous anti-racist feminist figure reshaped for science-studies analyses and feminist theory alike (Haraway 1985). Piercy developed her thinking about the cyborg as lover, friend, object, subject, weapon, and golem in *He, She, and It* (1991). Her cyborgs and mine became "trans" to their origins, defying their founding identities as weapons and self-acting control devices, thus trying to trouble U.S. cultural commitments to what counts as agency and self-determination for people—and for other organisms and machines.

Subsisting not in the vast reaches of interstellar space, where the 1950s rat cyborg was semiotically bound, but in the dark passages of a termite's gut, the humble *Mixotricha paradoxa* is perhaps most "trans" of all to standard natural history accounts of unity and agency in cyborg lives lived within the crevices and fluids of Gaia's multi-form flesh. Cyborgs are about particular sorts of breached boundaries that confuse a specific historical people's stories about what counts as distinct categories crucial to that culture's natural-technical evolutionary narratives. *Mixotricha* is a pro at transgressing just those sorts of boundaries. Like the other entities in this foreword, *Mixotricha* could not cohabit the *The Cyborg Handbook*'s world without all of the materializing instruments, discourses, and political economies of transnational technoscience—from scanning electron microscopes, to molecular genetic analysis, to theories of evolution, to circulations of money and people. Appropriately, Lynn Margulis, the University of Massachusetts biologist who introduced me to *Mixotricha*'s genre-confounding talents, is also one of the formulators of the Gaia hypothesis. The account of the nature of life by her and her son is a rich exposition of the travails of the auto-poietic earth (Margulis and Sagan 1994). These writers cross-stitch technology, organic beings, and inorganic nature into a cobbled together, profoundly materialist and dynamic biosphere. Their techno-biosphere is a kind of cyborg coyote or trickster, not an innocent being, not in our control, but not out of our control either (our practices matter and the cyborg is our flesh too), and in whom we are fatefully embedded, along with the multi-talented prokaryotes and odd protoctists that they describe so lavishly. They refuse both technological determinism, whether of a cultural-industrial or biological-genetic sort, and back-to-nature mysticism. Margulis and Sagan's *What Is Life?* is anemic, for my taste, in its account of the flows of capital and questions of politics and cultural specificity in the whole earth's story, much less in any sense of critique of the mechanisms of "planetary metabolism" that capitalism and technoscience have become.[3] Yet, *What Is Life?* is full of ways to avoid the traps in the tradition of Western natural history and its conjoined twin called political theory of methodological individualism: humanist arrogance, demonology of the machine, and boring certainties that we already know everything. The arguments that machines are indissociable human extensions (an extended phenotype), coupled with the insistence on the intimate joins of matter and feeling, consciousness and history, are all persuasive to me, who, it must be said, has long been a believer on these issues. Margulis and Sagan provide an historical narrative with a future that is full of metamorphoses, but without apocalypses. **"Our" bodies are indeed weedy and promiscuous, and the earth has always been going to seed**.

M. paradoxa is a particularly apt resident of this version of the whole earth. Using Lynn Margulis and Dorion Sagan's earlier book, *Origins of Sex: Three Billion Years of Genetic Recombination*, as my guide, I will close with a story of the promiscuous origins of cells that have organelles, in order to explore what counts as a unit, as one, in a promising, non-innocent Gaian-cyborg natural history practice. Cells with organelles are called "eukaryotes"; they have a membrane-bound nucleus and other differentiated internal structures. "Prokaryotes" like bacteria, do not have a nucleus to house their genetic material, but keep their DNA naked in the cell. Consider, then, the text given us by the existence, in the hindgut of a modern South Australian termite, of the creature named *Mixotricha paradoxa*, a mixed-up, paradoxical, microscopic bit of "hair" (*trichos*). This little filamentous creature makes a mockery of the notion of the bounded, defended, singular self out to protect its genetic investments. The problem our text presents is simple: what constitutes *M. paradoxa*? Where does the protist stop and somebody else start in that wood-eating insect's teeming hindgut? In the five-kingdom classification of life, a protist is a member of the Protoctista, which is made up of "microorganisms and their larger descendants composed of multiple heterologous genomes" (Margulis 1992:40). Not belonging to the plant, animal, fungus, or bacterial kingdoms, but constituting a kingdom of their own, protoctists include algae, slime molds, ciliates, and amoebae, among many others. The "multiple heterologous genomes" are the source of my pleasure in these abundant and baroquely elaborated beings.[4] Plants, animals, and fungi all descended from such beginnings. What does *Mixotricha*'s paradoxical individuality tell us about beginnings? Finally, how might such forms of life help us address the tendentious questions broached at the beginning of this foreword?

M. paradoxa is a nucleated microbe with five distinct kinds of internal and external prokaryotic symbionts, including two species of motile spirochetes, which live in various degrees of structural and functional integration with their host. About one million "individuals" of the five kinds of prokaryotes live with, on, and in the nucleated being that gets the generic name *Mixotricha*. The substantive seems to imply an individuality, a *basis* for the name, that must make any serious cosmic nominalist orgasmic. When the congeries reach a couple of million, the host divides; and then there are two—or some power of ten of two. All the associated creatures live in a kind of obligate confederacy. Opportunists all, they are nested in each other's tissues in a myriad of ways that make words like competition and cooperation, or individual and collective, fall into the trash heap of pallid metaphors and bad ontology. From Margulis and Sagan's "symbiogenetic" point of view, *Mixotricha*'s kind of confederacy is fundamental to life's history. Such associations probably arose repeatedly. The ties often involved genetic exchanges, or recombinations, that in turn had a history dating back to the earliest bacteria that had to survive the gene-damaging environment of ultra-violet light before there was an oxygen atmosphere to shield them. "That genetic recombination began as a part of an enormous health delivery system to ancient DNA molecules is quite evident. Once healthy recombinants were produced, they retained the ability to recombine genes from different sources. As long as selection acted on the recombinants, selection pressure would retain the mechanism of recombination as well" (60). I like the idea of gene exchange as a kind of prophylaxis against sunburn. It puts the heliotropic West into perspective.

Protists like *M. paradoxa* seem to show in mid-stream the ubiquitous, life-changing association of events that brought motile, oxygen-using, or photosynthetic bacteria into other cells, perhaps originally on an opportunistic hunt for a nutritious meal or a secure medium for their metabolic transactions. Some predators settled down inside their prey and struck up quite an energy and information-exchange economy. Mitochondria, oxygen-using organelles with respiratory enzymes integrated into membrane structures, probably joined what are now modern cells in this way. "With the elapse of time, the internal enemies of the prey evolved into microbial guests, and, finally, supportive adopted relatives. Because of a wealth of molecular biological and biochemical evidence supporting these models, the mitochondria of today are best seen as descendants of cells that evolved within other cells" (71).

The story of heterogeneous associations at various levels of integration repeated itself many times at many scales. "Clones of eukaryotic cells in the form of animals, plants, fungi, and protoctists seem to share a symbiotic history.... From an evolutionary point of view, the first eukaryotes were loose confederacies of bacteria that, with continuing integration, became recognizable as protists, unicellular eukaryotic cells.... The earliest protists were likely to have been most like bacterial communities.... At first each autopoietic [self-maintaining] community member replicated its DNA, divided, and remained in contact with other members in a fairly informal manner. *Informal* here refers to the number of partners in these confederacies: they varied" (72). Indeed, they varied. And this kind of variation relies on a different narrative structure from the Terminator's endless repetitions. *Mixotricha* is a logo for a very weedy version of Gaia, where the monocultures of transnational agribusiness and the heavily capitalized rush to convert biodiversity into biotechnology for sale runs into at least a narrative and a figural speed bump.

Undoubtedly, we will have to do more than mutate the stories and the figures if the cyborg citizens of the third planet from the sun are to enjoy something better than the deadly transgressive flexibility of the New World Order. I like to tell stories, and I regard biology as a branch of civics. I know that I am in a long tradition of natural historians, as well as laboratory scientists, in this pursuit. I also know that my stories, as well as those of my willing and unwilling scientist informants, are excruciatingly historically and culturally specific, whether acknowledged as such or not. And, naturally, my stories are all true, or at least they aim to be, and in several dimensions at once. **My hope is that this kind of truth is situated and accountable, and therefore able to be in power-sensitive engagement with other versions and materializations of the world.** My stories are not impartial; they are for some ways of life and not others. I think that characteristic puts my account right in the middle of technoscientific practice in general. Fact and fiction, rhetoric and technology, and analysis and story-telling are all held together by a stronger weld than those who eschew taking narrative practice seriously in science—and in all other sorts of "hard" explanation—will allow. Even so, mutating the stories is part of a much bigger task of engaging the apparatuses for producing what will count as "global" and as "us." I do not think that most people who live on earth now have the choice not to live inside of, and not to be shaped by, the fiercely material and imaginative apparatuses for making "us" cyborgs and making our homes into places mapped within the space of titanic globalizations in a direct line of descent from the cybernetic Gaia seen from NASA's fabulous eyes. **The global and the universal are not pre-existing empirical qualities; they are deeply fraught, dangerous, and inescapable inventions.**

The cyborg is a figure for exploring those inventions, whom they serve, how they can be reconfigured. **Cyborgs do not stay still. Already in the few decades that they have existed, they have mutated, in fact and fiction, into second-order entities like genomic and electronic databases and the other denizens of the zone called cyberspace.** Lives are at stake in curious quasi-objects like databases; they structure the informatics of possible worlds, as well as of all-too-real ones. Whether our attention, and our action, is addressed to labor systems, sexual configurations, circuits of disease and well-being, banking wizardry, trajectories of food and the means to get it, political organizing, religious visions, virtual realities and time-space compressions symbolized by the internet, racial formations, reality or the Reality Engine™, serious business or world-shaping play, cyborg figures have a way of transfecting, infecting, everything. This *Handbook* is a valuable guide to the cyborg worlds we willy-nilly inhabit, whether we want to or not. I think *The Handbook* is one instrument for achieving what Elizabeth Bird, on the staff of the Center for Rural Affairs in Nebraska, called for in her slogan: Cyborgs for Earthly Survival!

Notes

1. For an analytical catalogue of real-life military cyborgs, see Gray (1991). On machines and subjectivity in cyborg worlds, see Edwards (1995).

2. Chris Gray, an editor of this *Handbook*, first showed me Clynes and Kline's publication.

3. I thank Lynn Margulis for the opportunity to read *What Is Life?* in manuscript.

4. Never one for disembodied points, I note that, even as I write this preface, I am trying to evict one sort of amoeba from my own teeming gut, with the aid of a commodity, iodoquinol, for sale from a New Jersey pharmaceutical company and purchased by my health maintenance organization. We North American hominids, at least those rich ones with good medical insurance, are more socially fastidious about our organic symbionts than most of earth's residents can afford to be. We are, however, rather less fastidious about our cyborg commensuals, to the peril of us all.

References Cited

Bowker, Geof (1993) "How to Be Universal: Some Cybernetic Strategies." *Social Studies of Science* 23:107-27.

Campbell, Nancy (1994) Unpublished manuscript. History of Consciousness Board, University of California, Santa Cruz.

Clynes, Manfred E. and Nathan S. Kline (1960) "Cyborgs and Space." *Astronautics* September, 26-27, 75-76.

Downey, Gary Lee, Joseph Dumit, and Sarah Williams (1995) "Granting Membership to the Cyborg Image." In this volume.

Edwards, Paul N. (1995) *The Closed World: Computers and the Politics of Discourse in Cold War America.* Cambridge, Mass.: MIT Press.

Gray, Chris Hables (1991) *Computers as Weapons and Metaphors: The U.S. Military 1940-90 and Postmodern War.* Ph.D., University of California, Santa Cruz.

Haraway, Donna J. (1985) "Manifesto for Cyborgs: Science, Technology, and Socialist Feminism in the 1980s." *Socialist Review* no. 80: 65-108.

Harvey, David (1989) *The Condition of Postmodernity. An Enquiry into the Origins of Cultural Change.* Oxford: Basil Blackwell.

Lovelock, J. E. (1979) *Gaia: A New Look at Life on Earth.* New York: Oxford University Press.

Margulis, Lynn (1992) "Biodiversity: Molecular Biological Domains, Symbiosis and Kingdom Origins." *BioSystems* 27:39-51.

Margulis, Lynn and Dorion Sagan (1986) *Origins of Sex: Three Billion Years of Genetic Recombination.* New Haven: Yale University Press.

Margulis, Lynn and Dorion Sagan (1994) *What Is Life?* New York: Simon and Schuster.

Martin, Emily (1994) *Flexible Bodies. Tracking Immunity in American Culture from the Days of Polio to the Age of AIDS.* Boston: Beacon Press.

Piercy, Marge (1976) *Woman on the Edge of Time.* New York: Fawcett Crest.

Piercy, Marge (1991) *He, She, and It.* New York: Fawcett Crest.

Introduction

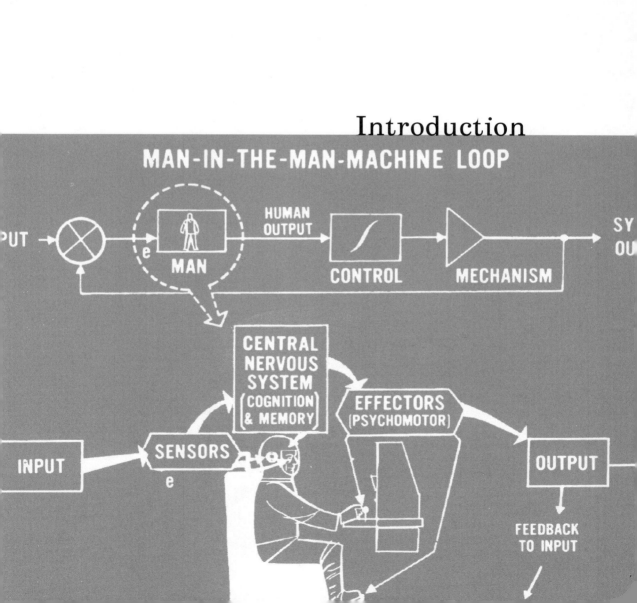

Cyborgology

Constructing the Knowledge of Cybernetic Organisms

Chris Hables Gray, Steven Mentor, Heidi J. Figueroa-Sarriera

Linguistically and materially a hybrid of cybernetic device and organism, a cyborg is a science fiction chimera from the 1950s and after; but a cyborg is also a powerful social and scientific reality in the same historical period. Like any important technology, a cyborg is simultaneously a myth and a tool, a representation and an instrument, a frozen moment and a motor of social and imaginative reality. A cyborg exists when two kinds of boundaries are simultaneously problematic: 1) that between animals (or other organisms) and humans, and 2) that between self-controlled, self-governing machines (automatons) and organisms, especially humans (models of autonomy). The cyborg is the figure born of the interface of automaton and autonomy.

—Donna Haraway

The Proliferation of Cybernetic Organisms

On December 8, 1993, there was a discussion of cyborgs on *The 700 Club*, the fundamentalist Christian news show hosted by Pat Robertson. While finishing a generally favorable discussion of prototype implantable ID chips that would allow people to turn part of their anatomy into a credit card, Debbie Terry, the commentator on the "Newswatch" section, asked about the possibility that such chips, or more elaborate neural implants, might be 666, the Mark of the Beast foretold in the Bible. The news director, who was making the report, agreed that, yes, there was a danger, but the Bible, fortunately, prophesied that the Mark would be worldwide and, as of yet, implant chips were only planned for Europe, North America, and Japan. The assembled Christians looked relieved. While this may not be completely reassuring for all literal interpreters of the Bible, it also shows just how complicated cyborgization is. Sure, it's a neato-keeno technology, but the cyborg just might be the Herald of the Apocalypse as well!

Cyborg. Cybernetic-organism.[1] **The melding of the organic and the machinic, or the engineering of a union between separate organic systems, is the subject of this collection.** This merging of the evolved and the developed, this integration of the constructor and the constructed, these systems of dying flesh and undead circuits, and of living and artificial cells, have been called many things: bionic systems, vital machines, cyborgs. They are a central figure of the late Twentieth Century.

As Donna Haraway points out, **this figure of the cyborg helps us bring together myths and tools, representations and embodied realities, as a way of understanding postmodernity**.[2] But this understanding will not come easily. This collection shows that the ramifications of today's proliferation of types of cyborgs and cyborgian relations are very difficult to determine at the moment because cyborgs are everywhere and multiplying. This *Cyborg Handbook*, far from being an answer to *the* cyborg question, is rather an initial map of the important cyborg *questions*, anxieties, problems and possibilities.

There is no one kind of cyborg. To borrow from the future/present world of science fiction, where most cyborg theorizing has taken place until recently, cyborgs can range from the barely organic Terminator, merely a human skin over a complete robot, to Chief Engineer Geordi LaForge of the liberal Federation of United Nations and Planets multicultural fantasy *Star Trek: The Next Generation* (ST:TNG), with his prosthetic visor. Cyborgs can be "rugged" individuals but they are usually trapped in intense corporate settings, like *The Six-Million-Dollar Man* of television who works for U.S. intelligence, and Robocop of the Detroit Police, a subsidiary of OmniConsumerProducts (OCP). This is only fitting, as most cyborg technology requires incredible institutional support. Every cyborg is part of a system (more accurately of overlapping systems). Or the cyborg can be the system itself, as with the group-mind totalitarian civilization of the Borg, also inhabitants of ST:TNG.

But the story of cyborgs is not just a tale told around the glow of the televised fire. There are many actual cyborgs among us in society. Anyone with an artificial organ, limb or supplement (like a pacemaker), anyone reprogrammed to resist disease (immunized) or drugged to think/behave/feel better (psychopharmacology) is technically a cyborg. The range of these intimate human-machine relationships is mind-boggling. It's not just Robocop, it is our grandmother with a pacemaker. Not just Geordi but also our colleague with the myloelectric prosthetic arm. Not just the cyberwarriors of a hundred militaristic science fiction stories, but arguably anyone whose immune system has been programmed through vaccination to recognize and kill the polio virus. Not just the fighter-bomber pilot in the state-of-the-art cockpit who can target enemies with the eyes, fire missiles with a word, and who uses computers to monitor his or her own body and to create a disembodied "God's Eye" view of the battle, but also the potentially billions of humans yet unborn who will be the products of genetic engineering.

Even if many individuals in the industrial and post-industrial countries aren't full cyborgs, we certainly all live in a "cyborg society."[3] Machines are intimately interfaced with humans on almost every level of existence not only in the West and Japan but among the elite in every country of the world. Cyborg society also refers to **the full range of intimate organic-machinic relations**, from the man-machine weapons systems of the postmodern military to the rat-cyborg portrayed in the article where the term was coined (see page 30), to the genetically engineered mice of today to biocomputers, artificial life programs, and any future extravaganzas like the plant-intelligent-machine symbiosis in Lois Gresh's "Digital Pistil" (in this volume). Cyborg technosciences aren't just about making individual cyborgs, they encompass a vast range of cyborgian relationships, which as Donna Haraway shows in the foreword to this volume, can extend from the smallest creature to Gaia, the whole web of all the life on this planet.

Where do cyborgian technologies come from? Most have military origins, although civilian medical research has become almost as important a source. The other major centers of actual cyborg creation are entertainment (print, film, games, and action figures) and work (the computer industry, certainly, but also the cybernetization of all industry). Together, these four cyborgology centers map another set of distinctions between types of cyborgs. Cyborg technologies can be **restorative**, in that they restore lost functions and replace lost organs and limbs; they can be **normalizing**, in that they restore some creature to indistinguishable normality; they can be ambiguously **reconfiguring**, creating posthuman creatures equal to but different from humans, like what one is now when interacting with other creatures in cyberspace or, in the future, the type of modifications proto-humans will undergo to live in space or under the sea having given up the comforts of terrestrial existence; and they can be **enhancing**, the aim of most military and industrial research, and what those with cyborg envy or even cyborg-philia fantasize. The latter category seeks to construct everything from factories controlled by a handful of "worker-pilots" and infantrymen in mind-controlled exoskeletons to the dream many computer scientists have—downloading their consciousness into immortal computers.

Cyborgian techniques in entertainment and more direct mind-control research underway since the 1960s offer the possibility of disquieting changes that *degrade* humans into addicts of direct neurostimulation or, the nightmare of cyberphobes, into the perfect will-less soldier/subjects like the Borg, who "assimilate" all. In general, the differences between restorative, normalizing, reconfiguring, enhancing, and degrading cyborg technologies seem particularly important in ethical terms, as we hope this collection demonstrates in detail.

Clearly, cyborgology is not simple. For one thing there is no consensus on what a cyborg is. The term has long since escaped Manfred Clynes' original formulation although it certainly continues to derive sustenance from it, which we find a healthy development, and one which this book, where definitions of cyborg proliferate as relentlessly as incarnations, supports. The range of human-machine couplings almost defies definition: even existing human cyborgs range from the quadriplegic patient totally dependent on a vast array of high-tech equipment to a small child with one immunization. The patient on a kidney machine twice a week and the combat pilot attached to his warcraft with sensors and complex interfaces for flights are both intermittent cyborgs and yet between them there is a tremendous difference. The patient uses cyborg technologies to maintain his or her human body; the pilot cyborg is an enhanced human, a man-plus. Other such distinctions become readily apparent and there is an incredible array of ways of categorizing cyborgs, and renaming them.[4]

For example, just in this volume alone, Manfred Clynes delineates Cyborgs I, II, III, IV, and V; Jennifer González distinguishes between machine cyborgs and organic cyborgs (monsters and transgenetic constructions); Mark Oehlert breaks down comic-book cyborgs into controllers, bio-tech integrators, and genetics; Monica Casper describes "Technomoms and Cyborg Fetuses" and Linda Hogle explains "Cadaver Donors."[5] David Hess, in his turn, discusses "Low-Tech Cyborgs." Two of the editors have also experimented with validating cyborg differences, specifically between neo-, proto-, multi-, ultra-, semi-, hyper-, retro-, omni-, pseudo-, mega- and meta-cyborgs.[6]

While lines are drawn between types of cyborgs, others have renamed them or have defined cyborgs as only part of a more general cyborgian transition in human history.

The Cyborg Age?

The transition of proto-human hunter gatherers into *homo faber*, humans

defined, determined even, as tool users, undoubtedly took place thousands or tens of thousands of years. The spawning of machine culture (civilization, living in cities), seems to have happened more quickly but in any event it has taken at least ten thousand years to go from the first cities, simple machines for living, to the machine-dominated culture we live in now. While those most ancient machines, armies of armed men, have probably played a major role in most human culture for even longer, it wasn't until two hundred years ago that biopower machines were supplanted by self-powered machines when the industrial revolution swept the globe.

It was Carlyle who labeled his own time, the Machine Age, noting the incredible proliferation of machines and the growing intimacy of the traffic between them and the humans. Since then the integration of machines into cultures, lives, and bodies, has become pronounced. There is no longer a "partnership" between machine and organism; rather there is a symbiosis and it is managed by cybernetics, the language common to the organic and the mechanical.

Norbert Weiner's elaboration of the idea of cybernetics, of a technoscience that explained both organic and machinic processes as parts of informational systems, was the culmination of many different currents in Western culture. The mechanization of war, the automation of work, the electronization of information, the commodification of culture, the triumph of mass media, the spread of global networks, and the hegemony of cybernetic metaphors in science and medicine all contributed.

Long before Manfred Clynes conjured "cyborg" from *cybernetic organism* at the behest of his friend, Nathan Kline, the idea of the human-machine living system was spreading. **Many see Mary Shelley's monster, Frankenstein's creature, as the first cyborg;** certainly he is among the most powerful. L. Frank Baum's Tin Man was also a true cyborg, as well as a metaphor for the effect the mechanization of work was having on workers. Later, especially during the 1940s, there were a number of science-fiction stories, most notably "No Woman Born" by C. L. Moore and "Camouflage" by Henry Kuttner, that described full cyborgs. Ten years earlier, the great British scientist J.D. Bernal had written in his *The World, the Flesh, and the Devil* that humans, especially those involved in colonizing space, would take control of their evolutionary destiny through genetic engineering, prosthetic surgery, and hard-wired electric interfaces between humans and machines that would allow them to attach "a new sense organ or ... a new mechanism to operate ..." (p. 22) as needed or desired.

By the end of World War II it was very clear that the mechanization of the human, the vitalization of the machine, and the integration of both into cybernetics was producing a whole new range of informational disciplines, fantasies, and practices that transgressed the machinic-organic border. This marks a major transition from a world where distinctions between human and tool, human and machine, living and dead, organic and inorganic, present and distant, natural and artificial seemed clear (even if they really weren't) to the present, where all of these distinctions seem plastic, if not ludicrous.

This watershed has been noted by a fair number of observers. Many mark it with the sign of the cyborg, the context of this book, but other labels are also used, including **the age of the vital machine, The Fourth Discontinuity, the posthuman, and the transhuman.**

One of the most interesting of these analyses is David F. Channell's *The Vital Machine*. Channell sees today's machinic/organic mergings as the synthesis of two central currents of Western culture: the mechanical and the organic worldviews. Inevitably, there are paradoxes. Organic systems are increasingly described in information-processing terms, while the more complex mechanical or informational devices (software, for example) are today usually explained in identical language. From artificial life programs to "living-dead" cadaver-organ donors the line between the organic and the machinic is becoming very blurred, indeed.

This is the central point of another important work of what we would call cyborgology, Bruce Mazlish's *The Fourth Discontinuity: The Co-evolution of Humans and Machines*. In Mazlish's story, Western intellectual history can be seen as the overcoming of a series of great illusions, termed discontinuities, because they posited as natural four artificial distinctions, those: 1) between humans and the cosmos (overcome by Copernicus); 2) between humans and other life (overcome by Darwin); 3) between humans and our unconscious (overcome by Freud); and 4) between humans and machines. Wheresoever we note the dissolving fourth discontinuity, cyborgs thrive.

But haven't people always been cyborgs? At least back to the bicycle, eyeglasses, and stone hammers? This is an argument many people make, including early cyborgologists like Manfred Clynes and J.E. Steele. The answer is, in a word, no. Certainly, we can look back from the present at some human-tool and human-machine relationships and say, "Yes, that looks very cyborgian," but this is only possible because of hindsight. Just as ancient humans, once they'd learned to wield the club, could see the tree limb as a tool. Before then it was only a stick. Cyborgian elements of previous human-tool and human-machine relationships are only visible from our current point of view. In quantity, and quality, the relationship is new. Yes, it is a direct development out of the human-tool and human-machine relationships, but it represents a fundamentally new stage, perhaps even culmination, of this history. "Cyborg" is as specific, general, powerful, and useless, a term as "tool" or "machine." And it is just as important.

We believe the figure of the cyborg helps us see more specifically whether other central stories of our age are accurate or useful. Many of these other stories are ancient, about gender and power, life, love and death. But others, intertwined with them, are themselves cyborg myths, **attempts to understand the broader implications of human/machine co-evolution,** which we hope our readers will develop, critique, and rewrite as they to learn to "speak" cyborg, without forgetting whatever human or machine languages they already might know.

Speaking Cyborg

Language, and especially stories and metaphors, reflect and direct culture, lived experience, and perception. A vast number of our most powerful metaphors come from our bodily senses and orientation: feeling "high" or "low", "seeing" what you mean, "understanding" or "overlooking", having "potent" of "fecund" metaphors, and so on. Inevitably, then, we are radically changing our senses with prosthetics, highly interactive technologies such as virtual reality and Waldos, and soon the widespread use of implants and direct neural connections to the brain already used experimentally. How will this affect the way we express the new sensations? If every important part of human life—birth, education, sex, work, aging, death—is transformed by intimate connections with technologies, then the language of technology will begin to "invade" the ways we express and perceive these experiences. Just as Frankenstein's monster and the "good" Terminator struggled to learn to speak as humans, we "humans" will struggle to speak as cyborgs, to find the words to express very new experiences.

This applies to stories and myths as well as metaphors. We have certain stories, like that of Frankenstein, which raise important questions about our relationship to the technological systems we unleash on the world. And we have an ever larger number of science-fiction stories about cyborgs, stories that help dramatize some of our fears and hopes as we visualize the emerging cyborg world. But within these stories, and in the culture at large, other stories shape the way we approach this change: stores about gender, race, class, the body politic, work, and play. Cyborgs can make these stories problematic (a woman in an exoskeleton might be 1000 times stronger than a man) but some cultural stories may affect who benefits from cyborg technologies (rich cyborgs might live ten times longer than poor humans; some technologies may be just for men, or for an elite group, or used by one group against another).

This doesn't just apply to our individual bodies, either. We live in a world that is changing before our eyes. Corporations transcend particular countries and are now global, no longer really "centered" anywhere. Nations are breaking apart and reforming, and peoples are often far flung in diasporas across different continents. It is no accident that the modern has become postmodern as human changes to cyborg. Nor that a cyberculture is spreading as exuberantly and insidiously as the Internet, into recreation (video games, drugs, music, raves), work, and politics.[7] All these changes depend on and reflect new telecommunications technologies. As these larger "bodies"—of people, business, and government—are more closely tied to vast technologies, they too become cyborgs and we struggle to find ways to understand and predict how they are shifting. As with our individual bodies, so with these: the changes are both good and bad because the technologies are themselves ambivalent, capable of many often contradictory uses. It may help us to confront these changes if we accept our new status as cyborgs and begin to look at these changes from a cyborgian point of view.

Cyborgs also remind us that we are always embodied, but that the ways we are embodied aren't simple. Some people imagine the future as bodiless: either as "brains in a vat" or as somehow downloaded into immortal computers as organic-artificial intelligences. Yet, while AI systems are still in the early stages of development, cyborg technologies are everywhere, affecting millions of people every day. Some of us may feel like "cogs" in a machine, but we are really bodies hooked into machines, and bodies linked to other bodies by machines. It may be that cyborgs will be neither male nor female, neither with nor without color in the far future, or some complicated version of these, but how we are affected by cyborg technology now still depends a great deal on what gender, race, and class we are. There is no one "cyborg" and no one benefit or drawback or evil; every person will respond differently to different ways technology invades or caresses her body. Cyborgs are "situated knowledges" (as Donna Haraway explains in her article of the same name) with embodiment, not a black box that defies understanding.

We call this book a "handbook" because it is set up to help the reader develop specific, and useful, understandings, as is the duty of all good Cyborg Citizens. But we are also playing with the word, making parody because we don't pretend to have compiled here the totality of cyborg knowledge. A "hand book" is a hybrid itself, a cyborgian technology, designed in this case to show in an explicit way the possibilities of fragmentation and hybridity as well as the impossibility of totalization.

The Cyborg Handbook

While the word cyborg was coined almost thirty-five years ago, for many years it was little used beyond the science-fiction subculture. At the time of the first printing of this volume, it will have been ten years since Donna Haraway's incredible essay, "A Manifesto for Cyborgs," was published in the *Socialist Review*, a little-read political-theory journal. Since then, cyborgism has become a central concept for many academics, not only people in science and technology studies, but also political theorists, military historians, literary critics, human-factors engineers, computer scientists, medical sociologists, psychologists, and cultural observers of all types.

Cyborgology is proliferating as profligately as its subject, but it is still a small enough field to be treated comprehensively. That is what we have tried to do here, bringing together some of the most important historical and theoretical documents on cyborgs. There are a handful of other books on cyborgs to which this *Handbook* has aimed to be complementary. Foremost among these are the works of Donna Haraway. It is particularly fitting that this book begin with her foreword. Cyborg-ology as an academic attitude started with her 1985 "Manifesto." Any serious student of cyborgology must explore her work directly and at length, and should certainly read her collection of essays *Cyborgs, Simians and Women* (it includes the "Manifesto"), if nothing else.[9]

We've also not given fiction its due. Although we have three pieces of fiction, including a science fiction story, the role of fiction in cyborgology has been, and no doubt will continue to be, much greater. The compleat cyborgologist must study science fiction as the anthropologist listens to myths and prophecies. Science fiction has often led the way in theorizing and examining cyborgs, showing their proliferation and suggesting some of the dilemmas and social implications they represent. And several important critics—Kate Hayles, Scott Bukatman, Fredric Jameson, Anne Balsamo, and Donna Haraway come to mind—have used these fictional resources to explore the cyborg and the ways he/she/it affects our ideas of the "human." Bukatman's *Terminal Identity* in particular explores fictional versions of many of the themes sounded by our contributors and is highly recommended.

This book is by and large limited to a Euro-American perspective despite the few articles that discuss Africa, Brazil, and the Middle East. It is particularly unfortunate that there is little on Japanese culture and cyborgs. Although much work is in progress on cyborgs in Japan and other parts of the world, often by contributors to this volume, only what is here was available for publication. In the future we are confident that perspectives from other cultures will increase our appreciation of the cyborg and therefore enrich our understanding of ourselves.

This book is organized into three main sections. First, in "The Genesis of Cyborg," which conceptually includes this introduction, the prehistory and birth of the cyborg figure are explored. This article is followed quite appropriately with a discussion of "African Influences on Cybernetics" by Ron Eglash. The rest of this section is made up of documents and interviews by Manfred Clynes, who coined *cyborg*, and J. E. Steele, who created the word *bionics*.

The second, and largest section, is "The Proliferation of Cyborgs." It is divided into three subsections that explore the major centers of cyborg production in our culture: science and engineering (particularly in space exploration and war promulgation), medicine, and the imagination.

Since "cyborg" was first used in a proposal to modify humans so they could live in space without spacesuits, **it is fitting that human-machine integration in space exploration is one of the most advanced sites of cyborg production in our culture.** In 1963 NASA even went so far as to commission a special "Cyborg Study," an excerpt of which we reproduce here. Interestingly enough, even though NASA's policy of human-machine integration, which dates back to its very beginnings, never changed, after this study the agency seemed almost allergic to the term "cyborg" and instead used more technical, and usually specific, locutions like teleoperators, human augmentation, biotelemetry, and bionics. Two other articles in this subsection come out of the space program: a history of "Teleoperators and Human Augmentation," from a NASA and Atomic Energy

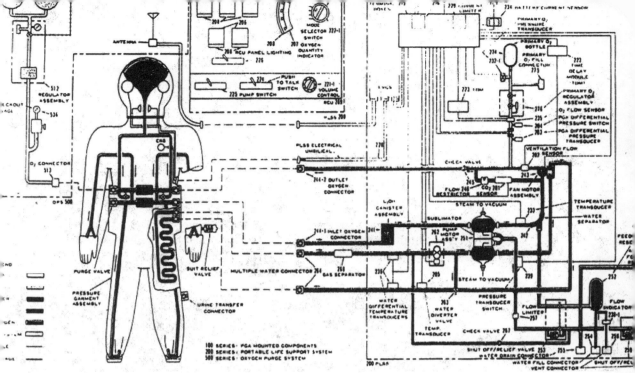

Commission study on this cyborgian technology and an interview with Dr. Patricia Cowings, head of NASA's Ames Research Center. As an African-American woman scientist doing cutting-edge biofeedback research she has an interesting point of view on cyborg technoscience.

NASA's commitment to the human-machine space-travel system was inevitable since much of its technoscience, especially in biomedicine, came out of the U.S. military, committed to what they call the man-machine weapon system since World War II. A huge part of the cyborg family tree is profoundly militarized. The anthropologist Hugh Gusterson tells a tale with a cyborg theme from his ethnographic study of nuclear protesters and weapon makers in California. There are several pieces on the Pilot's Associate by Chris Gray and DARPA, and there is an essay by Les Levidow and Kevin Robins on the implications of the militarized cyborg for the future. Levidow and Robins are the editors of *Cyborg Worlds: The Military Information Society*, the definitive collection of essays on militarism and cyborgs.

The subsection ends with Heidi J. Figueroa-Sarriera's analysis of Hans Morevec's fascinating book, *Mind Children*, which sings the praises of a future life-style organized around downloading human consciousness into machines, his favorite bearing a remarkable resemblance to a tumbleweed.

The next subsection focuses on medicine, a crucial locus for the production of many different types of cyborgs and cyborgian relationships. Adele Clarke, a medical sociologist, begins with an overview of cyborgian medicine called "Modernity, Postmodernity & Reproductive Processes, c. 1890-1990, or 'Mommy, Where Do Cyborgs Come From Anyway?'" This is followed by a fascinating, almost bitter, article about the experience of Barney Clark, the dentist who received the first artificial heart, as seen by the psychological staff that treated him during his acute and fatal cyborgian experience. Then there is an abstract of the most important official U.S. study of artificial organs, the Van Citters Report. It is followed by articles by active medical researchers, Motokazu Hori's "Artificial Liver: Present and Future" and Eli Friedman's revealing essay on some of the motivations for artificial organ developers.

George Annas, one of the foremost legal authorities on bioethics and medical cyborg issues, here imagines a legal opinion from the future on rationing artificial organs "Minerva vs. the National Health Agency." The subsection ends with essays by two of Adele Clarke's colleagues, Monica Casper and Linda Hogle, who analyze in turn, the "Fetal Cyborgs and Technomoms" at the start of the twentieth century, Euro-American cyborg's life span, and the donor cyborg or "living cadaver" status they may well achieve at the end.

The last, and perhaps most important, site of cyborg production today is the imagination. Not that militarized technoscience and medicine aren't fueled by imagination themselves, but there is a realm of pure fantasy production which has produced some of the most startling, and insightful, takes on cyborgs.

The first piece in this subsection is from "Captain America to Wolverine," a survey by Mark Oehlert, of some of the most revealing of the cyborg comic characters. In "Recalling Totalities," Jonathan Goldberg presents a Lacanian reading of Arnold Schwarzenegger. It is followed by David Tomas' look at the implications of his "Cybernetic Automaton" performance art. Jennifer González then offers five beautiful readings of cyborg iconography. Next comes Cynthia Fuchs' brilliant analysis of some contemporary cyborg images, especially the "Death is Irrelevant" Borg of *Star Trek: The Next Generation.* Philip K. Dick's classic science fiction tale, "I Hope I Shall Arrive Soon," has as its main character a cyborg spaceship. Then Katherine Hayles uses a close reading of a number of the most important cyborg fictional texts to describe "The Life Style of the Posthuman." Finally, the section ends, appropriately enough, with Lois Gresh's captivating story about the love life of cyborg plants.[10]

The third major division of *The Handbook* addresses the implications of cyborgs more than their specificities. It contains two subsections "Cyborg Anthropology" and "The Politics of Cyborgs."

The first is a series of anthropological interventions. Anthropologists have taken the cyborg figure particularly to heart, as illustrated in the first piece, a manifesto promulgated by Joe Dumit, Gary Lee Downey, and Sarah Williams which calls for "Granting Membership to the Cyborg Image." Joe Dumit follows with a meditation on the cyborgian implications of brain machines, followed by Gary Lee Downey's discussion of "Human Agency in CAD/CAM Technology." David Hess then defines "Low-Tech Cyborgs" while also describing his anthropological field work in Brazil. Finally Sarah Williams, who is involved in a long-term ethnographic study of anthropology itself, reflects on this work in "Visions of Cyborg Anthropology in Post-Cultural Worlds."

This section ends with a series of interventions about the socio-political implications of cyborgism. First, Sandy Stone muses on the tensions between subjectivity and virtuality. Chela Sandoval then analyzes the intersection of her reflections on oppositional consciousness with the work of Donna Haraway and the cyborg figure. Joseba Gabilondo, the noted Basque author, articulates the poetics of the post-colonial cyborg's politics. The team of Ray Macauley and Angel Gordo-López also explores the political ramifications of possible cyborg consciousness in "Cyborg Textualities." Lorne Falk and Mireille Perron put cyborgologists into perspective in their cheerful play, "The Conversion of Père Version." Finally, two of us (Chris Gray and Steven Mentor) give their own interpretation of "The Cyborg Body Politic."

At the very end come the appendices and the index, which in this case are not mere afterthoughts. There is a vast cyborg fiction, much of which is listed in the annotated fiction bibliography and the filmography. But, like the technical literature from computer science, medicine, genetics, and bionic engineering, there is too much of it to track completely. There is some technical literature in this volume, and technoscientific work is often cited at great length in many of the theoretical articles, but there has been no serious attempt to list all of the technical cyborg articles and books in the nonfiction bibliography. The bibliography here, while perhaps the most extensive on cyborgology yet put together, contains only major technical works and most of the English-language theoretical and descriptive articles on cyborgs and closely related phenomena, but it is not exhaustive.

Cyborgology

> I have always been told that we manipulate the system, but what's to keep the system from manipulating us? Symbionts. Soon, perhaps it will be impossible to tell where human ends and machines begins.
> —Maureen McHugh, China Mountain Zhang (p. 214)

> 'Change for the machines,' she sighed heavily. 'That's all we've ever done is change for the machines. But this is the last time. We've finally changed enough that the machines will be making all the changes from now on.'
> —Pat Cadigan, Synners (p. 334)

Cyborgology must go beyond traditional academic boundaries. While some of the articles are quite clearly from one particular discipline (particularly the medical works and some of the social science analysis) most of them are interdisciplinary and multidisciplinary. Many even transcend the hard boundaries between the humanities, the sciences, and the arts. To validate this mixing, as well as those tenacious pockets of disciplinarity, we have allowed the authors to keep their own citation style for their works. This has the added advantage of preserving the format of the historical documents, an important consideration when how something is cited can be just as important as what. For the rigorous academic reader this may be off-putting, but please use this small bit of heteroglossia in the spirit in which it is intended, to broaden our perspective.

Cyborgology, too, must be multicultural. While Western Culture has played a conspicuous role in the launching of the Cyborg Age, cyborgs are basically a cross-cultural phenomena just as tool and machine invention and promulgation were and are. This issue is discussed here but we do lack an extended treatment of the idea of the cyborg in other cultures. As noted above, this is a particularly glaring omission in the case of Asia, where China and Japan have a long history of making, and reflecting on, automatons and complex human-augmenting machinery and tools.

Today, Japan is an especially fertile nursery for cyborgs and cyborgologies. Frederik Schodt argues in his book *Inside the Robot Kingdom: Japan, Mechantronics, and the Coming Robotopia* that the Japanese have a different perspective from that of the West on robotics and cyborgs. It is striking that many Japanese corporate slogans are so cyborgian. Consider Mitsubishi's "sociotech," Hitachi's "humanication," and Matsushita's "human electronics." In addition to being a center for advanced computing and artificial-organ research, Japan has seen an incredible proliferation of cyborgs in its comics. Among scientists there is a great deal of speculation on these topics and Ichiro Kato, one of Japan's most important roboticists, believes the future will be a "cybot" society of robots, humans, and cyborgs.

Other countries are undergoing their own confrontations with the Cyborg Society, whether in Vietnam, where a number of prosthetics factories have been set up to deal with the aftereffects of the long war there, or in Guatemala, where a key part of Mayan cultural and political resistance takes place around the question of access to computers and international networks. Diane Nelson, who has been studying this resistance, concludes,

> The information revolution and generations of indigenous struggle have opened up a new arena where Mayan intellectuals can hack the Ladino power structure, i.e. overcome system limitations, decode and reprogram post-coloniality by pressing 'enter.' These activists are insisting on the appropriateness of their presence in the post-modern world by appropriating what they term universal culture for their own ends. One Mayan leader told me, "The Maya give thanks for food, for air, for the tools which serve us, the office machines, and the computers." The ALMG (Guatemalan Mayan Language Academy) maintains that the "decolonialization of the Maya begins with knowing how to use technology and not being used by it." [11]

These are just a few of the many possible examples that illustrate how ubiquitous cyborgization is becoming, and how multifaceted it is. But with so much happening in so many ways, what should we pay particularly close attention to?

While this book certainly doesn't offer any definitive answers, a glance at the cyborg questions and implications that seem to preoccupy the vast majority of the cyborgologists here is very revealing. Specifically, there is a fascination (but no consensus), with agency and subjectivity. Despite the many contemporary arguments for granting machines agency and for denying humans subjectivity the tenacity of the traditional view is measurable in the efforts to refute it. This is unsurprising, given that the ontology of cyborgology is embodiment. Without it the figure does not stand. Add to this the weight of our own embodiment and reconstructing this basic metaphor can seem very difficult indeed. Yet, bit by bit, the cyborg relationship is shifting it. As it shifts, so to do other meta-narratives, like the complicated didactic stories we call ethics.

Could there be a cyborg ethics? Yes, we think so. And not just one. Several systems are implicitly elaborated in the pages that follow. Clearly it will not be beyond good and evil, but new constructions of good and evil, new regimes of good and evil, to be Foucauldian, are inevitable.

David Channel has elaborated what he calls a "bionic" ethic:

> A bionic ethic must take into consideration both the mechanical and the organic aspects of the cybernetic ecology in order to maintain the system's integrity, stability, diversity, and purposefulness. Neither the mechanical nor the organic can be allowed to bring about the extinction of the other. (The Vital Machine, p. 154).

Perhaps his bionic ethics, or something like it will help with the real-life cyborg dilemmas more and more people are facing these days. However, it doesn't seem like it will work for all cyborgian problems. For example, the grandmother of one of the editors had a pacemaker installed in her chest a few decades ago. It allowed her easily a dozen or more good years of life. Then, one day, a blood vessel burst in her head. She was, in today's medical slang, "single dead." Now normally when this happens the signals from the brain that tell the heart to keep going cease, and the body dies, or achieves full death. She had insisted in her Living Will that no extraordinary measures be taken. But they already had been. She had been a cyborg for years. She had an electromechanical pacemaker that told her heart to keep beating. It could not be legally turned off. For a number of days she was kept in the neo-mort state (obeying Channel's maxim that neither organic nor mechanic was to bring about the extinction of the other), causing much emotional and financial pain. Finally, the heart stopped and she died (legally), quickly reaching "triple dead."

Her family, like the contributors to this volume, seek to understand the implications of the cyborg, because the more we understand the better we can predict, or even change, the results of our society's actions and fascinations. As Donna Haraway explains in her 1993 essay, "A Game of Cat's Cradle," this is a "messy" business.

> *What constitutes an apparatus of bodily production cannot be known in advance of engaging in the always messy projects of description, narration, intervention, inhabiting, conversing, exchanging, and building. The point is to get at how worlds are made and unmade, in order to participate in the process, in order to foster some forms of life and not others. If technology, like language is a form of like, we cannot afford neutrality about its constitution and sustenance. (p. 63)*

In any event, if your grandmother, or anybody you love, is thinking of getting a pacemaker you can't afford neutrality. Maybe it isn't so bad to "change for the machines" if we know what those changes offer, and cost. Maybe we need to know that in order to decide how we are going to change the machines ourselves. And, finally, perhaps there is as much hope as horror in the realization that China Mountain Zhang comes to in Maureen McHugh's story, **"Soon, perhaps, it will be impossible to tell where human ends and machines begin."** There are, after all, more important distinctions to make, between just and unjust, between sustaining and destroying, between stable and erratic, between pleasure and pain, between knowledge and ignorance, between effective and ineffectual, between beauty and ugliness.

All of these are dangerous dualities, to be sure, but spectrums we have to face in any event, even if only implicitly or by omission. Once, most people thought that artificial-natural, human-machine, organic and constructed, were dualities just as central to living, but the figure of the cyborg has revealed that it isn't so. And perhaps this will cast some light on the general permanence and importance of these dualities. After all the cyborg lives only through the symbiosis of ostensible opposites always in tension.

We know, from our bodies and from our machines, that tension is a great source of pleasure and power. May cyborg, and this *Handbook*, help you enjoy both and go beyond dualistic epistemologies to the epistemology of cyborg: **thesis, antithesis, synthesis, prosthesis.** And again.

The Editors

Notes

1 The term cyborg was first coined by Manfred E. Clynes, who co-authored, with Nathan S. Kline, the article "Cyborgs and Space," in 1960, and he has a particular and precise definition of cyborgs. [See the reprinted article, and the 1994 interview with Manfred Clynes, this volume. All works mentioned in this article are cited in full in the bibliography.]

2 The issue of (post)modernity is addressed in many of the contributions here, including our own, so suffice it to say that there is a startling temporal and geographical correlation between cyborgism and postmodernism.

3 The distinction between a Society of Cyborgs and Cyborg Society was first brought to our attention by our colleague Joe Dumit.

4 Among cyborg mega-stars one can clearly contrast the basically human "Six-Million-Dollar Man" with the gloriously cyborgian RoboCop and the almost totally robotic Terminator models. In *Star Trek: The Next Generation* there is another possible schema for classing cyborgs. There's Picard with his artificial heart, Geordi with his visor, Worf with a regenerated spine, Riker's clone, created through a transporter mishap, and Data with his downloaded human memories and emotions. The Borg culture is a particularly important cyborg type (see Cynthia Fuchs' article, this volume) but there have also been many other cyborgian variations from computer-generated life (including the ship itself giving birth) to holo-deck creatures with embodiment and consciousness.

The technical literature also produces complex cyborg typologies. Teleoperated systems, exoskeletons, virtual embodiments, biological androids, robots with biocomponents, genetically engineered organisms, artificial life forms, artificial intelligences, inert and interactive prosthetics, all have specific definitions and much wider connotations. In cyborgology, Mazlish, for example, has used the term "homo comboticus" to describe "computer man." Bolton writes of Turing's Man in his pro-cyborg book of the same name and Channell proclaims the age of the Vital Machine.

5 There are at least two more types of purely medical cyborgs as well: neomorts and persistent vegetative state (PVS) patients.

6 One possible reading of these might be:

•Large cyborg entities are *mega-cyborgs*, including gigantic infantrymen wearing mind-controlled exoskeletons (a Los Alamos Labs project), gigantic human-machine weapons systems (such as "Star Wars" in some of its more grandiose formulations), or even world-wide (empire or the UN) or galaxy-wide (the United Federation of Planets or the `Borg) cyborg body politic, good or evil.

•*Semi-cyborgs* are organisms that are only intermittently cyborgs, like dialysis patients linked to the life-giving machine 30 hours a week; or some small semi-industrial countries, which are only part of the world economy and world telecommunications culture at a limited number of specific places and moments.

•*Multi-cyborgs* are combinations of various types of cyborgs, or have the ability to shift among flavors of cyborgs.

•*Omni-cyborg*s make of everything they interface with a cyborg, like the omni-cyborgain theory of articles such as this one.

•A *neo-cyborg* has the outward form of cyborgism, such as an artificial limb, but lacks full homeostatic integration of the prosthesis.

•The *proto-cyborg* lacks full embodiment.

•The *ultra-cyborg* is an enhanced cybernetic organism, greater in its realm than any mere machine or all-meat creature, as with soldier cyborgs, literally, or with some athletes and mega-stars, transformed through drugs, foods, the body-sculpting of exercise, cosmetic surgery, or digital enhancement of their voice and image.

•A *hyper-cyborg* might be one where cyborg embodiments were layered or in some other way cobbled together into greater and greater cyborg bodies.

•A *retro-cyborg* would be one whose prosthetic-cybernetic transformation was designed to restore some lost form; in the case of a *pseudo-retro-cyborg*, a lost form that never was.

•The *meta-cyborg* is the non-cyborg citizen in cyborg society; it is cyborg society itself. They are not cyborgs in the strict definition of the technical term, but in context and process they are most certainly cyborgian.

7 Besides "surfing" the Internet constantly, the best way to monitor the spread of cyberculture is to read magazines like *Wired, Mondo 2000, Boing-Boing, Future Sex,* and *Extropy: The Journal of Transhumanist Thought.*

8 We prefer the term "attitude" to discipline because we reject (eschew) any claims to disciplinarity. We are interdisciplinary scholars, or multidisciplinary; how could we be otherwise and study cyborgs?

9 We also strongly encourage you to read, besides the works mentioned prominently in the text, Brahm and Driscoll's *Prosthetic Territories*, Dery's *Flame Wars*, Livingston and Halberstam's *Posthuman Bodies*, and the best collection of cyborg fiction yet assembled, Scortia and Zebrowski's *Human-Machines.*

10 This taut tale was the winner of our First, and Last, Annual Cyborg Short Story Contest.

11 There is a special relief agency that provides prosthetics for war victims, Handicap International, which is building a prosthetics workshop in Quan Tri hospital. See Malcolm Browne "They still die at Khe Sanh as farmers plow up shells," *The Oregonian*, May 15, 1994, p. A5. Diane Nelson's work is described in her article, "Maya-Hackers and the Cyberspatialized Nation State: Of Lizard Queens and Science Fiction in Guatemala," unpublished, 1994, from which the quote is taken. She, in turn, is quoting (and translating) from *Documentos del Seminario: Situación Actual y Futuro de la ALMG*, Guatemala: Patrocino del Ministerio de Cultura y Deportes, 1990, p. 42.

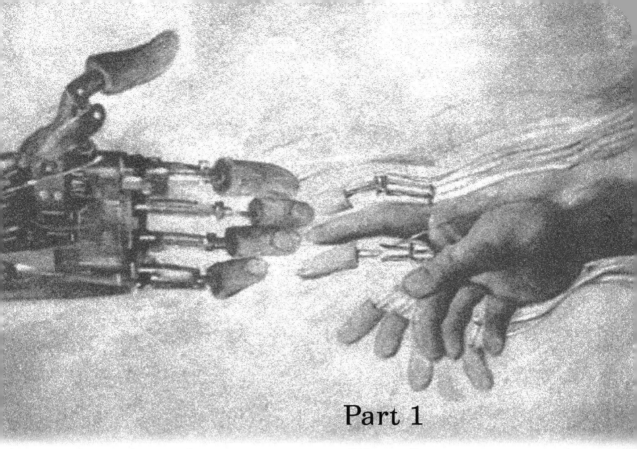

Part 1

The Genesis
of Cyborg

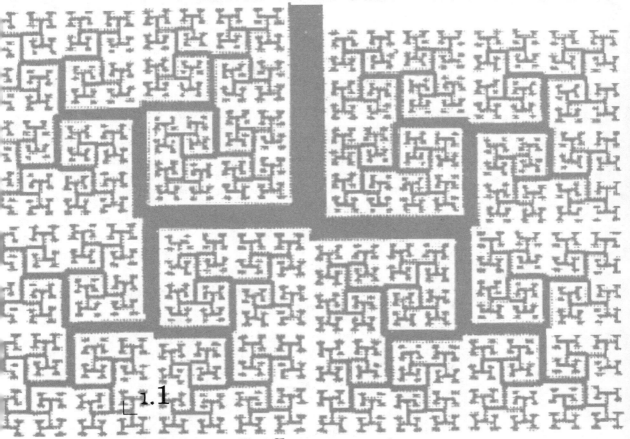

1.1

African Influences in Cybernetics

Ron Eglash

introduction

The problems of natural/artificial dualisms encountered by cyborgs are similar to those which plague activists and theorists in the long historical battles against racism. Primitivist racism operates by making non-western culture too concrete, and thus "closer to nature"—not really a culture at all, but rather beings of uncontrolled emotion and direct bodily sensation, rooted in an edenic ecology. Orientalist racism operates by making non-western culture too abstract, and thus "arabesque"—not really a "natural" human, but one devoid of emotion, caring only for money and an inscrutable spiritual transcendence. Racism on the African continent—tending towards Orientalism in the north, and Primitivism in the south—precludes any simple opposition that a category like "African cybernetics" might hold. An anti-racist characterization of African influences in cybernetics must be situated in ways which do not merely reverse or refute its claims, but address its historical construction.

Opposition to racism has often been composed through two totalizing, essentialist strategies: sameness and difference. For example, Mudimbe (1988) demonstrates how the category of a singular "African philosophy" has been primarily an invention of difference, having its creation in the play between "the beautiful myths of the 'savage mind' and the African ideological strategies of otherness." In contrast, structuralists such as Lévi-Strauss have attempted to prove that African conceptual systems are fundamentally the same as those of Europeans (both having their basis in arbitrary symbol systems). The problem of these unitary assessments of epistemological status is made particularly clear by the contradictions in the philosophic approach of Sandra Harding, where African conceptual views were at first characterized as the holistic opposite of Western reductionism (Harding 1989), and then soon after as having exactly the same analytic approach as Western science (Harding 1990). As Mudimbe notes, neither sameness nor difference will suffice.

This critique indicates that the analysis of interactions between cybernetic theory and the African diaspora should not be limited to a purely epistemological perspective. At the same time, however, socially grounded analyses of science have all too often presented a kind of "Realpolitik" approach to the social construction of cybernetics, **one in which the science of computation and control systems is merely a thin disguise for methods of social domination and control** (e.g., Lilienfeld 1974). Here any subaltern identity (female, non-white, working class, etc.) appears only as yet another powerless victim, and typically one for whom a previously natural existence is endangered by the intrusion of artifice. Thus the focus of this essay on African *contributions* to cybernetics is not an attempt to overlook the brutal tragedies enacted by that science, but rather to underscore the multifaceted aspects of its history, and thus possibilities for resistance and reconfigurations. By moving between questions of epistemological structure and social constructions of science, this essay will suggest some possible origins of cybernetic theory in African culture, ways that Black people have negotiated the rise of cybernetic technology in the West, and the confluence of these histories in the lived experience of the African diaspora.

information and Representation in Cybernetics

Cybernetic theory is based on two dimensions of communication systems. One is the information structure, the other the physical representation of that information. The most fundamental characteristic of an information structure is its computational complexity, which is a measure of its capacity for *recursion* (i.e., self-reference, reflexivity). This mathematical result agrees nicely with our intuition about the crucial role of reflexive awareness in our own "information structure." **The most fundamental characteristic of a representational system is the analog-digital distinction.** Digital representation requires a code table (the dictionary, Morse code, the genetic code, etc.) based on physically arbitrary symbols (text, numbers, flag colors, etc.). Saussure postulated this characteristic when he spoke of the "arbitrariness of the linguistic signifier." Analog representation is based on a proportionality between physical changes in a signal and changes in the information it represents (e.g., waveforms, images, vocal intonation). For example, as my excitement increases, so does the loudness of my voice. While digital systems use grammars, syntax, and other relations of symbolic logic, analog systems are based on physical dynamics—the realm of feedback, hysteresis, and resonance. This dichotomy is fundamental to current cybernetic debates concerning, for example, which type of representation is used by neurons in the human brain, or the type recommended for artificial brains.

In the first years of American cybernetics, analog and digital systems were seen as epistemologically equivalent, both considered capable of complex kinds of representation (cf. Rubinoff 1953). But by the early 1960s a political dualism was coupled to this representation dichotomy. The "counterculture" radicals of the cybernetics community—Norbert Wiener, Gregory Bateson, Hazel Henderson, Paul Goodman, Kenneth Boulding, Barry Commoner, Margaret Mead, among others—made the erroneous claim that analog systems were more concrete, more "real" or "natural," and therefore (according to this romantic cybernetics) ethically superior. In social domains, this converged with Rousseau's legacy of the moral superiority of oral over literate cultures.[1] Thus, for example, McLuhan (1966) writes:

> It was ... a considerable revelation when writing came to detribalize and to individualize man.... Cybernation seems to be taking us out of the visual world of classified data back into the tribal world of integral patterns and corporate awareness (McLuhan 1966, p 102).

For African-Americans this meant a debilitating valorization. They could use this ethical claim to combat some racism, but only in terms of identifying as unconscious, innocent natives in a lost past. Thus African modes of *representation* in the use of sculpture, movement and rhythm were often abandoned to modernist claims that Africa was the culture of non-representation, the culture of the Real. By the 1970s, widespread epistemological critiques of realism—noting that it is representation that allows self-consciousness and intentionality—resulted in interpretations which limited cultural analysis to arbitrary signifiers. African dance, for example, would be a set of movement symbols, not a waveform.

Subsequently, African cultural analysis became split between those who retained the modernist trope of African identity grounded in naturalist realism (recognizing analog systems but refusing to see them as representation), versus those who adopted the postmodern trope of textual metaphor (which avoids primitivism at the expense of abandoning recognition of analog systems)—**reggae versus rap**.[2]

Postmodern cybernetics, however, has shown that analog systems are capable of the flexible representation required to perform complex (Turing Machine-equivalent) computations, as demonstrated in both theory and experiment (Wolfram 1984, Touretzky 1986, Rubel 1989, Blum, Shub and Smale 1989). In particular, a new appreciation for analog systems was fundamental to the rise of fractal geometry, nonlinear dynamics, and other branches of chaos theory (Gleick 1987, see also Dewdney 1985, Pagels 1988). By viewing physical systems as forms of computation, rather than merely inert structures, researchers became open to the possibility of having infinite variation in deterministic physical dynamics. **Analog systems can achieve the same levels of recursive computation as digital systems; the two are epistemological equals.**

In other words, the appeal to digital systems in African culture may well have been a necessary antidote to the skewed social portrait of it, but it is not the only recourse for combating ethnocentric epistemological claims. African cultures have indeed developed systems of analog representation which are capable of the com-

Fig. 1. Branching fractals in Saharan cities

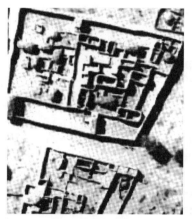

Fig. 2. Logone-Birni in Cameroon

Fig. 3. Songay village of Labbazanga

plexities of recursion, and there are indications that this indigenous technology has been in conversation with cybernetic concepts in the west.

Africa in the origins of the cybernetics

The use of African material culture as a form of analog representation is particularly vivid in cases of recursive information flow. In African architecture, recursive scaling—that is fractal geometry—can be seen in a variety of forms. In North Africa it is associated with the feedback of the "arabesque" artistic form, particularly in the branches of branches forming city streets (figure 1). In Central Africa it can be seen in additive rectangular wall formations (figure 2), and in West Africa we see circular swirls of circular houses and granaries (figure 3). This is not limited to a visual argument; the fractal structure of African settlement patterns has been confirmed by computational analysis of digitized photos in Eglash and Broadwell (1989).

Recursive scaling in Egyptian temples can be viewed as a formalized version of the fractal architecture found elsewhere in Africa, and is most significant in its use of the Fibonacci sequence (Badawy 1965; see Petruso 1985 for additional Egyptian use of the sequence). The sequence is named for Leonardo Fibonacci (ca. 1175–1250), who is also associated with an unusual example of recursive architecture in Europe (Schroeder 1991, p 85). The Fibonacci sequence was one of the first mathematical models for biological growth patterns, and inspired Alan Turing and other important figures in the history of computational morphogenesis. Since Fibonacci was sent to North Africa as a boy, and devoted his years there to mathematics education (Gies and Gies 1969), it is possible that this seminal example of recursive scaling is of African origin.

Benoît Mandelbrot, the "father of fractal geometry," reports that his invention is the result of combining the abstract mathematics of Georg Cantor with the empirical studies of H. E. Hurst. Cantor was a nineteenth-century Rosicrucian mystic, who often combined his mathematics with his religious belief. His cousin Moritz Cantor was a famous scholar in the geometry of Egyptian art and architecture. Given these facts, and the similarity of this first European fractal to the Egyptian architectural structure symbolizing creation (the lotus), an Egyptian origin is likely here as well. H.E. Hurst also has Egyptian connections, as will be discussed shortly.

Recursive scaling also occurs in the case of certain African sculptural forms, where it is often related to animist religious concepts. Although frequently reduced to "fetish worship" or "natural spirituality" in western descriptions, animism is, on the contrary, typically concerned with a cultural transfer of information or energy through physical dynamics. While animist religions are still active in Africa today, this conception of animated physical form is quite ancient, and is reflected in the myths of God creating humanity from clay. In some North African traditions certain spiritualists could create their own clay robots, "golems."

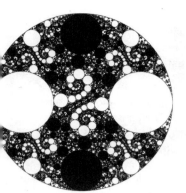

Fig. 4. Mandelbrot fractal

Fig. 5

Goldsmith (1981) reports golem legends going back to the fourth century B.C.E., and describes their continuing popularity in Jewish legend. Norbert Weiner, the Jewish founder of analog cybernetics, was quite influenced by this concept of information embedded in physical dynamics (Heims 1984, Eglash 1992). He made several references to the golem in his writing, and reported that even as a child he was fascinated by the idea of making a doll come alive. His religious identity was closely tied to *gashmuit*, the informal, physical (and traditionally female) side of Judaism, and he was particularly proud of his ancestry to famed Egyptian physician Moses Maimonides.

In addition to spatial analog representation, many African societies have developed techniques for the analog representation of time-varying systems, including transformation into frequency- or phase-domain representation. In figure 5 we see animist energy flow, drawn by a Bambara seer for the author, visualized as a spiral wave emanating from a sacrificial egg. The dashed lines inside the figure are a digital code symbolizing good fortune. Undulatory schemes in Egyptian art (Badawy 1959) show an understanding of motion as a rhythmic time series, and the transformation of time-series to a frequency-domain representation can be seen in African conceptualizations of circular time (figure 6). The extreme in African time-series analysis is the search for patterns in the Nile floods. The most recent data set, taken once a year for 15 centuries, became the basis for the work of H.E. Hurst mentioned previously. A British civil servant, Hurst spent 62 years in Egypt, and finally deduced a scaling law, based on this time-series, which Mandelbrot used to bring Cantor's abstract set theory into empirical practice.

The most common frequency analysis used by Weiner and others in modern cybernetics is the Fourier transform. Fourier began his work with an analysis of Descartes' theory of equations; he did not leave this static framework until his expedition to Egypt in 1798, where he analyzed the geometry of Egyptian architecture. It was here that he devised the basis for the Fourier transform. A comparison of Fourier's visualizations of convergence of a sequence with a diagram of Egyptian architecture (which, because of the Fibonacci sequence, also shows convergence to a limit), suggests that the African concept of recursive structure and dynamic form may have contributed to this analysis as well.

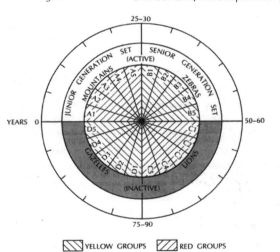

YELLOW GROUPS   RED GROUPS

Fig. 6 - Cyclic time in Africa. Cycling age-grade system of the Karimojong of Uganda. They recognize four fixed generation sets, encompassing a total span of 100 to 120 years. Each generation set is subdivided into five age sets. The Gazelles and Zebras, who are called "yellow" because of their brass ornaments, are associated in a grandfather-grandson relationship. A similar relationship exists between the "red" generation sets, the Lions and Mountains. In this diagram only the Zebras and the Mountains are active, the former in a position of authority and the latter of obedience. (in Zaslavsky 1973, p. 263)

African influence in American cybernetics

Related to these systems of analog recursion are studies on computational self-reference; these too have possible African influences. For example, Seymour Papert, a white computer scientist who championed hierarchical, non-recursive computing in the 1960s, made a dramatic conversion to decentralized computation following his U.N. work in

21 }

Africa in the mid-70s. Another white engineer, N. Negroponte, developed his conceptions for self-organized computing following his study of "vernacular architecture," most of which was African. Earl Jones, one of the first African-American computer engineers, was in innovator in decentralized data distribution.

Analog computing networks have become increasingly important in the post-modern phase of American cybernetics, where they are no longer a stronghold of holistic hippy science, but rather a promising (and well-funded) area of research for the military and industry (Eglash 1990, 1992). African influences in American science date back to the contributions in biological knowledge and metalwork by slaves; the biological (especially botanical) is particularly significant for cybernetics due to its involvement in models of information coding. While romantic accounts of cultural difference would use botanical expertise to emphasize the "naturalness" of African traditions, this is certainly not the only interpretation. George Washington Carver, for example, declared that not only did God create the Kingdom of Plants and the Kingdom of Animals, but that He also had a "Kingdom of the Synthetic." This spiritual legitimation of the artificial fits well into the African religious traditions of analog representation discussed previously.

A direct line for African influences in analog cybernetics can be seen in the work of E. E. Just, who used music as both a conceptual model for decentralized biological morphogenesis, and as a cultural basis for understanding his African heritage (Manning 1983, pp. 203, 261). Just's work, particularly that on information encoded in non-symbolic representation (based in part on Just's rebellion against the position that the only intracellular information is that of a "master code" in the cell nucleus), was taken up by Ross G. Henderson, an important influence in the General Systems Theory (GST) community (Haraway 1976), which in turn influenced the origins of cybernetics through studies of aggregate self-organizing phenomena and positive feedback loops.

Fig. 7. Many traditional African hairstyles use recursive procedures, often embedding layers of social meaning in their braids of braids. This style, "le fils a tresse" (from Cameroon) uses a fractal branching pattern.

As previously noted, the GST and related cybernetics community took a romanticist turn in the 1960s, which resulted in a disabling of the analog conception by Realism (cf. Varela's account of the "nonrepresentationist point of view" developed in the 1960s with McCulloch, Maturana, and others [Varela 1987, pp. 48-49]). What little involvement the Black community had in the cybernetics movement was, however, often opposed to this romantic tendency. For example, at the first Cybercultural Research conference in 1966, James Boggs, a Black political activist, suggested that the "new cybercultural society" would not be alienating to Blacks because (unlike whites) they could draw on a labor history in which their dual identity as both biological automatic machines and the makers/users of machines were deeply imbricated with their cultural identity (Boggs 1966, p. 172). Black identification with categories of the artificial are here political, but converge with the same conceptions that informed Carver and others; concepts that parallel the animist legitimations of the artificial in Africa.

The lived experience of African-Americans' interactions between these African diasporic innovations and their survival of American racism is particularly apparent in the work of African-American women. As Nakano Glenn (1992) argues for the case of service workers, gender and race cannot be reduced to "additive oppressions," and must be seen as the site of an interlocking or relational dynamic. For example, both the traditional work of African women (Hay and Sticher 1984), and specific labor locations for women of all ethnicities in America have contributed to the frequency of their involvement in biomedically related fields. From 1876 to 1969, over half of the Black women science Ph. D.s have been in bio-sciences (Jay 1971), and the Black women inventor, Clara Fry, specialized in health-care tools (James 1989, p. 80). The most relevant example in cybernetics is the work of Patricia Cowings, who makes cyborgs for NASA. In an interview in this volume, Cowings discusses her use of analog biofeedback as a method for reducing motion sickness in space, and notes several complex interactions between her identity as a Black woman and her successful career in cybernetics. Yet she has distanced herself from the claims for any simple mimesis of "African culture" in her construction of cybernetics. The contributions of African-American women to what has become modern cybernetics should be seen as a form of resistance that cannot be reduced to either the restoration of tradition or a relocation to universalism.

Black cybernetics in the postmodern era

The rejection of cybernetic romanticism by radical African-Americans was no longer necessary by the mid-70s, when youth sub-culture had turned from hippy naturalism to the urban affinity of punk-rock and hip-hop (Hall 1980, Hebdige 1987, hooks 1990). Thus the popular rap group Digital Underground displays an appreciation of cybernetics which is politically oppositional but no longer primitivist or naturalizing. While the impact of new cybernetic technologies on African-American communities has been part of a long history of labor displacement (Jones 1985, Hacker 1979), environmental racism, and other subjugations, here we can also see some hints for the appropriation of technology in new configurations. For example, the famous "scratch" sound in hip-hop came about when the normally silent back-cue of the dee-jay's turntable was amplified and moved in time to the beat, thus changing a passive reproduction into an active synthetic instrument; turning tables on the turntable.

To what extent is this subcultural cybernetics merely "bricolage"—reassembling available components for a practical goal—and to what extent is it a deeper understanding of abstract principles? First, we should note that "official" cybernetics is both; it used pre-existing abstract principles—feedback, information theory, etc.—for practical application in a new assemblage. Indeed, the divisions between bricolage and science in general are far more permeable than we have been led to believe. This point has been admirably made in Sherry Turkle's study of bricolage programming styles in the hacker community, where she also notes that the interaction between popular culture and the scientific community is an active source of ideas in both directions.

Let us pursue this question a bit further. Setting aside both the definition of cybernetics and its interaction with popular culture, **what kinds of technological capability does the vernacular cybernetics of the African-American community represent?** One clear illustration can be found in the striking utilization of the analog/digital dualism for the production of musical signifiers in the divisions between reggae and rap music. As previously noted, reggae is more aligned with the naturalizing trope of modernity, and rap with the artificial affinities of the postmodern. In reggae we see the language of analog representation. "Rastaman Vibration" lets us "tune into de riddem;" we become resonant nodes linked by the waveforms of a polyphonic beat. In rap music it is digital communication that signifies cultural identity. Natural harmonies are broken up by arbitrary soundbites and vocal collage, and the melody is subordinated to a newly spliced code; a mutant reprogramming of the social software.

From the viewpoint of cultural studies, the utilization of the analog/digital division in reggae vs. rap does indeed count as a technological capability. But would it also count from the view of a cybernetics engineer? The use of the scratch sound mentioned earlier is associated with the birth of rap, but phonograph records are analog devices. Similarly, reggae makes use of an array of both analog and digital audio equipment. Isn't the use of technological language by African diasporic subcultures merely linguistic play? The answer is no. Despite (in fact because of) the wide assortment of apparatus, rap and reggae artists have created a technology for signal processing that would indeed meet the specificities of current cybernetics engineering. The evidence for this begins in the work of Richard Voss, who first measured the fractal dimension for various types of acoustic communication in 1977. Voss discovered that the physical arbitrariness of digital signifiers meant that the waveforms of digital communication were a succession of fairly random signals, overall creating a "white-noise spectrum." In analog waveforms, on the other hand, long-term changes in information were reflected in long-term signal changes. Since there were similar information changes on many scales, the result was a fractal structure, or "1/F noise spectrum," in the case of analog communication. Thus the waveform created by pitch changes in speech, which are primarily due to the phonetic differences between words, tends toward a white-noise spectrum, while the pitch signal of music shows the fractal structure of analog representation.

Rap

Fractal Dimension	Source
1.246	Why is that? (Boogie Down Productions)
1.219	Hold Your Own (Kid Frost)
1.170	Eric B for President (Eric B)
1.274	The Bridge (M.C. Shan)
1.259	Supersonic (JJ Fad)
1.186	Queen of Royal Badness (Queen Latifah)
1.158	10% Dis (M.C. Lyte)

Reggae

1.454	Many Rivers to Cross (Jimmy Cliff)
1.286	Trench Town Rock (Bob Marley)
1.341	Pressure Drop (Jimmy Cliff)
1.329	Rivers of Babylon (Jimmy Cliff)
1.285	You Can Get It (Jimmy Cliff)
1.386	Sing Our Own Song (Judy Mowatt)
1.374	Rock Me (Judy Mowatt)

Figure 8: Fractal dimension differences in Rap vs. Reggae

Voss (1988) later showed that this relationship held for all types of music, both instrumental and vocal, with samples ranging from Indian ragas to Russian folksongs. My own studies (Eglash 1993) show that while reggae music also has this fractal structure, **rap is the only music** (aside from avant-garde experiments such as those of John Cage) **which violates this rule** (figure 8). The reason for this is the intentional violation of analog representation by digital coding, a violation that invokes rap artists' oppositional stance, but also offers a positive outlook in the possibilities for their cybernetic innovation. Moreover, the rap-reggae fusions that are now becoming increasingly popular (e.g. ragamuffin) have characteristics which indicate that their signals are likely to average a fractal dimension value half-way between the two. This precision of control over an abstract cybernetic principle indicates that it is not simply a matter of the adoption of terminology; African diasporic identity is expressed in these examples through a conscious manipulation of complex signal characteristics.

Applications to science education

One might think that such rich vernacular cybernetics would be an obvious resource for improving science education, but such opportunities have been ignored. For example, The National Assessment of Educational Progress reported in Anderson (1989) suggests that Black high-school students have cultural barriers to their participation in science, based on studies which supposedly indicate "fewer science-related experiences" (p. 45). But the examples of such experiences—planting a seed, watching an egg hatch—are primarily naturalistic; the artificial realms of video games and audio technology, which are surely "science-related," are completely excluded. Even more disturbing is the claim of "cultural barriers" based on reports that "a substantial portion of Blacks did not have confidence in the ability of science to solve most or some of our problems," and that they were "less convinced of the benefits of science to society." Here a potential route to involving Black youth in science education—by recognizing their critique as an intelligent understanding of science history—is instead dismissed as ignorance.

Similarly, an ideology of individualism is persistently portrayed as a neutral, universal characteristic of scientific style and rational thought (e.g., Pearson 1985, p. 174) which African-Americans must adopt. But like the turn to collective computation in cybernetics, collective scientific production can often be a robust path to success. Both this obligatory individualism, and the previously noted naturalistic assumptions, operate in the NAEP's report that African-American youth "did not believe so strongly as their national peers that individuals' actions can make a difference in solving societal problems." Reluctance toward "using an economy car, separating trash for recycling, or turning off lights" are symptoms of this pathology (p. 48). A better understanding of African-American cultural connections to science would suggest that such individualistic approaches are neither universal nor uniquely beneficial.

Conclusion

In summary: the history of African interactions with cybernetics does not revolve around a single essence. It includes white engineers bringing ideas from Africa and Black engineers who make no claims about inspiration from any ethnic tradition. A portrait of the multivariate dynamics between the African diaspora and the information sciences—from the celebration of popular culture to the struggle of minority scientists—must be brought together with an understanding of the lived experience of people, from a multiplicity of ethnic configurations, who have found themselves fused, networked and oddly interfaced in the evolution of cyborg society.

Notes

1. This was combated in different ways by structuralists and post-structuralists. According to Levi-Strauss, the arbitrariness of non-western symbolics (e.g., a fox stands for stupidity in one mythology and cunning in another) proves that they are just as digital as Europeans, with the exception of the oral/literate dichotomy. Derrida, while agreeing with this position, takes Lévi-Strauss to task for retaining the oral/literate dichotomy, and details how speech is just writing in air instead of paper—thus again using digitality as the justification for epistemological equivalence. Tragically, poststructuralists have adopted Rousseau's assumption that analog representation is not as abstract as digital.

2. That's not to say that the division is uniform (e.g., occasional use of digital motifs in reggae), nor that there are not instances of the third alternative, analog representation, on either side. For example, while Monique Wittig's *The Lesbian Body* used digital collage to create a European-centered self-birthing, Audre

Lorde's lesbian self-birthing in *Zami* was equally recursive, but based on analog representation.

References

Armstrong, R.P. *The Affecting Presence.* Urbana: University of Illinois Press, 1971.

Badawy, A. *Ancient Egyptian Architectural Design.* Berkeley; University of California Press, 1965.

Badawy, A. "Figurations egyptiennes à schéma ondulatoire." *Chronique d'Egypte.* 34 (68), July 1959.

Blum, L., Shub, M., and Smale, S. "On a theory of computation and complexity over the real numbers." *Bulletin of the American Mathematical Society* 21, no. 1, July 1989, pp. 1-46.

Boggs, J. "The Negro in Cybernation." in *The evolving society; the proceedings of the first annual Conference on the Cybercultural Revolution—Cybernetics and Automation,* 1966.

Butcher, E.L. and Petrie, W.M.F. "Early Forms of the Cross." *Ancient Egypt.* 1916, part III, pp 1-109.

Clark, G. *The Man Who Talks to Flowers.* St. Paul: Macalester Park Publications, 1939.

Clayton, P.A. *The Rediscovery of Ancient Egypt.* London: Thames and Hudson, 1982.

Cole, H.M. and Ross, D.H. *The Arts of Ghana.* Los Angeles: UCLA Museum of Cultural History, 1977.

Dewdney, A.K. "Building computers in one dimension sheds light on irreducibly complicated phenomena." *Scientific American,* (February 1985) pp. 18-30.

Derrida, J. *Of Grammatology.* Baltimore: Johns Hopkins, 1974.

Duly, C. *The Houses of Mankind.* London: Blacker Calmann Cooper, 1979.

Eglash, R. "Postmodern cybernetics: holistic military technology." Paper delivered at Social Studies of Science Society, Irvine Ca. November 1990.

Eglash, R. *A Cybernetics of Chaos.* Ph.D. Dissertation in History of Consciousness, University of California, Santa Cruz, 1992.

Eglash, R. "Inferring representation type from the fractal dimension of biological communication waveforms." *Journal of Social and Evolutionary Structures.* 16, no. 4, 1993.

Eglash, R. and Broadwell, P. "Fractal geometry in traditional African architecture." *Dynamics Newsletter.* June 1989, pp 1-10.

Gleick, J. *Chaos—making of a new science.* New York: Viking, 1987.

Gies, J. and Gies, F. *Leonardo of Pisa and the New Mathematics of the Middle Ages.* New York: Thomas Crowell, 1969.

Hall, S. (ed) *Culture, media, language: working papers in cultural studies, 1972-79.* London: Hutchinson, 1980.

Hambidge, J. *The Elements of Dynamic Symmetry.* New York: Dover, 1967.

Haraway, D. J. *Crystals, Fabrics, and Fields.* New Haven: Yale University Press, 1976.

Harding, S. *The Science Question in Feminism.* Ithaca: Cornell University Press, 1986.

Harding, S. *Whose Science? Whose Knowledge? Thinking From Women's Lives.* Ithaca: Cornell University Press, 1991.

Hay, M.J. and Stichter, S. (eds.). *African Women South of the Sahara.* New York: Longman, 1984.

Hebdige, D. *Cut 'n' mix: culture, identity, and Caribbean music.* New York: Methuen, 1987. *Negroes in Science.* Detroit: Balamp, 1971.

Jones, J. *Labor of Love, Labor of Sorrow: Black Women, Work and the Family from Slavery to the Present.* New York: Basic Books, 1985.

Lamy, L. *Egyptian Mysteries.* New York: Crossroad, 1981.

Lilienfeld, R. *The Rise of Systems Theory.* New York: John Wiley, 1978.

Lorde, A. *Zani: A New Spelling of My Name,* New York: The Crossing Press, 1982.

Mandelbrot, Benoît. *The Fractal Geometry of Nature.* San Francisco: W.H. Freeman, 1982.

Manning, K. R. *Black Apollo of Science.* Oxford University Press, 1983.

May, R. "Simple Mathematical Models with Very Complicated Dynamics." *Nature* no. 261 (1976), pp. 459-67.

McMurry, L. O. *George Washington Carver, Scientist and Symbol.* New York: Oxford University Press, 1981.

Museum of Primitive Art, New York. *Bambara Sculpture from the Western Sudan.* New York: University Publishers, 1960.

Negroponte, N. *Soft Architecture Machines.* Cambridge: MIT Press, 1972.

Pagels, H. R. *The Dreams of Reason: the Computer and the Rise of the Sciences of Complexity.* New York:

Simon and Schuster, 1988.

Perczel, C.F. "Ethiopian Crosses at the Portland Art Museum." *African Arts* 12, no. 3, 1975.

Petrie, F. "The Treasure of Antinoe," *Ancient Egypt* 1920, part 1, pp. 1-14.

Petruso, K. M. "Additive Progression in Prehistoric Mathematics: A Conjecture." *Historia Mathematica* 12 (1985), 101-106.

Pitt-Rivers, A. *Antique Works of Art from Benin.* New York: Dover, 1976.

Roössler, O. *Zeitschrift für Naturforschung* 13a, (1976), p. 259.

Rubel, L.A. "Digital simulation of analog computation and Church's thesis." *Journal of Symbolic Logic.* v.34, no. 3 (September 1989) pp. 1011-1017.

Rubinoff, M. "Analogue and digital computers—a comparison." *Proceedings of the IRE.* (October 1953), pp 1254-1262.

Ruelle, D. and Takens, F. "On the nature of turbulence." *Communications in Mathematical Physics* 20 (1971), pp. 167-92.

Schroeder, M. *Fractals, Chaos, and Power Laws.* New York: W. H. Freeman, 1991.

Sertima, I. V. *Blacks in Science.* New Brunswick: Transaction Books, 1984.

Thompson, R. F. *African Art in Motion.* Los Angeles: University of California Press, 1974.

Touretzky, D. S. "BoltzCONS: Reconciling connectionism with the recursive nature of stacks and trees." *Proceedings of the 8th Annual Conference of the Cognitive Science Society.* (1986), pp 522-530.

Vergis, A., Steiglitz, K., and Dickinson, B. "The complexity of analog computation." Technical report No. 337, Dept of Electrical Engineering and Computer Science, Princeton University (February 1985).

Voss, R. F. & Clarke, J. "1/F noise in music". *Journal of the Acoustical Society of America* 63, no. 1, (1978), pp. 258-263.

Wittig, M. *The Lesbian Body.* Boston, Beacon Press, 1973.

Wolfram, S. "Universality and complexity in cellular automata" *Physica* 10 D (1984), 1-35.

Zaslavsky, Claudia. *Africa Counts.* Boston: Prindle, Weber & Schmidt, 1973.

Cyborgs and Space

Altering man's bodily functions to meet the requirements of extraterrestrial environments would be more logical than providing an earthly environment for him in space...Artifact-organism systems which would extend man's unconscious, self-regulatory controls are one possibility

By Manfred E. Clynes and Nathan S. Kline

Clynes   **Kline**

Manfred E. Clynes has since 1956 been chief research scientist at Rockland State, in charge of the Dynamic Simulation Lab. A graduate of the Univ. of Melbourne, Australia, and holder of an M.S. from Juilliard School, he has for the past 10 years been engaged in the design and development of physiological instrumentation and apparatus, ultrasonic transducers, and electronic data-processing systems.

Nathan S. Kline has been director of research at Rockland State since 1952 and an assistant professor of clinical psychiatry at the Columbia Univ. College of Physicians and Surgeons since 1957. Author of more than 100 papers, Dr. Kline holds a New York Newspaper Guild Page One Award in science, the Adolph Meyer Award of the Assn. for Improvement of Mental Health, and the Albert Lasker Award of the American Public Health Association.

This article is based on a paper presented under the title of "Drugs, Space and Cybernetics" at the Psychophysiological Aspects of Space Flight Symposium sponsored by the AF School of Aviation Medicine in San Antonio, Tex., in May. The complete paper appeared in the Symposium proceedings, published by Columbia Univ. Press.

SPACE travel challenges mankind not only technologically but also spiritually, in that it invites man to take an active part in his own biological evolution. Scientific advances of the future may thus be utilized to permit man's existence in environments which differ radically from those provided by nature as we know it.

The task of adapting man's body to any environment he may choose will be made easier by increased knowledge of homeostatic functioning, the cybernetic aspects of which are just beginning to be understood and investigated. In the past evolution brought about the altering of bodily functions to suit different environments. Starting as of now, it will be possible to achieve this to some degree *without alteration of heredity* by suitable biochemical, physiological, and electronic modifications of man's existing modus vivendi.

Homeostatic mechanisms found in organisms are designed to provide stable operation in the particular environment of the organism. Examples of three successful alternate solutions provided by biological mechanisms to the body-environment problem with regard to operating temperature are man, hibernating animals, and poikilothermic fish (organisms with blood that take on the temperature of the environment).

Various biological solutions have also been developed for another problem—respiration. Mammals, fish, insects, and plants each have a different solution with inherent limitations but eminently suitable *for their field of operation*. Should an organism desire to live outside this field, an apparently "insurmountable" problem exists.

However, is the problem really insurmountable? If a fish wished to live on land, it could not readily do so. If, however, a particularly intelligent and resourceful fish could be found, who had studied a good deal of biochemistry and physiology, was a master engineer and cyberneticist, and had excellent lab facilities available to him, this fish could

(*Reprinted from* ASTRONAUTICS, *September*, 1960)

One of the first Cyborgs, this 220-gm rat has under its skin the Rose osmotic pump (shown in close-up below), designed to permit continuous injections of chemicals at a slow controlled rate into an organism without any attention on the part of the organism.

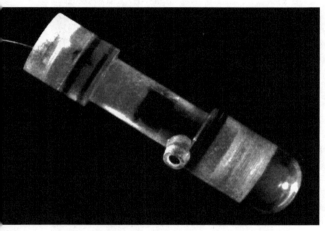

conceivably have the ability to design an instrument which would allow him to live on land and breathe air quite readily.

In the same manner, it is becoming apparent that we will in the not too distant future have sufficient knowledge to design instrumental control systems which will make it possible for our bodies to do things which are no less difficult.

The environment with which man is now concerned is that of space. Biologically, what are the changes necessary to allow man to live adequately in the space environment? Artificial atmospheres encapsulated in some sort of enclosure constitute only temporizing, and dangerous temporizing at that, since we place ourselves in the same position as a fish

taking a small quantity of water along with him to live on land. The bubble all too easily bursts.

The biological problems which exist in space travel are many and varied. Long-term space voyages, involving flights not of days, months or years, but possibly of several thousand years, will eventually be hard realities, and resultant physiological and psychological conditions must be considered.

These are reviewed below. In some cases, we have proposed solutions which probably could be devised with presently available knowledge and techniques. Other solutions are projections into the future which by their very nature must resemble science fiction. To illustrate, there may be much more efficient ways of carrying out the functions of the respiratory system than by breathing, which becomes cumbersome in space. One proposed solution for the not too distant future is relatively simple: Don't breathe!

If man attempts partial adaptation to space conditions, instead of insisting on carrying his whole environment along with him, a number of new possibilities appear. One is then led to think about the incorporation of integral exogenous devices to bring about the biological changes which might be necessary in man's homeostatic mechanisms to allow him to live in space *qua natura.*

The autonomic nervous system and endocrine glands cooperate in man to maintain the multiple balances required for his existence. They do this without conscious control, although they are amenable to such influence. Necessary readjustments of these automatic responses under extraterrestrial conditions require the aid of control theory, as well as extensive physiological knowledge.

Cyborg—Frees Man to Explore

What are some of the devices necessary for creating self-regulating man-machine systems? This self-regulation must function without the benefit of consciousness in order to cooperate with the body's own autonomous homeostatic controls. For the exogenously extended organizational complex functioning as an integrated homeostatic system unconsciously, we propose the term "Cyborg." The Cyborg deliberately incorporates exogenous components extending the self-regulatory control function of the organism in order to adapt it to new environments.

If man in space, in addition to flying his vehicle, must continuously be checking on things and making adjustments merely in order to keep himself alive, he becomes a slave to the machine. The purpose of the Cyborg, as well as his own homeostatic systems, is to provide an organizational system in which such robot-like problems are taken care of automatically and unconsciously, leaving man free to explore, to create, to think, and to feel.

One device helpful to consideration of the construction of Cyborgs, which is already available, is the ingenious osmotic pressure pump capsule developed by S. Rose for continuous slow injections of biochemically active substances at a biological rate. The capsule is incorporated into the organism and allows administration of a selected drug at a particular organ and at a continuous variable rate, without any attention on the part of the organism.

Capsules are already available which will deliver as little as 0.01 ml/day for 200 days, and there is no reason why this time could not be extended considerably. The apparatus has already been used on rabbits and rats, and for continuous heparin injection in man. No untoward general effect on health was noted when the injector was buried in animals. As long as five years ago, an injector 7 cm long and 1.4 cm in diameter, weighing 15 gm, was successfully buried under the skin of rats weighing 150-250 gm. The photo on page 27 shows a rat weighing 220 gm with an injector *in situ*.

The combination of an osmotic pressure pump capsule with sensing and controlling mechanisms can form a continuous control loop which will act as an adjunct to the body's own autonomous controls. In this manner, these controls can be changed to the desired performance characteristics under various environmental conditions. If these characteristics were determined, such a system would be possible today with the selection of appropriate drugs.

For example, systolic blood pressure may be sensed, compared to a reference value based on the space conditions encountered, and regulated by letting the difference between sensed and reference pressures control administration of an adrenergic or vasodilator drug. Of course, any such system presupposes that we would be cognizant of what optimum blood pressure would be under various space conditions.

While it is quite difficult to set up per limits to "natural" human physiological and psychological performance, we can take as minimal the capabilities demonstrated under control conditions such as yoga or hypnosis. The imagination is stretched by the muscular control of which even the undergraduate at a Yoga College is capable, and hypnosis per se may prove to have a definite place in space travel, although there is much to be learned about the phenomena of dissociation, generalization of instructions, and abdication of executive control.

We are now working on a new preparation which may greatly enhance hypnotizability, so that pharmacological and hypnotic approaches may be symbiotically combined.

Psycho-Physiological Problems

Let us now turn our attention to some of the special physiological and psychological problems involved in space travel, and see how Cyborg dynamics may help achieve better understanding and utilization of man's natural abilities.

Wakefulness. For flights of relatively short or moderate duration—a few weeks or even a few months—it would appear desirable to keep the astronaut continuously awake and fully alert. The extension of normal functioning through the use of that group of drugs known as psychic energizers, with adjunctive medication, for this purpose is a present-day reality. In flights lasting a month or two, no more than a few hours a day of sleep would be required in the normal environment if such drugs were employed. Tests indicate efficiency tends to increase, rather than decrease, under such a regime, and extended usage appears entirely feasible.

Radiation Effects. One subsystem of the Cyborg would involve a sensor to detect radiation levels and an adaptation of the Rose osmotic pump which would automatically inject protective pharmaceuticals in appropriate doses. Experiments at the AF School of Aviation Medicine already indicate an increase in radiation resistance resulting from combined administration of aminoethylisothiouronium and cysteine to monkeys.

Metabolic Problems and Hypothermic Controls. In the case of prolonged space flight, the estimated consumption of 10 lb a day for human fuel—2 lb of oxygen, 4 lb of fluid, and 4 lb of food—poses a major problem. During a flight of a year or longer, assuming that the vehicle was operating satisfactorily, there would be little or no reason for the astronaut to be awake for long periods unless some emergency arose. Hypothermia (reduction of body temperature) would appear to be a desirable state in such long voyages in order to reduce metabolism, and thus human "fuel" consumption. The use of external cooling, reduction of the temperature of the blood in an arterio-venous shunt, and hibernation (through pituitary control), alone or in combination with pharmaceuticals, all seem to offer possibilities in attempting to obtain and maintain such a state. Control of the temperature by influencing the heat-regulating center would be more desirable than changing the reference level.

Oxygenization and Carbon Dioxide Removal. Breathing in space is a problem because the space environment will not provide the necessary oxygen, and respiration eliminates needed carbon dioxide and involves heat and water losses. An inverse fuel cell, capable of reducing CO_2 to its components with removal of the carbon and recirculation of the oxygen, would eliminate the necessity for lung breathing. Such a system, operating either on solar or nuclear energy, would replace the lung, making breathing, as we know it, unnecessary. Conventional breathing would still be possible, should the environment permit it, discontinuing the fuel-cell operation.

Fluid Intake and Output. Fluid balance in the astronaut could be largely maintained via a shunt from the ureters to the venous circulation after removal or conversion of noxious substances. Sterilization of the gastrointestinal tract, plus intravenous or direct intragastric feeding, could reduce fecal elimination to a minimum, and even this might be reutilized.

Enzyme Systems. Under conditions of lowered body temperature, certain enzyme systems would tend to remain more active than others. The extent to which pharmaceutical or chemical agents could influence this enzyme activity has not been systematically investigated, but beyond question they will play an important role. Since metabolism is subject to enzyme control, several intriguing possibilities exist. For example, it may be possible through in vitro radiation to convert certain organisms from aerobic to anaerobic states and, by studying changes in the enzyme systems, to adapt them for eventual human use. In the same manner, selected atmospheres of other types could be investigated.

Vestibular Function. Disorientation or discomfort resulting from disturbed vestibular function due to weightlessness might be handled through the use of drugs, by temporarily draining off the endolymphatic fluid or, alternately, filling the cavities completely, and other techniques involving chemical control. Hypnosis may also be useful for controlling vestibular function.

Cardiovascular Control. The application of control-system theory to biology has already yielded sufficiently fruitful results in studies of the multiple homeostatic functions of the cardiovascular system to indicate the possibility of altering the system by the Cyborg technique. Administration of presently available drugs, such as epinephrine, reserpine, digitalis, amphetamine, etc., by means of Rose injectors, offers one possibility of changing the cardiovascular functions so as to fit them for a particular environment. Alteration of the specific homeostatic references within or outside the brain, and electric stimulation, either as a means of regulating heart rate or affecting selected brain centers in order to control cardio-

vascular functioning, are other possibilities.

Muscular Maintenance. Prolonged sleep or limited activity has a deleterious effect on muscle tone. While reduction of body temperature and metabolism may reduce the magnitude of the problem, further investigation of the chemical reasons for atrophy appears necessary to develop adequate pharmaceutical protection to help maintain muscle tone on prolonged space voyages.

Perceptual Problems. Lack of atmosphere will create markedly different conditions of visual perception than those with which we are familiar. Attention should be given to providing a medium which would recreate some of the distortions to which we are accustomed, and to which the astronaut could become acclimated before takeoff. Part of the problem would come from searching for an adequate frame of reference, and in this regard the factors which influence autokinesis (and illusory movement) may have an influence on space perception problems. Investigation of whether pharmaceuticals would influence autokinesis is therefore desirable.

Pressure. Under pressure lower than 60 mm Hg, man's blood begins to boil at his normal body temperature. Therefore, if he is to venture out of his space vehicle without a pressure suit, some means must be found of reducing his normal operating temperature to a point where the vapor pressure of his fluids is no greater than the internal tissue pressures. This is another reason why lowering of body temperature is essential to avoid the use of constricting pressure suits.

Variations in External Temperature. While man will require the protection of a space ship or station at the real extremes of temperature, there are also likely to be intermediate conditions within or close to the limits of human tolerance. By controlling reflection and absorption by means of protective plastic sponge clothing plus chemicals already in existence which produce changes in pigmentation and provide effective protection against actinic rays, it should be possible to maintain desired body temperature. Needed is a light-sensitive, chemically regulated system which would adjust to its own reflectance so as to maintain the temperature desired.

Gravitation. A change in the ratio of gravity and inertia forces to molecular forces will alter mobility patterns, among other things. Body temperature control and other uses of pharmaceuticals could possibly improve functioning under conditions of greater or lesser gravitation than that on earth.

Magnetic Fields. Chemicals and temperature alteration might also act to retard or facilitate the specific effects of magnetic fields in space.

Sensory Invariance and Action Deprivation. Instead of sensory deprivation, it is sensory invariance, or lack of change in sensory stimuli, which may be the astronaut's bugaboo. In most of the sensory deprivation experiments to date, it has been sensory invariance which has produced discomfort and, in extreme circumstances, led to the occurrence of psychotic-like states. Of even greater significance may be action invariance, deprivation or limitation, since in many such experiments subjects have mentioned a "desire for action." The structuring of situations so that action has a meaningful sensory feedback should reduce these difficulties. Here again drugs could play a useful role in reducing resultant tensions. Action without demonstration that such behavior is purposeful or sensory stimuli without opportunity for appropriate response are both highly disturbing.

Psychoses. Despite all the care exercised, there remains a strong possibility that somewhere in the course of a long space voyage a psychotic episode might occur, and this is one condition for which no servomechanism can be completely designed at the present time. While an emergency osmotic pump containing one of the high-potency phenothiazines together with reserpine could be a part of the complete space man's kit, the frequent denial by an individual undergoing a psychotic episode that his thought processes, emotions, or behavior are abnormal, might keep him from voluntarily accepting medication. For this reason, if monitoring is adequate, provision should be made for triggering administration of the medication remotely from earth or by a companion if there is a crew on the vehicle.

Limbo. The contingency of possible extreme pain or suffering as a result of unforeseen accidents must also be considered. The astronaut should therefore be able to elect a state of unconsciousness if he feels it to be necessary. Prolonged sleep induced either pharmacologically or electronically seems the best solution.

Other Problems

There obviously exists an equally large number of medical problems amenable to pharmacological influence which have not been discussed here for lack of space. Among these are such conditions as nausea, vertigo, motion sickness, erotic requirements, vibration tolerance, etc.

However, those selected for discussion offer an indication as to what the Cyborg can mean in terms of space travel. Although some of the proposed solutions may appear fanciful, it should be noted that there are references in the Soviet technical literature to research in many of these same areas. Thus we find the Russians proposing prior oxygen saturation as a solution to the problem of respiration during the first few minutes after space vehicle launchings; reporting on alterations of the vestibular function both by drugs and surgery; studying perception and carrying out research on the laws of eye motion in vision; finding that lowering of temperature can aid in solving pressure problems; etc.

Solving the many technological problems involved in manned space flight by adapting man to his environment, rather than vice versa, will not only mark a significant step forward in man's scientific progress, but may well provide a new and larger dimension for man's spirit as well.

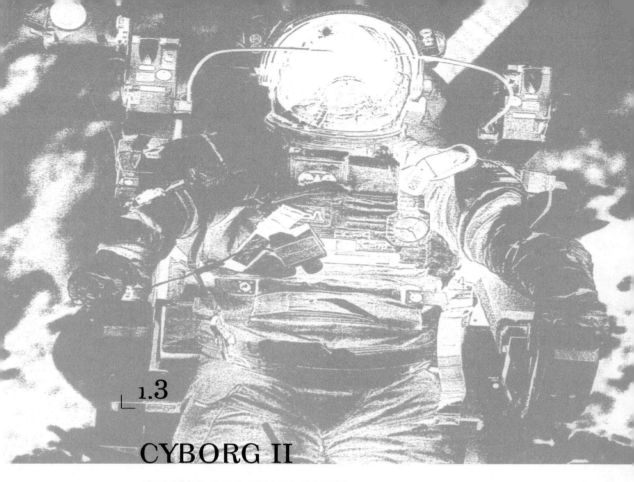

L 1.3

CYBORG II

SENTIC SPACE TRAVEL

Manfred E. Clynes, D. Sc.

Note: This article was written in 1970 on the invitation of the journal Astronautics *but they refused to publish it.*

In 1960 a new concept was created to denote the cooperation of man with his self-designed homeostatic controls in quasi-symbiotic union: the cyborg. Together with Dr. Nathan S. Kline of the Rockland State Hospital, we explored the implications of how man's ability to redesign his own homeostatic controls to fit a new environment of his choice would further his plans for space travel. **The concept of the cyborg was to allow man to optimize his internal regulation to suit the environment he may seek.** The point was exemplified by a fish who might wish to live on land: would such a fish take a bowl of water with him, encapsulate himself in that bowl, so that he would live as a fish on land, or would he not prefer to redesign his gills to breathe air as a lung could do, if he had the intelligence? ✻ Clearly, wherever possible, man would do far better by redesigning his physiological regulatory systems so that they could, in the new external environment also, near optimally regulate his internal environment without his conscious attention. How far have we come in the twelve years since the suggestion was made, in simplifying man's approach to space travel? Not very far yet. We are largely dependent on earthbound optimization of energy sources for the maintenance of life. We cannot yet use sunlight even like a plant for a source of organic chemical energy. We cannot automatically recycle the oxygen we require in our blood stream. And our regulatory systems are largely permitted to "float", i.e. to provide their own (mal) adjustments. ✳ And so rather than try to see where we stand today with the development of the early cyborg concept, in this paper we shall look at different and important aspects of man's functioning relevant to space travel, largely omitted in the 1960 paper: **dynamic forms for, and his need for, emotional communication.** ✳ Our work in the last few years in this subject, called **sentics**, makes it possible to look at those needs and functions in a new perspective and see how they can be fulfilled in the exigencies of space travel. We have come to realize that apparently innate modes of expression of emotion are also, among other things, innately very much related to the direction and strength of gravitation. Space travel changes man's ability to express emotion, and also affects his need for it. We shall look at the specific ways in which these changes occur and suggest new ways in which his needs may be satisfied. And it seems that in the course of studying such new forms of satisfaction, man's concept of his own nature shall be enlarged. ▶ Man's exploration of space has been successful from the technical point of view during the last decade, but his emotional exploration of his new experience and environment have not been spectacular. It may be too much to expect astronauts to provide us with a fully communicated view of their new enlarged experience: the exigencies of piloting their vehicles necessarily make great demands on them: so we must be satisfied with the language of "wows" and "man-oh-man" and similar expletives, whose implications we can only guess at from their contexts on good old earth. But communicating new emotional possibilities is only part of the story that remains to be developed. The other, perhaps in the long run more important, part is to provide for the emotional needs of the astronauts who are confined to such small spaces for such long periods of time, often without significant emotional contact with other human beings and/or at the same time, almost paradoxically, may be confined with another individual in a small space without respite for much longer periods than they could normally endure without severe emotional stress. ✳ **To plan for space travel adequately we need to understand man's psychological drives, needs and qualities of satisfaction,** as well as to provide for physiological homeostasis. We could call this aspect his psychologic homeostasis, but that tends to be misleading, since there is an indissoluble connection between his mental and physiologic functions. We are more advanced in understanding the processes of physiologic homeostasis than those that include psychologic homeostasis. ✳ Thus we crudely believe it to be desirable to be "creative", but we do not really understand the processes that produce the pressure to be creative, nor their satisfaction. We don't even have a generally clear concept of where our notion of creativity stops: if it is creative to write a symphony, we also say it is "creative" to perform a spontaneous, "authentic" gesture. A gesture that is not authentic, that is to some extent inhibited or distorted, is not called creative (although it may well create confusion and misunderstanding!) ✳ **How can man be authentic in space?** ✳ We do not adequately differentiate between the creativity of the engineer, the inventor, the scientist, the musician, and the artist, and the cook, the educator, and the writer, to name a few. For each, the emotional, aggressive, intellectual, relational mix of satisfactions are different. ✳ We recognize man's "creative needs" as far as we are able to understand this, but also, we are aware of so-called aggressive needs. The term aggression, however, is used with even greater confusion than creativity. There is a prevalent failure to distinguish between constructive aggression, such as manifested by an engineer who builds, and hostile aggression. ✳ In terms of sexual activity, the quality of satisfaction is determined not merely by a specific physiologic process, but through the context of relationship (real or fantasized).

● **We need, therefore, a branch of knowledge centered around the study of satisfaction,** comparable to branches of philosophy dealing with ethics, aesthetics, or phenomenology; for each sensation and emotion also have their own distinct satisfactions although they are usually not denoted by different names. The satisfaction of hunger is different from the satisfaction of thirst. The satisfaction of scratching an itch is different from the satisfaction felt after urinating. And although the satisfaction of defecation has been rather arbitrarily used as a prototype of creative satisfactions, yet it has its own specific character. ✳ If we send man into space, how do we provide for his satisfactions? The possibilities are in some ways more limited and in some ways more enlarged than on earth. ✳ During the last few years progress in the study of sentics, a branch of science dealing with the communication of emotions in the present moment, has made considerable progress, and in this paper we shall outline how its contributions can help provide for some of the creative and emotional experiential needs of the astronaut. ☘ Some outstanding components of the astronaut's emotional experience are exhilaration, boredom and anxiety. Exhilaration is fine, although at times it could be an element of danger, but we want to avoid the deteriorating effects of boredom, and at times of anxiety. We want to avoid the buildup of explosive needs, unsatisfied through long periods of deprivation. ■ Thus, the problem of the astronaut is not so very different from that of the inhabitants of earth. Man has a need for both order and variety. Nature has provided both, but in his trip into space he may well suffer from too much order and not enough variety. ✳ Every man when he dreams, has at his disposal an extraordinary faculty of imagination and fantasy. Even the "dullest" man, when he dreams, produces plays that he casts, directs, and acts in, and produces—plays we call dreams. In these he not only writes the lines and casts the actors, but designs the costumes and stage sets as well, complete in details. ✳ There is a strange technological imbalance between man's development of his tools and machines for the penetration of the nature of space, and his lack of progress in cyborg technology, even in the most obvious modification of his own nature for the environmental goals that he sets: the first thing he had to do on achieving the tremendous technological feat of landing on the moon was to sleep for eight hours! We do not know why man needs to sleep. If the spaceship had such pervasive unknown needs, it surely never would have made it to the moon! An essential part of sleep is to allow man his necessary dreams. But the quality of those dreams in a prolonged space trip might often become nightmares. It is fortunate that recently a method was developed allowing a person to generate and experience fantasy emotions reliably, and repeatedly, enjoy them creatively, and enable him to be "in touch" with his emotions. The process provides him with a reservoir of calmness and aspects of psychic energy, replacing hostile aggression, and constitutes a satisfaction in itself. This process is the development of sentic cycles. ✚ As inhabitants of earth we have been largely used to express emotion in specific contexts and situations. When we are angry, we are angry at someone or at a particular situation. When we are joyful, we generally are joyful about something, and when we love we are used to loving a particular person. Emotion is thus associated with specific people and situations. While this has been the preponderant manner of experiencing emotion, there has developed on earth another less practiced mode of experiencing emotion: a generalized mode not dependent on specific situations or individuals. This mode is exemplified by music. Music as auto- and cross-communication is capable of generating and discharging emotional states through its vibratory touch forms, which we call sound. The emotions that these forms denote are not directed at specific individuals or situations but can be very intense nevertheless. They are examples of generalized emotion. ‼ Only a small proportion of the population is able to use these forms creatively, and much hard labor and learning skills are required to permit this even for those who can. We shall see that in some ways doing sentic cycles is like composing music without the need for years of development of skills and concern about critical evaluation. It allows a person to create his own generalized fantasy emotion forms. It is easily learned, by practically any adult. It is a way in which the entire spectrum of emotions may be experienced in fantasy without need of specific external contexts and associations. Let us explain this in more detail. ◆ In expressing emotion, there are many optional output modes involving the musculature: we may use a gesture of the arm, the leg, the tone of voice, a dance step or even a musical phrase. Studies in our laboratories during the last few years, confirmed by other investigators, have shown that for each emotion there is a characteristic dynamic form element that is common to these output modalities, and it is this dynamic form that is recognized by the nervous system in the process of generating the emotion, or the sentic state. To prove this the measurement of expressive form was standardized to the mode of using the transient pressure of a single finger. Horizontal and vertical components of pressure were measured as functions of time. When this was done the resultant pressure-transient vector forms proved to be stable and similar across different cultures, including the United States, Japan, Bali, and Mexico. We call these spatio-temporal signatures "esssentic forms". A person sits in a chair, (with a straight back and without side arm rests) rests his arm on a finger rest placed at the level of the seat of the chair and expresses with a single transient pressure a particular quality of emotion. The person doing this knows when he has expressed the quality with the right form: he discovers the particular essentic form for each emotion rather quickly. ✳ The second important function in making the process possible is that **through repeated expression of a particular sentic state the state itself is generated.** There is a positive feedback. The bio-cybernetic approach allows one to consider emotion as a system comprising both the state and its expression as one entity. It permits one to study dynamic interaction of the expression with the state, unlike the traditional psychologic studies which have generally studied the state and its expression separately. ❏ The generating effect of repeated expression takes place effectively only if the repetition is not "mechanical"; that is, initiation should occur at unpredictable times. This important feature is incorporated into sentic cycles by providing an external initiating signal, as a soft tap recorded on tape occurring at unpredictable intervals. The intervals of time themselves are different according to what emotion is being generated. ✳ As a person sits in this manner and expresses a sequence of 30 to 40 expressive actions of a particular emotion, called E-actons, and experiences the emotion, the rest of his body becomes very quiet, almost as if asleep. At the end of such a sequence a word announcing the next emotion is heard on the tape and another sequence of E-actons begins. In this way a person can traverse substantially the entire spectrum of emotions. The standard sequence of sentic states that has been used consists of no emotion, anger, hate, grief, love, sex, joy, reverence. This sequence forming a sentic cycle takes about one-half hour. Two cycles are done at a session. **At the end of the cycle a person tends to feel**

calm, shielded, "put-together" and contented. ☉ While sitting still, only expressing with the pressure of one arm on a finger rest, the person undergoes a highly pervasive, and integrating experience. The application of this to space travel is obvious. ✿ While the sentic cycle experience provides calmness, the calmness is also combined with a sense of well-being and energy—it is not the calmness of a tranquilizer. Hostile aggression is strongly attenuated and there is a sense of belonging, of satisfaction of being, in itself. We have said previously that the experience of sentic cycles was like composing music. It is not like listening to music, because the person is creatively involved in every single action. Nor does it have the eventual monotony of the repetition of a piece of music, no matter how good. (We don't find dreams monotonous either, nor do we tire of dreaming throughout a lifetime.) Although sentic cycles can be emotionally draining if done to excess, in proper measure no boredom sets in. There is also a remarkable phenomenon of a collapse of the sense of elapsed time. A one hour sentic cycle experience is often judged to be only some twenty minutes long. *(Sentic Cycle Tapes and finger rests are available for a small fee from the Secretary, American Sentic Association, Box 143, Sonoma, CA 95476.)* ▲ All these attributes make sentic cycles interesting for possible use in space travel. ❍ But let us stay on earth for a while longer. Among the many uses of this process on earth are removing anxiety, improving sleep, and for emotional training and therapy. A particularly interesting aspect is illustrated by the case of a person who has been paralyzed for over twenty years with multiple sclerosis. This patient was severely depressed and suicidal before beginning sentic cycles in June, 1972. Her nurse wrote to say that she would like to experience the apparently beneficial effects of sentic cycles, but that, of course, she could not move her arms, her fingers or legs; and asked if there was any way she could have the experience. So instead of a finger rest, a chin rest was designed for her, and she has been doing sentic cycles, expressing with her chin every day since June, 1972. At the very first session she was able to experience emotions she had not felt for many years. It was a spine-chilling experience to see her express her accumulated resentment and grief. She could not feel joy at first at all, but by saying to her, "try to imagine you are perfectly well, and are playing outside in the sunshine!", she was then able to do it very well. Since then, she has experienced all these emotions every day. Within two weeks a marked change took place in her whole attitude and family relationships. When asked whether she would like to have "hope" as one of the emotions in the sentic cycles, she replied that she *has* hope now, through doing the other emotions and so does not need it as a separate period! She is interested in her surroundings, communicates readily, and her husband finds it pleasant to come home to her as she "smiles and is in pleasant moods." ✾ After nine months of doing this daily, she still looks forward to the experience every day and enjoys it. This, in spite of the worsening of her physical condition to the extent that her eyes are rolling independently without control and she cannot see at all without covering up one eye, and even then quite poorly. Although her body functions have been so seriously altered, **through sentic cycles she has come to realize that emotionally her capacities are unimpaired,** and she is "fully human" even though her environment does not now provide the situations creating emotion she would need as a normal human. ✿ This example of a person in Colorado is cited because in some ways it resembles the conditions of space travel. The paralysis of the patient causes her to be effectively confined in space. Many of the sensory inputs available to normal individuals are eliminated for her. Even her sleep pattern is affected by the requirement that she be turned over every hour-and-a-half all throughout the night, which her husband has been doing for all these years! The fact that sentic cycles have been able to make life not only tolerable but even pleasant for her, is not without relevance to the conditions facing the space traveler. ❖ Another aspect of the use of sentic cycles is that the mode of an action may in many cases be preferable to the use of various drugs, not only from the point of view that drugs may have side effects, but also of how long it takes the body to recover from the administration of drugs. But a suitable combination of sentic cycles with appropriate drugs should not be necessarily excluded. ✳ Earlier we have mentioned the fact that expression of emotions takes place very differently in the absence of gravitation. Studies with sentic cycles show that the position of the body and limbs in relationship to the direction of gravity is an integral part of the spatio-temporal forms of emotion expression. ✳ **For each emotion there is a bodily experience, which we call a virtual body image, characteristic of that emotion.** These virtual body images are closely linked to the force and direction of gravity. For joy, for example, there is a sense of lightness, of bounce. The essentic form of joy contains a rebound overshoot corresponding to a floating sensation. Grief, on the other hand, is characterized by a sense of heaviness of the limbs. The expression of grief includes a letting go, a collapse. The word 'grief' itself derives from the Latin root *grave*, meaning heavy. There is also a tilt of the head downward and to one side; for joy, the head tends to be tilted upwards. In anger too, the head is tilted slightly downwards and the expressive movement has a strong outward and downward direction. For example, expression of anger with the foot has a strong downward component. Courage is also expressed directly in relation to the direction of gravity. In the expression of love it is found that for a caress the surface of contact tends to be with palm downwards. The pressure-transient exertions necessary to effect a caress with the palm upward, pressing vertically upwards largely, are generally foreign to our programmed forms of expression, and tend to feel unnatural and, if attempted as a distortion of the form, block the feeling of the emotion associated with it. ✚ The question is then to what extent these inherent body images will be felt as missing in space travel, and to what extent they might be altered or retrained? If there is no gravity, how can the heaviness of grief find its expression? Will it no longer be heavy, or will it simply not be possible to express and even experience grief? Experiments in water tanks quickly point out the difficulties of the removal of the gravitational forces on the ability to communicate and express emotions. Floating in water, the dynamics of gestures are modified not only because of the resistance of the water but because of the layered kinesthetic experience. In accordance with the sentic principle of partial reciprocity, floating in water tends to be pleasant in itself. The absence of heaviness tends to counteract the possibility of the bodily images of grief and related sadness, and is in accordance with virtual body images associated with joy. **Much of the exhilaration of the experience of weightlessness is related to this characteristic of the essentic form of joy.** The experience is presaged in the experience of those who dream about flying with their own bodies. This is a very common dream. One pushes off with one's legs and then floats while usually looking down on the scene below with a delightful feeling. The author once had occasion to ask astronaut Cunningham if he had ever dreamt of flying in this way. He said he had on a number of occasions dreamt that. "And how does that feeling in the dream compare with your experience of weightlessness in space?" I asked. "Come to think of it, it was just like that feeling," was the reply! ✚

The ability of dreams to provide us with a precise perspective of feeling and to create preverbal concepts for us is a crucial human function. The particular essentic forms and bodily images accompanying specific emotions that have evolved in humans are in part common to the higher animals. (A dog understands the tone of voice, a caress, etc.) How do we account for the lightness of joy? What is it about joy that links it with lightness indissolubly and why does the shape of a caress have to be the way it is to express love, while a sexual caress in turn has a very different form? Would these forms be different in different parts of the universe? If each emotion has its own specific spatio-temporal form, what new emotions might we find some day among beings living elsewhere and what would their essentic forms be? Emotions which we regard as the highest developed on earth may well be surpassed by more highly developed beings. It is not merely in intelligence but also in the spectrum of emotions that evolution proceeds. ✗ The words of natural language only inadequately characterize and identify the distinct emotional entities, and their associated specific spatio-temporal virtual body images. The words joy and anger are familiar and reasonably identifiable existences. But what, for example, about that less generally familiar, but important emotion, for which there is no word—an emotion man has when he is searching for new ideas, not only curious, but ready to receive: we may describe it as an intellectual fervor, a focused openness, a listening, a receptivity to whatever may come to his awareness, an enthusiasm with an element of trust that when an idea comes, it is through an ongoing, "good" process? ❀ In that emotion, perhaps a prerequisite, a necessity for the discovery of new ideas, the head tends to be tilted slightly, and slightly upward, the body feels light, there is no anxiety and fear, but an enthusiastic, and yet still eagerness, which waits like an open shell, to receive; the face has a characteristic openness and intentness, even a rapt kind of attention. There is a sensation in the forehead between the temples. It is not the exhilaration of having found the idea, but antecedent to this! ✳ This nameless, but quite specific emotion (it is being named "apreene" by the author in another publication, in press at the moment) also involves gravity! We need to ask, is the specific angle of the head with respect to gravity no longer part of the innate spatio-temporal form of that emotion in space? Does that mean, then, that the lightness and strength experienced (a feeling of not being totally earthbound, but perhaps part of an infusing process) [cf. "the *flight* of the imagination"] will no longer have the sensation-aspect of newness, of being taken out of one's ordinary pedestrianism, in conditions of space where lightness is habitual? ☁ In addition to the virtual body images innately associated with experiencing sentic states, there are specific dynamic muscular patterns involved in the expression of each specific emotion. This is also manifest in the dynamic form of breathing. (The transient forms of breathing are modified, even when there is no voluntary intent to express the state.) The expression of anger and hate, for example, involves distinct abdominal-muscle contractions. The diaphragm also moves differently with each form of emotional expression. Joy favors inspiration, anger sharp expiration—an ejecting of the breath from the body. Grief favors respiratory pauses at the end of expiration, as in a sigh; reverence and love favor pauses at the end of inspiration. Sexual excitement too, has its own dynamic form of breathing, involving a special, late tension phase during expiration. ✖ In the absence of gravity, as well as to some extent in lower atmospheric density, these breathing patterns are modified in various degrees. Cyborg technology has even aimed to bypass the out-in tidal flow of the breath, and to oxygenate the blood with a fuel-cell device instead. Although emotion can be experienced and expressed without specific breathing patterns, modification of the breath does affect the quality of the experience. ✚ Yet, man is able to disassociate selective body functions in his state of dream-emotion. In dreams, the virtual body images and the patterns of muscular expression of emotion acquire another perspective, although many of the body functions remain connected in various degrees. Also, there is a different connection between the autonomic and the unconscious. In dreams we do seem to be able to imagine emotions we have never experienced, but even the emotions of our dreams may be quite incompatible with the realities of emotion in another part of the universe. ✳ The emotional-generating functions of our dreams make use of the essentic forms, and innate body images, that include the strength and direction of gravity. In the weightless condition of space, as also in conditions of different gravity, the traveler will find his emotional virtual-bodily images at variance with experience. The method of sentic cycles should allow him, nevertheless, to experience these fantasy emotion states and to allow him to use the pressure transients appropriate to his state. To what extent the essentic forms would be modified in prolonged space travel can now be investigated. The instrumentation necessary to do this is very simple and light. Accordingly the opportunity should not be missed, in coming space flights, to conduct these simple tests. ✳ The question is whether the virtual body images, which involve gravity and appear to be genetically programmed into man's nature, would be affected by prolonged weightlessness. There is a direct correspondence between the expressed form and the felt experience. If there is an alteration in the form, the experience felt also changes. If the exigencies of space travel were to alter the expressed form, our inbuilt nervous system integration of that form would also alter the quality of the corresponding emotional experience. In other words, it is possible that disassociation may occur between gesture and experience. This would present a serious problem for the emotional stability and long-term viability of the astronaut's mode of life. Sentic cycles provide a possibility both to study this condition and to ameliorate it, should it be of concern. ○ **The ability of man to express his emotions in accordance with his nature is indispensable for a prolonged existence in space.** In this paper we have tried to point out some of the difficulties he faces in venturing out from his gravitational home and to see whether in weightless condition his emotional nature can function in an unaltered manner or whether, like the elves and fairies of our myths, the dance of space necessarily requires him to transform his nature emotionally. ❖ The virtual body images associated with each emotion have an unconscious origin. They are not willfully created by each individual—they represent his heritage. So do essentic forms. This unconscious heritage travels with us into space. ✳ But we have seen that the autonomic and the unconscious meet. Through understanding our unconscious heritage consciously, we may be able to teach our autonomic systems to live in harmony with our old heritage, as well as with our new exploration of outer, and perforce, inner, space.

An Interview with Manfred Clynes

Chris Hables Gray

Chris Hables Gray: Where were you born?

Manfred Clynes: In Vienna, Austria in 1925.

CHG: And what did your parents do?

MC: My father was an engineer, inventor, a naval architect. My mother was a truly remarkable, beautiful woman, a writer and also a person of extraordinary intellect. She was a gifted amateur singer, and studied with my uncle Max Klein, who was a baritone at the Vienna Opera and later on taught Metropolitan Opera stars in New York.

My mother was very musical. When I was a small child she often sang lieder, especially Schubert and Mahler. In those days, the late twenties and early thirties. I used to love to crawl under the piano to listen, while she was singing, with an accompanist playing. Sometimes I was very scared. A few of the Mahler songs had images like "a hot glowing knife in my breast," things that scare a little child. And when the song talked about 'those two blue eyes in the sky,' I thought, looking at the blue sky, that I saw them.

CHG: Did you have any siblings?

MC: No, unfortunately not.

CHG: So your family left Vienna in 1938?

MC: Well, actually, Budapest in 1938. My parents moved to Budapest about 1930.

CHG: Did you grow up speaking Hungarian and German?

MC: I had to learn Hungarian, yes. Just when I managed to learn it so the other kids didn't laugh at me, we left for Australia and I had to learn English.

CHG: Is that where you went to college?

MC: First I went to work in a factory. When we first came there I was thirteen years old. My father literally kissed the ground when we arrived. We knuckled down and started a new life. I went to work in a factory and worked 48 hours a week for a wage of 15 shillings and 6 pence.

CHG: It must have been hard times.

MC: It was an interesting social experience. The paramount mood was of gratitude for having been saved to be with 'normal', decent, simple-minded (if foulmouthed) people; anything was small trouble compared to the horrific trials of my girl cousins, with whom I used to play, who were left behind and were gassed.

I went to school, after that stint of factory work, in a tradesman's school. Then I asked my father to send me to a high school for one year, and then I went to university.

CHG: Was your first degree there in engineering?

MC: I did music and engineering simultaneously, and science at the University of Melbourne. I was allowed to do it by special permission from the Vice Chancellor of the University. They had never had anyone request that before but he let me do it. He thought I could do it and he gave me a chance. So I remember in one year, the second year I think, I had 18 exams in one year, 18 subjects. But it was fun.

CHG: You stayed on there and got your upper degrees there?

MC: I got my undergraduate degrees there and then I went to Juilliard in the United States. I got my masters in music and piano at Juilliard. I had played with orchestras quite a bit as a soloist in Australia and I earned a fellowship to Juilliard by winning a nationwide competition.

CHG: Then what happened?

MC: I went to Juilliard for three years and got my Master's degree. Then I went to Wrightwood, California for six months and I studied music there by myself. This was 1949. Then I went back to concertizing in Australia and was appointed to the conservatory of music there in Melbourne, on the piano faculty, the youngest person ever to hold that position. I became well known as one of the foremost solo pianists in Australia. I did many broadcasts, and performed the *Goldberg Variations* there the first time they were played in Australia. That was in 1950, the 200th anniversary of Bach's death. I played that in all the capital cities. Then, two years later I got a Fulbright fellowship.

I was interested in the psychology of music and got a Fulbright to go to Princeton and study and also to teach there as a graduate assistant. I stayed in Princeton and also did concert tours in Europe. That was 1953. And I had the wonderful opportunity to meet Einstein there. I visited him five or six times and played music for him at his house. It was a marvelous thing. I even discussed with him the theory of relativity, believe it or not. Then I toured Europe. It was very successful. I played in the Royal Festival Hall, London, and in all of the capital cities. This was the fall of 1953. Then in 1954 I started to do this other kind of work. First as a control engineer working with an analog computer at an electrical manufacturing concern. And then I was invited by Rockland State Hospital's director of research to do medical research.

CHG: Nathan Kline.

MC: Nathan Kline. Yes. In 1955, I guess.

CHG: So this analog computer was at Princeton?

MC: No, that wasn't at Princeton, but at a place called Bogue Electric Manufacturing Company in Paterson, New Jersey. And then Nathan Kline bought a computer for me at Rockland State Hospital. I think it must have been in 1955 when I started there part-time, because in 1956 I decided to accept his offer to do that full-time and became chief research scientist. That's where I developed all these things like the CAT computer and discovered unidirectional rate sensitivity by 1960. That is a basic law of biologic systems for communication of information. Other inventions of that time included eight patents in the field of ultrasound, particularly color ultrasound; pulse frequency-modulation data tape recording; and silence duration modulation for telemetering. The latter invention allowed enormous savings of power because data were communicated by the duration of silence. Silence was the measure of the quantity. You just needed two pulses, one at the beginning of the silence and the other at the end and those would define the quantity of the variable. Silence passes at the same rate everywhere in the world so there was no problem about distortion. It is infinitely precise by the laws of nature.

CHG: So, since the period when you got you Ph.D...?

MC: Well, I have a D.Sc.

CHG: Oh, a Doctorate of Science.

MC: A D.Sc. is actually a higher degree than a Ph.D.

CHG: That's from Australia, the University of Melbourne?

MC: Yes. That's given only for a considerable body of work commensurate with that kind of degree, work which becomes a D.Sc. thesis, and is examined. It's not like a Ph.D. thesis. It's a British thing. There's nothing like it in the United States actually. England and Australia have it and they only give very few of those, maybe two or three a year, to anybody, in selected areas of science.

CHG: So then you were working at Rockland. When did you and Nathan Kline start thinking about space travel?

MC: That was in 1960. I had been there for about four years and worked on the organization of the body's nervous system and its cybernetic control.

I worked with the control of heart rate at the time, through respiration. It's called sinus arrhythmia. The changes in heart rate bought about by breathing. We solved that problem and published that in *Science* and in other journals. We had equations that simulated that non-linear control process very accurately. It was really a rather interesting piece of work, exciting for me as one of the first useful applications of computers to biologic-control systems. People were kind of excited about that. I got the Baker Award at that time for it, surprisingly. We did other things with pupil-rate dynamics and that was revealing. Pretty soon we saw that there was a general property there in the nervous system which we called unidirectional rate sensitivity, a really awful name and tongue twister, but later it was called rein control, and the first paper on it was published in 1960.

That law exists because molecular concentrations are used as analogs of information in the body and molecules can only arrive in positive numbers. There's no such thing as introducing negative numbers of molecules. They can only arrive in positive numbers. An increase in concentration therefore is easily accomplished, representing an increased value of a variable transmitted as information, e.g., sensing heat. But if you need to represent the information through decreasing the level, then you can't, as you can in electrical systems, just send a negative electrical signal. There are no negative molecules for a gland to inject into the blood stream, for example, to send a message, and so you need another chemical channel to interact with those molecules to reduce their number, to get rid of the molecules. And that has its own dynamics. It becomes two channels, and so it's called rein control, like the reins of a horse, each of which can pull but not push.

CHG: And was it around pupil dilation that you first noticed this?

MC: Well, in pupil dilation we found a paradoxical contraction with a pulse of darkness. It should have brought on a dilation but instead it actually caused a contraction. And then we saw that it was due to the trailing edge of the stimulus. It was the trailing edge when the light returned which caused the contraction. It didn't significantly respond as dilation, which was much slower; that channel is a much slower channel. So we noticed this, and it also appeared in touch. If you touch a pattern with a lot of little protuberances, say pins, with your hand or finger, and let's say you feel that there are five pins, then you very slowly remove several of those pins, so the person does not notice it. And when you then take your hand off, the act of taking your hand off, which is negative information, will not tell you how many pins are left. So we found the same property there.

Pretty soon we realized that this was due to a general principle. Then a few years later there was a conference by the New York Academy of Sciences on that subject, in 1967. It was several days long and many people presented data on various systems that exhibited this property. The keynote speaker was Warren McCulloch from M.I.T. Have you heard of Warren McCulloch?

CHG: Of course.

MC: A great man, very encouraging for my work in the early phases, the heart-rate work. He wrote me a handwritten letter saying it was the finest thing on nonlinear dynamics he had come across, in biologic systems. That's how I got to know him.

He was truly a remarkable person. I used to never understand what he said in his talks. At first I thought, 'Is he talking nonsense, is he pulling people's legs?' He had such a large view of things and he could express it in such powerful language not many people could easily understand it.

CHG: Yes, I've read _Embodiments of Mind_ and it is a very amazing work. There are definitely parts of it that go beyond my understanding.

MC: Yes, that's a beautiful work. When he died he wasn't even 68 or 69. I remember that for his 65th birthday I wrote a poem. A Festschrift was published in honor of his 65th birthday, and I contributed the little poem to that. Pretty soon after that he died.

CHG: A shame.

MC: Then I developed the CAT computer. That was very successful. It revolutionized the measurement of electrical events in the brain. All over the world they used the CAT computer, probably the first specific-purpose portable digital computer. It cost $10,000 at the time, in 1961. They even have one today, still, here at the University of California, in Berkeley. It still works after thirty years.

CHG: That's amazing. I didn't know that.

MC: They're still using it! I was amazed. I went there a couple of months ago and in this lab they still have it and are actively using it.

I made at the time a fair bit of money with that. Then it was time to go back to music. I studied with Pablo Casals.

CHG: When was this?

MC: This was 1966.

CHG: Let's backtrack a little to cyborg and your and Dr. Kline's cyborg article.

MC: That was in 1960.

CHG: Why exactly did you guys decide to write about space travel?

MC: Nathan Kline was the director of this research facility there at the Rockland State Hospital and one day somebody asked him... Dr. Kline was interested in the application of drugs for the treatment of mental patients.

CHG: Yes, psychopharmacology.

MC: Psychopharmacology. This man, I think Flaherty...

CHG: Yeah, he was with NASA.

MC: ... invited him to write something for us at NASA. So he talked to me and said, 'Would you like to write something jointly with me? I will write about the drugs and you write about other physiologic systems.' I said, 'What do I know about this? I know nothing.' Anyhow, we agreed. I thought about it for a few days and I wrote something up and we talked and compared ideas, and we decided to go ahead and write something. I thought it would be good to have a new concept, a concept of persons who can free themselves from the constraints of the environment to the extent that they wished. **And I coined this word cyborg. I remember he said, 'Oh, that sounds like a town in Denmark.'** Well, that seemed all right. The main idea was to liberate man from constraints as he flies into space—that's a kind of freedom—but it seemed necessary to give him the bodily freedom to exist in another part of the universe without the constraints that having evolved on earth made him subject to. For example, the level of gravitation that is here, the oxygen, the atmosphere. And some of the other things that have conditioned the physiology of man to be what it is.

CHG: I noticed you used the term participant evolution in that article.

MC: Yes. In other words man has now become conscious enough of the way he was built physiologically, and here, I emphasize physiologically, that he could now supplement the homeostasis with which he evolved. Are you familiar with the term 'homeostasis?'

CHG: Yes.

MC: So as to supplement it by his own imagination and through his own creativity. In such a way as to make it possible to exist, *qua* man, as man, **not changing his nature**, his human nature that evolved here. Not to change that but to simply allow him to make use of his faculties, without having to waste his energies on adjusting the living functions necessary for the maintenance of life. They become unconscious, automatic rather, the way they are here. You don't have to constantly adjust your blood pressure, for example.

CHG: What kind of reception did it get?

MC: Oh, it got a good reception. *Life* magazine wrote it up a little later. They had a big article with a picture of the cyborg. Did you know that?

CHG: No, I'll have to find that.

MC: I had a big photograph of that thing hanging on my wall for years.

CHG: Was that 1960?

MC: It must have been very near there.

CHG: But you didn't know that NASA went on to commission a whole study of cyborgs?

MC: Actually, I had heard of that.

CHG: What did you think when you noticed the term cyborg was being used a lot in popular literature, in science fiction?

MC: Well at first I was amused and then I was horrified because it was a total distortion. It gradually seemed to become more and more distorted. This recent film with this Terminator, **with Schwarzenegger playing this thing—dehumanized the concept completely**. This is a *travesty* of the real scientific concept that we had. It is not even a caricature. It's worse, creating a monster out of something that wasn't a monster. A monsterification of something that is a human enlargement of function; as if making a man who reads a book into an inhuman monster, just because he reads a book.

CHG: Well how about images like the Bionic Man?

MC: I could say to you in general that our 1960 paper concerning the physiologic adjustment of homeostatic systems did not deal at all with problems of man, or any alteration in the **nature** of man or woman at all.

CHG: But you talked about prosthetic organs.

MC: Yes, prosthetic organs, but for the maintenance of the person. It wasn't changing their nature. Like a kidney, for example, functions to maintain the internal environment, blood levels, but does not affect man's basic nature to any extent.

CHG: You didn't see that this might lead to what some people might call super-men? Kolff (inventer of the artificial kidney) used to argue that people with artificial organs wouldn't be allowed to compete in the Olympics.

MC: I would imagine that certainly these drugs they take in the Olympics are a form of alteration of the body functions, and that of course makes it unfair for the Olympics, but Olympics are made not for cyborgs but for people who are not taking drugs or other modifications of function. But I think they are allowed to wear glasses!

The important thing is that the Cyborg I paper was concerned with physiology. Then in 1970 *Astronautics* asked me to write a sequel. I wrote this and I pointed out that we had not dealt with the emotional nature of man in the Cyborg I paper. The Cyborg II paper[1] pointed out that there was an incompatibility in the emotional aspect of man's nature that didn't simply permit one to choose the environment willy-nilly, even with physiologic adjustments.

CHG: So when did you start focusing in on Sentics? When did you coin that term?

MC: I started working with that in 1967-68. The first paper was published in 1968.[2] Then there was a big AAAS conference in 1970 and another one in 1971. Then I started writing my book *Sentics* and I published a big article in 1973.[3] There I first stated the theory and the experimental data in a fairly full manner.

CHG: Do you think that with this deeper understanding of the emotions which you are pursuing human nature will stay the same, or will this be sort of a prosthesis to make people have better control, or perhaps a different type, of human nature?

MC: First of all the world of psychology until that time ignored the emotional nature of man—not only the Skinnerian, which is obvious, but even Freud himself. Although he was very interested in the inner life, he didn't concern himself with specific emotions like joy, anger, and love but rather with basic drives. The natural dynamic expressive forms, the nature of the expression of love, for example, of joy, of anger, of hate—we have isolated and measured their forms. And the forms of these expressions have a positive feedback-effect function in **generating** these states.

CHG: I'm curious about the implications of this improved understanding of human emotions.

MC: Well I think it has enormous possibilities. Actually the Cyborg II paper really focused on the problem of space flight from an emotional point of view and it suggested some exercise like the Sentic cycle that you could do to help you avoid boredom, avoid the desert of emotional nothingness. Even sexuality. By the way, parenthetically, **the idea of cyborg in no way implies an it. It's a he or a she.** It is either a male or female cyborg; it's not an it. It's an absurd mistake. The cyborgs are capable of the same emotional expression and experience as an uncyborg—what would you call them?

CHG: A *homo sapiens*, I guess.

MC: *Homo sapiens*, when he puts on a pair of glasses, *has* already changed. When he rides a bicycle he virtually has become a cyborg. Initially it's a little hard to learn to ride a bike but once you learn it you do all of these things automatically and the bike becomes almost a part of you. When *homo sapiens* walks he doesn't pay much attention to how he walks, it's natural. In the same way, when he is on his bicycle it feels natural to a person who knows how to ride a bike. You can call that, if you want, a simple cyborg right there.

CHG: Well, take for example the idea that Hans Morevec of Carnegie Mellon and other computer scientists have of downloading human consciousness into a machine. There, unless one goes to the effort of making sure the machine has sexual organs, gender becomes quite arbitrary or irrelevant. Do you think that's impossible?

MC: No, no. This question is improperly posed. It is the brain circuitry that engenders sexual feelings; the organs are just the buttons you press to turn it on and they could be replaced by more direct inputs. The genes and chromosomes already determine sex, and the brain circuitry expresses that sexuality, among other things. I'd like to come to that but in a more systematic way. It would take quite a bit to answer that. But right now I'd like to say—that the cyborg, per se—talking now of men or women who have altered themselves in various cyborgian ways—in no way has that altered their sexuality. In no way has that altered their ability to experience emotions, no more than riding a bicycle does. And even more importantly, it hasn't altered their essential identity.

CHG: I was struck, actually, that in your sentic research males and females seemed to have the same basic emotional response and ability to read these emotions.

MC: Most of the basic communicative expressive forms, including, for example, of sex, are the same. Laughing and yawning, likewise contagious, are, too. Actually if they weren't, it would make it hard for them to communicate with each other. That doesn't mean that their sex organs are the same.

CHG: But sex organs can be changed, we now know. Some people are paraplegic and quadriplegic, their sex organs are, for all intents and purposes, dead. They only exist through cyborg technologies.

MC: They can be paralyzed, but the sexual nature of man isn't just the sex organs. It is something very much in the identity of the person and in the environment. These include unconscious things. What excites one sexually is determined by the kind of sexual person you are. If you are a man certain shapes would tend to excite you and if a woman, other ones. Or if you are a homosexual it is a different matter, but I'm talking right now of heterosexual persons. Those are not arbitrary things. You cannot change them easily.

But now, I would like to come to what I call Cyborg III, that is achievable today. I also have a Cyborg IV, but lets talk about Cyborg III, first. I have to criticize a little what seems to be a great lack of appreciation of molecular biology among cyborg studies. The great things that are happening today in the scientific world are advances in molecular biology along with computers. Those are the two regions of our scientific world that are growing very rapidly, and compared to them psychology is dead in the water completely.

It already is known that the emotional world of men is fashioned through molecules like neuropeptides. Many peptides in the brain affect, and really control, the emotional aspects. Not just what used to be called the old messengers like hormones, which travel throughout the body, but more specifically and more powerfully these peptides, that in minute quantities exert very specific effects, often entirely on the brain side of the blood-brain barrier. There are receptors for these various peptides and undoubtedly each basic emotion has their own peptide. Many of these have not yet been identified. These peptides have receptors scattered throughout the brain, and the question is what happens to the other side of these receptors? That is largely not known yet. However, it is known that the emotional world can be affected now by designer molecules. That's where the computers and molecular biology will intermarry, they already have flirted with each other quite strongly. They will be able to have computer-designed molecules, designed along the lines of naturally occurring molecules, that will naturally work inside the brain and will be able to change the emotional aspects.

CHG: Is that Cyborg III?

MC: Yes, that is part of it. Our knowledge of DNA and how the genes function is such today that we can see that genes are not just a blueprint but they are functioning in the present moment. They continually are making gene products, some are turned off, some are turned on, and which and how much each thing is turned on and off is constantly changing. Every thought has an effect, even on that. So that by controlling and knowing how to control the natural products, and turning the genes on and off **we will have tremendous power to change the emotional world of man.** For example, I will tell you one of the least things: to change the percentage of time it will be possible to have orgasms. A man's refractory time can be altered.

Also, we don't know for example why we need to sleep, and sleep also means dreams. All of that is part of the emotional nature and it is necessary to man to be able to sleep; we don't know why. These questions will be answered within ten or fifteen years.

CHG: Do you ever worry that humans might not have the moral capabilities of dealing with the increased chance of structuring our own evolution?

MC: That's a different question on a whole different level. We have trouble enough already with nuclear bombs. Every invention brings about a possibility for both good and bad. It is very, very difficult to be a futurologist. We just don't have the imagination to imagine even beyond 20 years. Today, if you ask me what will happen fifty or a hundred years from now, it boggles the mind. I cannot imagine. Everything will be different and surpass what can be imagined. That's the wonder of it. But we need to be cautious and careful, and test every step along the way, as surely will be done. I only wish I could be alive a couple of hundred years from now just for a week or two just to see what will be done. **Maybe I'll freeze myself.**

CHG: Have you thought of that seriously?

MC: I've thought about it. I haven't done anything about it.

CHG: What is this Cyborg IV idea?

MC: Let me just finish a little bit the Cyborg III. The Cyborg III makes use of the abilities we have found now to alter the products of the genes, and also to insert new genes into existing DNA. We can now, in an adult person, insert fragments of a new gene that finds its way into adult cells, creating new gene function, new products, without, of course, changing heredity, and in the latest experiments, even through simple intravenous injection.

CHG: Right, they've done that already.

MC: They're just starting to do that. It's beginning with animals, adult animals, and they'll do that with humans more and more in a couple of years. That is a wonderful thing, because first of all diseases that are a result of genetic malfunction can be fixed.

See, we live in a world of puritanical science where you're allowed to get rid of pain from minus to zero but you aren't allowed to go beyond zero to plus, ie., pleasure. Nobody will give you a grant for that. Again I'll just say that part of the reason why people who have been writing about cyborgs have failed to understand the human aspect of it is possibly, in my view, that they're still hanging on to the one-dimensional characterization of emotions by psychologists on the pain-pleasure axis. The pleasure-pain axis is a one-dimensional thing, whereas pleasure is multi-dimensional and can't be expressed as a one-dimensional thing. We are programmed by nature, by our evolution, to have many many different types of satisfactions. The pleasure of feeling love is not commensurate with that of a hot bath.

Today, however, in Cyborg III, we shall be able to use the molecules and design them, making use of our knowledge of what types of emotion we have and how we want to improve man's emotional nature to make him less destructive and more creative, enjoying the various satisfactions of life. To better the quality of life, not in a hedonistic way alone. Not chiefly in a hedonistic way.

CHG: Well, reverence was one of the emotions you concentrated on.

MC: I'm the only one, I think, in the whole of psychology who has measured the expression of reverence! One person who writes about cyborgs says a cyborg doesn't feel reverence. Well, that is simply false. There is no reason in the world why cyborg can't feel reverence as much as any other human.

CHG: What about Cyborg IV?

MC: Cyborg III, you see, is making use of all the knowledge of molecular biology to improve man without changing heredity. Now Cyborg IV will come maybe fifty or a hundred years from now, when we know enough about the relationship between these molecules and the mind, consciousness and emotions, so they will no longer be afraid to change something, even in heredity. So that they will be able to improve, clearly, without the possibility that this could be damaging. And then participatory evolution at that point will really change human nature, and for the better.

CHG: Do you see a proliferation of different types of humans? Because everyone won't be changed in the same way, I imagine.

MC: Let's say at present you can remember seven digits of a number.

CHG: Short-term memory.

MC: The average person now. With certain changes you could make it go to nine or whatever. Or, let's say there will be a way to implant into the brain actual learning.

A computer can do two things a human can't do. One, it can forget perfectly, and two, if it learns one thing, a bit of information, a program, then all computers in the world have learned it, assuming that the operating systems are compatible. You work out a program for one computer and you can run it on all of them. If one learns French then they all know French. Eventually it should be possible to tap human memory in such a way that you can make people learn some things without the effort of learning.

CHG: And the emotions too, I would imagine.

MC: Well, emotions are mostly not learned. They grow in us; they're part of our biological heritage. You see, they are not arbitrary. They are part of the gifts we are born with, just like organs. You have hearts, you have kidneys, and you have all these sets of emotions. Like laughter, for example. You can't teach anybody to laugh who doesn't know how to laugh. You can say, "First you do 'ha'. Practice that. Next week you do 'ha, ha, ha'. When you can do that well, then you may try 'ha ha ha.'" It will never work. This sort of, thing you can never introduce into a human from outside.

CHG: I was struck that in several places your book talks about a new kind of laughter you sort of discovered.

MC: It's the same laughter, but done in a very different way. It's laughter, but instead of the voice you substitute another motor output. It was a prediction of the theory. The first time that an emotional function could be predicted before it was ever experienced.

CHG: So it is not a new emotion?

MC: It's not a new emotion. In fact it feels identical. The interesting thing is precisely that it feels the same, but it's done in a totally different way. Not the usual way: "Ha, ha." I press my arm and my fingers on my knee at the rate of the "ha, ha," and no "ha, ha" and tears will come to my eyes in the same way as if I laughed with the voice.

We can't invent new emotions unless we can change things radically in molecular biology. The human genome is being analyzed now. This will take some time, but decades are nothing on a larger scale. Eventually we will know the difference, let's say, between a dog nature and a cat nature. How are cat's emotions different than dog's? The dog wags his tail very readily and is generally very happy and jumps up and down when his master comes home.

CHG: Right, cats are very different.

MC: Cats are very different. But emotions also would not necessarily have to change with age in the way that they largely do now.

Even with Cyborg IV there is no likelihood of being able to invent new emotions. The link between an emotion gene and the specific feeling is a fundamental equation that is still far from being solved, even at the stage of Cyborg IV. That is a fundamental mystery that goes to the heart of being. It may take several hundred or even thousand years to understand that. But that is not long.

I think I should mention that some people writing about cyborgs talk about machines that are virtually invisible because they are made of what they call sunshine, electromagnetic light, electromagnetic waves, and they make a big deal of that. But what in fact is visible to us by nature? We live in a **real virtual reality**. That is, our senses give us a real virtual reality. For example, there are no colors. They don't exist. How would the Good Lord see colors? Wouldn't he have to have three receptors like we do, and our *qualia* as designed into our brains? There are no colors in `nature`, there's no sweet, there's no sound. There's none of that stuff. It's all filtered with active filters, our senses. We, our brains, create the sensory world. *We* create this. This is a virtual reality that we create. It is a real virtual reality and is our common home, derived from our sensing—and our feeling.

Feeling warm or cold defined by *our* comfort zone. And it's the `invention` of feeling itself *that* we need to understand, how that marvel happened.

Even beyond this, importantly, when you see anything, you see it out in space, even though the light touches your retina. You don't feel it at the retina. You (your nervous system, of course) *project* it out into space. When you hear a sound coming, you don't feel it normally at your eardrum, unlike when your body is touched. Evolution has figured out a **projected** virtual reality, that your brain creates for you. Enjoy it! That too is part of the real virtual reality.

When you create this cyborg so that you can see a person 1,000 miles away you are changing things very little from what nature magically did for us. Of course, there is no "nature" either: there is no localized earthian "Nature," only the universe.

Eventually, millennia from now, our brains may perhaps exist for thousands of years or more, rich in illusion, concentrated and powerful, with multiple sensors, and may not really need the body for its existence. The pleasures of the body, and striving of the spirit, learning, creating and inquiring and communicating could be available without the body, and then some, as they are to us in dreams today. That would be Cyborg V. Man's essence survives the vicissitudes of the body, with a brain of expanded functionality, with more highly evolved feeling, with further developed empathy. By the time that happens the very materials of the brain will have been changed to a degree, with a new freedom because its organization will be less taken up with its own maintenance, and more with its consciousness, with communicating to other consciousnesses, and communicating with sources of information, music, art, experiencing new emotions. The web of Internet will truly become a body politic, loneliness banished for all, while maintaining individuality, privacy. People will not fall in love because of their appearances, but will love for its own sake, as foreshadowed in the music of Beethoven, of Bach. What will such people talk about? Serial language will have been replaced by parallel language. (I don't mean here parallel computing which is going on in the brain all the time, but language itself.) Time consciousness too, will be choosable, to encompass various rates of time flow, at will. And what is will, or rather what will be will? There we have to leave you with something to ponder, in case everything else has been taken care of!

When we dream in sleep today we give up our will, we dream to ourselves, we don't know what we'll be dreaming next, yet we are also effortlessly creating the dream. Moreover, in dreams our sense of time is transmuted. We shall know enough then to be able to chose the pace of our time consciousness. **We are presently programmed biologically for a certain rate. There is nothing *absolute* about that rate**. A being might exist for whom day and night is like a flicker; and for a fly a second may be a lot longer than a second is for us now. Modifying our own rate of time consciousness as we desire will very likely become possible at some stage after Cyborg IV. Our dreams already point to that possibility.

After all we need to dream now, and often, mysteriously to us, we may be wiser in our dreams than we think. **Evolution is more than survival of the fittest.** And participant evolution can make fit the adventurous, the self-chosen unfit, and probably improve the qualities of life more effectively, even in the long run, than by just waiting for the less fit to become extinct. Let us pay homage to those adventurous fish who ventured unto land. Without them we would not be here. Their less adventurous cousins are fit and still survive today, in water.

Notes

1. Rejected without explanation by *Astronautics,* it is published for the first time immediately preceding this interview.

2. "Essentic form-aspects of control, function, and measurement." *Proceedings of the 21st ACEMB Conference,* 1968.

3. "Sentics, Biocybernetics of Emotion Communication." *Annual of the N.Y. Academy of Sciences* 220, pp. 55-131, 1974.

HOW DO WE GET THERE?

Major Jack E. Steele, USAF, MC

Wright Air Development Division

Where are we, where are we going, and how do we get there? These questions are obviously interrelated. Apparently we are going to design devices and systems which to the naive observer might appear to be alive. They will employ processes and techniques and accomplish functions which hitherto have existed only in living systems. Where are we now? We are on the threshold, or some would say slightly beyond the threshold, of an era of scientific and technical development in which such achievements are possible. We are here because we are consciously aware of, and have had some practical experience with the methods necessary to such achievement. We have given the name "Bionics" to the recognition and practice of these methods.

The techniques employed, drawn from three scientific or technical disciplines—biology, mathematics, engineering—are represented by the symbol with which you are familiar. Present-day computers, with all their shortcomings, are some of the most 'vital' devices man has ever produced. A short review of their heritage is in order. It will serve to illustrate the method of contribution of each of the three areas. It begins with Aristotle's study of man. His contribution was his logic, a verbal description of the processes of thinking and of speaking which he considered to be a manifestation of thought. The next important step in the sequence was the work of George Boole, a mathematician who published, about a century ago, a book titled *The Laws of Thought*. In this book he demonstrated that the essence of classical logic could be expressed as an algebra, now known as Boolean algebra. And finally we have in this century the engineer Claude Shannon, who showed that Boolean algebra could be applied very practically in the design of switching circuits and networks. And today there is a host of engineers applying that algebra to the design of those switching networks known as digital computers.

These relationships so expressed seem fairly clear and obvious. But, they have not always been so obvious to everyone. I have met computer designers who said they had no use for biology, that mathematics alone was adequate for their design problems. They employed Boolean algebra, of course, but obviously were unaware of or had forgotten its origins. On the other hand, I have heard designers discuss the implementation of ideas which they attributed to Piaget, a child psychologist. I trust they will graduate eventually to borrowing from adolescent and eventually adult psychology. The greatest hope of bionics is that something has been learned about the human mind since the days of Aristotle, that modern mathematicians can formalize this knowledge and that modern engineers can utilize it.

Now to discuss the greatest difficulty, organization. The three disciplines are competent to handle their proper portion of the problem, but how is the effort to be combined? All combinations of the same three things are not equivalent.

These three techniques or disciplines no more constitute bionics than a box full of transistors, condensers, resistors and wire forms a radio. The relationships existing among the components is the deciding feature. The same components yield systems of widely differing function, depending on their interconnections. These interconnections are more difficult to trace in human organization. When we see a team composed of biologist, mathematician and engineer working together we may easily misinterpret the function of the group. Considering a single directed relationship such as who offers advice or assistance to whom, there are 51 discrete ways to organize such a three-man group without excluding any man from the group activity.

Of these many possible structures for such a group some are so traditional and common that many people can conceive of no other. The engineer builds equipment with which the biologist collects data for the mathematician to analyze. This is as obvious and natural a relationship as the sun rising in the east, setting in the west and thus revolving around the earth once a day, but it is not bionics. This traditional limitation is unbelievably severe. I know of *not one* biologist whose main activity is that of applying biological principles in the aid of machine design. There may be a few attempting to formalize biological data so that it may be ultimately applicable.

Consider the quantitative aspects of the problem. Four rather large corporations with over 400,000 employees and expressing great interest in bionics employ among them in their research and design activity five life scientists. Any small biological or neurophysiological laboratory may employ this many physical scientists, engineers or technicians. But still more serious, in each of these corporations, the relationship is such that the engineers are helping the biologists *study* life. The biologists are not helping the engineers with their problems. The attitude of the biologists—that they know nothing of value, and that only at some future date, after having received still more assistance from the other two disciplines, will they acquire marvelously useful knowledge—is one of the greatest impediments to successful collaboration.

This situation is the consequence of natural selection. A man with a primary passion for synthesis or creative design simply does not become a biologist. The problems and attractions of biology are not those of synthesis and design, but of observation and analysis. Lest you think I am over-critical of the biologist I shall remind you of the problems brought to the collaboration by the engineer and the mathematician.

The engineer typically resents the sloppy amorphous quality of biological knowledge, its lack of precision and its multivariate complexity. The engineers often feel they have nothing to learn from this messy science and that mathematics is adequate to their needs. This means that someone like Boole must convert the biological principles into nice neat equations so the engineers will not be offended.

Finally to the mathematician. He enjoys manipulating symbols. If these symbols stand for nothing recognizable to anyone else, biologist or engineer, then the mathematician refers to the manipulation as Pure Mathematics. The mathematician prefers abstractions, the less he abstracts from, and the more he can reject of, reality, the happier he is. The mathematicians "neuron" is stark indeed. He quickly strips it of all its biologically interesting features to get on more quickly with the more enjoyable occupation of symbol manipulation. He strips his problems of these features which would make them interesting to others to make them rigorously solvable and therefore of more interest to himself.

Well, how do we get there? What is to be done about these problems of tradition, disposition, and organization? Tradition can be overcome only by education and demonstration, at worst by the education of a new generation of scientists differently oriented because they gained their experience and training by working on problems of a different type and in a different environment than that which molded their predecessors. The problems of the biologist, the mathematician and the engineer referred to previously exist because in the caricatures drawn the man was "only a biologist," "only an engineer," or "only a mathematician." When one man is all three he cannot hold these provincial attitudes in regard to communicating with himself. He can bring a blend of the attitudes of all three to bear on the same problem.

Herein lies part of the motivation behind the generation of the term bionics. Interdisciplinary effort, cross-fertilization is approved by all, but the product, the half-breed is often socially acceptable to neither parent group.

He who chases two rabbits catches neither. A man half trained in several fields is well trained in none. However, he serves a useful purpose, that of translator. The easiest way to make such training acceptable, both to the man who must acquire it and to the institutions which must provide it is to define a new area precisely covering it. The trick has been used before, often successfully. In the meantime we must make do by continuing the education of existing specialists, by teaching biology to the engineers, mathematics to the biologist, and an appreciation of messy, nonlinear, probabilistic reality, both biological and technological, to the mathematicians. For those who can stand it, the insight afforded to their traditional problems by the broadened conceptual system so acquired is well worth the effort. Further they are then qualified to participate in one of the most fascinating and rewarding challenges of modern technology, the creation of the true servomechanism, the true slave-machine transcendent in strength and intellect, subservient in will.

Though this goal is great and distant, we need not sacrifice to reach it. Each step of the route affords rich rewards more than sufficient to repay the effort necessary to achieve it. This becomes increasingly evident to those working in the field and helps provide part of the answer to the final problem, how to gain the organizational and financial support from the nontechnical portions of the organizations in which such activities as bionics must always be embedded.

There is always opposition of greater or lesser degree, of various types and of many motivations. "Men were not meant to fly." "Wheels are better than feet." "Airplanes don't flap their wings." Many fear the fate of Prometheus and Arachne. Some simply consider the task too difficult and all effort wasted. The answer is unceasing education and explanation, and gadgets, simple solutions, soon delivered. Identified as the offspring of bionics they will bring honor and support to their parent and make the greater achievements possible. Other organizational problems are not specific to bionics and their solution will not be discussed here.

Finally having acquired personnel of adequate education and attitude, and having acquired financial and organizational support, the technical approach is relatively simple and straightforward. Of utmost importance is to keep the goal in mind, the solution of some engineering design problem, not the conduct of experiments, not the formulation of theories, not the publication of technical reports. These are ancillary to the solution of an engineering problem. Problem selection is based on several criteria:

> 1. *Utility. The solution of the problem must yield something of practical value, not a symbolic reward.*

> 2. *The problem must be common to both synthetic and living systems.*

> 3. *The problem must appear solvable in all three areas.*

>> a. *Biological understanding must be well developed.*

>> b. *The requisite mathematics must be available or under development.*

>> c. *Engineering ability must exist to exploit the answer when available. Having selected a problem, the biological system and processes responsible for its solution are analyzed. The information is formalized or described mathematically and applied to the solution of the engineering problem. This is the analysis, formalization and synthesis represented in the bionics symbol.*

The manner in which bionics will make its greatest contribution to technology is not through the solution of specific problems or the design of particular devices. Rather it is through the revolutionary impact of a whole new set of concepts, a fresh point of view. Engineers are not considering systems of organizational complexity far beyond their past experience and present ability to comprehend. Such systems are the natural domain of the biologist. It would appear strange indeed if the concepts developed during their centuries of study do not provide profitable insight to those men presently laboring at the synthesis of similar systems.

(From the Bionics Symposium, Dayton, Ohio, September 1960. Thanks to Frank L. Palazzo for tracking Dr. Steele down.)

⌐ 1.6

An Interview with Jack E. Steele

Chris Hables Gray

Chris Hables Gray: Can you tell me when you were born and your parents names?

Jack E. Steele: 27 January 1924 in Lacon, Illinois. My father was Maurice Steele. His family left England as a result of the War of the Roses. My mother was Ruth Feller. Her parents were Pennsylvania Dutch.

CHG: Where did you go to school?

JES: Many places. 12 years in my father's school system in Mendota, Illinois. Then one year at the University of Illinois in Champaign. I was drafted in 1943. I was in the ASTP, the Army Specialized Training Program. The Army sent me, after basic training, to the Illinois Institute of Technology for two quarters of engineering and then to the University of Minnesota for a year of pre-medicine. After 9 months working in an Army hospital I was sent to Northwestern University Medical School. I was discharged in the spring of 1946 because the Army didn't need doctors. I finished medical school with the help of the G.I. Bill and a 40-hour-a-week night job. Then in 1951 they decided that they did need doctors and I was drafted again.

During medical school I spent one summer at the University of Indiana and one at the

University of California at Berkeley. Fermi and Oppenheimer were visiting professors. I audited their courses and took a course in atomic physics. I had been studying semiconductors and metallic-oxide films because I thought they could be used to make small solid-state analogues of vacuum tubes and I realized that many such would be needed to build my thinking machine.

CHG: Didn't you also get a master's degree in 1977?

JES: Right, that was from Wright State. I had nightmares in medical school if I didn't continue studying engineering. While in the Air Force at Wright-Patterson Air Force Base, I took courses in missile guidance, servomechanisms, computer programming and mathematics. By the time I retired from the Air Force I had the equivalent of a B.S. in engineering and was accepted in the Wright State master's program.

CHG: Before the Army drafted you the second time you were researching neuroanatomy.

JES: After interning at Cincinnati General Hospital I returned to Northwestern University Medical School and asked Dr. Ray Snider for permission to work in his laboratory. When he understood that I was not asking for employment he agreed. After two months he found a fellowship for me and I was given enough to live on. During the following months my mother sent me a quotation from Edison, one of my boyhood heroes. He said, in effect, that any man can work for any man he wishes if he offers to work and does not demand payment. Furthermore, if he is worth anything he will get paid. I am the only person I know who actually did this.

In Dr. Snider's laboratory I studied the effects of drugs on the electrical activity of the rabbit's brain, I may have been the first to observe that DDT affected the brain. Alcohol does also. They were the two largest effects.

At the end of that year another doctor and I were accepted to work at Mantino State Hospital, with a population of over 20,000 psychiatric patients. We had the use of a laboratory and hoped to test some of our theories about schizophrenia, but I was drafted again.

CHG: When was the first time you were drafted by the U.S. Army?

JES: In 1943 for World War II. I was drafted again in 1951 (in spite of being over the draft age and having had more than the required time in service).

CHG: You were then an officer because of your medical training.

JES: Right. I was a first Lieutenant in 1951. I retired in 1971 as a Colonel.

CHG: I was going to ask you about the exact genesis of the term 'bionics.' I guess it was first publicized in 1960, but you coined it in 1959?

JES: Probably, in August, 1958. The first printed example I can find is June, 1959 in a note to the Committee on Bioelectronics. We more readily recognize the existence of something if we have a name for it. Bioelectronics, biophysics, biomechanics, biochemistry were all names for other disciplines in the service of biological research. There was almost no recognition of biology in the service of design engineering or the solving of design problems in general. This reverse flow of information has occurred for centuries but only in the work of individual creative men. There was no organized effort as in other disciplines.

I sought Greek roots as the best source for a scientific name and most easily translated to other languages. The dictionary defined 'bion' as a unit of life with emphasis on function, as opposed to 'morphon' with the emphasis on form. '-ics' is a common ending for an area of intellectual or other activity as in mathematics, physics, athletics, politics. **Bionics is the discipline of using principles derived from living systems in the solution of design problems.** Similar problems may be solved by similar techniques. Bionic is the adjectival form and refers to things which are lifelike in function or the efforts to produce such things.

CHG: You were saying that your earliest interest was in the human brain.

JES: I knew about thought before I knew there was a brain. "Why do other people think so funny?" was a big question in my mind as a preschooler exploring the world. It is actually easier to analyze a system through its failures than when it is functioning well. The nature of the mistakes it makes is determined by its structure and function.

At that time I was collaborating with Leonard Butch. He was a major in the Electronics Technology Laboratory. When the bionics project was split between the two laboratories we began to work closely together.

I did know Warren McCulloch quite well. In fact I shocked my bosses when we were planning the first symposium. In a meeting one day they said it would be nice to have him and Von Foerster in our symposium. The next day I told them that the men had agreed to come. They wondered how I had done it. I simply called them up and asked them. I had known them for years.

CHG: How did you know them?

JES: The year I worked with Dr. Snider he introduced me to Dr. McCulloch who was at the University of Chicago. I actually can't remember where I first met Von Foerster. It was probably through them.

I visited McCulloch's farm near Old Lyme, Connecticut. I tried to explain what was wrong with his "A Logical Calculus of The Ideas Imminent in Nervous Activity," the digital logic, etc. He sort of pooh-poohed it and said I should go study logic. So I studied logic for a couple of years and so was better able to explain why it was wrong. The information in a signal is carried by the part of the signal that varies. Neural pulses are remarkably alike. It is the spaces in-between which vary and they of course are analog. Others I met include Norbert Wiener, when he spoke at a brown bag lunch at M.I.T. I had read his book, *Cybernetics*, when it first came out. What impressed me most about him was his recognition that there is no reason to believe that mathematics may ever represent reality exactly, that at best it is probably an approximation. People too readily accept logical, formal descriptions of things as totally accurate representations.

CHG: That's a good point.

JES: He is the first person I met who really understood this.

CHG: At some point you did research for NASA on space sickness?

JES: No. Twice they requested my transfer and I agreed but twice it was blocked by my supervisor. I did, however, work on motion sickness.

CHG: Lately, NASA's been using biofeedback as a way of dealing with space sickness. Would that fit into your model?

JES: You can control a lot of things by feedback, even the pain of a burn and certainly blood pressure. Basically I think that motion-sickness symptoms are a problem of vascular control. For example, when I was doing zero-G rides, I got sick. Not during the zero part but during the increased G. I began to get a little nauseated. I opened up one of the bags just in case, stuck my hand in, and found that someone had already used it. My nausea vanished immediately.

CHG: Because your blood pressure went up?

JES: Yes, I got angry. Later that same day, I was standing in a crowd waiting to see some dignitary visiting the art museum. I got so nauseated and faint just standing there that I had to leave. Because I'd over exercised my vascular control system apparently. You see, getting blood to the brain is important. We have to tune the muscles in our veins and arteries in such a way as to do it. And that's part of the adaptation to a changing inertial environment.

The problem in motion sickness is not overload of the sense organ but overload of the data processing required for adaptation to a novel inertial environment. There is no sickness when adaptation is achieved or if there is no attempt to achieve it.

CHG: I was going to ask if the first time you ever heard about cyborgs was when the writer Martin Caidin came by?

JES: Yes. I think so.

CHG: And how did he hear of you? Do you know?

JES: I don't know. I'm not sure I know what you mean by a cyborg.

CHG: Well, Clynes and Kline had a specific definition but if you've ever read Caidin's book *Cyborg*...

JES: Oh, yeah. Specifically an amplifier of human beings? That was one of the things I was interested in. At that time servomechanisms were designed using feedback to control either the force or the position of the actuator. Living systems fed back both force and position information. This is necessary when your actuators are working against a load having variable impedance. I had a simple little device built to try that in our lab but it's amazing the things I couldn't get my bosses interested in. That was one of them.

CHG: Doesn't the Air Force still actually have bionic symposiums? Do you know of any bionics associations?

JES: I know of no recent symposiums nor of any associations, though there are laboratories of bionics in other countries.

CHG: Well, the term is used. I come across it.

JES: What does it mean when you come across it?

CHG: Well, it's often in terms of engineering. Actually it's sort of become the engineering term for working on the idea of cyborgs. Mechanical systems that imitate living systems, living systems made mechanic, or actual systems involving both. Biomechanical. Work done in medicine. You might come across the term bionics as an engineering discipline.

JES: There is a big difference between using the principles of living things, such as dual feedback, so that you can feel what sort of resistance you are meeting, in order to avoid shaking things like airplanes apart, versus making something that looks like an arm that can lift something and move it. One is imitation where it just sort of looks like and acts like, and the other is a design process. The end product may not look like anything. But when you borrow design features from a living thing, that to me is bionics. Of course, a word is like a child. You launch it into the world and it develops a life of its own.

One thing that makes me kind of happy is to see an eight-year-old kid hobbling along on leg braces and crutches grinning and saying, 'I'm bionic! I'm bionic!' I get a chuckle out of that.

CHG: You were telling me how Universal Studios was trying to buy....

JES: They bought the rights to *Cyborg*.

CHG: Yeah, Martin Caidin's book. And then they tried to copyright and trademark bionic.

JES: They tried to keep other people from using the term. Apparently they did copyright a few combinations like "bionic dog" or "bionic woman."

CHG: Did this ever go to court?

JES: Oh yes. I looked up cases on bionics and I found quite a few. Mainly it was Universal Studios trying to prevent others from using the term. A rubber-heel company wanted to make bionic heels, a knife company wanted a bionic knife, and so forth. And generally, Universal Studios lost, not because it wasn't their term, but because nobody would confuse a rubber heel with a bionic man.

Incidentally, the hidden agenda behind my promotion of bionics was to legitimize and obtain support for building a thinking machine, my life ambition. I found there was a lot of resistance to it. I put down thinking machine as a long-range goal in the research plan. My bosses crossed it out. I was not allowed to work toward a thinking machine.

CHG: But the term bionics didn't scare them?

JES: No. That was life; they were biologists. We were in an aeromedical laboratory, a biological laboratory. Bio didn't scare them. Neuromime networks were acceptable.

Col. Butch (he was finally made a colonel) described what we were trying to do to one of the Brothers at the University of Dayton, a Catholic institution. He was told, "If you succeed, it will have to be baptized." That alerted me to the source of a lot of the resistance. Human egotism, the need to feel unique and superior. There's a lot of emotional resistance to a thinking machine. Only men can think; machines can't. **It is ridiculous the way people keep redefining thinking in order to keep themselves ahead of machines.** So I started giving speeches all over the country, in Minneapolis, Minnesota, in Texas, Washington, New York, and Virginia. "Machines Who Think and People That Don't."

Telling about how clever machines are and how people keep putting them down. Like we aren't animals. "God made us superior to animals." If we are made in the image of God, you can see the blasphemy some would see in our making a machine in our image.

CHG: So you actually think that in some ways we are machines and we are animals.

JES: Of course we are animals and machines. If we and other animals didn't share some properties with machines, bionics would be impossible.

Most designers of intelligent machines tend to follow Aristotle. He made a great error in his logic. He said he intended to analyze human thought, but since we thought in Greek, he would just analyze the Greek language. The purpose of language is communication, not thought. That has misled almost everyone who has worked on thinking machines. Words are tricky. People who think with words don't think very well. Formal logic is kind of ridiculous. The thinking is all done by the time you get the formal logic going. Most psychologists and logicians agree that we do not think with logic. It is not natural and must be learned. Formal logic deals with the form of statements, not their content. Our thinking is mainly by content logic. Formal logic may be used to check the results.

I call the logic we actually use 'protologic'. I developed it before trying to design neuromime networks to implement it. At first I called it "fuzzball logic" because of its multidimensional and fuzzy properties. I was pleased when Zadah started promoting fuzzy logic. It was very similar. That's what machines will have to use if they're going to think. Some of the networks are approaching that a little bit.

CHG: So from the very beginning when you heard of digital computers—and maybe you heard of Turing's article in 1950 in *Mind*?

JES: Oh, yeah.

CHG: You assumed that the digital approach wasn't going to be the right approach?

JES: I always believed that thinking was analog. As I learned more about digital computation I realized that for computational purposes they're equivalent, but I have never seen the real differences between digital and analog discussed.

Essentially a digital system uses some subset of all possible signals. Not every possible signal is recognized as an acceptable signal. In speech every sound is not a legitimate speech sound. We have a set of sounds, maybe fifty, that we recognize as speech signals. Different languages use slightly different sounds. Accents are due to our programming as children to hear only our own set of speech sounds. However, when we hear sounds near one of them we tend to interpret it as if it were that sound. When you hear a foreign language you tend to hear sounds in your own language that are near what they say. It's sort of a noise-correcting thing. Digital basically is a noise-correcting system wherein signals that are a little bit off are interpreted as being the nearest acceptable signal. That's the difference between digital and analog. An analog signal is infinitely continuous. It makes error detection and correction difficult.

CHG: What was the first computer you came across?

JES: Good question. I read about Vannevar Bush's Differential Analyzer, an analog machine. The first digital one was the IBM machine on the base. I remember my surprise when it ran the same problem twice and got identical answers. Thinking like an engineer I always expect a little slop and error. When you repeat an experiment you get nearly the same results. I started collecting pieces to build my own computer. We had a computer club in Dayton, but before I got enough parts, Commodore came out with a computer for about $600. It sat on the kitchen table for several years.

CHG: Then after you left the Air Force, your M.D. was already in psychiatry?

JES: Psychiatry is a medical specialty.

CHG: You had to go through analysis?

JES: No. Three years are required. A year of didactic instruction, a year of research, and a year of supervised practice. You are then eligible to take speciality board exams. That's one way to get to be declared a specialist. In Ohio I'm legally a psychiatric specialist not because I took the board exam but because I limited my practice to psychiatry for ten years. The reason I didn't take a residency is I could do impossible things as an intern and I didn't want to spend three years being told it couldn't be done.

CHG: For example?

JES: Getting a catatonic-schizophrenic out of her catatonia and talking normally in about an hour-and-a-half or two. Getting a paranoid-schizophrenic, who was too paranoid to eat the food, claimed it was poisoned and so forth, able to return home in ten days.

CHG: What is your approach to psychiatry? Is it very much neurological?

JES: No. Ideological. Logical if you want. Personality. Remember since age five I've been trying to figure out how people think. By 1943, when I was in the Army in engineering school, I experimented with implanting a memory in a man. Very successful.

CHG: Through hypnosis?

JES: No. That's a misunderstood condition or term. Indirectly, I set it up so that it was to his advantage to remember. He protected his ego by remembering. So his own internal parts juggled things around to remember because it would have been too painful to him not to remember.

We were in a school that failed out twenty percent per quarter and they went out to be shot at. Losing your memory could be fatal. So I emphasized that he didn't remember and this was a sign of mental weakness. I never once told him what to remember. That isn't how you suggest things. Anyway that confirmed that my theories were coming along pretty good. In doing psychiatry I felt that I was modeling clay using tools of clay. I had to get an internal ally. Instead of emphasizing their sickness I'd emphasize the part in there that was well. You strengthen the part you interact with. Instead of making a lame man hop on his lame leg, you teach him to walk with crutches on his good leg. Then you have an ally to help you solve the problem. Fifth-column therapy, if you want.

CHG: Is that what it's called in psychiatry?

JES: I don't think anybody calls it anything. Some refer to 'the answers within'. People heal themselves with the therapist's coaching.

CHG: Well some psychologists have emphasized thinking about what makes

people well. People like Maslow. I don't know psychiatry that well.

JES: I did not take a residency because I did not want to be told for four years the impossibility of doing what I could already do. Had I known about Milton Erikson I would have sought a residency with him. You asked how did I deal with those patients? In retrospect it seems I was using Eriksonian indirect hypnosis. The reason I really miss not getting to know him was he arrived at it by years of experience. I arrived at it by theory. He always eschewed theory. Most theories aren't very good. Theory got me to the same clinical-type activity as his nontheory. I think we would have made a good pair.

CHG: Are you now thinking of working more on your original project, of a thinking machine?

JES: You know what model neurons are I suppose?

CHG: Yes.

JES: I didn't even call mine a neuron because I figured it was much more simple. But it had about five different types of input. Just one or two types of inputs seemed totally inadequate. In order to accomplish the logic I thought people used in thinking they had to have at least five different types of input. Incidentally, now they've discovered 15 or 20 different chemical communicators in the brain, possibly closer to 100. I anticipated that there were more than they knew at the time because they were necessary to accomplish the logic.

CHG: Are you going to go back and play around with neurons?

JES: For one thing, now that everybody knows more I won't have to explain as much when I write. People have stumbled along with a lot of stuff, fuzzy logic, for example. That is much like the protologic I was trying to implement in the 60's. I get kind of irritated with people who make a neuron and say, 'Well, if we hook enough together it will think.' Like, 'birds fly with feathers. Let's glue a bunch of feathers on a board and it will fly.' That's not the right way. The task comes first and then the tool. You've heard about the doctors who invented a cure and thought surely they would find a disease for which it would work? That's the approach of these guys with their networks. To me the proper approach, and the bionic approach, is not 'What does the brain do?' but 'What is the logic that the brain uses?' You see, we don't have to have the same hardware or the same signal, but if we use the same logic system we can get it done. And incidentally, neither the logicians nor the psychologists will claim that we think with formal logic. That's Aristotle's analysis of language. And Boole claimed rules of thought but he just formalized Aristotle. And, as far as I know, I'm the first one who ever really looked at the logic of the brain. I get frightened sometimes. I think, 'Gee, am I the first one who ever did this or ever did that?' I can feel less proud when I realize that protologic, a content logic, could have had no application before the advent of computers. It simply requires too much information processing.

CHG: Someone has to be first.

JES: Yeah, I guess so. You know what happened to the first guy to fly across the Atlantic?

CHG: No.

JES: Lindbergh. His son was murdered.

CHG: Oh, right, he was kidnapped and murdered.

JES: This impressed me about the time I was learning to read. He was my hero and then when I'm reading the newspapers I hear about what happens to people who are famous and well known. It's always been rather repellent. My ambition has always been to have my work well known, and not my person.

CHG: That reminds me of that story you wrote in your letter. Your mother fell and you had a dream.

JES: Yeah, that was the dream.

CHG: That your mother fell and her head came open and it was full of wheels. And that was a relief?

JES: Yes.

CHG: Because you realized that her brain worked the same way as yours?

JES: No. I realized that was why she was so rigid in her thoughts. She was programmed. Automatic. She couldn't adapt to circumstances. I couldn't reason with her any more than you can reason with a clock.

CHG: That's interesting.

JES: If a person is foolish you think, 'Gee, maybe they're crazy or something?' But if you find out that they are merely programmed then there may be nothing wrong with their thinking. They are just poorly programmed. People would ask at the hospital why I never got angry at the patients. I'd think of them as malfunctioning machines. It's stupid to get angry at machines. And other people say, 'Oh, don't you care about people?' Certainly, I happen to love machines.

CHG: That's very interesting. Um, to go back to a more contemporary issue ... Have you ever read Marvin Minsky's book, *A Society of Minds*?

JES: I don't think so. Is that a multimind kind of thing?

CHG: He actually looks at a lot of different approaches used in artificial intelligence. Everything from scripts to McCarthy's fascination with common sense and so on to neurological models. He says, "Well, they're all sort of true."

JES: Well, they're all symbol manipulations rather than representations of reality.

CHG: So you would say they're all sort of false?

JES: Yes. They are all Aristotelian in that sense of manipulating the names of things instead of a more information-rich representation. When I get to feeling proud about being the first to figure out this protologic logic I put myself down, saying, 'Well, what good is it? You can't write it down? It takes a computer to realize.' There was no use for it before computers. Other logic had good use, but protologic was a content logic, or at least a large part of it was content. To illustrate: If two men can paint a house in a week, ten of them can paint it in a day, a thousand of them can paint it in under thirty seconds? Formal logic would say yes, that's so. But you laugh at it because of the content. You have knowledge of houses, men, and the operation of painting. That's the way we think.

CHG: Zeno's paradox shows the fallacy of that kind of logic ... the arrow only gets half-way there, then half-way again ...

JES: The fallacy is in the term 'never', a temporal concept. Each step goes half the remaining distance but in half the remaining time. The ancients weren't too good at summing infinite series. Well, of course, Zeno's paradox is evidence of poor thought. Any paradox shows you are using a poor model. Reality has no paradoxes, only models of it do. Whenever you encounter a paradox there is an error in your model.

CHG: Still, you must accept Gödel's Theorem that any model that's at a certain level of complexity is then either limited or does have paradoxes?

JES: Certainly. All models are limited. They are abstract. Ultimate prediction is impossible because the only total model of reality is reality itself. Any other predictor is a small subset and has to be abstracted and leave something out.

CHG: So I'm curious about several other issues. Did you ever read much science fiction?

JES: Yes. I did last night. I did this afternoon.

CHG: I meant originally ... When you were younger.

JES: Oh, yes. I started in the forties. Not my forties, 1940, 1939, in there.

CHG: Do you remember any of the things you read?

JES: *Astounding* mostly. I remember a story about Waldos, remote manipulators. They were a sort of telepresence for manipulation. They could be made large and strong or small and delicate. There was one story about rewiring a brain. They just hooked things up and figured the person would learn to use the new connections, which was rather fascinating and rather forward looking at the time. There's a limit to how far you can relocate connections. If an auditory input is hooked to a visual area you will see sounds. This occurs sometimes in human development.

CHG: Asimov's robots?

JES: Yeh. Incidentally, there must be eight or a dozen consciousnesses in the mind running things. I mean, it takes a thousand men to run a battleship. A captain couldn't do it with a lot of buttons. There is too much information processing involved.

CHG: Is this related at all to multiple-personality disorder?

JES: Of course it is related to multiplicity. We all are multiple. But we're a little more tightly organized than the multiple personality. We all have things we've forgotten, areas we don't remember. Different parts do different things. In different circumstances we're different people. I'm thankful for all my tumbling and athletic and combat training because when I'm in a dangerous physical situation I react so rapidly that only in retrospect can I realize what I've done. A motorcycle accident, for example, I came out of totally uninjured. Just by very fast responses.

Multiple personalities develop for protective purposes. Some suffer the trauma but keep the others unaware of it. Thus the person can keep functioning. **It becomes a disorder only when the person has escaped the traumatic situation but has not reorganized the crew or cared for the injured parts.**

CHG: So what science fiction have you been reading more recently?

JES: I subscribe to *Analog* and *Fantasy* and *Science Fiction*. I'm getting a little disgusted at the PC-ness of it. Political Correctness.

CHG: How so?

JES: Well, they just have to have a female black homosexual for a hero. Or some variation thereof. I get a chuckle from *Star Trek* sometimes, when they seem to show great cooperation among different species. You know everybody gets along with everybody. And then poor old Data wants to be human. That's not getting along. Its just another example of human egotistical chauvinism. As if being human is good, somehow super-virtuous.

CHG: I was also wondering since you watch a lot of science fiction what do you think of some of these cyborgs you see on TV, like the Borg on *Star Trek*.

JES: They were intended to be villainous, but their villainy is not due to their mechanical augmentation but to their biologic traits, those of colonial insects, bees or ants.

Of course my favorite is Data. He's a great guy. People so easily overlook that we're all sort of cyborg. We wear false teeth or have metal or plastic implants in our natural teeth. And clothing. Clothing is so obvious that we don't see it. All of us are cyborgs walking around with synthetic fur, synthetic skin on the bottoms of our feet. Many wear lenses in front of their eyes or amplifiers in their ears and in these modern times many another artificial but well-functioning part.

CHG: Yeah, it certainly is a continuum. Humans have always been...

JES: We've always been cyborgs, more or less!

CHG: In some sense I think that's certainly true...

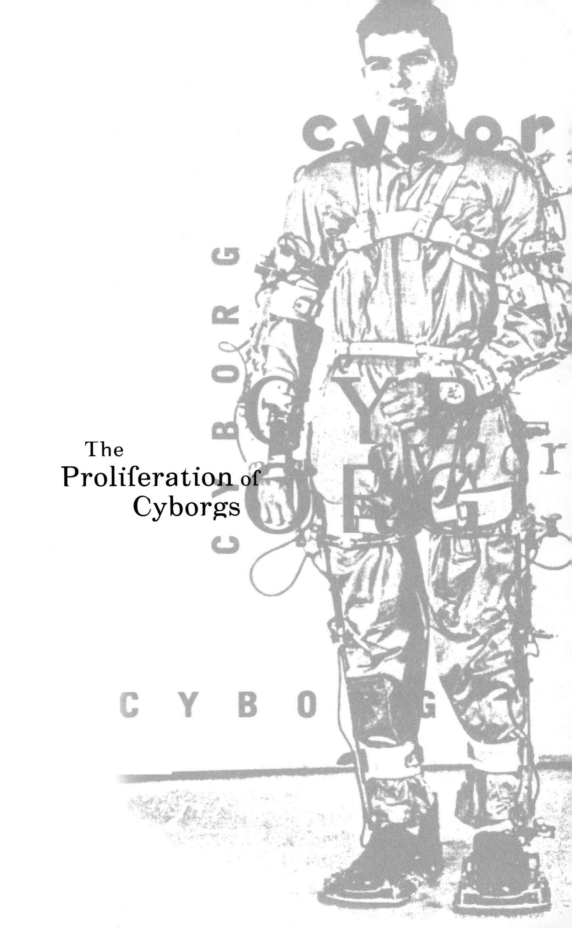

The
Proliferation of
Cyborgs

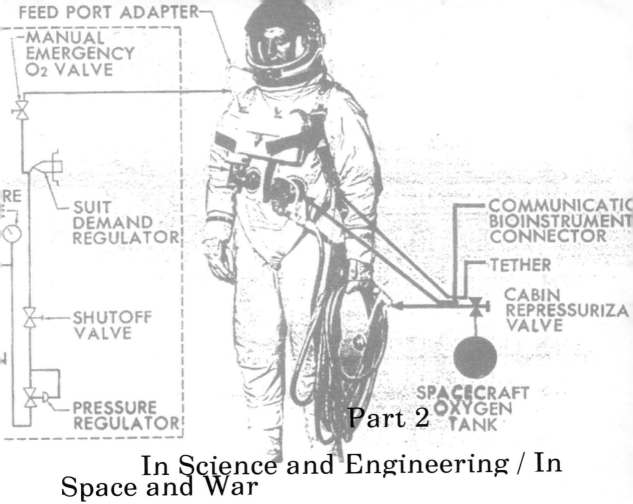

FEED PORT ADAPTER

MANUAL EMERGENCY O₂ VALVE

SUIT DEMAND REGULATOR

SHUTOFF VALVE

PRESSURE REGULATOR

RE

COMMUNICATIO BIOINSTRUMENT CONNECTOR

TETHER

CABIN REPRESSURIZA VALVE

SPACECRAFT OXYGEN TANK

Part 2

In Science and Engineering / In Space and War

Engineering Man For Space
THE CYBORG STUDY

FINAL REPORT
NASw-512

TO: NASA (OART) BIOTECHNOLOGY AND HUMAN RESEARCH
WASHINGTON, D.C.

MAY 15, 1963

SUBMITTED BY: ROBERT W. DRISCOLL, CYBORG PROGRAM
APPROVED BY: RICHARD J. PRESTON, MANAGER, BIO-SCIENCES AND TECHNOLOGY

UNITED AIRCRAFT
CORPORATE SYSTEMS CENTER
FARMINGDALE, CONN.

The CYBORG study is the study of man. It concerns itself with the determination of man's capabilities and limitations under the unpredictable and often hostile conditions of space flight, and the theoretical possibility of incorporating artificial organs, drugs, and/or hypothermia as integral parts of the life support systems in space craft design of the future, and of reducing metabolic demands and the attendant life support requirements. By this approach it is hoped that the efficiency and longevity of the life process on board space flights may be increased. It covers these new areas in detail in order to determine whether their application or utilization can assure the continued contribution of man to the success of prolonged space flights or interplanetary exploration without threatening his safety during such flights. The idea of modifying man is an advanced concept which must supersede conventional thinking and which will, in the long run, provide us with basic research data in the fundamental physiology of man during the conditions of space travel.

The Phase I CYBORG study has two principal task areas. Task A is a detailed consideration of the availability and practicability of using artificial organs, hypothermia and/or drugs in adapting man to a space environment.

Task B is the collection and study of data relating to the operation of the human heart in a space environment. This has included the development of a mathematical and physical dynamic model.

This report is divided into seven major sections. The sections on artificial organs, hypothermia, drugs, sensory deprivation, and cardiovascular models represent the detailed discussion of the roles each may play in space flights of the future.

Section II thoroughly analyzes the history, development, state-of-the-art, and future directions in the fields of the artificial lung, the artificial heart, the artificial kidney and extracorporeal pump oxygenating equipment. All of the problems associated with the development of such units, physical, mechanical, and physiological, are considered in detail. Various existing models of each of the units used in present-day clinical procedures are illustrated and evaluated. Conclusions based on this information indicate limited application of artificial organs to space craft life support system design, with certain reservations however.

Section III follows the same general plan of analysis with great stress being placed in the physiologic aberrations and responses to artificially reduced body temperature. Methods by which body temperature can be lowered either by external means or electrical neurologic stimulation are covered thoroughly. The effect of this temperature reduction on the major organ systems and their physiologic functions is carefully analyzed. This work appears to indicate a potential role for hypothermia as a metabolic retarding element, both from the standpoint of space applications and terrestrial medical research contributions. The metabolic reducing effects of a hypothermic situation have been clearly demonstrated in many areas of clinical research. The ability, at some point in this research, to "suspend animation" by hypothermia becomes a significant possibility. In the preservation of red blood cells for instance, work under Navy contract has already shown that the storage of the erythrocyte is possible for periods up to four years. Tagging and reinjection of these stored cells into living systems has indicated that their predetermined life cycle of approximately 120 days has remained unchanged by the lengthy period of hypothermic preservation.

Section IV deals with a pharmacologic approach to the problems possibly to be encountered by space travelers. The use of drugs as adjunct or protective agents in human physiology for space flight considerations is not new. Extensive work has been done on the radioprotective properties of a variety of chemical agents. The section on drugs in this report limits itself, however, to a study of those agents considered applicable only in the areas of anxiety, depression, fatigue, acceleration protection, thermo-protection, metabolism reduction and motion sickness.

The use of chemical agents to alter physiologic function in space flights enables the operators to eliminate many variables in physiologic function and maintain precise and predictable control over these functions. However, although there is a great wealth of information on literally thousands of such agents, there is no central information source where the complete and varied effects of these agents, over and beyond those for which they were produced, may be obtained. It is felt that such an information base should be established immediately to fill this need. This agency would not only help the medical profession, but would also make its data available to those engaged in all forms of biomedical research.

The section on Sensory Deprivation (V) was heavily investigated because it is felt that this area can cause potentially debilitating effects on research pilots engaged in space exploration. It is considered a serious limitation on man's adaptability to space flights and, therefore, it has been emphasized in the CYBORG final report. In this area there has been extensive research and even the most preliminary analysis indicates that in hypodynamic situations where there is minimum sensory input, depending on the conditions, serious psychophysiologic deviations may occur in periods of less than one hour. This section discusses the aberrations resulting from exposure to hypodynamic conditions, identifies the environmental events associated with such effects and the sensory modality most susceptible to them, evaluates the characteristics of individuals most resistant or susceptible. In addition, it investigates methods of identifying and evaluating such characteristics and analyzes the hypodynamic aspects or possibilities of the space capsule and a space environment. It cannot be over-emphasized that the area of sensory deprivation must be actively pursued and that this area is worthy of continued, penetrating CYBORG research.

Section IV discusses the operation of the human heart in a space environment. Complete understanding of the multitude of complex interactions of organs and organ systems in the human will be a long time in coming. However, careful analysis of several of the more obvious characteristics of these systems has shown that their properties can, in many cases, be expressed in mathematical terms. The subsequent ability to duplicate and simulate any or all of these functions in terms of mathematical analogues will lead to an improvement in our understanding of the basic mechanisms and controls which affect the human system operation. By employing hypothetical, mathematical equivalents for computer simulation and high-speed input variation analysis, we can begin to understand some of the complexities of human organ systems, their interface relationships, and, accordingly, be in a better position to predict function as influenced by new and changing environments.

Although the CYBORG study (NASw-512) has dealt specifically with hypothermia, drugs, artificial organs, and cardiovascular modules, we have expanded this concept to include other fields which cannot justifiably be reported in this document. However, it is felt that the area of calcium mobilization, a potentially severe limitation on man's physiologic adaptability to a space environment, should be investigated in detail. As was discussed in the interim CYBORG report presented to NASA-OART in January of this year, the calcium-excretion levels evidenced by the three U.S. orbital man space flights were significantly elevated to arouse the interest of United Aircraft's Bio-Science group into an active pursuit of the reasons for this phenomenon. It has been proposed that mineral dynamics, along with mathematical and physical models of biological systems and sensory deprivation, be continued in subsequent phases of the CYBORG program.

VII. Future Directions of the Cyborg Concept

A. Introduction

The NASw-512 Contract is a biological design study of man, particularly in alien or extraterrestrial environments. It concerns itself with the systems requirements for the optimum life support, man monitoring control, and spacecraft configuration design which will insure his safe and continued contribution to extra-terrestrial and space explorations. By thorough study of man's systems and subsystems when subjected to the simulated and actual conditions of extraterrestrial environments, we will be able to make significant progress toward the better understanding of man as a space voyager.

In long-term space flights, the physiologic well-being of the pilot is of primary concern to the earth-bound medical monitors. While on such flights, the pilot/astronaut must be protected not only from all of the known hazards of the space environment, but must in addition receive protection from those that are suspected to be of a debilitating nature. By the same token, the conquest of space by man must not be delayed by hyperprotective measures adopted through an overcautious approach to the unknown which require elaborate and unnecessarily redundant system designs. Only by a complete understanding of man's psychophysiological reactions to these hazards can we be permitted to let such flights take place, and be in a position to predict with any degree of reliability the probable success of a given flight.

As this report indicates, only selected areas merit detailed experimental efforts in the Phase II portion of the CYBORG Program. These are mathematical models (Biocybernetics), Sensory Deprivation, and Mineral Dynamics.

B. Biocybernetics

The ability to determine the performance of several aspects of the human organism while it is subjected to the stresses of space flight, without risking an astronaut's life, can be accomplished with a large measure of success by terrestrial simulation. Careful analysis of many aspects of human functions has shown that in many cases even the seemingly most complex systems can be reduced to mathematical relationships. By computer simulation and mathematical models of these systems we can develop an actual physical dynamic analog of the system under consideration. By subjecting these analogs to the environmental stresses of a space flight in terrestrial simulation laboratories we may be better able to gather a thorough understanding of the system dynamics involved and generate the design requirements for this aspect of manned space flight.

Phase I of the CYBORG Study has been concerned with the basic problem of conceptualizing and defining specific system components of man and the functioning of these components in an extra-terrestrial environment.

As part of CYBORG, considerable effort has been devoted to the synthesis of a non-linear mathematical model of the human cardiovascular system designed to reproduce the salient features of its functioning under several environmental conditions and, possibly, under certain types of psychological inputs. In the continuation of the CYBORG concept in Phase II, efforts will continue to be devoted to the development and exploration of a cardiovascular system model and will be extended to other human systems and subsystems. It is recognized that the experimental verification of this analytic model in all detail cannot be undertaken without access to a gravitation-free environment. It is possible, however, to perform significant experimental work in animals which have been subjected to surgery in which their carotid sinuses and other baroceptors have been denervated. These animals can be thus regarded as "pseudoweightless" from the cardiovascular viewpoint, and hence can be used in studies designed to evaluate the response of the cardiovascular system to certain standard inputs such as would be encountered in rapid re-entry from a deep space mission.

Since one ultimate objective of this program is the design of sensing and processing systems, it must be emphasized that ultimately some aspects of this work must be performed under actual operational conditions in man. It is not possible or desirable at this time, however, to do more than point out the necessity for this ultimate test. Additional understanding of human cardiovascular dynamics can be expected to improve the precision with which we can specify more nearly optimum sensor-processing systems. For example, blood flow or vascular current is an important but difficult to measure physiologic parameter. It is conceivable, as shown by F. Cope, that blood flow can be determined indirectly from data on blood pressure and blood-vessel compliance.

Relationships such as the one indicated above have been investigated as part of Phase I and should certainly be further studied in this proposed program. The availability of molecular integrated circuit techniques makes it entirely conceivable that once a set of rational requirements has been generated, small sensor-processor units can be designed which will handle the data in a manner which will permit the display of more meaningful cardiovascular variables. Even in those cases where it is not feasible or desirable to incorporate the data processing elements in the sensor packages themselves, the processing methods can still be incorporated in suitable computing devices for remote handling and display. After this objective is accomplished, studies will be undertaken to explore the utility of preparing analog packages of the human vascular system. Such packages, once developed, would prove useful in both terrestrial experimentation and in the preliminary exploration of the extra-terrestrial environment.

C. Sensory Deprivation

This area has been included in the CYBORG Study because many reported effects of sensory deprivation constitute a serious modification of normal functioning, and there are grounds for supposing that the space capsule constitutes a restricted environment which provides significantly less sensory stimulation than that to which humans are usually accustomed. A major contingency which must be guarded against on any extended space mission is the induction of hypodynamic conditions as a result of a failure of any component. For example, loss of power could result in the cutting of communications with earth station. In order to maximize the probability of survival, it is essential that design requirements be specified and devices be incorporated which will maintain the sensory environment at a high dynamic level.

The major purpose of the proposed study is the identification and evaluation of the means by which man can be prepared to cope successfully with the many psychological stresses which may affect him during long-term space missions. The need for this work arises because man is basically a biological organism designed to operate within the parameters defined by the earth environment. Despite a remarkable degree of overdesign, there are many areas in which man's capabilities fall short of requirements posed by such missions.

On the basis of the present analysis, time-structuring events such as programs of moving displays, sound, and recorded material of interest to the crew seems to merit investigation. Other activities such as problem-solving requirements and sequential tests may be promising. The design requirements of such devices should receive the highest priority. By presenting to the pilot changing patterns of sensory inputs, we may be able to control his possible lapse into a state of sensory deprivation and prevent its attendant incapacitating effects from ever occurring. In addition, it is felt essential that means be formulated which will have the capacity to monitor the status of the Central Nervous System. Such a device would be able to determine the level of Central Nervous System reactivity to a marginal signal input and determine whether quite unconsciously the pilot is gradually losing control of his conscious mental processes.

D. Mineral Dynamics

On each of the three United States manned orbital flights, collected in- and post-flight urine specimens showed significantly elevated levels of excreted calcium. This is a phenomenon which has been frequently observed in the past in cases of hospital patients subjected to extended periods of immobilization, in sensory-deprivation studies, certain stress situations, and in simulated weightlessness experiments involving water immersion. It remains to be determined, however, whether this increase reflects potentially serious drainage of calcium from the skeletal system. In order to monitor and appraise the significance of alterations in calcium output, it is necessary that a detection system be devised which will permit the tracing of the mineral through the several metabolic compartments.

It can be unequivocally stated that no method is known today for determining calcium movement other than those methods involving some type of tracer. It is to be emphasized that passive neutron-activation methods are capable only of "static estimates of calcium." The elucidation of the dynamics of the mineral requires the use of distinguishable but chemically identical atomic species. Therefore, a suitable system for the detection of calcium dynamics must involve:

1. The use of a tracer,
2. A suitable sensor, and
3. The application of correct data processing techniques to the information collected.

In the course of this proposed program, we shall continue the investigation of calcium dynamics in man and animals from the viewpoint of the changes which occur as a result of immobilization and/or psychological stress and establish the requirements for a detection system to determine and display changes and predict trends in the pilot's calcium dynamics.

The CYBORG program is expected to be a long-range program of study and experimental efforts. The experimental phases are intended to develop both mathematical and physical-dynamic models of important human systems. These will include the cardiovascular, endocrine, gastrointestinal, cutaneous, and pulmonary systems. The physical models will be verified by actual laboratory experiments and relating mathematical formulae will be developed to describe interaction of the systems. These models will be simulated in the UAC computer facility and dynamically tested, ultimately, in space environmental extremes. Firm design requirements will be established for an optimized physiologic monitoring system as well as for the design requirements for a life-support environmental control system. Such systems will be integrated to provide a total man-machine complex with man in the control loop as the forcing function. Space-capsule design requirements will be delineated, as well as a result of sensory-deprivation experiments and man-augmentation mechanism design constraints.

These design requirement "groups" will be developed in such a way that a relatively simple modification scheme will allow the requirements to change and update the state of the art as time progresses. This will prevent the necessity of having to fund an entirely new program every few years to redevelop design requirements as the changing state of the art makes existing requirements groups obsolescent.

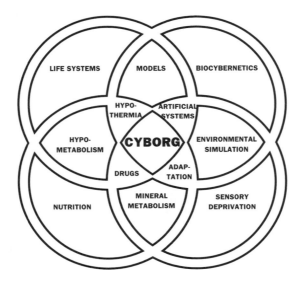

Out of the CYBORG program we will be able to understand considerably more about man, his systems and his subsystems. Methods for augmenting and extending his limitations, which will be compatible with the state of the art and the applicability of man in a space mission will be derived from CYBORG in an effort to obtain the maximum integration of man into a man-machine complex.

Hopefully we will evolve a model of the central nervous system during this period. This is an ambitious task, but must be earnestly assaulted if such a worthy undertaking is ever to be completed.

A significant number of experiments will be performed on animals and man throughout this program to verify the modeling concepts which have evolved from the CYBORG theory. In this way, CYBORG will accomplish its mission by providing a better understanding of the biological design of man and relating the impact of this understanding to compatible hardware systems.

AN AEC-NASA TECHNOLOGY SURVEY

TELEOPERATORS AND HUMAN AUGMENTATION

Edwin G. Johnsen
William R. Corliss

TECHNOLOGY UTILIZATION DIVISION

NATIONAL AERONAUTICS AND SPACE ADMINISTRATION

INTRODUCTION TO TELEOPERATORS

Early in the nineteenth century, Napoleon sat across a chessboard from a ferocious-looking automaton swathed in the robes of a Turk. Napoleon moved his chessmen into battle; the Turk did the same. Then, when Napoleon blundered three times in succession, the audacious machine swept the board clean with an iron hand.

The chess-playing Turk was constructed by Baron Von Kempelen; it took on all comers until Edgar Allen Poe deduced that beneath the Turk's chess table there was a midget chess expert who manipulated the various controls that gave "life" to the machine. Those were the innocent times when man believed that he could build anything—not the least of which was a chess-playing robot.

Now that man must work in outer space, ocean depths, and other hazardous environments, he is building machines that recall Von Kempelen's intricate "automaton." These machines perform as appendages of man, particularly his arms, hands, and legs. Radio links, copper wires, and steel cables replace nerve fibers and muscle tendons. We shall call these man-machine systems "teleoperators," whether they are the tongs used by the old-fashioned grocer to retrieve a cereal box from the top shelf or the mechanical hand that may repair some future nuclear-powered space vehicle. The basic concept is portrayed in fig. 1, where man's bodily dexterity is shown communicated across a barrier to mechanical actuators that can operate under loads too great for an unaided man, or in an environment too hostile or too far away for him to conquer in person. A teleoperator augments a normal man, or, in the case of prosthetics, helps a handicapped man become more nearly normal.

NASA is concerned with the development of teleoperators because many astronautical targets are so far away that they must be explored by proxy. Yet the amplification and extension of man via the teleoperator concept transcends

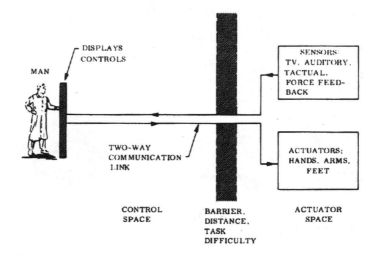

FIGURE 1.—Generalized schematic of a teleoperator incorporating dexterous actuators in the actuator space. The "barrier" between the control and operating spaces may result from distance, a hostile environment, or the sheer physical magnitude (weight, for example) of the task to be done.

space exploration. A survey of this fascinating technology must also embrace many advances made in the nuclear industry, in undersea exploration, in medicine, and in the engineering of "man amplifiers."

A teleoperator is a *general purpose, dexterous, cybernetic machine.* These adjectives separate teleoperators from other machines. The adjective "cybernetic" excludes all preprogrammed machinery, such as timer-controlled ovens, record-changing phonographs, and much of the machinery on automatic production lines. A teleoperator, in contrast, *always* has man in the control loop. The other adjectives—"dexterous" and "general purpose"—sharpen the focus further. These semantic sieves trap human-controlled, but undexterous, machines such as remotely controlled aircraft and telephone switching circuits. The man-machine systems that fall through our sieves allow man to:

—Pick up and examine samples of the lunar surface while remaining on Earth.
—Repair an underwater oil pipeline from a surface ship.
—Manipulate radioactive nuclear fuel elements in a hot cell.
—Regain dexterity with an artificial limb (the prosthetics concept).
—Lift a ton-sized load (the man-amplifier concept).

The prefix "tele" in teleoperator describes the ability of this class of man-machine systems to project man's innate dexterity not only across distance but through *physical barriers as well*.

When an area of technology with latent commercial potential approaches

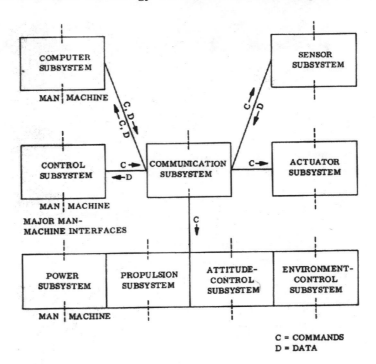

FIGURE 2.—Schematic of a general purpose, dexterous, cybernetic teleoperator, showing the nine subsystems. A man-machine interface may be created in any of the subsystems.

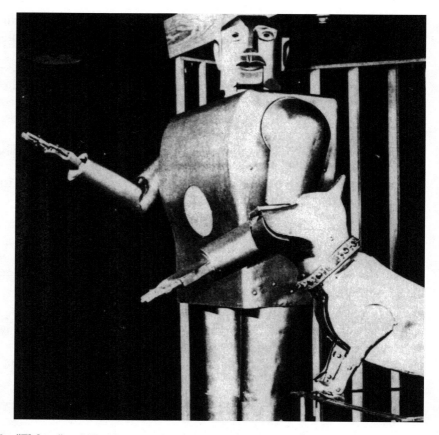

FIGURE 3.—"Elektro" and "Sparko," automatons shown at the 1939 New York World's Fair. (Courtesy of Westinghouse Electric Corporation.)

that point where exponential growth appears imminent, engineers invariably become word testers. Because no unified discipline welds the technical innovators together, synonyms and overlapping words proliferate. The following glossary should dispel some of the confusion:

—*Telepuppet.* A word coined in the 1950's by Fred L. Whipple, now director of the Smithsonian Astrophysical Observatory, to describe his concept of how sophisticated machines could take the place of man on spacecraft. The word has not become popular, presumably because "puppet" implies toys and entertainment rather than science and engineering.

—*Telechirics.* John W. Clark synthesized this word from Greek roots while at Battelle Memorial Institute in the early 1960's. Literally, telechirics means "remote fingers." It is descriptive, but unfortunately excludes walking machines and man amplifiers.

—*Telefactor.* The idea of making or doing something at a distance is intrinsic in this word conceived by William E. Bradley, at the Institute for Defense Analyses. It is semantically sound, but many people do not immediately recall that "factor" implies doing or making as well as algebra.

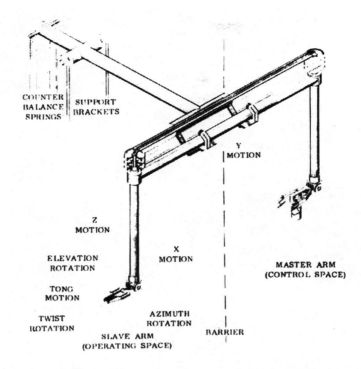

FIGURE 4.—The ANL Model-1 experimental mechanical master-slave manipulator. Motions of the master arm are mechanically communicated to the slave arm. Because the reverse is also true, this is termed a "bilateral" manipulator. (Courtesy of Argonne National Laboratory.)

—*Cybernetic anthropomorphic mechanism* (*CAM* for short). Ralph S. Mosher, at General Electric, has often used this term in his papers on walking machines, but it excludes many nonanthropomorphic mechanisms included in this survey. Mosher now refers to the field as *mechanism cybernetics,* a term that omits only the desired attributes of dexterity and versatility.

—*Master-slave.* Originated by Ray C. Goertz at the Atomic Energy Commission's Argonne National Laboratory in the late 1940's, this term is generally applied only to the common mechanical and electronic manipulators that have long been used in hot cells.

The terms "manipulator" and "remote control" are also often associated with the telemechanism field. The first term is too narrow a concept, since it excludes walking machines and exoskeletons. "Remote control" is too broad because it includes everything man does at a distance, even to changing a TV channel from his armchair.

A compact, accurate synonym for general purpose, dexterous, cybernetic machines may evolve as the field matures. Meanwhile, "teleoperator" will serve in this book.

Four of the nine subsystems deal directly with machine augmentation of man. These four are:

FIGURE 5.—An early manipulator at Brookhaven National Laboratory. Motion was communicated over a lead-brick wall by various mechanical linkages. Note mirrors in viewing scheme. (Courtesy of L. G. Stang, Jr., Brookhaven National Laboratory.)

—*The actuator subsystem* that carries out the manipulations and other dexterous activities ordered by the human operator. The actuators may be stronger, more dexterous, and faster than the operator.

—*The sensor subsystem* that permits the operator to see, feel, hear, and otherwise sense what the actuators are doing in the actuator space and what their environment is.

—*The control subsystem*, which includes the human operator, analyzes information fed back by the sensors in the actuator space and compares this with the operational objectives. The result is a series of commands to the actuator subsystem.

—*The communication subsystem* is the information hub of the teleoperator. It transmits commands and feedback among the various subsystems.

The supporting roles of the other five subsystems shown in fig. 2 are apparent from their names.

While the system diagram may seem somewhat involved, it is sufficiently general to include simple tongs for handling radioactive samples and extremely complex systems.

FIGURE 6.—The ANL Model E1 electric-master slave. Used only for experimental purposes, this bilateral manipulator was developed in 1954. (Courtesy of Argonne National Laboratory.)

RECENT HISTORY

The chess-playing Turk was preceded by the marvelous automatons of the Jaquet-Droz father-son team in the late 1700's. Controlled by grooved, rotating disks, the Jaquet-Droz automatons could play music and write out compositions: one in particular, "The Draughtsman," astounded King George III and Queen Charlotte by sketching them on the spot—or so it seemed. (Such a machine would be called pre-programmed today.) A "Steam Man," built by a Canadian, Professor George Moore, in the 1890's, was powered by a half-horsepower, high-speed steam engine; this primitive walking machine could puff along pulling light loads behind it. The Westinghouse automatons exhibited at the New York World's Fair in 1939, "Elektro" and "Sparko" (fig. 3), could walk, talk, and distinguish colors. The word "robot" means "worker" in Czech and gained popularity from Karel Capek's 1923 play "R.U.R." (for "Rossum's Universal Robots").

Today a robot is generally considered to be an automaton made in the shape of a man. Robots are usually preprogrammed or, in science fiction particularly, self-adapting and intelligent, not requiring and even disdaining help from humans. In contrast to robots, man is always intimately in the loop in the teleoperators discussed in this book.

Taking the historical road labeled "teleoperators," let us pass over the early and well-documented developments of television, cybernetics à la Norbert Wiener, radio control, and the supporting technology of prosthetics, and begin with master-slave manipulators built under the impetus of the atomic energy program. These were the

FIGURE 7.—A working model of a lunar walking machine. This six-footed walker can negotiate terrain impossible with ordinary wheeled vehicles. A solar-cell panel is mounted on top for power; and a claw-like sample collector is shown below. The walking motions are preprogrammed. (Courtesy of Space-General Corporation.)

first really sophisticated machines to project man's manipulative capability into a hazardous environment.

The chronology runs like this:

—1947. Mechanically and electrically connected unilateral[1] manipulators were developed at the Atomic Energy Commission's Argonne National Laboratory (ANL).

—1948. Ray Goertz and his coworkers at ANL developed the Model-1 bilateral mechanical master-slave manipulator (fig. 4).

—1948. John Payne built a mechanical master-slave manipulator at General Electric and many AEC installations subsequently acquired a great variety of mechanical manipulators (fig. 5).

—1948. General Mills produced the Model-A unilateral manipulator in which

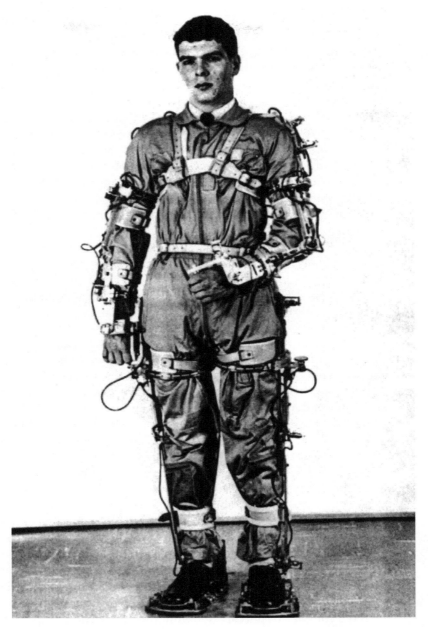

FIGURE 8.—An unpowered exoskeleton built by Cornell Aeronautical Laboratory under Department of Defense contracts. Actuators are not simulated. The exoskeleton would be a "man amplifier." (Courtesy of Cornell Aeronautical Laboratory.)

the arms and hands were driven by switch-controlled motors rather than by direct mechanical or electrical linkage to the operator (as in the true master-slave). The Model-A became a "workhorse" of the nuclear industry in tasks requiring more strength and working volume than possible with master-slaves.

—1950. ANL experimented with master-slaves coupled with stereo TV.

—1954. Development of the Argonne Model-8 mechanical master-slave manipulator was completed. This manipulator is still predominant in the atomic energy industry and is manufactured commercially.

—1954. Ray Goertz built an electric master-slave manipulator incorporating servos and force reflection (sense of touch or "feel") (fig. 6). The master-slave position control of the manipulator arms and hands plus force reflection made this the first bilateral electric manipulator.

—1954. The General Purpose Robot (GPR) was built at the AEC's Savannah River Plant. This was the first general-purpose manipulator-equipped vehicle.

—1957. Professor Joseph E. Shigley, at the University of Michigan, built a primitive walking machine for the U.S. Army. Although many walking machines were built earlier, Shigley's inaugurated the present-day Army program in "off-road" locomotion.

—1958. First mobile manipulator with TV was built at ANL. This teleoperator was called a "slave robot."

—1958. Ralph S. Mosher and coworkers at General Electric built the Handyman electrohydraulic manipulator incorporating force feedback, articulated fingers, and an exoskeletal control harness. This equipment was built for the joint AEC-USAF Aircraft Nuclear Propulsion Program.

—1958. William E. Bradley, Steve Moulton, and associates at Philco Corporation developed a head-mounted miniature TV set that enabled an operator to project himself visually into the operating space.

—1961. The first manipulator was fitted to a manned deep-sea submersible when a General Mills Model 150 manipulator was installed on the *Trieste*.

—1963. The U. S. Navy began deep-submergence projects, including the development of underwater manipulators.

—1963. R. A. Morrison and associates at Space-General Corporation constructed a lunar walking vehicle (fig. 7). This machine was later converted into a "walking wheelchair" for handicapped children.

—1964. Neil J. Mizen and coworkers at Cornell Aeronautical Laboratory reported on the construction of a "wearable exoskeletal structure." The Cornell exoskeleton was not pwered (fig. 8).

—1965. Ray Goertz and his associates at ANL combined the ANL Model E4 electrical master-slave manipulator with a head-controlled TV camera and receiver.

—1966. ANL combined the Model E3 electric master-slave with the Mark TV2, head-controlled TV, which added translational motion to the viewing system.

—1966. Case Institute of Technology, working under a NASA grant, demonstrated a computer-controlled manipulator that can perform preprogrammed subroutines specified by the operator.

This chronology gives little hint of the imminent and intimate man-machine partnership that many believe essential to the large-scale exploitation of space and the oceans. Many of the most important developments listed were made under the aegis of the Atomic Energy Commission. Further developments are likely from many sources.

Notes

1 "Unilateral" means that there is no kinesthetic or force feedback as there is in a "bilateral" system. See pages 86 & 87 for definitions of the various kinds of teleoperators.

This excerpt is from the report by Edwin G. Johnsen and William R. Corliss, Washington, D.C.: 1967.

An Interview with Patricia Cowings

Ron Eglash

The following is an edited interview with Patricia Cowings, director of the Ames-NASA Psychophysiology Laboratory, on September 10, 1993.

Ron Eglash: How about introducing yourself.

Patricia Cowings: Well, I'm the director of the psychophysiology lab; we study the relation between brain and behavior. Our lab has been working on developing methods for getting people to adapt more quickly to micro-gravity, and to re-adapt to earth.

RE: And it's specifically motion-sickness that you're concerned with...

PC: Motion-sickness is the first indication your body gives you that something's wrong here. Because we didn't evolve in a micro-gravity environment, an awful lot of things go to heck in a handcart in short order. Space motion-sickness is the first overt sign of maladaptation to that environment.

RE: And your approach to a solution?

PC: As psychophysiologists, we have to monitor physiology and behavior of the subject in a specific environment that causes him or her to stress. So first thing we do when we bring people here is we make them sick, using a variety of insidious devices made by NASA specifically for that purpose. We do that because motion-sickness per se is a completely artificial disease. The subject is

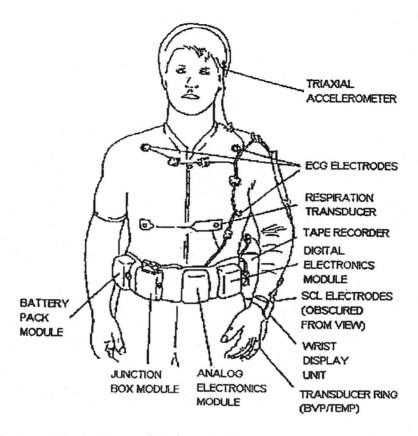

TRIAXIAL ACCELEROMETER

ECG ELECTRODES

RESPIRATION TRANSDUCER

TAPE RECORDER

DIGITAL ELECTRONICS MODULE

SCL ELECTRODES (OBSCURED FROM VIEW)

WRIST DISPLAY UNIT

TRANSDUCER RING (BVP/TEMP)

BATTERY PACK MODULE

JUNCTION BOX MODULE

ANALOG ELECTRONICS MODULE

The Autogenic-Feedback System-2 (AFS-2). An ambulatory monitoring system as worn by crewmembers.

perfectly well when he comes in the door, usually better than average health. We systematically make them sick so we can see how their body responds to the onset of the stimulus, and how their response levels change as you increase stimulus intensity (I hope I don't sound sadistic). When they say, "Turn this thing off or I'm going to throw up," you turn it off and see how rapidly they return to their own baselines. No two people respond in exactly the same way. A single person will always respond this way. He produces a kind of physiological fingerprint. I can go through a few hundred records and identify John Doe, because that's how he responds—in the motion-sickness environment, or darned near any environment that causes him emotional distress.

RE: And these are autonomic nervous system parameters you record?
PC: Yes, we call the data—a picture of the person if you will—an "autonomic stress profile." You may see people making larger-magnitude changes in the cardiac system than in the gastrointestinal system for example; it's a hierarchy of response magnitudes and latencies.

RE: Could you describe the apparatus that's hooked up to these people?
PC: In our research we developed for space, we devised a physiological monitoring system called AS2; we told the crew it's the latest thing in astronaut underwear. Its a wide stretch garment that has holes where ECG electrodes are placed. All electrodes and transducers are tied to a single umbilicus cable and are tied down to the garment with velcro, including measures of ECG, respiration, skin conductance, and peripheral blood flow, as well as three axes of head acceleration. We designed this to be very comfortable; around the waist there are 3 x 1 inch squares that have

{ 94

analog electronics, digital electronics, and a battery pack—sort of like Batman's utility belt-and a nine-track tape recorder that's good for 24 hours. Its an intelligent system: on the wrist is a very small computer display that continuously shows the subject their own heart rate, respiration, blood flow, skin conductance, and tells them if the machine is malfunctioning, like if an electrode fell off. Plus it tells time.

RE: So they can use this as biofeedback?

PC: Well, that's an instrument used in space. In the laboratory we teach our subjects to control up to 20 different physiological responses simultaneously. They sit in front of a wide-screen oscilliscope that can display four analog signals at a time, like the raw respiratory waveform for example. Mounted above are 12 digital meters that show the information in numeric form. In addition to giving them both digital and analog visual displays, we have two auditory tones. We spend quite a bit of our time just teaching subjects how to utilize this much information without having sensory overload. And part of my job is to see which kinds of parameters John Doe responds to better. Some people look at a visual display and all of their attention leaks right out of their heads. Some people want you to talk to them continuously; some want you to shut up. Part of what I do is very much like being a conductor in a band. I see all the feedback all the time. And I direct the subject's attention by turning the display on and off. So in the first two hours we gradually introduce more and more feedback displays in different combinations to see how this person responds. Part of the training is in teaching them to cross-reference these signals to get a feel for how they're doing. For example, you can see breaths per minute by looking at the meter, but you can also see volume by looking at the analog signal.

RE: There was a 1989 National Research Council Report that was very critical of biofeedback, but they singled out your studies as an exception, a case of clearly successful use.

PC: Well, I noticed that too. But you know, nobody else in the world noticed it!

RE: So why are you singled out as the successful biofeedbacker?

PC: Unlike people in academia, or even in the clinical world, I've been working for the last 21 years on one problem—and I've been required to demonstrate an objective basis for what I'm saying (*laughter*). Seriously, I've performed large-scale formal experiments over and over again...

RE: So basically were talking about a lot of sweat here.

PC: Yeah, a lot of work; we also have a somewhat unique methodology. Neal Miller, my co-investigator, has often said that there are as many different methods for doing biofeedback as there are clinicians. We've tried to find the right combination of methods, and see if we could refine it and standardize it. NASA only gave us 5 hours to train each astronaut. I've told my methods to clinicians and they say "What, am I in a hurry?" We had to demonstrate that we could make it work in a large population, under a variety of stimulus conditions. I'm glad you mentioned that; other people have said "Oh, but the NIH said that biofeedback is bunk," and I have to show them that one page that said "But Pat's OK."

RE: Could you say something about that *Washington Post* article—you talked about a contrast between conventional medicine and behavioral medicine.

PC: Contrast or contest? You mean within the agency?

RE: Well, I was trying not to make it sound like a leading question, but.... Let's start outside the agency.

PC: I don't know about the rest of the world—I've lived with this agency since I was a baby, you know what I mean? I came here full-time when I was 23, and I worked as a grad student before that. Within NASA, when I first came on board, it was in the fat days. They had known for twenty years that they had a big problem with space motion-sickness, and nothing worked. So they said "let's try anything—acupuncture, whatever." So that's how I got my foot in the door.

RE: And were you the one who suggested biofeedback?

PC: Yes. In my first year in grad school I had a course in the applied school of engineering. The class was to design some feature into a space shuttle from the point of view of the future user. The course was inundated with engineers designing zero-gravity tables and such. **I told the instructor that he had to let me in the class, because there were no women, and so who was going to design the curtains?** And he had no life-sciences people in the class, and as far as I knew astronauts were alive (although I've since worked with quite a few of them and now I wonder about that). I spent a year researching the literature to see the current biomedical problems, and motion-sickness was at the tippy-top. And my doctoral thesis work was on combining autogenic therapy with biofeedback to get more effective control of cardiovascular responses. So I wrote a paper for him on possible applications of "visceral learning" (that's what we called it in those days) to problems in manned space flight. He turned out to be the director of Ames Research Center. And every time we did a study, the critics would say "Yes, but you didn't show men and women," so we would test that, and they would say, "Yes but you didn't control for age," so we would test that, and so on. By the time the NIH study came out we had done everything on the face of the planet.

RE: I read that previous studies had shown women being more susceptible to motion-sickness, but that your results were pretty much equal between men and women.

PC: (*laughing*) Yeah, it's funny. Every reference says, "We all know women are more susceptible to motion-sickness than men." Finally you go back, and the original source is only two papers: one from a shipboard physician in the 1800s (and women used to faint a lot in the 1800s, I think it was those corsets); the other study was by the Navy. They ran 15 women and 15 men, and the women were more susceptible than the men. But the men were all active-duty military, in excellent physical condition, and the women were all secretaries and housewives. They did no matching for physical fitness.

RE: Didn't that study claim there was no pulse change during motion sickness?

PC: Yes, that study was absolutely astonishing. When I went to Russia they were all having a big laugh over it. Because you'll get a pulse change, y'know, just from a telephone conversation (*laughter*). So we assumed the methods were flawed.

RE: Seems like a reasonable assumption. Now let's go back to that conventional versus behavioral-medicine contrast. That's just about pharmaceuticals versus the biofeedback?

PC: No it isn't—unfortunately its much more than that. I'm not a Christian Scientist: I don't think there's anything wrong with conventional medicine. And I certainly don't think there's anything wrong with pharmaceuticals. They were ineffective in space because we don't metabolize things in space the way we do on earth. The positive fluid shift and diarrhesis causes electrolyte imbalance, so one can't predict how it will be metabolized from one day to the next. The current motion-sickness drug is really nothing more than an anti-histamine, and the dose that they give you is enough to put an elephant to sleep. It helps if you're suffering from intractable vomiting, but all it does is put you out. That's an operational fix; its not solving the problem of adapting to that environment, nor examining why one person adapts and the other doesn't.

RE: Yes, the idea of individual responses, each of us with our own stress profile, seems like a completely different picture of human physiology than we get from, say, a commercial pharmaceutical that is supposed to help some sort of

"average" response.

PC: It is the reason why conventional medicine, even vestibular physiologists, were unable to see the effects of motion-sickness on the autonomic nervous system. Ken Money did a study, 1970, I think, where some people's heart rate went up, some went down, one person didn't respond the same from one test to another. That's because they didn't see that the individual was consistent within him or her self. Yes, maybe one test takes 15 minutes to make you sick, and the other test takes 95 minutes to make you sick, but if you look at the physiology at the point where they have become sick it's the same.

RE: Would it be possible to have the pharmaceutical industry use something like this? Have drugs that are specific to particular categories of stress profiles?

PC: Up to a point. Pharmaceutical companies can't make money if they're trying to tailor an aspirin to each individual. And perhaps a physician could combine drugs in a more efficient way for the crew members. But, say, a scopolamine and dexedrine combination won't affect you the same on one day and another, depending on whether or not you've exercised that day, or depending or whether or not you're depressed that day. Drugs by their nature have a systemic effect on an individual. But you could use it to say, "This category of drug is no good for this individual."

RE: So the conventional/behavioral medicine contrast is more a question of group versus individual?

PC: I'll tell you for your tape recorder. The problem is much more fundamental than that. They went to medical school, and we did not. And we have the cheek—the temerity!—to try and solve a biomedical problem. And I'm sure you'll see this across the board in other clinical applications in biofeedback. But within this agency, where we have a bunch of aeronautical engineers and hard-headed rocket jockies, biofeedback seems like California tofu. The first time I met with a shuttle commander, he said (*imitating a Texas drawl*) "So whaddya all do, sit in the corner in a lotus position and chant?" So with the astronauts we present it as an exercise regimen, "You're learning to control other muscles." And because they can see them going up and down they say "Oh yeah, that's muscles."

RE: It seems like the causal chain of the pharmaceutical is very Newtonian. You have this chemical and then a reaction to it. Whereas with biofeedback its more complex.

PC: Well, there's ways of looking at a problem. In this country, if you have a problem you have a headache you take an aspirin. And if there is a pill for your problem, then by all means go find it. But what we are dealing with is a body cast in an alien environment. Rapidly de-adapting to earth and re-adapting to space has somewhat traumatic effects on organ systems.

RE: Let me try a philosophic question. We are often told that it's symbolic systems like speech and writing that are the only significant conveyors of knowledge. That view leaves our bodies as inert blobs of mechanics or chemistry. Does the body get to have the status of an information-processing system in your work?

PC: I don't know what you're talking about. Look, all of your organs are attached to your nervous system; your spinal cord, etc. is attached to your cerebrum. Nobody knows where volition is in the brain. The only way I have of communicating with these people is verbally. I can't talk to monkeys or to my dog. This is considered a reliable...

RE: Whoa, wait—I wasn't trying to imply some kind of mystical interpretation. I just wanted to know if you're storing all this information on a computer: what's the baud rate of these autonomic parameters?

PC: You have to think of it a little differently. What I'm storing is evidence of something that has already happened. That's what people see as the subjective evidence of the effect. But what is the effect? **You have to think of the brain as wetware.** I have trained over three hundred people, and have never come across anyone that couldn't control their responses up to some point. Neal Miller said he has never come across an animal that couldn't control their responses up to some point. The difference between working with rats, even dogs or monkeys, is that when you work with people they are very, very complicated animals, and they can all arrive at the same place by completely different paths. **So I think of the subject as a black box, as a sensory organism, a data-processing organism.** I modify the information that goes in through his senses, and look at the output. I have no idea how he's getting that, but until I get the output I want I keep modifying the input. And it works.

RE: Why is it we can't just take our own pulse, or breathing rate? Why do we need a machine to monitor our bodies for biofeedback?

PC: It's just a function of paying attention. Most people aren't aware of bodily sensations that reflect autonomic changes. I can teach you to control the blood flow to the little finger of your left hand, only. Can you sense changes in the blood flow to the little finger of your left hand?

RE: Well, no, not unless I had a nice machine hooked up to it.

PC: Well if you have a nice machine hooked up to it you could detect shifts of tenths or hundredths of a degree. Then you could learn to focus your attention tightly enough. "What am I feeling here that reflects blood flow to the periphery?" And yes, some people can hear their own heartbeat, faintly, but if you're trying to teach a person to control a pattern of physiological responses, you have to provide them with information on twenty things simultaneously. It's very difficult for him to feel without first being instructed on how to feel it. Part of our training was to sort out how to provide this much information in a useful manner.

RE: So it's not just a human-machine interface; it's a machine-mediated coupling between the autonomic nervous system and the central nervous system.

PC: Yes, you could think about it that way—it serves as a prosthetic for the nervous system.

RE: Before we end, I'd like to know a bit more about your own history and background.

PC: Well, I'm a Black woman, I'm married, and I'm short—five-foot-two—and I'm not telling my weight. I have a six-year-old son, a brother who's a two-star general, another who's a jazz musician, and the third is a disk jockey—yeah, he's having a lot of fun with that...

RE: How about your early influences, growing up?

PC: I grew up in the South Bronx. My mother was a teacher's aide, my father was a grocery store owner. I was the only girl in a family with three brothers. I noticed that men got to do everything: fire*men*, police*men*. I also noticed that white people got to do everything. None of my teachers were Black: none of the policemen were. So I figured there really wasn't much that I could be. One day 1958 I think, I was about 9 years old, I went to my dad, and I said, "I'm never going to be able to have a job." He said "No, what you are is a human being, and the human being is the best damned animal on the whole damned planet. A human being is just a little animal. It doesn't have much fur, it doesn't have claws, and it doesn't have teeth. But what he has that sets him apart from the other animals is a whole huge brain up on the end of his neck; it's like an information factory. One day someone looked at a bird and said, `I wish I could fly.' Now humans can fly higher and faster than any bird. Because a human being can learn, it can learn to do anything, and you can do anything other human beings can do." It's the same story I tell my six-year-old. And I literally started studying human potential at that point. I guess that might have sparked my interest in science fiction to some extent.

RE: You must have been a major _Star Trek_ fan.

PC: Sure, but the first for me was Robert Heinlein. Also Le Guin, Asimov, and Andre Norton. That was why I took a class on engineering space environments, even though I was a psychology major. And from there to NASA and I've loved it ever since. I even met my husband here. He's one of the rare people who can't get motion sickness. It turns out he has no osteolyths, a dysfunctional inner ear, and … you can guess the rest. I was also the first woman to take the space training test. And I helped with the training for Mae Jemison. I really felt when I came to work for NASA that what we were doing was some of the most important work that a human being could do. We're the first animal to evolve enough to actually leave the planet of our origin.

RE: How have you negotiated the "minorities in science" stuff?

PC: Oh, seems like every official who comes by wants to drag me out for a dog and pony show. "Look, minorities in science. See? There goes one now." And I'm always being invited somewhere to make another unpaid speech.

RE: What do you think about using science fiction to help students get interested in science?

PC: Oh, that's great. I've been writing science fiction myself for about 100 years. They've turned down my stories so many times I get rejection letters on a first-name basis.

RE: In folklore studies we find that there are lots of American stories that turn out to have origins in West Africa. Do you think your father's story could have had an African origin?

PC: I honestly don't think so. My father ran a grocery store, but his father was a lawyer. And his father was a slave. They came to those kinds of conclusions from the society they were raised in. I don't think so; there's never been any such mention.

RE: Let me ask another question in that same area. Your brother is a jazz musician. Now jazz is something new, it was invented here in America. But it also has some African roots to it. Its not a symbolic code, like story-telling, but there is information there in the waveform.

PC: Oh, well, I know all about waveforms! But I think it would be a real stretch to say that reading sheet music is like reading a polygraph printout.

RE: Well, you look at sheet music and you can see a waveform of pitch over time.

PC: I can see patterns in the polygraph, but then, I was trained to look for them. Sure, we're always looking for patterns in our data. But an analogy between that and music—I think that's a real reach. I don't know—none of my brothers and I have anything in common with each other. It's actually kind of amazing that we all sprang from the same parents. We're all different colors too, but that's beside the point.

RE: One last question. You said that you write your own science fiction stories. Are any of them in the cyborg theme? Blurring the boundary between the natural and the artificial?

PC: Yeah, in fact, just about everything I've written does that.

PILOT'S ASSOCIATE

Combat pilots make split-second, life-or-death decisions based on rapidly changing and often incomplete and conflicting information. Fighter pilots engaged in combat must integrate information from many sources, make instantaneous decisions, and aggressively seek mission accomplishment in a hostile environment. The Pilot's Associate will relieve the pilot of numerous lower-level functions and present to him, for ultimate decision, the best courses of action. The Pilot's Associate will integrate four expert systems dealing with system status, mission planning, situation assessment, and tactics planning through an expert pilot-vehicle interface. The program will stress machine intelligence, advanced computing, and pilot-vehicle interfaces as a means of focusing the research on critical mission demands. This innovative application of advanced computer technology will greatly enhance pilot capability and survivability in a most stressing environment.

The systems that comprise the Pilot's Associate are not intended to replace the pilot or to act as computerized crew members. Rather, the goal is to assist the fighter pilot with managing information, making decisions, and performing a wide range of tasks in order to optimize his flying and fighting skills. Instead of saturating the pilot with large quantities of data, the Pilot's Associate will integrate and prioritize information based on the situation at hand. Significant information will be presented to the pilot in an orderly manner, allowing him

Mock-up of Cockpit with Pilot's Associate

to assess the situation with regard to mission requirements and to his own tactical preferences. The pilot will then either accept the Pilot's Associate's recommendation, override it, or request more information.

The Pilot's Associate program will exploit progress in AI and related computer technologies. Expert systems, parallel processing, and speech input and output systems will receive primary attention for this program. The Pilot's Associate will produce a set of four cooperating expert systems operating at very high speeds. The computing requirements are expected to be met by new parallel processor architectures, as well as advanced software for symbolic processing. The resulting system will be a hybrid of computing concepts, including symbolic processing within expert systems, numeric processing of sensor data and control systems, and predictive processing for trajectory planning. Intent-driven interfaces with pilots will utilize techniques such as speech, natural language, and specialized sound and graphics. Additional system development constraints will continue to arise from interfaces with other avionics systems and from projected size, weight, and power requirements for flight systems.

In keeping with the fundamental goals of the Strategic Computing Program, Pilot's Associate is structured to provide a high potential for technology transfer to future aircraft systems. A program office has been established at the Air Force Wright Aeronautical Laboratories to provide an association with related work at the various laboratories, and visibility to the system acquisition community. In addition, the schedule is punctuated with several demonstrations which will serve as technical and operational tests that will provide feedback to both DARPA and the Air Force.

Planning for the Pilot's Associate program and definition of the initial system has been underway since late 1984. A study, conducted by Perceptronics, Inc. provided task requirements analyses, advanced machine-intelligence technology assessments, task and technology matching, and the distillation of these assessments into a functional design. In a second effort, requirements for program demonstrations, as well as performance metrics, were developed in a study by the C. S. Draper Laboratory, Inc. Acceptable levels of system evaluability, completeness, and clarity were defined for the Pilot's Associate's system construct. Initial concepts for evaluating the Pilot's Associate's performance and for the verification of knowledge bases were also provided. A final study, conducted by Titan Industries, Inc., addressed the information required by pilots for various mission segments, and the relative importance of information-presentation time, format, media, and content. Also, this study produced a systematic method for generating information requirements for a variety of mission segments and combat scenarios.

In 1985, a set of four demonstrations are conducted for the purpose of indicating the feasibility of applying artificial intelligence capabilities to assist combat pilots. This series of demonstrations produced prototype expert systems addressing portions of the Pilot's Associate subsystem functions. Four contractor participants applied these prototypes to assist pilots who flew short mission segments in flight simulators.

The demonstration conducted by Boeing Military Aircraft Company, with Advanced Decision Systems, Inc., addressed tactics and mission replanning for an air-to-ground engagement, where the force was attacked by interceptors. The General Dynamics Corporation in conjunction with Bolt, Beranek, and Newman, Inc., demonstrated the use of sensors and the tactical prioritization of aerial targets in a beyond-visual-range engagement, including pop-up threats. The Northrop Corporation demonstration provided critical tactical trajectory planning for evading surface-to-air missiles, including multiple launches. Finally, the Systran Corporation demonstration produced proper reactions to in-flight emergencies to assist the pilot with multiple failures of aircraft systems. In total, these demonstrations provided important insights into the challenges of developing the entire Pilot's Associate system.

Specifications for the first major developmental phase were provided to industry in early 1985, and a competitive procurement was held to select two development contractors. A major selection philosophy was to chose two differing approaches to capitalize on the technology "pull" while also minimizing uncertainty. The two contractor teams selected were: (1) Lockheed Georgia Company with subcontracts to General Electric Company, Goodyear Aerospace Corporation, Teknowledge Federal Systems, Search Technology, Defense Systems Corporation, and Carnegie-Mellon University; and (2) McDonnell Aircraft Company with subcontract to Texas Instruments. In addition to providing parallel technical approaches, these teams are cost-sharing in the project to leverage DARPA's investment.

(From the *Strategic Computing Second Annual Report*. DARPA. February 1986.)

Science Fiction Becomes Military Fact

McDonnell/Douglas hires workers for a Pentagon R&D fantasy (With a nod to *Harper's Magazine*)

Chris Hables Gray

McDonnell Aircraft owes its commanding position to the largesse of the Pentagon which has made its parent company, McDonnell/Douglas, one the top recipients of Department of Defense contracts in the second half of the twentieth century. They were awarded a cool $7.7 billion in 1987, for example. In 1986 McDonnell/Aircraft and Texas Instruments were given $4.2 million for phase I work on the Pilot's Associate. Another $6.7 million went to a team headed by Lockheed Georgia and including Lockheed-California, General Electric, Teknowledge Federal Systems, Goodyear Aerospace Corp., Search Technology, Inc., Defense Systems Corp., and Carnegie-Mellon University.

The Pilot's Associate is actually five different expert computer systems networked together: situation assessment, mission planning, system status, tactics, and the pilot/vehicle interface. These expert systems will evaluate the input from external sensors as well as monitor and diagnose all of the aircraft's on-board subsystems, including the pilot. The Pilot's Associate will not only try to predict what the pilot will ask it to do, it will also initiate actions of its own when it deems it necessary, including firing weapons and even taking over the aircraft from the pilot.

Neural Networks is a promising computer field that simulates organic mental processes on a crude level that allows machines to develop some learning and recognition abilities not possible with traditional programming. While decades away from any practical application it is a fertile new concept for those seeking military funding just as the failures of older artificial intelligence techniques have become too obvious for even the Pentagon dreamers to ignore.

No doubt. McDonnell/Douglas has a great fondness for job applicants with "familiarity with the DOD" as can be seen by its hiring of Melvyn R. Paisley as a consultant right after he retired as Assistant Secretary of the Navy for Research, Engineering, and Systems. The FBI has accused Mr. Paisley of the "illegal disclosure of information and exertion of influence," including revealing classified data to McDonnell/Douglas management. Most of the information the FBI says Mr. Paisley sold was about "high performance fighter-aircraft" standards and bids, which indicates one method used by McDonnell/Douglas to become the "world's leading designer and producer" of this deadly product. According to the FBI he also passed on information on the Advanced Tactical Aircraft Program, of which the Pilot's Associate is a part. Other examples of the importance McDonnell/Douglas gives to hiring candidates who have a "familiarity with the DOD" can be seen in the appointment of former Secretary of the Air Force Edward Aldridge, Jr. as the president of McDonnell/Douglas Electronic Systems in 1987.

Meeting th Technical C of Tomorr

The strategic application of advanced technologies is our lifeblood—and the pulse is quickening. McDonnell Aircraft Company is the world's leading designer and producer of high performance fighter aircraft. Our engineering oriented artificial intelligence solutions ensure that we meet the technical challenges encountered in the design and development of tomorrow's aircraft systems. To achieve ever increasing product performance and capability, we "push the technology envelope" in such areas as:

- Pilot Decision Aiding and Automatio (Pilot's Associate)
- Integrated Diagnostics
- Intelligent Sensor Management
- Advanced Avionics Architectures
- Biocybernetics
- Neural Networks

Artificial Intelligence Opportunities

We are seeking highly qualified, experienced app for manager of our Intelligent Computing S Group.

Responsibilities- Strategic planning and manag of intelligent computing technologies to enhanc ity, productivity, performance, availability, and ability of our products. Includes expansion of contract R&D activity and internal/external cu interface.

Qualifications- The ideal candidate will have vanced degree in Computer Science/Engineerin cessful experience in managing intelligent system neering applications, and familiarity with th Source Selection Process. Aerospace experience o

Biocybernetics is one name for research aimed at developing better communications, even integration, between computers and humans. It includes various forms of pilot-state monitoring, such as systems reading human brain waves, following eye movements, and testing the conductivity of sweaty palms, all in order to gauge his or her mental states. The computer network will theoretically know how to improve communication between the pilot and the pilot's associate, when to take specific actions on its own, and when to assume control of the aircraft from the human pilot. Brain-wave research that dates back at least to the early 1970s has advanced to the point where scientists at Johns Hopkins have managed to sort out enough brain waves to predict when a monkey will move its arms by reading its electrical mental patterns before it acts. The next step is to play back these readings to the monkey so it will raise its arm at the command of the programming. Such techniques should work on humans as well, thus insuring fast and resistance-free responses even to the most unpleasant orders.

The arrows here represent a number of different communications links including the computer talking and listening to the pilot, the pilot's aiming weapons with his or her eyes and flying/fighting the plane with verbal commands, and a number of hardware connections for monitoring the pilot's brain waves and galvanic skin responses. Eventually the military hopes for an even more intimate integration of the human with the machine if current research on implanting silicon chips in dogs' brains (to give them an extra sensing organ) and growing neurons into silicon chips (to improve communication between humans and machines by allowing the chips to be activated by hormones and neural electrical stimulation as well as to send hormonal and electrical signals directly to the human body and brain) pans out.

The "big picture" is actually the information that is filtered through the various computer programs and sensors of the aircraft. The real "big picture" is the military's dream that turning pilots into cyborgs will lead to military superiority and keep the tradition of humans (or almost humans) as pilots alive. A key resource in this fantasy are science-fiction writers who have often prefigured projects such as the Pilot's Associate in their stories. The Air Force has formalized this relationship and now pays science-fiction writers to meet with Air Force officers to help set research and development priorities.

McDonnell's St. Louis headquarters were raided by FBI agents on June 15, 1988 looking for documents Melvyn R. Paisley passed on to his employers. Before his six-year stint in the Pentagon Paisley worked for Boeing for 23 years. He was hired as an Assistant Secretary of the Navy by his friend and patron, former Secretary of the Navy John Lehman, who also used to work for Boeing. As one official describes the Paisley-McDonnell Douglas relationship, it was a classic revolving-door syndrome: guys in the Pentagon and guys who have left the Pentagon scratching each other's backs.

Short Circuit

Watching Television with a Nuclear-Weapons Scientist[1]

Hugh Gusterson

introduction

Cyborgs, Weapons Scientists, and Anthropologists

As an anthropologist I spend more time watching people than watching television. When I was doing my fieldwork, however, I sometimes combined the two pursuits, watching some quite lowbrow popular films on television with one of my "informants," Ray,[2] who loved nothing more than to spread out on the couch with the remote control and a pizza, chatting intermittently with me as we watched a film or surfed between channels. I was a former anti-nuclear activist, now turned anthropologist, doing an ethnographic study of a nuclear-weapons laboratory where Ray worked as an engineer. After he befriended me at a church social event,

I ended up spending a fair amount of time with him and his television.

At first I was annoyed by Ray's fondness for television. I shared the perception, common among academics and humanists, that watching television is often a waste of precious time and an evasion of real human communication. I was trying to understand Ray's cultural world, and I saw the television, which Ray rarely turned off when I came to visit, as an electronic barrier against my attempts to understand him—a Maginot Line in his living room for me to transgress.

In fact, however, it was by watching television with Ray that I came to some of my subtler and most counterintuitive insights into his world. I eventually realized that television, especially science-fiction fantasies on television, offered all kinds of commentaries, both oblique and direct, on Ray's world—a social world in which, as in much science fiction, the star character was often either technology itself or the sort of cyborg characters that achieved mass marketability in the decade of *The Terminator, Bladerunner,* and *Robocop.* In this context watching television with Ray was, far from being an impediment to our relationship, a low-key but effective way of getting to know him, since the playful flow of images, stories, and fantasies on television catalyzed casual but revealing conversations about problematic issues in his life that could be discussed more freely in relation to the dreamworld of television than in the context of a formal ethnographic interview where, relentlessly searching for structure and consistency, I might make over-zealous and reductionist attempts to pin down the underlying logic of Ray's life. That life, like most human lives and despite my academic attempts to make it otherwise, was obstinately complex and contradictory. The informal conversations and confidences evoked by the fantasy world of television helped me to see that complexity in a way that no formal interview could have, making me realize that the contradictions and inconsistencies in Ray's discourse were not "noise" that I had to filter out in distilling the essence of his world but were, in fact, an integral part of that essence.

In this article I want to briefly describe Ray's world, and then explain how watching television with him helped illuminate that world. My account will focus principally on one film we watched together, *Short Circuit.* Although the film at the time seemed a little silly to me, and although my conversation about the film with Ray was comparatively brief, that conversation was like an intellectual electric shock for me—**a vital moment of recognition in my fieldwork that disrupted many of my presuppositions about both nuclear-weapons scientists and a Hollywood film that had seemed so transparently simple before we got to discussing it.** Ever since that conversation both nuclear-weapons scientists and the cultural products of Hollywood have seemed more interesting and more complex to me.

The star character, and in many ways the most interesting character, of the film *Short Circuit* is a cyborg: the robot called "Number Five" which (who?) acquires human consciousness and becomes a pacifist. The machine that transcends its programming and becomes autonomous is a common figure in contemporary science fiction, though it usually appears as a frightening, dangerous figure like the computer Hal that turns on the spaceship crew in *2001,* the replicants that menace humanity in *BladeRunner,* and the artificial intelligence Wintermute which ruthlessly manipulates and kills in order to secure its autonomy in William

Gibson's cyberpunk novel *Neuromancer*. These are all retellings of a story first told by Mary Shelley in her book *Frankenstein* and, as Langdon Winner (1977) has observed, this recurring story is about our profound anxiety that we have lost control of, and may even be destroyed by, the technology we have created in the modern age. The film *Short Circuit* retells this cyborg story yet again, but this time as comedy rather than as tragedy.

We are clearly quite fascinated by cyborgs at this moment in our history. Donna Haraway, who put cyborgs on the map of cultural criticism, defines a cyborg as "a hybrid of machine and organism, a creature of social reality as well as a creature of fiction" and "a kind of disassembled and reassembled, postmodern collective and personal self" (Haraway 1990:191, 205). Calling cyborgs "the illegitimate offspring of militarism and patriarchal capitalism, not to mention state socialism" (p.193), Haraway declares that:

> By the late twentieth century, our time, a mythic time, we are all chimeras,
> theorized and fabricated hybrids of machine and organism; in short, we are
> cyborgs. The cyborg is our ontology; it gives us our politics.
> (Haraway 1990:191).

One of the key characteristics of the cyborg for Haraway is its fundamental ambiguity. The cyborg has a dark side, but it also has utopian possibilities:

> From one perspective, a cyborg world is about the final imposition of a grid of
> control on the planet, about the final abstraction embodied in a Star Wars
> apocalypse waged in the name of defense, about the final appropriation of
> women's bodies in a masculinist orgy of war. From another perspective, a
> cyborg world might be about lived social and bodily realities in which people
> are not afraid of their joint kinship with animals and machines, not afraid of
> permanently partial identities and contradictory standpoints.
> (Haraway 1990:196).

My conversations with Ray emphasized that the cyborg is indeed an ambiguous figure, **more ambiguous than I had realized.** In this article I want to show how that ambiguity became manifest in our conversations, and how the ambiguous, shape-shifting figure of the cyborg helped me see more clearly the ambivalence and complexity at the heart of Ray's world-view. My approach here is strongly, if obliquely, influenced by Janice Radway's (1991) beautiful study of a group of suburban American women devoted to reading romance novels. Adopting Stanley Fish's (1980) notion of "interpretive communities," Radway argues that the same text may mean quite different things to different readers bringing different identities and social locations to the act of reading. She quotes Dorothy Hobson's (1982:17) argument that a text "comes alive and communicates when the viewers add their own interpretation and understanding" and that "there can be as many interpretations of a programme as the individual readers bring to it" (quoted in Radway 1001:9). Radway argues that we cannot understand the meaning of a text simply by analyzing its plot by ourselves. Instead she calls for ethnographies of reading—sociological studies of the multiple ways particular individuals and communities read particular texts.[3] In this article, which is focused on television rather than print, I show how the film *Short Circuit,* and in particular the cyborg character at the heart of it, **signified quite different things to Ray and me because we viewed the film from different social and political standpoints,** and I show how the cinematic cyborg can function as a

Rorshach to provoke and focus debates on the politics of technology at the end of the second millennium.

Ray's World

Ray worked at the Lawrence Livermore National Laboratory, one of two nuclear-weapons design laboratories in the U.S. (The other is the Los Alamos National Laboratory in New Mexico.) The Livermore Laboratory, set amidst vine-yards and rolling hills about forty miles east of San Francisco, was founded in 1952.[4] Since then its scientists have designed eighteen nuclear weapons, including the neutron bomb and the warheads for the MX, Minuteman, and Poseidon missiles. They have also worked on such SDI technologies as the X-ray laser and Brilliant Pebbles. With about 8,000 employees and an annual budget of a little over $1 billion, the Laboratory devoted roughly two-thirds of its resources to weapons work throughout the 1980s, though it also sponsored research in such areas as new energy technologies, environmental cleanup, and the Human Genome Project.[5]

The 1980s were difficult years for the Laboratory. In the early years of that decade, as the Nuclear Freeze movement swept across the country, the Livermore Laboratory became the local target of mass demonstrations organized by an anti-nuclear movement that was exceptionally strong in Northern California.[6] Meanwhile America's mainstream churches, especially the Catholic Church, for the first time became vocally critical of the nuclear-arms race. Laboratory scientists, many of whom are committed Christians, had to contend with the spectacle of priests, nuns, even a bishop, getting arrested for civil disobedience at the Laboratory gates.[7] Then, in the late 1980s, the new Soviet Government headed by Mikhail Gorbachev made increasingly strenuous efforts to end the cold war which, for nearly forty years, had provided the Laboratory's principal *raison d'etre*. It was in this conflictual historical context that, in 1988, I met Ray.

Ray had a Master's Degree in electrical engineering and worked maintaining and reconfiguring some of the immensely expensive and delicate experimental equip-ment at the Laboratory. He did not work directly on nuclear weapons research, but he was quite candid that his work contributed to nuclear weapons development. In the course of my research I found that many Livermore scientists believed they thought much more than their colleagues about the ethics of working at a nuclear weapons laboratory, and Ray was no exception.[8] "They [his co-workers] don't think very much about the ethics of what we do," he told me, adding that many of his colleagues even persuaded themselves that, since they were not working directly on nuclear weapons design, there was no ethical issue to confront. "I have no illu-sions about my work," he said tersely.

I once commented to Ray that some of his colleagues seemed so wrapped up in the technical problems they were trying to solve that they had lost sight of what nuclear weapons could do to human beings. He surprised me by nodding and say-ing that was why some of them came up with some "really sick ideas" for new nuclear weapons, such as, for example, the neutron bomb—a weapon that excited considerable controversy when it was produced in the 1970s because it was designed to kill human beings with an intense burst of radiation while doing rela-tively little damage to buildings.

At the time that I met him Ray had been forced to look again at the ethics of his work because of his membership in the Catholic Church, which he took seriously. The Catholic bishops had in 1983 issued a much publicized pastoral letter criticizing the nuclear arms race and appealing for its prompt cessation (National Conference of Catholic Bishops 1983). Ray had even had the experience when he went to worship at a church in a nearby town, where the priest knew nothing about his work, of being asked why he was not helping to plan a protest against the Laboratory! When he explained to the priest that he worked at the Laboratory there was, he said, "an uncomfortable silence." He added, "I had the feeling he really wished he could throw me out."

At the time I first knew Ray, from 1988-89, he was quite sure that his work was ethical. He believed that the development of American nuclear weapons was, on balance, still more likely to stabilize than endanger the world. This conclusion derived largely from his deeply held belief that the Communist regime in the Soviet Union was historically a ruthless, aggressive threat to world peace that was being contained by a democratic United States forced to arm in defense of itself and allied nations. He worried that the Gorbachev regime was essentially no different from its predecessors except in its aptitude for public relations and, one evening when a news clip about Soviet arms control policy came on television, he told me that if I thought Gorbachev had unilaterally suspended Soviet nuclear testing for 18 months "because he's a nice guy, then I've got some real estate for you in the Arizona desert." At one point he even articulated a concern that the Soviets might be pursuing global nuclear disarmament because they had designed a secret non-nuclear weapon with which they would be able to seek global domination in a non-nuclear world. Still, he told me,

> if Gorbachev's sincere—which I doubt because it's all been too slick—but if he's sincere, then five years from now there won't be any need for this lab and I'll quit. I'm not saying that the Government will see that there's no need for the lab. I'm saying I'll quit because the work will no longer be justifiable.

In Ray's discursive world, if the Soviets abroad were dangerous and malevolent, anti-nuclear activists at home were naive. He did not dispute their good intentions, but he was quite adamant that, whether they knew it or not, much of their funding came surreptitiously from the KGB, whose goals they furthered whether or not they intended to. "I'm not saying that anti-nuclear protesters are all bad. But they're naive about where their money comes from and whose interests they're serving. You'd be surprised how much of their money comes from the KGB."[9]

Ray's belief that his nuclear weapons work was ethical and appropriate was grounded, however, not just in his fearful mistrust of the Soviets but also in a positive faith in technology, particularly American technology, as a solution to human problems. It was this faith in technology more than his anti-Sovietism (which, in any case, was far from universally shared by scientists at the Laboratory, many of whom were political liberals) that bonded Ray with his colleagues. Ray's house was full of gadgets, and he loved to tell me about the amazing things Livermore machines were capable of doing. He was impatient with people who opposed nuclear power plants and genetic engineering, since he strongly believed that technology under rational and beneficent human control made the world a better and safer place. His attitude to gun control, which he and I often disagreed about, illustrates the point: where I saw guns as a menace to everyone's safety, he believed that people had the right to own guns and were safer with than without guns, but only if they had been properly trained so that they did not, for example, point them at people or keep them loaded in the house. I worried about guns, I worried about nuclear weapons, and I worried about the plutonium facility only two miles from my house. He said he worried about guns and nuclear weapons only in the wrong hands, and the only time he worried about the plutonium facility was when they found one of the operators there was smoking marijuana. As long as technology was in the hands of reliable experts—a category of person of whose existence I was skeptical—Ray felt safe.

Watching Television With Ray

In Ray I had met someone profoundly different from myself. In the rest of this article I want to outline how the differences between us were made clearer by watching television together, but also to give some sense of the ideological ambiguities and conflicts built into Ray's world—a world that can too easily be reduced to a set of linear consistencies by a thumbnail sketch such as the one above.

The otherness of Ray's world became dramatically clear to me one evening in the spring of 1989 when I was visiting him and we ended up watching the film *Short Circuit* on television. In view of the conversation that ensued I hesitate to even describe the film, since it became clear that the film I saw and the film Ray saw were not the same, even though we sat in front of the same television. Still, as I saw it, the film goes as follows.

It concerns a brilliant but naive young scientist called Dr. Newton Crosby who, while working for the Nova Laboratory,[10] invents a new kind of super-intelligent robot capable of going behind enemy lines with nuclear weapons and prosecuting a nuclear war. During a demonstration of the new robots to the top Pentagon brass one of them, Number Five, in a scene that recapitulates Frankenstein as comedy, gets struck by lightning and somehow acquires consciousness and free will. Number Five escapes from the Laboratory and the military, afraid of an armed, super-intelligent robot it cannot control, spends most of the rest of the film chasing it and trying to blow it up. Number Five, meanwhile, terrified of being "disassembled", befriends Stephanie, a young and beautiful animal-rights activist, who becomes his (the robot is clearly male) protector. Stephanie contacts the Laboratory ("Can I speak to your head warmonger, please?") and tries to convince the army and the scientists that Number Five is harmless and is a life-form rather than a robot, but the military, which tricks her into revealing Number Five's whereabouts, is intent on one thing only: blowing up its robot. Meanwhile the scientist who has also befriended Stephanie, refuses to believe what has happened, saying, "It's a machine. It doesn't get happy. It doesn't get sad. It just runs programs ... It's malfunctioning and needs to be repaired." "Life," replies Stephanie, "is not a malfunction." Number Five, who has been reading the encyclopedia, learning to cook and watching television, also becomes a pacifist and, when Crosby asks him who told him it was wrong to kill, he replies "I told me. Newton Crosby, Ph.D. not know killing is wrong?" "Are all geniuses as stupid as you?" Stephanie asks Crosby not too long before they fall in love and, having outwitted the military, disappear into the sunset with Number Five in their van to live as a happy cyborg family in the Edenic wilderness of Montana.

As I watched the film its moral seemed transparently clear to me: the military just seeks to destroy and cannot be trusted; brilliant scientists are often naive and allow their work to be misused by an unscrupulous military; an enjoyment of love and life is antithetical to military and scientific life; and scientists and military men need to be brought to their senses by strong, activist women with big hearts. In short the film seemed to me a searing indictment of Ray's life. Only one thing puzzled me: why was Ray enjoying it so much that he almost fell of the sofa laughing at one point?

"You enjoyed that film?" I asked, bemused.

"Wasn't it great? I've seen it before, but I love it," he answered, grinning from ear to ear.

I felt the way the first Newton must have felt when the apple fell on his head, but before he had any idea why. I was sure I was onto something important here, but I was not sure what. I told Ray my interpretation of the film, emphasizing what I took to be its critique of the military and of weapons scientists. There was a moment of silence as Ray looked first perplexed, then tired. I had taken him by surprise. He told me that the film, as far as he was concerned, may have poked some good-natured fun at the military and at scientists, but its central theme had to do with the fact that machines are enchanted and magical, and that people are unnecessarily afraid of them. "People are afraid of what they don't understand," he said. "That's what the film was about. It was making fun of people's fear of technology."

I realized that Ray and I had been watching different films. The film revealed in stark relief the different cultural worlds inhabited by Ray and I. If ever I had been inclined to doubt the palpable force of culture in human affairs, here was my evidence of its determinative influence. Where I had read the film as a transparent (almost embarrassingly so) warning about the evils of scientific militarism, and had been unable to see any other possible interpretation, Ray had seen it as a technological fantasy mocking popular fears of technology and celebrating the possibility that machines might be alive, magical, and essentially harmless. Separated by our initial attitude to technology, we had understood the film in fundamentally different ways. Ray's reading of the film was completely invisible to me as a possibility until our conversation.

Ideology and Popular Culture

An incident such as this prompts important questions about the relationship between hegemony and popular culture. One way of reading the event described above would be to say that, in a situation where (as Janice Radway and Stanley Fish tell us) texts are susceptible to multiple interpretations while dominant discourses and ideologies are (as Foucault tells us) overwhelmingly powerful, then texts and films that appear from one perspective to be counter-hegemonic can easily be recuperated and their message disarmed by the dominant discourse. Here the internal fissures and ambiguities of texts so celebrated by the deconstructionists become just one more means of enabling webs of power to maintain themselves.

Although this is a plausible interpretation of this single instance, it is one that we should treat with caution—and not only because it would seem, in the world of political practice where human beings endeavor to persuade each other about right and wrong, to lead to the bleak conclusion that hegemonic systems are hopelessly immovable once established. It seems to me, instead, that ambiguity and internal contradictoriness cut both ways, affecting dominant discourses as well as counter-hegemonic texts and artifacts. Thus I want to add an account of another conversation I had with Ray, this one provoked by a different film he and I watched together on television—a film that apparently caught him in a different mood than *Short Circuit* did.

The film in question is *Splash,* which like *Short Circuit,* **stars a boundary-confusing creature persecuted by the military,** only in this case a mermaid rather than a (male) robot. The mermaid in *Splash* falls in love with a man but is then found and captured by Pentagon researchers, who keep her imprisoned in a tank so they can experiment on her. Her lover spends much of the film trying to rescue her. This film, initiating a chain reaction of associations, prompted Ray to tell me about yet another film he had seen with a similar theme: *Starman. Starman,* as Ray described it, is about an alien who accepts an invitation to visit earth and is captured and dissected by the authorities. "There are governments in the world that would do that sort of thing, you know," Ray commented knowingly to me. I expected him to follow up this pronouncement with a commentary on Soviet human rights abuses but, to my surprise, he said, "I wouldn't even put it past some people in the U.S. Government ... The scientists in the film remind me of the attitude of some scientists you see at the lab, doing things without being alive to the human consequences." He even likened these to German scientists in World War II who did experiments in the concentration camps and mused that he wondered how history would judge the Laboratory's scientists if nuclear weapons were ever used.

What are we to make of this? Ray's response to *Splash* and *Starman* clearly fits with his perception, mentioned earlier, that some of his colleagues at the Laboratory were less concerned about ethics than he. It also suggests that critical popular films about militarism are sometimes able to penetrate the dominant discourse, opening up fissures and enabling the articulation of doubts and queries that might otherwise remain unvoiced. While these doubts may only overwhelm a particular subject in unusual circumstances, that does not mean that they can easily be put to rest. Thus, if I have a quarrel with Janice Radway's approach to the ethnography of reading, it is that articulating a fundamentally post-structuralist insight about the multipleness of the world with a structuralist sensibility, she assigns too much stability to her readers' responses, discerning in them a clearly consistent set of beliefs about the world that ultimately correlates with the social position of the readers. As I have tried to suggest here by exploring Ray's contradictory responses to different films we watched together, people's ideology may be unstable and fissured in its own way, just like the texts through which we strive to discern that ideology. After all, as Raymond Williams (1977:112) remarks, hegemony is never finally stable but "has continually to be renewed, recreated, defended, and modified."

Conclusion

This article has sought to probe the fractal multipleness of human social and cultural life by analyzing a scene from my fieldwork at a nuclear-weapons laboratory. In this scene I thought I understood a film I saw and I thought I understood an informant I had come to know quite well, but once the film and the informant were combined I found myself in a situation where I could no longer be sure of my understanding of either—though both now seemed much more interesting to me than before. The fact that it does not all fit together neatly in the end, that systems electrical and hermeneutic are always vulnerable to short circuit, is what makes cultural analysis an impossible but vitally important and exciting project. Films may have more than one meaning, depending on the viewer and the context of viewing; informants may articulate fragments of different ideologies, depending on the situation that evokes their speech; cyborgs may be utopian or dystopian, tragic or comedic, depending on whether they appear in *BladeRunner* or *Short Circuit*.

I have tried here to weave my story about the fractal quality of texts, ideologies, and people around the enigmatic, liminal, shape-shifting, tricksterish figure of the cyborg. In doing so, I have taken my cue from Donna Haraway herself, who, arguing against the totalizing discourses of Marxism and eco-feminism, insists in her "Manifesto for Cyborgs" that the cyborg's only true politics lie in its opposition to disambiguating closure: "the cyborg ... has no truck with ... seductions to wholeness through a final appropriation of all the powers of the parts into a higher unity" (Haraway 1990:192). In her final paragraph Haraway claims that "cyborg imagery can suggest a way out of the maze of dualisms in which we have explained our bodies and our tools to ourselves. This is a dream not of a common language but of a powerful infidel heteroglossia" (Haraway 1990:223). Taking these ideas a little further and refracting them back on Haraway's own work, I want to conclude with a warning against an over-romantic view of the cyborg among some contemporary writers that threatens to turn into a fatal attraction.

Paradoxically, and problematically, in insisting so vocally that the cyborg's politics are anti-essentialist, **Haraway herself essentializes the cyborg,** thus denying it the full extent of its shape-shifting ability. Thus, for example, Haraway tells us that the cyborg is "oppositional, utopian, and completely without innocence" (p.192). She goes on to say that:

> the cyborg does not expect its father to save it through a restoration of the garden, that is, through the fabrication of a heterosexual mate, through its completion in a finished whole, a city and cosmos. The cyborg does not dream of community on the model of the organic family, this time without the Oedipal project. The cyborg would not recognize the Garden of Eden; it is not made of mud and cannot dream of returning to dust.
> (Haraway 1990:192).

I am struck by this passage because almost every clause of it is belied by the particular cyborg that is Number Five in *Short Circuit*. Number Five appeals to audiences precisely because of his quality of childlike innocence; he does expect his "father" (Newton Crosby) to save him, and the process of salvation involves a heterosexual union between Crosby and Stephanie that consummates Number Five's own romance with Stephanie and suggests a new covenant between science, society, and technology; Number Five *does* dream of returning to dust—he is haunted by the fear of being "disassembled"; finally, Number Five *does* indeed "dream of community on the model of the organic family, this time without the Oedipal project:" in the final scene Number Five, Newton Crosby, and Stephanie escape to the Eden (Montana) that supposedly holds no appeal for cyborgs as a single family in which Number Five is a sort of robot-child that, by virtue of its mechanical inability to couple with humans, is freed from the Oedipal hex and able to complete a seamless, conflict-free family.

I offer this slightly heavy-handed exposition of both the film *Short Circuit* and Donna Haraway's prose in order to emphasize that, despite its liminality, the cyborg can easily be worked into the "maze of dualisms" that is so powerful in structuring Western thought. **We can have unabashedly military cyborgs, liberal cyborgs, and feminist cyborgs just as easily as we can have cyborgs that undermine such categories.** To think otherwise is to underestimate the power of the grand narratives of Western thought and to substitute a romanticized vision of the cyborg (based, paradoxically, on its supposed immunity to romance) for older romantic salvation narratives organized around either a return to nature or a surrender to technology. Just as nature cannot save us, technology cannot save us, and the working class cannot save us, so also the cyborg cannot save us. **We created the cyborg, just as we created nature, technology, and the working class, and only we can save ourselves.**

Notes

1. I am grateful to Jane Caputi, Michael Fischer, Chris Gray, and anonymous reviewers for the *Journal of Popular Film and Television* for comments that helped me revise this article. As always, responsibility for remaining idiocies is mine alone. The research upon which this article is based would not have been possible without the financial support of a Mellon New Directions Fellowship at Stanford University and an SSRC-MacArthur Fellowship in International Peace and Security.

2. Ray is not "Ray's" real name. I have also taken the liberty of disguising some of the circumstantial details I give about "Ray's" life in order to make it harder to identify him. In accordance with the prevailing, but unfortunate, convention in anthropology, and for want of a better word, I call Ray an "informant," though I dislike this word's connotations of surveillance and betrayal.

3. Besides Radway, my approach here is also influenced by a classic anthropological article by Laura Bohannon (1966), who explored the different ways she and her African Tiv hosts understood Shakespeare's *Hamlet*. The present article can be read as an updating of Bohannon's argument for the age of film and video.

4. The founding and early history of the Laboratory is best described in the writings of Herb York, its first director (York 1975, 1987: 65-72).

5. For overviews of the Laboratory's programs, see Cochran *et al.* (1987:44-52) and a special issue of the Laboratory's *Energy and Technology Review* (1990). An excellent but unpublished overview appears in Senate Policy Committee (1984).

6. On the rise and fall of the Nuclear Freeze Campaign, see Solo (1988) and Waller (1987). For a more general portrait of the anti-nuclear movement in the 1980s, see Loeb (1987). Barbara Epstein (1985, 1988) gives an excellent description and analysis of the Livermore Action Group, which organized the mass blockades of the Laboratory, one of which attracted about 5,000 participants. 1300 people were arrested for civil disobedience at this protest in 1982, making it one of the biggest civil-disobedience actions in American history. For an account of one of the mass blockades, see Cabasso and Moon (1985).

7. For an exploration of the growing opposition to the arms race within America's mainstream churches, see the interviews in Wallis (1983). The Bishop who was arrested at the gates of the Laboratory was Leontine Kelley, a Methodist.

8. For a more detailed exploration of Livermore scientists' thinking about nuclear ethics, see Gusterson (1995: chapter 3).

9. In my writing I usually treat nuclear-weapons scientists' political statements as material for cultural analysis, bracketing the contentious question of whether these statements should be seen as "true" or "false." In this case, however, I feel compelled as commentator to make an exception to my own policy in order to refute what must in all candor be described as disinformation about the anti-nuclear movement promulgated by the Reagan Administration. Based on my experience first as a participant in and later as a researcher on the Northern California anti-nuclear movement of the 1980s, I am quite sure that this movement was not funded by the KGB. I spent a year of my life deeply involved in fundraising for the San Francisco Nuclear Freeze and got to see first-hand, when the mail was opened, where the money came from. (Mostly lots of small donors.) I also spent years watching anti-nuclear organizations sink into debt,

fall behind in paying their employees' minimal salaries, and keep having to neglect their political goals in order to organize fundraising events to keep themselves afloat. This was a movement that was starved of resources (cf. Gusterson 1993).

10. Ironically, the crown jewel in the Livermore Laboratory's technological crown in the 1980s was its Nova laser—the most powerful laser in the world—used for both military and alternative-energy experiments.

References Cited

Bohannon, Laura "Shakespeare in the Bush." *Natural History,* August/September,1966.

Cabasso, Jackie and Susan Moon *Risking Peace: Why We Sat in the Road.* Berkeley: Open Books, 1985.

Cochran, Thomas; Arkin, William; Norris, Robert; and Hoenig, Milton *Nuclear Weapons Databook, Volume II.* Cambridge, Mass.: Ballinger, 1987.

Energy and Technology Review "The State of the Laboratory." *Energy and Technology Review,* Lawrence Livermore National Laboratory, July/August, 1990.

Epstein, Barbara "The Culture of Direct Action." *Socialist Review* 82/83:31-61, 1985.

Epstein, Barbara "The Politics of Prefigurative Community: The Non-Violent Direct Action Movement." In Mike David and Michael Spriker (eds.) *Reshaping the U.S. Left: Popular Struggles in the 1980s.* London: Verso Books, 1988, pp. 63-92.

Fish, Stanley *Is There a Text In This Class? The Authority of Interpretive Communities.* Cambridge, Mass.: Harvard University Press, 1980.

Gibson, William *Neuromancer.* New York: Ace Books, 1984.

Gusterson, Hugh *Testing Times: A Nuclear Weapons Laboratory at the End of the Cold War.* Berkeley: University of California Press, 1995.

Gusterson, Hugh "Exploding Anthropology's Canon in the World of the Bomb: Ethnographic Writing on Militarism." *Journal of Contemporary Ethnography* 22 (1):59-79, 1993.

Haraway, Donna "A Manifesto for Cyborgs: Science, Technology, and Socialist Feminism in the 1980s." In Linda Nicholson (ed.) *Feminism/Postmodernism,* New York: Routledge, 1990.

Hobson, Dorothy *Crossroads: The Drama of a Soap Opera.* London: Methuen, 1982.

Loeb, Paul *Hope in Hard Times: America's Peace Movement and the Reagan Era.* Lexington, Mass.: Lexington Books, 1987.

National Conference of Catholic Bishops *The Challenge of Peace: God's Promise and Our Response.* Washington D.C.: U.S. Catholic Conference, 1983.

Radway, Janice *Reading The Romance: Women, Patriarchy, and Popular Literature.* Chapel Hill, N.C.: University of North Carolina Press, 1991.

Senate Policy Committee, Berkeley Division of the Academic Senate, University of California. The University of California, the Lawrence Livermore National Laboratory, and the Los Alamos National Laboratory. Unpublished background paper, 1984.

Shelley, Mary *Frankenstein.* Oxford: Oxford University Press, 1969.

Solo, Pam *From Protest to Policy: Beyond the Freeze to Common Security.* Cambridge, Mass.: Ballinger, 1988.

Turkle, Sherry *The Second Self: Computers and The Human Spirit.* New York: Simon and Schuster, 1984.

Waller, Douglas, C. *Congress and the Nuclear Freeze: An Inside Look at the Politics of a Mass Movement.* Amherst: University of Massachusetts Press, 1987.

Wallis, Jim (ed.) *Peacemakers: Christian Voices From the New Abolitionist Movement.* San Francisco: Harper and Row, 1983.

Williams, Raymond *Marxism and Literature.* Oxford: Oxford University Press, 1977.

Winner, Langdon *Autonomous Technology.* Cambridge: MIT Press, 1977.

York, Herbert "The Origins of the Lawrence Livermore Laboratory." *Bulletin of the Atomic Scientists* 31 (7): 1975, pp. 8-14.

York, Herbert *Making Weapons, Talking Peace: A Physicist's Odyssey From Hiroshima to Geneva.* New York: Basic Books, 1987.

2.7

SOCIALIZING THE CYBORG SELF

The Gulf War and Beyond

Kevin Robins and Les Levidow

The cyborg self can be characterized as follows: through a paranoid rationality, expressed in the machine-like self, we combine an omnipotent phantasy of self-control with fear and aggression directed against the emotional and bodily limitations of mere mortals. Through regression to a phantasy of infantile omnipotence, we deny our dependency upon nature, upon our own nature, upon the "bloody mess" of organic nature. We phantasize about controlling the world, freezing historical forces, and, if necessary, even destroying them in rage; we thereby contain our anxiety in the name of maintaining rational control (Levidow and Robins, 1989, p. 172).

Vision and image technologies mediate the construction of the cyborg self. The so-called Gulf War highlighted their role. **In a very real sense, the screen became the scene of the war:** the military encountered its enemy targets in the form of electronic images. The world of simulation somehow screened out the catastrophic dimension of the real and murderous attack.

As the Gulf War also brought home to us, it was not just military personnel who became caught up in this technological psychosis. The "Nintendo war" involved and implicated home audiences, who took pleasure in watching the official images of war, often compulsively so. How was it possible to achieve this popular engagement? How were viewers locked into the war through their TV screens? How is the cyborg self generalized to the society at large?

The Military Cyborg

War converts fear and anxiety into perceptions of external threat. It then mobilizes

defenses against alien and thing-like enemies. In this process, new image and vision technologies can play a central role. Combat is increasingly mediated through the computer screen. Combatants are involved in a kind of remotely exhilarating tele-action, tele-present and tele-engaged in the theatre of war, sanitized of its bloody reality. Killing is done 'at a distance', through technological mediation, without the shock of direct confrontation. The victims become psychologically invisible. The soldier appears to achieve a moral dissociation; **the targeted "things" on the screen do not seem to implicate him in a moral relationship**.

Moreover, by fetishizing electronic "information" for its precision and omniscience, military force comes to imagine itself in terms of the mechanical or cybernetic qualities that are designed into computers. **The operator behaves as a virtual cyborg in the real-time, man-machine interface which structures military weapons systems**. A new "cyborg soldier" is constructed and programmed to fit integrally into weapons systems. By training for endurance, the soldier attempts to overcome biological limits, better to respond to real-time 'information' about enemy movements. By disciplining his 'mindware', and acting on the world through computer simulations, the soldier can remain all the more removed from the bloody consequences of his actions (Gray, 1989).

In the Gulf War, the cyborg soldier was complemented by new "smart" weapons. Although the view from a B-52 bomb bay already distanced the attacker from any human victims, new weapons rationalized military vision even further. Paradoxically, the Gulf video images gave us **closer visual proximity between weapon and target, but at the same time greater psychological distance.** The missile-nose view of the target simulated a super-real closeness which no human being could ever attain. This remote-intimate viewing extended the moral detachment that characterized earlier military technologies (Robins and Levidow, 1991, p. 325).

It was the ultimate voyeurism: to see the target hit from the vantage point of the weapon. An inhuman perspective. Yet this kind of watching could sustain the moral detachment of earlier military technologies. Seeing was split off from feeling; the visible was separated from the sense of pain and death. Through the long lens the enemy remained a faceless alien, her/his bodily existence de-realized (Robins and Levidow, 1991). Military attack took the form of thing-like relations between people, and social relations between things, as if destroying inanimate objects. Perversely, war appeared as it really was (Levidow, 1994).

In targeting and monitoring the attack, a real-time simulation depended upon prior surveillance of the enemy, conceptualized as a "target-rich environment." In the five months preceding the January, 1991 attack on Iraq, the US war machine devoted laborious "software work" to mapping and plotting strategic installations there. The concept of "legitimate military target" extended from military bases and the presidential palace, to major highways, factories, water supplies and power stations. The basic means of survival for an entire population were reduced to "targeting information." **Enemy threats—real or imaginary, human or machine—became precise grid locations, abstracted from their human context.**

This computer simulation prepared and encouraged an omnipotence phantasy, a phantasy of total control over things. At the same time, the phantasized omnipotence required the containment of anxieties about impotence and vulnerability. The drive for electronic omniscience both evoked and contained anxiety about unseen threats. Designed to prepare real-time attacks, an electronic panopticon intensified the paranoiac features of earlier omnipotence phantasies. Through these technological attempts at ordering a disorderly world, uncertainty was rendered intolerable.

Any attempt to evade penetration by the West's high-tech panopticon simply confirmed the guilt and irrationality of the devious Arab enemy. Any optical evasion became an omnipresent, unseen threat of the unknown which must be exterminated. This paranoid logic complemented the U.S. tendency to abandon the Cold War rationales for its electronic surveillance and weaponry, now being redesigned explicitly for attacking the Third World (Klare, 1991).

In the Gulf episode, the U.S. military portrayed the Iraqi forces as in hiding. When Saddam decided to avoid a direct military confrontation with the U.S. coalition's air force, he was described as 'hunkering down', almost cheating the surveillance systems of the West's rational game plan (Levidow and Robins, 1991). Iraq's caution was personified as the backward Arab playing the coy virgin: "Saddam's armies last week seemed to be enacting a travesty of the Arab motif of veiling and concealment ... [Saddam] makes a fairly gaudy display of mystique" (*Time* magazine, February 4, 1991, pp. 12-13). Such language updated an earlier cultural stereotyping of the mysterious Orient (Said, 1985).

The racist logic emerged more clearly after the U.S. massacre of civilians in the Amariya air-raid shelter. In this case, unusually, TV pictures showed us hundreds of shrouded corpses. In response, the U.S. authorities insisted that they had recorded a precise hit on a "positively identified military target;" they even blamed Saddam for putting civilians in the bunker (Kellner, 1992, pp. 297-309). The U.S. continued to cite its surgical precision as moral legitimation, even though it was the precise targeting which allowed the missile to enter the ventilation shaft and incinerate all the people inside the shelter.

Constructing the Viewer

This combined logic of fear and aggression is not just a military phenomenon. The Gulf War showed how much we, **the home viewers of the Nintendo war, were also implicated in the logic of fear, paranoia and aggression.** Seen on network TV, the video-game images were crucial in recruiting support for the U.S.-led attack.

The images evoked audience familiarity with video games, thus offering a vicarious real-time participation. Video games in the wider culture are also about the mastery of anxiety and the mobilization of omnipotence phantasies; these psychic dimensions correspond to the cyborg logic of the military "game." The parallel with weapons systems runs deep; after all, some innovators have alternated between designing military and entertainment versions of interactive simulation technology.

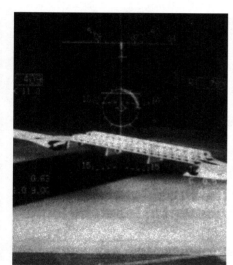

Where the Gulf massacre publicly enacted phantasies, video games privatize them. The processes of anxiety and control are actively structured by the computer-video microworld, with its compulsive task of achieving 'perfect mastery' (Levidow and Robins, 1989, pp. 172-175). In particular, the video game is a psychodynamic process of projecting and managing internal threats: "The actual performance required of us in the video game is like being permanently connected to broadcast television's exciting live event." Video games elicit young boys' phantasies of exploring the damage done inside the mother's body; here the male 'fears both his own destructiveness and a fantasized retaliation from the object of his destructive fantasies' (Skirrow, 1986, pp. 121-22).

Video games can thus be understood as a paranoiac environment that induces a sense of paranoia by dissolving any distinction between the doer and the viewer. Driven by the structure of the video game, the player is constantly defending himself, or the entire universe, from destructive forces. The play becomes a compulsive, pleasurable repetition of a life-and-death performance. Yet the player's anxiety can never be finally mastered by that vicariously dangerous play. He engages in a characteristic repetition, often described as "video-game addiction" (*ibid.*, pp. 129-33).

While the video game simulates a real-time event, the Gulf episode took such images as its reality. The Gulf War was "total television", **an entertainment form which merged military and media planning** (Engelhardt, 1992). "The Pentagon, and its corporate suppliers, became the producers and the sponsors of the sounds and images, while the 'news' became a form of military advertising" (Stam, 1992, p. 112). How, then, did this infotainment engage its audience, and even construct the viewer?

The home audience, which seemed to take great pleasure in its viewing, was also implicated in collective phantasies. Primitive anxieties were evoked and structured by a pervasive cultural rhetoric, which gave specific meanings to the electronic images. The Iraqi state, even an entire society, was personified as an irrational monster, 'a new Hitler', from whom we must be saved. The sadistic 'rape of Kuwait' posed a threat of symbolic buggery against the West, even a threat to civilization itself. Saddam seemed to personify a sadistic, unpredictable, limitless violence. He was a "madman" who transgressed the combined rules of morality and rationality. By exaggerating claims about Iraq's nuclear weapons development and speculating on its chemical weapons, the mass media portrayed a regional aggressor as a threat of global annihilation.

In the face of these perceived threats, viewers were infantilised, leading them to welcome a strong saviour who was apparently wielding a civilized violence on behalf of international law. When the West's attack transparently went beyond the official mission to 'free Kuwait', the ensuing destruction resonated with popular wishes to remove the source of primitive anxiety—by civilized means only, of course. In contrast to Saddam's sadistic Scuddish violence, the West was imagined to be inflicting a morally based violence; **'our' missiles, by virtue of their precision and rationality acted as exterminating angels.** This good/evil split permitted western TV audiences to deny the barbarism within their own civilization, to deny the internal sources of its violence, and to treat its destructive hatred as an enemy threat (Aksoy and Robins, 1991). Western rationality became inseparable from a paranoid projection which conflated, and confused, internal and external threats.

Bombed facilities were rhetorically personalized as Saddam's military machine. In this way, 'the media turned Iraq into one vast faceless extension of their demonized leader' (Stam, 1992, p. 114). The mass media also adopted U.S. military euphemisms which further reified the massacre. This language denied the human qualities of the victims, while attributing such qualities to inanimate objects: for example, 'smart' bombs 'killed' Iraqi equipment. Home viewers could thereby detach themselves morally from the human consequences of surgical strikes against the evil, non-human forces personified by Saddam (Kellner, 1992, p. 247).

The images did far more than to sanitize death. The video-game war also combined viewer and doer: 'telespectators were made to see from the bomber's perspective' (Stam, 1992, p. 104; cf. Levidow and Robins, 1991). With missile cameras "the sectors of destruction and information became almost completely synonymous" (Wark, 1991, p. 15). The images involved us as vicarious participants in destroying perceived threats to our bodily integrity, our physical existence, and our social order. Indeed, we could feel a pleasurable identification with high-tech violence against a barbaric enemy (Broughton, 1993).

In this paranoid rationality, the problem is less about people accepting the literal "truth" of propaganda images, than about seeking refuge from anxiety. 'The danger is that people will choose fantasy, and fantasy identification with power, over a threatening or intolerably dislocating social reality' (Rosler, 1991, p. 63). As an anti-war poster warned, "You are the Target Audience: When you watch the news, you are invited to enter into a pact. You are expected to believe in the same system, share the same values and goals."

Even those disposed to be critical could find certain parts of themselves consenting to this pact. The war images both evoked and contained primitive anxieties in all of us. We were confronted with invasive and induced feelings, and found ourselves experiencing feelings and thinking thoughts that were in an important sense not entirely our own. We had to reckon with feeling-states that seemed to inhabit and impose themselves on us, irrespective of our conscious desires. As Baudrillard (1991, pp. 12-13) puts it, 'we were all held hostage by the intoxication of the media'.

The Social Cyborg

The Gulf massacre brought home to us **the role of high-tech systems in mass psychopathology.** This episode belied the naive hopes of those who have idealized electronic information—as an instrument of participatory democracy, as a social prosthesis, or even as inherent resistance to the commodity form. Rather, electronic systems constituted a paranoiac environment; mediating an omnipotence phantasy, they converted internal threats into thing-like enemies, symbolizing rage at our bodily limitations.

In the paranoid-schizoid mode, 'the self is predominantly a self as object, a self that is buffeted by thoughts, feelings, and perceptions as if they were external forces or physical objects occupying or bombarding oneself' (Ogden, 1989, pp. 21-22). The fear and pain immanent within ourselves is evacuated and experienced as danger immanent within the other. Once they are externalized in this way, 'the establishment can get to work, offering its protection, keeping the threat at bay, zapping intruders, policing the boundaries' (Hoggett, 1992, p. 346).

Screen, surveillance and simulation technologies have become fundamental to this 'protection'. It now involves new global networks of sensors keeping track of worldwide targets in real time. Vision technologies appear to enhance security through continuous monitoring of the globe as a danger-rich environment. With the spread of such defense systems, 'real enemies' become elusive and ominpresent. The technologies now monitor an unidentified and amorphous threat 'out there', both within and beyond the boundaries of the western world.

For example, Britain has an estimated 200,000 video-surveillance cameras, many of them continuously monitoring main streets and shopping centres. It is argued that the cameras not only help police to identify criminals, but also make people feel safer. If so, then the cameras compensate for—and even intensify—the social isolation which makes us feel vulnerable in the first place. This form of 'security' further constructs our lives as social relations between things, just as a Nintendo war 'protected' us from any human relation with its victims.

The Other is an unseen and invisible threat, detectable only through electronic surveillance and mediation. The technological systems generate a structural paranoia: their panoptic vigilance requires the existence of a virtual enemy. It is not only the state which is caught up in this logic of paranoid rationality. Its psychic defense, which underlay the 1980s Star Wars project, became a mass-culture recruitment drive during the Gulf War. As in that 'virtual war', the whole society is now caught up in 'this visualization of things, this hypervisibility, this hyperpredictability and programming, hyperprogramming, of things' (Baudrillard, 1993, p. 251).

Through electronic mediation, this aspect of war pervades wider areas of our lives, thus socializing the cyborg self. We fear ourselves and each other, while identifying with an omnipotence phantasy of technological power. The question remains: instead of infantilizing us, can electronic mediation help us to handle our fears and to identify with fellow targets of the paranoid panopticon?

References

Aksoy, A. and Robins, K. (1991), 'Exterminating angels: morality, technology and violence in the Gulf War', *Science as Culture*, 12:322-337.

Baudrillard, J. (1991), *La Guerre du Golfe n'a pas eu lieu*, Paris, Editions Galilée.

Baudrillard, J. (1993), 'Hyperreal America', *Economy and Society*, 22 (2): 243-252.

Broughton, J. (1993), 'The pleasures of the Gulf War', pp. 231-246 in R. Stam (ed.), *Recent Trends in Theoretical Psychology III*, New York, Springer.

Engelhardt, T. (1992), 'The Gulf War as total television', *The Nation*, 11 May: 629-632.

Gray, C.H. (1989), 'The cyborg soldier', pp. 43-72 in L. Levidow and K. Robins (eds.), *Cyborg Worlds: The Military Information Society*, London, Free Association Books/New York, Columbia University Press.

Hoggett, P (1992), 'A place for experience: a psychoanalytic perspective on boundary, identity and culture', *Environment and Planning D: Society and Space*, 10 (3): 354-356.

Kellner, D. (1992), *The Persian Gulf TV War*, Boulder, Co, Westview Press.

Klare, M. (1991), 'Behind Desert Storm: the new military paradigm', *Technology Review*, May-June: 26-36.

Levidow, L. (1994), 'The Gulf massacre as paranoid rationality', in T. Druckrey and G. Bender (eds.), *Ideologies of Technology*, Seattle, Bay Press.

Levidow, L. and Robins, K. (1989), *Cyborg Worlds: The Military Information Society*, London, Free Association Books/New York, Columbia University Press.

Levidow, L. and Robins, K. (1991), 'Vision wars', *Race and Class*, 32(4): 87-92.

Ogden, T. (1989), *The Primitive Edge of Experience*, Northvale, New Jersey, Jason Aronson.

Robins, K. and Levidow, L. (1991), 'The eye of the storm', *Screen*, 32(3):324-328.

Rosler, M. (1991), 'Image simulation, computer manipulations', *Ten 8*, 2(2): 52-63.

Said, E. (1985), *Orientalism*, Harmondsworth, Penguin.

Skirrow, G. (1986), 'Hellivision: an analysis of video games', in C. MacCabe (ed.), *High Theory, Low Culture*, Manchester, Manchester University Press.

Starn, R. (1992), 'Mobilising fictions: the Gulf War, the media and the recruitment of the spectator', *Public Culture*, 4(2): 101-126.

Wark, M. (1991), 'War TV in the Gulf, *Meanjin* 50 (1): 5-18.

2.8

CHILDREN OF THE MIND WITH DISPOSABLE BODIES

Metaphors of self in a text on artificial intelligence and robotics

Heidi J. Figueroa-Sarriera

Just as water, gas and electricity are brought into our houses from far off to satisfy our needs in response to minimal effort, so we shall be supplied with visual or auditory images, which will appear and disappear at a simple movement of the hand.

—Paul Valéry

When texts are conceived of as socio-semiotic units, certain assumptions come into play: 1) within texts, phrases lose their ambiguity; 2) texts incorporate assumptions and implications from the phrases that construct them; 3) there are various possibilities to paraphrasing a text. Every textual articulation germinates within a chrysalis of particular historical coordinates that anchor the possible significations of that text. One must take into consideration not only the textual character of discourse but also its extratextual character when considering discourse as a structuring form, for the discourse constitutes social practices within a historical context. Every text, therefore, implies a certain discursive fabric, woven about the intersection of the syntagmatic axis and the paradigmatic axis.

The force of metaphor resides precisely in the fact that as a rhetorical tool simultaneously exploring similarity and difference, it functions primarily along the paradigmatic axis of linguistic production. **Metaphor enables us to understand and experience one sort of thing in terms of another.** In its daily use, according to Lakoff and Johnson (1986), what we experience with a metaphor is that a kind of "reverberation" is felt "down through the network of entailments that awaken and connect our memories of our past ... and serves as a possible guide for future ones" (140). These memories and experiences, however, cannot be conceived except from a point of view that is necessarily political and ideological.

In considering the self as a socially and historically constructed category, we must look back to the Enlightenment and the beginnings of capitalist industrial development. Traditionally, the characteristics associated with the self in modern times stem from a particular re-articulation of legal discourse, beginning with the French Revolution and the consolidation of Christianity as a religion of salvation and confession, in which the notions of equality and liberty are broadened (Foucault, 1985, 1990). At that historical moment, a particular social being was gradually produced, a "self" which was the bearer of certain rights and responsibilities, and whose existence required a sort of interior cavity that assumed the responsibility for the person's acts and that might easily be converted into an object of the various normalization programs that accompanied industrial development. The notion of self that gradually takes shape in modern times makes that self both the center of "self-consciousness" and a unit of self-contained and integral action. This self claims, paradoxically, simultaneous difference from and equality with the "other."

Although in antiquity the psyche was conceived of as an impersonal and transcendent entity whose most remarkable characteristic was its categorical opposition to the body, and thus its total exemption from the limitations on the physical existence of that body, the psyche of modern times is seen as the counterpart of that other, bodily substance. According to the Cartesian dualism that emerges in the seventeenth century, body and soul are two substances that mutually depend upon each other.

Today, late-capitalist society is advancing toward new modes of capital accumulation, which leads us to consider the need to articulate a new notion of the self, one which takes shape, though in contradictory ways, within these new historical and social conditions. David Harvey (1987) has pointed out that as a result of the collapse of the Fordist system of production, a new system of political and social order has arisen, based on flexibility. This new mode of accumulation demands flexibility with respect to labor processes, the labor market, production and more recently differentiated patterns of consumption.

Flexible production systems put emphasis on product innovation and the exploration of small-scale markets. New technologies—robotics, information technology, visual technologies, genetic engineering, etc.—serve to accelerate the temporal processes leading toward this new mode of accumulation. This phenomenon translates into accelerated compression of space/time. The repercussions of these new modes of production are reordering the threads for a new design of the social fabric in post-Fordist late-capitalist society. These new articulations point out the need to sew back together the so-called "fourth discontinuity" in the human/machine relationship (Mazlish, 1993).[1] We might also speak of a human/machine compression, this compression signifying a new qualitative leap in the evolutionary process, as some researchers have suggested, Moravec (1988) and Ursua (1988) among others. This suturing of the human/machine dichotomy implies a new notion of self that, in turn, would respond, although in contradictory ways, to the goals of the globilization of the economy.

This paper is an analysis of Hans Moravec's *MIND Children: The Future of Robot and Human Intelligence* (1988).[2] Two discourses predominate in this text: the *biological* and the *magical*. Between them, they generate a matrix of statements that would appear to argue in favor of the suturing of the "fourth discontinuity" and the forging of new modes of capital accumulation in the historical moment at which we now find ourselves.

First of all, Moravec characterizes the human/machine relationship with the metaphor of "symbiosis," specifically alluding to the concept of the interface between human being and the machine. The word "symbiosis" fundamentally signifies "the living together in more or less intimate association or close union of two dissimilar organisms; the intimate living together of two dissimilar organisms in a mutually beneficial relationship." Two assumptions may be seen in this metaphor. **First, that symbiosis is a cooperative relationship, and second, that the relationship is one between two entities conceived of as organisms.** Both "reverberations" have several implications, as we will see.

Furthermore, **the term "interface" itself means a surface forming a common boundary, a meeting-point or area of contact between objects, systems, etc.** This view of interface as a common boundary implies an inexorable machine/human connection, and thus we see that all the textual instances that mention or imply interfaces have a particular relevance to this discussion.

When Moravec narrates the history of the development of interfaces, he calls upon two metaphoric formulations that recall the two discursive modes previously mentioned: the organic and the magical. For example, Moravec says that the first interfaces were "rat's nests." As a vehicle of significance, one of the acceptations for the word "rat" is "a miserable or ill-looking specimen," and thus Moravec reiterates the primitive and somewhat tedious and daunting nature of those first interfaces, predisposing the reader to the "new" advances over the "old." A second metaphor used by Moravec is that of the "hacker's habitat," which is the work-space in which programmers develop better and better software. This metaphor clearly has organismic connotations, since the word "habitat" is associated with the dwelling-places or environments of organic life forms. In the passage in question, the machine appears to widen, organize, and facilitate the user's habitat. These rearrangements of the habitat are aimed at new and better modes of communication between users, achieved thanks to the employer's machines. The work-space is re-thought, and becomes a natural, organic environment in which social relationships emerge spontaneously and ludically. Thus, the signs of exploitation and domination characteristic of salaried jobs are occluded or omitted.

On the other hand, in this chronological account of the development of interfaces, another sort of clerk or scrivener begins to appear—the "hacker." Hackers are very similar to medieval scribes, for they are the possessors of the skill of writing (in this case, writing software), they associate in guilds of a sort (support groups, user groups, and other types of associations and networks), and they have secret signs (the particular programming languages and access-codes and passwords they use). The notion of "network" changes subtly into an "arcanum"—an occult or recondite secret or mystery—to be revealed only to certain initiates or adepts.

Through this metaphor, Moravec brings the legacy of alchemy into the modern world of the development of interfaces. In several passages he alludes to magical, enchanted, and mysterious or occult aspects of these new technological advances. Especially well-articulated is a magical conception of image-production. Images appear as privileged forms (the religious word "icon" is used), and become the dominant mode of representation, producing a new sort of interface that, in popularizing "writing" on a video screen and conveying that writing to a mass audience, establishes a hypertext. There is, then, a secularization of icono-graphic writing, similar in many ways to the general secularization of writing in modern times. For Moravec, "the icon interfaces proved effective and easy to use for novices and experts alike, probably because they tapped the nonverbal object-manipulation skills of humans" (Moravec, 1988, 84).

The image of self implied here picks up the concept of self present at earlier stages of development, and fits the image of user/machine interaction as ludic activity. This type of vision (and approach) leads eventually to the production of those extremely "user-friendly" microcomputers and software that mushroomed in the 80s.

In spite of the importance and profusion of this sort of hypertext, Moravec presents us with yet another sort of interface, one providing even greater interactivity. Moravec calls this interface "magic glasses," once again employing the magical metaphor. These glasses may be accompanied by "magic gloves" and even, in time, by a "magic rope." This equipment produces an artificial or "virtual" reality that, in interactivity with a person, functions as a hypertext or hyper-reality.

Kim Sawchuk (1987) has pointed out that in late capitalism, power resides in the "imaginary," where as Sawchuk says, "subjects are maintained in a circuit of desire and anxiety." Here, creating an abstraction is no longer an exercise that produces a sort of mirror-phenomenon, more or less isomorphic with reality, but it is the generation of models of reality that do not take their origin from reality. We are dealing, then, with a hyper-reality.

Likewise, models of proxy-robots have been designed, one in 1986 at the Naval Ocean Systems Center in Hawaii. The motions of the operator can be copied by the robot at the same time as images from the robot's camera-eyes are delivered to the operator's "magic glasses." This sophisticated equipment gives the operator the subjective sensation of being in the robot's body.

"Magical" interfaces can put limitless experiences at a person's disposal, even without the person's having to leave the comforts of home. Moravec promises that eventually the difference between transportation and communication will be moot. A person will be able to interact with other life-situations in several ways: by remote control (receiving sensory experiences from a robot), or by simulators, or by way of equipment which produces virtual realities. Or, of course, any combination of these.

In Moravec's text, the image that underlies this vision of the near-future is the prosthesis, which in turn generates a vision of a protean self at two distinct levels of that metaphor: First, technological equipment becomes the user's prosthesis, **and at the same time the body itself becomes a hyperpragmatic prosthesis in a world of virtual realities.** The word "prosthesis" is used to indicate an artificial device to replace a missing part of the body, but also a device which extends the radius of action of an organism.

This prosthesis metaphor contrasts favorably with Gianfranco Beltetini's notion. He speaks of the experience of the viewer of a film, arguing that the addressee's body is a "symbolic prosthesis." The subject of the enunciation, Beltetini says, has no body yet, but enters a text as a bodiless simulacrum into which is introduced, in disguise, a subject-addressee that does have a body. The viewer's body participates, then, in a symbolic production whose symbols come from the realm of the fantastic or illusory. The addressee's sense organs have no contiguous relationship with the signals from the screen. There is an "empty space" that the viewer fills by means of a symbolic production:

> It is precisely this lack of satisfaction, physically determined by the space
> which separates the viewer's body from the phantasms of the signifier, which
> allows the images to enter the order of discourse and allows the viewer to be
> located in turn in a discursive dimension, to perform the role of producer of
> symbols. One might say that the viewer's body "extends" its action
> constructing for itself a real symbolic prosthesis of its own (p. 35).

But what happens in the case of interaction with virtual realities? In this case there is indeed sensory continuity, provided by the "magic glasses," "magic gloves," etc. The viewer has no "empty space" to fill in the sense described by Beltetini. All is "presence," the presence of discourse not from the boundaries of the real but rather from the borders of the hyper-real. In this case, the body would be a prosthesis that did not "extend" but "spilled out of" the boundaries of the real organism. As we shall see in a moment, **this technological discourse at last implies the possibility of the ultimate "replacement" of the body.**

It is important to note that these advanced interfaces are given metaphorical names of clothing—gloves, coat, glasses—worn on the body. Julia Emberley (1987) says that the metaphor of clothing for designating the interface between the self and the rest of the world, in the post-modern image, implies that the body has been turned inside-out, exploding towards the surface where experience has been transformed into an ornament that inscribes the body with new signifieds.

At first glance the body is to be conserved and preserved:

> The magic glasses allow you to see through the robot's eyes, the coat and
> gloves permit you to feel, gesture, and act through the robot's manipulators,
> and foot controls on your armchair let you drive the robot around. By renting
> proxies at remote locations, you can visit, talk, and work at widely scattered
> projects without incurring the physical risks of dangerous locations or the
> boredom of long trips (Moravec, 1988, 1991).

In this passage we are presented with technology as protection for the body against physical harm, thereby implying the need to preserve the real physical body. This image, however, enters into a contradiction with the assumption of the body's obsolescence that appears in other passages, in which the author hints at the possibility and desirability of the transmigration of the mind into a synthetic body. In these passages, **the biological body assumes a character fundamentally scatological and disposable.**

In Moravec's text, we can identify some peculiarly modern continuities and discontinuities. Among these, there is the Platonic recreation of the "soul" (conceived of as mind) inhabiting a body, and functioning as the generator of life. The brain is displaced, as the heart was previously, as the generator or nucleus of life. Through the metaphor of transmigration, the myth of the separability of "soul" and "body" is rewritten, and there emerges the possibility of a "reincarnation" (a notion inherited from the Orient, later forming part of the Judeo-Christian tradition and also appearing in certain syncretic religions). The image of eternal life also survives here, since we would no longer suffer the physical limitations of the flesh, and in a kind of reworking of the Paradise Lost myth, here and now, on earth, not in some vague "hereafter." This discursive construction points toward a trend in modernism that privileges the subject as the forger of the subject's own destiny. Then, there is a re-articulation of the myth of life-as-electrical-charges (in this case, electromagnetic charges that may be reproduced or replicated in a computer simulation) that came into vogue during the eighteenth century with the vitalist movement led by Franz Anton Mesmer, who held that bodies contained an internal "fluid" of a magnetic nature, and that the flow of this fluid maintained the health of the body (Darnton, 1968). This myth is masterfully worked out in Mary Shelley's famous nineteenth-century work Frankenstein.[2] However, unlike Dr. Frankenstein's great achievement, life is now generated in inorganic matter. **In other words, the machine, and not a biological body, becomes the repository of mind.**

Another great discontinuity with modernism occurs when the body is taken to be disposed of. There is no doubt that there is a negative valuation of the biological body. In his text, Moravec says that the cerebral tissue—now simulated—is disposable and can be sucked up by a "vacuum." This negative valuation can be seen more clearly in later paragraphs, where he outlines other methods of achieving transmigration without having to appeal to what he calls "messy surgery."

In their article on the disappearing body in the hyper-modern condition, Arthur and Marilouise Kroker (1987) recall Foucault's prophecy that the bourgeois body tends to become an empty locus of the dissociated ego, within a "volume in disintegration" defined and permeated by the technologies of power. The Krokers propose that the current insistence on the recuperation of subjectivity indicates that hyper-subjectivity is the condition within which power will be operating at the end of the millennium. I am talking, then, about a superfluous, disposable, changeable and even interchangeable, plastic body wherein resides a fragmented and multiple hyper-subjectivity.

For control and domination, the person would require not the flagellation of the body (as in the ascetic tradition), nor the propadeutic four square walls of the confessional (whether the confessional booth itself or the psychotherapeutic equivalent), but rather the possibility of its total reconstitution following the dictates of the "new" order, and in extreme cases, its total replacement. **In summary, we are talking about a plastic body which is the offshoot of the aesthetic of the technologization of the body.**

On the one hand, the technologization of the body generates a sort of double bind for the development of capitalism and the globalization of the economy. On the other hand, the body is subordinated to functionalism, yet it resists this subordination. **The body has shown itself to be necessary yet superfluous for the functioning of the economic system of technological society.** This double bind is reflected in several passages of Moravec's text.

Sometimes the body appears as material to be conserved, while at other times it is stuff that one might even wish to get rid of, for it restricts possibilities that the self, held within the body and inhibited to a greater or lesser degree by the fact (fear) that the body could be annihilated, can only yearn after: the possibility of "transmission" (by way of cables conducting electronically digitalized signals), the possibility of being duplicated (generating a multiplicity of memories simultaneously), and finally the possibility of being shared by multiple bodies.

It has been said that the assumption of hardware/software separability that underlies these ideas is a reformulation of Cartesian dualism. We need to look more carefully, however, at the philosophical discourse implied in this text. I would suggest that more than Descartes, it is Plato that is present here. For Plato, the empirical subject (the body and its experiences) is imperfect matter, and the authentic subject of knowledge is the soul (Braunstein, 1979). For Moravec, it is not acceptable to assume that personal identity is defined by the "stuff," as he calls it, of which the body is made. Opposed to this view of "body-identity," Moravec proposes the concept of "pattern-identity," and defines this concept as follows:

> Pattern-identity, conversely, defines the essence of a person, say myself, as the pattern and the process going on in my head and body, not the machinery supporting that process. If the process is preserved, I am preserved. The rest is mere jelly (17).[3]

The dualistic implications of this idea are clear. The mind is independent of the body. For Moravec, although the mind is a consequence of interacting stuff, the ability to be copied from one storage medium to another confers independence and an identity separate from the machinery that processes it. Personal identity conceived of as "pattern identity" offers the possibility of rearticulating the ancient myth of Proteus, the sea-god who possessed the ability to change shape at will.

For Moravec, furthermore, **the mind not only has no reason to be tied to a single body, it has no reason to be tied to one particular pattern.** It may be represented in an infinite number of patterns, which are only equivalent in the abstract or mathematical sense of the word "equivalent."

The archaic and apparently still untiring search for the fountain of youth and immortality swings between control of the protean body and the inevitable unpredictability of that body's fate as it is subjected to the avatars of life that inflict uncontrollable changes on it. Moravec contemplates the possibility that some parts of our bodies will be discarded and replaced by others, as the conditions of our

133 }

individual lives change. With the precariousness of the physiological substrate as a given, **the disappearance of the body and the externalization of the mind are proclaimed to be inevitable phenomena in the evolutionary process.**

In the fabric of Moravec's text there emerges a new self, one that transcends biological limits via a post-biological self. Still, there is the contradiction that this cybernetic progeny will be subject to all the calamities to which the biological body was prey. It would appear that the text wants, at one and at the same time, to both preserve and discard the organic paradigm.

Interestingly, it is the inevitability of the life/death contradiction, the precariousness and plasticity of the biological and social substrate, that permits the creation of a common substrate for the human-machine suture through symbiotic cooperation. The metaphor of the "symbiotic path" returns us, once again, to the biological discourse.

According to John Broughton (1985), the organic metaphor (as used in discourses concerning computer literacy) provides instrumental reason with an ontology that knits together the domains of the physical, the vital, and the human. This metaphor creates the illusion that the rigid automatic processes inherent in machines are transcended. In Moravec's text, notions like "organization," "habitat," and "symbiosis" become ontological metaphors **that see "life" not in contradistinction to "machine" but rather as a quality of that machine,** so that it becomes a common substrate underlying both human and mechanical.

In conclusion, the notions of self in this text point toward a reconstitution of the transcendent subject, a subject articulated with qualities similar to those of decentering: plasticity, multi-referentiality, the constitutive precariousness of the subject, etc. Its metaphors are fundamentally spatial and structural and provide the ontological infrastructure for the creation of an ultra-human condition (prophesied by Nietzsche at the end of the nineteenth century). Another quality peculiar to this reformulation of the self is that its characteristics are suitable to the suturing of Mazlish's "fourth discontinuity." Seen from this perspective, the processes through which subjectivity is formed would have to be conceived in relation to an "other" that could be the machine.

Finally, **I emphasize the need to see technological discourses as space—in this case, spaces for struggle**—in the same sense in which Michel de Certeau (1985) presents social spaces as "spaces for enunciation." These discourses become privileged spaces so that the domination/resistance contradiction can be carried to its limit; they propose modes of social existence that are unforeseen and unpredictable—frightening qualities offering important challenges to normalization at the same time as they appeal for the articulation of new forms of political consensus.

Notes

This paper was presented at the Second Discourse Analysis Workshop/Conference, July 10-12, 1991, at Manchester Polytechnic Institute, England.

1. In the eighteenth lecture of his *Introduction to Psychoanalysis* (in Vienna between 1915 and 1917), Freud suggested that in the history of thought his work stood as the third instance of the wounding of humanity's self-esteem. The first instance was the work of Copernicus, who established that Earth, and therefore humanity, did not occupy the center of the Universe but rather a tiny speck within a system

whose magnitudes could hardly be conceived. The second instance was the work of Darwin, who stripped humanity of its privileged origin within divine Creation and made it a simple descendant in the animal kingdom. The third instance was Freud's own work, which demonstrated that the "ego," to which we tended to ascribe such power, "is not even master in its own house."

2. Robert Melone (1978) says that the automaton created by Jaquet-Droz in the nineteenth century (a writing-machine with a human figure that could write any message of no more than forty characters and that functioned through a complex clockwork mechanism) was the inspiration for Dr. Frankenstein and his creation. The automaton's creator, Jaquet-Droz, was arrested and accused of witchcraft.

3. A slightly more classical version of this motif appears in John Pollock's book *How to Build a Person* (1989), in which he defends the thesis that a person is fundamentally a conative-cognitive machine, an intelligent machine, and as such, added to a body: "My claim is that instead of being identical with their bodies, people are physical objects that supervene on their bodies" (32).

References

Beltetini, G. (1986). El cuerpo del sujeto enunciador. In *La conversación audiovisual*. Madrid: Cátedra, pp. 21-62.

Braunstein, N. (1979). El problema o el falso problema de la relación "del sujeto y el objeto". In Braunstein, et. al. *Psicología, ideología y ciencia*. México: Editorial Siglo XXI, pp. 233-260.

Broughton, J. M. (1985). The Surrender of Control: Computer Literacy as Political Socialization of the Child. In D. Sloan (ed.) *The Computer in Education*. New York: Teachers College Press.

Darnton, R. (1968). *Mesmerism and the End of the Enlightenment in France*. New York: Schocken Books.

de Certeau, M. (1985). Practices of Space. In M. Blonsky (Ed.) *On Signs*. Baltimore: The Johns Hopkins University Press, pp. 122-145.

Emberly, J. (1987). The Fashion Apparatus and the Deconstruction of Postmodern Subjectivity. In A. and M. Kroker (eds.) *Body Invaders*. New York: St. Martin's Press, pp. 47-60.

Foucault, M. (1988). *Discipline and Punish: The Birth of the Prison*. New York: Vintage.

Foucault, M.(1990). *Technologías del yo y otros textos afines*. Barcelona: Editorial Paidós.

Harvey, D. (1990). *The Condition of Postmodernity*. Cambridge, Mass.: Basil Blackwell, Inc.

Kroker A. and M. (1987). Thesis on the Disappearing Body in the Hyper-Modern Condition. In A. and M. Kroker (Eds.) *Body Invaders*. New York: St. Martin's Press, pp. 20-34.

Lakoff, G. and Johnson, M. (1980). *Metaphors We Live By*. Chicago: The University of Chicago Press.

Lozano, G., Peña-Marin, C. and Abril, G. (1989). *Análisis del discurso. Hacia una semiótica de la interacción textual*. Madrid: Ediciones Cátedra.

Malone, R. (1978). *The Robot Book*. New York: Jove Publications, Inc.

Mazlish, B. (1993). *The Fourth Discontinuity: The Co-evolution of Humans and Machines*. New Haven: Yale University Press.

Moravec, H. (1988). *MIND Children: The Future of Robot and Human Intelligence*. Cambridge: Harvard University Press.

Pollok, J. (1989). *How to Build a Person: A Prolegomenon*. Cambridge: The MIT Press.

Sawchuck, K. (1987). A Tale of Inscription: Fashion Statements. In a A. and M. Kroker (Eds.) *Body Invaders*. New York: St. Martin's Press, pp. 61-77.

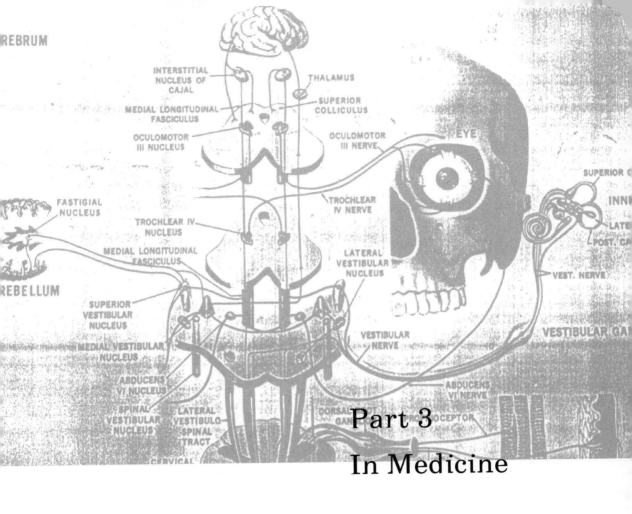

Part 3

In Medicine

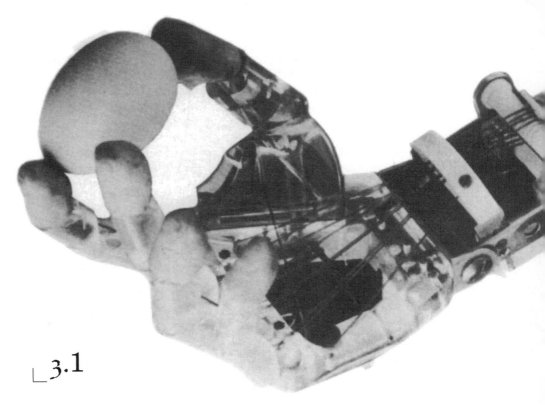

L 3.1

Modernity, Postmodernity & Reproductive Processes *ca.*1890-1990
or, "Mommy, where do cyborgs come from any-way?"

Adele Clarke

> *"Science, more than any other investigative and descriptive activity, creates and conceals the context from which it arises" (Duden 1991:20).*
>
> *"Cyborg anthropology is a dangerous activity" (Downey, Dumit and Williams 1992:4).*[1]

Valerie Hartouni (1991:30) recently examined the stories behind two headlines about medical cyborgs from the late 1980s, "Brain-Dead Mother Has Her Baby," and "Orphan Embryos Saved." She asks:

> *What makes these headlines make sense? Why might they seem sensible today when only twenty years ago they would certainly have been preposterous? ... What beliefs, assumptions, and expectations allow them to be coherently rendered, taken seriously, understood as "fact" rather than "fiction"? What is the world they simultaneously construct and contain? What are the stories they tell about reproductive possibilities, relations and relationships in late twentieth century America, and what is the terrain they occupy and contest in that telling?*

In response, **I will argue that modern approaches to reproductive bodies and processes were and remain centered on achieving and/or enhancing *control over* those bodies and processes** (Clarke 1988).[2] In contrast, postmodern approaches are centered on re/de/sign and *transformation of* reproductive bodies and processes to achieve a variety of goals. In short, I argue that the common distinction embodied in the term "the *new* reproductive technologies" which appears in scholarly as well as popular media constitutes a constructed, conceptual as well as a practical—in practice—boundary.

However, there is tremendous variation within both modernist and postmodernist approaches to reproductive phenomena and considerable traffic across the varyingly constructed boundaries between them, some of which I shall try to unjam. I begin by deconstructing reproduction into its component processes, and then lay out what I mean by modernist and postmodernist approaches to them. Next I work some of the border problematics including the robustness of the boundary, the simultaneity in time and space of modern and postmodern approaches, and how the ending of the human/nonhuman distinction is being framed. While centered on reproductive bodies, the paper has implications for thinking about bodies in general some of which I note in concluding.

i. Deconstructing Reproduction:

In order to grasp the nature of modern and postmodern reproductive practices, we must deconstruct reproduction into its component processes as those processes have themselves been constructed culturally and historically by scientists, clinicians, technologists and the rest of us. Only then can we empirically analyze the specific concrete technical and organizational practices associated with each of these processes across very different times and circumstances. Today the major reproductive processes or categories of study and intervention include: menstruation, contraception, abortion, assisted conception, pregnancy, heredity/clinical genetics, childbirth, menopause, and male reproductive processes. In terms of organizational and technical practices, each of these processes has been developed differently, by different constellations of scientists, technologists, clinicians, manufacturers, consumers and so on. These differences are central to my argument.

We must also deconstruct the body. When I say control over and transformation of bodies, I am speaking of bodies in the multiple, drawing specifically on the framework of the three bodies provided by Nancy Scheper-Hughes and Margaret Lock (1987:6):

> *1) body(ies) viewed as phenomenally experienced, lived individual body(ies)/self(ves);*
>
> *2) social body(ies), what anthropologists term a natural symbol for thinking about relationships among nature, society and culture; and*
>
> *3) body(ies) politic, artifacts (and I would add inscriptions) of social and political control.*

Thus my framing of the modern qua *control over* and postmodern qua *transformation of* the reproductive body is exercised across all three bodies. I would add to Scheper-Hughes and Lock's framing that all three bodies are also economic bodies.

That is, the distribution of resources for life are of concern individually, socially and politically. The economics of bodies is of central concern here.

How have control over and transformation of reproductive bodies and processes been achieved over the past century? First, the expanding legitimacy of and invest-ment in the scientific study of reproductive processes have, in a tandem co-con-structive fashion, supported and been supported by the legitimacy of intervention in reproductive processes. Here representing in the "lab" is almost immediately fol-lowed by intervening (Hacking 1983) in the field, coop, sty, pasture, operating room and bedroom. The legitimacies of both representing and intervening in specific reproductive processes were and remain varyingly contested (Clarke 1990a; Clarke and Montini 1993). But technoscientific capacities for intervening have quite dra-matically expanded from control over reproductive processes to "manipulation" (e.g., Austin and Short 1972, 1987) and transformation of both processes and prod-ucts. Crucially, the human/nonhuman distinction is of decreasing relevance to reproductive and genetic scientists.

Second, individuals and collectivities of various sorts of both women and men have sought to control and transform their own reproductive processes, sometimes through the use of technoscientific products and other times not. It is important to remember that attempts to control reproductive processes have likely been made throughout human history and, moreover, many premodern as well as modern attempts were likely more scientific (read empirical) and much more effective than has heretofore been understood (e.g., Riddle 1992; Ginsberg and Rapp 1991).

ii. Modernity and Reproductive Processes

> *"The body is the first and most natural tool of man"* *(Marcel Mauss in Scheper-Hughes and Lock 1987:6).*

> *"You should always be in control of your tools"* *(*The Handyperson's Guide to Household Repair *1981).*

One definition of modernization offered by the National Academy of Science in 1963 is the "extension of deliberate human control over an increasing range of the environment." Enhancing control over reproductive phenomena was of consider-able and widespread concern much earlier in the U.S.—by the late nineteenth cen-tury—embedded in ideologies of science as progress, technologies as liberatory, and the West as leading the way into a secure future through (self/bodily) control and careful management. This is the model of development exported then and still.

The basic social process through which *modern* control over reproductive processes was and is today achieved is industrialization (Clarke 1988). Here I mean what Harvey (1989) would call a Fordist emphasis on the production of goods, technolo-gies, and services and their (re)organization to achieve and enhance control. Bodies too are organized around Fordist principles of centralized control (Martin 1992) in terms of reproduction and more generally. Modern industrialization has occurred at both the most public social and political levels and the most private individual lev-els and these are inextricably enmeshed. I must note, however, that neither human nor agricultural reproduction has been at all thoroughly industrialized, although rationalized approaches have guided developments for over a century (Rosenberg 1979).

By the turn of the twentieth century, the stage was set for the explicit application of the concepts and technical innovations of modernity/industrialization to be applied to human reproduction. The most important factor was the industrial revolution and subsequent reduction in the value of child labor (e.g., Lancaster et al. 1987). Known as the demographic transition, a secular trend toward small families began to be reflected in the U.S. in declining birth rates after about 1810.[3] By the turn of the twentieth century, a significant minority of the U.S. population was affected and the economic costs of having children were articulated in startlingly familiar ways among the upwardly mobile, non-agrarian, white middle classes. One physician said in 1903, "The fittest to survive in our civilization are the trained and educated," and the President of Harvard said that one should have only the number of children you can afford to raise well (Gordon 1976:150, 153). This has become a dominant if not the predominant ideology in the U.S., where children are now commonly viewed as ends in themselves, not means to other ends (Blake 1980:197). This distinctively secular ideology assumes the decline of religious explanations of the natural and social world, grants legitimacy to an array of interventions in making life, and reflects a shift in the economic meanings of human reproduction.

On the darker side, children are themselves becoming commodities. As people drastically limit their quantities of children, they seek to improve the chances for high quality according to their own standards, including heredity and sex preselection. **Through postmodern approaches, one can now *supplement* quantity control with quality control.** I would frame this as a *re*/commoditization. (We can no longer claim innocence, and romanticization of the past will buy us nothing.) That is, historically (and still) children have been valued for their labor power as substitute and supplement to social security and state welfare, especially for the aged and infirm. Their labor power was commoditized. Today among the affluent, the value of children may lie in different social securities of identity, embodiment, enmindment, achievement. This advertisement for Barbara Walters' television show (Figure 1) is a popular culture icon of desirably engendered and perfected embodiment as child. Beingness is commoditized: racialized white (Frankenberg 1993), gendered male, tall, athletic, healthy and smart (as implied by IQ).

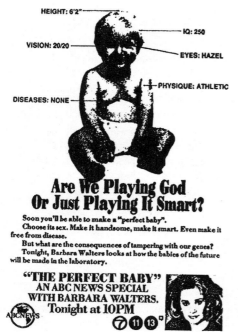

HEIGHT: 6'2"

IQ: 250

VISION: 20/20

EYES: HAZEL

PHYSIQUE: ATHLETIC

DISEASES: NONE

Are We Playing God Or Just Playing It Smart?

Soon you'll be able to make a "perfect baby".
Choose its sex. Make it handsome, make it smart. Even make it free from disease.
But what are the consequences of tampering with our genes? Tonight, Barbara Walters looks at how the babies of the future will be made in the laboratory.

"THE PERFECT BABY"
AN ABC NEWS SPECIAL
WITH BARBARA WALTERS.
Tonight at 10PM
⑦⑪⑬

Fig. 1

Historically and still, ideological support for small families served as the foundation for the explicit application of the concepts and technical innovations of modernization and postmodernization to be applied to human reproduction. But what do I mean by the term modern *industrialization* of reproductive processes? First, it was and remains embedded in an economic market system. Yet it is more than the factory system, more than mass production and an elaborated division of labor. Modern industrialization is a set of approaches to achieve *a high degree of control over (re)production processes*, including rationalization (segmentation of a larger process into smaller sub-parts more amenable to

manipulation), standardization, efficiency, planning, specialization, professionaliza-
tion, commodity and technological development, and profitability (Clarke 1988).

The major initial investor in modernizing human reproductive processes through
industrialization was the Rockefeller Foundation which, through financing the
National Research Council's Committee for Research on Problems of Sex (Aberle
and Corner 1953), supported the "heroic age of reproductive endocrinology"
(Parkes 1966) between the world wars. This Committee "virtually paid for the development of [reproductive] endocrinology in the United States during the period
when the female sex hormones were identified and clinicians began to use hormone extracts to treat disease" (Reed 1984:313). In 1934, Warren Weaver, head of
the Natural Sciences Division of the Rockefeller Foundation, wrote what we might
today frame as an ode to modernity. He asked:

> *Can man gain an intelligent control of his own power? Can we develop so*
> *sound a genetics that we can hope to breed, in the future, superior men? Can*
> *we obtain enough knowledge of the physiology and psychobiology of sex so*
> *that man can bring this pervasive, highly important, and dangerous aspect of*
> *life under rational control? ... Can man acquire enough knowledge of his own*
> *vital processes so that we can hope to rationalize human behavior? Can we, in*
> *short, create a new science of man?* [4]

Weaver was comparing the rationalized control man was developing over his physical environment to hopes for such control in the future governing "man as a conceiving, child-bearing, thinking, behaving, growing and finally dying organism."[5]
Genetics, reproductive sciences, endocrinology, nutrition, psychobiology and psychology composed Weaver's "new science of man."[6]

Looking at the summary chart (Figure 2), modern approaches to reproductive
processes center on control for various purposes via monitoring, planning, limiting,
bounding, setting up barriers. The means are Fordist emphases on development and
mass production of new consumer goods (e.g., commercial menstrual products);
development and mass production of new technologies (e.g., hormones, contraceptives, pharmaceuticals like "twilight sleep" used in childbirth); and the organization
and mass distribution of basic reproductive services including obstetrics, functional
(i.e., non-surgical) gynecology, and "family planning." Expanding production, distribution and consumption—widening, deepening and lengthening the consumer
pool—was a means of achieving those goals. Payment derived from individuals and,
increasingly, the welfare state.

One of the distinctive features of modern approaches is their universalizing tendencies. They were and remain aimed at the masses while they operate, for the
most part, in/on individual women's bodies. Nelly Oudshoorn (1993) recently analyzed the "one size fits all" approach to making scientific contraceptives such as the
Pill and IUD. Diversities among women from weight, height, and nutritional condition to social situation and access to health care were and are largely erased. They
are replaced by disembodied universalizing abstractions such as "woman-years of
use" and "woman-cycles." "One size fits all" is viewed as requisite for *mass* distribution (see also Bell 1994).

Modern approaches focus on specific reproductive processes. Here, for brevity's
sake, I merely list these in the chronological order of application of industrialized
approaches to them: childbirth, menstruation, pregnancy, menopause, contracep-

APPROACHES TO REPRODUCTIVE PROCESSES

MODERN	POSTMODERN
Goal: *control over* reproductive processes bodies via universal technologies;	**Goal:** *transformation* of reproductive processes for a variety of specific and often highly local, individual, and differentiated goals;
Means: Fordist emphases on	**Means:** emphasis on flexible accumulation via

1) development and mass production of new goods (e.g. commercial menstrual products); new technologies (e.g. hormones, contraceptives);
 2) organization and mass distribution of basic reproductive services (e.g. obstetrics, functional gynecology, "family planning")
 3) "one size fits all" approach to mass product and technology development
 4) universalizing of women and technologies
	1) elaboration of specific services (re)organized for selectively targeted delivery:
	   infertility services
	   sex preselection services
	   fetal treatments and surgeries
	 2) elaboration of specific services (re)organized for mass delivery toward targeted individuals/families:
	   —genetic screening and counseling
	   —fetal screening and counseling
	 3) individually tailored technological alternations
	 4) differentiation of women, men and technologies

Reproductive Processes focused on:	**Reproductive Processes focused on**
childbirth menstruation pregnancy contraception abortion menopause	conception/infertility pregnancy heredity/clinical genetics male reproduction
Lived body: to be controlled (ideally across the full life span); changes and new directions to be planned **Social body:** naturalized "traditional nuclear family" to be created and maintained via rationalized management **Body politic:** population control via contraception; enhanced legitimation and legalization of interventions in reproductive processes.	**Lived body:** to be transformed and customized/manipulated; cyborg with "tailor-made specificities" **Social body:** transformed and/or reconstructed heterogeneous "families" with new meanings for gender, mother, father and family (biological/social/surrogate/donor/other) via constructing cyborgs **Body politic:** "deconstruction of motherhood"? "family" as a new industry/market and policy niche; surveillance strategies; the state confronts cyborgs

Note: simultaneity of premodern, modern and postmodern approaches sustained through present moment.

Fig. 2

tion, and abortion. Each of these modernist processes is framed and experienced in the three bodies. The modernist lived body is to be controlled and changes are to be planned. Ideally control can be exercised across the life course from birth through menopause (Clarke 1990b). For the modern lived body is Elias's (Duden 1991:14; see also Bordo 1993; Glassner 1990) self-controlled body. It is not an unchanging body, but rather changes derive from the exercise of individual willpower to shape that body (Crawford 1985), rather than application of technoscientific transformatives—one shot cures. There is a low-tech vigilance requisite for the modern body to be maintained (in contrast to high-tech postmodern transformations).

The modern social body is the traditional heterosexual nuclear family, maintained via an array of management efforts (e.g., Banta 1993). That is, exertion of control over reproductive processes is framed in terms of achieving the ideal nuclear family in as safe and secure as possible fashion. The major technical innovation of modernity in terms of the social body lay in the area of contraception, for the goal is smaller and planned/controlled families. This goal is not necessarily shared across the diversities of class, race and culture, but it is ideologically pervasive. The means of achievement here disaggregate/disassociate sex from reproduction. Thus (hetero)sexuality was/is framed or assumed to be ubiquitous and, quite radically, was NOT to be the focus of control. In Adrienne Rich's (1992) terms, heterosexuality was "compulsory." However, sex need not be resisted and only certain consequences of sexuality are to be controlled: pregnancy and sexually transmitted diseases.

In terms of the body politic, modernity is centered on population control via contraception and enhanced legitimacy of intervention in reproductive processes. Initially the legality of exercising control over some reproductive processes needed to be established. For example, in the U.S. the legality of contraception was not guaranteed nationally until a 1966 Supreme Court decision (Griswold versus Connecticut). In 1970 contraceptives were taken off the obscene devices list of the Comstock Law. Not until 1972 did the Supreme Court guarantee the unmarried the same right to contraception as the married. The U.S. Agency for International Development began distribution of contraception in 1963; shortly after this President Johnson's "War on Povery" (which poverty won) allowed a local option policy for publically-funded family planning services (Reed 1984:377–8).

Let me note here that both the social body and the body politic seem to drag their heels in terms of modern control over reproduction. Also, modern approaches are sustained through the present postmodern moment.

iii. Postmodernity and Reproductive Processes

> *"The body is the first and most natural tool of man" (Mauss cited in Scheper-Hughes and Lock 1987:6).*

> *"If it is not 'the right tool for the job,' practices can be devised to make it the right tool" (Casper and Clarke, 1990).*

Let me return here to Hartouni's (1992:30) analysis of the two headlines about the brain-dead mother and the orphan embryos:

> *Conceptually, both headlines produce a kind of mental astigmatism; meanings temporarily blur, lose definition, appear distorted, and are resolvable only with some sort of conceptual retraining or adjustment. They require us to do conceptually, it seems, what lenses would do optically ... But just as lenses may enable us to see the world, they also transform the world we see ... The headlines ... engage us in the making of [the world]...*

I am asserting that the world to which she refers is postmodern. In postmodernity, specific reproductive processes are transformed for a variety of highly local, individual and heterogeneous goals. The reproductive body is transformed by customizing, tailoring, re/de/sign/ing. The means of achievement emphasize late twentieth-century approaches which Harvey (1989) calls flexible accumulation via two overarching strategies. First is the *elaboration of specific services* (re)organized for selectively targeted delivery. Here we find infertility services aimed at those who can afford them; sex preselection services aimed at those who can afford them and at specific cultural groups constructed as desirous of such services (Thobani 1992); and fetal treatments and surgeries likely to be aimed at those who can afford them. Fetal research and treatment sponsors may focus on the state as well as a source of funds for both research and service delivery (Casper 1994b).

The second strategy is ultimately centered on *case-finding*. It involves the elaboration of screening protocols (re)organized for mass delivery to locate individuals/families targeted for specific interventive services. Here we find genetic screening and counseling seeking problematized hereditary traits, and fetal screening and counseling seeking both hereditary and congenital problems for fetal treatments. In postmodernity, capital has fallen in love with difference.

The reproductive processes focused on in postmodernity center around assisted conception and infertility treatments, the "new" reproductive technologies, only recently widely available in the US in terms of both technological innovations and organized service delivery.[7] Earlier there was little potential for mass production and only a limited though constant distribution market for such services (e.g. Corner, 1957; Kelly, 1928; American Foundation, 1955). The "new" techniques include artificial insemination (AI) available on a limited basis since the 1930s[8] in vitro fertilization (IVF),

embryo transfer (ET), gamete intra-fallopian transfer (GIFT), and an array of hormonal and other infertility treatments. While most were pioneered in the 1930s in animal agriculture (Biggers 1981; 1984; 1987), a 1955 assessment of the infertility field (American Foundation, 1955:137) found that "literal application of the results of animal research to correction of human infertility has been thus far disappointing." This is no longer the case as whatever boundaries between reproductive agriculture and medicine existed collapse (Austin and Short, 1987).

Fig. 3
Signe Wilkinson,
Philadelphia
Daily News

Helping make babies when none was thought possible is miracle medicne. Unlike services to prevent (at least some significant proportion of) infertility in the first place (such as sex education, STD education, appropriate birth control education, and so on), current infertility research and services are high-tech, "cutting edge" biomedicine. They are also what has been called "boutique medicine"—medicine mostly for the wealthy—as most such procedures are not covered by private health insurance much less by Medicaid.[9] The term "boutique medicine" also gets at the specialty "tailor-made" specificities of such cyborg services. Ruzek (1988) has found a continuity of focus since the nineteeth century on ensuring that middle and upper-class women do have children, and we can see the "new reproductive technologies" as sustaining such concerns.

In postmodernity, pregnancy is the focus of an increasingly wide array of new surveillance technologies (e.g., Terry 1988; Stanworth 1987), including fetal surveillance related to potential surgical interventions *in utero* (Casper 1994a, b, 1995).

We saw in modern approaches the universalizing of women and their bodies so that "one size fits all." In the postmodern lies the moment of the disembodiment of women. Pregnant women's bodies are erased to make way for the one true person—the fetus (e.g., Petchesky 1985, 1987; Duden 1993; Casper 1994a). Heredity is also increasingly addressed via clinical genetics (Beeson 1983; Paul 1993; Wertz and Fletcher 1987). Male reproductive phenomena are now being increasingly studied and a medical specialty, andrology, has emerged focused on nonspermatic functional physiology (Pfeffer 1985). Sperm banking is organized around the construction and maintenance of male difference (Moore and Schmidt 1994). Reproduction in outer space is also a focus of concern (Casper and Moore 1995).

The postmodern lived reproductive body is transformed, manipulated, customized—often involving the creation of cyborgs with what Emily Martin (1992) has called "tailor-made specificities." The postmodern lived body is neither stable nor singular. Like multiple selves and appearances, it is transformed and transformable (e.g., Finkelstein 1991; Bartel 1988; Bordo 1993). It is cyborg, described most hopefully by Haraway (1992a) as a body with "prosthetic devices, intimate components, friendly selves, an aspect of our embodiment." Cyborgs flexibly accumulate desired characteristics and capacities as Hogle (1994a,b, 1995) points out, and can delete the undesired. Bodies are customized—to fit fashion and to fit (re)constructions of "family" or other framed goals via reproductive technologies. Postmodern bodies can shapeshift. In many cyberspace games, players are invited to configure their bodies and identities themselves from a selection of parts. In some games the most interesting body parts cost more. Art reflects life.[10]

Analytically here we need to see the postmodern lived body not only in terms of reproduction but across its many contexts. The [manipulated] body is social performance—performance art in all its temporality. Bodily modifications flow across many zones. Once one is breached then others seem to follow. For example, a significant proportion of women who have breast implants for cosmetic reasons proceed to have face-lifts and so on downstream (Bordo 1993; Wepsic 1993). Plastic surgery has been called psychiatry by other means (Haiken 1992; and see Goldsmith 1993), and is certainly pervading a much wider market (e.g., Japenga 1993; Balsamo 1992). It is now about a $1.75 billion-a-year industry in the U.S., with about 1.5 million people per year undergoing plastic surgery of some kind (Bordo 1993:25).

But we need to note that the manipulation of body parts and the creation of cyborgs also includes many kinds of transplantations, joint replacements, implantations, coronary bypasses, angioplasties, and so on. Linda Hogle (1994a,b, 1995), who is studying the procurement of biological materials for transplantation and research, discusses how body parts are becoming widgets—standardized items to replace as needed—or desired. Her research focuses on how the organization of procurement and delivery has itself been transformed from an altruistic patient service provided by tertiary hospitals to an increasingly international for-profit market-based industry. Technical developments are centered on preservation of the materials for transportation, such as fast acting liquids for freezing the contents of the entire peritoneal cavity while the family can then be asked to donate organs. Workers used to sell their labor, a supposedly renewable resource, but now at least in Egypt they are also selling their organs—assuredly non-renewable (Hedges 1991). Animal organs—such as baboon hearts—have also been used and transformed for use.

147 }

Thus our conceptualization of cyborg needs to be revised. We have had a human/technology continuities model which needs to be augmented with human/technology/human models (denoting technological mediations among human body parts, some of which were not born together) and human/technology/animal models as well. We also need to begin thinking about some of the implications of these new models for manipulating reproduction. **When will there be transplantable wombs and fallopian tubes? Which women's bodies would seem most likely as donors of wombs, tubes, life? Will families be approached to donate whole brain-dead women's "living cadavers" to serve as free-standing wombs to be implanted via IVF? Postmortem maternal ventilation has already been ethically justified** (Elias and Annas 1987:261).[11] **Will free-standing technoscientific wombs be cyborgs?** Will baboons or other primates be used for gestating selected humans instead, bred specially for such purposes? Keller (1989) has argued that artificial wombs will be developed because of their appeal to a great variety of interests—including those of some women as well as scientists and those romantically involved with eugenics (e.g., Kevles 1985).

In postmodernity one goal is to transform the currently lived body into the desired lived body aligned with a desired social body. The social body can also be transformed and/or reconstructed multiple times with new meanings for mother, father and family (biological/social/surrogate/donor/other). Certainly the discourses and vocabularies of kinship in the U.S. and other Western countries have been undergoing dramatic elaboration. Postmodern social bodies can be "designer" "families," "artificial families" (Snowden and Mitchell 1981), or postmodern fragmented families (Stacey 1990). We can view the "family" as a new industry/market niche (Strathern 1992). Chico's (1989) study of the letters people wrote inquiring about sex preselection in the U.S. found a strong conceptualization of the "complete [heterosexual] family," minimally including children of both sexes and sometimes much more delimited. Transformative technologies now permit a much wider range of such designed or engineered conceptualizations, and people also create new families from diverse communities—such as the houses of voguers in the film *Paris is Burning* by Jenny Livingston. Designer cats and other pets are under construction, opening the concept of family more clearly to the nonhuman (Rowland 1992).

Postmodern familial design capacities allow a new disaggregation. If in the modern framework, heterosexuality could be set free from its reproductive consequences, in the postmodern frame, gender, sex and sexuality can all be disaggregated from reproduction. For example, there was a billboard in San Francisco of two women standing close together, one pregnant and the other with a hand on her belly. The caption was, "Another traditional family." One possible reading is that it honors Roberta Achtenberg, a lesbian San Francisco Supervisor nominated and approved for a post in the Clinton administration, the first "out lesbian" to go through U.S. Senate confirmation hearings. She is "married" to a judge and they have one child (Lynch 1993a, b). They too constructed their version of a complete family.

In terms of the body politic, on the critical end, postmodern reproductive technologies can be implicated in the "deconstruction of motherhood" (Stanworth 1990), to the disadvantage of women. Yet others (e.g., Casper 1995, 1994a,b) assert that both de/ and re/constructions occur—that the former imbricate the latter. Certainly we are seeing the privatization of the costs of achieving a "complete family" if new reproductive technologies are needed. Also, the "deconstruction of motherhood" requires legal and political (re)interpretations (e.g. Cohen and Taub 1989; Blankenship et al. 1993), since even doing the census is affected. Politically we know that surveillance strategies will be utilized. To date, it is largely poor women and women of color who have been surveilled (Terry 1988); but will other women as Rowland (1992) has noted, perhaps especially elite women (Ruzek 1988), become the objects of intensive surveillance as they are already the marketing targets for "new" reproductive technologies? How will nation-states address which kinds of cyborgs? Who/what will need a passport? Or will cyborgs [continue to] float unregulated and flexibly accumulating, micro-versions of multinationals?

In sum, I believe we are just moving into postmodernity regarding reproductive processes and that social bodies and bodies politic are the laggards. These domains will also be sustained sites of major contestation. One rationale articulated for the desirability of transforming individual bodies is that it is easier to change the individual than to change society—our social and political frames of action (Haiken 1992).

iV. Porous Boundaries/Border Crossings

Now that I have created something of a master narrative, I can begin to problematize and deconstruct it. First, a core argument of this paper is that what is "new" in the "new" reproductive technologies is *recognition* of their transformative capacities. What they are transforming is conceptions of what it is to be human, male, female, reproductive, parent, child, fetus, family, race, and even population. That is, the "new" reproductive technologies in their postmodern splendor are constitutive of what Paul Rabinow (1992:8) termed the remaking of life itself. I have chosen to "name" modes of *control over* reproductive phenomena "modern," and modes of *transformation of* reproductive bodies and relations "postmodern," and I find this effectively captures an important distinction. But it is the *distinction* that is most important, especially the economics of the distinction—the shift from Fordist mass production and distribution to targetted niches for flexible accumulation.

For modern approaches, race is the tacit trope and racism as sets of practices live, for example, in the technologies of contraception created and in the uneven, unequal and unjust techno-organizational mechanisms of their distribution (e.g., Rutherford 1992:267). For postmodern approaches, class is clearly and commonly involved for the "new reproductive technologies" are mostly very expensive, usually uncovered by private or state health plans, and also very unevenly distributed (e.g., Giminez 1991). Yet both race and class can be manifest in both and, of course, gender is everywhere implicated.

My second key boundary crossing point concerns the simultaneity of premodern, modern and postmodern approaches to reproductive processes. Modern modes of *control over* reproductive processes as I have framed them are requisite for and generally presumed by postmodern approaches which *transform* reproductive processes and bodies. There is an historically cumulative but not exclusive relation.[12]

Third, one of the major distinctions of the western enlightenment has been the planet-wide distinction between humans and everything else (the nonhuman), a dualism which has been defended vociferously, including contestation regarding who/what counts as human, often posed in terms of race. Elsewhere[13] I discuss at length some of the problematics of how the collapse of the distinction between the human and nonhuman is being framed and addressed, including the work of Haraway (1989, 1992b), Latour (1993), Casper (1994a) and my own studies of American reproductive sciences. What the collapse makes visible is a stunningly heterogeneous array of cyborgs and hybrids, along with the vulnerabilities of other co-habitants. The implications of this collapse for matters of ongoing life, especially reproduction, are momentous and need to be addressed.

VI. Conclusions

Reproductive technologies must be understood not only within the broader structural context of the postmodernization of human reproduction but also within their more immediate contexts of service delivery—medicine and other biomedical technologies. The comparative question is whether the development of such new reproductive technologies is fundamentally different from other medical technologies—or do they fit the same basic pattern? I would argue for both positions. First, new reproductive technologies are *different* because most have been so deeply targeted at a select subset of only half the population—women. They are exceptionally highly gendered cyborg makers. Second, they are *like* other medical technologies in that they enhance control over human life and death. The means are very sophisticated technologies which permit successful intervention *at the individual level* —classic late capitalist Western biomedicine qua privatized "boutique medicine" (e.g. Roth and Ruzek, 1986; Riessman, 1983). Like other medical technologies in the U.S., these have been relatively unregulated (e.g. Blumenthal, 1983), although this may change (Eichler 1989).

The modern/postmodern model seems to me to hold water/hold meanings but requires futher exploration of actual conditions of concrete practice and application. I would argue that one major social issue continues to be the overall *legitimacy of intervention* in reproductive processes. Another controversial issue concerns *access to interventions:* who decides who uses which means of control and under what conditions? There has been considerable coercion in the U.S. and elsewhere around modernist approaches. There are also resistances for many reasons—against genocidal activities, against racism, against the wanton distribution of unsafe drugs and technologies, and so on (e.g., Arditti et al., 1984).

Postmodern approaches are vividly portrayed but are not yet very common practice. Selective distribution and the need to "afford" them limit access. Yet there also seem to be moments of possible coercion here—such as convincing women to endure the rigors of IVF or forcing mothers of prospective fetal patients to undergo multiple surgeries and literal confinements—which will lead to contestation. There is also the risk that people will be inadvertently enrolled by such technologies because of the "revolutionary" hype surrounding them. On the one hand these technologies can bestow pomo chic.[14] Yet on the other hand a retreat into what Haraway termed organicist romanticism is also dangerous.

But I anticipate even more intense debate about the legitimacy of transformations enabled by these technologies: it is not only lived bodies but also social bodies which will require changes in the bodies politic to make these postmodern transformations "practical." Mary Douglas (1966) noted many years ago that things that fall outside cultural systems of classification are often perceived as dangerous abominations. Certainly postmodern reproductive lived bodies, social bodies and bodies politic are and will likely continue to be so perceived by at least some segments of society.

We have already reached a fundamental crisis in the West regarding death. How will we redefine life, human/nonhuman boundaries and cyborgian/hybrid continuities with respect for the nonhuman and the other/once-human? Along the way we must come to better understandings of how nature, life, justice and reproduction are co-constructed, co-constitutive. Reproduction has been, is, and will in all likelihood continue to be charged with intensifying politics of hope and despair, pleasure and danger for individuals, collectivities and societies. It is a site worthy of our sustained concern.

Notes

1. This paper is an abstracted version of one slated to appear in *Making Sex, Fabricating Bodies: Gender and the Construction of Knowledge in the Biomedical Sciences*, edited by Joan Fujimura and Anni Dugdale. It is dedicated to the memories of my colleagues Barbara Rosenblum and Anna Hazan who helped me with a much earlier version in a writing group. I want to thank Kathy Charmaz and Marilyn Little (the other members of that group), Carol Conell (my faculty sponsor in the NIMH Postdoctoral Program in Organizations and Mental Health at Stanford University which provided early support), Joan Jacobs Brumberg (formal discussant of the paper at the Conference "Between Design and Choice: The Social Shaping of New Reproductive Technologies" sponsored by the Department of Science and Technology Studies, Cornell University), Carolyn Acker, Susan Bell, Monica Casper, and Peter Taylor for detailed comments. The Rockefeller Archives provided access to important data for related projects (Clarke 1985/1995).

2. A most provocative discussion of "control" is offered by Vanderwater (1992); see also Dixon-Mueller (1993) on reproductive rights in developing countries.

3. Ginsberg and Rapp (1991) provide an important overview of recent work on the demographic transition which argues that it is not universal, and that there are a variety of transitions locally determined by economic as well as cultural and historical phenomena. See also Horn (1991).

4. This is from a Progress Report to the Board of Trustees in support of his program for sponsoring scientific research (Kohler, 1976:291).

5. Quoted in Kimmelman (1983:68); from Weaver's paper on "The Science of Man," 29 November 1933, RF 3.915.1.6. Max Mason of the Rockefeller Foundation went on to note that much of sex research had real social applications and could be effectively coupled with work done in sociology. Mason was also quoted in Kimmelman (1983:68): from Max Mason's diary, 2 September 1929, RF 1.1.216.8.103.

6. Certainly up to World War II, and in many areas after it, the Rockefeller Foundation was the primary funding source for such scientific research—including the psychology of sex (Aberle and Corner, 1953; Abir-Am, 1982; Hall, 1977, 1974; Kay 1993; Kohler, 1976, 1978). A strong focus of the Rockefeller and other foundations was from the outset on the applicability of research to solving human problems (Kohler, 1991) which Kay (1993) interprets as seeking science-based mechanisms for social control.

7. Crowe (1993) presented an excellent analysis of premodern, modern and postmodern framings of infertility in terms of rhetorics about the individuals, who is construed as the patient, and so on.

8. We might argue that AI was not "appreciated" as the radically socially transformative technology it now is understood to be. Note the lateness of policy debates about it in Sweden and England, for example (Liljestrand 1990; Mulkay, 1993).

9. The term "boutique medicine" was used by Uwe Reinhardt (Eakins 1987).

10. Thanks to Sandy Stone for this point, and to Alex Pang for its generalizability.

11. Casper (1993) provoked my thoughts on this wonderfully.

12. In contrast, Martin (1992:121), focusing on bodies, asserts the end of one kind of body and the beginning of another. I plan to discuss the premodern approaches in subsequent work.

13. This discussion is in the much longer version of this paper; see footnote 1.

14. I thank Peter Taylor for this insight.

References

Aberle, Sophie D. and George W. Corner. 1953. *Twenty Five Years of Sex Research: History of the National Research Council Committee for Research in Problems of Sex, 1922-1947*. Philadelphia: WB Saunders.

Abir-Am, Pnina. 1982. The discourse of physical power and biological knowledge in the 1930s: a reappraisal of the Rockefeller Foundation's Policy in Molecular Biology. Social Studies of Science 12:341-82.

American Foundation, The. 1955. Medical Research: A Midcentury Survey. Vol. II: Unsolved Clinical Problems in Biological Perspective. Boston: Little Brown for the American Foundation.

Arditti, Rita, Renate Klein and Shelley Minden (Eds.) 1984. *Test-Tube Women: What Future for Motherhood?* Boston: Pandora Press/Routledge and Kegan Paul.

Austin, C.R. and R.V. Short (Eds.) 1972. *Artificial Controls of Reproduction.* Cambridge: University Press [First Edition].

Balsamo, Anne. 1993. The Virtual Body in Cyberspace. Research in Philosophy and Technology 13:119-39.

Banta, Martha. 1993. *Taylored Lives: Narrative Productions in the Age of Taylor, Veblen and Ford.* Chicago: University of Chicago Press.

Bartel, Diane. 1988. *Putting on Appearances: Gender and Advertising.* Philadelphia: Temple University Press.

Beeson, Diane and Rita Douglas. 1983. Prenatal Diagnosis of Fetal Disorders. Part I: Technological Capabilities; Part II: Issues and Implications. Birth 10(4):227-241.

Bell, Susan E. 1994. Translating Science to the People: Updating the New Our Bodies, Ourselves. Women's Studies International Forum 17(1):9-18.

Biggers, John D. 1987. Pioneering Mammalian Embryo Culture. In Barry Bavister (Ed.) *The Mammalian Preimplantation Embryo.* New York:s i70 Plenum.

Biggers, John D. 1984. In vitro fertilization and embryo transfer in historical perspective. In Alan Trouson and Carl Wood (Eds.) *In Vitro Fertilization and Embryo Transfer.* London: Churchill Livingstone.

Biggers, John D. 1981. In Vitro Fertilization and Embryo Transfer in Human Beings. New England Journal of Medicine 304:336-42.

Blake, John B. 1980. Anatomy. Pp. 29-47 in The Education of American Physicians, edited by Ronald L. Numbers. Berkeley: University of California.

Blankenship, Kim M., Beth Rushing, Suzanne A. Onorato, and Renee White. 1993 Reproductive Technologies and the U.S. Courts. Gender and Society 7(1):8-31.

Blumenthal, David. 1980. Federal Policy Toward Health Care Technology: The Case of National Center. Health and Society 61(4):584-613.

Bordo, Susan. 1993. *Unbearable Weight: Feminism, Western Culture and the Body.* Berkeley: University of California Press.

Casper, Monica J. 1995. Fetal Cyborgs and Technomoms on the Reproductive Frontier. In this volume.

Casper, Monica J. 1994a. Constructions of `Human' in Experimental Fetal Surgery: Reframing and Grounding `Non-Human Agency.' American Behavioral Scientist fix.

Casper, Monica J. 1994b. At the Margins of Humanity: Fetal Positions in Science and Medicine. Science, Technology and Human Values forthcoming.

Casper, Monica and Adele Clarke. 1992. Turning the Wrong Tool for the Job into the Right One: The Pap Smear 1941-1900. Under revision.

Casper, Monica and Lisa Jean Moore. 1995. Inscribing Bodies, Inscribing the Future: Gender, Sex and Reproduction in Outer Space. Sociological Perspectives 38(5):forthcoming.

Chico, Nan Paulsen. 1989. *Confronting the Dilemmas of Reproductive Choice: The Process of Sex Preselection.* Dissertation in Sociology, University of California, San Francisco.

Clarke, Adele E. 1995. *Disciplining Reproduction: American Life Scientists and `the Problem of Sex.'* Berkeley: University of California Press.

Clarke, Adele E. 1990a. Controversy and the Development of Reproductive Sciences. Social Problems 37(1):18-37.

Clarke, Adele E. 1990b. Women's health over the life cycle. In Rima Apple (ed.), *The History of Women, Health and Medicine in America: An Encyclopedic Handbook.* New York: Garland.

Clarke, Adele E. 1990c. A social worlds research adventure: the case of reproductive science. In Thomas Gieryn and Susan Cozzens (eds.), *Theories of Science in Society.* Bloomington: Indiana University Press.

Clarke, Adele E. 1988. The industrialization of human reproduction, 1889-1989. Keynote Address. Conference on Athena Meets Prometheus: Gender and Technoscience. U.C., Davis.

Clarke, Adele E. 1987. Research materials and reproductive science in the United States, 1910-1940. Pp. 323-350 in Gerald L. Geison (ed.), Physiology in the American Context, 1850-1940. Bethesda: American Physiological Society/Waverly.

Clarke, Adele E. 1985. Emergence of the Reproductive Research Enterprise, c1910-1940: A Sociology of

Biological, Medical and Agricultural Science in the United States. Dissertation in Sociology, University of California, San Francisco.

Clarke, Adele E. 1984. Subtle sterilization abuse: a reproductive rights perspective. Pp. 188-212 in Rita Arditti, Renata Duelli Klein and Shelly Minden (eds.), *Test Tube Women: What Future for Motherhood?* Boston: Pandora/Routledge and Kegan Paul. Second edition published 1989.

Clarke, Adele E. and Joan H. Fujimura (eds.) 1992. *The Right Tools for the Job: At Work in Twentieth Century Life Sciences.* Princeton, NJ: Princeton University Press.

Clarke, Adele and Theresa Montini. 1993. The Many Faces of RU486: Tales of Situated Knowledges and Technological Contestations. Science, Technology and Human Values. 18(1):42-78.

Cohen, Sherrill and Nadine Taub (eds) 1989. *Reproductive Laws for the 1990s.* Clifton, NJ:Humana Press.

Corner, George W. 1957. Laboratory and Clinic in the Study of Infertility. Fertility and Sterility 8(6):494-512.

Crawford, Robert. 1985. A Cultural Account of 'Health': Control, Release and the Social Body. IN John B. McKinlay (ed) *Issues in the Political Economy of Health Care.* London: Tavistock.

Crowe, Christine. 1993. Changes in the Perception of Infertility. Presented at conference on Sex/Gender and Technoscientific Worlds, University of Melbourne.

Dixon-Mueller, Ruth. 1993. *Population Policy and Women's Rights: Transforming Reproductive Choice.* Westport, CT: Praeger Pubs.

Douglas, Mary. 1966. *Purity and Danger: An Analysis of Concepts of Pollution and Taboo.* London: Routledge, Kegan & Paul.

Downey, Gary Lee, Joseph Dumit and Sarah Williams. 1992. Granting Membership to the Cyborg Image. Paper presented at meetings of the American Anthropological Association, San Francisco. In this volume.

Duden, Barbara. 1991. *The Woman Beneath the Skin: A Doctor's Patients in Eighteenth Century Germany.* Translated by Thomas Dunlap. Cambridge, MA: Harvard University Press.

Duden, Barbara. 1993. *Disembodying Women: Perspectives on Pregnancy and the Unborn.* Translated by Lee Hoinacki. Cambridge, MA: Harvard University Press.

Eakins, Pamela. 1987. Study of 'Natural Experiment in History' Completed. Americal Sociological Association Newsletter: Footnotes (December) 15(9):6.

Eichler, Margrit. 1989. Some Minimal Principles Concerning New Reproductive Technologies. Pp. 226-235 in Overall (Ed.)

Elias, Sherman and George J. Annas. 1987. *Reproductive Genetics and the Law.* Chicago: Yearbook Medical Publishers.

Finkelstein, Joanne. 1991. *The Fashioned Self.* Philadelphia: Temple University Press.

Frankenberg, Ruth. 1993. *The Social Construction of Whiteness: White Women, Race Matters.* Minneapolis: University of Minnesota Press.

Gimenez, Martha. 1991. The Mode of Reproduction in Transition: A Marxist-Feminist Analysis of the Effects of Reproductive Technologies. Gender and Society 5(3):334-350.

Ginsburg, Faye and Rayna Rapp. 1991. The Politics of Reproduction. Annual Review of Anthropology 20:311-343.

Glassner, Barry. 1990. *Fit for Postmodern Selfhood: Symbolic Interaction and Cultural Studies*, eds. Becker, Howard S. and Michael M. McCall. Chicago: The University of Chicago Press.

Goldsmith, Olivia. 1993. *Flavor of the Month.* New York: Poseidon Press.

Gordon, Linda. 1976 [1990]. *Woman's Body, Woman's Right: A Social History of Birth Control in America.* New York: Penguin.

Hacking, Ian. 1983. *Representing and Intervening.* Cambridge: Cambridge University Press.

Haiken, Beth. 1992. Plastic Surgery and American Beauty at 1921. Paper from history dissertation at UC Berkeley, presented at the UC/Berkeley and UC/San Francisco History of Medicine and Culture Group.

Hall, Diana Long. 1977. The Social Implications of the Scientific Study of Sex. The Scholar and the Feminist IV. New York: The Women's Center of Barnard College.

Hall, Diana Long. 1974. Biology, Sex Hormones and Sexism in the 1920s. Philosophical Forum 5:81-96.

Haraway, Donna. 1992a. Situated Knowledges: The Science Question in Feminism and the Privilege of Partial Perspective. Pp. 183-201 in *Simians, Cyborgs and Women: The Reinvention of Nature.* London: Routledge & Kegan Paul.

Haraway, Donna. 1992b. The Promises of Monsters: A Regenerative Politics for Inappropriate/d Others. Pp. 295-337 in *Cultural Studies*, edited by Lawrence Grossberg, Cary Nelson and Paula Treichler. New York: Routledge.

Haraway, Donna. 1989. *Primate Visions: Gender, Race and Nature in the World of Modern Science*. New York: Routledge.

Hartouni, Valerie. 1991. Containing Women: Reproductive Discourse in the 1980s. Pp. 27-56 in Constance Penley and Andrew Ross (Eds.) *Technoculture*. Minneapolis: University of Minnesota Press.

Harvey, David. 1989. *The Condition of Postmodernity: An Enqury into the Origins of Cultural Change*. Cambridge: Basil Blackwell.

Hogle, Linda F. 1995. Tales from the Cryptic: Technology Meets Organism in the Living Cadaver. In this volume.

Hogle, Linda F. 1994a. Breadboarding, Finetuning and Interpreting: "Standard" Medical Protocols at the Level of Everyday Practice. Science, Technology and Human Values forthcoming.

Hogle, Linda F. 1994b. Dead, Double-dead, Triple-dead: Technoscientific, Legal and Economic Definitions of "Life" and Human." Paper presented at the meetings of the Society for Social Studies of Science, New Orleans.

Hogle, Linda F. 1993. Margins of Life: Boundaries of the Body. Presented to the Society for Applied Anthropology, San Antonio, Texas.

Horn, David G. 1991. Constructing the Sterile City: Pronatalism and Social Sciences in Interwar Italy. American Anthropologist 18(3):581-601.

Japenga, Ann. 1993. Face Lift City. Health. March/April.

Kay, Lily. 1993. *The Molecular Vision of Life: Caltech, the Rockefeller Foundation and the Rise of the New Biology*. New York: Oxford University Press.

Keller, Evelyn Fox. 1989. Feminism, Science and Postmodernism. Cultural Critique (Fall):5-32.

Kelly, Howard A. 1928. *Gynecology*. New York: D. Appleton and Co.

Kevles, Daniel J. 1985. *In the Name of Eugenics: Genetics and the Uses of Human Heredity*. Berkeley: University of California.

Kimmelman, Barbara. 1983. The American Breeders' Association: Genetics and Eugenics in an Agricultural Context, 1903-1913. Social Studies of Science 13:163-204.

Kohler, Robert E. 1991. *Partners in Science: Foundations and Natural Scientists 1900-1945*. Chicago: University of Chicago Press.

Kohler, Robert E. 1978. A Policy for the Advancement of Science: The Rockfeller Foundation, 1924-1929. Minerva 16:480-515.

Kohler, Robert E. 1976. The management of science: the experience of Warren Weaver and the Rockfeller Foundation programme in molecular biology. Minerva 14:279-306.

Lancaster, Jane B., Jeanne Altman, Alice S. Rossi and Lonnie R. Sherrod (Eds.). 1987. *Parenting Across the Life Span: Biosocial Dimensions*. New York: Aldine De Gruyter.

Latour, Bruno. 1993. *We Have Never Been Modern*. Translated by Catherine Porter. Cambridge, MA: Harvard University Press.

Lilijestrand, Petra. 1990. Rhetoric and Reason: Donor Insemination Politics in Sweden. Doctoral Disseration at the University of California San Francisco.

Lynch, April. 1993a. Achtenberg Rebuts Critics—Says She's Religious, Not Mean. San Francisco Chronicle, May 27:A-6.

Martin, Emily. 1992. The End of the Body? American Ethnologist 19(1):121-40.

Martin, Emily. 1990. Science and Women's Bodies: Forms of Anthropological Knowledge. *Body/Politics. Women and the Discourses of Science*, ed. Mary Jacobus, Evelyn Fox Keller, and Sally Shuttleworth, pp. 69-82. New York: Routledge.

Moore, Lisa Jean and Matt Schmidt. 1994. "The Spermatic Economy: Marketing Technosemen and the Construction of Male Difference." Paper presented at meetings of the Pacific Sociological Association, San Diego.

Mulkay, Michael. 1993. Rhetorics of Hope and Fear in the Great Embryo Debate. Social Studies of Science 23:721-42.

Oudshoorn, Nelly. 1994. *The Making of the Hormonal Body*. New York: Routledge.

Oudshoorn, Nelly. 1993. For Better or Worse: Scientists' Quest for Universal Reproductive Technologies. Paper Presented at Between Design and Choice: The Social Shaping of New Reproductive Technologies Conference, Cornell University (April).

Parkes, A.S. 1966. The rise of reproductive physiology, 1926-1940. The Dale Lecture for 1965. Endocrinology (Proceedings of the Society): xx-xxxii.

Paul, Diane. 1993. Eugenic Origins of Clinical Genetics, In Historical and Philosopical Perspectives in

Medical Genetic, E. Juengst. Ed. (D. Reidel, forthcoming).

Paul, Diane. 1991. The Rockefeller Foundation and the Origins of Behavioral Genetics Pp 263-283 in K. Benson, J. Maienschein and R. Rainger (eds) *The American Expansion of Biology*. New Brunswick, NJ: Rutgers University Press.

Petchesky, Rosalind Pollack. 1987. Fetal images: the power of visual culture in the politics of reproduction. Feminist Studies 13:263-92.

Petchesky, Rosalind Pollack. 1985. Abortion in the 1980s: feminist morality and women's health. Pp. 139-73 in Ellen Lewin and Virginia Olesen (eds.), *Women, Health and Healing: Toward a New Perspective*. New York: Tavistock.

Petchesky, Rosalind Pollack. 1984/1990. *Abortion and Woman's Choice: The State, Sexuality and Reproductive Freedom*. New York: Longman.

Pfeffer, Naomi. 1985. The Hidden Pathology of the Male Reproductive System. In The Sexual Politics of Reproduction, edited by Hilary Homans

Rabinow, Paul. 1992. Studies in the Anthropology of Reason. Anthropology Today 8(5): 7-10.

Reed, James. 1984. *The Birth Control Movement and American Society: From Private Vice to Public Virtue*. Princeton: Princeton University Press, Second Edition. Reinhardt 1987

Rich, Adrienne. 1982. *Compulsory Heterosexuality and Lesbian Existence*. Denver: Antelope Pubs.

Riddle, John. 1992. *Contraception and Abortion from the Ancient World to the Renaissance*. Cambridge, MA: Havard University Press.

Riessmann, Cathrine Kohler. 1983. Women and Medicalization: A New Perspective. Social Policy (Summer):3-18.

Rosenberg, Charles E. 1979. Rationalization and reality in shaping American agricultural research, 1875-1914. In The Sciences in American context: New Perspectives, ed. Nathan Reingold, Washington, DC: Smithsonian Institution:143-63.

Roth, Julius and Sheryl Ruzek (eds). 1986. *Research in the Sociology of Health Care. Vol 4:The Adoption and Social Consequences of Medical Technologies*. Greenwich, CT:JAI Press.

Rowland, Robyn. 1992. *Living Laboratories: Women and Reproductive Technologies*. Bloomington: Indiana University Press.

Rowland, Robyn. 1987. Technology and Motherhood: Reproductive Choice Reconsidered. Signs 12(3):512-28.

Rutherford, Charlotte. 1992. Reproductive Freedoms and African American Women. Yale Journal of Law and Feminism 4(2):255-290.

Ruzek, Shery Burt. 1988. Gender and Medicine. In Health and Human Values Supplement, Pennsylvania Humanities Council, Pittsburg Post Gazette. November 22.

Scheper-Hughes, Nancy and Margaret Lock. 1987. The Mindful Body: A Prolegomenon to Future Work in Medical Anthropology. Medical Anthropology Quarterly. New Series:6-41.

Snowden, Robert and G.D. Mitchell. 1981. *The Artificial Family: A Consideration of Artificial Insemination by Donor*. London: Unwin Paperbacks.

Stacey, Judith. 1990. *Brave New Families: Stories of Domestic Upheaval in Late Twentieth Century America*. New York: Basic.

Stanworth, Michelle (Ed.) 1987. *Reproductive Technologies: Gender, Motherhood and Medicine*. Minneapolis: University of Minnesota.

Stanworth, Michelle. 1990. Birth Pangs: Conceptive Technologies and the Threat to Motherhood. In *Conflicts in Feminism*, ed. Evelyn, Fox, Keller, pp.288-304. New York: Routledge.

Strathern, Marilyn. 1992. *Reproducing the Future: Anthropology, Kinship and the New Reproductive Technologies*. New York: Routledge.

Terry, Jennifer. 1990. Lesbians Under the Medical Gaze: Scientists Search for Remarkable Differences. The Journal of Sex Research 27(3):317-339.

Thobani, Sunera. 1992. From Reproduction to Mal(e)production: The Promise of Sex Selection. Presented at meetings of the American Anthropological Association, San Francisco.

Vanderwater, Bette. 1992. Meanings and Strategies of Reproductive Control: Current Feminist Approaches to Reproductive Technology. Issues in Reproductive and Genetics Engineering 5(3):215-230.

Wepsic, Rebecca. 1993. Silicone Breast Implants: Cosmetic Responses and Rhetorics of Choice. Presented at Qualitative Research Forum, University of California, San Francisco.

Wertz, Dorothy C., John C. Fletcher and John J. Mulvihill. 1987. *Medical Geneticists Confront Ethical Dilemmas: Cross-Cultural Comparisons Among 18 Nations*. Springer Verlag.

Barney B. Clark, DDS

A View From the Medical Service

F. Andrew Gaffney, MD, Barry J. Fenton, MD

Very few people within or outside the medical profession failed to follow the saga of the courageous and dedicated Barney B. Clark, DDS, the world's first recipient of a mechanical heart implantation. Dr Clark suffered from end-stage congestive cardiomyopathy but, because of his age and overall medical condition, was ineligible for heart transplantation. The preoperative psychiatric evaluation of this patient and his family, along with a detailed description of Dr Clark's postoperative course ending with his death 112 days later, is provided in this issue of the *Archives* by Berenson and Grosser.[1] The heroic and noble efforts of Dr Clark and his family have been superbly detailed and many interesting questions about assessing the severely ill patient have been raised. Although the focus of their case report was to have been the process by which the patient was selected for this well-publicized experiment, it is their problems surrounding the psychiatric assessment of a seriously ill medical patient that prompt this discussion.

Dr Clark's preoperative examination was compromised by his generally debilitated state, and many of the formal tests commonly used to screen for organic brain dysfunction were not performed. Nonetheless, Dr Clark's prior episodes of unconsciousness and hypotension during periods of recurrent ventricular tachycardia probably produced some neurologic damage.[2] The relevant questions preoperatively were as follows: (1) Could Dr Clark give an informed consent? (2) Once given, would and could he cooperate with his physicians in their experiment? The first question has been discussed widely without resolution;[3-6] the second question is answered by this case study, although the meaning of the word "cooperation" may still be debated. The problems that limited the authors' preoperative evaluation played an important role in the patient's postoperative course as well.

A situation analogous to that faced by Drs Berenson and Grosser is often seen by internists or cardiologists. The authors asked Dr Clark's family about any change in his mental function, but such changes often occur slowly in patients with end-stage heart disease. This slow deterioration tends to lessen the awareness of disability for both the patient and his family. Only by careful, specific questioning about the patient's activities and level of functioning in the past can one really determine what changes have occurred.

Similar pitfalls exist in interpreting clinical tests in these patients. Tests of baseline function provide little information about how an organ or system will function during stress. For this reason, many of the tests commonly used in medicine involve some form of stress. In cardiology, the method of stress testing varies according to the patient's condition and their ability to exercise. Pacing of the heart or the administration of drugs that increase the heart rate are sometimes used in patients who are unable to exercise. With these tests, one is usually able to estimate the functional state of the cardiovascular system and its reserve capacity. It is likely that, prior to being considered for surgery, Dr Clark had lost considerable brain reserve. The psychologic stress of a long and debilitating illness, severe congestive heart failure, and the pharmacologic agents used to treat this condition could have, alone or together, caused Dr Clark to be delirious at times prior to surgery.[7] Neuropsychologic testing would have been useful to assess this loss of brain reserve. The authors' assessment that Dr Clark was too ill to undergo formal psychiatric testing strongly suggests that there was very little functional or reserve capacity present for handling stress. It is not surprising that Dr Clark's psychiatric course was as stormy as his medical one.

The multiple reasons for Dr Clark's prolonged confusional state after surgery are discussed by the authors. The neurologic problems surrounding prolonged cardiopulmonary bypass (over four hours in this case) were well reviewed and consist mainly of cerebral injury due to a variety of embolic sources including air, platelet aggregates, and foreign bodies from the perfusion apparatus itself. Dr Clark was said to have had an adequate cardiac output since this could be "chosen" by setting the pump at the desired level. Unfortunately, this does not guarantee an appropriate distribution of the cardiac output once it leaves the heart. It is impossible to determine whether cerebral perfusion and oxygenation were high, low, or normal, given the coexistence of acid-base problems, chronic hypercarbia, uremia, anemia, sepsis, and multiple transfusions. All of these factors could affect cerebral blood flow as well as oxygen and nutrient transport across the blood-brain barrier. However, Dr Clark's mental status probably reflected his grave overall condition and not simply "hypoperfusion."

Patients with multiple medical problems and confusion are common in medical intensive care units.[8] In fact, it would be unusual to find an alert, oriented patient as ill as Dr Clark was.[9] Psychiatrists are rarely, if ever, consulted for such patients, since a confused, or at least poorly alert patient, is considered "normal" in an intensive care unit setting. Focal neurologic findings, or seizure activity, as in this case, would probably produce a neurology consultation. A hemiparesis or dysarthria may represent a new stroke; but it is sometimes only the reappearance of an old deficit in a patient who can no longer compensate for what may have been subtle clinical deficits prior to the stress. Patients who are minimally compensated prior to stress can be expected to do worse with stress, whether their problem is diabetes, ischemic heart disease, an old stroke, or a mild organic brain syndrome.

The magnitude of stress in this case has probably been substantially underestimated by both the surgeons who often view their procedures as "routine" and the authors who may not have been involved in the hour by hour care of the patient. The "half hour surgical procedure" on the third day was a thoracotomy performed with Dr Clark under general anesthesia, followed by prolonged endotracheal intubation. The "emergency surgery procedure that was performed for repair of a fractured mitral valve" was another thoracotomy. A tracheostomy that was performed for the relief of continued respiratory distress probably required the administration of more anesthetic, and produced more pain, an inability to speak normally, and connection to another machine. Additional insults included significant epistaxis requiring nasal packing, and hemarthrosis, usually painful bleeding into the joint. The surgical teams' acceptance of Dr Clark's confused state as "normal for the situation" was evidenced by their decision not to honor the patient's expressed wish to die. Not mentioned in this case report is the fact that hospital officials also considered Dr Clark to be mentally incompetent. Mrs Clark signed all of the consent forms for implantation of the artificial heart.[10]

The exact link between severe psychologic and physical stress and decreased alertness in critically ill patients is unknown and probably multifactorial. One can, however postulate a patient's withdrawing to conserve energy in such a situation.[11] Despite these tremendous complications Dr Clark showed his remarkable resilience and characteristic adaptability in a number of ways, both physiologically and psychologically. The problems that were associated with the use of the mechanical heart were largely overshadowed by the other medical problems, but some interesting observations were made. The inertial forces associated with such a device are substantial and cause the patient's entire body to vibrate with each "heart" beat, similar, but lesser, vibration occurs in everyone, but it is sensed normally. However, persons with normal vision who wear prism glasses that reverse the usual right-left orientation of the visual field become aware of each cardiac pulsation and complain of it just as Dr Clark did Charles Oman, PhD, Cambridge, Mass, Massachusetts Institute Technology, personal communication). Likewise, with time these people readapt and are again unaware of their heartbeat. Dr Clark's decreased awareness of his body's vibrations was not due to an abnormal mental status, but was an appropriate adaption, thought to be a function of the vestibulo-ocular system. Dr Clark's attempts at humor about his "machine" are a further example of his adjustment to a new stress. His personality and the basis for commitment clearly aided him throughout the vicissitudes of his clinical course.

The patient eventually died of sepsis. An autopsy shows only mild atherosclerosis (his heart disease was not due to atherosclerosis) and multiple microinfarcts of the brain. Neither the location of the microinfarcts nor their extent totally explain Dr Clark's mental status. In fact, there is no real explanation for Dr Clark's mental status change except that he was critically ill for a prolonged period, profound changes in mental status are commonly found that setting. One case provides insufficient data to develop implantation selection and screening criteria as Drs Berenson and Grosser had hoped. Their suggestion that a less ill patient "would have been a better choice" is true, but does not address the fact that a less ill patient probably would not have been considered for the implantation at all, given the current state of development. Hopefully, any remaining controversy in this particular case will be focused on the procedure, and not on the man.

Accepted for publication July 24, 1984.

From the Departments of Internal Medicine (Dr Gaffney) and Psychiatry (Dr. Fenton), University of Texas Health Science Center, Southwestern Medical School, Dallas.

Reprint requests to Division of Cardiology, H8.122, University of Texas Health Science Center, Southwestern Medical School, 5323 Harry Hines Blvd., Dallas, TX 75238 (Dr Gaffney).

Notes

1. Berenson CK, Grosser BI: Total artificial heart implantation. *Arch Gen Psychiatry* 1984;41:910-916.

2. De Vries WC, Anderson JL, Joyce LD, Anderson FL, Hammond EH, Jarvik RK, Kolff WJ: Clinical use of the total artificial heart. *N Engl J Med* 1984;310:273-278.

3. Woolley FR: Ethical issues in the implantation of the total artificial heart. *N Engl J Med* 1984;310:292-296.

4. Galletti PM: Replacement of the heart with a mechanical device: The case of Dr Barney Clark. *N Engl J Med* 1984;310:312-314.

5. Fletcher JC: Cardiac transplants and the artificial heart: Ethical considerations. *Circulation* 1983;68:1339-1343.

6. Strauss MJ: The political history of the artificial heart. *N Engl J Med* 1984;310:332-336.

7. Lipowski ZJ: Transient cognitive disorders in the elderly. *Am J Psychiatry* 1983;140:1426-1436.

8. Hackett TP, Cassem NH, Wishnie HA: The coronary-care unit: appraisal of its psychologic hazards. *N Engl J Med* 1968;279:1365-1272.

9. Katz NM, Agle DP, DePalma RG, DeCosse JJ: Delirium in surgical patients under intensive care. *Arch Surg* 1972;104:310-313.

10. Annas GJ: Consent to the artificial heart: The lion and the crocodile. *Hastings Cent Rep* 1983;13:20-22.

11. Weiner MF: Conversation withdrawal and mental retardation in medical-surgical patients. *Psychosomatics* 1983;24:41-43.

Artificial Heart and Assist Devices

Directions, Needs, Costs, Societal and Ethical Issues

Robert L. Van Citters, Catherine B. Bauer, Lois K. Christopherson, Robert C. Eberhart, David M. Eddy, Robert L. Frye, Albert R. Jonsen, Kenneth H. Keller, Robert J. Levine, Dwight C. McGoon, Stephen G. Pauker, Charles E. Rackley, Vallee L. Willman, and Peter L. Frommer

Working Group on Mechanical Circulatory Support, National Heart, Lung, and Blood Institute, National Institutes of Health, Bethesda, Maryland, U.S.A.

Abstract: A Working Group appointed by the Director of the National Heart, Lung, and Blood Institute (NHBLI) has reviewed the current status of mechanical circulatory support systems (MCSS), and has examined the potential need for such devices, their cost, and certain societal and ethical issues related to their use. The media have reported the limited clinical investigative use of pneumatically energized total artificial hearts (which actually replace the patient's heart) and left ventricular assist devices (which support or replace the function of the left ventricle by pumping blood from the left heart to the aorta with the patient's heart in place). However, electrically energized systems, which will allow full implantation, permit relatively normal everyday activity, and involve battery exchange or recharge two or three times a day, are currently approaching long-term validation in animals prior to clinical testing. Such long-term left ventricular assist devices have been the primary goal of the NHLBI targeted artificial heart program. Although the ventricular assist device is regarded as an important step in the sequence of MCSS development, the Working Group believes that a fully implantable, long-term, total artificial heart will be a clinical necessity and recommends that the mission of the targeted program include the development of such systems. Past estimates of the potential usage of artificial hearts have been reviewed in the context of advances in medical care and in the prevention of cardiovascular disease. In addition, a retrospective analysis of needs was carried out within a defined population. The resulting projection of 17,000-35,000 cases annually, in patients below age 70, falls within the general range of earlier estimates, but is highly sensitive to many variables. In the absence of an actual base of data and experience with MCSS, projection of costs and prognoses was carried out using explicit sets of assumptions. The total costs of a left ventricular assist device, its implantation and maintenance for a projected average of 4½ years of survival might be approximately $150,000 (in 1983 dollars). The gross annual cost to society could fall in the range of $2.5-$5 billion. Ethical issues associated with use of the artificial heart are not unique. For individual patients these relate primarily to risk-benefit, informed consent, patient selection, and privacy. However, for society as a whole, the larger concern relates to the distribution of national resources. Issues of primary importance to clinical investigation have been examined and special guidelines for the clinical investigative phase of artificial heart research have been set forth. The Working Group believes that, except as part of NHLBI research protocols, public funds should not be available for clinical use of MCSS until their clinical effectiveness and reasonable cost-effectiveness are demonstrated. The Working Group affirms the position of the 1973 panel in establishing "medical" suitability of the recipient (which is more complex than simply medical characteristics) as the primary criterion for decisions regarding the distribution of this costly and scarce resource. However, it is the judgment of the Working Group that cost and cost-effectiveness are legitimate considerations in entitlement and reimbursement decisions. The issues of cost, distributive justice, and patient selection are not unique to artificial heart and ventricular assist device development, but highlight the need to direct attention to the issues often associated with increasingly complicated medical care.

Received June 1985.

Address correspondence and reprint requests to Dr. P. L. Frommer, National Heart, Lung, and Blood Institute, Building 31, National Institutes of Health, Bethesda, MD 20892, U.S.A.

Reprinted from NIH publication 85-2723, with minor stylistic changes, e.g., retitling the Executive Summary as Abstract, renumbering the references, and numbering the footnotes.

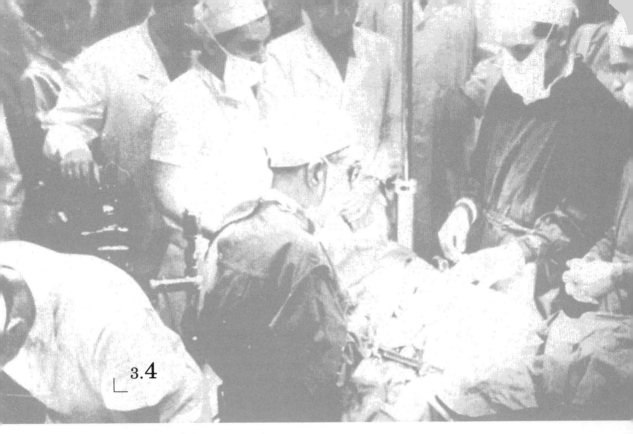

3.4

Artificial Liver

Present and Future

Motokazu Hori

Department of Surgery, Institute of Clinical Medicine, University of Tsukuba, Japan

Abstract: Early in 1956, the first model of a biological artificial liver, using a live dog's liver incorporated in a cross-hemodialyzer, was placed in an experimental animal with portocaval encephalopathy. This "biological artificial liver," a hybrid liver in the present terminology, was the first in the world. In October 1958, the first human patient, a young male patient in hepatic coma due to liver cirrhosis, was placed on the laboratory-made biological artificial liver composed of four parabiotic cross-hemodialyzers connected with four live dogs' livers to which the "hepatic reactors" for ammonium adsorption and acid-base balance were additionally equipped. This first case was very successful, resulting in the patient's recovery from coma. This article introduces the past history of the artificial liver, research of which has mainly been conducted in Japan since the early 1950s by the author, M. Mito, and Y. Nosé. Until recently, little progress had been made in this field through the application of blood purification principles such as hemoadsorption, plasma-pheresis, and other modifications and combinations. Accumulation of clinical experiences with such conventional methods has stimulated the third generation of the artificial liver to a return to a hybrid organ applying modern science and technology. A concept of hybrid organs in comparison with organ transplants is introduced. The Japanese national project of developing a new artificial liver system, as conducted by the author as the chairman and his associates, is introduced.

The artificial liver research of Yukihiko Nosé, Michio Mito, and the author started as a dreamful challenge in Japan in the early 1950s.

Early in 1955, the author, during his first year as a surgical resident at the University of Tokyo Hospital, had a sad experience with a middle-aged woman who had fallen into a deep coma due to postoperative hepatorenal syndrome complicated with jaundice and anuria. This patient, who had shown some recovery from anuria and temporarily from coma following repeated hemodialysis, had died.

Because this case was the first case of a patient treated with an artificial kidney in Japan, it was an impressive but also disappointing experience. However, it inspired the author toward the further development of artificial liver supports. Until the first model was applied to an experimental animal with portocaval encephalopathy one year later in 1956, the name artificial liver had not existed.

In October 1958, the first laboratory-made biological artificial liver was placed in a 20-year-old male patient in hepatic coma due to cirrhosis. This artificial liver was composed of four units of parabiotic cross-hemodialyzers connected to the hepatic circulation of a live dog, each with the hepatic reactors of pretreated ion exchange resin columns for ammonium adsorption and acid-base balance. This first application, 55 minutes in duration, resulted in a dramatic recovery from Grade 4 coma. Later, two more patients were placed on the biological artificial liver. These cases were reported by Professor Kimoto at the 1959 annual meeting of the American Society for Artificial Internal Organs held in Atlantic City.[1] These first cases of the clinical application of an artificial liver were also the first artificial organs with complex functions. In the early 1960s, there were two groups studying the artificial liver in Japan, or for that matter in the world: one group in Tokyo (M. Hori) and the other in Sapporo (M. Mito and Y. Nosé). Both groups worked on a hybrid artificial liver in different ways.

In the history of the artificial liver there have been three streams of development: the biological, the artificial, and the combined hybrid approaches (Table 1).

To the present, a purely "artificial" liver has been impossible to realize even with the most advanced science and technology available. According to the accumulated experiences, artificial blood purification techniques in patients in hepatic coma permit the return to consciousness in many cases, but do not save the life of the patient. It has become very clear that not only the purely passive functions such as plasma separation, adsorption, and dialysis are needed; but also some metabolic function derived from hepatocytes or liver tissue in order to relieve the toxic or deficient conditions of the brain and of liver regeneration is needed, as well as the addition of both known and unknown substances to the patient (Table 2).

To date, and probably until the 21st century, we will have to depend on the biological components to solve the difficult problems. Thus, an integration of "artificial" and "biological" elements is needed for the artificial liver (Table 3).

Because it is not possible to play the "almighty" in the development of a complete artificial organ whenever a difficulty is encountered, a way must be found to apply the concepts and specific technologies of a hybrid system. Technology is oriented in the development of the blood detoxification apparatus, biological structures (from whole body to molecular components), and the interface between the two. As for the biological components, the source, procurement, prevention of contamination and degradation, protection of immune rejection, preservation, maintaining viability and industrialization are the problems to be solved.

There has been an empirical and practical concept of a two wheels of a cart relationship between artificial organs and organ transplants in replacement and substitution. For example, the artificial kidney and kidney transplantation and artificial heart and heart transplantation go hand in hand. As far as the liver is concerned, however, the situation is quite different. At the present stage, the artificial liver, or hepatic assist systems available, are not sufficient to support the liver transplant recipient. However, the liver can often regenerate within 2 weeks or so even in case of fulminant hepatic failure, unless the brain is irreversibly damaged. Thus the need may only be temporary.[2]

The Japanese national project of developing a new artificial liver system started in 1979 with the goals and working hypotheses shown in Tables 1 and 2. The major component in the system is the metabolic unit composed of the isolated, frozen-preserved hepatocytes packed and perfused in the polymethylmethacrylate hollow fiber devices (Table 3). In this project, Dr. M. Mito and his associates have played a major role in the development of this most important metabolic unit.

Dr. Mito is one of the 1955 graduates of the Hokkaido University School of Medicine. He trained in surgery at the Hokkaido University hospital, did surgical research at Harvard Medical School and at Boston City Hospital, and was appointed Professor and Chairman of Surgery at the Asahikawa Medical College in 1975. Not only regarding the artificial liver but also in transplantation and academic surgery in general,[3,4] he is a real leader in Japan and has been a very good friend of the authors since 1957.

Notes

Originally appeared in *Artificial Organs*, Volume 10, Number 3, 1986, pp. 211-13.

1. Kimoto S. The Artificial Liver: Experiments and Clinical application. *Trans Am Soc Artif Interns Organs* 1959:5:102-12.

2. Hori M. Artificial Liver. The Concept and Working Hypothesis of Hybrid Organs: From a 25 year old anecdote to the 21st century model. *Trans Am Soc Artif Interns Organs* 1982:28:639-41.

3. Kusano M. Mito. Observations on the fine structure of long-survived isolated hepatocytes inoculated into rat spleen. *Gastroenterology* 1982:82:616-28.

4. Mito M., Ebata H., Husano M, et al. Morphology and function of isolated hepatocytes transplanted into rat spleen. *Transplantation* 1979:28:499-505.

Table 1

The Goal of an Artificial Liver

To relieve the patient with fulminant hepatic failure in more than two of three cases

To be used continuously or intermittently for 2 weeks until the liver regenerates

To substitute the liver function, not only of blood purification but also of metabolism, even in part

Table 2

Working Hypotheses of an Artificial Liver

Not only blood purification (detoxification) but also some metabolic function is required in an artificial liver.

Hepatic coma is a toxic and deficient condition of the brain acutely affected by ill blood due to fulminant hepatic failure.

Liver cells and tissue can be regenerated in many cases within 2 weeks unless the brain is irreversibly damaged.

Toxic substances to the brain and inhibitory substances to liver regeneration can be removed from blood and deficient substances can be added to blood through the used membrane.

The isolated, cultured, and stored animal hepatocytes remain viable and function closely like normal human hepatocytes for hours while perfused with oxygenated plasma.

Separated plasma can be more efficiently treated in the system than can whole blood.

Table 3

Artificial liver development: 1956-1985

	Principle	**Components**	**Membrane**
1956	Cross-hemodialysis	4 live dog livers	Gel cellulose
	Hepatic reactor	Ion exchange resin	
1970s	Hemoperfusion	Charcoal	
	Plasma separation		Cellulose acetate, PVA, PMMA hollow fiber
1980s	Plasma separation		PMMA hollow fiber
	Metabolism	Isolated xenogenic hepatocytes	PMMA hollow fiber
	Adsorption	Charcoal, Ionex	

ISAO Proffers A Marvelous
Cover for Acting Out Fantasies

Eli A. Friedman

Each of us attempting to advance medical science—whether an engineer, chemist, theoretician, or physician—depends on personal enthusiasm to sustain our work. Optimistic, self-driven investigators succeed beyond the point where the pessimist, convinced that the project cannot be done, has given up. Commitment to the design, construction, and implanting of artificial internal organs requires a positive, romantic, and unrestrained view of what may be attainable. Members of our society share a bond gained by the belief that fantasy can be transformed to reality.

While no data substantiate the point, I consider it safe to speculate that a high proportion of ISAO members were enthralled by science fiction as restless adolescents, and still recall how Wells, Heinlein, van Voght, and Asimov told of a world in which imagination was unrestricted. Future ISAO members walked on other planets, regressed or advanced in time, and watched as the dead were restored to health by cloning individuals from cell parts. A recurrent theme in "SciFi" is the acceptance of medical facilities termed "cosmetics" in which severely wounded Starpersons receive spare parts permitting normal vigor. As we near the close of this century, many of these hopes for tomorrow have been absorbed into daily life. Thousands of diabetics receive daily injections of insulin manufactured by specially instructed bacteria. The anemia of uremia yields to erythropoietin made by recombinant DNA synthesis in tissue cultures of ovarian cells from

Chinese hamsters. Islets of Langerhans from a rat function for a year or longer in a mouse. Paraplegics have taken halting steps using muscles driven by an Apple computer. Implanted artificial hearts serve as a "bridge to transplantation" for subsequent cardiac allograft. Twenty-first century medicine is foreshadowed in the abstracts submitted to our biennial meeting.

I believe in the likelihood of multiple near-term workable bionic implants. By the turn of the century, I envision the permanent cure of simple hormonal deficiencies by implanted endocrine cells encased within either an inert coating or hybrid device. There is no question in my mind that a permanent implantable artificial heart is achievable soon. Building on Kolff's lesson that an artificial organ need not replace all of that organ's missing metabolic functions to forestall death due to organ absence, I consider fabrication of both a bionic kidney and a bionic lung to be a solvable problem—soon.

Having lived through the time of the "giants" in our field, when things were done one person's way alone, I currently recognize the importance of cross-fertilization, by several investigators, to the long-term function of a complex device. Kolff, who built his artificial kidney by himself, found it necessary to assemble a team to undertake the design and testing of his concept for an artificial heart. Even the advanced thinker building a new body part needs biomaterial expertise to prevent internal clotting, as well as the skills of a surgeon to implant the device. Toward the end of facilitating information exchange between scientists building artificial organs, ISAO has established this journal. Fast publication of original articles in *Artificial Organs* and other journals shrinks distances between laboratories, but does not substitute for personal interchange of ideas, the hallmark of ISAO meetings. Our rapid growth in membership and attendance at conventions affords support for ISAO's key function as a catalyst furthering our field. ISAO convenes an extraordinary admixture of mavericks, "marchers to different drums," and very smart scientists capable of converting "what if" to "why not." During my term as President, I will do my best to stay out of the path of creative ISAO members who cannot wait for tomorrow.

George J. Annas

Minerva v. National Health Agency
53 U.S. 2d 333 (2020)

SUPREME COURT OF THE UNITED STATES
No. 111-252

Minerva et al.,
Petitioners,
v.
National Health
Agency

}

On Appeal from the United
States Court of Appeals for the
District of Columbia.

[Argued November 12, 2019—Decided April 10, 2020]

Synopsis

In 2016 the National Health Agency ("the Agency") promulgated regulations which provided for the allocation of artificial hearts in the United States under the authority of the National Health Insurance Act of 1996 (P.L. 104-602). The regulations prohibited the manufacture, sale, or implantation of an artificial heart without a permit from the Agency; prohibited individual purchasers from being recipients of artificial hearts without a permit from the Agency; and provided that permits to recipients be issued only by the Agency's computer, which would pick qualified applicants at random from a master list. This regulation is challenged by P. Minerva, a thoracic surgeon, and two of her patients, Z. Themis and Z. Dike. Themis did not meet the Agency's qualification standards as he is less than fifteen years old; Dike, while meeting the standards, has not yet been chosen by the computer. The plaintiffs challenge the regulations as a violation of their right of privacy, and challenge both the qualification criteria and the random selection procedure and due process under the Fifth Amendment to the U.S. Constitution. This appeal is taken from a decision in favor of the Agency by the Court of Appeals for the District of Columbia. *Minerva v. National Health Agency*, 294 F.3d 28 (D.C. Cir. 2018). Additional relevant facts are set forth in the opinion of the Chief Justice.

CHIEF JUSTICE CLIO delivered the opinion of the Court.

When Congress passed the National Health Insurance Act it granted exceptionally broad powers to the National Health Agency ("the Agency"). One of these powers was the exclusive authority to allocate scarce and expensive medical resources. The Agency has been granted the authority to suspend and revoke medical licenses—all of which have been issued exclusively under federal authority since 1996—of individuals who violate, aid a violator, or conspire to violate the allocation regulations promulgated by the Agency. These provisions of the Act have been previously challenged and upheld by this Court in *Arusha v. National Health Agency,* 29 U.S.2d 124 (2008). In that case, which involved an agency decision to prohibit the use of kidney dialysis machines and ordered all existing kidney dialysis clinics shut down based on a cost-benefit analysis, this Court found such action permissible. Our decision was grounded on a finding of a compelling governmental interest in containing costs and properly allocating resources under the National Health Insurance Program, and a finding that no other reasonable alternative was available to the Agency with regard to this technology. The authority of the Agency to make allocation decisions and to enforce these decisions through licensing sanctions is thus no longer open to challenge.

After three decades of frustration, the implantable artificial heart, powered by a battery, was developed and widely tested in the late 1990s. By 2014 more than 10,000 of these devices were being implanted annually in the United States at a cost of approximately $200,000 each (in terms of 2000 U.S. dollars). The 2014 projections of the National Health Agency were that the annual demand for such hearts would reach approximately 100,000 by the year 2025, and that the National Health Service did not have sufficient funds, personnel, or facilities to implant and maintain such a large number of devices. For example, while the devices are serviceable, they do break down, and all are equipped with a monitoring and warning system that advises the wearer when to get to an emergency department (ED) for service and repair. Up to 20 percent of all ED visits may involve such maintenance in twenty years time. Moreover, a Social Security study found that unlimited use of this device could result in people living longer and this would have the effect of drastically increasing Social Security payments without increasing tax revenues.

Accordingly, the Agency decided, after more than a year of public hearings, to make available annually a maximum of 20,000 artificial hearts. The Agency was statutorily established as the exclusive controller of supply in an effort to ensure both adequate quality control and fairness in patient selection procedures. The allocation scheme promulgated by the Agency and challenged by the plaintiffs provides:[1]

(1)To be placed on the National Waiting List for Artificial Hearts, the candidate must meet the following criteria: He or she must

    (a)be more than 15 years old but less than 70 years old;

    (b)be capable of living at least 10 additional years if the implant procedure is successful; and

    (c)not be a chronic alcoholic or a drug addict.

(2)Individuals certified as meeting the criteria in part (1) by a physician certified by the National Health Agency as a qualified thoracic surgeon shall have their names immediately placed on the National Waiting List for Artificial Hearts. Individuals will be selected from this list at random at the rate of 400 a week. Individuals will be notified of their selection by hologram which will indicate the data and place of the implant procedure. All transportation costs will be paid by the National Health Service. Individuals shall remain on the list until they die, or until such time as they fail to meet any of the criteria set forth in part (1).

I

Plaintiff Minerva's initial argument is that these regulations have "no rational connection with a patient's needs and unduly [infringe] on the physician's right to practice." *Doe v. Bolton,* 410 U.S. 179 (1973). She argues that her patients should be permitted to purchase artificial hearts with their own funds and have her implant them without any interference from the Agency. This argument need not detain us. When the National Health Insurance Act was passed, Congress made it a national priority to provide all its citizens with unlimited access to a specified amount and type of medical care. Any other care was to be rendered at the discretion of the National Health Agency and pursuant to its regulations. So long as such regulations are consistent with the Act and are reasonable methods of rationing expensive and scarce medical resources, they will not be found by this Court to violate a physician's right to practice.

The National Health Agency has permitted a private market in many types of health care—although not in any area of thoracic surgery. This is because after the publication of numerous studies in the late 1990s demonstrating a gross oversupply of surgeons, residency positions in this specialty were sharply curtailed. As a result, by 2010 the supply of surgeons in general, and thoracic surgeons in particular, was deemed to be near optimal. The supply, however, was at a point where the shifting of a significant number of surgeons out of the National Health Service would have severely restricted the ability of the Health Service to provide adequate surgical services to the population.

Accordingly, the Health Agency prohibited private surgical practice except under very restrictive conditions. This prohibition was upheld by the court in 2014 in *American Medical Association v. National Health Agency,* 48 U.S.2d 10 (2014). The basis for this decision was that failure to restrict private surgical practice would endanger the health of the members of the public who could not afford private surgical services, since the supply of surgeons and surgical services in hospitals was not adequate to permit elective procedures to be performed on a large scale without a significant decrease in the supply of surgical services to the Health Service. The same rationale, of course, applies to the present case. If a private market in artificial hearts were permitted, a significant percentage of the one million patients a year who need such hearts would purchase this procedure. These purchases could take more than half of all existing thoracic surgeons out of the Health Service, leaving the remainder of the population without sufficient services in this vital area. These effects were felt as early as 2012 when, with fewer than 10,000 implant procedures being performed annually, the average waiting time for other thoracic surgery increased from four to six months. Justice Melpomene argues that a black market in artificial hearts will be produced by these regulations. This is sheer speculation, and in any event the potential existence of such a market should not prevent the federal government from adopting a policy it believes is right and just.

We cannot allow the avarice of a few to jeopardize the health of the many, especially in view of the fact that the many subsidized the training of all currently practicing physicians, continue to subsidize all hospital and surgical facilities, and almost completely subsidized the development of the AH777 model of the artificial heart. The private market in health care is a fiction to which this Court will not subscribe. The physician's "right to practice medicine" properly is regulated and circumscribed by the National Health Agency for the benefit of the public. The regulations properly seek to extend the lives of as many citizens as possible—within the fiscal, personnel, and facility realities of the National Health Service.

II

Plaintiffs Themis and Dike challenge the regulations as a denial of Fifth Amendment due process and equal protection of the laws. The due process argument can be disposed of easily. Plaintiffs argue that they have a right to a hearing, a right to be represented by counsel, a right to an appeal, a right to access to all of the information on file at the National Health Agency concerning each qualified candidate, and a right to challenge the qualifications or comparative qualifications of each candidate.

While the arguments put forth are interesting, they are not persuasive. The allocation scheme is not adversarial. It does not seek to pit the plaintiffs against all other candidates. Indeed, it is possible that *all* the candidates in a given year will be found to be qualified. The scheme is merely an exclusionary one, designed to deny the operation to those who would not derive a sufficient benefit from it to warrant the societal expenses involved. Moreover, the issues are not based on facts personal to the applicant, as in other cases requiring an adjudicatory hearing, but are much more in the nature of applying general policy guidelines. Davis, *Administrative Law* ¶7.03. Therefore, no procedural due process safeguards, other than the certification of the examining physician, are constitutionally required. Furthermore, such additional due process mechanisms, if utilized, could do more harm than good. By delaying the implantation process and by involving the certifying physicians in court battles, time would be lost that could more effectively be spent in screening and treating patients. All potential recipients would suffer.

The equal protection argument is stronger; but, for the reasons set forth below, we reject it. The plaintiffs correctly assert that, although the federal government has not directly created the scarcity in artificial hearts, when it attempts to regulate their distribution the government is bound by the mandate of equal protection. Under the equal protection doctrine of the United States Constitution it also "seemingly makes no difference that the threatened interest is a privilege rather than a right. Even a privilege, benefit, opportunity, or public advantage may not be granted to some but withheld from others where the basis of the classification and difference in treatment is arbitrary."[2] To deny artificial hearts to a group of citizens, the federal government must demonstrate that the classification is based on reasonable grounds in light of the purpose sought to be attained by the Congress, and is not arbitrary and does not cause invidious discrimination. Plaintiffs have urged us to declare the right to an artificial heart a "fundamental interest," or to declare the qualifications for selection "suspect" so that the federal government must demonstrate a compelling state interest to uphold the regulations. We decline to construe the issues at stake so broadly. While the right to life is certainly fundamental and worthy of constitutional protection, the individual's interest in obtaining specific scarce and expensive medical devices is not. Likewise, while the criteria do establish a certain category of qualified recipients, they are drawn narrowly and with a rational relationship to a legitimate governmental purpose. This Court has been very reluctant to expand either the list of fundamental interests or of suspect classifications, and we find no necessity to do so in this case. We do note, however, that even if we concluded otherwise, we would find that the federal government had a compelling public well-being interest in promoting the allocation scheme outlined in the regulations, and that the scheme was reasonably related to this interest.

In general, this Court will not interfere with government-mandated allocation schemes. Thus, in *Dandridge v. Williams,* 397 U.S. 471 (1970), we upheld Maryland's AFDC program even though in setting an absolute maximum of $250 per family it discriminated against members of larger families. Likewise, in *Belle Terre v. Boraas,* 416 U.S. 1 (1974), we found a regulation which limited the number of unrelated persons living in a household to be a valid means of controlling vehicular traffic and overcrowding. However, in *Dept. of Agriculture v. Moreno,* 413 U.S. 528 (1973), we struck down a food stamp regulation requiring all members of a household to be related. Even though the federal government argued that this requirement was necessary for the prevention of fraud, we could find no rational relationship between this regulation and the purpose of the statute: to feed the poor. The distinctions between these cases are worth emphasizing. In no instance in *Dandridge* was any family completely deprived of a fundamental requirement of life, and the issues in *Belle Terre* did not involve necessities of life.

This Court will not permit the federal government to deprive its citizens of life's necessities. It will, however, permit the allocation of resources that, while important, are not commonly thought of as necessities of life, provided that the allocation scheme is based upon a valid governmental interest, is for a legitimate purpose, is reasonable, and is not invidiously discriminatory.[3] As applied to the National Health Agency, we conclude that the state cannot deprive its otherwise healthy citizens of "life's necessities" such as emergency medical services. However, when an expensive medical technology can properly be labeled a luxury, even though it does sustain life, the state need not provide it to all citizens.

We find that an artificial heart is no more necessary to an individual than a castle or dinner at Maxim's. Individuals need food, shelter, and medical care—but they may not convert the shield against starvation, exposure, and sickness that the federal government may decide to provide into a sword with which to extract luxuries that society cannot afford. Nature, not the federal government, takes the lives of those who are unsuccessful in the artificial heart lottery. The purposes of maximizing lives within resource constraints and of preventing the destruction of the National Health Service are valid, and the rationing scheme adopted is reasonably related to accomplishing these purposes.

We find that the current regulations are not constitutionally objectionable. There seem to be only two ways to avoid rationing: universal treatment or universal non-treatment. The first option is simply not feasible. Congress has refused to vote the more than $20 billion (in terms of 2000 dollars) in funds annually required for universal treatment, and through this Congressional refusal the taxpayers have indicated that they would rather retain the money necessary for this program for their own discretionary use than to pay for the tax increases necessary to finance it. The second option, universal nontreatment, makes sense only if it is in fact impossible to make nonarbitrary distinctions among competing applicants, or impossible to devise an equitable rationing process. We find neither to be the case, and therefore conclude that the federal government has a right to enforce its rationing scheme.[4]

III

Plaintiffs have raised the following objections to the Criteria for Placement on the National Waiting List for Artificial Hearts: (1) by specifically denying treatment to most applicants, the regulations cheapen human life and undermine society's belief in the equality of life; (2) the criteria are not medical at all, but are based on "social worth," a criterion specifically denounced in the Conference Committee Report on P.L. 104-602, and a criterion which also undermines our belief in the equality of life; and (3) the artificial heart lottery provisions are unnecessarily imprecise and lead to squandering the federal government's resources since they fail to take into account the relative life expectancy of one applicant versus another or the degree to which one applicant desires the implantation as opposed to another. Thus, the scheme inherently is inequitable and irrational, and only significant modifications in it would make it constitutionally acceptable.

We shall deal with these objections in the order in which they were raised. The first is a general argument against any attempt to ration scarce medical resources, and we reject it outright. By attempting to save as many lives as possible, society does not cheapen life. On the contrary, it attempts to the best of its ability to protect and prolong life. The fact that all will not benefit from this new technology does not mean that no one should.[5] All citizens cannot live within ten miles of an emergency department equipped to deal in the most efficient way with cardiac arrest. This does not mean we must close these facilities. It only means that they should not be permitted to discriminate arbitrarily among patients who present themselves for treatment.

Themis' argument focuses on the age limitations utilized. We find, however, that they are reasonably related to the purposes of the regulation and, therefore, are proper. The fifteen year cut-off reflects both the age of majority (lowered from eighteen to fifteen in 2012) and thus of consent to medical procedures, and the fact that the thoracic cavity will not, in general, be large enough to house the standard AH777 model of the artificial heart currently in use. The rationale for not implanting the heart in anyone incapable of giving informed consent, is sufficiently dealt with in the concurring opinion of our sister Justice Melpomene.

Parenthetically, we note that the seventy-year age limit reflects the overall judgment of the Agency that individuals beyond this age are so likely to be afflicted with other conditions that could prove fatal that it makes more medical sense simply to eliminate them entirely from the process rather than to spend the resources to screen them. One may disagree with these reasons, but Themis has failed to demonstrate to the satisfaction of the Court that these age limitations are so arbitrary as to erode our belief in the equality of human life.

The second objection is more serious. Social worth criteria are properly condemned because they are so imprecise as to maximize the probability of arbitrary decisions based on personal biases of the decisionmaker. We believe, however, that the criteria formulated by the Agency are essentially medical in nature and as such are capable of precise and nonarbitrary application by qualified thoracic surgeons. All of the screening surgeons must meet the strict requirements for certification by the Agency, and we must assume that they will honestly and fairly perform their functions under the regulations. *Withrow v. Larkin,* 421 U.S. 35 (1975). Moreover, the criteria are reasonable in that they preclude from allocation those who will gain only marginally from the implant, and thus help to maximize society's benefits as compared to the costs of this program. Age, prognosis with the implant, drug addiction, and alcoholism are all characteristics that are readily ascertainable by a qualified physician and all can be considered strictly medical criteria.

The third argument is somewhat troublesome, but inasmuch as the plaintiff Dike has not suggested any way in which desire can be quantified and measured on a comparative basis, we need not deal with it.

IV

Additional support for the type of rationing scheme chosen by the Agency is found in law and custom. An 1842 case, for example, involved an American ship which was near Newfoundland, en route from Liverpool to Philadelphia, when it struck an iceberg. The crew and half the passengers escaped on two overly filled lifeboats. One contained forty-one individuals and after about twenty-four hours it became clear that unless some went overboard, all would perish. The first mate instructed his crew (eight in number) to throw fourteen passengers overboard, using the rule "not to part man and wife, and not to throw over any women." At the trial of one of the seamen for homicide, the court instructed the jury that under extraordinary circumstances the "law of necessity"[6] may justify taking a life, but that in choosing who shall live and who shall perish "there should be consultation and some mode of selection fixed, by which those in equal relations may have equal chance for life ... for ourselves we can conceive of no mode so consonant both to humanity and justice [as casting lots]."[7]

Not only was a lottery approved, but the court also concluded that the first mate and as many of the crew as were necessary to run the boat were not required to take part. Thus, the court sanctioned the exclusion, based on specified criteria, of certain members of society from a lottery scheme. While this case involved choosing individuals to die, not to live, as is the case in allocating artificial hearts, the same standard applies in the latter case. The traditional rule of the sea when a ship is sinking has always been "women and children first." This principle seems to rest on the belief that women are necessary for the survival of the species, and that children have more years left to contribute to society than adults. Both this traditional principle and the lifeboat case sanction "social worth" criteria under certain extreme cases, the arguments of our sister Justice Urania notwithstanding.[8]

The decision of the Court of Appeals of the District of Columbia is accordingly

Affirmed

Calliope, Terpsichore, and Polyhymnia, JJ. join in THE CHIEF JUSTICE'S opinion.

JUSTICE MELPOMENE, concurring in the result.

While I join my sisters in upholding these regulations as valid and constitutional exercises of authority by the National Health Agency, I feel compelled to pen a separate opinion. In my view, there should be *no* allocation scheme whatsoever mandated by the federal government: artificial hearts should simply be outlawed in this country. I come to this conclusion even though I myself have such a device pumping blood through my arteries. It never gives me peace. When I am alone in my bed at night I hear it. It reminds me both of my mortality and of my humanness—but it also taunts me. I am no longer fully human; I am already partially dead.

Furthermore, how can one give informed consent to receive such a device? I did, or so I thought, but when faced with death, people are likely to consent to anything. We all know this. It is ancient history that Christiaan Barnard noted of the first recipient of a human heart that consent to this procedure was not heroic but to be expected:

> He was ready to accept it because he was at the end of the line. What else was there to say? ... For a dying man, it is not a difficult decision because he knows he is at the end. If a lion chases you to the bank of a river filled with crocodiles, you will leap into the water convinced you have a chance to swim to the other side. But you would never accept such odds if there was no lion.[9]

Likewise, Denton Cooley wrote of the first human ever to receive an implanted artificial heart: "He was a drowning man. A drowning man can't be too particular what he's going to use as a possible life preserver. It was a desperate thing and he knew it."[10]

Currently, implants are no longer experimental, and the situations of patients are no longer so "desperate." Nevertheless, it is my experience that a significant number of candidates feel they *must* have an artificial heart, and will do almost anything to gain access to one.[11] This impulse may be based solely on the irrational desire to live forever.

It is my view that any attempt to ration artificial hearts, even one so carefully drawn as the regulations under consideration, will fail to prevent significant black markets in such hearts; will encourage surgeons in the National Health Service (who consider themselves grossly underpaid) to operate in this market; and will encourage patients to attempt to bribe health officials and physicians, and to commit other crimes in an effort to obtain an artificial heart.

For these reasons—because the artificial heart is fundamentally inhuman and inhumane, because informed consent can never be obtained, and because allocation will lead to many undesirable side effects in society—I would outlaw these devices altogether. Nevertheless, since I believe this is properly a legislative decision, I would uphold regulations that at least attempt to limit their distribution.

JUSTICE URANIA, with JUSTICE THALIA and JUSTICE ERATO join, dissenting.

The Supreme Court today approves an allocation scheme that is inherently inequitable and unjust, that undermines society's view of the sacredness and equality of human life, and that makes social worth the standard for longevity in our society. The majority asserts that the allocation scheme reflects the application of rational and exact medical criteria. In fact, however, the regulations permit individual physicians to make arbitrary decisions based solely on their own views of social worth. Since physicians in general, and thoracic surgeons in particular, are likely to have a white upper-middle class male bias in this area,[12] such a classification scheme is inherently violative of the equal protection mandate of the Fifth Amendment.

I

The true character of the regulations may be seen in a recent study of the persons who were accepted and those who were rejected for places on the National Waiting List for Artificial Hearts for the year 2018 (the only full year for which statistics are available).[13] In that year more than two million persons applied for the Waiting List. Of that number, one million, or fifty percent, were rejected. Of these, more than ninety percent were rejected on the basis of criteria (b) (incapable of ten additional years of life), or criteria (c) (chronic alcoholism or drug addiction). The statistics also indicate that at least seventy percent of each of the following categories of individuals were rejected:

> I.Q. lower than 80: 98%
> History of mental illness: 80%
> Criminal record: 75%
> Indigency: 80%
> Unemployed: 70%

The generality of the statistics does not permit further breakdown into more specific income level, I.Q., or type of mental illness. Nonetheless, I submit that these figures are sufficient to warrant the conclusion that the scheme mandated by the regulations discriminates invidiously and unconstitutionally against the mentally deficient, the mentally ill, those with prior criminal records, the poor, and the unemployed. While the regulations, as written, are difficult to attack, they are clearly *not* the criteria that surgeons have actually been using to select patients. There is *no* rational connection between such invidious discrimination and the state's purpose; thus, the regulations must fail a constitutional test. Although the majority concludes that the classification established by these regulations should not be considered suspect, these figures clearly indicated not only that it should, but that it is. Accordingly, the state should be required to demonstrate a compelling interest to permit these regulations to withstand an equal protection challenge. Whether the interest in maintaining the viability of the medical care delivery system is compelling or not depends in large part on one's view of its credibility. In my view, the government has failed to demonstrate adequately that a less restrictive allocation system would lead to a total breakdown of the National Health Service. Until such evidence is forthcoming, I would rule that the compelling interest test has not been met, and therefore find the regulations constitutionally deficient.

In addition, the legislative history indicates that Congress intended that only objective medical criteria be permitted to enter the decisionmaking process. There was testimony, for example, concerning some of the initial methods used to screen patients for kidney dialysis forty years ago. One lay member of a screening committee in Seattle testified that

> *The choices were hard.... I remember voting against a young woman who was a known*

prostitute. I found I couldn't vote for her, rather than another candidate, a young wife and mother. I also voted against a young man who, until he learned he had renal failure, had been a ne'er-do-well, a real playboy. He promised to reform his character, go back to school, and so on, if only he were selected for treatment. But I felt I'd lived long enough to know that a person like that won't really do what he was promising at the time.[14]

All members of the Conference Committee found these types of social worth judgments disgusting. In their final report to Congress they quoted the following language from a study of the Seattle committee of which this woman was a member:

The descriptions of how this committee makes its decisions ... are numbing accounts of how close to the surface lie the prejudices and mindless cliches that pollute the committee's deliberations.... What is meant by "public service," a phrase so difficult to define in a pluralistic society? Were the persons who got themselves jailed in the South while working for civil rights doing a 'public service'? What about working for the Antivivisection League? Why should a Sunday-school teacher be saved rather than Madalyn Murray? The [decisions] paint a disturbing picture of the bourgeoisie, of the Seattle committee measuring persons in accordance with its own middle-class values. This rules out creative nonconformists, who rub the bourgeoisie so much the wrong way but who historically have contributed so much to the making of America. The Pacific Northwest is no place for a Henry David Thoreau with bad kidneys.[15]

The regulations are so loosely drawn, especially subsections (b) and (c), that they permit physicians to exercise completely unbridled discretion in making their choices, and permit them to make these choices not on the basis of fixed medical criteria, but on the basis of their own, sometimes warped, views of social worth. The results of the study support the conclusion that this is precisely what has been occurring. It is apparent that physicians are basing their survival estimates on such things as "cooperativeness," "rehabilitation potential," "self-esteem," "low intelligence," "impulsive, irresponsible behavior," "self-destructive wishes," "difficulty relating to authority figures," and so on. A demonstrated "connection between the favored traits severally considered and ability to survive"[16] should be demanded if such criteria are to continue in use. No such connection has been demonstrated. Accordingly, the regulations should be struck down.

II

The Agency has convinced the majority that its age limitation is reasonable, but it has not convinced me. A youth of twelve or thirteen, such as plaintiff Themis, may have a body capable of receiving the artificial heart and should not arbitrarily be denied it simply because most other children his or her age could not be fitted with the AH777. Likewise, is it reasonable to reject a seventy-one-year-old applicant with a life expectancy of twenty years, while accepting a sixty-nine-year-old with a life expectancy of ten years? Such an allocation scheme is de facto irrational. Since it could be much more fairly drawn, it cannot stand constitutional challenge. I would much prefer to have simply a first-come, first-served scheme than to set such patently arbitrary criteria. While the first-come, first-served system would also discriminate arbitrarily, such discrimination would be more in the nature of "acts of God" rather than explicit acts of government, and thus would not serve to cheapen our view of human life and the equality of man.[17]

III

Further, to characterize the artificial heart as a "luxury"—which the majority does—is playing with words. Today's luxury is tomorrow's necessity. The heroic or extraordinary treatments of the late 20th century are today commonplace in our hospitals. Artificial hearts are prolonging lives. They could prolong far more lives both now and in the future if more resources were allocated to this critical field. When, in fifteen or twenty years, all the other civilized nations of the world routinely implant such devices in their citizens, will the majority change its mind? Will artificial hearts then become "natural" or at least necessary for life? If so, why must we sacrifice the present generation for the next?

IV

The allocation scheme is a threat to our values and an insult to our intelligence. We need not be guided in our decision by the unwritten rules of sailors who prowled the sea in their sail-drawn ships almost two centuries ago. How much better to learn from the more advanced planets with whom we have recently established contact. On Zeno, for example, all are eligible for artificial organs—but must make the election by their twenty-fifth birthday and accept permanent sterility as the price. In this way, they both lengthen life and control total population size (and thus the cost of the program).[18] While I do not propose that we accept such an alternative without study or legislative mandate, I do reject the current scheme and the majority's endorsement of it.

JUSTICE THALIA, dissenting.

I join with my sister Urania in her dissent. Nonetheless, I write to argue that her analysis leads to an additional and inescapable conclusion: the regulations violate a candidate's right to due process. It is apparent that no matter what criteria are utilized, fairness is enhanced when there is more than one decisionmaker. It is inappropriate and unfair to expect a patient to dispute the findings of the examining physician to the physician herself. A procedure requiring the concurrence of two of a board of three physicians would be much fairer and presumably would lead to much more consistent and accurate decisionmaking. In addition, if the criteria specified in the regulations are to be applied, and "survivability" is defined as I believe my sister Justice Urania accurately indicates it is presently defined, then many more due process protections than currently exist are mandated by the U.S. Constitution. Contrary to the majority's view, the types of facts at issue in the screening process are extremely personal, and ones that are unique to the candidate. Due process, therefore, requires that the candidate be given a full adjudicatory hearing upon request. Davis, *Administrative Law* ¶7.03.

Additional safeguards are also necessary. The patient's life is at stake, and Congress has mandated a system that excludes social worth from consideration so that the fundamental belief of our society in the equality of human life is not destroyed. To insure that each potential patient has a fair opportunity of being included in the National Waiting List for Artificial Hearts it is essential that at the minimum he or she be permitted (1) to examine in advance all records in the hands of the decisionmaker; (2) to have an opportunity to refute their accuracy and to supplement them; (3) to have an opportunity to call and cross-examine any individual who has presented information that might disqualify the applicant from consideration; (4) to have a record of the reason for the decision; and (5) to have an opportunity to appeal the decision to an appeals board. Unless these minimal procedural safeguards are provided (and I also favor mandatory representation by counsel upon request, but it is not constitutionally required), it is my opinion that these regulations are constitutionally deficient and must be struck down.

JUSTICE EUTERPE, dissenting.

I find the arguments of my colleagues all very interesting but, with the exception of Justice Melpomene, irrelevant. Have we progressed so much in this country that we have lost sight of our purpose as a nation? The unsubstantiated communications from Zeno notwithstanding, surely no one in their right mind will argue that we can make our citizens immortal. Even if we can produce an artificial heart that will last forever, the other tissues and organs will continue to deteriorate. While reading is not currently in fashion in our society, some will recall *Gulliver's Travels* and Swift's description of the Struldbrugs, creatures who did achieve immortality, but whose minds and bodies suffered from the decay of old age nonetheless:

> At ninety they lose their teeth and hair; they have at that age no distinction of taste, but eat and drink whatever they can get, without relish or appetite. The diseases they were subject to still continue without increasing or diminishing. In talking, they forget the common appellation of things and the names of persons, even of those who are their nearest and dearest friends and relations. For the same reason, they never can amuse themselves with reading, because their memory will not serve to carry them from the beginning of a sentence to the end; and by this defect, they are deprived of the only entertainment whereof they might otherwise be capable.... They are despised and hated.... They were the most mortifying sight I ever beheld.... Besides the usual deformities in extreme old age, they acquired an additional ghastliness in proportion to their number of years, which is not to be described.

The energies of the National Health Agency should be directed toward the young and the middle-aged and toward making life more enjoyable and richer. It should not be directed toward prolonging the agony of death and the miseries of old age. If we are unwilling as a society to pay for the implantation of an artificial heart into each of our citizens who can reasonably benefit medically from it, then we should have the courage to adopt a rule which says that *no one* shall have such a device implanted. Such a rule promotes equality and fairness. It is also an attempt to allocate resources toward medical and health measures that make our lives worth living, rather than ones that prolong lives that are not worth living. I would rather deprive all of the aid of the artificial heart, as did Conrad's Lord Jim and the rest of the crew who deserted the passengers of the Patna, than to arbitrarily choose who shall live, as the first mate did in the lifeboat case summarized by the Chief Justice.

Even if one were determined to implant artificial hearts in some, surely the market system is a better allocator of 20,000 hearts a year than the administratively clumsy and arbitrary scheme envisioned in the regulations. Although ability to pay is itself somewhat of a social worth criterion, when coupled with a strong desire to have an implant and a willing physician, I believe it is a proper characteristic to use for deciding who will receive a medical device which is of dubious value to either the individual or society. It might also be appropriate to create a "distinguished citizen" award, the recipients being individuals of tremendous importance to our society whose lives should be prolonged for the good of us all without respect to their financial ability or even their desire for an implant.

Finally, I do not think it purely a coincidence that all five Justices in the majority are recipients of artificial hearts, while none of the four in the minority applied for one either before or after the regulations under question went into effect. While the decision on disqualifying oneself because of a conflict of interest or bias in a particular case is for each individual Justice, I cannot help but observe that the decision would have been unanimously decided against these regulations had these Justices taken the step of disqualifying themselves from hearing this case.

Notes

1. 21 C.F.R. 324.885 (1)-(2) (2015). The government has had similar schemes under study for more than a half century. *See, e.g.,* Dept. of Health, Education, and Welfare, Pub. No. (NIH) 74-191, The Totally Implantable Artificial Heart: A Report of the Artificial Heart Assessment Panel of the National Heart and Lung Institute (June 1973); J. Katz and A. M. Capron, *Catastrophic Diseases: Who Decides What?* 184-196 (1975); and F. Moore, *Transplant: The Give and Take of Tissue Transplantation* 107, 287 (1972). For some early thoughts on how this opinion should be written, see Annas, G. J., Allocation of Artificial Hearts in 2002: *Minerva v. National Health Agency, 3 Am. J. Law & Med.* 59 (1977).
2. Van Alstyne, The Demise of the Right-Privilege Distinction in Constitutional Law, 81 *Harv. L. Rev.* 1439, 1454-55 (1968), citing *Weiman v. Updegraff,* 344 U.S. 183, 192 (1952).
3. *See generally* Note, Developments in the Law—Equal Protection, 82 *Harv. L. Rev.* 1065 (1969). Congress exempted allocation determinations of the National Health Agency from the Americans with Disabilities Act.
4. *Cf. Ross v. Moffitt,* 417 U.S. 600 (1974) (equal protection does not require absolute equality, only freedom from unreasonable distinctions).
5. As our predecessor Oliver Wendell Holmes so aptly stated, "the law does all that is needed when it does all it can." *Buck v. Bell,* 274 U.S. 200, 208 (1927).
6. For a brilliant discussion of this concept, see Fuller, The Case of the Speluncean Explorers, 62 *Harv. L. Rev.* 616 (1949).
7. *United States v. Holmes,* 26 F. Cases 360, 367 (Cir. Ct. Pa. 1842). See also *Holmes v. N.Y. City Housing Authority,* 398 F.2d 262 (2d Cir. 1968) (the court indicated it would approve an allocation scheme in public housing based on a first-come, first-served basis with certain specified exceptions).
8. *See* Dukeminier & Sanders, Legal Problems in Allocation of Scarce Medical Resources: The Artificial Kidney, 127 *Arch. Intern. Med.* 1133, 1134 (1971).
9. C. Barnard & C. B. Pepper, *One Life* 311 (1969).
10. *Quoted in* J. Thorwald, *The Patients* 402 (1972).
11. In this regard it is my view that while a deductible of one year's income would help to measure "desire," it would not significantly reduce the number of applicants since money becomes less meaningful as the time available to spend it decreases.
12. The plaintiff, Minerva, is one of the few exceptions to this rule.
13. Glantz, Patient Selection for Artificial Hearts: The First Year, 46 *Am. J. Law & Med.* 232 (2019).
14. R. Fox & J. Swazey, *The Courage to Fail,* Chicago: U. of Chicago Press, 1974. See also R. Fox & J. Swazey, *Spare Parts,* New York: Oxford U. Press, 1992.
15. Sanders & Dukeminier, Medical Advance and Legal Lag: Hemodialysis and Kidney Transplantation, 15 *U.C.L.A. L. Rev.* 357 (1968). *And see* Annas, The Prostitute, the Playboy, and the Poet, 75 *Am. J. Public Health* 187 (1985).
16. Note, Patient Selection for Artificial and Transplanted Organs, 82 *Harv. L. Rev.* 1322, 1339 (1969).
17. *See, e.g.,* Childress, Who Shall Live When Not All Can Live? 53 *Soundings* 339, 247-53 (1970). *See generally* G. B. Shaw, *The Doctor's Dilemma* (1905).
18. Communication from Zeno II Tracker Station, NASA Classified Document 2119652 (level of classification is classified) (quoted with permission of the Director).

3.7

Fetal Cyborgs and Technomoms
on the Reproductive Frontier

Which Way to the Carnival?

Monica J. Casper

Envisioning Fetal Cyborgs and Technomoms: Some Cultural Scenes

In the popular television series *Star Trek: The Next Generation,* a particularly scary episode involves Captain Picard's capture and physical transmogrification by the Borg. The Borg, as any Trekkie knows, are an alien race of cyborgs linked via an elaborate neural network originating in their immense technological cube of a spaceship. Their mission is to incorporate organic life forms into their own hybrid system and, as they inform their human quarry, "Resistance is futile." While somewhat resembling human bipeds, the Borg are distinctive for the technologies attached to and protruding from their bodies (see p. 281). This is the fate which befalls the intrepid Captain Picard during a routine mission. When, in an act of resistance, members of the Enterprise crew (the "away team") board the Borg ship to rescue the captain, they stumble upon a sort of incubation room, where human babies are being gradually transformed into Borg. The babies lie in metal drawers and have small pieces of technology, such as brain implants, attached to their bodies. Whenever I view this episode of *Star Trek* (one of my favorites), I identify these embryonic creatures as "fetal cyBorgs" or "technofetuses."

Fetal cyborgs also inhabit Katherine Dunn's (1989) *Geek Love,* the funny, fascinating, and ultimately tragic tale of a traveling carnival family. For the strange yet oddly compelling Binewskis, the carnival represents their collective livelihood. But in order to sustain it they must continually configure themselves and each other as carnivalesque. Thus, Lillian and Al Binewski make every effort to produce "perfect" babies—perfect, that is, for the Binewski's Carnival Fabulon. The more monstrous the offspring, the more valuable they are to the family enterprise. Assisted by Al and his special recipes, Lil ingests massive quantities of teratogenic substances during her many pregnancies including drugs (cocaine, amphetamines), insecticides, arsenic, radioisotopes, and more. Sometimes the experiments are successful, often they are not.

The Binewskis clearly love all of their surviving children—Arturo the Aqua Boy (with flippers where his arms and legs should be); Siamese twin girls, Iphy and Elly; Olympia, a bald, albino, hunchbacked dwarf; a grotesquely huge and strong baby boy, aptly named Mumpo; and Chick, a "normal" looking male child with extraordinary mental powers, whose physical appearance provoked disappointment and near-abandonment until his "gift" was revealed. Each child, by virtue of her or his unique difference, has a place in the family business. Yet Lil Binewski's reproductive "failures" are also important to her and she has saved their remains after miscarrying. She displays these monstrous fetal cyborgs in glass jars in the Chute, "A Museum of Nature's Innovative Art," and their loss is keenly felt.[1]

Uranus the giant, Londy the giantess, and Simone the dwarf

What do these fictional accounts of fetal cyborgs have in common? Both *Star Trek* and *Geek Love* represent popular cultural visions of the intersections of organic bodies with technologies and technological practices in the realm of "human" reproduction. In *Star Trek,* human neonates and adults are cyborged via neural networks to create another kind of being altogether, although usually against their will. In *Geek Love,* the Binewski fetuses are cyborged via teratogenic substances to create humans with a difference, offspring who will serve a useful purpose in the family trade. Both stories describe possible visions of human/technological interfaces, now and in the future, one characterized by force and domination and the other characterized by economic and familial desires. Yet fetal cyborgs are not solely creatures of the twentieth-century popular imagination. The cultural visions of *Star Trek* and *Geek Love* also represent and (re)interpret practices of contemporary technoscience through which a multitude of cyborgs have been and are produced. The cyborg figure is indeed becoming ubiquitous in our "postmodern," "posthuman" world.

A number of people have commented on the degree to which we are now living in a "cyborg society," surrounded by other cyborgs of all shapes, colors, sizes, and technical specifications (Haraway 1985; Downey, Dumit, and Williams 1992; Gray 1995). While it is certainly the case that cyborgs, like television talk-shows hosts, seem to be popping up all over, describing this phenomenon as a cyborg society poses some limitations on analysis. If we are all cyborgs, then the analytic value of this concept in differentiating *cyborg* from other identities and subject positions becomes diminished. Further, despite a proliferation of cyborgs, there are many ways in which contemporary social actors both accept and resist the cyborg image. By suggesting that we are all cyborgs, there is a danger in losing sight of these resistances, as well as of possible differences among cyborgs.

Some useful questions in analyzing a "society of cyborgs"[2] might be: Under what conditions (social, cultural, political, economic, technical, and other) are cyborgs configured? By whom? In whose interests? For what purposes? Also, when isn't an entity not a cyborg? By whom and under what conditions does resistance to cyborgism occur? For whom and in whose interests are cyborgs "pleasurable"? For whom and in whose interests are cyborgs "dangerous"? Who or what is implicated (bodily, economically, technically) in the production of cyborgs? **In short, I am arguing that cyborgs need to be (re)situated within the conditions of their origin in order to make sense of them analytically *and* politically.** By doing so, we can begin to address some of these questions. Cyborgs in our accounts should not float in space like the fetus in the movie *2001* because they do not do so in actual practice. Our representational practices should include situated framings (Haraway 1991; Clarke and Fujimura 1992), and resistances should also be represented in our accounts.

I explore these issues through an analysis of fetal cyborgs and technomoms on what I call the reproductive frontier. More specifically, I suggest that our social, political, and technical landscapes are characterized by a proliferation of technofetuses and other fetal cyborgs, such as those envisioned in fictional accounts. Across multiple and diverse social worlds, fetuses and technologies are being combined in diverse ways by social actors to produce new and different fetal bodies and subjectivities.[3] One key difference between fiction and its milieu, however, is that "real world" accounts of fetal cyborgs have a distinct—and often urgent—political edge, particularly in the U.S. Unlike the Borg, whose offspring develop in metal drawers, but like Lil Binewski whose progeny are home-grown, most of the fetal cyborgs which I discuss here are embodied; they occupy the highly contested uterine space of a pregnant woman's body.[4] **Thus, to talk about fetal cyborgs and technofetuses is necessarily to talk about maternal cyborgs, or what I call technomoms,**[5] not all of whom are as well-served as Lil Binewski by transformations in fetal ontology and corporeality.

Below, I first discuss some heterogeneous fetal cyborgs and technomoms located at the intersections of organic bodies (fetal and female) with contemporary scientific, technological, and medical practices. I then focus more concretely on experimental fetal surgery, a set of practices in which fetuses are transformed into patients and subjects via technological intervention, with often profound consequences for the pregnant women involved.[6] Last, I return to the issues raised above and consider some theoretical "pleasures and dangers" of using cyborg approaches to conceptualize and analyze the substantive issues raised here. Fetal cyborgs may indeed be "monstrous and illegitimate," but whether they also serve as sites for "resistance and recoupling" (Haraway 1985:154)—and if so, for whom—remains to be seen.

A Carnival of Fetal Cyborgs and Technomoms

In the Museum of Science and Industry in Chicago there is an exhibit of human embryos and fetuses, pickled and floating in jars for daily public viewing by those with access to the museum. Dating from the 1930s, the fetal remains supposedly are there to teach museum-goers, many of whom are school-age children, about human development, life, and other grand topics. I remember being fascinated by this display as a child on countless field trips to the museum. Although I have not seen these pickled fetuses in over a decade, reading the description of the Chute in *Geek Love* vividly reminded me of the exhibit.

It is my memories of this exhibit, coupled with aggressive public displays of alleged fetal parts by anti-abortion zealots, the emergence of technologies for visualizing fetuses, and the increasing public displays (on billboards, bottles, and buses) warning pregnant women to avoid "anti-fetal" behaviors such as smoking and drinking, that have prompted my use of the term *carnival* here. Although this term has a significant and fertile theoretical usage in cultural studies and anthropology (see, e.g., Bakhtin, 1984/1968; Morson & Emerson, 1990; Reiss, 1988), I am using it more simply here to refer to the American carnival tradition in which the strange, the monstrous, and the grotesque, geeks and freaks alike, have been subject historically to public visual consumption. From Siamese twins to bearded ladies, this tradition has created economic and cultural capital out of human difference, as is richly conveyed in *Geek Love.*

The term carnival used in this sense captures two elements of reproductive cyborgs that are crucial for my analysis. First, many reproductive practices (re)configure pregnant women and fetuses in startling new ways that challenge pre-existing moral, technical, and ontological boundaries. The production of strange, monstrous, and grotesque fetal cyborgs and technomoms, while fascinating, serves to remind us of just how different they are and, more importantly, of what is lost or gained in the translation. Second, the carnival metaphor marks visualization as an important aspect of these practices. In the late twentieth century, pregnant women and their fetuses are visual objects, not just in terms of optically viewing them but also in the degree to which they are embedded within a range of material and discursive practices. Fetuses, uterine spaces, pregnant women's bodies, and "woman's place" are all highly contested, intently and intensely visualized, and multiply configured and reconfigured. What follows is an attempt to make some sense of the carnival of fetal cyborgs and technomoms.

A host of contemporary technological practices in both science and medicine have made possible the emergence of a plethora of fetal cyborgs and technomoms. Because of the bodily location of fetuses, maternal and fetal transformations are intersecting components of the same process of hybridization. All of these technologies (re)configure fetuses and pregnant women, transforming them from "naturalized" organic entities into something else. Yet the shape of that "something else" is contingent upon the specific technological practices involved and the social relations within which these cyborgs are produced and situated.

The technologies I discuss include fetal visualization technologies; fetal diagnostic technologies; technologies which enable a fetus to live inside a brain-dead woman's body; technologies which transform aborted fetuses into materials for scientific research and biomedical therapy; technologies which provide physiological knowledge about fetuses; and an array of fetal treatment technologies.[7] In the realm of "human" reproduction, each of these technologies represents a possible response to the question, "Mommy, where do cyborgs come from anyway?" (Clarke, 1993). The categories I use below to organize these technologies and their fetal and maternal products are porous; there is considerable traffic in fetal cyborgs and technomoms across these different practices, and multiple simultaneous transformations are common.

Technologies of "Vision"

Technologies of vision allow a fetus *in utero* to be seen by those outside of a woman's uterus; these technologies transform embodied fetuses into symbolic film images.[8] The most significant of these technologies is ultrasound, originally developed as a technique for detecting submarines during WWII (Oakley, 1984).[9] Using sound waves to take a picture of the fetus, ultrasound enables physicians to "render the once opaque womb transparent, letting the light of scientific observation fall on the shy and secretive fetus" (Harrison 1991:3). How does the technology work? A pregnant woman, having consumed massive quantities of water, lies on her back with her abdomen exposed. A technician coats her belly with a jelly-like substance (usually shockingly cold), and then runs a scanner back and forth across her abdomen. The scanner bounces sound waves off of her "insides," including the fetal being lodged in her uterus. Sometimes, in order to get a "better" picture, the newer technique of vaginal ultrasound is used, in which a phallic condom-covered wand is inserted into a woman's vagina; the wand bounces sound waves through the cervix and into the uterus.

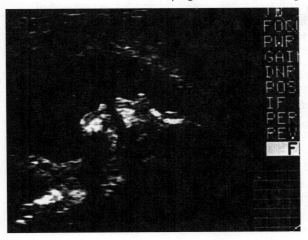

Ultrasound view at 19 weeks

Ultrasound's main use is in diagnosing fetal abnormalities which can be seen sonographically, usually structural and/or organic problems rather than genetic defects. Ultrasound is, in the U.S., a routine part of prenatal care, at least for women who have access to it. Ultrasound images are used to detect anomalies in fetal growth, to expose birth defects, to "see" how many fetuses there are, to determine gender, and to otherwise ascertain "normality" in pregnancy. It does these things by transforming an embodied fetal entity into a series of photographic images on film. Clinicians focus on these images in making treatment decisions, eschewing more "traditional" forms of fetal diagnosis involving direct physical contact with a pregnant woman's body. For example, at fetal treatment meetings at one institution where clinicians discuss problematic cases, there are no pregnant patients in the room; all eyes focus on the ultrasound images which ostensibly represent the fetus in question. The ultrasound image does not "show" the mother but rather symbolically and visually excerpts and isolates the fetus from her body. In the domain of clinical decision making, these visual fetal cyborgs replace the organic fetal beings still inside their mother's bodies in another part of the hospital or at home. The representation *becomes* the phenomenon.

The impact of visualization technologies is not limited to biomedical domains; often these images seep into public consciousness via cultural channels. For example, ultrasound provides "snapshots" of a developing fetus for a pregnant woman; in this sense it becomes a high-tech method of getting baby's first picture for the family album. Such images are also deployed by political groups intent on granting fetuses personhood in an effort to restrict abortion rights (Petchesky, 1987; Rapp, 1990). Anti-abortion groups display these images publicly, as in the propaganda film *The Silent Scream,* using their "erasure" of pregnant women to reframe the maternal-fetal relationship as one of opposition.[10] Ultrasound works in this sense because "the maternal space has, in effect, disappeared and what has emerged in its place is an environment that the fetus alone occupies" (Stabile 1992:180).

Of course, within a capitalist framework, once these images become part of the cultural landscape they may also penetrate economic domains. Taylor (1993:602) documents the use of ultrasound images in an automobile advertisement, with accompanying text asking "Is something inside telling you to buy a Volvo?" As she points out, this public exhibition of the fetus (or technofetus, in my framing) speaks to multiple interpretations about abortion, life, and so on, depending on the situation of the reader/viewer/consumer. In this sense, fetal images become part of the cultural repository from which economic actors can draw to sustain capitalism. Ironically, women who have limited access to ultrasound are also unlikely to purchase a Volvo, vehicular icon of the middle-class family.

In short, visualization technologies like ultrasound reconfigure fetuses as cyborg images, gray-scale "baby pictures" on high-resolution photographic film. These images become "immutable mobiles" (Latour, 1987) which convey fetal cyborgs across multiple domains. The "power of visual culture" (Petchesky, 1987) is indeed on display in these practices.

Technologies of "Diagnosis"

Other prenatal diagnostic technologies—amniocentesis, chorionic villus sampling, and blood tests are discussed here—also configure fetuses but in quite different ways. These technologies transform fetuses into streams of quantitative clinical data rather than visual images. In this sense, they might be conceptualized as "digitalization" technologies (Mesman, 1993).[11] Of course, as with ultrasound, access to these diagnostic technologies may be contingent on other factors such as class and race.

In amniocentesis, fluid is withdrawn from a pregnant woman's amniotic sac transabdominally using a large needle, usually during the second trimester of pregnancy. The fluid, which contains fetal cells, is then cultured and analyzed, particularly for chromosomal anomalies and neural tube defects. The newer technique of chorionic villus sampling (CVS) can be used in the first trimester, and is thus often seen as an alternative to amniocentesis. In CVS, a catheter is inserted through a woman's cervix and directly into the chorion, the outermost fetal membrane. Villi, or small hair-like projections on the surface of the membrane, are removed using a syringe, then separated from maternal tissue and cultured. Like amniocentesis, CVS is a technique for diagnosing genetic abnormalities. Significantly, both amniocentesis and CVS are invasive diagnostic technologies, and may cause a pregnant woman to miscarry her fetus. These technologies are thus implicated in issues of maternal and fetal safety and risk.

The third diagnostic technique, a simple blood test of the pregnant woman, is still experimental but could potentially avoid the risk of spontaneous abortion because there is apparently little danger to the fetus. In this technique, clinicians sift through a sample of maternal blood using cell sorters to find the small number of fetal cells that migrate through tiny fissures in the placenta. The fetal cells are then examined for genetic abnormalities using a technique called fluorescent in-situ hybridization (FISH), which marks certain chromosomes for viewing under a special microscopic light. Unlike amniocentesis and CVS, which are common but not yet routine, a diagnostic blood test could easily become an integral part of prenatal care. It would likely be less expensive (and thus more accessible to women of lower economic classes), could be done earlier in pregnancy, and may be used in conjunction with other blood tests to determine the health status of a pregnant woman and her fetus.

Just what information does prenatal diagnostic data, or digitalized fetuses as constructed by these technologies and interpreted by medical personnel, offer pregnant women? Most significantly, it tells them (or at least claims to tell them) whether or not their fetuses are genetically defective or monstrous. Yet because there are currently very few treatment options for genetic diseases, prenatal diagnosis leaves most pregnant women with only two "choices": abort or carry a potentially "defective" baby to term, often with significant clinical and social ramifications. We are, after all, a culture which values "perfect" rather than "monstrous" babies, unlike the traveling Binewskis.[12] Last, testing also discloses fetal sex/gender, prenatal diagnosis is perhaps one of the first social attributions of "female" and "male."

Prenatal diagnostic testing may also profoundly affect a pregnant woman's experience of pregnancy and of her fetus. Rothman (1986) has argued that amniocentesis transforms pregnancy into a "tentative" event, contingent on the outcome of testing. Pregnant women often do not allow themselves to define their fetuses as potential babies until they have been given a digital seal of approval. Ironically, until a fetus has been transformed into a type of fetal cyborg via prenatal diagnostic testing, it is less "real" for the pregnant woman carrying it, although this may vary by race, ethnicity, and class differences among women. As Rapp (1990:41) has pointed out, "amniocentesis and other new reproductive technologies open a Pandora's box of powerful knowledge." However, it is not only knowledge that is produced by these new technological practices; fetal cyborgs also spring out of the box when it is opened, with critical consequences.

Technologies of "Life"

With prenatal diagnostic technologies, pregnant women's experiences of their digitalized fetuses are affected because the women are living, acting subjects. In postmortem maternal ventilation (PMV) (Murphy, 1989), the women are neither. PMV uses relatively "simple" life-support technology to sustain pregnancies in brain-dead women so that their fetuses may grow to viability, at which point the fetuses are "delivered." *Pregnant cadavers* are brain-dead women whose fetuses are still alive, while *ventilated pregnant cadavers* are bodies to which ventilation must be applied in order to sustain the fetus (Murphy 1989). Unlike non-ventilated cadavers, ventilated pregnant bodies retain a fleshy skin color, are warm to the touch, and lack the stiffness of dead bodies, thus simulating the state of being "alive." They are, however, lacking in all consciousness.

What kind of fetal cyborg is created by PMV? After all, these fetuses are not trans-formed by an external technology into something else; they are still in their dead mothers' wombs, "safe" from intervention. How, then, is a PMV fetus different from a "natural" fetus? In this practice, it is the pregnant woman (or the organic part of her body that remains alive) who/which is transformed into a cyborg via elaborate life-support and/or ventilation technologies. Yet a funny thing happens on the way to the morgue: *the pregnant woman's body becomes the technology which trans-forms the fetus.* The dead pregnant woman—and thus the fetus which is part of her body—become different entities than when pregnancy began. That which sus-tains the fetal cyborg is no longer the warm touch of a living and conscious woman's womb; it is technomom and the various "technologies of life" pumping through her "dead" body. In PMV, the fetus is like an astronaut (or uteronaut?), an organic passenger inside the space capsule of a dead woman's body.[13]

Hartouni (1991) has argued that the discourse around PMV reflects the view that motherhood is a "natural" condition and a state of bodily being, rather than a deliberate social activity.[14] She suggests that only in a context in which pregnant women are reduced to "biological tissue and process"—or technomom in my fram-ing—does a headline such as "Brain-Dead Mother Has Her Baby" make sense. Discursive representations of PMV in which brain-dead women are reported to "have" babies delete "the third-party intervention, the hand that reaches into a surgically opened uterus and removes the fetus, the technology that permits the crossing of a hitherto uncrossable border" (1991:32).

The fetocentric/fetophilic practice of PMV thus blurs distinctions between the physiological event of pregnancy and women's experiences of it. As Hartouni points out, this lends credibility to the idea that being brain-dead and having a baby are not necessarily mutually exclusive states. Yet such a practice is possible only under conditions in which both fetuses *and* pregnant women are transformed into cyborgs, one vitally/virtually dead and the other alive but not yet born.

Technologies of "Death"

While PMV is (claimed to be) a technology of fetal life but in fact sustains maternal death, abortion is claimed (by some) to be a technology of fetal death but is in fact a technology of maternal life. It all depends on how we define "life," one of the most contested identities in the late twentieth century. Abortion—whether using saline solution, suction and catheter, or surgical tools—transforms a living, embodied (and sometimes impaired) fetus into a mass of tissue, cells, and possibly organs (depending on the technology used and the stage of development). For the most part, aborted fetal material is destroyed in a manner consistent with other organic biomedical waste, particularly if it is "defective" in some way.[15] Anti-abortion activists' claims and public displays notwithstanding, aborted human fetal tissue rarely ends up in Mason jars on the front lines of the U.S. abortion wars.[16] Yet under particular ethical, economic, and political conditions, abortuses (dead fetal cyborgs) are used in fetal tissue research, a fairly broad category of biomedical practices including fetal physiological research, development of fetal cell lines, tissue trans-plantation, and other basic scientific research, such as the Human Genome Project.[17]

Significantly, unlike fetuses which are transformed *by* diagnostic and other technologies, fetal cyborgs in tissue research are transformed *into* tools for research and therapy.[18] These fetal cyborgs, disembodied and "dead" but nonetheless organic, are used as therapies for diseases such as Parkinson's and Alzheimer's, in which fetal cells are directly transplanted into patients' brains (Kopin, 1993) and in fetus-to-fetus transplantation for genetic and other defects (Zanjani, 1993). They are also used as research tools in the establishment of fetal cell lines to study differentiation and growth, in the replication of viruses for developing and testing vaccines, and in screening pharmaceutical agents to determine whether or not they create "monsters" (see, e.g. Redmond 1991).

Fetal tissue is an ideal research material because fetuses have a limited immune system, grow rapidly, and are extremely biologically plastic—all of which enable fetal tissue to be integrated physiologically into another organism with little or no adverse response from the host. Fetal tissue is also unlikely to be contaminated or pathological, and it can be preserved and then reanimated, as in cryopreservation where it is frozen and subsequently revived. For these reasons, fetal tissue is like Play-Doh™ for many scientists, easily manipulated and shaped into all sorts of baroque cyborganic configurations.

Most fetal tissue originates in abortion practices, which are highly contested in the U.S. at this historical moment. Because of this fetal tissue is seen as tainted, both politically and ethically. Scientists thus work very hard at attempts to distinguish their research from the political domain. Their strategies have included, for example, investigating the use of alternatives to "fetal cyborgs" in tissue research such as using tissue from spontaneous abortions and ectopic pregnancies (both "natural" events), using yolk sac or placental tissue, and developing fetal cell lines using biotechnologies. Many scientists also advocate xenogenic transplantation, or the use of animal fetal cyborgs, to avoid the political and ethical problems of human research.[19] In short, although dead fetal cyborgs are standard material in fetal tissue research and transplantation, their production has been constrained and their use is hotly contested because of their direct relationship to abortion practices.

Technologies of "Pain"

Fetuses (both "human" and "non-human") are transformed also through basic biomedical research geared toward understanding fetal physiology. One example is research focused on fetal wound healing mechanisms, originally related to how fetuses heal without scars following prenatal surgery (Adzick & Longaker, 1992). Adult wound healing is generally understood as a series of specific events, including wounding, inflammation, cell proliferation, and formation of fibrous tissue. Fetal wound healing occurs without inflammation or the formation of such tissue and is thus more akin to *regeneration* than to the scarring process in adults. Indeed, the younger a fetus is at the time of surgery, for example, the more likely it is to regenerate and to be born without post-surgical scars. As one fetal surgeon remarked, "the only way we could find the incisions on some of these babies was because the stitches were still in place."

As with much fetal research, political and ethical constraints on practice have led scientists to investigate two major alternatives to experimenting on human fetuses outside of fetal surgery, both of which vividly illustrate constructions of fetal cyborgs: animal models and in vitro models. In addition to human fetuses, fetal wound healing research has been carried out on chick embryos, opossums, guinea pigs, mice, rats, rabbits, sheep, and non-human primates (Adzick, 1992; Krummel & Longaker, 1991). Despite a short gestation, the rabbit is the most widely used animal model, while non-human primates are considered the most rigorous in terms of applicability to human fetuses.[20] In all animal models, wounds and lesions are simulated and examined by researchers using assay systems, wire mesh cylinders implanted under animals' skin, and other "wounding" technologies, thus physiologically transforming fetal bodies and likely causing a great deal of pain and eventual death for fetuses and the pregnant females in which they exist.

Avoiding some of these issues, *in vitro* models are used to study the effects of local biochemical factors on fetal wound healing. In this type of research, wounded tissue is surgically removed and isolated from the rest of the organism and maintained in laboratory conditions using cultural media. Scientists investigate the role of circulating cells which migrate to the wound site and are incorporated into the wound healing process. One example of the *in vitro* technique is the sheep explant model, in which pieces of fetal sheep skin are placed on gauze in culture dishes and combined with different substances. Different combinations of fetal sheep skin and growth factors are then analyzed for effects. Both models permit manipulation of fetal wound healing "in a controlled fashion," allowing scientists to "elucidate some of the individual components that participate in the phenomenal process of scarless fetal skin repair" (Burd, Longaker et al. 1992:262).

Not only are fetal cyborgs created via these practices but, unlike the other fetal cyborgs discussed, these are *scarless,* evoking the phantasma of contemporary science fiction.[21] This unique quality means, for example, that the production of fetal cyborgs at this particular site is of potential interest to actors outside of biomedical domains, such as the cosmetics industry. Here, as in areas discussed above, we see the interpenetration of science and medicine with both cultural and economic interests, lending a capital twist to notions of the "traffic" in fetal cyborgs. It also means that fetal wound healing provides scientific justification for prenatal treatment; if surgeons can repair a fetus prior to its birth, recovery is claimed to be faster and cascading disabling conditions and diseases may also be prevented.

Technologies of "Healing"

Last, an array of biomedical technologies have been used to transform fetuses into clinical patients, beginning with the administration of penicillin to pregnant women with syphilis in the 1930s. Pharmacological intervention has remained a staple in the fetal treatment arsenal since that time for problems ranging from biochemical defects to premature labor (Schulman & Evans, 1991). Other fetal therapies include nutritional supplements for fetal growth and development (Harding & Charlton, 1991); fetal blood sampling (FBS), also called percutaneous umbilical blood sampling (PUBS), for treatment of Rh incompatibility, chronic maternal/fetal hemorrhage, infections, and other problems (Moise, 1993); selective termination of a "defective" fetus, particularly when there is more than one fetus per pregnancy; the use of corticosteroids in preventing respiratory distress syndrome in premature infants and in facilitating fetal growth and development; the use of catheters and other needles to drain fluids from malformed organs, such as blocked urinary tracts (Harrison & Filly, 1991); and many other forms of fetal treatment.[22]

Potential *future* treatments currently under investigation include gene therapy *in utero,* in which genes are inserted into a living fetus in order to correct genetic deficiencies (Karson and Anderson 1991); fetus-to-fetus transplantation, in which fetal cells from a dead fetus are transplanted into a living fetus *in utero* (Crombleholme, Zanjani et al. 1991); and experimental fetal surgery for a variety of structural defects (discussed below). These future treatments also invoke ideas from contemporary science fiction. Genetic therapies are especially touted as the wave of the future given current scientific and economic investments in mapping the Human Genome. One of the selling points of the project has been the claimed downstream biomedical and clinical applications in treating diseases.

Like many of the other technologies discussed, fetal treatments require intervention not only into fetal bodies but also into maternal bodies. Accessing the fetus necessarily means somehow getting through or around a pregnant woman's body. Unlike ultrasound diagnosis, where access is gained visually, access in fetal treatment is physical, material, and corporeal. With pharmacological therapies or nutritional supplements, this may involve something as "low-tech" as a pill or intravenous access. Yet many fetal therapies require major sustained intrusion into a pregnant woman's body, ranging from catheterization to suction to surgical penetration via cesarean section. Further, in most fetal treatment cases, with the exception of Rh incompatibility and a handful of other disorders, there is *nothing* physiologically wrong with the pregnant woman. This has significant implications, I argue, for how pregnant women and their fetuses are perceived culturally and clinically.

Below I focus my analytical lens more directly on fetal surgery as a site at which both fetal and maternal cyborgs are produced via the "healing" practice of experimental fetal surgery. By discussing this particular practice in greater depth, I hope to more fully illustrate the argument I have been making about technofetuses and fetal cyborgs. I use the fetal surgery case as a springboard for a broader discussion of some theoretical issues which I have raised here, including the need to situate cyborgs within the sites and conditions of their production in order to adequately analyze them.

Experimental Fetal Surgery: Fetal Cyborg, "Human" Patient

Surgical fetal cyborgs are situated within a broader domain of heterogeneous medical cyborgs. As Gray (1995) points out in a discussion of artificial implants and organs, "a quick tour of the human body, from the head to the toes, will offer some idea of how many ways medicine can turn humans into cyborgs." Medical cyborgs are not created solely by implants and organs, however, they may also be produced through surgery and other biomedical interventions claimed necessary for healthy bodies. I add the uterus and its contents, the "final frontier" in medicine according to some of my informants, as a relatively new site of medical cyborgization.

As part of an array of medical practices which produce cyborgs, fetal surgery is also embedded within the economic and political context of the U.S. health care system. Who gets access to this practice shapes what kinds of cyborgs are produced and with what consequences. Because of the dynamics and politics of health care, moreover, investing in fetal surgery as a therapeutic option may divert resources from other clinical practices, such as routine prenatal care which is already unavailable and/or inaccessible to many women under the current system. Questions also remain about whether fetal surgery will compete with other high-tech practices such as PMV, IVF, and the like.

Despite their commonalities, cyborgs in experimental fetal surgery differ from other medical cyborgs in a fundamental way: *during surgery fetuses remain inside and attached to a pregnant woman's body.* **Thus, in fetal surgery there are two "patients" inside one body.** This, I argue, fosters the simultaneous production of both fetal cyborgs *and* maternal cyborgs, as seen in the other practices discussed thus far. Yet where the object of fetal surgery is to "heal" the fetal patient, the *only* object of maternal surgery in this practice is to access the fetus. Pregnant women become "technomoms," cyborganisms whose biomedical maintenance and management are claimed to facilitate fetal well-being.

Fetal surgery, a relatively new biomedical procedure still considered experimental, is aimed at "saving" sick fetuses who might otherwise die. Building on animal research in sheep and monkeys done in the 1960s (Adamsons, 1966; Liley, 1963), surgeons at the University of California, San Francisco, successfully performed the first open fetal surgery in 1981. They removed a 21-week old fetus from a pregnant woman's body, operated on the fetus surgically, and replaced it for subsequent delivery via cesarean section. Although the baby died four months after birth, this operation marked the beginning of more than a decade of clinical experience with fetal surgery. Since then, use of fetal surgery has expanded to include a range of structural diseases, such as congenital diaphragmatic hernia,[23] sacrococcygeal teratoma,[24] chylothorax,[25] congenital hydronephrosis,[26] congenital heart disease, cystic adenomatoid malformations,[27] and craniofacial defects. Fetal surgery has also been proposed for cardiac malformations, central nervous system disorders, and a handful of other diseases (Harrison, Golbus, and Filly 1991). In all these cases, structural defects are initially diagnosed via ultrasound, illustrating the imbricating nature of fetal practices in medicine.

In basic terms, fetal surgery involves surgically opening a pregnant woman's abdomen and uterus via cesarean section, opening and draining the amniotic sac, exposing and partially removing the fetal body part which requires surgery, operating on and then closing the fetus, replenishing the amniotic fluid, and then resealing the woman's uterus and abdomen. Throughout the procedure, the fetus is monitored via a small telemetric device placed inside its chest via one of the incisions. Both patients are anesthetized through the maternal body. A variety of fetal technologies are in place to ensure the success of the operation, which is defined in terms of fetal and maternal mortality and morbidity.[28] These include elaborate visualization and recording technologies which enable surgeons to determine fetal health status, specialized surgical technologies which allow surgeons to clinically access the fetus, and special materials such as Gortex, used for example to contain the organs of a fetus with a congenital diaphragmatic hernia.[29] In many instances, these technologies and materials remain attached to the fetal body until it is delivered, sometimes up to three months later, when it then undergoes additional postnatal treatment.

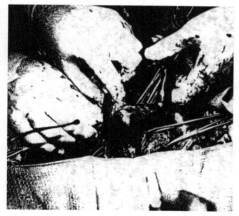

Fetal Surgery

Perhaps the most important "technology" in fetal surgery, however, is the pregnant woman, or technomom, who is referred to by surgeons as "the best heart-lung machine available." As mentioned, surgeons must penetrate a pregnant woman's body in order to access their fetal patient. This involves surgically slicing through multiple layers of skin, tissue, fat, and muscle to reach and expose the uterus, which is then held open during surgery with large metal clips. Maternal and fetal anesthetic is applied via intravenous access into the woman's vascular system. A variety of pharmacological agents to prevent pre-term labor, called tocolytics, are also used. Throughout surgery, the pregnant woman is as carefully monitored as the fetus via an arsenal of imaging and recording technologies. Thus, fetal surgery, like post-mortem maternal ventilation and other practices, transforms pregnant women into maternal cyborgs for the maintenance of technofetuses.

These practices continue in the post-surgical period, when premature labor continues as a major threat and fetuses are defined as being at particularly high risk. Because pregnant women and fetuses are so intimately linked, maternal clinical management is considered a priority in fetal surgery. The overriding goal is to ensure the survival of the fetal patient which has been so "painstakingly" repaired. Thus, pregnant women are subjected to considerable technological intervention throughout the remainder of their pregnancies. For example, immediately following surgery they may be whisked off to a Fetal Intensive Care Unit (FICU), where high-tech medical care is provided to the fetus through its mother's body. In the post-operative period and up until birth, premature labor remains the most critical problem surgeons face. The pregnant women must administer tocolytics to themselves every day through IV lines which have been semi-permanently inserted into their bodies. Technological intervention continues at birth, when cesarean section is invariably used to deliver the fetus.[30] In short, multiple technological practices both during and after surgery produce maternal cyborgs, technomoms whose health status is claimed to profoundly affect fetal outcome.

The degree to which fetuses and pregnant women are transformed into cyborgs in fetal surgery is striking. Fetuses become cyborgs through the application of various technologies, including the transformation of pregnant women into technomoms. Yet what is also distinctive about fetal surgery is the way in which fetuses are configured as *human* subjects in what is currently defined as an experimental treatment (Casper, 1994). Fetuses are continually referred to by surgeons and others in both humanist and gendered terms, as "he," "the kid," and so on. Yet the most significant way in which fetal humanity is accomplished is by configuring fetuses as distinct patients amenable to treatment. *Patient,* in this framing, becomes a subject position contingent upon certain ontological assumptions about what it means to be human.

Ironically, then, technologizing fetuses, turning them into cyborgs, may serve to make them seem more "naturally" human.
Recognizing that both a fetus and a pregnant woman must first be transformed into cyborgs *before* the fetus can be defined as an individual patient counters biomedical notions of fetuses as natural entities, nestled in the womb awaiting clinical treatment. Fetal status is relational, both socially and culturally constructed, rather than inherently given by nature. This is the case whether the person forming the relationship is a pregnant woman (Rothman, 1989; Sherwin, 1992) or a fetal surgeon. Conversely and simultaneously, pregnant women are dehumanized by being constructed as cyborgs within fetal surgery; they are construed as technical components of a fetal surgery unit and become "maternal intensive care units" rather than patients or actors. Thus, while both pregnant

women and fetuses are transformed into potent cyborg figures through surgical practices, the consequences for each may be quite different because they become very different types of cyborgs.

Resituating Cyborgs: Some Analytical Possibilities and Limitations

I have discussed an array of heterogeneous fetal practices, ranging from visualization technologies such as ultrasound to experimental fetal surgery. Throughout, I have drawn attention to the various ways in which both fetal and maternal bodies are transformed into cyborgs. On display in the carnival I have described are organic, embodied fetuses reconfigured as photographic images, as digital data, as "uteronauts" inside brain-dead technocapsules, as pliable research materials and biomedical therapies, as wounded and scarless research objects, as biomedical patients, and as "human" subjects in experimental treatments. Simultaneously, pregnant women appear in the carnival of cyborgs as technomoms, as bodies made transparent by imaging technologies, as bodies made tentatively symbolically non-pregnant by diagnostic technologies, as living dead technocapsules for fetal uteronauts, as mother lodes for fetal parts to be used in science and medicine, and as technologies of healing on behalf of fetal patients. How are we to make some sense out of this grotesque, carnivalesque display of fetal cyborgs and technomoms?

In attempting to do so, I again turn to the stories with which I began. While fetal cyborgs figure prominently in both *Star Trek* and *Geek Love,* there is a fundamental difference in how they are represented. The Borg are not interested in finding out whether organic life forms actually desire to become cyborgs; their battle cry is, after all, "resistance is futile." This particular cultural vision of cyborgism is one in which cyborgs, "personified" by the Borg, are threatening, scary, and downright mean. Yet totalization is not complete, despite the Borg credo; resistances do occur and Captain Picard is eventually rescued by his loyal crew. But the Borg remain a long-term threat to the Federation and its (mostly organic) members. In *Geek Love,* on the other hand, Lil Binewski appropriates several technologies for her own familial and economic purposes. Indeed, given her family's unique set of physiognomic characteristics in an otherwise "normal" society, continuing to configure her fetuses as carnivalesque may itself be an act of resistance.

On the reproductive frontier, fictional or otherwise, where do pregnant women and their fetuses fall along the continuum between resistance *to* cyborgism and recoupling *by* cyborgism? In other words, when do we choose to be cyborgs, when do cyborgs choose us, and when is it inappropriate to speak of choice in what is fast becoming the age of cyborgs? Let us return (figuratively speaking) to the uterine spaces of pregnant women's bodies, to fetal cyborgs. Cyborg perspectives are highly useful in pinpointing the multiple ways in which fetuses are (re)configured technologically in the late twentieth century. As Haraway (1985) has argued, cyborg are important precisely because they resist being encoded as natural. Positioning fetuses as I have in this essay allows for a critique of the social and technical relations which produce fetal and maternal cyborgs. This analytic strategy thus enables us to recognize that fetal cyborgs are, or were at one time, embodied although not necessarily natural entities. Fetal cyborgs are produced by women's bodies and, in many cases, are transformed *within* women's bodies. Thus, the cyborg image shows us that part of the process of making fetal cyborgs is turning pregnant women into technomoms, into originators and maintainers of technofetuses.

And what about these technomoms, the pregnant women in whose bodies fetal cyborgs are engendered? The new subjectivities produced via cyborg transformations are often seen as potential sites for political action (Haraway 1985). In the cyborg carnival, however, women's agency (unlike their bodies) is often *not* on display. Yet in many of the technological practices discussed above, pregnant women must exhibit some agency in using certain technologies for specific reasons. For example, many women "choose" to use prenatal diagnostic technologies to prevent babies with genetic diseases. Women also "choose" abortion technologies for a variety of reasons and often in the face of considerable resistance. And a growing number of women are "choosing" to submit their own bodies to biomedical intervention for the benefit of their fetuses, as in experimental fetal surgery or to get fetuses in the first place through infertility services.

On the other hand, brain-dead pregnant women are incapable of making any choices; for these living cadavers, resistance is not merely futile but impossible. And women from whom fetal tissue is removed and subsequently used for research and therapy have no say in how such materials will be used. This diversity of practices tells us that for pregnant women, choice is contextual, both enabled and constrained by the options and technologies available. Thus, while for some women the subject position of technomom may indeed be a site for political action, for others it may be a position of severe pain and oppression.

Stabile (1992:200) has argued that "the promise of monsters and of the cyborg should not blind us to the cyborgs being forced upon us." Although this cautionary statement is compelling, it is nonetheless important to insist on the cyborg figure. Cyborg perspectives provide an analytical lens into the making of cyborgs on the reproductive frontier and elsewhere. While cyborg positions are not necessarily sites for political action for some "subjects" (obvious cases are fetuses and dead pregnant women), it is almost certainly a political act for social and cultural analysts to identify something/someone as cyborg and thus to raise some possibilities and dangers of that positioning. For example, by focusing on a multitude of fetal cyborgs and technomoms, I have paved the way for asking: Under what conditions are pregnant women able to resist becoming cyborgs and, conversely, when are pregnant women able to derive pleasure and economic benefit in being transformed into cyborgs, like Lil Binewski? The cyborg figure as an analytical tool allows us to ask these and other critical questions by situating the actual practices and their products at the center of attention.

Yet it would be a mistake to apply this tool indiscriminately by beginning with an assumption that we are all cyborgs. To do this lessens the analytical value of the concept, as well as poses limitations on our understanding of resistance. As illustrated in the carnival of fetal cyborgs and technomoms displayed above, there are a range of positions representing different dimensions of human/technological interface. I suggest the proliferation of cyborgs might best be conceptualized as a continuum, with "choice" at one end and "no choice" at the other. As a way of avoiding the potential dichotomy this sets up, I acknowledge at the outset that most cyborgs will fall somewhere between these two options. Analytically, our task is to place cyborgs along this continuum and attempt to resituate them within their conditions of origin. This enables us to see the actual cyborg-making practices, as well as any resistances to these.

When it comes to cyborgs, and to understanding our own position(s) within a society of cyborgs, it is important to remember that despite the Borg's attempt at hegemonic political discourse, resistance is *not* futile and does occur in diverse ways at multiple sites. Like the Binewski's Carnival Fabulon, there is a place for the monstrous, the illegitimate, and the grotesque. Yet somebody needs to make sense of the carnival of cyborgs, technomoms, and other contemporary hybrids located on the reproductive frontier and other landscapes. Perhaps it is up to cyborg analysts, conditioned to seek out heterogeneous intersections of the organic and the technological, to go where no one has gone before. Which way to the carnival?

Notes

1. "The jars were Al's failures. 'And mine,' Lil would always add. She would spray the big jars and polish them. She would talk softy, all the while, to the things floating in the jars or to whoever was with her. She remembered the drug recipe Al had prescribed for her pregnancy with each one, and reminisced about the births. There were four who had been born dead: Clifford, Maple, Janus, and the First. 'We always say Arty is our firstborn but actually Janus was the first,' Lil would say as she peered into the fluid that filled up the jar, examining the small huddled figure that floated upright inside" (Dunn 1989:53).

2. The distinction between "cyborg society" and a "society of cyborgs" belongs to Joe Dumit. See Gray (1995) for a detailed discussion of these terms.

3. Some fetuses may well be conceptualized as *semi-cyborgs,* to borrow Gray's (1995) framing. Semi-cyborgs are characterized by intermittent or temporary human-machine symbiosis. "Unlike a pure cyborg where the artificial body part(s) are permanently attached, semi-cyborgs are perfect examples of the spreading cyborg society which involves the simultaneous and progressive linking and unlinking with various machines such as automobiles, computers, and telephones" (1995:8). Fetuses are excellent candidates for semi-cyborg status, as they are in transition from one stage of development to another. Because of this fluid, emergent, and transitory state, fetuses are particularly malleable, and the shape of their development is easily influenced by technological intervention. A not-yet-finalized entity is perhaps the best kind to transform.

4. Throughout this paper I use the term "embodied fetuses" to refer to fetuses located within pregnant women's bodies. I am *not* using it to describe fetal bodies themselves.

5. A quick note on the origins of this term. In fetal surgery, where most of my field work has been done, medical actors invariably refer to the pregnant women as "Mom." In their usage it becomes a technical term, but one which also represents the relationship between pregnant women and their fetuses as "natural." Yet as feminists have long argued, mother/mom is a social rather than a natural category, shaped by familial, economic, political, and cultural relations. Drawing on these perspectives, I have coined the term "technomom" to counteract the tendency in clinical and scientific practices to naturalize relationships between pregnant women and their fetuses. Plus, the first part of the term specifically points to the highly technologized ways in which pregnant women are constructed through these various practices.

6. The empirical work presented in this essay comes from my dissertation (in progress), entitled *The Making of the Unborn Patient: Gender, Work, and Science in Experimental Fetal Surgery, 1960-1993.* Methods include ethnographic fieldwork in a fetal treatment unit at a major urban medical center, interviews with key actors, observations of fetal surgery, participation in weekly staff meetings, and attendance at clinical presentations and conferences.

7. I should say a few words about technologies I will *not* discuss in this paper. In vitro fertilization (IVF), for example, aids in the production of embryos and fetuses. Although I could include IVF here as a source of fetal cyborgs, I am limiting my discussion to the post-conception period. Neonatal technology is also intriguing in that it enables "babies" to live who are the same age as some fetuses, thus blurring boundaries between what constitutes "fetus" and "baby." Indeed, rather than being a "natural" category, fetal/neonatal viability is in part constructed through technological practices. Electronic fetal monitoring (EFM), another practice which transforms fetuses into clinical data, has been analyzed by Oakley (1984) and others. I would also like to have included a discussion of "future" fetuses promised by current technologies, but do not have room to do so. For example, technofetuses appear in contemporary discourses about sexuality and reproduction in outer space (Casper & Moore, 1993). Because space flight poses serious risk to astronauts' bodies via radiation and a zero-gravity environment, pregnancy is seen as a potentially problematic experience in space. Fetal development may be adversely affected and fetuses may adapt physiologically to a technospace environment; thus a baby born in space may not be able to survive on Earth. This would not only transform astronauts' experiences of pregnancy, but may also radically alter

child-rearing practices, giving new meaning to "Dr. Spock's" advice. Future accounts of fetal cyborgs and technomoms may well include discussions of space babies.

8. Feminist analyses of ultrasound and other visualization technologies are indebted to Petchesky's (1987) groundbreaking and insightful discussion of fetal images and their cultural deployment.

9. An early obstetrical proponent of ultrasound remarked, "There is not so much difference after all between a fetus and a submarine at sea" (quoted in Oakley 1984). Other visual technologies include fetoscopy and magnetic resonance imaging (MRI). The latter is increasingly being used in pregnancy, although ultrasound remains the most widely used technology.

10. A common refrain among the anti-abortion ranks is that if pregnant women's abdomens were made of glass, there would be no abortions, attesting to the perceived power of the visual in contemporary culture (Stafford, 1991).

11. Hogle (this volume) makes a similar argument concerning the transformation of donor-cyborgs into data bases and data displays.

12. Imagine how useful Lil and Al Binewski would find prenatal screening technologies. In an ironic "fiction is stranger than truth" twist, they would likely screen *for* appropriate monsters, precisely the kind of entities that most people in the "real" world attempt to screen out.

13. A number of feminist theorists have commented on the space metaphor to describe pregnancy in which the uterus represents the space capsule and the fetus is the astronaut. In PMV, a pregnant woman's body may seem even more like a space capsule because it is dead and therefore less "human."

14. Yet this may vary depending on the woman in question. In 1993 a pregnant African-American woman was shot, allegedly while attempting to burglarize somebody's home. She died, but some attempts were made to save her first-trimester fetus. In the media coverage surrounding this event, her race, economic class, and the fetus' possible future were invariably mentioned, leading readers to wonder whether this particularly baby was "worth" saving. Such demographic "facts" rarely appear in media coverage of white, middle-class brain-dead women serving as incubators for their fetuses.

15. Defective fetal tissue is of little use in scientific research, particularly for development of fetal cell lines.

16. Yet in the contemporary U.S., fetuses do end up in the strangest places, as illustrated by the headline "S.F. Police Confiscate 5 Fetuses from Haight Street Garage Sale" (Rojas, 1994). According to the article, police took custody of five human fetuses at various developmental stages but were surprised to learn that they had no legal grounds upon which to arrest the salesman, who had hoped to get $100 for the fetuses. Apparently police took the fetuses despite the absence of a legal basis because they were afraid children might see the fetuses and become upset. This provides a striking contrast to the fetal exhibit at Chicago's Museum of Science and Industry, which is seen by many children daily. It raises the question of when it is acceptable to publicly display fetuses, under what circumstances and by/to whom?

17. For a more elaborate discussion of the material on fetal tissue research presented here, see Casper (1994). As I was writing this essay, controversy erupted over a British scientist's claim that he had successfully transplanted ovaries from aborted mouse fetuses into adult female mice. The ovaries eventually produced eggs in the adult mice. Based on this experimental work, the scientist suggested that it may be possible to transplant ovaries from fetuses to adults in humans as a solution to (female) infertility. Comments from leading ethicists, many of whom usually support fetal tissue transplantation research, ranged from "the idea is so grotesque as to be unbelievable" to "these are major mutations ... in public morality" (Kolata, 1994). Clearly, mining fetuses for the materials to make more fetuses crosses some boundary of morally acceptable reproductive practices. This controversy also calls to mind the public response to doctors' reports that they could make post-menopausal women pregnant via IVF practices. Here the boundary that was violated had to do with taken-for-granted understandings of what a mother is, and how old she should, and should *not*, be.

18. See Hogle (this volume) for a discussion of the production of cyborgs outside the confines of individual human bodies, particularly in relation to organ donation.

19. Of course, these scientists, as well as many ethicists, do not consider animal research and the use of animal body parts to be morally objectionable.

20. See Haraway (1989) and Brans & Kuehl (1988) for more explicit discussions of how non-human primates are used in scientific and biomedical research.

21. Indeed, when I mentioned the science fiction-like aspects of scarless fetuses to one of my informants, he laughingly remarked, "We like *Star Trek* here!"

22. See Harrison, Golbus, and Filly (1991) for a comprehensive discussion of the diagnosis and treatment of fetal diseases.

23. Congenital diaphragmatic hernia (CDH) is a condition in which there is a hole in the diaphragm, causing fetal organs to migrate upward into the chest and impairing lung development. Many fetuses with CDH die at birth; those who live and undergo pediatric surgery after birth generally have respiratory and

other problems for the rest of their lives. Fetal surgery for CDH is designed to repair the diaphragm *in utero* and reposition the organs in the fetal abdominal cavity, thereby making room for subsequent lung development.

24. Sacrococcygeal teratoma refers to a tumor located on both the sacrum, or the part of the vertebrae directly connected to the pelvis, and the coccyx, or the end of the spinal column.

25. Chylothorax is a condition in which there is an accumulation of milky fluid in the pleura, or the serous membrane enveloping the lungs, and lining the walls of the pleural cavity. It usually causes severe respiratory problems.

26. Hydronephrosis refers to an excess build-up of fluid in the kidneys caused by an obstruction to the flow of urine; untreated, it generally results in renal failure and death.

27. Cystic adenomatoid malformations refer to tumors in the connective tissue surrounding the urinary bladder or gallbladder. Like hydronephrosis, this condition can cause severe kidney damage and/or renal failure. According to one informant, treatment of this condition has been more successful than for any other fetal disease.

28. One fetal surgeon remarked that "we either take them out dead or put them back in alive," suggesting that there is no middle ground in determining the success of an operation. Another stated proudly, "We haven't lost a mom yet."

29. In most CDH cases there is not enough room in the fetal abdominal cavity to simply replace the organs that have migrated into the chest area. The current procedure is to replace the hernia to enable lung growth, while leaving the abdominal organs outside the fetus' body sewn inside a Gortex sac. Because of the unique regenerative properties of fetuses, the remaining time in the womb after surgery engenders the formation of additional space in the abdomen. After birth, these organs are surgically replaced inside the fetus' body.

30. Vaginal delivery has *never* been used following open fetal surgery, thus ensuring that pregnant women undergo at least two cesarean sections, sometimes within weeks of each other. The consequences for women's health may be quite grave, as a c-section is major surgery. Usually designed to take fetuses out at birth, in fetal surgery the first c-section is used to access the fetus, potentially causing significant problems related to pre-term labor.

References

Adamsons, Karliss, Jr. (1966). Fetal Surgery. *New England Journal of Medicine*, 275, 204-206.

Adzick, N. Scott (1992). Fetal Animal and Wound Implant Models. In N. Scott Adzick and Michael T. Longaker (Eds.), *Fetal Wound Healing* (pp. 71-82). New York: Elsevier Science Publishing Co.

Adzick, N. Scott and Michael T. Longaker (Eds.). (1992). *Fetal Wound Healing*. New York: Elsevier Science Publishing Co.

Bakhtin, Mikhail (1984/1968). *Rabelais and His World* (Helene Iswolsky, Trans.). Bloomington: Indiana University Press.

Brans, Yves W. and Thomas J. Kuehl (Eds.). (1988). *Nonhuman Primates in Perinatal Research*. New York: John Wiley and Sons.

Burd, D., Andrew R., Michael T. Longaker, and N. Scott Adzick (1992). In Vitro Fetal Wound Healing Models. In N. Scott Adzick and Michael T. Longaker (Eds.), *Fetal Wound Healing* (pp. 255-264). New York: Elsevier.

Casper, Monica J. (1994). At the Margins of Humanity: Fetal Positions in Science and Medicine. *Science, Technology, and Human Values*, 19(31).

Casper, Monica J. and Lisa Jean Moore (1993). Inscribing Bodies, Inscribing the Future: Sex and Reproduction in Outer Space. Paper presented at meetings of the California Sociological Association, Berkeley, CA, October 15-16.

Clarke, Adele E. (1993). Modernity, Postmodernity and Reproductive Processes, ca 1890-1990: or, `Mommy, Where Do Cyborgs Come from Anyway?'. Paper presented at the conference Between Design and Choice: Social Shaping of New Reproductive Technologies, Cornell University, Ithaca, NY.

Clarke, Adele E. and Joan H. Fujimura (1992). What Tools? Which Jobs? Why Right? In Adele E. Clarke and Joan H. Fujimura (Eds.), *The Right Tools for the Job: At Work in Twentieth-Century Life Sciences*. Princeton: Princeton University Press.

Crombleholme, Timothy M., Esmail D. Zanjani, Jacob C. Langer, and Michael R. Harrison (1991). Transplantation of Fetal Cells. In Michael R. Harrison, Mitchell S. Golbus, and Roy A. Filly (Eds.), *The Unborn Patient: Prenatal Diagnosis and Treatment* (pp. 495-507). Philadelphia: W.B. Saunders Company.

Downey, Gary Lee, Joseph Dumit, and Sarah Williams (1992). Granting Membership to the Cyborg Image. Paper presented at meetings of the American Anthropological Association, San Francisco, CA.

Dunn, Katherine (1989). *Geek Love*. New York: Warner Books.

Gray, Chris Hables (1995). Medical Cyborgs: Artificial Organs and the Quest for the Posthuman. In Chris Hables Gray (Ed.), *Technohistory: Using the History of American Technology in Interdisciplinary Research.* Melbourne, FL: Krieger Publishing, forthcoming.

Haraway, Donna (1985). A Manifesto for Cyborgs: Science, Technology, and Socialist Feminism in the 1980s. *Socialist Review,* 80, 65-107.

Haraway, Donna (1989). *Primate Visions: Gender, Race, and Nature in the World of Modern Science.* New York: Routledge.

Haraway, Donna (1991). *Simians, Cyborgs, and Women: The Reinvention of Nature.* New York: Routledge.

Harding, Jane E. and Valerie Charlton (1991). Experimental Nutritional Supplementation for Intrauterine Growth Retardation. In Michael R. Harrison, Mitchell S. Golbus, and Roy A. Filly (Eds.), *The Unborn Patient: Prenatal Diagnosis and Treatment* (pp. 598-613). Philadelphia: W.B. Saunders Company.

Harrison, Michael R. (1991). The Fetus as a Patient: Historical Perspective. In Michael R. Harrison, Mitchell S. Golbus, and Roy A. Filly (Eds.), *The Unborn Patient: Prenatal Diagnosis and Treatment* (pp. 3-7). Philadelphia: W.B. Saunders Company.

Harrison, Michael R. and Roy A. Filly (1991). The Fetus with Obstructive Uropathy: Pathophysiology, Natural History, Selection, and Treatment. In Michael R. Harrison, Mitchell S. Golbus, and Roy A. Filly (Eds.), *The Unborn Patient: Prenatal Diagnosis and Treatment* (pp. 328-402). Philadelphia: W.B. Saunders.

Harrison, Michael R., Mitchell S. Golbus, and Roy A. Filly (Eds.). (1991). *The Unborn Patient: Prenatal Diagnosis and Treatment* (2nd ed.). Philadelphia: W.B. Saunders Company.

Hartouni, Valerie (1991). Containing Women: Reproductive Discourse in the 1980s. In Constance Penley and Andrew Ross (Eds.), *Technoculture* (pp. 27-56). Minneapolis: University of Minnesota Press.

Karson, Evelyn M. and W. French Anderson (1991). Prospects for Gene Therapy. In Michael R. Harrison, Mitchell S. Golbus, and Roy A. Filly (Eds.), *The Unborn Patient: Prenatal Diagnosis and Treatment* (pp. 481-494). Philadelphia: W.B. Saunders Company.

Kolata, Gina (1994, January 6). Fetal Ovary Transplant is Envisioned. *New York Times,* A10.

Kopin, I.J. (1993). Parkinson's Disease: Past, Present, and Future. *Neuropsychopharmacology,* 9(1), 1-12.

Krummel, Thomas M. and Michael T. Longaker (1991). Fetal Wound Healing. In Michael R. Harrison, Mitchell S. Golbus, and Roy A. Filly (Eds.), *The Unborn Patient: Prenatal Diagnosis and Treatment* (pp. 526-536). Philadelphia: W.B. Saunders Company.

Latour, Bruno (1987). *Science in Action: How to Follow Scientists and Engineers Through Society.* Cambridge: Harvard University Press.

Liley, A.W. (1963). Intrauterine Transfusion of Fetus in Hemolytic Disease. *British Medical Journal,* 2, 1107-1109.

Mesman, Jessica (1993). The Digitalization of Medical Practice: Uncertainty in the Neonatal Intensive Care Unit. Paper presented at meetings of the Society for Social Studies of Science, West Lafayette, IN.

Moise, Kenneth, Jr. (1993). Percutaneous Umbilical Blood Sampling. Paper presented at the Institute of Medicine Conference on Fetal Research and Applications, Irvine, CA, June 20-22.

Morson, Gary Saul and Caryl Emerson (1990). *Mikhail Bakhtin: Creation of a Prosaics.* Stanford: Stanford University Press.

Murphy, Julien S. (1989). Should Pregnancies Be Sustained in Brain-Dead Women?: A Philosophical Discussion of Postmortem Pregnancy. In Kathryn Strother Ratcliff (Ed.), *Healing Technology: Feminist Perspectives* (pp. 135-159). Ann Arbor: University of Michigan Press.

Oakley, Ann (1984). *The Captured Womb: A History of the Medical Care of Pregnant Women.* Oxford: Basil Blackwell.

Petchesky, Rosalind Pollack (1987). Fetal Images: The Power of Visual Culture in the Politics of Reproduction. In Michelle Stanworth (Ed.), *Reproductive Technologies: Gender, Motherhood, and Medicine* (pp. 57-80). Minneapolis: University of Minnesota Press.

Rapp, Rayna (1990). Constructing Amniocentesis: Maternal and Medical Discourses. In Faye Ginsburg and Anna Lowenhaupt Tsing (Eds.), *Uncertain Terms: Negotiating Gender in American Culture* (pp. 28-42). Boston: Beacon Press.

Redmond, Eugene (1991). The Critical Need for Fetal Tissue Transplantation Research. In National Abortion Rights Action League Foundation (Eds.), *The Politics of Abortion: The Impact on Scientific Research* (pp. 13-14). Washington, DC: Bass and Howes.

Reiss, Timothy J. (1988). *The Uncertainty of Analysis: Problems in Truth, Meaning, and Culture.* Ithaca: Cornell University Press.

Rojas, Aurelio (1994, January 10). S.F. Police Confiscate 5 Fetuses from Haight Street Garage Sale. *San Francisco Chronicle,* A18.

Rothman, Barbara Katz (1986). *The Tentative Pregnancy: Prenatal Diagnosis and the Future of Motherhood.* New York: Penguin Books.

Rothman, Barbara Katz (1989). *Recreating Motherhood: Ideology and Technology in a Patriarchal Society.* New York: W.W. Norton & Company.

Schulman, Joseph D. and Mark I. Evans (1991). The Fetus with a Biochemical Defect. In Michael R. Harrison, Mitchell S. Golbus, and Roy A. Filly (Eds.), *The Unborn Patient: Prenatal Diagnosis and Treatment* (pp. 205-209). Philadelphia: W.B. Saunders.

Sherwin, Susan (1992). *No Longer Patient: Feminist Ethics and Health Care.* Philadelphia: Temple University Press.

Stabile, Carol (1992). Shooting the Mother: Fetal Photography and the Politics of Disappearance. *Camera Obscura,* 28, 179-206.

Stafford, Barbara Maria (1991). *Body Criticism: Imaging the Unseen in Enlightenment Art and Medicine.* Cambridge: MIT Press.

Taylor, Janelle Sue (1993). The Public Fetus and the Family Car: From Abortion Politics to a Volvo Advertisement. *Science as Culture,* 3(4), 601-618.

Zanjani, Esmail (1993). Transplantation of Fetal Liver Hematopoietic Stem Cells in Utero. Paper presented at the Institute of Medicine Conference on Fetal Research and Applications, Irvine, CA, June 20-22.

⌐3.8

Tales from the Cryptic

Cadaver ## Technology meets Organism in the Living

Linda F. Hogle

A 32-year-old man, in excellent health, sits at his computer and "talks" with colleagues over the Internet.[1] He logs off, hops on his bike, custom-built with the latest technology. He heads for the health club, where machines will grow his muscle mass and sense his body parameters. One could say he is an average modern-day cyborg, functioning with the help of everyday technologies. But on the freeway headed home, he is hit by a motor vehicle. Rushed to the emergency room, he is scanned, wired and tubed, sampled and fed into diagnostic equipment. Artificial materials will substitute for blood and bone, and his body will produce and be produced by medical data. He is taken to surgery, where lasers coagulate ruptured vessels, and prosthetic devices are inserted. His final stop is the intensive care unit, where he requires technology to breathe, to pump blood, to feed, to urinate. By now it is clear that his brain is no longer functioning on its own—no longer produces electrical signals large enough to be considered "activity". His brain is dead, therefore, he is dead.

Is this man more of a cyborg than before, or less? Progressively he is sustained by more mechanical and chemical devices and technologies, while the organic parts of him are destroyed, removed or substituted. But if he is no longer alive, if he is only a cadaver and no longer "human", can he be considered to be a cyborg at all? How much of the human needs to remain in order to call an entity "human?" and the integrated whole "cyborg?"

Now suppose this body is not disconnected after death is declared, rather its physiological functions are artificially supported and some of its characteristics changed and enhanced through more biomedical technologies. By employing specially developed techniques, components of the cyborg can be preserved and improved for use in other bodies (or for pharmaceuticals or for medical research). This cyborg will exist only for a limited time, and for a specific purpose: to process and store materials for other uses. A new set of actors will be involved in controlling and determining its fate. External managers will define the parameters, determine the admixture of organic and technological components, and set the pace. Is this body-chemical-mechanical machine now a different kind of cyborg—a production cyborg? Are there differing types of cyborgs, depending on their uses, proportion of human to technology, social contexts or other variables?

Situations like this force us to reexamine a core anthropological question: **how do we define and produce "humanness", and what exactly is "technological"?** Centering cyborgs as study objects allows us to explore cultural meanings and social relations around evolving life-technology forms. But cyborgs are not static; in capturing the cyborg, we have to look at how it is constituted in its various environments. Cyborg identities, I suggest, are produced simultaneously in many locales by many different agents for many different purposes (see Marcus 1992 for a discussion of identity construction which can be applied to cyborgs). Various types of machine-human composites have their own histories, contexts and purposes which must be understood in order to find utility in the concept of Cyborg.

Cyborgs as study subjects often appear as bodiless identities existing in virtual spaces, or as bodies which walk around with their technologies embedded. It is mainly in fiction where we find cyborgs which were previously living humans continuing to exist after their 'human' existance was over. The cyborg described above, on the other hand, is animate but not legally 'alive', organic but chemically preserved, a mechanical and chemical object that breathes. It is a human cadaver kept functioning ("living?") with technologies in order to process and supply human biological materials.

In order to grant cyborg membership to the living cadaver, then, a new social space must be created in which it is allowed to exist. Without cultural mechanisms to make this rather extraordinary border creature appear to be consistant with what we think are our cultural norms, it could not survive. These mechanisms, particularly the notion of "brain death", are attempts to classify and order the cyborg so we can apprehend what this entity is, what it is used for, and how it "fits" within the **human** social schema. (We have not yet been willing to overtly place it in the machine continuum.)

At the same time, these mechanisms allow us to use the cyborg as a production technology itself. The materials contained within the cadaver—organs, corneas, connective tissue, bone, skin, heart valves, cells—are used for a variety of therapeutic, research and commercial purposes. As such, they have considerable value. Enormous investments of money and effort go into creating and maintaining these entities toward this end. Therefore, there are vested interests in how cyborgic boundaries are defined and used; where they are placed, for what purpose, for whom and around which bodies.[2]

However, constructed distinctions do not necessarily function as intended in our practices around certain cyborg entities. With this particular type of cyborg, and within its social milieu, its uncertain status and conflicting cues create persistant ambiguities and challenge our cultural assumptions. As a result, the donor cyborg is differentially constructed by those who interact with it in various social and technical contexts. This is better understood by first sketching its social history.

Living Cadavers, Donor-Cyborgs, or Gifts of Life?

This is my body which is broken for you.
—Luke 19:22

Cyborg Genesis,
Alebar

In the German language, the words 'Leib' and 'Laib' sound identical. The substitution of a single culturally-recognized code changes the meaning from 'body' (including a dead one) to 'loaf', as in bread. Similarly, by using social technologies, a cadaver can be reinterpreted as a source of sustenance.

The idea of using human bodies after death is certainly not new or shocking. For centuries bodies and their parts have been used for knowledge production (anatomy labs), for symbolic purposes (as in the display of Lenin's remains), and for commercial purposes (in pharmaceuticals, sales of relics, and a plethora of other products). In each case, body materials come to be seen as existing in another state; another category from the whole person. But this state is explained differently by the various actors involved. With the donor-cyborg, these include medical research scientists pushing the boundaries of knowledge, practicing physicians who must balance needs and resources, health economists seeking alternatives to long-term care, family members of the dead who need to find a purpose in the loss, and health professionals who must attend to this patient who now requires a different sort of care. The interests and interactions of these actors tell the story of the birth of this very particular cyborg.

With the development of heart-lung bypass devices in the 1960's, patients whose bodies could not breathe or circulate blood on their own could be kept physically functioning as long as they were connected to so-called "life-assisting" equipment. This introduced a significant controversy, as many of these patients would never "recover", but could not "survive" without their machine counterparts.

Meanwhile, another cyborgic technology, organ and tissue transplantation, was being improved in parallel fashion. The need for viable tissue provided practical significance for the ability to keep human organic material oxygenated, functioning and available. The partially-live body in combination with "technology that helps life to work" (Strathern 1992, p. 60) thus had distinct advantages: it provided a materials supply source, a processing unit and storage container all in the same place. Seen as the power of biomedical technoscience to conquer the failures of nature, the transfer of materials from these otherwise no longer useable bodies was represented as the 'miracle of life' for others whose deaths could be postponed. The physical and symbolic conversion of body materials was thus construed not only as a social virtue, but as an efficient use of valuable resources. As bioethicist Joseph Fletcher (1985) put it, it is a "shameful waste of human tissue" to let bodies go to a coffin without tapping the resources within. With the social sanctioning of the concept of using bodies as sources of "spare parts" (Fox and Swazey 1992), **the donor soon became a routine cyborg**, unremarkable because of its work and role in society.

This is possible in a late-capitalist age in which commodification has reached into hithertofore unimaginable realms of life (Jameson 1984). However, it meant that ideas about the boundaries of the body as well as boundaries between human and nonhuman had to change. In order to accomplish this, new social interventions were required. The first and most important was a new definition of "death". The cessation of certain brain functions using specific diagnostic protocols is now accepted as the legal and medical category "death" in many countries. Brain death allows the suspension of time, which in turn allows cultural and bodily processes to be fragmented and reconfigured. Significantly, it allows the process to be staged by biomedical 'managers' and experts. This boundary marker was constructed to make the distinction between life and death, human and technology, natural and artificial distinct. **Instead, this medical-legal construction left us with an even more ambiguous entity; the "living cadaver".**

In attempting to reduce ambiguity, it is necessary to deconstruct the subject (the person), and reconstruct an object (the production unit). The first step is the recasting of the death experience. The patient is dead, but has not died. This must be explained in a way understandable and acceptable to both family members and professionals. One method of coping with this and allowing the body to be further used is to reorder or suspend the sequencing of events, as in the use of "decoupling": first a grave prognosis is given, then the announcement of death (brain death), then later the request for organs and tissues from the "remains"[3] These phases are independent of the timing of the actual events themselves.

Throughout the process, cultural meanings must be stripped from the person (Hogle 1992). Identity must be erased. Once brain death is declared, the term "patient" is dropped, along with the name, and the potential donor is referred to as the cause of death, the age, or simply as "the donor" (for example: "the 24-year-old drive-by shooting at XX Hospital). Reference to the body changes from 'patient' (used until permission to donate is secured) to 'donor' (used sometimes before permission is secured and up until time of procedure). As the procurement procedure nears, there may be no reference to the body or person at all, rather to the specific materials that are to be removed (the heart at XX Hospital). Descriptions of the circumstances surrounding the death or personal information about the person, significant in potential donor selection, is completely deleted (Hogle 1993).

While these processes can be called social technologies, the core technologies used to transform the cadaver into a donor cyborg are chemical and mechanical. Through these, the physical body is reprogrammed and retooled for new uses. The nature of the body right down to the cells must be changed to the extent that the conditions are incompatible with "life" for the body in which they exist, yet will artificially extend life for another body. In essence, chemical and mechanical technologies become an integral part of the human body, as well as the bridge to the new body.

The Management of Cyborgs and Good Manufacturing Practice

Turning a 'person' into a 'donor-cyborg' requires not only wiring and plumbing connections, but specific techniques to manage the integrated whole. Standardized protocols have been developed toward this end, with the goal "to produce prime, quality organs", as one informant put it. When it appears that a patient will become brain-dead, a change in medical routines occurs. Care of the patient as a whole being becomes care of biological materials contained within and the technological components that convert them into useable products. There are two parts to the process; the maintenance of the body as incubator and storage container for the human materials, and the preservation and conversion of the specific materials themselves.

It is important to note that this process can begin long before the patient is declared legally 'dead'. Ranging in time from a few hours to perhaps two or more days, the duration can be quite plastic, depending on a number of logistical, social and technical variables. These include location of end-users of the materials, resolution of legal matters and the process of procuring permission from relatives. This has major implications in terms of materials and labor costs, staffing patterns (often a 2:1 staff to patient ratio is used) and certainly stress to the family of the donor.

Converting the body to a production site

Once the brain ceases to function, the central operating system which monitors and regulates internal physical function and participates in external social functioning is lost. The body is no longer a self-regulating system. But the organic material in the rest of the body retains its ability to function; to "live". Physiological functions can be maintained for some time after the brain "dies", but this requires external control from human and technical "others". A specialized group of professionals, called procurement coordinators, is trained in techniques to maintain these functions, in addition to related functions, such as securing permission to use the organs and tissues. These technologists then not only control the process, but also participate as a part of the cyborg itself through their interactions with the various human body and the machine components.

By this point, therapeutic interventions to prevent further brain damage have been halted. Diagnostic tests and clinical measurements, however, are continued, often at an increased pace, and aim to determine specific organ function and status rather than its function within the system as a whole. To monitor the function and quality of the tissues and organs, the cadaver undergoes a plethora of diagnostic tests, including CAT scans, ECHOcardiograms, and even cardiac catheterizations, in addition to the full panel of chemistry tests, often made every two hours. The cadaver and its array of equipment may even be moved to another hospital where more high-tech equipment is available to view its interiors.

To achieve optimal preservation and condition of the materials as well as mainte-nance of the body-container calls for the employment of a varity of mechanical, chemical and social technologies. In many cases it is far more than would be used if the patient had been expected to survive. In fact, it is sometimes difficult to 'locate' the body through the forest of ventilating equipment, thermosensor warm-ers, electronic biosensors and automatic intravenous fluid pumps.

Massive amounts of fluids, blood and pharmaceutical agents are circulated through the body-machine system to keep physiological systems in balance. Cyborg mechan-ics must replace brain functions: the body can no longer regulate its temperature, fluid balance and blood pressure, heart rate and chemical balance. Chemical tech-nologies, such as colloids and crystalloids, dopamine, manitol, lasix, electrolyte prod-ucts, fibrin and other materials must be constantly administered and monitored closely (Kaufman 1986; Soifer and Gelb 1989). Depending on how far the concept of a cyborg as an inter-species entity can be carried, it must be remembered that human bodies are inhabited by other life forms; bacteria, viruses and fungi. Powerful and toxic antibiotics not commonly used in living patients are used to hold these colonizers in check. But the body, after all, is only casing at this point.

Raw materials into finished goods

While patient resuscitation protocols switch to body maintenance routines, tech-niques designed to preserve the tissue are also employed. The change in the use of the term "preservation" during the evolution of organ/tissue substitution technolo-gy is an indicator of a shift in medical practices around donor bodies. Previously, the term referred to the storage of materials after explantation and during trans-port to the end user. Now, however, preservation begins much earlier; within the body itself.

Recognizing the considerable market potential of the human materials industry, pharmaceutical and medical supply companies have developed new products and entire new industries designed specifically for use in donor cadavers. These include free-oxygen scavengers, "hibernation hormones", new perfusion and preservation fluids, and other chemicals to preserve targeted tissue cells while still in the donor body. The goals of these new products are to preserve tissue integrity before being removed, and to make the materials more "immunologically silent" to prevent problems later when they are re-placed inside another body. In essence, the human materials are being structurally, chemically and functionally transformed to make them more universal. In this way, they become not only substitutable mechanical parts, but more like off-the-shelf reagents, available for use in a variety of end-users.

But while these technologies mechanize the parts and make them more interchangeable, there are additional techniques for ensuring optimal performance. Tissue preservation protocols are increasingly geared toward specific tissue types; there are certain combinations used to target liver cells, for example, and others which selectively maintain kidney function. As the production of human organs and tissues has become routinized, parallel processes have developed to create "product-specific" handling, marketing and even accounting systems.

What is interesting about this process is that procedures used to preserve certain kinds of tissue often interfere with the function and preservation of other tissues. For example, chemicals to maintain fluid balance may affect vascular tone, which may be more damaging to heart tissue than say, kidney. This can lead to conflicts between parties who are to receive the end products for use in their patients, and territorial disputes on the precise way the donor-cyborg is to be "managed".

Cyborg production ... and reproduction

Through the processes of body conversion, the human recedes as more and more of the organic is technologized. In this altered state, is there really any difference between an artificial organ and a biological one which has been technologically altered? The kidney has been ontologically changed to become a kidney through technique. It is now in a sense more of a kidney than a "real" kidney. It will be implanted into its new container in a primed, prepped and hyped state, fully data-encoded with both old and new codes.

In this way, transplanted human body parts become the seeds that replicate new cyborgs. When the cyborg reaches its almost-total-technology state, its parts are dispersed and distributed to numerable other bodies. With the large variety and numbers of parts that can be used for replacement therapy (Kimbrell 1992), a single cyborg can easily breed dozens of new ones. In many respects this recalls the sexual linking of which Sandy Stone (1993) speaks. The gestated human material literally transcends space and time, but the exchange is not just that of data points. A human body is impregnated with new material which changes the character and arguably the identity of the bearer, the newly-created cyborg.

The Cryptic: Ambiguity and the Cyborg

You do not die all at once. Some tissues live on for minutes, even hours, giving still their little cellular shrieks, molecular echoes of the agony of the whole corpus. Here and there a spray of nerves dances on. True, the heart stops; the blood no longer courses; the electricity of the brain sputters, then shuts down.

Death is now pronounceable. But there are outposts where clusters of cells yet shine, besieged, little lights blinking in the advancing darkness. Doomed soldiers, they battle on.

—*Richard Selzer, in* Mortal Lessons

The redistributable donor cyborg is the culmination of a variety of techniques used to strip the human and the cultural away from the biological. The standardized protocols, the mechanical and chemical technologies have all been employed to this end. It would seem that the cyborg is quite literally a docile body which at the end stage, retains little of its humanness.

But in directly observing practices around this entity, it is evident that cultural meanings around the body adhere stubbornly. Interactions of humans with donor-cyborgs suggest that there is extensive ambiguity which persists. The donor-cyborg is clearly an organic-mechanic-data composite. Still, in comparison with either "living" cyborgs or cyborgs that are mostly hardware infused with human programming, the status is uncertain. The "living cadaver" creates ambiguities that disturb normal social relations around bodies and deaths of bodies.

Death in the cyborg era

The problem stems in part from the fact that humans have both biological *and* cultural bodies. The biological death event thus requires an attendant social death. In the case of brain-dead persons, this becomes problematic.

Usually, the line between life and death is clear. There is no breath or heartbeat, no response to touch, the flesh becomes cool and hard. These signals cue participants in various societies as to what to do; to prepare the body in certain ways, to gather together a "public" of relatives and friends to overtly mark the occasion, to redistribute belongings to other members of the social group. Throughout these activities the identity of the person as occupying certain roles is articulated through rituals particular to various cultures. Rituals of disaggregation serve to detach former social and cultural meanings from the physical body. Rituals of reinstallation then create a new social identity within a different social space.[4]

As deaths increasingly occur in the highly technological environment of the hospital, however, this passage point is more difficult to recognize. Body parts can die at different rates, as various technological nursemaids are enrolled to take over body functions (Muller and Koenig 1988). In the case of severely brain-injured patients, the biological body only partially dies; hair and nails continue to grow and metabolism continues until it converts to catolysis. So cues must be created: laboratory data, an electroencephalogram printout or technological devices must signal a threshold situation incompatible with continued functioning. A decision must be made to "turn off the machines", or orders given to stop medical care and sustenance. Alternatively, the decision can be to maintain the organic body and merely declare the death.

The biological person at death now no longer has a place except within a technological milieu. Traditional ways of dealing with the death experience and the dead body don't work any more. The timing and flow of activities which serve to convey a person from one domain to another are disrupted by the unique status of the brain-dead cyborg. This is true not only for family and friends who knew the person rather than the object, but for the staff who begin the conversion process of the patient into a donor. These caregivers first experienced the body as a live patient. Then they must participate in the symbolic recategorizing of the body as a brain-dead cadaver, and the physical conversion of the cadaver into a source of useable materials. Fully accustomed to working with patients in symbiotic relationships with equipment, the use of technology with cadavers stimulates different responses. Evidence for this lies in the way these workers interact with the various body and machine components of the cyborg, and in the verbal and textual representations.

Cyborg social relations

In the new, changed relations around the body, visual inspection, normally heavily relied upon in intensive care unit protocols, is eschewed in favor of data representations. In fact the entire body is usually covered with electronic warmers and/or towels, so that all that can be seen is the equipment itself with lines connected to a form on the bed. The face and genitalia are also carefully kept covered, even during various manipulations and procedures, and body parts are very gingerly, but quickly handled. By covering the markers of human-ness, the body becomes a more anonymous part of the equipment; literally faceless and genderless.

The treatment of patients as nonpersons is no surprise to those who have long observed aspects of patient care in clinical settings. Neither is the anthropomorphizing of equipment to those who have studied human-machine interactions. But the juxtaposition of the human and nonhuman parts under these special conditions clearly makes it more comfortable for participants to work with the mechanical parts than the organic parts of the cyborg.

This differential reaction can be observed when one component gets out of 'spec' (that is, outside desired parameters for operation, either through malfunction or imbalance of other components). Signalled by a shrill alarm, the person managing the system looks first to the mechanical devices to understand what's just happened, rather than to the body, even though the body is generally the site of the change (for example, the heart rhythm may change or the intubation tube may dislodge). It is also common for the body manager to talk to the equipment; "I know, hon, I know. Just hang in there for a little longer." I have never heard anyone talk to the body in this way. In fact, rarely will they look at or touch the body, other than very quickly for specific purposes, such as creating or adjusting entry/exit portals for equipment connections.

Yet if anything goes wrong, it is the body, not the equipment or the operators, which gets blamed. Take the example of a donor which was lost due to circulatory arrest:

> What happened was his potassium was normal but I said he needed bicarb. The nurse gave him 2 amps-boom, boom, right behind each other. Then he coded and we didn't know why. We found out his potassium was 2.2 so what happened was he pushed all his potassium intracellular, so he had a deficit. I'm not sure we could have ever changed things.

The coordinator describing this case was quite certain of her interpretation of events; there was no possibility that the first laboratory test was inaccurate, or that she had ordered bicarbonate inappropriately, or that some other system was failing. Another case was described by a procurement coordinator:

> He did really well at correcting his acid/base problem ... We had a PT problem and some labs were bad, but that didn't matter—it was OK. He was looking good. I said let me look at my labs. I mean, this guy was like a rock. Then I turned around, looked at the screen and there it was: (she draws a pattern with her finger in the air indicating the patient was coding).[5]

Here again, the "labs" (visual representations of "facts" about the status of the body) were "bad", but were rejected in terms of their importance to the overall function of the cyborg system. In the discussion which followed, several explanations of the "systems failure" were offered by other coordinators:

> Maybe he had an adrenic surge, or a global M.I.
> Or maybe he ruptured his septum?
> He could have been a little irritable. Could have taken some lidocaine.

When the donor is being blamed, it is always referred to as 'he' or 'she': "she peed out her brain" (i.e. cells in the brain allowed fluid to escape, creating edema and the need to quickly control fluid output), or "he crashed right before we had an O.R. time scheduled."[6]

This sort of discomfort and awkwardness around the donor-cyborg is exhibited in other ways. Physicians are often unsure of themselves and feel uncomfortable handling donors, as do the nurses who normally work with living patients. Indeed, most of the time the attending physician for the patient disappears from the scene by the time brain death is declared, often relinquishing control of the case to physicians, technicians and nurses who specialize in the procurement and transfer of human materials. But even these professionals, who work with donors on a regular basis, display unease.

Nursing staff who have just previously been working to keep the patient alive must now perform other types of duties, more akin to materials processing or equipment monitoring in a manufacturing setting. Sometimes nurses will refuse to perform duties normally expected for patients, such as washing the body. The film, *Ich Pflege Toten Patienten* (I Take Care of Dead Patients) (Stengl 1988), explores caregivers' feelings about this work, including doubts that the patient is dead, or **irreversibly** dead. While they verbally acknowledge and accept the concept of brain death, it is obvious that the constructed categories aren't so clearcut after all. This is compounded if the body has spinal reflexes. When this occurs, the arms may raise, eyes may open, or other parts move spontaneously, making the person appear alive. The definitions of animation, movement and capacity for life are blurred in these moments.

It is easy to see, then, why language usage in reference to donor-cyborgs also reflect an unsure status. Procurement coordinators often describe potential donors as "dead", "double dead" and "triple dead". This corresponds to circulatory arrest, brain death and dead-so-long-it-can't-even-be-used-for-its-tissues (i.e., 24 hours).

The term "resuscitation" is used both for therapies to restore cellular functions and to "revive" donors should their heart stop beating. This is done just as it would be for a live patient ("coding"): physicians and nurses rush to the scene, perform heart massage and/or shock and use drugs to restart the heart. The necessity to code the patient is a negative event because of potential damage to organic material, and requires a great deal of extra effort. Here again, the organic body rather than technical components are blamed. It is almost always perceived as a malfunction in the organic system, such as the heart or the electrolyte balance, rather than mechanical failure.

References to the materials themselves are also ambiguous. While everything possible has been done to remove cultural meanings from them, and turn them into off-the-shelf reagents, 'human' labels still persist. When trying to match organs from a donor to a recipient, for example, a heart will be called "generous" rather than large, and a liver "hardy" rather than functioning or in good condition. The heart always carries more symbolic content: when the time comes in the operating room to clamp the major aorta and stop the heart ("cross-clamp time"), there is a countdown to the moment, then virtually all activity comes to a standstill until the organ is removed.[7]

While the donor-cyborg is meant to be handled as a single, integrated unit, then, it appears that interactions with the mechanical-chemical components of the cyborg are less problematic than the human. Is it that the mechanical parts are considered to be more reliable, predictable and controllable? Or is it that the organic constituents retain too much of the human? And if it is too close to our conception of human, does the unease come from the violation of what we think we believe as "the Whole"? or simply that the death event has been suspended in limbo? I suggest it is in part due to the fact that the human has been decentered and redistributed within the cyborg machine. The human has been reduced through commodification and objectification, but a residual essence remains. Otherwise, the boundaries of death and life, technology and human would not be an issue.

Toward a Theory of Cyborg identities

The donor-cyborg can occupy various social spaces: it is text, container and producer of data, and a reification of the social values of altruism and the belief in a common social good. Donor-cyborgs are reproduceable, as their components are re-installed in other social bodies. They are robust enough to exist in cyberspace, transcending space and time. Yet these are unstable entities. They possess former attributes of human, body, machine, chemical, but the composite exists only under artificial conditions and within certain contexts. Attempts to control this instability are seen in the devising of new rituals such as clinical management protocols and agreed-upon definitions which script the roles of the cyborg and cyborg managers. Still, stability is elusive as we consider the equilibrium of human-organic-chemical-mechanical parts.

The challenge to cyborg studies is to learn how to capture the formation of cyborg identities, keeping in mind the equilibrium dynamics. This will push the question of how much human-ness needs to remain in order for the entity to be a cyborg and not merely a commodity.

Are brain-dead bodies only cyborgs when they are "jacked in?" Can bodies phase in and out of cyborgism depending on momentary positions in social, physical and textual space and time? Or is there an ontological change once the process is begun, which becomes a permanent part of who and what we are? If we have crossed the border already, is there movement within the cyborg realm in which we are "more" or "less" cyborgic, depending on how many fragments of the human are present? If there are varying "degrees" of cyborgism, is it reversible (whether or not we want it to be)? Can we not say there are differing conditions which create varying types of cyborgs and are they transient in character? The questions are not trivial. There are profound implications for how we treat bodies and persons for various purposes, depending on how we answer.

In Western cultural thought, at least, we cling to the idea that the body is more than organic matter and that this matter contains something that is somehow "us". A number of studies on personhood and the organ/tissue transplant recipient attest to this. There is a persistant notion that the "person" lives on in someone else. However, as Rabinow points out, in late modernism it is less the body than its fragments which have value to science, industry and the individual. In and of itself the fragmentation of the body and identity is not the problem. Where this becomes troubling, says Rabinow, is "when efforts are made to fit it into other value spheres where different narratives of responsibility and personhood are found" (Rabinow 1992).

Cyborgs are human bodies fragmented and re-configured in another sense. **If we are to study cyborgs, the technoscience that makes them possible and the phenomenon around them, we must examine our romanticism for the "Whole", our desire for the transcendant, and our notions of the human.**

Postscript

I write these thoughts from the heart of Germany, where there is much to say about romanticism, technoscience and the use of human bodies. Stories about Golems can handily be set in Prague (Piercy 1991), Hollywood-real cyborgs easily imagined in Los Angeles projected forward in time (*BladeRunner* 1982) and hard-edged, upgraded-version humans 'fit in' in the Manhattan-Boston sprawl (Gibson 1984).

But what of post-war, post-rational Germany, where the transgression of human body integrity and the idea of experimentation with 'the natural' now elicits violent opposition? This neo-romanticism regarding the condition of "nature", along with the opposition to certain types of scientific rationality, has impacted the use of human materials for a variety of purposes, as well as the way they are collected. Remembering past projects meant to extend the capabilities of select humans acts as a prophylactic to projects with familiar-looking profiles.

Still, this thread co-exists with the conservative movement away from social welfare models and towards development of technologies that will salvage an ailing economy. Within the past year, prohibitively restrictive regulations applied to biological technologies have been relaxed to allow more research to be done within German borders. Monolith corporations like Siemens and Hoechst have already invested heavily in cyborgic research and development, and bionics researchers are actively researching new materials and human cell lines.

The guilt and horror of memory mingle with the desire to re-member; to supplement bodies in a rapidly aging society, and to reconstruct an economic miracle out of revered German technology. But 'promises of monsters' means something quite different in the context of a culture which some claim has Faust as its central cultural mythos. Without explicating further the particular case of Germany, the point for cyborg studies is that if we are indeed to grant membership to this image (Downey, Dumit and Williams 1992) we must consider not only the concept that "humans and human subjectivity are as much a function of machines, their relations and their information transfers as they are machine producers and operators", but also the contexts in which these symbiotic relationships exist. Haraway's question of who gets to have what kind of body is very much a product of the historical, political and social context in which these entities are birthed.

While it may be true that many of us are living in cyborg societies, we have to remember that those are also plural societies. So what happens when cyborgs are created from members of cultures for which the seat of the soul is the eyes? When their corneas are treated and removed does the body retain its humanity? In countries like Japan, the creation of donor-cyborgs and use of their materials is completely condoned, with one exception. Until very recently removing the heart was considered to be murder, since heart standstill rather than brain function loss was accepted as the sign of death (Lock and Honde 1988). How does this difference in bounding life and death affect the use and understanding of this cyborg? Does this also mean there are 'right' and 'wrong' uses of these cyborgs across cultural or national lines?

Future cyborg studies will hopefully attend to cultural beliefs and practices, and the ways in which they are transformed and transforming. Studying cyborgs and their social relations means not only learning where and how bodies exist in relation to machines, but also what types of bodies they are, and where they are situated. As Stone (1994) has pointed out, bodies and communities constitute each other.

Notes

1. The descriptions and quotations regarding organ and tissue procurement come from ethnographic fieldwork among procurement coordinators, primarily in the U.S., but also in Germany. While I refer to these organic-technologic composites as donor-cyborgs, I recognize that the use of the term 'donor' is a political strategy by those who create and manage them. It calls to mind altruism and the "gift of life" for other bodies whose lives can be extended (or their deaths forestalled). I would also like to thank Ingo Braun for discussions which contributed to this paper.

2. Individuals and societies often invest enormous amounts of money and technology in order to place social members on different sides of cyborgic boundaries. In contrast, there are, of course, many who would pay to be able to keep the indeterminate status, as for example couples who freeze embryos for possible later implantation, or individuals who have their bodies cryopreserved in hopes that they will later be reanimated.

3. Decoupling is a term used for the deliberate separation of the notification of death from the request for donation of the materials. Organ procurement organizations have found this staging of the death and donation process very successful in "getting to yes"; i.e. receiving permission to donate.

4. For a fuller description of death rituals, taboos and the importance of the phasing of the death period, see, for example, Hertz, Bloch and Perry.

5. PT is a laboratory test which indicates bleeding/clotting time. 'Coding' means a patient's heart has stopped beating.

6. 'Crash' can refer either to rapid oxygen drop and/or electrolyte imbalance with heart arrhythmia or more commonly to circulatory arrest. The word crash is often used for equipment, like an airplane or automobile, which may have actually been the technology counterpart which brought the person into the brain-dead cyborg condition.

7. This is more than the surgical team members standing back while the heart is electrically shocked into passivity; rather, a number of ritualized markings of the event occur before the rest of the team resumes its activities.

References

Blade Runner, a film by Michael Deely and Ridley Scott, 1982.

Bloch, M. and J. Perry, *Death and the Regeneration of Life* (Cambridge: Cambridge University Press, 1982).

Downey, G., J. Dumit and S. Williams, "Granting membership to the cyborg image", Paper presented to the American Anthropological Association, San Francisco, 1992. In this volume.

Fox, Renee and Judith Swazey. *Spare Parts*. (New York, Oxford University Press, 1992).

Gibson, William, *Neuromancer* (New York: Ace, 1984).

Hertz, R., *Death and the Right Hand* (London: Cohen and West, 1960).

Hogle, Linda, "Margins of life, boundaries of the body." Paper presented to the Society for Applied

Anthropology, San Antonio, Texas, 1993.

Hogle, Linda, "Body repairs and social reparations." Unpublished manuscript, 1992.

Ich Pflege Toten Patienten (I care for dead patients), a documentary film by Dieter Stengl, 1988.

Jameson, Frederic, "Post Modernism, or the Cultural Logic of Late Capitalism," *New Left Review*, July/August 1984, 53-94.

Kaufman, H. Brain death. *Neurosurgery* 1986: 19:850-856.

Kimbrell, H. *The Human Body Shop* (New York: 1992).

Locke, M. and C. Honde, "Reaching consensus about death: heart transplants and cultural identity in Japan" in Weisz, G. (ed.) *Social Science Perspectives on Medical Ethics*, (Philadelphia: University of Pennsylvania Press, 1990).

Maschine Traume, a film by Peter Krieg (1988).

Muller, Jessica and Barbara Koenig, "On the boundaries of life and death: the definition of dying by medical residents" *Biomedicine Examined*. Margaret Lock and Deborah Gordon (eds.) (Boston: Kluwer Academic Publishers, 1988) pp. 19-57.

Piercy, Marge, *He, She and It* (New York: Knopf, 1991).

Rabinow, Paul, "Severing the ties: fragmentation and dignity in late modernity," *Knowledge and Society: The Anthropology of Science and Technology*, Vol. 9 (New York: JAI Press, 1992).

Selzer, Richard, *Mortal Lessons* (New York: Touchstone, 1987) p.136.

Sharp, Leslie, "Surgical alterations of bodies and selves: organ transplantation in the contemporary U.S.," Paper presented to the American Anthropological Association, New Orleans, 1991.

Soifer, B. and Gelb, A. The multiple organ donor: identification and management. *Annals of Internal Medicine* 1989: 110:814-823.

Stone, A.R. "Will the real body please stand up? Boundary stories about virtual culture," pp. 81-118, in Benedikt, M. (ed), *Cyberspace: First Steps* (Cambridge, Mass: MIT Press, 1992).

Strathern, Marilyn. *Reproducing the Future: Anthropology, Kinship and the New Reproductive Technologies.* (Cambridge: Cambridge University Press, 1992).

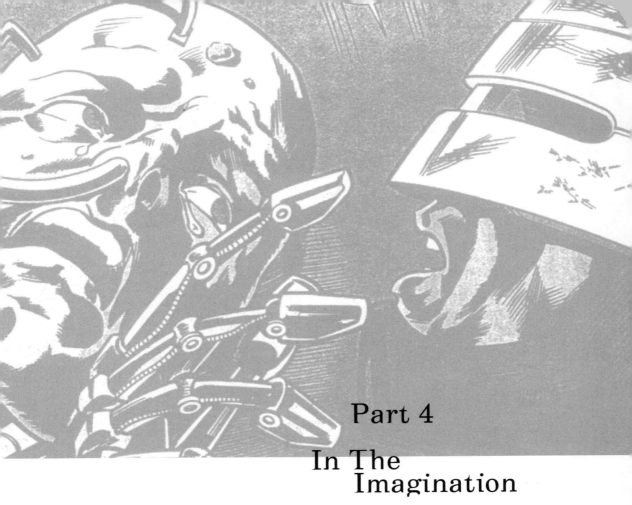

Part 4

In The Imagination

FROM CAPTAIN AMERICA TO WOLVERINE

Cyborgs in Comic Books, Alternative Images of Cybernetic Heroes and Villains

Mark Oehlert

This paper is dedicated to Jack Kirby.
One of the earliest and greatest comic book artists ever.

Current comic book cyborgs reveal much about how these characters are perceived. In addition to movies, comic books represent the most prevelant medium in which many children and adults are forming their impressions of cyborgian culture. One of the more interesting characteristics of this culture is the divisions that comic book cyborgs can be sifted into. These categories are, in order of increasing complexity, simple controller, bio-tech integrator and genetic cyborgs. Comic book cyborgs also expose some of the psychological reactions that these characters evoke in us, ranging from a deep ambivalence towards violence and killing to issues of lost humanity and, finally, to new conceptions of the nature of evil.

Golden Age to Marvel Age

Comic book cyborgs have a myriad of ancestors. The comic books that we know today can be traced to the 1930's, when Harry Donenfeld, a pulp magazine publisher, bought *New Fun Comics* from its originator, Major Wheeler-Nicholson.[1] Donenfeld's company would eventually become *DC (Detective Comics)* and would go on to publish *Superman* in 1938. To avoid an attempt at a history of the comic book, which would not only shortchange the medium but which is beyond the scope of this essay, it is sufficient to say that *Marvel,* the company that would come to dominate the comic book market, was also born during this time, the "Golden Age" of comics (1939-1950).

This "Golden Age" started at *Detective Comics* with the most well-known hero ever, *Superman.*[2] Interestingly enough, this first hero was not even from Earth but was an alien and an illegal one at that. *Detective Comics (DC)* continued to dominate the early market with their release of *Batman* in 1939.[3] This time *DC* went to the other end of the spectrum from *Superman. Batman* had no super powers and was the son of wealthy parents who were slain in a mugging. The first hero that could be classified as cyborgian[+] appeared two years later.

In 1941, with the world at war, *Marvel* (then called *Timely*) created the super-soldier *Captain America.*[4] *Captain America's* secret identity was Steve Rogers, a 98-pound weakling who was rejected for Army service until he was injected with a "super-soldier serum."[5] This hero's first villain was none other than Adolf Hitler himself. Another anti-Nazi, cyborg-like hero was the *Human Torch.*[6] The original *Torch* was an android that was created in a lab and then rebelled against his creators. The *Torch,* like most of his comic book contemporaries, immediately went to work battling the Nazis.

After World War II ended and the Cold War began, the emphasis of the heroes shifted from Germany and Japan to Russia and China. The very title of *Captain America's* comic book became "*Capt. America ... Commie Smasher.*"[7] While *Capt. America* was fighting Soviet efforts, *Marvel* created a Chinese communist villain known as the *Yellow Claw* who dabbled in magic and had created a potion to extend his life.[8] A multitude of other heroes and villains were created during this time but these examples illustrate the fairly simplistic origins and conflicts that early characters were involved in. Stories would soon become much more revealing.

Science plays a dominant role in creating both heroes and villains during this time (1961-1970) known as the "Marvel Age."[9] The *Fantastic Four* were a group of heroes who were created by accidental exposure to radiation, a central theme in many of the comics of the time. The *Hulk, Spider-Man* and *DareDevil* were all heroes created by different forms of radiation. This was a definite reflection of the public's fears concerning radiation in the aftermath of World War II. This era also saw the creation of some characters that are discussed below such as the *X-Men, Dr. Doom* and *Iron Man.* The conflicts that these heroes and villains were involved in also took on a cosmic nature. Instead of defending the United States from communism, characters were now trying to save the entire planet.

During the twenty intervening years from 1970 until 1990, comic books were awash with a multitude of super-powered characters. The *Marvel* personas ranged from the *Swamp-Thing* (a swamp creature created by toxic waste), to *Ghost Rider* (half biker/half demon) to the *Punisher* (a Vietnam vet fed up with crime.)[10] These individuals not only fought larger external battles but also began to deal with a bagful of personal problems. A shining example of this "realistic" superhero character development came in issue #128 of *Iron Man,* in which a powerful super-hero is forced to come to grips with alcoholism.[11] This maturing of heroes and their problems brings the comic timeline up to the present age, which could almost be known as the "cyborg age," considering their ubiquitous nature.

This section is intended to put to rest any lingering illusions that the comic book industry is still just a kid's game. *Wizard,* a comic industry magazine, reported that U.S. comic book sales for 1993 were over $750,000,000.[12] This same magazine received 285,000 pieces of mail from its readers during the same year.[13] *Wizard* also noted that, as of 1994, in addition to the ongoing animated shows of the *X-Men* and *Exo-Squad,* plans were in the works for a *Youngblood* series as well as a new *Spider-Man* animation.[14] *X-Men* were also the best-sellers in the toy market in 1993.[15] A new journal named *Inks* is being published by the Ohio State University Press, which is devoted to research on cartoons, comic strips, and comic books. *Wizard* lists, from 12/1/93 until 1/15/94, hundreds of shows and conventions in 32 states from Vermont to California, the sheer numbers of which indicate a thriving subculture.[16]

Marvel is the company that has the largest market and dollar share of the comic market and the *Marvel Universe* is a place replete with cyborgs.[17] There will also be several characters examined who are in *Image Comics,* a newer, smaller company but one in which almost every hero or villain is in some way a cyborg. *Detective Comics,* which is the second largest comic company, simply does not seem to have the same variety of cyborgs that are present in the others.

No doubt there are many other comics with cyborgs but the cyborgs that are covered in this paper, by most accounts, are among the most popular comic characters of the mid-1990s and therefore they make ideal subjects for analysis.

Current-Day Cyborgs

Contemporary cyborg comic characters can be grouped into three broad categories; simple controllers, bio-tech integrators and genetic cyborgs. The rationale for these divisions can be found in the work of Chris Gray, in which the levels of integration are similarly described as;

> *1) With informational interfaces including computer networks, human-computer communications, vaccinations and the technical manipulation of genetic information. 2) With simple mechanical-human relationships as with medical prosthesis, vehicle or weapon man-machine systems, and more general human-tool integration. 3) With direct machine-human connections such as the military's state-of-the-art attempts to hard-wire pilots to computers in DARPA's "pilot's associate" and the Los Alamos Lab's "pitman" exoskeleton. Plans to "download" human consciousness into a computer are part of this nexus as well.[18]*

One thing that makes grouping characters into categories difficult is that many of the heroes and villains fit into multiple divisions, so for the purposes of this analysis the cyborgs are grouped by their primary system.

The first broad category of cyborg is the simple controller group. This label is used to denote cyborgs of two smaller subsets; Implants and Suits. These cyborgs are characterized either by the simplicity of their system or its removability.

Controller

A perfect example of the simple controller/implant cyborg is a *Marvel* character known as *Wolverine.* He is a member of the mutant team, *X-Men,* but his primary cyborg system is surgically attached metal. *Wolverine* was a Canadian mercenary who underwent a series of experimental operations in order for Canada to begin creating its own team of super-heroes. His implants consist of adamantium (the fictional hardest metal in the *Marvel* universe) grafted onto his skeletal structure with some very long, very sharp adamantium claws implanted in his hands.[19] Considering his mutant abilities of super-fast (almost instantaneous) healing and super-sharp senses coupled with a beserker rage, *Wolverine* is a prime example of the newer, darker cyborgs that populate current comics. One of *Wolverine's* most infamous enemies is also a wonderful illustration of the simple controller/implant type.

Omega Red is a creation of the old Soviet Union and when he was developed he so terrified his creators that they placed him in suspended animation.[20] While *Omega Red* is a powerful villain he is also a cursed one. His cyborg structure is crafted with an artificial metal known as "carbonadium" in order to prevent his "death spore" affliction from killing him.[21] This affliction forces *Omega Red* to drain the life force from others in order to live. While he is not quite remorseful about this, it is a weakness that he would like to correct. While his infection reflects a complicated biologi-

Captain America

Iron Man

Cyber

cal problem, *Omega Red's* cyborg weapons are still fairly simple. He possesses cables that are similar to *Wolverine's* claws. These are grafted directly onto and into his nervous system and so are controlled by thoughts, a common cyborgian system. The final character in this category also governs his abilities by thought.

In the *Image* comic, *StormWatch,* the United Nations sends teams of super-powered agents to various trouble spots to act as peacekeepers. The man coordinating these many teams in various global locations is codenamed *Weatherman One.*[22] The *Weatherman* has the ability to "consider huge amounts of data and to make quick, calm decisions" helped along by "cybernetic implants which link his cerebral cortex directly to the SkyWatch computer net."[23] The *Weatherman* is a classic implant/controller who utilizes cyber-technology in concert with the data-processing and decision-making ability of the human brain. The next category are the controller/suit cyborgs, who represent the outermost layer of cyborg culture. These are cyborgs whose abilities are for the most part removable. They may possess some inherent powers but those powers are profoundly augmented by their technological additions.

The first and probably most well-known of this type is *Iron Man* who debuted in 1963 from *Marvel Comics*.[24] In Les Daniels' history of *Marvel*, he mentions that *Iron Man* is not a cyborg simply because of the exo-suit that he wears but he also has additional medical problems.[25] Daniels' recounts how *Iron Man's* armor is not just for battle but was also "created to keep his damaged heart beating" and that a microchip was implanted to correct a later problem insuring that "even without his high-tech costume, Tony Stark is a mixture of man and machine, what science fiction writers call a cyborg."[26] *Iron Man* controls his suit via his thoughts and some form of a cybernetic link. The armor has jets in the feet which allow it to fly, "repulsor beams" that shoot from the palms of the hands and servo-mechanisms which increase the wearer's strength by several orders of magnitude. The present day suit is also modular and can be fitted with several different weapons packages depending on what the immediate mission may be.[27] A testament to *Iron Man's* continuing popularity is the fact that now there is even a spinoff comic based on a character that had to fill in as *Iron Man* while Tony Stark (the regular *Iron Man*) was indisposed. This character, aptly named *War Machine*, is a younger more violent model of a controller/suit.[28] One of the most infamous villains in the comic world also

Deathlok

Sentinels

Omega Red

belongs to this category, namely *Doctor Doom*.

Victor von Doom is described as "a crazed scientific genius who hid his scarred face behind a mask" and who used his position as the "ruthless ruler of a small country ... to cloak his plans for world conquest."[29] *Doom* not only exists technologically, within his suit, but he is also a mystic, the ruler of a nation, and a psychotic bent on ruling the world. The final controller/suit in this category is also one of the newest.

Battalion is a super-hero from *Image Comics*, *StormWatch* series. The suit that he wears is referred to as a "cyber-tran suit" which amplifies his own psionic power a "hundred-fold."[30] Additionally the suit is also to be equipped with the "new, experimental tri-kevlar body armour as well as an integrated communication system."[31] This is one of the new directions that suits are taking in comics. Where once the suits of *Iron Man* and *Dr. Doom* simply multiplied their human strength or abilities or allowed them access to a man-machine weapon system, this new suit goes a step beyond. In *Battalion* there is a character whose mental facility is amplified by his suit and his greatest enemy, *Deathtrap*, is a villain whose mental power can focus and improve the performance of machines.[32] These suits then would seem to be the equivalent of mental Waldos.

Other notable controller/suit characters include *Doctor Octopus, Cyber* and *Ahab.* The next category to be discussed is the bio-tech integrator.

Bio-Tech Integrator

Compared to the controller cyborgs mentioned above, the bio-tech integrators are much more complex. Their systems can not be removed and often they are not fully explained either. They are, however, very popular cyborgs. One of the most popular is codenamed *Cable.*[33]

Cable is a character whose very existence is difficult to describe. To make a convoluted story short, *Cable* is the son of two members of the *X-Men.* As a baby, *Cable* is infected with a "techno-organic virus", and is sent into the future in hopes that a cure could be found for his disease.[34] The disease is arrested and *Cable* is left with "techno-organic but not sentient" portions of his molecular structure that can be altered at will.[35] This means that *Cable* can re-configure parts of his body to either a machine or an organic state. As a rule, some visible portion of his body is always portrayed as a machine and when asked about why he would do this, when he could look entirely human, his response is "to get where you want to go ... it never hurts to remember where you've been."[36] It is obvious that the relationship between *Cable* and his cybernetic system is a more intimate and symbiotic one than exists for the class of controller cyborgs. This is also true for another cyborg member of the bio-tech integrator class named *Weapon X.*

The term *Weapon X* is a confusing element in at least three different comic book series. In its most general term, *Weapon X* is the Canadian government's top secret program for building superheroes, unfortunately for Canada it seems that once imbued with super powers, most of their creations do not feel like working for the government anymore.[37] *Weapon X* was also *Wolverine's* original designation. The current *Weapon X* is a character named Garrison Kane.[38] The present *Weapon X's* capabilities include increased strength and the ability to actually shoot parts of his body at opponents as projectile weapons (i.e. a fist or an arm).[39] Again the cybernetic connection is made at a very basic systemic level. A controller such as *Wolverine* can not alter his cyborg system at will but an integrator like *Weapon X* certainly can.

Genetic Cyborgs

This is the third category of comic book cyborgs and one of the most interesting. Characters in this class may or may not have artificial implants but their primary power rests in a purposeful alteration of their genetic code. The issues of purposefulness and intent are critical and defining ideas for this group. It is intent that distinguishes the genetic cyborg from the comic characters that have been created by accident. These accidental individuals include such notable figures as *Superman, Spider-Man, Flash* and the *Hulk.*

The first constructed genetic cyborg was one of the comic world's most recognized heroes, *Captain America.* The *Captain* was a product of World War II and his debut, fighting against Hitler, in March of 1941, preceded Pearl Harbor.[40] In the first issue of *Captain America,* the doctor who injected skinny Steve Rodgers (*Capt. America's* alter ego) with the "super-soldier serum", declares that the serum "is rapidly building his body and his brain tissues, until his stature and intelligence increase to an amazing degree."[41] During the course of one adventure, *Captain America* was thrown into the icy waters of the North Pole, thanks to the cold and the serum he was preserved until the mid-1960s when he was discovered and revived by the super-hero team, the *Avengers.*[42] Just recently, this original genetic cyborg received the bad news that the serum was beginning to adversely affect his health and that if he continued to perform his super-hero activities, he would eventually become paralyzed.[43] While *Captain America* remains a popular character, his views on violence in comics have become antiquated and mark him as a throw-back to a different era.

Whereas *Captain America* is arguably the first genetic cyborg, the character known as *Supreme* is one of the newest. *Supreme* and *Captain America* are an interesting pair for comparison since these two radically different characters were conceived fifty-three years apart, but in their respective comic universes they were created at essentially the same time. Steve Rodgers (a.k.a. *Capt. America*) volunteered for his experiment out of his sense of patriotism but *Supreme* remembers a government that "was playing with civilian lives as usual and I was offered a position with them that I was unable to refuse."[44] During this experiment *Supreme* was given pills and he recalls his handlers "shot me full of experimental drugs, exercised me, exposed me to all sorts of radiation" until they hit upon the right mix which began to increase his strength, mass and weight.[45] When the scientists connected him to computers which "were able to accelerate what had already been started", he became a "genius ten-fold" and eventually realized that he had been "divinely selected for omnipotence ... to be a supreme being."[46] Not only is *Supreme* portrayed as much more powerful than *Captain America* but his attitude is diametrically opposed to the *Captain*'s understated style. *Supreme* has also evidenced the ability to, within a time span of nanoseconds, scan an opponent's weapon and then alter his own biological structure to provide a natural defense against that specific weapon, much like a super-powerful, consciously directed immune system.[47]

Marvel comics has always had a knack for designing characters that were bittersweet and they managed to do it again when they created a mercenary codenamed *Deadpool. Deadpool* was facing terminal cancer and had already been "on chemo twice and radiation three times" before he submitted to *Weapon X*'s (the government program) "bio-enhancing" experiments.[48] The results included increased strength and an immune system that is constantly healing him while it is, ironically, horribly scarring his body and disfiguring his face.[49] *Deadpool* also fits right in with *Weapon X*'s other projects. As soon as he is cured, he becomes a mercenary and goes freelance.

These three categories represent the most popular and populated classes of cyborgs in comics today. However, they do not encompass all of the characters that could possibly be classified as cyborgian, nor is the listing of heroes and villains in these groups anything more than a representation of entire groups of cyborgs. The current comic book world of *Marvel, Image, DC* and others is literally packed with individuals that could be classed as cyborgs.

A Cyborg's Greatest Fears or Our Fears of Them

Any current hero or villain in comics today faces a multitude of problems that the characters of yesteryear never even dreamed of. Today's super-powered individuals worry about rent, careers, stable relationships, dysfunctional childhoods and even the HIV virus. *Shadowhawk*, a character from *Image* comics, is HIV positive and his creator states that AIDS will cause his death.[50] Among the issues comic book cyborgs confront are violence, consciousness downloading, lost humanity, corporations as evil avatars and the view that obviously robotic creatures are almost entirely evil. Violence is probably the easiest problem to discuss and is certainly the most graphic.

In his classic science fiction novel, *Starship Troopers*, Robert Heinlein's main character declares that the clearly cyborgian "Mobile Infantry" has made future war and violence "as personal as a punch in the nose."[51] Comic book cyborgs are taking that violence and making it as personal as ripping your spine out. In the November 1993 issue of *Bloodstrike*, over a space of six pages, *Supreme* singlehandedly crushes a ribcage, smashes someone's arms off, crushes a hand, gouges eyes out, hits a character in the stomach with such force that his opponent's intestines fly out his back and to finish up breaks a spine.[52] While this is an extreme example of violence, committed by a cyborg against other cyborgs, it is certainly not an isolated instance.

Violence, as a cyborg issue, is a double-edged sword. One edge cuts into society's fears and desires concerning the present level of crime. These cyborg heroes are taking on the drug lords and the terrorists who are keeping us up at night worrying for our safety. Not only are they meeting them head on, but with regenerative tissue and psionically-created weapons, they are violently and graphically destroying these criminals. Instead of waiting or negotiating in a hostage situation, the character *Supreme* simply waded in and chopped them to death with his bare hands.[53] This is cyborg justice. No Miranda rights, no crowded court dockets, no criminals going free on a technicality. If you attract the attention of a cyborg hero, you can probably expect to be killed or maimed.

The opposing edge of the blade lays open our own fears concerning the cyborgs themselves. Are these images of our post-modern Frankenstein monsters? If these cyborgs are so powerful, then how do we, as normal (?) homo sapiens, stand a chance if they ever turn on us? In comic books creatures have been created that are beyond the control of anyone. The fictional *Weapon X* program is a prime example. The very ambiguity with which many of the cyborg heroes and villains are portrayed, good guys become bad guys and vice versa, is indicative of our unease with these creations. The violence depicted on the pages of these comic books may be perceived as warnings as to what might happen if we pursue this line of technology. *Wolverine*, once said, "I can't be one hundred percent sure he's lying, but I have to be one hundred percent sure because if I kill him, then he's one hundred percent dead."[54] In the March 1994 issue of *Captain America*, there was a scene involving *Captain America* in civilian clothes intervening in a child's theft of comic books from a local store. *Captain America* looks at the comics and then asks the store owner if he reads them:

> **Store owner:** *"Of course I do! I love super-heroes ... they're at the cutting edge of the counter-culture! I wish I knew some personally! I'd have the Punisher break this punk's hands or I'd have Wolverine carve the word 'thief' on his forehead!"*

> **Capt. America:** *"Those heroes are your favorites?"*

Store owner: *"Yep, the more violent they are the better I like them! The better they sell too!"*[55]

This is an issue that clearly separates this very cyborgian comic era, from previous epochs.

Lost Humanity

In his article on cyborg soldiers, Chris Gray notes that while current military thought is "moving towards a more subtle man-machine integration", the vision is still one of "machine-like endurance with a redefined human intellect subordinated to the overall weapons system."[56] While this reflects current military thinking, it is not reflective of the man-machine control issues in comic books.

The hero or villain of today's cyborg comic book is likely to be in control of his weapon system to a greater degree than ever before. A prime example of this would be the character *Supreme*. Here is a genetic cyborg who exercises control over his system at a cellular level.[57] In their article on knowledge-based pilot aids, Cross, Bahnij and Norman, approach the issue of control from the aspect of human capabilities. Specifically they state that "Humans have finite capabilities. They are limited by the amount of information they can process and the amount of time required to process that information."[58] Here they seem to be arguing for a preponderance of machine control in a man-machine system because of a lack of human attention span. Cyborgs in comic books seem to be unfettered by this problem and the reason is fairly clear, these characters are participating in Old West shootouts with post-modern weapons. They are not attempting to place a five-hundred-pound bomb on a particular building in a large city while avoiding collateral civilian damage, they are up close and personal.

There also is some disparity between this article and the comic book world in terms of which human capabilities are the lowest limiting factors in a man-machine system. Bahnji, Cross and Norman make it clear that they feel the limit is on "CA ... cognitive attention." They go on to break down "CA" into "CAs= the cognitive attention required for task accomplishment at the skill-based level, CAr= the cognitive attention required for task accomplishment at the rule-based level and CAk= the cognitive attention required for task-accomplishment at the knowledge-based level."[59] Comic book cyborgs are not constrained here because their cyborg system allows them to make a quantum jump forward in skill, their rules are extremely simplified (stop your target before they stop you) and all the knowledge they need is the location of their opponent. As opposed to pilots of fighter aircraft who require a great deal of their attention to be focused on the operation of their system, cyborgs whose systems are managed intuitively require little of their attention to be diverted from the actual combat. The issue of humanity with comic book cyborgs then is not if the machine will take over the human side of the equation but what will the human half choose to do with his new abilities.

The concept of looking and acting like a man and Moravec's more advanced idea of downloading consciousness have both been dealt with in the world of the comic book cyborg. The issue of how much machinery a person must integrate before he becomes a machine however, has not drawn nearly as much attention as the consciousness issue has. Perhaps the best example of this is a character named the *Vision*.

A *Marvel* comic describes the *Vision* as "a unique form of android known as a syn-thezoid, who is both composed of mechanical parts and an unknown material that mimics the properties and functions of human tissue and bone but is far stronger and durable."[60] The *Vision* has a long and interesting cybernetic history. He was created by another robot, a villain known as *Ultron*, who originally used him to attack the heroic *Avengers*.[61] The *Vision's* consciousness was based on "encephalograms from the brain of *Wonder Man* who was then believed to be dead ... in later years the *Vision* and *Wonder Man* came to regard themselves as 'brothers' of a sort."[62] If all this was not enough, the history of this android becomes even more complicated. Over time the *Vision* managed to develop human emotions and he even married a fellow super-heroine known as the *Scarlet Witch*, which in the comic world "evoked the unreasoning hatred of bigots who would not accept the *Vision's* claim to be human."[63] Once, due to damage sustained in a battle, he was connected to a giant computer and through this connection came to believe that the way to save humanity was for him "to take absolute control of the planet through linking himself to all the world's computers."[64] Finally, the *Vision* had this connection severed, returned to normal (a hero), was abducted by the government who now feared him, was disassembled, his programming erased (killed?), was rescued by his friends, was reassembled but lost his capacity for emotions, was divorced and is now a reservist for the *Avengers*.[65] From his marriage on there were arguments over whether or not the *Vision* was alive, what relation he had to *Wonder Man* since they shared brain patterns and whether or not he could be trusted. This would be an interesting point to bring up to Moravec. If consciousness could be downloaded and "backup copies" could truly be made, what would happen if a couple of you were in existence at the same time?[66] The question of the *Vision's* loyalty and the fact that he was created by the evil robot, *Ultron*, brings up the issue of the nature of robots and androids in the comic world.[††]

Evil, Inc.

The great evils in the comic world are the multi-national corporations. In their article on the growth of new cyborgian political entities, Gray and Mentor assert that "the age of the hegemony of the nation state is ending."[67] They go on to speak of nation states being "drained of sovereignty by multinational corporations on one side and nongovernmental organizations and international subcultures sustained by world-wide mass telecommunications on the other."[68] This is exactly the situation that has come to pass in comics, especially in the world of *Image* comics. In one particular comic, aptly name *CyberForce*, the great evil is a corporation, again with the appropriate name of *CyberData*. This scenario has *CyberData* implanting its *S.H.O.C.* (Special Hazardous Operations Cyborgs) troops with a micro-circuit implant that forces the recipient's personality into more and more aggressive and lethal pathways.[69] The idea behind the super-hero team is that a doctor, employed by *CyberData*, uncovers its scheme and develops a method for removing the chips. He is promptly killed but by then the team is formed and they still possess the removal method.[70]

Two other teams that were formed by corporate interests were *YoungBlood* and *Heavy Mettle*. These two groups are both genetically engineered humans who are employed by a corporation known as G.A.T.E. International and who are contracted to the government.[71] Gray, in his article on war cyborgs, asserts that "the very possibility of cyborgs is predicated on militarized high technology". While this continues to be true in comic books it is not the government that is in control of this technology.[72] While most of these super-powered teams seem to work for the good of society, there is always the possibility, indeed the implicit danger, that a member or an entire team may go renegade.

The arms race is also clearly present in this new generation of comic books. The twist is that this time the arms are people. In *StormWatch* the race is for "seedlings", children who may have been genetically altered by the close passing of a strange comet.[73] This type of race is in line with the prediction by Gray and Mentor that "the body politic of the future will be those cyborg industries which meld great skill at information processing and personnel management into tremendous profits and powers" as well as their observation that "cyborgs are also the children of war and there is a real chance that the dominant cyborg body politics of the future will be military information societies much like the U.S."[74] It seems that the comic book vision of the future has that dominant body politic resting within the corporate veil.

These issues of violence, downloading, and evil corporations are just a few of the myriad of problems being discussed in cyborg-oriented comics.[†††]

Concluding Thoughts

> The poet's eye, in a fine frenzy rolling,
> Doth glance from heaven to earth, from
>   earth to heaven;
> And, as imagination bodies forth
> The forms of things unknown, the poet's
>   pen
> Turns them to shapes, and gives to airy
>   nothing
> A local habitation and a name.[75]

In Shakespeare's time it was the poet who gave wings to visions of the future, later writers such as Verne and Wells took up the burden. More recently, Asimov, Pohl, Clarke and Card have all provided us with their unique interpretations of what the future will look like. Today, science fiction writers still provide a large part of future scenarios but they are also being helped along to a growing extent by comic book artists and writers.

Where those future visions include cyborgs, comic books have seized them tightly. On those multi-colored pages of what were once considered kid's toys are some of the most graphic and vivid images of what cyborgs might look like. Not only are their potential shapes explored but their potential uses as well. The popularity of comic book cyborgs also attests to the growing acceptance and interest in the possibility of such creations. If a search is on for a medium in which cyborgian futures are being explored with great vision and energy, a researcher need look no further than the local comic book store.

Notes

[†]For the purpose of this paper a key factor in determining whether or not a hero or villain is a cyborg will be based on design. Changed humans who were created by accident, i.e., *Daredevil*, *Spider-Man*, will not be considered cyborgs, they are more properly mutants.

[††]If cyborgs in comics seem ambiguous in nature, more overtly robotic creatures do not. A quick look at the

most obviously robotic characters such as *Vision, Ultron, Sinsear, Nimrod* and the *Sentinels,* reveals that all at one time were villians and that all but the *Vision* are still considered evil. The question seems to be why do comics regard the creatures that humans should be able to control to the greatest extent, as the creations most likely to run amok? These villians are constantly creating more evil robots and *Ultron's* plans have grown to include his intention of obliterating not just humanity, but all plants and animals—all organic life on Earth. Since the focus here is on cyborgs, suffice it to say that the robotic position is at least as interesting as that of cyborgs.

†††Some other problems include:

Anti-mutant Hysteria: Glance at any of the pages of comic books involving mutants, particularly in the *Marvel* universe, and examples will be found of sinister-sounding mutant registration programs, and grass-roots bigotry against mutants, also known as "homo superior."

Gender/Race/Handicaps: A multitude. The leader of the *Avengers,* one of the oldest super-hero teams, is a woman, the current *Captain Marvel* is a black woman and there are also blind, paraplegic heroes as well as HIV-positive characters and characters fighting cancer.

Comic books also dive into cyberspace, virtual reality addicts, multiple uses of holographic technology and artificial intelligence racing out of control.

1. Les Daniels, *MARVEL.* (New York: Harry N. Abrams Inc., 1991) 17.

2. Robert M. Overstreet, *The Overstreet Comics and Cards Price Guide* (New York: Avon Books, 1993) p. 48.

3. Ibid., p. 49.

4. Les Daniels, op. cit., p. 39.

5. Ibid., p. 39.

6. Ibid., p. 31.

7. Ibid., p. 71.

8. Ibid., p. 80.

9. Ibid., p. 83.

10. Ibid., p.163.

11. Robert M. Overstreet, op. cit., p. 206.

12. Jon Warren, "1993: The Year in Review," *Wizard* January 1994: p. 217.

13. Gareb S. Shamus, "Forward Thinking," *Wizard* January 1994: p. 12.

14. Barry Layne, "The Hollywood Beat," *Wizard* January 1994: p. 153.

15. "From the Best of 1993," *Wizard* January 1994: p. 189.

16. "Shows and Conventions," *Wizard* January 1994: p. 291.

17. Jon Warren, op. cit., p.221.

18. Chris Gray, "Cyborg Citizen: A Genealogy of Cybernetic Organisms in the Americas," Research Proposal for the Caltech Mellon Postdoctoral Fellowship: p. 2.

19. Les Daniels, op. cit., p. 191.

20. Fabian Nicieza, *CABLE,* Vol.1–No.9 (March 1994): p. 7.

21. Fabian Nicieza, *CABLE,* Vol.1–No.10 (April 1994): p. 1.

22. Jim Lee, *STORMWATCH SOURCEBOOK,* Vol.1–No.1 (1994): p. 1.

23. Ibid., p. 1.

24. Les Daniels, op. cit., p. 101.

25. Les Daniels, op. cit., p. 101.

26. Les Daniels, op. cit., p. 101.

27. Ken Kaminski, *IRON MAN,* Vol.1–No.300 (January 1994): n. page.

28. Scott Benson, *WAR MACHINE,* Vol.1–No.1 (April 1994): p. 1.

29. Les Daniels, op. cit., p. 88.

30. Brandon Choi and Jim Lee, *STORMWATCH,* Vol.1–No.0 (August 1993): p. 20.

31. Ibid., p. 20.

32. Jim Lee, et al., *STORMWATCH SOURCEBOOK,* Vol.1–No.1 (January 1994): p. 27.

33. Matt Ashland, Owner, Matt's Cavalcade of Comics, Cards and Collectibles, Corvallis, OR, personal interview, February 1, 1994.

34. Fabian Nicieza, *CABLE,* Vol.1–No.8 (February 1994): p. 15.

35. Fabian Nicieza, *CABLE*, Vol.1—No.9 (March 1994): p. 14.

36. Ibid., p. 15.

37. John Byrne, *ALPHA FLIGHT*, Vol.1—No.1 (August 1983): n. page.

38. Rob Liefeld, *X-FORCE*, Vol.1—No.10 (1992): n. page.

39. Joe Madureira and Fabian Nicieza, *DEADPOOL: THE CIRCLE CHASE*, Vol.1—No.4 (December 1993): n. page.

40. Les Daniels, op. cit., p. 37.

41. Les Daniels, op. cit., p. 38.

42. Peter Sanderson, *AVENGERS LOG*, Vol.1—No.1 (February 1994): p. 8.

43. Mike Grell, *CAPTAIN AMERICA*, Vol.1—No.424 February 1994): n. page.

44. Rob Liefeld, *SUPREME*, Vol.1—No.424 February 1994) p. 10.

45. Ibid., p. 11.

46. Ibid., p. 13.

47. Rob Liefeld, *SUPREME*, Vol.1—No.2 (February 1993): pp. 14-15.

48. Joe Madureira and Fabian Nicieza, *DEADPOOL: THE CIRCLE CHASE*, Vol.1—No.3 (November 1993): n. page.

49. Joe Madureira and Fabian Nicieza, *DEADPOOL: THE CIRCLE CHASE*, Vol.1—No.4 (December 1993): n. page.

50. Brian Cunningham, "Out of the Shadows," *WIZARD* April 1994: p. 40.

51. Robert A. Heinlein, *STARSHIP TROOPERS* (New York, N.Y.: Ace Books, 1959): p. 80.

52. Keith Giffen, *BLOODSTRIKE*, Vol.1—No.5 (November 1993): pp.16-19.

53. Rob Liefeld, *SUPREME*, Vol.1—No.3 (June 1993): p.17.

54. Peter David, *X-FACTOR*, Vol.1—No.85 (1993): n. page.

55. Mike Grell, *CAPTAIN AMERICA*, Vol.1—No.425 (March 1994): n. page.

56. Chris Gray, "The Cyborg Soldier: The U.S. Military and the PostModern Warrior," in L. Levidow and K. Robins, eds., *Cyborg Worlds: The Military Information Economy*, London: Free Association Press, 1989, pp. 43-72.

57. Rob Liefeld, *SUPREME*, Vol.1—No.4 (July 1993): n. page.

58. Stephen E. Cross, et al., "Knowledge-Based Pilot Aids; A Case Study in Mission Planning" in *Lecture Notes in Control and Information Sciences: Artificial Intelligence and Man-machine Systems*, Berlin: Springer-Verlag, 1986: p. 147.

59. Ibid., p. 148.

60. Peter Sanderson, *AVENGERS LOG*, Vol.1—No.1 (February 1994): pp. 24-25.

61. Ibid., p. 44.

62. Ibid., p. 24.

63. Ibid., p. 25.

64. Ibid., p. 25.

65. Ibid., p. 26.

66. Ed Regis, op. cit., p. 167.

67. Chris Gray and Stephen Mentor, "The Cyborg Body Politic Meets the New World Order," in this volume.

68. Ibid., p. 11.

69. Walter Simonson, *CYBERFORCE*, Vol.1—No.0 (September 1993): p. 8.

70. Ibid., p. 9.

71. Rob Liefeld, *SUPREME*, Vol.1—No.1 (April 1993): n. page.

72. Chris Gray, "The Culture of War Cyborgs: Technoscience, Gender, and PostModern War," in *Research in Philosophy and Technology*, special issue on feminism, ed. by Joan Rothschild, 1993: p. 1.

73. Jim Lee, et al., *STORMWATCH SOURCEBOOK*, Vol.1—No.1 (January 1994): p. 2.

74. Gray and Mentor, op. cit., pp.12 and 14.

75. *The Concise Oxford Dictionary of Quotations* (New York: Oxford University Press, 1981) p. 227.

76. Peter Sanderson, *AVENGERS LOG*, Vol.1—No.1 (February 1994): p. 4.

77. Jim Lee, et al., *STORMWATCH SOURCEBOOK*, Vol.1—No.1 (January 1994): p. 4.

78. Ibid., p. 7.

79. Fabian Nicieza, *CABLE,* Vol.1—No.9 (March 1994): p. 6.

80. Chris Claremont, *X-MEN,* Vol.1—No.253 (1989): n. page.

81. Marv Wolfman, *TALES OF THE NEW TEEN TITANS,* Vol.1—No.1 (June 1982): pp. 15-16.

82. Walter Simonson, *CYBERFORCE,* Vol.1—No.0 (September 1993): n. page.

83. Rob Liefeld, *SUPREME,* Vol.1—No.10 (February 1994): p. 10.

84. Les Daniels, op. cit., p. 191.

85. Fabian Nicieza, *CABLE,* Vol.1—No.9 (March 1994): p. 7.

86. Joe Madureira and Fabian Nicieza, *DEADPOOL: THE CIRCLE CHASE,* Vol.1—No.4 (December 1993): n. page.

87. Jim Lee, et al., *STORMWATCH SOURCEBOOK,* Vol.1—No.1 (January 1994): p. 1.

88. Simon Jowett, *NIKKI DOYLE:WILD THING,* Vol.1—No. 1 (April 1993): n. page.

89. Jorge Gonzalez and Bob Layton, *X-O MANOWAR,* Vol.1—No.0 (August 1993): n. page.

90. *Archangel,* Fleer Ultra—Marvel Comics X-Men Trading card, (1994) #12.

91. *Deathlok,* Sky Box—Marvel Masterpiece Trading Cards, (1993) #71.

Recalling Totalities
The Mirrored Stages of Arnold Schwarzenegger

Jonathan Goldberg

"It is, under any circumstances, a remarkable story. The shy boy, who is afraid of his father, too timid to seek the comfort of others ...

A remarkable story? my story re-marked; *my* story? It's the one I read at the back of the comics; the one in which I recognized myself, and refused the trajectory being offered, the way out of being "shy," "timid," rejected without knowing consciously what the code was, what the appeal, the solicitation of the ad: there is a way not to be gay, a way not to appear gay, a way to be the father you fear, a way to overcome the need of the comfort of others, and it is all in you, it is all up to you, all inside of you, if you take control of yourself.

My story? The story of a generation of men, growing up on certain images, and desiring *through the image* to be transformed; or to *have* the image rather than to be it; or to refuse the system entirely. Impossibilities, any way, despite the promise

233 }

of the comic books, the culture.

> *... turns to lifting weights and builds on a dream to be best in the world. He wins all the body-building titles worth winning, then sets about turning those titles into cash (Carcaterra 28).*

Whose story? What trajectory of identification and its refusal remarks these pages? The story of Arnold Schwarzenegger ... or THE PHALLUS.

i. Pumping ironies

Pumping Iron, first a book, then a movie, then, fulfilling the destination of postmodernity—repetition, nontermination—a second edition of the book, and a film sequel, *Pumping Iron II: The Women.*[1] These texts provide a first entrance into the subject of this essay, sites to test the tautological phallic identification broached above. They suggest another trajectory as well, a parallel path to be pursued: from Arnold to the women, from the Terminator to Sarah Connor.

In the film (George Butler & Robert Flore 1977), nothing would seem more foreclosed than phallic identification. Structured as a series of parallel plots, *Pumping Iron* follows the contestants for the 1975 Mr. Olympia competition (a contest that constituted, until Schwarzenegger's surprise re-entry in 1980, his final bodybuilding competition, and the initiation of his career as a "serious" movie star). The movie narrows down to Schwarzenegger's only real competition among those his size, Lou Ferrigno. (First parallel: after his defeat, Ferrigno also chose stardom—on the small screen, but as the Incredible Hulk.) The difference between the two men is marked in a number of ways: Lou is presented as, to understate, rather slow; most importantly, he is in the constant company of his father, Mattie, who retired from the NY police force to become his son's trainer. The movie includes shots of little Louie, a young man straight out of the Charles Atlas ads, immensely awkward, wearing thick glasses and, in one shot, posing next to his father; biceps compared, Lou falls short. (These stills can be found in the second edition of the book.) In the film, the theme of paternity is played out too in the hulking figure of Mike Katz, the one bodybuilder actually pictured as a father. Katz is shown with his children (never with his wife), inviting his little daughter to feel her brother's bicep ("isn't that hard?" he croons), and then, her father's: "how about Daddy's?" In the movie Schwarzenegger is presumably not only the hardest, he is also explicitly in the father's position. At breakfast with Lou and his parents before the competition, a scene of psyching out (or, to put it in terms to be recalled later, of

Figure 1: Charles Atlas advertisement. "Mac, the 97-pound weakling about to take the Atlas plunge."

From Comics Journal *144 (1991):87.*

mindfucking), Arnold addresses Mattie rather than Lou; as Barbara Correll has noted (294), the discussion between men keeps Lou in the child's (or mother's) place. Finally, Schwarzenegger counsels Mattie: "Help him. Don't screw him up this time...." Of his only other serious competitor, Franco Columbu, he has this to say: "Franco is a child and when it comes to the day of the contest, I'm his father; he comes to me for advices, so it's not that hard for me to give him the wrong advices."[2] Arnold-the-father is, his lines aver, the father that screws up his son.

If this makes him Mattie, it also places him in the position of his own father, as the biography presents the feared parent (and Nazi, it is claimed [Leigh 5]). About his father, site of (refused) identification, Schwarzenegger is more circumspect: his repressive life in Graz made him yearn, he says, from the age of ten on, to be (as he puts it) "different," and to go to America, desires played out, it seems, in building muscles. Arnold's father, like Lou's, was a policeman, another line of identification that further suggests that however much the movie (and its hero) seek differentiation from the Incredible Hulk, their relationship is a specular one. Schwarzenegger tells the story of his father's death (in a scene following his breakfast put-down of Mattie)—his mother's phone call, asking him to come to the funeral, and his refusal (the rationalization: it was two months before a competition and it would have broken his training). If the mother's call is refused, the mother is not quite, however; in the second edition of *Pumping Iron*, for instance (written after Schwarzenegger's stardom had become the book's topic), there are childhood shots of "the Austrian Oak," as Gaines and Butler fondly name their subject: Infant Arnold with mother, overdeveloped Arnold with mother. The hiatus between shots effaces the "remarkable" story—recalled only in the repudiated others that populate the film.

This is how Arnold occupies the father's place: total recall ... or amnesia?

The occupation of the father's place in every possible locale (with Franco, with Mike Katz, with Lou) and the *effacement* of the father displaces the "remarkable" Arnold—the Arnold made by re-marking—in these various, and uncontrollable, simulacra. Displacing the father also displaces the Symbolic. Moreover, the built body offers the spectacle of the made body, the artificial, "different" body (becoming a statue is the favored trope in the bodybuilder's discourse) as a locus of Imaginary identifications. If, to return to our initial tautology, this (displaced) paternal body "is" the phallus, it cannot simply secure the Symbolic.[3]

To locate this displaced phallus, we need only listen to Schwarzenegger on the "pump," the feeling that accompanies the engorged muscle, filled with blood, short of oxygen:

> ... the greatest feeling, or the most satisfying feeling you can get, is the pump....
> It's as satisfying as coming, as having sex with a woman and coming. So can
> you believe how much I am in heaven? I'm like getting the feeling of coming in
> the gym, I'm getting the feeling of coming at home, I'm getting the feeling of
> coming backstage when I pump up, onstage when I pose in front of 5000
> people, so I'm coming day and night. That's terrific, right? So, I'm in heaven.

As Correll comments, this sounds like female orgasm.[4] Indeed, Schwarzenegger's second thought, defining coming as if it only could occur in sex between a man and a woman, seems pointedly irrelevant to his compulsive and repetitive syntax. Repetition here, as in the structure of the film, rides over difference. Father/son; man/woman. Or, to follow Leo Bersani's suggestion (in "Is the Rectum a Grave?"), were we to site this "female" pleasure *on Arnold's body* its location might be less phallic than anal.[5]

Arguably, if at first glance paradoxically, that displacement of the penis answers to an ideal of bodybuilding. **Making every inch of the body hard, having erections everywhere, entails a massive denial of**

the adequacy of the penis. By this, I do not mean to endorse the familiar supposition that bodybuilding is compensatory, that penile inadequacy is the sub-text in the posing and picturing of hard male bodies.[6] Building the body to experience the pump is not a way of compensating for having a small dick; more to the point, the pump locates an inadequacy within the Symbolic, a lack at the very site of the realization of the equation of penis and phallus, for, as excessive coming, the pump disconnects phallus and penis. In such dispersal, *the* body itself is shattered, even as it is built. The male bodybuilder's body aspires to other than bodily limits, to a hypermasculinity that falls, insofar as it exceeds, to guarantee the gender category it means to secure.

This can be seen as well if one considers the two aims of bodybuilding: bulk and definition, pumping up and sculpting/cutting/ripping. The latter, Schwarzenegger reports (*Encyclopedia* 187), can produce worries about smallness. (Size replaces gender, and big and small are controlling adjectives, and not only as categories of competition; in the film Arnold addresses virtually everyone as "Big": "Big Mike," "Big Lou," etc.) Mike Katz, quoted in the book, handles the fear of "smallness": "You see your deltoids and you've got things in there, and you could stick who knows what in there and it would get lost. That's muscularity" (168). Of the thing, Schwarzenegger is quoted earlier saying: "You don't really see a muscle as part of you, in a way. You see it as a thing. You look at it as a thing and you say well this thing has to be built a little longer.... And you look at it and it doesn't even seem to belong to you. Like a sculpture" (52).

Non-belonging part, movable thing, concave and convex, big and small, receptive and penetrative: if this is the phallus it is everywhere, and no longer sutured to gender or identity, but to the artificial built body, monstrously, unnaturally, always coming.

This communicates with yet another ideal of bodybuilding, the dream of immortality (the theme song of *Pumping Iron* intones: "Everybody wants to live forever. Everyone wants to be bigger than Dad"): these bodies know no age, or refuse to reveal the process of aging. The claim, reiterated in the second edition of *Pumping Iron*, is that as builders get older, their bodies get younger (240). Time travel. Although Mike Katz worries about a limit to bodybuilding—the possibility "to infinitely become unreal" (68), as he puts it—that "unreal" nonetheless defines the aim of bodybuilding. "I confess I loved it when they called me a monster," Schwarzenegger writes (*Education* 77). Such are the monster ambitions announced in the closing pages of the second edition of *Pumping Iron*, to go from being a "giant" bodybuilder to equal mega proportions as movie star or even as politician. With the opening of *Terminator 2*, Schwarzenegger announced his political intentions, following in the path of "*Ronald Reagan*," *the Movie*. For there is a political path of the bodybuilder, time travelling backwards and forwards at once. It is suggested by lines in *Pumping Iron* that follow the reminiscences about the father he wished to escape: "always dreaming about very powerful people. Dictators and things like that. I was just always impressed by people who would be remembered for hundreds of years, or even like Jesus, being for thousands of years remembered." **Re-membered: the body of iron, timeless, ageless, finds its ideal locus in "the endless possibilities in this country"** (*Pumping Iron* 250). At the end of this speech in the movie, Arnold, who has been carrying his picture (like Jesus carrying the cross?) is seen posing in the southwest desert, a final shot recalled at the end of *Total Recall*. Totalitarianism recalled, as the image of Arnold in another desert also might suggest: posed as a statue, a Greek victory, with three black African boys clinging to his legs. Shades of Leni Riefenstahl.[7]

These images give pause (to put it mildly); the frightening hold that they may exert, and the atavistic longings which they can unleash, however much they participate in political realities (after Desert Storm, it would be naive to claim otherwise), remain, for all that, less deterministic, capable, I would argue, of being read and received otherwise. With Schwarzenegger politics is science fiction (Star Wars taught us to take this seriously); he embodies an "unnatural" sex too. ("Infinite" agelessness—time/space travel—is another version of coming all the time, and places the body in its "remarkable" narrative.) The body, however, has become a cyborg, a machine of simulation that gives mind and body a different ontology.[8] "Pumping iron, nobody's going to be bigger than I am," the chorus of *Pumping Iron* concludes, phonically equating "iron" and "I am." It is this body that *Pumping Iron* reproduces in its parallel plots, a structure of simulations of the image that resist determination. For the body of the bodybuilder is produced by the mirror, in the mirror. Flexing for himself, building on the basis of the image and the reflection, what desire is reflected? Narcissism? Ego-ideal? Ego trip (to recall *Total Recall*)? What gaze is solicited?

Against the path of totality, recalling it (in both senses of the word), the image can be read not only for the complicities that might, securing the image for the Symbolic, hand it over to a regressive politics, but in terms of other desires less readily amenable to such constructions. One scene in *Pumping Iron* suggests what these might be: shown visiting the prison on the aptly named Terminal Isle, Schwarzenegger kisses one of the women inmates, and a male voice asks for a kiss too. "I've heard about people like you here," Arnold jokes, but then offers a kiss if the man will come out of the crowd and identify himself. The scene is glossed by remarks in the book, about how the "general public doesn't know how to look" (93); Schwarzenegger depends not only on the gaze of his fellow bodybuilders, but on another gaze as well:

> When a homosexual looks at a bodybuilder, I don't have anything against that. I would probably stare the same way if Raquel Welch or Brigitte Bardot walked by. If I see a girl with big tits, I'm going to stare and stare. And I'm going to think in my mind what I'm going to do with her if I would have her. The same is true with the homosexual—he's looking at the bodybuilder and picturing what he would do with him. You have to face it if you have a good body, and it is somehow a compliment to a bodybuilder. Sometimes girls are attracted to your body; sometimes homosexuals are attracted to your body. (92)

How to read this? Within the heterosexual/sexist construction of gender, in which gender opposition defines gender difference, it would mean that Arnold is a woman when a gay man looks at him—and this is how Arnold articulates it, equating himself with a female pinup, site of the gaze. Yet, of course, the analogy also posits his straight looking (at a woman) as the way in which a hemosexual looks at him. And it insists, even as it evacuates the category, on the masculinity of the place he occupies.

Bodybuilding is haunted by the spectre of homosexuality; it is basically dismissed by the book, flicked off on Terminal Island.[9] Yet, one biographer has suggested,

Schwarzenegger may have been a boytoy, allowing the look, if nothing else (Leigh 50-51, 60-65). It is in the looking that these bodies are constituted, in the mirror. End of a good session (to be recalled later as a good scene):

> ... he walks over to one of the big mirrors and takes off his shirt. The gym goes even quieter than it was before, and everyone still in it stops whatever he is doing.... The men standing behind him watch the mirror in the same elated, adrenalized way you watch a fight as Arnold checks himself through five or six quick poses, his face now grinning and appraising wolfishly. They are all bodybuilders ... and they have all seen Arnold pose before, yet they stare at the reflection like the ladies on Santa Monica Beach when they see a builder for the first time. (52)

It is the space of this gaze that the second edition of *Pumping Iron* seeks to refuse to the women who are part of the "The Terrain, 1980," denying that there could be anything sexual in women bodybuilders (by which the authors mean any way a man could desire such a woman; their analogy with the women on the beach [dis]avows their desire for the male body). *Pumping Iron II: The Women* (George Butler 1984) is even more conflicted in its presentation. If, as Christine Holmlund has argued, the film is troubled by the possibility that the most muscular woman in the movie only could be soliciting the gaze of gay men or of lesbians ("In each case, the stereotypes of what kinds of bodies gay men and lesbians find attractive are constructed around the phallus: gay men are assumed to be wimps who worship "he-men," while lesbians are assumed to be women who *are* "he-men" or women who worship "he/she-men" [42]), her argument suggests rather that the phallus is the symbolic totem of a failed and impossible heterosexuality. The spectacle of bodybuilding, in which female bodybuilders bring to a crisis patriarchal definitions of femininity, points too to the fact that hypermasculinity always transgresses, refuses, and exceeds the phallic measure. The excesses on both sites defuse the heterosexual imperative even as an attempt is made to install it—forever. If these bodies *are* the phallus, the phallus has been so dispersed that it is the proper name of nothing but a scandal—a scandal that I would seek to mobilize politically.

ii. indeterminations

The site on which I would focus, *The Terminator* (James Cameron 1984),[10] Schwarzenegger's star-making vehicle, admittedly, is not all that easily amenable to such a progressive reading. (To anticipate my argument, it should be noted that the reading of *Pumping Iron* offered above has been guided by a logic of simulation in *Terminator* as well as later Schwarzenegger films that continues to provide the trajectory of this essay.) The efforts of one feminist commentator (Necakov) to read the film's heroine as a challenge to Hollywood representations of women—largely on the basis of the final tableau of Sarah Connor, gun across her lap, riding alone in a jeep across the Mexican desert into the storm that symbolizes the approaching apocalypse—has (still in the name of feminism) been dismantled.[11] As Margaret Goseilo argues, however progressive the film may appear—"any popular action film featuring the demise of an Arnold Schwarzenegger character at the hands of a woman merits attention," her essay opens—its slasher and sci-fi conventions are reinforced by a series of stereotypical gender representations. Sarah Connor is first a targeted victim, then a damsel in distress, and her salvific mission is couched in terms of her abilities *as a mother* to bear a male child; in short, "she is a mere conduit of male power and supremacy between her son and her lover, assigned her role by their male discourse, most specifically John Connor's message from the future and Reese's directives in the present" (46).

Her maternal role makes the film, Goscilo argues, a pro-life document (the police psychologist, one recalls, characterizes the Terminator's mission as a "retroactive abortion"); indeed, the child of the holy family that must be saved has the telling initials J.C.. He will save humanity from the machines that seek to destroy all people.

Nonetheless, the pro-life *Terminator* is also, in its engagement with and representation of this future, a Star Wars fantasy of invulnerability, a mechanical triumph over human failure. This contradiction about technology intersects with Sarah's role. As a number of commentators have remarked, Constance Penley most notably, *Terminator* seems to be a resolutely anti-technological film; its present is overrun with machines, many of which fail to work when they are wanted—Sarah gets a recording when she tries to contact the police; her message on the answering machine tips off the Terminator that the woman he has just killed is Sarah's roommate Ginger—and Ginger, of course, plugged into her walkman, almost misses her date's (obscene) phone call, does miss Sarah's call, and fails to hear the arrival of the Terminator and the mayhem in the next room. As Goscilo comments, the theme of the machine in *The Terminator* is, especially through the figure of Ginger, gender inflected—machines fail women. Thus, while to Penley the critique of the machine is a progressive aspect of the film, offering in her words, a "critical dystopia" (68) in which machines have gone wrong thanks to their misuse, the critique can, like the image of Sarah, the strong woman, as easily be denied. While the movie evidences a yearning for a time before the machine (it can be found in the post-apocalyptic moments in Reese's memory, for instance the one in which a mother and daughter are seen huddling before a TV set which now, rather than housing an image, is the site of a flame keeping them alive), such yearnings are patently regressive. This future looks like the past, as it does too in other films in this genre, most stunningly so in the Mad Max films (one further sign: only dogs can smell out the difference between humans and terminators). Penley's argument with technology as a *human* failure repeats this regressive plot, as if the human were an unideological or ungendered term. The refusal of the machine is, patently, an ideological lure: at the simplest level, sci-fi movies appeal through their special effects, the mark of their complicity with advanced technology. Need it be said that the star of *The Terminator* is The Terminator? (If this suggests that the pro-life aspect of the movie also is a ruse, a cover for the destructivity the movie celebrates, the ordinariness of this connection, this ideological slippage, has been demonstrated by Zoe Sofia, who ably shows the nuclear exterminist aims of those who declare themselves pro-life.[12])

These remarks about technology allow us to begin to see that *The Terminator* is a more conflicted site than the either-or positions of the commentaries on the film's politics. Without denying the force of the arguments that regard the film as regressive, and certainly with no desire to argue that it is in any simple sense politically progressive, it seems possible—and politically valuable—to argue that the film cannot be reduced to monolithic ideological effects. Between the claims of a feminism that would appropriate the film for its agendas, and a feminism that would deny the film, one would need, I would think, to pose the question of what feminism is, whether the concept itself is not divided, and, if so, whether something other than a weighing of counter-claims is required. Here, I would only invoke the arguments of Teresa de Lauretis in her (for these purposes) aptly titled *Technologies of Gender*,[13] in particular her sense that the ways in which bodies are made by ideology will never exhaust or fully coincide with them. De Lauretis is most telling when she labels as one of these ideologies the very concept of feminism in the singular; this is to suggest an argument fully as useful and as complex as the by now far more familiar deconstruction of Woman as the singular object of feminist inquiry. To dismiss *Terminator* as simply, as entirely, regressive is a move of despair[14]: it imagines popular culture as fully co-opted by backward social forces; it places the (homogenized) audience for these films in an entirely passive position; in its reading of female victimization, it hands over to a reified patriarchy the power fully to subjugate women. In a word, to do this concedes the symbolic value and the full efficacy of the phallus.

Pumping Iron has suggested a different trajectory, and I turn now to the question of the paternal in *Terminator*, its mode of (re)inscription and the possibilities for deconstructive—and political—analysis thereby offered. I would begin by recalling Goscilo's characterization of Sarah's place *between men* (between her son and his father), italicizing the term to signal the importance of Eve Kosofsky Sedgwick's book of the same name in the analysis that follows. If (as in the bodybuilding genre), the paternal and the heterosexist are to be displaced, or, at least, shown to be less secure than might be imagined, the networks of relationship in the film that cut across and interfere with the paternal line must be explored. It is therefore worth stressing that there is no single narrative line in the film, and not only because it describes a loop in a time travel plot. In the two accounts he offers for his mission in 1984 Los Angeles, Kyle Reese gives two contradictory explanations; that he volunteered; that he was chosen by John Connor. This is a prevarication along one of the fundamental thematic lines of the film (and the genre of time travel), the question of determinism. But it also suggests the possibility that the determinist plot (the teleological narrative that maps onto the biological/paternal imperative) is/may be disturbed. It co-implicates the plot of the Terminator to terminate the future in John Connor's determination of the future.

One way of seeing that is to note a certain fatality that hangs over Reese, as in his resolute declaration of the nexus of his relationship with John Connor—"I'd die for John Connor." It is easy to see that sentence as (among other things) the emotional core of his life; more to the point (since such *human* evaluation may be precisely what in its most progressive aspects the film works to evacuate), if the line represents some kind of Oedipal fantasy (in which the father willingly, accommodatingly dies before but also at the command of the son), it also serves as the annunciation of a homoerotic relation that is not, I would argue, readily assimilable to the heterosexual plotting of the film; rather, it recasts its ostensible plot and, with it, the supposedly inevitable psychic support of the Oedipal. One sign of this might lie in Reese's description of John Connor to Sarah: about *his* height but with *her* eyes. The phallic measure, and the site of castration both appear here, but in fantasmatic ways: in which father and son are equal in height (size), mirror reflections, and in which the son's sight—including, presumably, the way he sees his father, is *as his mother sees*. Reese's desire to die for John Connor is, like so much else in the representation of the character, eerily anticipatory: each of Kyle's "memories" of the future ends with his death. This father of the future is death-marked in every locus of his existence (indeed, as Sarah muses at the end of the film, it is difficult to say where or when he does exist). If this signals the death of the paternal even as it is being fulfilled, it is also how Reese can "have" John Connor.

What this relationship between men might look like can only be read through Reese's relation with his specular other in the film, the Terminator, itself specularly related to John Connor. The two plot Reese's destination, Connor in the future, the Terminator in the present of the film. The quasi-Oedipal plot in which the son kills the father is doubled by the exterminating anti-paternal Terminator; this doubling also is, in the present, a site of erotic identification, as fully as in that future in which Reese is the worshipful follower of John Connor (this reversal of father and son serves, too, as a sign that the opposition of Reese and the Terminator may be read in reverse). Paths of cross-identification mark the relation between Reese and the machine he pursues.

As the film begins, the arrival of the Terminator is seconded with the arrival of Reese: painless arrival and easy ascendency is, the second time round, anything but (there are scars on Reese's back, perhaps the result of the space trip, perhaps from the camps in which he has served—camps which, it should be noted, also cast the future retroactively, this time as Nazi concentration camps, a connection that will also shape the image of the Terminator). What the two bodies share, of course, is nudity. Undeniably, that is a source of their appeal, part of the way, too, they seem made for each other, or made from each other. The pumped body of the Terminator is echoed in the smooth, developed, but much smaller, musculature of Kyle; paternity is replaced by mirroring, the Terminator as much an image of where Kyle comes from as where he is headed (the timeloop plot is the bodybuilder's eternity). (There is a further echo of Kyle's body in Matt, Ginger's boyfriend, killed in post-coital bliss by the invading Terminator, a scene that first suggests male-male violation before it moves to the murder of the last of the Sarah Connor duplicates in the film.) In the opening sequence of the film, all the way to the Tech Noir, the bar in which the Terminator attempts to kill Sarah and is stopped by Reese, the film cuts from one to the other, and in ways that only retrospectively (if then) serve to distinguish the Terminator (the opponent of the paternal) from the father. (*Terminator 2* plays this simulation in reverse.)

This complicity helps to downplay the oppressive patriarchal part, to make it, let us say, something of a surprise that Reese is the father of the future. He doesn't exactly seem suited to the heroic part (in this, then, he also doubles Sarah, his blond double, who declares herself a totally improbable candidate as mother of the future). As others have noted, Reese is, in many respects, coded as a "sensitive" type in the film[15]—a 1980s men's movement man, ready to be written up in the "About

Men" column in *The New York Times Magazine:* virgin, worshipper of Sarah, slight, blond, and wounded, his narratives are not only self-destructive but full of self-pity. What has to be asked here, though, is whether the coding isn't also a (deniable) way of suggesting that Reese is gay. Sarah's pity for his sexual inexperience perhaps too quickly heterosexualizes—or presses Reese into *nominally* heterosexual service (*hers* as well as his)—his relation to women, who are, to him, rather, "good fighters." If Reese imagines women *in the position of John Connor*—if this is what makes Sarah attractive to him—her disappearance between men (or her assumption of a role *as a man*) need upset only a feminism that operates within the invidious terms of a compulsory heterosexuality. The heterosexual markings of the lovemaking scene are minimal: Sarah's "feminine" response to Reese's story of a "loveless" life allows Reese his one "sexual" experience. Moreover, the sex scene, as Goscilo notes, is filmed in the slow motion used when the Terminator kills the various Sarah Connor substitutes in the film, and the shot immediately following has the Terminator in full leather astride a motorcycle. The filming of the scene of the conception of John Connor suggests how close Reese is to the Terminator: even as he "is" the father, he is in the position of the embodiment of the antipaternal, the Terminator. To the argument that the Terminator is *nothing but the phallus,* one would have to ask therefore, for whom? and in what scenario? The image of the Terminator that follows suggests a site to respond to such questions, which will be pursued in a moment—the leather scene.

It helps, however, to see that Reese is in the film **to get Sarah pregnant as expeditiously as possible, and then to be gotten out of the way: to function as efficiently as a machine**. One mechanism he serves is as the enunciator of the plot: Reese's story is nothing but the story of the film, the explanations interspersed in its chase scenes. After his death, retrospectively, and for the first time, Sarah will occupy this narrative position, dictating into her tape recorder, filling their moment together with a "lifetime," a gesture, like many in the final moments of the film, towards giving her an interiority that she has hitherto lacked. The false consciousness supplied is stereotypically feminine; the best that can be said for it is that it rings utterly false, and is contradicted by the image we have already recalled, of her riding off into the storm, alone, without a man. (Having consciousness, while it may *humanize* Sarah, runs counter to the gestures of the movie upon which this reading builds: those that dehumanize, mechanize, but also go beyond the imperatives of the biological, the differentiation of the sexes along the axis of heterosexuality and within the inevitability of procreation.) Sarah's destiny, as I will argue further, involves a reproduction of reproduction that also signals its termination. Reese's sacrifice to/for the patriarchy is one sign of it. Another way of putting the case about him: Reese is an unappealing or, let us say, an *impossible* character in the film. Much as he functions to save Sarah, to instruct her, to fuck her, he is also aptly diagnosed by the police psychologist as psychotic. For Reese fills the paternal role and also vacates it, leaving that position to what the anti-paternal Terminator and Sarah make of it.

One cannot, of course, speak of the Terminator's place without recalling that one also is speaking about Arnold Schwarzenegger. The "new order of intelligence" that the Terminator inhabits—marked by its ability to simulate the human—arguably alludes to the ways in which the cyborg involves a remaking of the image of the bodybuilder as mindless beefcake. If, as I have been suggesting, Reese doubles the cyborg, the cyborg doubles the "real" Schwarzenegger. Within the movie, the moment when the Terminator and Reese come together—and also can then be differentiated as potential murderer and savior—is when Arnold riffles in Sarah Connor's drawer to find her picture. This brings him to the point that Reese already occupies, since knowing what the "real" Sarah Connor looks like is the single piece of information that Reese has that keeps him one step ahead of the Terminator. Reese once had a picture of Sarah Connor (given to him—when?—by John Connor); he has memorized it and it defines his mission and his erotic trajectory. What it means to fall in love with a picture rather than a person—and especially *this* picture of Sarah alone *after his death* and on the road to becoming a good fighter—is amenable not only to a reading via the Imaginary. It suggests that Reese is connected to Sarah by image reproduction, by the photograph. Once again, this aligns him with the cyborg and other than biological modes of reproduction; if these are—even in the Imaginary—linked to technologies that exceed the body, so much the better. It is this conflation at the site of the body of the bodybuilder, the star, and the machine that replaces the paternal.

In this context, the relentless opposition to biological reproduction represented by the Terminator is capable of a reading that suggests more than its complicity with (and exposure of) a Star Wars mentality. The Terminator embodies a "new order of intelligence" that is resolutely anti-human and anti-reproductive. The mission to destroy Sarah Connor (and thus John Connor) is nothing less than a mission to ensure the end of the human race. Yet, part of the undeniable appeal of the Terminator lies in the fact that he is Arnold Schwarzenegger, that the end of the human is therefore the end of a particular form of the human. On the one hand, this new order of intelligence is a calculated and ideological misnomer: a primitive mentality is being celebrated, one reduced to mindless destructivity (generically, this feature marks *Terminator* as an action movie like *Conan* or *Commando* or the rival Rambo flicks). But also, thanks to certain punk signifiers—it is to them that the Terminator turns for his first "image"—what might be termed a new stupidity at the center of various forms of popular culture also is affirmed. It is declared early in the film, at the punning moment when Arnold responds, in a thick Germanic accent, to the charge that one of the punks makes; he finds something "wrong" with the "picture" of the naked form approaching them, assumes he is "a couple of cans short of a six pack"; "Your clothes"/"You're close," Arnold wittily/unwittingly replies. The artificial intelligence of the machine ruthlessly exposes supposedly "higher" human intelligence; stupidity is revalued, as it is in punk culture, as a resolutely anti-humanist gesture.

This "dumb" machine is plugged into resources in cultural energies opposed to prevailing orders: the police are the target, blasted away at every opportunity, and especially in the scene that fulfills the promise: "I'll be back." If, as social psychopath, the Terminator seems simply outlaw, the figure also taps into right wing fantasies of vigilante control (the weapons "purchased" are for home defense); but also, underclass opposition to police oppression (he gains admiration from the Black man that he passes, armed and beleathered, in the SRO hotel—the single moment in the film that looks to ally the Terminator with Blacks); even Left distrust of the police. Everyone loves to see the police massacred. Besides the massacre in the police station, there is one at the Tech Noir where the target is yuppie culture.[16] The bar scene brings to a close a path launched in the slaughter of Matt and

Ginger, that mindless, body-toned pair, who embody the pornography of a self-absorbed heterosexuality. Those who play with technology—the technologies of body building, of (hetero)-sexual allure, of militaristic/policing intelligence—are blasted away by a machine of a futurity of quite another kind.

Where do cyborgs come from? What reproductive technology do they represent? The answer lies in a repudiation of biological reproduction. The cyborg body—the bodybuilder's body—is "grown," Reese explains (he is, like the replicants in *Blade Runner,* a "skin job," and the trailers for *Terminator 2* showed his reconstruction, the hardware, and then the genetic machine that produces the body). If the body that surrounds the machine somehow "humanizes" it (in the time machine, as Reese explains, only living tissue can be transported; since the Terminator can travel too, the machine and the human are inextricably linked in the cyborg), the "human" that the cyborg represents is the product of quite other technologies—a human produced through and succeeding as simulation. If Reese already throws the Oedipal into a certain fantasmatic relation to the ordinary psychological dynamics that go under that rubric, that is the case too in a parallel Oedipal moment, in which Arnold cuts into his own arm to expose the mechanism beneath (the muscle is a machine), and then removes his eye. The arm has replaced the phallus, a displacement of more than one kind: if it speaks to the ways in which the gun extends the arm, it also is linked to writing. This is not a farfetched or merely theoretical point: the Terminator knows only the alphabetic trace of Sarah Connor; he and Reese first locate her in a phonebook, making clear that writing precedes speaking, that the technologies of the telephone and telecommunication are writing effects.[17] Were he human, these operations would be castrative/blinding; rather, they are revelatory of another order of being. The simulated "real" eye is displaced by another "real," the red light that will signal life to the end of the film. This artificial life realizes a dream of the bodybuilder.

And not his alone: if Arnold is a cyborg, so are we all. I fetch my argument from Donna Haraway's crucial manifesto, and endorse her claims against those who would see in the Terminator an "embodiment" of the postmodern condition as inevitably destructive. Haraway's argument explicitly rejects the sentimental humanism that marks many of these responses to postmodernity and fosters recognition of the ways in which a post-humanist ideology is necessary for the kinds of "new people" who demand a place in the political—women of color, people with AIDS, etc.—people whose "novelty" lies precisely in the ways in which their (*our*) identities fracture the human/biological/heterosexual imperatives. It is this position of the Terminator in the movie that rewrites both the maternal and paternal, the positions of both Sarah and Reese. If she *is* a photograph at first—and if her time loop takes place within that mode of reproduction—we last hear her voice dictating. That is to say that the voice *we hear* is a recording, and on two counts at least: from that perspective, her displays of consciousness are false in the sense that all consciousness is as it passes through the circuits. Sarah may remain "femininely" incompetent in any number of ways (there is bafflement as well as romanticism in her dictation), but in the final moments of the film she is not being menaced by machines and they are not failing her. They are, rather, producing her. For, finally, the cyborg/Terminator explains the generation of John Connor. At the level of telecommunications, the cyborg is the equivalent of time/space travel;

what electrical impulses do is what the Terminator is, and the way in which he reproduces is the way in which John Connor comes to exist in a moment in which past and future fuse in the present that is not, that is only the space of differentials, of protensions and retentions, the space of the trace, of the program and of the image. Of simulation. It is here that the dream of *Pumping Iron* meets the machine of its realization, *The Terminator:* in the image of Schwarzenegger.

From this perspective one can put pressure on Constance Penley's argument that time travel, and especially the fantasy of being one's own father, is resolutely Oedipal, indeed, by way of one of her own examples, David Gerrold's *The Man Who Folded Himself.* The story involves a boy named Dan whose uncle Jim bequeaths him a time travel belt. When Dan travels, he comes upon his duplicates—possible future or past versions of himself that do and do not coincide with himself (the narrative marks temporal differences between subjects alphabetically—Dan finds Don; Diana, Donna—and often does the same scene twice from each identical/different point of view). Dan, facing all these alternatives, insists on his identity even though he cannot locate its point of origin or of identification. In the course of the novel, he makes love to his simulations, declaring himself homosexual; a normative psychoanalytic definition (narcissism) is deformed since there is always a difference among these duplicate selves. Seeking a double that represents an alternative future/past, one with which Dan cannot identify (a structure that resonates with *Terminator* and with the possibility that it holds open and realizes in its sequel, of changing the past/future), Dan lights upon his female (i.e., lesbian) equivalent at a point of origin thousands of years in the past. They produce offspring, the Dan of the opening pages of the novel in fact; he, in turn, becomes the father who calls himself the uncle, or who, rather, *is* the uncle if that place represents a configuration outside or in excess of the Oedipal. His place matches those of the novel's duplications that put homosexuality/lesbianism in (non)relation to and at the fantasmatic origin of heterosexuality.[18]

In making her Oedipal claim, Penley ignores the anti-, extra-, and post-Oedipal articulations of these time travel stories. The moment of origination in Gerrold's time loop plot, the nominally heterosexual intercourse of Dan and Diane, poses questions to the sex scene between Kyle and Sarah (which Penley herself finds rather lackluster): **what form of sex is it when a gay man and a lesbian have sex? when a man and woman who are simulations of each other have sex? when what they simulate is a simulating machine?**[19] **These questions, of course, take us back to the cyborg.** Here we might notice, for instance, that in addition to Arnold's "natural" voice (Germanic recall of the concentration camp that marks the past/future and traces complicities the movie cannot entirely escape, and which mark its regressions), are his simulated voices: he does the police, and he does Sarah's mother. He simulates the paternal and the maternal and disposes of them.

If the machine exceeds the regulatory regimes of heterosexual gender, the donning of leather can be read in this context too. As leatherman, Arnold is the (anti)police. "Most leathermen," Geoff Mains writes, "accept the premise that government has no role whatever in the regulation of private life" (23). If this statement suggests a complicity between leathermen and right-wing anti-government ideology, it is (or can be) inflected in quite other directions. "Our political system," Pat Califia comments, *cannot digest the concept of power unconnected to privilege. S/M recognizes the erotic underpinnings of our system and seeks to reclaim them. There's an enormous hard-on beneath the priest's robe, the cop's uniform, the president's business suit, the soldier's khaki. But that phallus is powerful only so long as it is concealed, elevated to the level of a symbol, never exposed or used in literal fucking.(21)*

Does Pat Califia *literally* have a phallus? The "literal" she speaks of is anything but; rather, it literalizes the symbolic, demystifies it by refusing to separate power from sex or sex from power. Insisting on that connection, Califia's point would seem to involve a double order of simulation, what she calls the symbolic (based on hiding) and the literal (based on showing). What is shown is the simulation; the leatherman dressed as a cop or a Nazi stormtrooper is not really one. **Leather sex exposes sex where it isn't supposed to be, but it also is a refusal of sex where it is supposed to be.** Arguably, to return to Mains's point, the government enters the bedroom in heterosexual sex; by sanctioning marriage as the only possible legal sexual arrangement/institution, it makes private sex (of the legal kind) a public act. The Terminator blasts the yuppie fuckers. As the relentless refusal of heterosexual imperatives, he embodies—or bears the image of—leather culture, displaying a machismo with a difference. That difference lies beyond heterosexist gender as Califia, for example, explains when she remarks that although lesbian in her orientation she would sooner be banished to a desert island with a leatherman than with a vanilla sex lesbian. Because leather sex is not about orgasm but about boundaries and their transgressions; its scandal, as Jeffrey Weeks notes tellingly, is that it is about pleasure located beyond pain, beyond coupling, beyond compulsion. Its simulations of domination are all the more real by virtue of the fact that while they borrow from the world of the military, or, most Terminator-like, from bikers or Nazis, the images have been decontextualized, relocated; they are plugged into bodies and to pleasures linked inescapably (as pleasure is) to power.[20]

The cyborg, Constance Penley remarks, **establishes difference: crossing human and machine, past and future, the figure displaces the question of sexual difference,** marks it elsewhere and otherwise (76); for Penley the lines crossed serve only to remark gender difference as the only difference, compulsory heterosexuality as an ineffaceable boundary line in being. The figure can, however, be read otherwise, troubling differences in gender as they follow from the instability of sexual difference. The route is sado-masochism, and not only as it writes a film like *The Terminator*.[21] Here the theoretical work of Laplanche is crucial, since it roots sexuality in an "originary" masochism (scare quotes are needed since this primal moment is, as in the film, a looping back and a self-dividing self-simulating). Important too is the valuation given to an "other" sexuality in Bersani's *The Freudian Body*, which argues that even in Freud there is, alongside the teleological genital plot, another story that involves the shattering of boundaries, and whose pleasures are pre- or post-coital; for them, coital ejaculation is not the point.[22]

Sexuality manifests itself in a variety of sexual acts and in a variety of presumably nonsexual acts, but its constitutive excitement is the same in the loving copulation between two adults, the thrashing of a boundlessly submissive slave by his pitiless master, and the masturbation of the fetishist carried away by an ardently fondled silver slipper. (Freudian Body 40)

What is the same in all these is the confluence of pain and pleasure, the sado-masochistic experience of the transgressed boundary. "Shattering," Bersani's word for this, can also be found in Mains: "Leather is a sub-culture in which the austerity of image reflects a purification by constant shattering" (27). Bersani's theorization, even as it deforms the Freudian model, remains closeted (the leather connection goes undeclared). Why this is so is suggested in the more openly gay version of these arguments in "Is the Rectum a Grave?" There Bersani holds up a leather ideal that only can be occupied by a "real" (i.e., straight) man: gay men in leather are always, in his formulation, sissies; at best (at best?) they testify to gay self-hatred in their donning of macho gear, even when that gear is their flesh and muscles. In that essay, Bersani deflects the powerful and important insight that would link sexuality and power to the rather less salient argument that gay male sex is infused with self-hatred and misogyny (since the gay man in Bersani's account yearns for the hated straight male oppressor and identifies with and as a woman).

In *The Terminator*, Schwarzenegger might appeal in that way to his self-identified straight male audience or to his self-hating gay male spectators: providing them assurance that he "must be" straight (look at those muscles, listen to that taciturnity). But if so, the assurance is everywhere transgressed and evacuated in the Terminator's relentless opposition to the category of heterosexual. The film after all does make Arnold the apogee of simulation, and the masculinity—the straight masculinity—that he might be taken to represent has opted out of every scene in which it would "normally" find itself located. Rather, the image presented is pure Tom of Finland, purveyor of images of bikers and policemen for a gay audience, but with a telling difference. Whereas Tom's fantasmatic leathermen are huge everywhere —especially between the legs—one doesn't look there to find Arnold (the one shot of him frontally nude obscures his genitals). **It is not that he doesn't have a penis, simply that it isn't the point.** "A good scene," Califia comments, "doesn't end with orgasm." S/M, Foucault comments,

> *has the effect of intensifying sexual relations by introducing a perpetual novelty, a perpetual tension and a perpetual uncertainty which the simple consummation of the act lacks. The idea is also to make use of every part of the body as a sexual instrument. (20)*

Or, as he also says: to make sure there will never again be post-coital sadness: hence the murder of Matt in the movie, the man caught in such a pose of tristesse, of a pathetic satisfaction. Perhaps leather offers a further way to think about Kyle and to revalue the scenes in which he shows his scars ("so much pain," Sarah responds, beginning to be initiated). The marked body—the body that has been in pain—is the site of an ecstasy that does not have to do with coming. "To leathermen pain is no second-rate substitute; pain is enjoyment because it is pleasure" (Mains 51).

The boundary of pleasure/pain is crossed by Arnold's simulation of gay leather-space, in Reese's time travel, and in Sarah's strange mode of conception. For, in addition to her existence as photograph and as tape recording, there is a second impregnation, the one that perhaps takes, when a piece of the machine enters her leg. She and the Terminator are identified, each rendered legless (in *Terminator 2*, Arnold will be if not in fact yet in Sarah's fantasy and desire the father of her son; "of all the would-be fathers who came and went over the years," she muses, "this thing, this machine, was the only one who measured up"[23]). In her final fight, she is plugged in, even as she opts out—"You're terminated, fucker," she says to the machine Reese calls, before he dies, a "motherfucker." No more men for her (prom queen's got a gun). When she returns in *Terminator 2* she has a new body. Arnold's body? "She has become a terminator," the script notes more than once (158, 166). Or, to adopt Carol Clover's term, she is the Final Girl of the slasher movie—the girl who also is a boy and who answers the sexual indeterminacy and duplicity of the slasher.[24] Who was Sarah's first and only declared love in the film, before the time travellers entered on her scene? Not the date with the Porsche who drops her, but her pet reptile. She mothers that coldblooded, leatherskinned creature until the "real" one comes along (she has just listened to her mother's voice on the answering machine, and fondles her pet instead), a man after her own heart. That is why, for this viewer, the Terminator is at his best when, much later, he repeats that call, and in the mother's voice says: "I love you too, sweetheart"—a moment of—dare it be said?—lesbian identification.

iii. Recalls

There is another such moment, totally gratuitous, it seems, in *Total Recall* (Paul Verhoeven 1990), when Schwarzenegger hides his hulk under a huge female form, a crossdressing that transforms him into a latter-day Divine.[25] Gratuitous, yet echoed earlier, when a first attempt to reclaim, to recall a lost identity, finds him, turbaned ("You look beautiful," the agent on the phone tells his former co-worker), fighting with a bag lady over a suitcase. "Fuck you, you asshole," she says, mouthing (with the slight variation of doubling "you") the one line we see the Terminator learn in the earlier movie. If this suggests cross-gendered identification, it is not unrelated to the main plot, in which the attempt to suture identities (to recall the lost one, which finally turns into its opposite, to call it back, to erase it) takes Doug Quaid to Mars, to join forces with a revolutionary prostitute. Can it be ignored that her name, Melina, is Mel for short, and that knowing what sex goes with that name is at least as complicated as determining gender when the leader of the revolution, Kuato, is a shrivelled and infantile male form who sprouts from another man's abdomen. Kuato could, arguably, come from Quaid, alphabetically, which is to say, along the route of the signifier. The dream logic of the film promotes such speculations in the repetition with a difference of the doubled "you," in the strange routes of an ego trip—self-duplication—in which recall is spelled Rekall, Inc.

There is no way of knowing where that trip ends, or whether it has begun when the movie opens inside of a dream of Quaid and Melina on Mars (the closing shot as well). The opening shot: two spacemen (it appears), holding hands.[26] Quaid's ego trip is launched with a question asked by Dr. Love (NB): "Sexual orientation," she snaps. And looks quizzical as he replies, "Hetero." We'll see the scene again, at the end, as Quaid is strapped into the chair, protesting his transformation back into Hauser, the patsy of the dictator, Cohaagen. "He's a fucking asshole," Quaid protests, about the identity he once occupied. "Get your ass to Mars," Hauser addresses Quaid in the mirror—the computer screen. His mission, in the double agency of this plot, to get Cohaagen, to "nail the son of a bitch who fucked you." The next time we see this scene—of Quaid looking at his Hauser reflection in the mirror, on the screen, Cohaagen will have his arm around Hauser, and will call him "my boy." Get dad.

In *Total Recall*, everything happens twice; the man who folds himself, attempting to recall, and then erase the past, is the man who has, from the start, been attempting to recall what has been erased. "The best mindfuck, yet," Quaid compliments Cohaagen, and it works even after the implant has been removed from his head (the scene in the film most evocative of the "castration" scene in *Terminator*, this time, Schwarzenegger appears to put his mechanical hand—supplied in the suitcase by Hauser—up his nose, in order to extract the bug implanted as the sign of the mindfuck). Duplicates everywhere (he's got a holograph), the aim is to be the identical image (the screen speaks) and yet to repudiate its past associations. Not the dictator's boy ... and yet, the film offers no other image of politics but the totalitarianism recalled—on earth as well as on Mars.[27] The only instituted political agency in the film is the Agency (CIA?); and all agents are, like Hauser/Quaid, double agents (the infiltrating taxi driver, Benny, black and a mutant, who works for Cohaagen, is Arnold's double too, the recall and recoil of the racism that marks this film). Revolutionaries are mutants—Arnold's body ("Still bulging, Hauser?" Mel asks, groping him) is the site of this monstrosity, and it, like everything, reads in two directions at once. Right on the surface of the body, the screen, the image.

The movie is an attempt—like *Twins,* like *Kindergarten Cop*—to recall, to reclaim, the image; to recall it in a process of erasing it. Arnold the savior of the world, or the proponent of nuclear explosion? The last images seem post-apocalyptic or, like much of the Mars footage in the movie, a reconstruction of 1950s sci-fi sets and their clean energy ideology. Where is Arnold? In the image, or displaced by the very attempt to control it? One can ask similar questions about *Terminator 2: Judgment Day* (Cameron 1991), Arnold remade in the mold of a kinder, gentler America—no murderer, now, just a maimer. The film seems, at first glance, the replay we desire, beginning with the naked male bodies. And when it inverts everything—giving, this time, Sarah Connor, a consciousness, a revolutionary goal, and palpably Left connections among the Mexicans, giving her too the pumped up body that could be read as lesbian even more than as Ginger-chic (she's been mishandled by psychiatry, as gays and lesbians have been, and it is in an asylum—a Terminal Island, not in a gym—that she has been working out), giving her feminist separatist and man-hating lines that make "our savior," teenage John Connor wince ("Mom, Mom, we need to be more constructive here. I don't see this as a gender-related issue" [177])—it leaves room for Arnold only in the weirdest reconstitution of the family. The film may believe that it has reconstituted the family (cf. *Twins*), **but father is a cyborg, mother perhaps a lesbian, and the kid is part juvenile delinquent, part computer hacker, a bushytailed white version of the black computer technician that the movie abjects**, and whose destruction also happens to mean that the future upon which the films have built, no longer obtains. *Terminator 2* succeeds in altering the future by an act of violent erasure: it allows us to see—in the most horrific and convincing special effects in the movie—the nuclear holocaust, and then erases that future (upping the nuclear fantasy of *Total Recall;* in this imagined holocaust the machines won't triumph but a humanized Terminator will, the loveable maimer, killer of blacks who aspire to a place in the middle class). Arnold the goodguy (a cross, in the telling description of Adam Frank, of the old Terminator with Kindergarten Cop[28]) is now so palpably on the side of everything bad (everything the movie calls good) that the only hope the movie leaves is that having been made from the reversals that *Terminator* permitted, reversal remains a possibility for the future. The image is not set.

iv. identifications

A final shot—*Terminator 2* sent on the path of *Total Recall*. Bill Zehme describes the scene, at the close of a piece in *Rolling Stone:* Schwarzenegger appears to judge an Arnold look-alike contest—Terminator look-alike, that is, beleathered—a look-alike of the sort the Terminator becomes when replicated in *Terminator 2,* that Arnold becomes when recalled:

> ... the look-alike proceedings.... At last, five contestants march out to stand before the man who represents all they dream of becoming. Arnold stares them down slowly, then taps one particularly sullen finalist as his choice ...

> "Congratulations, Scott," he says, slowly, "You look cool." Scott shuffles modestly. Arnold continues his appraisal. "I like those sexy lips of yours," he says, teasing, "It's true, Scott. They're driving me wild, I tell you!" (79)

Notes

1. This seems the appropriate place to note that I first saw these films thanks to Barbara Correll, and to acknowledge the centrality of her "Primary Text" in what follows. In the same vein, I record my gratitude to the Usual Suspects, Michael Moon and Eve Kosofsky Sedgwick, who read early drafts and screened films with me; to Andrew Parker and Marcie Frank, for helpful comments on a later draft, not all of which I was able to use in this one; and to Jonathan Brody Kramnick, who helped at every stage.

2. Columbu wins the preliminary competition among men of his size—"small" men—but then is defeated by Schwarzenegger in the final round. Columbu is also Schwarzenegger's preferred training partner and, in the film, his "roommate"—their beds are right next to each other. Training partners seem to be the closest to a sexual relationship between men that the film admits; there is, for instance, the opening scene between Schwarzenegger and Mike Katz, in which Katz says "You remember Joey," introducing his training partner. The film "forgets" Joey, and his ilk, though the commands often being shouted at the bodybuilders—"up, up" is a favored one—record these voices, whose job is, it seems, to keep their partners "up."

3. In asking these questions, I am, of course, attempting to displace the terms of Metz's classic account, which takes as its project the installation of the Imaginary in the Symbolic, and which has dominated film criticism, even of a feminist psychoanalytic cast. Thus, for instance, Holmlund is so intent upon showing the ways in which the sequel positions women as consumable items in capitalist culture that she denies the extravagant questioning of femininity that, as Correll argues, makes the film resist such a totalizing reading. Holmlund points, valuably, to the unnatural nature of bodies in these films, but then allows the unnatural to become the commodity. It is the inevitability of such trajectories that my argument seeks to resist. In doing so, I follow, of course, a trajectory arguably enunciated by Irigaray, whose rigorous insistence on the Phallus as the support of mystification and pretense could be taken to say that the Phallus, rather than securing heterosexual difference, is a product of the heterosexist imaginary.

4. "A man who achieves multiple orgasms—and who displaces the phallus to his perfect pecs and his 23-inch biceps—is obviously capable of some impressive feats" (Correll 295). In *Pumping Iron*, the book, Schwarzenegger is quoted as describing the pump as "better than coming," although he claims this is a joke (48). The disavowal, of course, attempts to ward off various sexual possibilities that cannot be reduced to heterosexuality: masturbation and homosexuality in particular. The authors of the book try to evade the pumping/coming equation by likening the feeling to quick motion camera shots of a flower blooming (42). The attempt fails, of course, not only because one kind of seed replaces another, but also because the "natural" image (attempting to supplant the "unnatural" suggestions) is linked to a technology (of the camera) congruent with the artifices of bodybuilding and its dependence upon looking, to which I will turn.

Pumping has been connected to Heideggerian being by Sandau; this move to make the pump an almost metaphysical concept—to imbues physicality with a virtual transcendentality—is fully in line with such idealizations as the insistent use of sculpting, of the body become art. Perhaps also to the point is the Germanic/Aryan/Nazi connection that Sandau keeps approaching and avoiding.

In his *Encyclopedia*, in line with the much tamed down image he cultivates as a movie star (the book *Pumping Iron* casually mentions his use of steroids, while the film shows him smoking a joint; the Chairman of the President's Council on Physical Fitness and Sports needs to efface this past), Schwarzenegger redescribes the pump as "nearly sexual" (79).

5. That this is also, for Bersani, the site of pleasurable pain might well be connected to the regimes of bodybuilding, to "the (almost) enjoyable pain of an intense workout" (*Encyclopedia* 81).

6. E.g., "The penis can never live up to the mystique implied by the phallus. Hence the excessive, even hysterical quality of so much male imagery" (Dyer 71). Dyer's wording almost gives the show away: "hysterical" codes these hard, erect bodies as female, suggests that the spectacle they offer—of being the phallus—rather than confirming masculinity denies it, and in the denial breaks the penis/phallus connection. The point I am making here seems to me congruent with Butler's "The Lesbian Phallus."

7. The image appears in the second edition of *Pumping Iron* (84), and is reproduced in Dyer (64).

8. Schwarzenegger's writings are filled with refusals of the machine—Nautilus machines and their lik—in favor of free weights. What is warded off is, clearly enough, a version of the artificial that threatens the favored trope of the statue/art; also resisted is the possibility that these are machine-made rather than mind-made bodies (Schwarzenegger insists over and over again that concentration and imagination can put muscles where one wants them).

9. The "Introduction" to *Pumping Iron* presents itself as aimed against the widespread belief that bodybuilders are "narcissistic, coordinatively helpless muscleheads with suspect preferences" (8). These charges are less engaged than ignored, although late in the book, one bodybuilder is quoted saying his life would be easier if he were kept by a homosexual (162), and there is a alluring reference to those who sully the sport by appearing with erections (174); mainly, however, a woman named Virginia is introduced as viewer (along with the boys, the male authors), to voice the worry that the men at whom she is gazing only have eyes for each other, and to be assured that they "like girls" (166); her response: " 'It would be such a waste.' 'What would?' 'If they didn't like girls' " (168).

In *Pumping Iron*, a history of bodybuilding is offered, from strongmen to muscular definition, from the circus to the athletic spectacle, from Germanic body worship to its statuesque realization. Nowhere in this account is the "other" history of bodybuilding mentioned in which the male pinups of such magazines as *Physique Pictorial* solicited a gay male gaze; Dyer takes up a bit of this history, as does Ischar, who reviews the work of Mapplethorpe and the venom directed at his "pornographic" images by the Right; Ischar argues that the sole value of the attack is the way in which it refuses Mapplethorpe's formalist aestheticizing, and suggests the affinities between some of his photos and those directed at gay male desires. In this context, it is worth mentioning Chapman's *Adonis*, a collection of photos of the sort that can be found in *Pumping Iron*; the difference lies in the book's publisher, and the assumptions that follow from that piece of information.

10. For those who have not seen the movie, a brief summary of the plot of *The Terminator* follows.

In 2029, humankind is in danger of annihilation by machines; a Terminator (a cyborg used to infiltrate and destroy humans) is sent back to 1984 Los Angeles to kill Sarah Connor, future mother of John Connor, who, in 2029, leads the humans against the machines; he, in turn, has dispatched Kyle Reese to save Sarah Connor, and to stop the Terminator. Depending on the phone-book listings, the Terminator kills two Sarah Connors and, in his final mistake, kills Ginger (the real Sarah's roommate), as well as her boyfriend, Matt. It is only then that he discovers her picture in a photo ID and pursues her to the Tech Noir bar, where a terrified Sarah has spotted Reese as her pursuer (it is a message she leaves on her answering machine, unheard by Ginger, but heard by the Terminator, that tips him off to the fact that he has not eliminated the final Sarah Connor). Sarah finally manages to contact the police, but not in time: Reese rescues Sarah in the bar, and begins to tell her the story of her part in the future as they are pursued by the Terminator and by the police, who finally capture them. The Terminator enters the police station and, in the ensuing massacre, only Reese (branded as crazy by the police psychiatrist) and Sarah escape. In the motel, thinking she is speaking to her mother on the telephone (in fact, it is to the Terminator, who has killed her and is simulating her voice) Sarah reveals where they are hiding. Continuing to fill her in on the future, Reese shows Sarah her picture, given to him by John Connor, and declares his love; they have sex. The Terminator arrives on a motorcycle, and a final chase sequence follows, in which the cyborg first appears to have been defeated, but survives without his human skin, pursuing Reese and Sarah to an electronics factory, where Reese is killed by the machine, and Sarah, wounded in the thigh, terminates the legless Terminator in a hydraulic press. At the end of the film, she flees to Mexico in a jeep, dictating her story for the baby she is carrying; stopping at a gas station, her picture is snapped; it is the photo that John Connor handed Reese when he dispatched him.

11. A similar, and fuller debate has been occasioned by the character of Ripley (played by Sigourney Weaver) in *Alien* (Ridley Scott 1979) and, to a lesser extent, in its James Cameron sequel, *Aliens* (1984); a good selection of these essays is offered in Kuhn.

12. "It seemed at first," Sofia concludes, "that a contradiction existed between the ruling conservatives' interest in military escalation and their espoused desire to protect fetal life, but both positions turn out to be articulations of the collapsed future.... [E]ach is part of the ideological apparatus of exterminism, which collapses the future onto the present and prepares for the ultimate science-fiction spectacular" (59), the nuclear holocaust. Sofia's terms—especially her use of extermination—resonate (before the fact?) with *The Terminator*, and her description of these complicities of nuclear family and nuclear war uncannily match the film.

13. I have in mind, in particular, the essay "The Technology of Gender," and its call for the recognition of

"contradiction, multiplicity, and heteronomy" (26), the opening of a space as it were between or within the overpowering determinations of patriarchal ideology.

In line with de Lauretis would be the comments of Kuhn in the various prefatory sections in *Alien Zone* which point towards an agenda that is marxist/feminist/intertextual, and which does not settle for single determinations or for readings that reduce films to singular effects.

14. It would bring one to the bathetic close to Jameson in which "political groups which seek actively to intervene in history"—and, as Jameson makes clear, those groups might be on the Left or on the Right—are stymied by the postmodern scene with its "deplorable and reprehensible ... image addiction" (85). Jameson's opposition to the present for its lack of presence could be called humanist; his lack of any engagement (in that essay or elsewhere) with feminism reveals a barely disguised masculinism.

It is, I would argue, when gender either is ignored, or is treated as if its relation to questions of sexuality could be ignored, that such evaluations of the culture of the present—including popular culture—can go on. Such views are countered in many essays in Modleski; Jameson's essay is used by Sobchack in *Screening Space* to provide a typology of 1980s sci-fi films.

15. By Goscilo (43), as well as by Mann in a narratological reading that perhaps too easily falls for the voice of the narrator—Reese, throughout most of the film; at any rate, Mann warms to the "emotional" and "cognitive" roles that Reese plays. For a reading of some current sci-fi films in relation to a replacement of patriarchal scenarios with, as she construes them more benign versions of the father, in family melodramas, see Sobchack, "Child/Alien/Father" (esp. 26-27), for a validation of Reese as a new style father as opposed to the Terminator as a figure for "invincible patriarchal power" linked to nuclear destruction. Sobchack fails to consider the links between these supposedly opposite figures in the film; she is more acute, on pp. 30-31, about the fantasmatic nature of the single-female-parent solution that the film appears to offer in Connor.

16. The machine is about as venomous as Bersani in "Is the Rectum a Grave?" when he remarks that "TV treats us to nauseating processions of yuppie women announcing to the world that they will no longer put out for their yuppie boyfriends" (202), an instance, undeniably to be deplored, of the ways in which the media have presented AIDS, dividing the population into an "innocent" general populace (invariably straight and white) and victims who are also viewed as murderers (gays and drug users, the latter invariably imagined as people of color). It has to be noted, however, that Bersani's example carries a fair dose of misogyny, as if the women so represented were responsible for the media. It might also be said that the representation of the Terminator (especially when characterized as an infiltrator who cannot be distinguished from a "real" human) conflates two gay thematics; one, the Terminator as the HIV virus; second, the Terminator as gay man passing as straight. I will comment on a version of the latter below.

17. The linking of gun and writing instrument is a long-established one, going back to the nineteenth century, Remington as maker of rifles and typewriters.

18. The theoretical points to be made here should almost declare themselves: the novel can be read by way of Rubin to be positing an originary/prohibited homosexuality at the origin of culture; moreover, as Butler argues, putting pressure on Rubin, the "prohibition" can also be read, by way of Foucault, as the *productive* site of sex/gender, making impossible the stability of the hetero-homo divide as unbreakable, denying either label the ability to deliver subject positions fully saturated with self-identity. Gerrold's anthropology also resonates with Mitchell's arguments about "The Holy Family" that seek to restore the avunculate—the mother's brother—as a fourth term that would displace the Oedipal triangle. If this reconfigures the place of women in culture, it also has been used by Owens in his important "Outlaws" to argue for the place of gay men *in the law* when the law is no longer understood in stereotypical Oedipal ways. Sedgwick, in recent (unpublished) work that it has been my privilege to read, has been extending the figure of the avunculate in order to offer non-Oedipal, non-phallic models for gay male relations.

19. These questions bear comparison to those asked by Patton; influential on my thinking here has been Moon's work on questions of sexual *dis*orientation.

20. Weeks (236-41, esp. 240-41); Weeks also emphasizes that S/M features a degenitalization of sex and of pleasure.

21. I approach here an argument that I would want immediately to distinguish from Silverman's work on male masochism, whose clinical language continues to pathologize the condition and to specularize "the homosexual." Much as Silverman commendably seeks a post-paternal, post-phallic disruption in masochism, she locates her frisson vis-à-vis the heterosexual man who submits to a dominating woman. Her conclusions, that is, are subsumed within the law of compulsory heterosexuality. It is, as it were, from this position of would-be "strong" woman lambasting straight male inadequacy that Smith, in work which I find even less useful on this subject, subsumes male masochism within the phallic law, leaving men only hysteria as that which exceeds the law; Smith seems to "get" his men by declaring them to be women.

22. Bersoni's arguments could also be compared to Adams, who finds two stories in Freud which he conflates and which she seeks to separate; "the story concerning the Law and the phallus" and "the story about the oscillation of the drive" (28).

23. *Terminator 2* screenplay (154). Cameron refers to this elsewhere as the "improbable family" motif (see, e.g., 133-34).

24. Positing that the Final Girl shares qualities of the slasher ("Just as the killer is not fully masculine, she is not fully feminine ..." [204]), Clover first presents this in terms of the pathology of the slasher (a pathologization of and defense against homosexuality), but her account, rather than taking sexuality seriously, plays off notions of gender. In a preliminary conclusion, Clover argues that the Final Girl really is a (stand in for) a boy, "a male surrogate in things oedipal, a homoerotic stand-in" (213). She then abandons, or modifies this thesis (dictated by the arguments of Mulvey) but continues to follow Mulvey to argue that the Final Girl isn't *really* a boy, but the locus for boys to become girls and girls boys. The syntax here maintains heterosexual difference (the imperative of the slasher genre, Clover contends) rather than seeing the ways in which such cross-identifications baffle the male-female opposition that structures Clover's account.

25. I owe this association to Butler; to begin to fill in what such a gesture might mean, one's guide would be Moon and Sedgwick's "Divinity."

26. While the revelation of their faces heterosexualizes the scene, it also works, even before then, to dispel the notion of the virginity of astronauts, to recall the title of an essay by Sobchack. That male-male sci-fi couples (especially Spock and Kirk from *Star Trek*) have been the site for a prodigious amount of female pornographic investment (K/S zines) is the subject of Russ.

27. The best discussion of the mixed political themes of the film is offered by Glass.

28. Personal communication, 3 July 1991.

References

Adams, Parveen. "Per Os(cillation)." *Camera Obscura* 17 (1988): 7-30.

Bersani, Leo. *The Freudian Body: Psychoanalysis and Art.* New York: Columbia UP, 1986.

_____"Is the Rectum a Grave?" *AIDS: Cultural Analysis/Cultural Activism.* Ed. Douglas Crimp. Cambridge: MIT P, 1987.

Butler, Judith. *Gender Trouble: Feminism and the Subversion of Identity.* New York: Routledge, 1990.

_____"The Lesbian Phallus and the Morphological Imaginary." *differences: A Journal of Feminist Cultural Studies* 4.1 (1992): 133-71.

Califia, Pat. "Unravelling the Sexual Fringe." *Advocate* 27 Dec. 1979: 19-21.

Cameron, James. *Terminator 2: Judgment Day.* New York: Applause, 1991.

Carcaterra, Lorenzo. Rev. of *Arnold: An Unauthorized Biography* by Wendy Leigh. *People Weekly* 28 May 1990: 28-29.

Chapman, David. *Adonis: The Male Physique Pin Up 1870-1940.* London: Gay Men's, 1989.

Clover, Carol. "Her Body, Himself: Gender in the Slasher Film." *Representations* 20 (1987): 187-228.

Correll, Barbara. "Notes on the Primary Text: Woman's Body and Representation in *Pumping Iron II: The Women* and 'Breast Giver.' " *Genre* 22 (1989): 287-309.

de Lauretis, Teresa. *Technologies of Gender: Essays on Theory, Film, and Fiction.* Bloomington: Indiana UP, 1987.

Dyer, Richard. "Don't Look Now." *Screen* 23 (1982): 61-73.

Foucault, Michel. "Sexual Choice, Sexual Act: An Interview with Michel Foucault." *Salmagundi* 58-59 (1982-83): 10-24.

Gaines, Charles, and George Butler. *Pumping Iron.* New York: Simon, 1974; revised and updated, 1981.

Gerrold, David. *The Man Who Folded Himself.* 1973, New York: Bantam, 1991.

Glass, Fred. "Totally Recalling Arnold: Sex and Violence in the New Bad Future." *Film Quarterly* 44 (1990): 2-13.

Goscilo, Margaret. "Deconstructing *The Terminator.*" *Film Criticism* 12 (1987-88): 37-52.

Haraway, Donna. "A Manifesto for Cyborgs: Science, Technology, and Socialist Feminism in the 1980s." *Coming to Terms: Feminism, Theory, Politics.* Ed. Elizabeth Weed. New York: Routledge, 1989, 173-204.

Holmlund, Christine Anne. "Visible Difference and Flex Appeal: The Body, Sex, Sexuality, and Race in the *Pumping Iron* Films." *Cinema Journal* 28 (1989): 38-51.

Ischar, Doug. "Endangered Alibis." *Afterimage* 17.10 (1990): 8-11.

Irigaray, Luce. "Commodities among Themselves." *This Sex Which Is Not One.* Trans. Catherine Porter with Carolyn Burke. Ithaca: Cornell UP, 1985, 192-97.

Jameson, Fredric. "Postmodernism, or The Cultural Logic of Late Capitalism." *New Left Review* 146 (1984): 53-92.

Kuhn, Annette, ed. *Alien Zone: Cultural Theory and Contemporary Science Fiction Cinema*. London: Verso, 1990.

Laplanche, Jean. *Life and Death in Psychoanalysis*. Trans. Jeffrey Mehlman. Baltimore: Johns Hopkins UP, 1976.

Leigh, Wendy. *Arnold: An Unauthorized Biography*. Chicago: Congden, 1990.

Mains, Geoff. *Urban Aboriginals: A Celebration of Leathersexuality*. San Francisco: Gay Sunshine, 1984.

Mann, Karen. "Narrative Entanglements: *The Terminator*." *Film Quarterly* 45 (1989): 12-27.

Metz, Christian. *The Imaginary Signifier: Psychoanalysis and the Cinema*. Trans. Celia Britton, et al. Bloomington: Indiana UP, 1982.

Mitchell, Juliet. *Psychoanalysis and Feminism*. New York: Vintage, 1974.

Modleski, Tania. *Studies in Entertainment: Critical Approaches to Mass Culture*. Bloomington: Indiana UP, 1986.

Moon, Michael. "A Small Boy and Others: Sexual Disorientation in Henry James, Kenneth Anger, and David Lynch." *Comparative American Identities*. Ed. Hortense Spillers. New York: Routledge, 1991, 146-56.

Moon, Michael, and Eve Kosofsky Sedgwick. "Divinity: A Dossier/A Performance Piece/A Little Understood Emotion." *Discourse* 13 (1990-91): 11-39.

Mulvey, Laura. *Visual and Other Pleasures*. Bloomington: Indiana UP, 1980.

Necakov, Lillian. "The Terminator: Beyond Classical Hollywood Narrative." *Cineaction* 8 (1987): 84-86.

Owens, Craig. "Outlaws: Gay Men in Feminism." *Men in Feminism*. Ed. Alice Jardine and Paul Smith. New York: Routledge, 1986, 219-32.

Patton, Cindy. "hegemony and Orgasm - or the Instability of Heterosexual Pornography." *Screen* 30.1/2 (1989): 100-12.

Penley, Constance. "Time Travel, Primal Scene, and the Critical Dystopia." *Camera Obscura* 15 (1986): 67-84.

Rogin, Michael. *"Ronald Reagan," the Movie, and Other Episodes in Political Demonology*. Berkeley: U of California P, 1987.

Rubin, Gayle. "The Traffic in Women." *Toward an Anthropology of Women*, Ed. Rayna Rapp. New York:Monthly, 1975, 157-210.

Russ, Joanna. "Pornography By Women For Women, With Love." *Magic Mommas, Trembling Sister, Puritans & Perverts*. Trumansburg, NY: Crossing, 1985.

Sandau, Jerry. "Heidegger and Schwarzenegger: Being and Training." *Philosophy Today* 32 (1988): 156-64.

Schwarzenegger, Arnold. *The Education of a Bodybuilder*. New York: Simon, 1977.

Schwarzenegger, Arnold. *Enclycopedia of Modern Bodybuilding*. New York, Siman, 1985.

Sedgwick, Eve Kosofsky. *Between Men: English Literature and Male Homosexual Desire*. New York: Columbia UP, 1985.

Sedgwick, Eve Kosofsky. "Tales of the Avunculate." Unpublished ms.

Silverman, Kaja. "Masochism and Male Subjectivity." *Camera Obscura* 17 (1988): 31-66.

Smith, Paul. "Action Movie Hysteria, or Eastwood Bound." *differences: A Journal of Feminist Cultural Studies* 1.3 (1989): 88-107.

Sobchack, Vivian. "Child/Alien/Father: Patriarchal Crisis and Generic Exchange." *Camera Obscura* 15 (1986): 7-34.

Sobchack, Vivian. *Screening Space*. New York:Ungar, 1987.

Sobchack, Vivian. "The Virginity of Astronauts." Kuhn 103-15.

Sofia, Zoe. "Exterminating Fetuses: Abortion, Disarmament, and the Sexo-Semiotics of Extraterrestrialsim." *Diacritics* 14 (1984): 47-59.

Weeks, Jeffrey. *Sexuality and its Discontents: Meanings, Myths and Modern Sexualities*. London: Routledge, 1985.

Zehme, Bill. "Mr. Big Shot." *Rolling Stone* 21 Aug. 1991:38-39, 41-42, 79.

ART, PSYCHASTHENIC ASSIMILATION, AND THE CYBER-NETIC AUTOMATON

David Tomas

*Sharing in the trickery of the automaton is merely another way to define
ourselves as human, that is, as both being and nothingness, presence and
absence: the automaton is, in a way, our mirror ... or our evil eye.*
—Jean-Claude Beaune

In the following pages I will present some conditions and
mechanisms that transform an art practice into a laboratory for the production and exploration of one kind of
quasi-mechanized human body. The approach is based on an ongoing
series of 'performed installations', the first of which was produced in 1983 and the
most recent in 1995, which explored one aspect or another of the relationship
between modern imaging systems (photography, closed circuit television, cable
television and, most recently, virtual reality technology), modes of
transportation/communication (in particular railways) and historical transformations in western vision.[1] My body functioned in these works as a passive mecha-

nized component in the sense that its parameters of operation and its own conscious and unconscious spaces were always defined by its ultimate subordination to a machine system and repetitive mode of mechanical reproduction. And yet this mechanized body served as a key point of articulation in a three-dimensional commentary, perhaps even a meta-discourse, modeled on the idea of a 'text' whose coherence was guaranteed by the human body's role of sensory transducer between different experiential domains.

The fact that I was a conscious component in a machine-like system allowed me to privately reflect *in situ* on my privileged status as working mechanical element in a performance that could last for a period of one hour in the case of a short presentation to approximately eight hours per day over a period of three weeks in the case of a longer work. Because of my anthropological interests, this reflection often took an auto-ethnographic turn without, however, any of the trappings of conventional fieldwork since the linkages between the activity I was engaged in and the position from which I was observing seemed, at the time, to be completely incompatible. Thus, with the exception of a few brief comments made during slide presentations in university based art departments, the consequences of my transformation into a machine component have been for the most part confined to a few unexplored personal reflections. [2]

Lately, however, I have begun to reevaluate the kinds of bodily experiences and psychological transformations that I encountered in my role as a 'quasi-mechanized' component. Evaluation has focussed, in particular, on my use of an early nineteenth century drawing instrument, William H. Wollaston's camera lucida: a simple and ingenious optical tool that allows the eye to perceive the image of a scene or 'view' virtually superimposed onto a drawing surface in such a way as to allow an amateur or professional draughtsman to produce a more or less accurate delineation of the scene.

For a number of years it was not obvious to me why I was so fascinated with this archaic instrument apart from its historical relationship to the 'invention' of photography and the fact that it allowed me to interface in a fairly simple yet rigid optical fashion with a given view: an overexposed photograph or, recently, live cable television. Indeed, the camera lucida's use in works that clearly focussed on modern imaging systems such as photography or television tended to exacerbate the contradiction that lay at the root of my body's reduction to machine element since the camera lucida's contemporary use as a primary means of image production was focussed in the opposite direction: on a pre-modern and largely unmediated activity—namely, pencil drawing.

However, the camera lucida's use in a short, strenuous performed installation in 1991 that dealt specifically with late twentieth century body/technology transformations[3] has prompted me to reexamine and clarify its enigmatic status as interface mechanism as well as its peculiar role in generating body/consciousness transformations in the context of a performed installation. The following observations on the relationship between art, psychasthenic assimilation and the cybernetic automaton are the result of this reexamination.

A Cultural Mechanism to Reimage the Body and Refashion the Eye

Performed installation is a peculiar hybrid of performance art and installation art.

As its name suggests, it is predicated on an installation form of art practice, that is, a practice which emerges by way of a materialized dialogue between an artist and a particular physical/symbolic environment. However, performed installation differs from more traditional forms of installation art practice in its use of a living human body. As opposed to the active use of the human body in performance art, or its absence in conventional object-based installation art forms,[4] **performed installations use a human body, but restructure its presence in such a way as to reduce it to the status of a mere component in an economy of artifacts and environment.** The human body is transformed, under these circumstances, into an unusual entity since its new spatial position, its *site specificity* or 'installed' sense of situated and objectified self, is the direct product of this economy.

Depending on the intensity of its assimilation, the body's new site specificity engenders an increasingly novel yet contradictory existence. The presence of mechanical supports, machine elements or advanced imaging systems can highlight its distinctiveness as an autonomous organic entity. On the other hand, this context can reduce the body to the status of a component because its subjectivity is increasingly infiltrated by an object-like or mechanized aura as organic mobility is constrained by mechanical integration and a regime of clearly defined machine-like actions. Thus, although the body-as-object is still metabolically alive, it seems to hibernate in its representational shell as if to camouflage its subjectivity in terms of its objectness.

Mimetic implosions of this type were originally explored by Roger Caillois in a classic paper 'Mimicry and Legendary Psychasthenia'. A performed installation's version of complete mimetic integration or psychasthenic fusion consists, in Caillois' descriptive terms, of a "*depersonalization by assimilation*" to an objective model of the body's own representational space which, because of its incorporation of object-like attributes, promotes a simultaneous "*generalization of* [physical/artifactual] *space* at the expense of the individual" body's subjective autonomy.[5] A condition of photostasis is thus achieved: a 'living death' resulting from the body's psychasthenic assimilation to the performed installation's immediate artifactual environment.

Caillois has also described how psychasthenia can promote a separation of body and consciousness as "the individual breaks the boundary of his skin and occupies the other side of his senses." Indeed, his description of what it means to occupy 'the other side of one's senses' provides a key insight into the bizarre turn that consciousness can take as it is turned inside out of a human skin to find a new home in another and foreign environment since his explanation allows one to picture the ethereal shape of its perceptual logic. In Caillois' words:

> He tries to look at himself from *any point whatever in space. He feels himself becoming space*, dark space where things cannot be put. *He is similar, not similar to something, but just* similar.[6]

If Caillois' theory of psychasthenia sheds general light on the mechanics of identities that are situated *beyond* the frontiers of visibility, then it does so because it maps the effects of a logic of similarity's absorption of all questions of difference within a common *perceptual* frame of reference. And if Caillois' theory of psychasthenia provides a plausible scenario for the formation of physical identities that are cast in invisible terms then it does so because it pinpoints the mechanism for their creation. Therein lies its descriptive power, for psychasthenic spatial dissimulation allows one to locate this new form of (self)-consciousness's governing logic as well as the source of its emergence **at the physical interface** of an organic human body and a given machine system.

The body's identity **as an installed and performed organism** is, as such, more accurately portrayed through its physical relationship to its new conditions and specifications of existence. Indeed, it is perhaps most accurately grasped through a system of *technicity* whose pattern of similarities and differences are rooted in the technical specifications of the artificial environments that serve as its new breeding ground. [7]

A performed installation can therefore be considered, from the point of view of its systemic powers of representational/perceptual transformation, as well as through its power to separate body and consciousness, **to function as a special kind of mimetically integrated** *technology*—ultimately, a complicated imaging system through which a living human body is radically refashioned.

Body in the image of Technology

A performed installation integrates, in its most extreme and evocative form, a living human body in a pure technological environment of machine elements, electronic components, advanced imaging systems. Under these conditions, the body's new systemic status creates novel communicational possibilities as it begins to extend its immediate sensory universe through technology's ability to link radically different spaces and places. A performed installation is thus a useful imaging system in its own right inasmuch as the history in which it operates is not strictly its own history or even that of art but rather those of the inner and outer spaces of technology, or the spaces that technology creates and the spaces of which it is composed. It being understood, of course, that all such spaces are constructed with the body in mind.

Technology maps the world according to its own particular array of spatio-temporal logics (here one thinks of the way the railway system has rewritten the landscape and in the process has not only changed the world but also our spatio-temporal position and view of that world[8]). Insofar as performed installations are three-dimensional narratives that are built on these initial maps or narratives, systems and metasystem, technology and performed installation, form a complex network for new kinds of 'spatial practices' and 'practiced places.' [9] First and foremost among these practices is that of an aesthetics of invisibility which is promoted in terms of psychasthenia and the new mechanized space and practiced place of the body itself.

Performed installations can be used, according to the degree of their systemic integration in a wider culture of technology, to actively explore the physical and tropological possibilities of this particular culture's nest of systems, networks and spaces; and, according to the transparency of the human body's technological integration, they inevitably explore these possibilities within the more or less sharply defined parameters of psychasthenic logic. Should these parameters be sufficiently strong they would also automatically map what it means to exist in close proximity to a zero degree of human consciousness as the body is transformed according to this logic and its aesthetics of invisibility into a boundary phenomenon balanced at the *technological* edge of conscious extinction.

Such a balancing act would no doubt open the way for an investigation into the consequences of a transformation in the body's powers of vision as its sense-organs are generalized through mimetic assimilation and prosthetic extension and its field of vision is absorbed by a series of interconnected imaging systems (photography, film, television, virtual reality). Should this balancing act prove subtle enough to actually bracket and suspend an instant in a body's conscious existence over the abyss of its extinction then one could imagine a situation in which a subjective consciousness might be dislocated, however briefly, but also perhaps forever, from all moorings of place to be suspended in a petrified state of pure non/existentiality. Perhaps it is only at this "razor's edge of non/existence" as consciousness comes 'face to face' with its negation that an answer might be found to a rather strange question which is nevertheless of more than passing interest in connection with a technology-intensive performed installation's peculiar operationally-based psychasthenic logic—namely: 'Can images exist *without* a corporeal reference point?'

While all photochemical, electronic and computer-generated virtual images share the psychasthenic body-as-object's disembodied representational status of suspended animation, they remain phantom imprints of the retinal images from an original human eye. Such images therefore remain rooted in the human body's presence as key reference point for their existence. Since all imaging systems retain their human coordinates, the spaces of a performed installation also preserve the multiple traces of human presences which circulate as so many lost souls around the body-as-object. **Escape from these phantasms is perhaps only possible at the *technological* edge of conscious extinction when a body becomes machine** and a human consciousness mutates into something radically different from a self that has been constructed on the bedrock of a common human form, the first step toward a shared humanity.

Finally, a technology-intensive performed installation can explore the *preconditions* for its own existence **as an *art* practice because it is composed of *two* interconnected cultural systems: a culture of imaging systems and a culture of images.** One is composed of a weave of local economies—photography, film, television, video, etc.—that feed into a larger second-order global system which determines the production, distribution and circulation of western and non-western images. The other consists of the images themselves with their often obscure lives and social patterns. This doubling of representation provides the means to map the mutations of a human consciousness as it moves from one kind to another kind of body. The one frame of reference for this movement corresponds to a body's surface and hence to its status as psychasthenic 'object' and the other to its interior (conscious and unconscious) spaces. For it is the interconnections between these two frames that determine the relationship between a performed installation's function as imaging system and its aesthetics of psychasthenic invisibility.

Cybernetic Automaton

In technology-intensive performed installations machine systems become, as in the case of space capsules or advanced fighter planes, the determining factor in the definition of the body's physical installation, the material foundations and psychasthenic grounds for its site specificity. In fact, the ultra-modern fighter plane's cockpit provides a good model for the way a human body can be almost completely integrated into an environment that consists of advanced imaging technologies such as sophisticated navigational and targeting systems.

A modern fighter plane is a technological breeding ground for a new kind of site-specific 'self'. This new subject position and subjectivity that operates under the name of 'fighter pilot), is, however, not solely the product of its own unique institutional apparatuses, specialized domains of knowledge and technologies. It is also the product of a psychasthenic logic. For the fighter pilot's model body and its technologically articulated consciousness exist in their purest state at the site (the fighter plane's cockpit) of a fundamental disturbance of perception, that of a schizophrenic implosion of self and place, the result of an organism's almost perfect assimilation to its surrounding space.

However, in contrast to the military/industrial crafting of new bodies and forms of consciousnesses, one can imagine that other socio-logics, other kinds of social bodies, might also be generated by similar kinds of implosive processes. Although these as yet undefined subjectivities could be radically different from their military/industrial counterparts, they nevertheless share a common root and myth of origins: the automaton.

Jean-Claude Beaune provides a useful overview of different stages in the development of automata. The first is represented by the **mythical** automaton which "maintains a relationship with the cosmos, with the totality of things"; the second by the **mechanistic** automaton which represents "an attempt to dissect and copy the human body and the body of other living creatures"; the third by the **mechanical** automation which "groups together concentrations of machines, workshops and factories, in accordance with very inflexible rules"; the fourth by the **cybernetic** and **computing** automaton with its "links with neomechanisms endowed with at least a semiautonomous intelligence or the ability to adapt, making it equivalent to a new kind of living creature"; and, finally, the fifth by synthetic **live matter**. [10]

Although the most common designation for a mid- to late-twentieth century hybrid human/machine organism is the *cyborg* or cybernetic organism, a term that was initially coined to describe 'man'/machine couplings designed to ensure human survival in outer space,[11] I favour Beaune's term 'cybernetic automaton' to describe the type of hybrid organic/machine entity that I am suggesting is the product of a body/technology fusion in a performed installation. In contrast to a 'cyborg', the cybernetic automaton does not necessarily suggest a military/industrial function. Furthermore, my use of the name presupposes an inversion in its terms of reference. In contrast to its normal use to denote the *physical* product of a fusion of living organism with machine system, I am using 'cybernetic automaton' in reference to a hybrid creation at the level of the *representation* of a human organism that has been transformed into a boundary phenomenon which is the effect of a special kind of imaging technology: the performed installation.

An installed and performed cybernetic automaton is thus a kind of transparent *representational* interface and threshold between an organic world and the world of machines. But this representational transparency is more than the simple product of a functional interface with the world of machines since it is also the result of a techno-mythological and perceptual *excess*.

At one level of its representational logic, the image of a cybernetic automaton continues to represent, as the classical automaton has always represented, a *"techno-mythological idea"*—"the mythic distillation of technical processes and machines and, by extension, of tools or instruments."[12] But at another more fundamental level it is a mythic *excess* whose roots reach to the cultural bedrock of a social Imaginary where a concept of the human can, and indeed has been, radically reimaged. For inasmuch as the human body and automaton coexist at a single representational interface as mirror images in a western history of what it means to be human, these roots nourish an extraordinary perceptual excess at the pregnant point at which the visible is the condition of invisibility and, through psychasthenic logic, where the inverse is also true, where invisibility (ie., perfect assimilation) is the condition of a new kind of visibility.

Furthermore, as Beaune has pointed out, the automaton "is not just a machine" or a mechanical mode of mapping the cosmos, organic body, mind, or life itself, it is "also the language [and mytho-language] that makes it possible to explicate" its own (mytho-)logic as machine system. This language marks, at any one time, a "limit of technology" and thus a limit of "the language of the techno-structure" itself as well as marking the limits of a vision that might operate in its terms.[13] Today that language has begun to penetrate and fuse with the human body with the promise of turning its architecture inside out and disseminating the fictions of its representational autonomy and identity as a living organism throughout the techno-structure. This is the promise that a psychasthenic logic and aesthetics of invisibility fulfills.

Beaune is therefore correct to suggest that "the social and intellectual automaton nowadays makes up the 'third type of world' we inhabit, a world **in which the frontiers and the limits between body and mind, as well as those between nature and culture, and between life and death, have grown so thick, so enduring and so dense that when we look in the mirror each day we confront portraits of the living dead**." [14] Beaune's living dead are the products of this simple, yet fundamental, mirror-stage where a western concept of the Human and a western concept of Death collude in transparent conspiratorial silence. [15]

The history of automata has produced a compelling spectrum of human/machine images. Lately, popular cinema has, through its own brand of magic, surpassed the evocative power of these earlier images with a series of its own visions of how the post-organic body should be conceived in films that range from the *RoboCop* and *Terminator* series to *Blade Runner* and *Hardware*. Although these visions are rooted in a conventional image of the cyborg as product of a military/industrial complex, there are other ways of conceptualizing body/technology transformations and their resulting hybrid forms, as well as other means of achieving such transformations besides those that are conventionally associated with a Hollywood-based Imaginary, advanced pharmaceuticals, high technology, and intelligent or semi-intelligent weapons systems. Insofar as performed installation is a concrete practice which binds the human body and technology according to a psychasthenic logic, it provides one way, among many others, of exploring the various facets of what it might mean to exist at or beyond the body/technology threshold.

Toward a Politics of the Senses at the Body/Technology interface

Marshall McLuhan pointed out in 1964, the heyday of cybernetics, that human consciousness could be considered to be a function of shifting sense ratios. He argued, moreover, that inasmuch as media technologies were only extensions of the human senses, patterns of consciousness could be mapped through the trans-formations and redeployment of the human senses in the form of new media.[16] Thus human consciousness was not only rooted in the parallel, if everchanging ratios of technologically extended senses and technology's extended senses but it was also rendered visible in their terms. The history of western media was, as a consequence, also a *visual* history of western human consciousness.

McLuhan's insights suggest that the transformative powers of a technology-inten-sive performed installation's imaging capabilities can be traced to its pattern of sensory organization and the way this pattern operates to reconfigure conscious-ness in parallel with the body's refashioning as machine element. Thus our atten-tion is drawn to the critical fact that one must also take account of a history of the senses as well as the present-day culture of imaging systems when one is engaged in the production of performed installations that are designed to alter sense ratios through the creation of different sensory economies. This important point brings us back to a question of why one should use a camera lucida as the primary means of investigating other sensory regimes and practices in the late-twentieth century. But in doing so it transforms it into a *political question.*

The use of an instrument like the camera lucida, an instrument in other words that links eye and hand through an embodied economy, produces a fundamentally dif-ferent experience of the senses of sight and touch than is normally experienced in an era which is now more then ever dominated by electronically televised images. As any comparison between a camera lucida drawing and television image reveals, and as the use of a camera lucida demonstrates, this kind of instrument resurrects the body's corporeality as a prerequisite for the forging of a laboring relationship (as defined in the act of drawing itself) between the eye and hand. Moreover, the fundamental role of the body as sensory transducer in the production of images is foregrounded in no uncertain terms when one begins to conceive of the relation-ship between the eye and the body in a new *virtual* manner, that is in terms of the absolute transformation of the body's sensorium into a pure digital medium as in the case of virtual reality technology's dream of pure disembodiment. For it is at this point that one realizes the extent to which a body's presence can be sensuous-ly transferred and even remapped onto the surface of a second skin, a piece of paper, through the humble medium of a simple pencil.

To use the camera lucida today as an interface with advanced late twentieth cen-tury imaging systems in a performed installation does not by any means automati-cally imply that one is resurrecting a so-called 'archaic' artisanal practice—drawing —in the interests of preserving academic standards, old models of the artist or artistic production. Rather, it is to highlight the existence of a particular counter-practice and its sensory space, a particular domain of tactile experience, by spatial-ly and temporally displacing this practice from the nineteenth to the late twentieth century. This spatio-temporal transposition ensures that the camera lucida is repositioned in history—a relocation which is consummated through its contacts with a late twentieth century optically governed, electronically propelled imaging culture. The contact and clash of old and new sense ratios, their respective imaging cultures and mode of graphic or electronic imaging 'draws' attention to what Michel de Certeau once described as "non-discursive practices"—activities, in other words, which have "not been tamed and symbolized in language." [17]

The camera lucida is an exceptionally interesting imaging device from the point of view of a non-discursive practice because it provides a world-view which is mediated by the 'touch of graphite'—a 'touch' that enacts a fundamental transformation in the relationship between the senses. Inasmuch as this instrument vehiculates the eye by means of a tactile logic that is geared to the production of an accurate optico/mechanical reproduction it compounds this logic by extending and disciplining the hand's touch by means of the eye's restructured powers of vision. Therein lies the power of its peculiar operational logic. For this intertwining of eye and hand, touch and vision, extends and multiplies the powers of each sense-organ—but only in terms of the other's power of representation and, moreover, only in terms of the camera lucida's prismic logic. Extension and multiplication ends up, however, in producing a sensuous condition of representational excess inasmuch as the instrument's combined sensory power transcends the individual powers of each sense-organ in a way that allows it to function beyond their traditional frontiers and, indeed, to combine each distinct sensory mode into a practice which produces a 'third' type of experience. In doing so, it can forcefully and yet sensuously remind us that there are other ways and dimensions of experience through which one might travel in search of the boundaries of what it means to be human in the late twentieth century.

If non-discursive practices are created as a consequence of the camera lucida's reorganization of the senses then they would appear to be confined to the level of an individual body's sensory apparatus and consciousness. In actual fact, however, they manifest themselves in a blended manner since the camera lucida creates new private sensations in the shape of a personal tactile experience as well as a public expression of that experience: a drawing. In the context of a performed installation, a camera lucida can also function as an interface and pivot between the twin representations of a human body and a cybernetic automaton. Hence, it is through a specific merging of private sensations and public gestures that one must search for a visible manifestation of the collective significance of a deep-rooted organic/sensory transformation. And one must do so precisely because the camera lucida registers the eclipse and transformation of the human body and its consciousness through an expanding field of graphite which doubles as a second skin; a graphite skin which, moreover, is 'shed' onto a piece of paper in the interests, it seems, of acquiring a new techno-logical shell and set of sense-organs. Thus, the camera lucida is more than a simple optical interface and interspace. It is also a powerful transducer that recalibrates the ratios between the senses of vision and touch and promotes, through this process of recalibration, the transformation of a human consciousness which is registered in a quasi-symbolic gesture: the shedding of (graphite) skin through the public display of an emergent drawing.

Inasmuch as the camera lucida 'draws' attention to such non-discursive activities in the specific context of a dominant late twentieth century televisually propelled mode of apprehending the world, its tiny optical interface functions as a means to transform (tele)visual representations into virtual images thereby allowing for their reproduction according to the tactile logic of pencil drawing. In doing so, this apparatus serves not only as an interface but also as a threshold mechanism through which an excess of touch is generated through the virtualization of (tele)vision—a vision whose ultimate present-day expression is to be found in the texture and flow of electronic images.

As the foregoing discussion has suggested, there are at least two reasons why one should adopt a *chronotopic* stance in connection with the present-day use of imaging systems like the camera lucida. [18] First, alternative economies that emerge through the use of new, marginal or even archaic instruments can not only replace or displace history at the level of their use values, they can also alter the relationship between the body conceived as an array of sense-organs and a visually-based culture of technology thereby producing significant, if marginal, shifts in the history of western perception and representation. Second, such alternative economies can provide important opportunities to renegotiate the body's position in a world whose mode of operation is governed by technology.

An Art of the Cybernetic Automaton

Vision has played a dominant role in late twentieth-century western speculations concerning body/technology transformations. Since the early 1980s, the image culture that has provided the most fertile ground for popular speculations on the body/technology interface has been a cyborg-based science fiction film culture in which late twentieth-century transformations of the human body are linked more or less directly to the development of advanced imaging systems. Recent big-budget Hollywood science fiction films such as the *Terminator* and *RoboCop* series or the British cult classic *Hardware* have presented different military models of the cyborg as a lethal, enhanced imaging system. We have, moreover, become sensitized to the power of sophisticated quasi-autonomous organs of vision which encircle the globe as a result of the widespread use of sophisticated surveillance and targeting systems during the 1991 Persian Gulf War. Meanwhile, the extraordinary powers of artificially enhanced vision have recently been celebrated through the trials, tribulations, and triumphs surrounding the operation of the Hubble Space Telescope.

A late twentieth-century commonplace would, no doubt, be to point to television, photographic and videographic cameras, photographic reconnaissance satellites of various kinds and other advanced imaging systems as the principal vehicles for a western 'culture of distance's' modes of production and dissemination. [19] However, this routine observation masks another: It is this culture's simulated and increasingly digitized photographic and cinematic space(s) which also sets the stage for the death and transformation of the human body. The key figure in these real-life or cinematic dramas is the 'human' eye and the scenario it follows is that of a dislocation of human vision, its redeployment in a televisual or cinematic space and subsequent transformation into cyborg vision—a transformation that doubles through metonymic displacement as a sumptuous requiem for the death of the human body as it too is absorbed by new forms of industrialized space or is simply destroyed as a direct consequence of their deployment. Hence, to focus on the question of technologically enhanced vision at this moment in history is to confront the actual or fictional possibilities of this transformation *on its own terms.*

A performed installation can enact a similar transformation of the body in the context of its own technology of vision. Inasmuch as one is 'fixed' in a technology-based psychasthenic system, one enacts one's own death—the death of an organic, living human body—according to a similar transformation in one's vision and visual field as one's consciousness is grounded through an optical interface into the body of technology. A performed installation can, in other words, plot a parallel transformation from one kind of body to another type of body as sense ratios change, as one sense-organ is enhanced at the expense of the others, as one organ is industrialized at the expense of the others, and as one type of consciousness is transformed into another.

However, the scenario of a body that succumbs to psychasthenic logic and its powers of perceptual re-representation can also be used to promote the existence of other ratios of the senses. These other ratios might challenge and pollute cyborg vision with a more subtle and dangerously intimate sensuality that is directly rooted in the human body itself. One scenario as to how this might be achieved begins with the camera lucida's use in a performed installation.

As I have suggested, an exploration of the limits of western vision, its logic and socio-political consequences must begin with the 'death' of the organic body and the western anthropological and engineering logics that are creating, that have already created, the cyborg. **It must begin with the cyborg because this entity, more than any other, holds the promise of other forms of intelligence and other worlds that might exist beyond the human body/machine interface.** However, this exploration must engage the future of a disembodied and invisible body in the name of the past, in the name of a visible, embodied, indeed, corporeal body that still inhabits much of the globe under the sign of difference. But it must not plunge uncritically into the past, just as it must resist the simple, ultimately fatal, solution of a nostalgic return to a past in the interests of the present. Instead, it must take shape, as Nietzsche once argued, through a diligent and critical *use* of the past in the service of a future. And, as he was at pains to point out, this use must be grounded in a tenuous balancing act between past and future.[20]

Perhaps an art of the cybernetic automaton is nothing more than this 'art' of balancing between a past history of the body and the future of a different kind of body. From this viewpoint, this art is not, and can never be, the pure product of the present; just as its practice cannot be rooted completely in the present, or directed solely towards the future. Its product is always a 'dirty' product, the result of a 'soiled' practice—a practice soiled by history, the history of a body and technology, the history of an interface. If the art of the cybernetic automaton is, finally, nothing more than a balancing act at the edge of conscious extinction and at the brink of the invisible, then this art is nonetheless a rebellious practice. It is rebellious because of its everchanging positions on the horizon of a chronotopic interface whose historical chimeras and techno-mythologies link past and present bodies in the service of future bodies whose invisible shapes and sensory universes are still open to speculative interpretation. The camera lucida stands in its capacity as interface mechanism, in its chronotopic role, as well as in its historical marginality, as a strange and idiosyncratic, yet particularly suitable symbol for these new and tenuous bodies.

An earlier version of this paper was presented at the Universities Art Association Conference, University of Windsor, in November 1993.

Notes

1. The performed installations include: 'Photography: A Word,' Yajima/Galerie, Montreal, 1983; 'Behind the Eye Lies the Hand of William Henry Fox Talbot,' S.L. Simpson Gallery, Toronto, 1984; 'This is What You Want, This is What You Get,' Walter Phillips Gallery, Banff, Alberta, 1991; Museum Moderner Kunst Stiftung Ludwig Wien, Vienna, 1992; 'Time Transfixed IV,' Oakville Galleries, Oakville, Ontario, 1994; and 'This is What You Want, This is What You Get,' California Institute of the Arts, Santa Clarita, 1995.

2. The exception is an interview, 'Pour Une Pratique Negative de la Photographie,' published in *Parachute* No. 37, 1984/5, pp. 4-8.

3. 'This is What You Want, This is What You Get,' Walter Phillips Gallery, Banff, Alberta, 1991.

4. In both cases I am, of course, referring to the body's use as an element *in the work of art* as opposed to the way a work of art might seek, as part of its visual or spatio-temporal strategy, to actively manipulate or situate a spectator.

5. Rogger Caillois, 'Mimicry and Legendary Psychasthenia,' *October* No. 31, 1984, pp. 30, 31 (emphases in the original). Caillois' article contains a full discussion of psychasthenia and its connections to a psychopathology of social spaces. Some important connections between psychasthenia and postmodern urban experiences are explored in relation to the formation of cyborg identities in Celest Olalquiaga, *Megalopolis: Contemporary Cultural Sensibilities*, (Minneapolis: U of Minn. Press, 1992), pp. 1-18. Olalquiaga's chapter does not, however, explore obvious connections between formation of a cyborg consciousness, psychasthenia and technology. Indeed, this is a striking omission in her otherwise excellent discussion of postmodernity and the urban psychasthenic experience. Rosalind Krauss has note various connections between Caillois' theory and automatons in her essay 'Corpus Delicti' in *L'Amour Fou: Photography and Surrealism* (Washington D.C.: The Corcoran Gallery of Art/New York:Abbeville Press, 1985), pp. 70, 85-86, 95. Although highly informative and often provacative, her observations do not extend beyond a surrealist frame of reference. Finally, for a discussion of psychasthenia in the graphic arts see my 'Mimesis and the Death of Difference in the Graphic Arts,' *SubStance*, no. 70, 1993, pp. 41-52.

6 Caillois, ibid., p. 30 (emphases in the original).

7. For a discussion of technicity see my 'The Technophilic Body: On Technicity in William Gibson's Cyborg Culture,' *New Formations* No. 8, 1989, pp. 113-129, and 'Technicity and the Future of Their Bodies,' *Bioapparatus* (Banff: The Banff Center for the Arts, 1991), p. 30.

8. See, for example, Wolfgang Schivelbusch, *The Railway Journey: Trains and Travel in the 19th Century*, trans. Anselm Hollo, (New York: Urizen Books, 1980).

9. Michel de Certeau, 'Spatiol Stories,' in The Practice of Everyday Life, trans. Steven Rendall, (Berkeley, Los Angeles, London: U of California Press, 1988), p. 115.

10. Jean-Claude Beaune, 'The Classical Age of Automata: An Impressionistic Survey from the Sixteenth to the Nineteenth Century.' In *Fragments for a History of the Human Body*, Michel Feher, Ramona Naddaff, Nadia Tazi (eds.), (New York: Zone Books, 1989), Part 1, pp. 443-434 (emphases in the original).

11. Manfred E. Clynes and Nathan S. Kline, (1960) 'Cyborgs and Space,' in this volume.

12. Beaune op cit., p. 431 (emphases in the original).

13. Ibid., p. 435.

14. Ibid. Rethinking photography in the shadows of Roland Barthes's *Camera Lucida* Krauss notes: "The automaton, the double of life who is death, is a figure for the wound that every photograph has the power to deliver." Op. cit., p. 95.

15. The connection between Caillois' concept of psychasthenia and Lacan's concept of the mirror stage is registered by Krauss in 'Corpus Delicti,' op. cit., p. 74.

16. Marshall McLuhan, *Understanding Media: The Extensions of Man* (New York: Mentor, 1964). pp. 33, 54.

17. De Certeau, op. cit., 'The Arts of Theory,' p. 61.

18. For the seminal discussion of chronotopes see Mikhail Bakhtin, 'Forms of time and of the chronotope in the novel,' in *Mikhail Bakhtin, The Dialogic Imagination*, Michael Holquist (ed.), Caryl Emerson and Michael Holquist (trans.), (Austin: University of Austin Press, 1981).

19. On a culture of distance and its consequences see Raymond Williams 'Distance,' *What I Came to Say* (London: Hutchinson Radius, 1989), pp. 36-43.

20. Friedrich Nietzsche, *The Use and Abuse of History*, trans. Adrian Collins, Indianapolis: Bobbs-Merrill, 1979, pp. 8, 12.

4.4

Envisioning Cyborg Bodies

Notes from Current Research

Jennifer González

> *The truth of art lies in this: that the world*
> *really is as it appears in the work of art.*
> —*Herbert Marcuse*

The cyborg body is the body of an imagined cyberspatial existence. It is the site of possible being. In this sense it exists in excess of the real. But it is also imbedded within the real. The cyborg body is that which is already inhabited and through which the interface to a contemporary world is already made. Visual representations of cyborgs are thus not only utopian or dystopian prophesies, but are rather reflections of a contemporary state of being. The image of the cyborg body functions as a site of condensation and displacement. It contains on its surface and in its fundamental structure the multiple fears and desires of a culture caught in the process of transformation. Donna Haraway has written,

> *A cyborg exists when two kinds of boundaries are simultaneously problematic:*
> *1) that between animals (or other organisms) and humans, and 2) that*
> *between self-controlled, self-governing machines (automatons) and*
> *organisms, especially humans (models of autonomy). The cyborg is the figure*
> *born of the interface of automaton and autonomy.*[1]

Taking this as a working definition, one can consider any body a cyborg body that is both its own agent and subject to the power of other agencies. To keep to the spirit of this definition but to make it more specific, **an *organic cyborg* can be defined as a monster of multiple species, whereas a *mechanical cyborg* can be considered a techno-human amalgamation** (there are also conceivable overlaps of these domains). While images of *mechanical cyborgs* will be the focus of the short essays that follow, both types of cyborgs, which appear frequently in Western visual culture, are metaphors for a third kind of cyborg—a cyborg consciousness.[2] This last, is both manifest in all the images included here, and is the invisible force driving their production, what Michel Foucault might call a "positive unconscious."[3] This unconscious is reflected in the spatial and political agency implied by a given cyborg body. Unlike some of my contemporaries, I do not see the cyborg body as primarily a surface or simulacrum which signifies only itself; rather the cyborg is like a symptom—it represents that which cannot otherwise be represented.

The following group of eclectic commentaries is meant to address a sample of the issues which may arise in the consideration of representing cyborg bodies. The images here were chosen not because they are the most beautiful, the most frightening or the most hopeful of the cyborg visions I have found, but because they incarnate what seem to be important features for any consideration of a "cyborg body politics."[4] This is only a beginning.

Mechanical Mistress

Fig. 1 L'Horlogère

Flanked by rows of cypress, demurely poised with a hand on one hip, the other hand raised with a pendulous object hanging from plump and delicate fingers stands "L'Horlogère" (The Mistress of Horology) (Fig. 1). From above her head stares the circular face of time, supported by a decorative frame through which her own face complacently gazes. Soft feminine shoulders descend into a tightly sculpted bust of metal. Cinched at the waist, her skirts flounce into a stiffly ornamental "montre emboeté" which rests on dainty feet, toes curled up to create the base. An eighteenth-century engraving, this image by an unknown printer depicts what we today might call a cyborg. The body of the woman is not merely hidden inside the machine (despite the two tiny human feet that peek out from below), nor is the organic body itself a mechanical replica, rather the body and the machine are a singular entity. In contrast to, but within the context of, the popular depictions of entirely mechanical automata—the predecessors of our modern-day robots—this image represents an early conception of an ontological merging of "cultural" and "natural" artifacts.

Taken as a form of evidence, the representation of an amalgam such as this can be read as a symptom of the pre-industrial unconscious. *L'Horlogère* substantiates an ideology of order, precision, and mechanization. French philosopher Julien Offray de La Mettrie, in his essay "L'Homme Machine" (1748) wrote "The human body is a machine which winds its own springs. It is the living image of perpetual movement."[5] The beating hearts of many Europeans at this time no doubt sounded an apprehensive ticking. Wound up to serve the industrial impulse, the human model of perfection culminated in a mechanized identity. Variations of this ideal continued into the nineteenth century with the expansion of large-scale industrial production. Scholar Julie Wosk writes,

> ... artists' images of automatons became central metaphors for the dreams and nightmares of societies under-going rapid technological change. In a world where new labor-saving inventions were expanding human capabilities and where a growing number of people were employed in factory systems calling for rote actions and impersonal efficiency, nineteenth-century artists confronted one of the most profound issues raised by new technologies: the possibility that people's identities and emotional lives would take on the properties of machines.[6]

But was this not exactly what was desired by one part of the population—that another part of the population become mechanical? Was this not also exactly what was feared? The artists, depicting an experience already lived by a large portion of the population, were reflecting a situation in which the relation—and the distinction—between the machine and the human became a question of gender and class. Those who had access to certain machines were privileged, those who were expected to behave like certain machines were subjugated. The same is true today.

The pre-industrial representation of *L'Horlogère* thus functions as an early prototype of later conceptual models of the cyborg. The woman is a clock, the clock is a woman—complex, mechanical, serviceable, decorative. Her history can be traced to automatic dolls with clockwork parts dating back to at least the fifteenth century in Europe[7] and much earlier in China, Egypt and Greece.[8] Of the examples which I have found of such automata, a decided majority represent female bodies providing some form of entertainment.

> The idea of automatons as useful servants and amusing toys continued in the designs of medieval and Renaissance clockmakers, whose figures, deriving their movements from clock mechanisms, struck the hours ...[9]

The history of the automaton is thus imbedded in the mechanical innovations of keeping time, and *L'Horlogère* undoubtedly derives much of her status from this social context. She is clearly an embodied mechanism, but she has the privilege of her class. The imaginative engraver who produced this image undoubtedly wished to portray *L'Horlogère* as aristocratic; as one who could acquire, and therefore represent, the height of technological development. As machine, she displays the skill and artistry of the best engineers of her epoch. The fact that she represents a female body is indicative of the role she is meant to play as the objectification of cultural sophistication and sexuality. Her gender is consistent with the property status of an eighteenth-century decorative artifact.

L'Horlogère is not merely an automaton. As part human, she should have human agency, or some form of human being. Her implied space of agency is, nevertheless, tightly circumscribed. This cyborg appears more trapped by her mechanical parts than liberated through them. If a cyborg is "the figure born of the interface of automaton and autonomy," then to what degree can this cyborg be read as a servant and toy, and to what degree an autonomous social agent? In order to determine the character of any given cyborg identity and the range of its power, one must be able to examine the *form* and not merely the *fact* of this interface between automaton and autonomy. For, despite the potentially progressive implications of a cyborg subject position,[10] the cyborg is not necessarily more likely to exist free of the social constraints which apply to humans and machines already. "The machine is us, our processes, an aspect of our embodiment,"[11] writes Donna Haraway. It should therefore come as no surprise that the traditional, gendered roles of Euro-American culture are rarely challenged in the visual representations of cyborgs—a concept which itself arises from an industrially "privileged" Euro-American perspective. Even the conceptual predecessors of the cyborg are firmly grounded in everyday social politics; "Tradition has it that the golem first did housework but then became unmanageable."[12] The image of *L'Horlogère* thus provides a useful ground and a visual tradition from which to explore and compare more contemporary examples of cyborg bodies.

Signs of changing consciousness

The image of the cyborg has historically recurred at moments of radical social and cultural change. From bestial monstrosities, to unlikely montages of body and machine parts, to electronic implants, imaginary representations of cyborgs take over when traditional bodies fail. In other words, when the current ontological model of human being does not fit a new paradigm, a hybrid model of existence is required to encompass a new, complex and contradictory lived experience. The cyborg body thus becomes the historical record of changes in human perception. One such change may be reflected in the implied redefinition of the space the cyborg body inhabits.

Taking, for example, the 1920 photomontage by Hannah Höch entitled *Das schöne Mädchen* (The Beautiful Girl) (Fig. 2) it is possible to read its dynamic assemblage of images as an allegory of modernization. Allied with the Dadaists of the Weimar Republic, Höch provided a chaotic vision of the rapid social and cultural change that followed in the wake of World War I. In *Das schöne Mädchen* the figure of a woman is set in the midst of a disjointed space of automobile and body parts. BMW logos, a severed hand holding a watch, a flying wig, a parasol, a hidden feminine face and a faceless boxer leaping through the tire of a car surround the central figure whose head has been replaced with an incandescent light bulb—perhaps as the result or condition of her experience.

*Fig. 2
Hannah Höch,
Das schöne Mädchen
(The Beautiful Girl),
1919-20, 35 x 29 cm.,
photomontage, private
collection.*

Many of Höch's early photomontages focus on what might be called the "New Woman" in Weimar Germany. These images are not simply a celebration of new, "emancipated" roles for women in a period of industrial and economic growth, they are also critical of the contradictory nature of this experience as depicted in the mass media. "Mass culture became a site for the expression of anxieties, desires, fears and hopes about women's rapidly transforming identities," writes Maude Lavin in her recent book *Cut With the Kitchen Knife: The Weimar Photomontages of Hannah Höch.* "Stereotypes of the New Woman generated by the media could be complex and contradictory: messages of female empowerment and liberation were mixed with others of dependence, and the new consumer culture positioned women as both commodities and customers."[13] Existing across several domains, the New Woman was forced to experience space and presence in new and ambiguous ways.

Traveling through and across this space could therefore be both physically and psychologically disorienting. The experience of a disjointed modern space takes form in Höch's collage as a cyborg body suspended in chaotic perspective (the hand-held parasol in the image is reduced to one-tenth the size of the figure's floating hair), with body parts chopped off, and with new mechanical/electric parts added in their place (the missing hand severed at the figure's wrist reappears holding the watch in the foreground). It is impossible to tell exactly which spatial plane is occupied by the body and of what sort of perception this body is capable. Yet, despite her Dadaist affiliation, Höch's work tends not to be random. Her images produce a discordant but strikingly accurate appraisal of an early twentieth-century experience of modernism. Here, existence as a self-contained humanist subject is overcome by an experience of the body in pieces—a visual representation of an unconscious state of being that exceeds the space of the human body. **Perception is aligned to coincide with the machine.** The effects of such an alignment are made alarmingly transparent by Virginia Woolf in her 1928 novel *Orlando.* In her description of the uncanny event of experiencing the world from the perspective of the automobile, her metaphor of torn scraps of paper is particularly appropriate to Höch's use of photomontage.

> *After twenty minutes the body and mind were like scraps of torn paper tumbling from a sack, and indeed, the process of motoring fast out of London so much resembles the chopping up small of body and mind, which precedes unconsciousness and perhaps death itself that it is an open question in what sense Orlando can be said to have existed at the present moment.*[14]

The questionable existence of Orlando, Virginia Woolf's protagonist who changes gender and who adapts to social and cultural changes across many centuries and continents, is not unlike the questionable existence of the cyborg. It is the existence of a shifting consciousness that is made concrete only in moments of contradictory experience. The attempt to represent and reassemble—but not to repair—the multiple scraps of body and mind that are scattered at such historical junctures has, in fact, been a central activity of modernism.

Photomontage has served as a particularly appropriate medium for the visual exploration of cyborgs. It allows apparently "real" or at least indexically grounded representations of body parts, objects and spaces to be rearranged and to function as fantastic environments or corporal mutations. Photographs seduce the viewer into an imaginary space of visually believable events, objects and characters. The same can be said of assemblage—the use of found or manufactured (often commonplace) objects to create a three-dimensional representational artifact. The common contemporary practice of representing a cyborg through photomontage or assemblage resembles the poetic use of everyday words: the discrete elements are familiar, though the total result is a new conceptual and ontological domain.

Fig. 3 Raoul Hausmann, Tête mécanique. L'Esprit de notre temps. ca. 1921 Assemblage of wood, metal, cardboard, leather and other materials, 12 1/2 x 7 1/2 x 7 1/2 inches. (Musée National d'Art Moderne, Centre Georges Pompidou, Paris. Photo: Musée National d'Art Moderne, Paris)

One of Höch's compatriots, Dadaist Raoul Hausmann, pictured this new ontological domain in several of his own photomontages and found-object assemblages. Unlike Höch's representations, however, Hausmann's images represent a more cerebral concept of the modern experience. Rather than a body in pieces, he depicts a mechanical mind. His assemblage *Tête Méchanique* (Mechanical Head) (Fig. 3) is a particularly appropriate example of a cyborg mind. Also called "The Spirit of Our Times," this assemblage consists of the wooden head of a mannequin to which are attached diverse cultural artifacts. A wallet is fixed to the back, a typographic cylinder in a small jewel box is on one side of the head, a ruler attached with old camera parts is on the other side, the forehead is adorned with the interior of a watch, random numbers and a measuring tape, and a collapsible metal cup crowns the entire ensemble. Timothy O. Benson writes that this assemblage depicts a man imprisoned in an unsettling and enigmatic space, "perceiving the world through a mask of arbitrary symbols."[15] At the same time it functions as a hyper-historical[16] object collection; a testament to Hausmann's own contemporary material culture. The cyborg in this case is not without origins, though it is without origin myths. Donna Haraway contends that cyborgs have no natural history, no origin story, no Garden of Eden and thus no hope of, nor interest in, simplistic unity or purity. Nevertheless, given their multiple parts, and multiple identities, they will always be read in relation to a specific historical context. According to scholar Matthew Biro,

> ... by fashioning his cyborgs out of fragments of the new mass culture which he found all around him, Hausmann also believed he was fulfilling the primary positive or constructive function he could still ascribe to dada: namely, the material investigation of the signs and symbols bestowed on him by his historical present.[17]

Until the desire to define identities and the power to do so is lost or relinquished, even the most spontaneous cyborgs cannot float above the lingering, clinging past of differences, histories, stories, bodies, places. They will always function as evidence.

The new spatial relations of the human body are thus traced onto the cyborg body. Höch's figure is fragmentary and dispersed, floating in an untethered perspective. Hausmann's figure implies a calculable context that is linear, a cerebral space of measurement and control. **Each cyborg implies a new spatial configuration or territory—a habitat.** For Höch's *Beautiful Girl*, the world is a space of multiple perspectives, consumer goods, lost identities and fleeting time. The world in which Hausmann's *Mechanical Head* operates is one that links identity to material objects, and is simultaneously an environment in which knowledge is the result of a random encounter with the world of things. Hausmann himself described this assemblage as representing an everyday man who "has nothing but the capacities which chance has glued to his skull."[18] Sense perception itself is accounted for only to the degree that appears in the image of the cyborg body. Sight, hearing, and tactile senses can only be implied by the body's exterior devices. The *Mechanical Head,* for example, has no ears to "hear" with, only a mechanical ruler and jewel case. *The Beautiful Girl* has neither eyes nor ears, nor mouth to speak with, only a light bulb for illumination. The human head which gazes from the corner of this image is at best the memory of what has been displaced. A new social space requires a new social being. A visual representation of this new being through an imaginary body provides a map of the layers and contradictions that make up a hyper-historical "positive unconscious." In other words, the cyborg body marks the boundaries of that which is the underlying but unrecognized structure of a given historical consciousness. It turns the inside out.

White Collar Epistemology

Turning the outside in, Phoenix Technologies Ltd. produced an advertisement for their new Eclipse Fax in 1993. The advertisement's lead-in text reads: "Eclipse Fax: if it were any faster, you'd have to send and receive your faxes internally." The text floats over an image of a pale woman's head and shoulders. It is clear from the image that the woman is on her back as her long hair is splayed out around her head. Her shoulders are bare, implying that she is unclothed. Mechanical devises comprised of tubes, metal plugs, cables, hoses and canisters appear to be inserted into her ears, eye sockets and mouth. Two electrodes appear to be attached to the woman's forehead, with wires extending out to the sides, almost like the antennae of an insect. A futuristic Medusa's head of wires, blinded with technology, strapped to the ground with cables and hoses, penetrated at every orifice with the flow of information technologies, this is a subjugated cyborg. Her monstrous head is merely a crossroads. All human parts of the image are passive and receptive. Indeed it seems clear that the blind silence of this clearly female creature is the very condition for the possibility of information flow. This is not a cyborg of possibilities, it is a cyborg of slavery. The advertisement promises that the consumer will be able to send and receive faxes "without being interrupted," and concludes that "... to fax any faster, you'd have to break a few laws. Of physics." Here the new technology is not only seen as always available, but also as somehow pushing the boundaries of legality—even if only metaphorically—in the use of the body. This is the bad-boy fantasy prevalent in so many images of feminized cyborgs. The textual emphasis on speed in this advertisement is but a thin veil through which the underlying visual metaphor of information flow as sexual penetration bursts forth. For many, this is already an apt metaphor for cyborg body politics: knowledge as force-fed data.

What *are* the consequences of a montage of organic bodies and machines? Where do the unused parts go? What are the relations of power? Is power conserved? Is the loss of power in one physical domain the necessary gain of power for another? Who writes the laws for a cyborg bill of rights? Does everyone have the "right" to become any kind of cyborg body? Or are these "rights" economically determined? These are questions that arise in the attempt to figure a politics of cyborg bodies. A visualization of this hypothetical existence is all the more important for its reflection of an already current state of affairs.

The power of plenitude

Robert Longo's sculpture/installation entitled *All You Zombies: Truth before God,* (Fig. 4) stages the extreme manifestation of the body at war in the theater of politics. The glow of many painted lights hang within the frame of a semi-circular canvas—an opera house or concert hall—that surrounds a monstrous cyborg soldier who takes center stage on a revolving platform. The chasm between the implied context of cultural refinement and the uncanny violence of a body that defies any and all such spaces, visually enunciates the collaboration that is always found between so-called civilization and its barbarous effects. The central figure is a cultural and semiotic nightmare of possibilities; an inhabitant of what Hal Foster has described as "the war zone between schizoid obscenity and utopian hope."[19] In a helmet adorned with diverse historical signs (Japanese armor, Viking horns, Mohawk-like fringe and electronic network antenna), the cyborg's double face with two vicious mouths snarls through a mask of metal bars and plastic hoses that penetrate the surface of the skin. One eye is blindly human, the other is a mechanical void. A feminine hand with razor sharp nails reaches out from the center of the chest, as if to escape from within. With arms and legs covered in one-cent scales, clawed feet, legs with fins, knee joints like gaping jaws, serpents hanging from the neck, insects swarming at the genitals, hundreds of toy soldiers clinging to the entrails and ammunition slung across the body, this beast is a contemporary monster—what Longo has called "American machismo."[20] The

cyborg might be what Robert Hughes saw in the Dadaist obsession with war cripples, **"the body re-formed by politics: part flesh, part machine."**[21] In this light, it may seem to embody the very "illegitimate offspring of militarism and patriarchal capitalism" that Haraway problematizes in her "Cyborg Manifesto."[22] But in fact Longo's sculpture describes a rebellion against these institutions, who are better represented by the familiar corporate or government-owned, sterile, fantasy figures such as RoboCop.

Instead of an asexual automaton, Longo's creature represents a wild manifestation of human, animal and mechanical sexual potency and violence. With one artificially-rounded bare breast, and one arm raised, holding a torn flag to a broken pole, the figure is remarkably reminiscent of Delacroix's *Liberty Leading the People*. Her incongruous presence has the power to capture the imagination

*Fig. 4 Robert Longo
All you Zombies: Truth
before God
L.A. County Museum of
Art, Rizzoli, NY 1990*

of the viewer through an embodiment of a maternal wrath and revolutionary zeal. At the same time the creature is not without his penis, protruding but protected in a sheath of its own armor (the wings of a powerful and no doubt stinging insect). Whether the cyborg is bisexual or not, it certainly has attributes of both human sexes. Interestingly, none of the three critics writing about this work in the exhibition catalogue mention this fact. Indeed, they all fail to acknowledge that the creature has any female attributes at all. Although the body overall has a masculine feel of weight and muscular bulk, this is clearly not a single-sex being. It storms across several thresholds; that between male and female, life and death, human and beast, organic and inorganic, individual and collective. To a certain degree then, this might be considered a hybrid body; a body which "rejoices" in "the illegitimate fusions of animal and machine."[23]

Historically, genetic engineering and cyborg bodies have produced similar fears about loss of human control—if there ever was such a thing—over the products of human creation. Barbara Stafford in her book *Body Criticism: Imagining the Unseen in Enlightenment Art and Medicine*, writes that in the eighteenth century,

> *The hybrid posed a special problem for those who worried about purity of forms, interfertility, and unnatural mixtures. Both the plant and animal kingdoms were the site of forced breeding between species that did not amalgamate in the wild. The metaphysical and physical dangers thought to inhere in artificial grafts surfaced in threatening metaphors of infection, contamination, rape, and bastardy.[24]*

Robert Longo's sculpture functions as an iconography of this metaphysics. It appears to be the very amalgamation of organic and inorganic elements that is the result of a dangerous and threatening mutation. But what makes this "hybrid" fusion "illegitimate"?

Fraught with many contradictory cultural connotations, the term "hybrid" itself demands some explanation before it can be used in any casual way—as it has been—to describe a cyborg body. The term appears to have evolved out of an early seventeenth-century Latin usage of *hybridia*—a crossbred animal.[25] Now the word has several meanings, among them: a person or group of persons reflecting the interaction of two unlike cultures, traditions, etc.; anything derived from heterogeneous sources or composed of elements of different or incongruous kinds; bred from two distinct races, breeds, varieties, species or genera. These definitions reveal a wide range of meaning, allowing for easy application, but little semantic substance. What makes the term controversial, of course, is that it appears to assume by definition the existence of a non-hybrid state—a pure state, a pure species, a pure race—with which it is contrasted. It is this notion of purity that must, in fact, be problematized. For if any progress is to be made in a politics of human or cyborg existence, heterogeneity must be taken as a given. It is therefore necessary to imagine a world of composite elements without the notion of purity. This, it seems, is the only useful way to employ the concept of the hybrid: as a combination of elements that, while not in themselves "pure" nonetheless have characteristics that distinguish them from the other elements with which they are combined. Hybridity must not be tied to questions of legitimacy or the patriarchal lineage and system of property which it implies. Rather, it must be recognized that the world is comprised of hybrid encounters that refuse origin. Hybrid beings are what we have always been—regardless of our "breeding." The visual representation of a hybrid cyborg thus becomes a test site for possible ways of being in the world. Raging involuntarily even against its own existence, the hybrid figure in *All You Zombies: Truth before God*, stands as its own terrible witness of a militarized capitalist state. As a body of power, active within its multiple selves, though mercenary in its politics, this cyborg is as legitimate as any other.

Passing

When I began to explore visual representations of cyborg bodies, I was originally motivated by a desire to unravel the relationship between representations of cyborgs and representations of race and racial mixtures.[26] I was brought to this point by the observation that in many of the texts written about and around the concept of cyborgs the term "miscegenation" was employed. Not only that, there seemed to be a general tendency to link the "otherness" of machines with the otherness of racial and sexual difference. I encountered statements such as the following:

> But by 1889 [the machine's] "otherness" had waned, and the World's Fair audience tended to think of the machine as unqualifiedly good, strong, stupid and obedient. They thought of it as a giant slave, an untiring steel Negro, controlled by Reason in a world of infinite resources.[27]

> Hence neither the identification of the feminine with the natural nor the identification of the feminine with the cultural, but instead, their uncertain mixture—the miscegenation of the natural and the cultural—is what incites, at once, panic and interest.[28]

The history of a word is significant. While the word "hybrid" has come to have ambiguous cultural connotations, words such as "illegitimate" and "miscegenation" are much more problematic. The latter is believed to have been "coined by U.S. journalist David Goodman Croly (1829-89) in a pamphlet published anonymously in

1864."[29] "Miscegenated" unlike "hybrid" was originally conceived as a pejorative description, and I would agree with scholar Stephanie A. Smith that "This term not only trails a violent political history in the United States but is also dependent on a eugenicist, genocidal concept of illegitimate matings."[30] At the same time, this may be the very reason that certain writers have employed the term—**to point out the "forbidden" nature of the "coupling" of human and machine.** (But, as others have made quite clear, this dependency upon metaphors of sexual reproduction is a problem of, rather than the solution to, conceptions of cyborg embodiment.) Lingering in the connotations of this usage are, of course, references to racial difference.

Silent Mobius

While there are several images I have encountered of cyborgs that appear to be racially "marked" as not "white" (*Cyborg* by Lynn Randolf being among the better known and more optimistic of these images) none struck me as so emblematic of the issues with which I was concerned as those found by my colleague Elena Tajima Creef in the 1991 Japanese comic book *Silent Möbius* (Fig. 5).[31] In part one, issue six, there is the story of a young woman of color. (Her hair is green, and her face is structured along the lines of a typical Euro-American comic-book beauty with big eyes [that not insignificantly fluctuate between blue and brown] and a disappearing nose and mouth. Yet, her skin is a lovely chocolate brown. **She is the only character "of color" in the entire issue and she is clearly a "hybrid."**) When we encounter her at the beginning of the story she is identified as a member of a futuristic feminine police force who is rehabilitating in the hospital. She is then seen racing off in a sporty jet vehicle after some dreaded foe. After pages of combat with an enemy called "Wire," it appears that she has won by default. She then declares that she must expose something to her love interest, a white young man with red hair. She disrobes, pulls out a weapon of some kind and proceeds to melt off her beautiful skin (looking more and more like chocolate as it drips away from her body), revealing to her incredulous and aroused audience that she is in fact a cyborg. Her gray body underneath looks almost white. She says, "This is my body Ralph. Seventy percent of my body is bionic, covered with synth-flesh. Three years ago, after being cut to pieces, I was barely saved by a cyber-graft operation. But I had it changed to a combat graft." "Why?" Ralph asks. "So I could become as strong as Wire, the thing that destroyed my life." But she goes on to say, "Eventually I started to hate this body. I wasn't feminine anymore. I was a super-human thing. I hated this body even though I wanted it. I didn't want to accept it. I kept feeling it wasn't the way I was supposed to be." As she speaks the reader is given more views of her naked body with gray, cyborg parts laid bare beneath disappearing brown skin. In the end she says, "I think I can finally live with what I have become."[32]

"Kiddy," for that is her diminutive name, **is typical of contemporary (mostly male-produced) cyborg fantasies: a powerful, yet vulnerable, combination of sex toy and techno-sophisticate—in many ways not unlike *L'Horlogère*.** But she is not an awkward machine with tubes and prosthetics extending from joints and limbs. She is not wearing her power on the outside of her body, as does Robert Longo's sculpture, nor is she broken apart and reassembled into disproportionate pieces, as in the case of Hannah Höch's photomontage. Rather she is an "exotic" and vindictive cyborg who passes—as simply human. It is when she removes her skin that she becomes the quintessential cyborg body. For in the Western imaginary, this body is all abut revealing its internal mechanism. And Kiddy is all about the seduction of the strip tease, the revelation of the truth, of her internal coherence; which, ultimately, is produced by the super-technicians of her time. Her "real" identity lies beneath the camouflage of her dark skin—rather than on its surface.

Silent Mobius

"Passing" in this case has multiple and ominous meanings. Initially this cyborg body must pass for the human body it has been designed to replicate. At the same time, Kiddy must pass for the feminine self she felt she lost in the process of transformation. Staging the performance of "true" identity, Kiddy raises certain questions of agency. Must she reveal the composition of her cyborg identity? Which seventy percent of her original self was lost? Which thirty percent was kept? Who is keeping track of percentages? (The historical shadow of blood-quantum measurement and its contemporary manifestations looms over these numerical designations. Still serious and painful, especially in many communities of color, are the intersecting meanings of percentage, passing and privilege.)[33] What are the consequences of this kind of "passing," especially when the body is so clearly marked with a sign—skin color—of historical oppression in the West? Why does Kiddy feel her body is not the way it is "supposed to be"? Has it been allowed unusual access to technological freedoms? Is the woman of color necessarily a cyborg? Or is Kiddy also only "passing" as a woman of color? What are the possible consequences of this reading? I leave these questions open-ended.

From my encounter with the world of cyborgs, and any cyberspace that these bodies may inhabit, I have seen that the question of race is decidedly fraught. Some see cyborgs and cyberspace as a convenient site for the erasure of questions of racial identity—if signs of difference divide us, the logic goes, then the lack of these signs might create a utopian social-scape of equal representation. However, the problem with this kind of e-race-sure is that it assumes differences between individuals or groups to be primarily superficial—literally skin deep. It also assumes that the status quo is an adequate form of representation. Thus the question over which so much debate arises asks: **are there important differences between people (and cyborgs), or are people (and cyborgs) in some necessary way the same?** The answers to this two-part question must be yes, and yes. It is the frustration of living with this apparent contradiction that drives people to look for convenient alternatives. As industrialized Western cultures become less homogeneous, this search intensifies. Cyborg bodies will not resolve this contradiction, nor do they—as yet—function as radical alternatives. It may be that the cyborg is now in a new and progressive phase, but its "racial" body politics have a long way to go. At best, the configuration of the cyborg, which changes over time, will virtually chart human encounters with a contradictory, lived experience and continue to provide a vision of new ontological exploration.

Notes

Acknowledgements: I would like to thank all of the friends and colleagues who have helped, and continue to help, in my search for images of cyborg bodies, and who have pointed me in the direction of useful literature on the topic; especially Elena Tajima Creef, Joe Dumit, Douglas Fogle, Chris Hables Gray, Donna Haraway, Vivian Sobchack and the Narrative Intelligence reading group at the MIT Media Lab.

1. Donna Haraway. *Primate Visions: Gender, Race and Nature in the World of Modern Science.* New York: Routledge. 1989. p. 139.

2. Donna Haraway alludes to such a consciousness in her essay "A Cyborg Manifesto," in *Simians, Cyborgs and Women: The Reinvention of Nature.* New York: Routledge. 1991.

3. Michel Foucault. *The Order of Things: An Archeology of the Human Sciences.* New York: Vintage Books. 1973. Foucault explains his project in this text as significantly different from earlier histories and epistemologies of science by suggesting that he wishes to reveal a "positive unconscious" of knowledge—"a level that eludes the consciousness of the scientist and yet is part of scientific discourse." p. xi. This "positive unconscious" can be thought of as "rules of formation, which were never formulated in their own right, but are to be found only in widely differing theories, concepts, and objects of study." p. xi. One might also think of this notion as akin to certain definitions of ideology. It is useful for my purposes to the degree that it implies an unconscious but simultaneously proactive and wide-ranging discourse, in this case, of cyborg bodies.

4. See "The Cyborg Body Politic Meets the New World Order" by Chris Hables Gray and Steven Mentor. In this volume.

5. Julie Wosk. *Breaking Frame: Technology and the Visual Arts in the Nineteenth Century.* New Brunswick: Rutgers University Press. p. 81.

6. Ibid. p. 79.

7. Ernst Von Bassermann-Jordan. *The Book of Old Clocks and Watches.* Trans. H. Alan Lloyd. London: George Allen & Unwin Ltd. 1964. p. 15.

8. "The delight in automatons extended back even earlier to ancient Egyptian moving statuettes with articulated arms, and to the automatons of ancient Chinese, ancient Greek and medieval Arab artisans, as well as to European clockmakers of the medieval and Renaissance periods. [...] Homer in *The Illiad* described two female automatons who aided the god Haphaestus, the craftsman of the gods. The women were 'golden maidservants' who 'looked like real girls and could not only speak and use their limbs but were endowed with intelligence and trained in handiwork by the immortal gods.'" See Julie Wosk, pp. 81-82.

9. Wosk. p. 82.

10. "From another perspective, a cyborg world might be about lived social and bodily realities in which people are not afraid of their joint kinship with animals and machines, not afraid of permanently partial identities and contradictory standpoints. [...] Cyborg unities are monstrous and illegitimate; in our present political circumstances, we could hardly hope for more potent myths for resistance and recoupling." Donna Haraway. "A Cyborg Manifesto," p. 154.

11. Ibid. p. 180.

12. Patricia S. Warrick, *The Cybernetic Imagination in Science Fiction.* Cambridge, MA: MIT Press. 1980. p. 32.

13. Maude Lavin. *Cut With a Kitchen Knife.* New Haven: Yale University Press. 1993. p. 2.

14. Virginia Woolf. *Orlando.* New York: Harcourt Brace Jovanovich Publishers. 1928. p. 307.

15. Timothy O. Benson. *Raoul Hausmann and Berlin Dada.* Ann Arbor: University of Michigan Research

Press. 1987. p. 161.

16. I use the term hyper-historical to connote an object or existence that appears to be synchronous with a very specific moment in history, but that seems to have had no coherent evolutionary past, nor developing future. The concept was originally conceived in order to salvage the seemingly a-historical status of the cyborg in Donna Haraway's description of this term (see *Simians, Cyborgs and Women: The Reinvention of Nature*). She writes that the cyborg has no myth of origin, but I do not think she means to imply that it has no historical presence. Rather it has a presence that is so entirely wrapped up in a state of contemporary and multiple being that it is an exceptionally clear marker of any given historical moment—even when it makes references to the past.

17. Matthew Biro. "The Cyborg as New Man: Figures of Technology in Weimar and the Third Reich." Unpublished manuscript delivered at the College Art Association Conference, New York 1994.

18. Benson. p. 161.

19. Hal Foster. "Atrocity Exhibition," in *Robert Longo,* ed. Howard N. Fox. Los Angeles: Los Angeles County Museum of Art and New York: Rizzoli. 1989. "It is in the war zone between schizoid obscenity and utopian hope that the art of Robert Longo is now to be found," p. 61

20. Howard N. Fox. "In Civil War," in *Robert Longo.* Los Angeles: Los Angeles County Museum of Art and New York: Rizzoli. 1989. "Longo describes the monster as an image of 'American machismo,' a confusion of vitality and vigor with warlike destructiveness," p. 43.

21. Robert Hughes. *The Shock of the New.* New York: Alfred A. Knopf Inc. 1980. p. 73.

22. Haraway. "A Cyborg Manifesto," p. 151.

23. Haraway. "A Cyborg Manifesto," p. 154.

24. Barbara Maria Stafford. *Body Criticism: Imagining the Unseen in Enlightenment Art and Medicine.* Cambridge, MA: The MIT Press. 1991. p. 264.

25. Random House Dictionary. Unabridged edition. 1993.

26. The term "race" is itself problematic and relies upon a history of scientific and intellectual bias. I use it here because the term has come to have a common-usage definition referring to genetic phenotype. Regardless of my distaste for this usage, I nevertheless recognize the real relations of power that are structured around it. It would be naive to ignore the ways in which this concept is employed and deployed. Here I try to point out the role of the idea of "race" in the conception of cyborg bodies.

27. Hughes p. 11.

28. Mark Seltzer. *Bodies and Machines.* New York: Routledge. 1992. p. 66.

29. Random House Dictionary. Unabridged edition. 1993.

30. Stephanie A. Smith. "Morphing, Materialism and the Marketing of *Xenogenesis,*" in *Genders,* No. 18, winter 1993. p. 75.

31. Elena Tajima Creef is Assistant Professor of Women's Studies at Wellesley College. She discusses *Silent Möbius* in relation to issues of race and representation in, "Towards a Genealogy of Staging Asian Difference," a chapter of her dissertation "Re/orientations: The Politics of Japanese American Representation."

32. Kia Asamiya. "Silent Möbius," Part 1, No. 6. Trans. James D. Hudnall and Matt Thorn. Viz Communications Japan, Inc. 1991. pp. 34-36.

33. For a good discussion of passing see "Passing for White, Passing for Black," by Adrian Piper in the British journal *Transition.*

"Death Is Irrelevant"

Cyborgs, Reproduction, and the Future of Male
Hysteria

Cynthia J. Fuchs

> *If the cyborg is anything at all, it is self-difference.*
> —Donna Haraway, "Postscript"[1]

> *I'm not going to knuckle under to any do-jigger I put
> together myself.*
> —Isaac Asimov, I, Robot[2]

> *Before you can read me, you've got to learn how to see me.*
> —En Vogue, "Free Your Mind"

Mind and Borg

The 1991 season finale of *Star Trek: The Next Generation* cliff-hung on the abduction of Captain Picard (Patrick Stewart) by the Borg. A neosocialist cyborg "community" which is interconnected through bioengineering and other advanced technologies, the Borg appear to be androgynous humanoids. In spite of their individual bodies, however, they constitute a single consciousness. Ruthless and emotionless (like all who oppose the optimistic imperialism of the USS *Enterprise*), the

Borg reproduce themselves by assimilating bodies, Picard's for instance, by literal physical penetration.

Transported to the Borg ship, Picard is surrounded by resolute figures in black rubber suits with tubes and wires piercing their faces and torsos. As he faces the vast and mystified ship's interior, he raises his voice in protest: "I will resist you with my last ounce of strength." The Borg's sourceless multivoice replies, "Strength is irrelevant. Resistance is futile. We wish to improve ourselves. We will add your biological and technological distinctiveness to our own. Your culture will adapt to service ours." Picard asserts that such absorption is "impossible" because of human beings' investment in "freedom and self-determination." He asserts, "We would rather die." **The Borg responds, "Freedom is irrelevant. Self-determination is irrelevant.... Death is irrelevant."**

The episode ends looking both backward and forward: Picard reappears, reconstructed as Locutus, liaison for the Borg. Dressed in a Borg bodysuit with a massive prosthesis on his right arm, he looms on the *Enterprise* viewscreen to address his former crew. Profoundly challenging the notion of an embodied and discrete masculine identity, this image of a penetrated, ungendered, and unfamiliar Picard collapses conventional binary terms of difference: self and other, desire and repulsion, culture and nature, death and life. Simultaneously absorbing and punctured by multiple inorganic implants, Picard's is a white male body in crisis, contestable, without desire or agency, and spectacularly incorporated.

That Picard is, by the end of the next season's premiere episode, returned to "himself" is surely inevitable, given the series' devotion to resolution and repeatability.[3] But there's more to primetime cyborg imagery than this particular closure would suggest. To date the Borg have appeared in four "ST:TNG" episodes, with promises of other and stranger Borg manifestations to come.[4] Continuing and shifting, the Borg are exemplary mass media cyborgs, increasingly unfixed and available for eclectic—recuperative as well as conflicted or negative—readings.

This diversity of readings implies a crisis of unified white masculine subjectivity. It is a crisis which is repeated and expanded in the following texts: *Robocop* (Paul Verhoeven, 1987), *Robocop 2* (Irvin Kershner, 1990), James Cameron's *Terminator 2: Judgment Day* (1991), *Eve of Destruction* (Duncan Gibbins, 1990), and *Hardware* (Richard Stanley, 1989). The cyborg is a paradox of penetrability and reproduction, visible in the simultaneously pierced and projected Locutus, Picard's double and replication as well as his self-consuming "other." It offers an alternative, nonbinary model of subjectivity, one that allows self-relation and self-transgression in the creation of a new, incongruous, and multiple subjectivity.

The cyborg's instability is located in its paradoxically hard and permeable body; the interface of flesh and technology is both thrilling and awful, the consummation of individual potency (an always-loaded weapon), as well as the consumption and production of consciousness. Cyborgs incarnate two contradictions of masculine identity. **First, they combine phallic masculinity and body permeability. Second, they contradict sociobiological constructions of paternity and maternity.** That is, the cyborg's multiple acts of penetration (of self or, more destructively, others) offer no promise of procreation; instead, they reiterate the cyborg's own indeterminate self-identity.

This essay examines three cyborg paradigms which respond to this crisis of straight white male subjectivity—constructed through penetration and reproduction—which is represented by the Borg. The first is the triumphant **machocyborg**, like Robocop or the Schwarzenegger-Terminator; the second is the threateningly **androgynous cyborg**, like Robocop 2 or the fluid-metal T1000; and the third is the **human forced to function as a cyborg**, enacting the radical performativity that Judith Butler describes as "gender trouble."[5]

Current cyborg imagery hardly sustains a progressive or feminist politics ("ST:TNG" and *Robocop* certainly operate otherwise in their devotion to resolution and masculinist victories). But cyborg representations cannot help but disrupt what Butler terms the "heterosexual matrix," where gendered identity and "the construction of stable bodily contours rel[y] upon fixed sites of corporeal permeability and impermeability" (*GT*, 132). That is, the cyborg offers unfixed contours and repeatable performances. And, Butler writes, "if every performance repeats itself to institute the effect of identity, then every repetition requires an interval between the acts, as it were, in which risk and excess threaten to disrupt the identity being constituted."[6] The "intervals"—those breaks in cyborg identity encoded by their "divided" selves, as well as by movie sequels and television episodes which go into syndication and "out of (temporal) order"—refute the cultural conditions of wholeness, linearity, and hierarchy. If, as Butler persuasively argues, "gender attributes are not expressive but performative," cyborgs offer imaginative sites for more radical performativity: nothing in a cyborg body is essential (*GT*, 141).

The performativity of cyborgs represents a future that collapses medical, technological, and political spheres of action. This future speaks directly to identity anxieties addressed in debates over essentialism versus constructionism. If Butler's argument appears to unhinge an authoritative, embodied experience of difference, the cyborg body refracts and reinscribes the boundaries which are apparently lost in constructionist social theory. In particular, macho-cyborg imagery celebrates technology's potent penetrations: like his precursor Rambo, Robocop recovers an ostensibly transcendent masculinity through what Susan Jeffords calls an "aesthetic of technology ... a fragmented collection of disconnected parts that achieve the illusion of coherence only through their display as spectacle."[7] But for the cyborg, the illusion is always-already transparent: Robocop's serial story is one of disunity.

Still, the macho-cyborg's incoherence differs significantly from the transgressive, nonlinear political project outlined in Donna Haraway's "Cyborg Manifesto."[8] But there are connections to be made (and such a narrative must be *made;* it is not essential). While Haraway's cyborg incarnates a "world-changing fiction" and an irony "outside of salvation history," it also relies on a next generation's dynamic myth of multiplicity ("CM," 148, 150).[9] Her "new" narrative contests the linear narrative of conventional, biological reproduction, much as the Borg's ongoing storyline reduces death (and birth) to irrelevance. Haraway writes, "Ideologies of sexual reproduction can no longer reasonably call on notions of sex and sex role as organic aspects in natural objects like organisms and families" ("CM," 162).

That is, the human-historical narrative must betray its reproductive fictions. By challenging the heterosexual matrix with a body that is self-reproducing but not reproductive, the cyborg also threatens the coherence offered by what Mary Ann Doane calls the "guarantee of a history." "Reproduction," she writes, "is the guarantee of a history—both human biological reproduction (through the succession of generations) and mechanical reproduction (through the succession of memories)."[10]

The cyborg's threat to this guarantee is perpetual, as its "memories" are reprogrammed and its body is (re)produced. But when Haraway describes the cyborg's limitlessness, its status as a "creature of the post-gender world ... a kind of disassembled and reassembled, postmodern collective and personal self," her own political and rehistoricizing agenda is also at risk ("CM," 163). This postmodern "self" is caught in time, re-presented through popular cyborg imagery, which challenges faith in a "postgender world." If Robocop is postmacho (with a large automatic weapon in his thigh), and Eve VIII (in *Eve of Destruction*) is postfeminist (with a nuclear bomb where her uterus should be), the terms at risk include "identity," "culture," and "politics." The reality of postnationality only realigns the unreality of embodied differences: even as race, class, and gender are reconceived in theory, their existence in the world—which is, of course, in the movies—seems deathless. I argue here that Haraway's poetic map of a cyborgian present is extended and recoded in these popular texts as an activist and immediate politics.

i, Robocop

Much like the genres it alludes to (earlier sci-fi films, action flicks, *films noirs*, and cyberpunk), Verhoeven's Reagan-era *Robocop* portrays a nostalgic struggle for gendered subjectivity through sexuality and violence. If, as Bruce Sterling writes, "for the cyberpunks ... technology is visceral," it is also a way to conceive bodies differently, to represent them as simultaneously transcendent and contained, excessive and entropic, virtual and densely physical.[11] This fluidity of a technologically mediated subjectivity also implies incessant delirium, a sense of disorientation and difference from the individually sexed and self-contained body. Simultaneously meat and matrix, Robocop is manifold, charged up, violently dislocated from himself.

Robocop represents the pernicious threat of industrial-to-electronic reassembly, rewriting it as ruthless and deceptive corporate paternalism gone wild. *Robocop's* Omni Consumer Products (like the *Terminator* movies' Cyberdyne Systems or the *Alien* series' Company) is an overwhelming, postnationalist hybrid of profit-minded government and business, the military-industrial complex grown to international proportions. This corruption of the political "body" is related to Robocop's excessive male body.

Though Andrew Ross juxtaposes cyberpunk's unmuscular, "technomasculine" heroes with the "unadorned body fortress of the Rambo/Schwarzenegger physique," in fact the hard-bodied Robocop is always an inconsistent (if highly unlikely) underdog, the site of intersecting cultural anxieties and social disruptions.[12]

Robocop is both too hard and too soft. Hardly "well adjusted" or at ease with his robotoid status, he is repeatedly shot up, bloodied, exploded, and dismembered. His explicitly self-penetrating body overstates and parodies what Ross calls "masculinity in retreat." Enacting what Ross terms the "technomasculine" character's "exciting softness," a penetrability that subverts conventional notions of hard potency and paternal legacies, Robocop represents the failed distinction between organic masculinity and implanted hardware (*SW*, 153).

The violence of this failure is reflected by what might be called "cyborg viewers," the spectators whose empathetic anxiety recalls what Lynne Kirby describes as cinematic "male hysteria." Engendered by a condition of "assault," these spectators endure "a certain pleasure of pain" **derived from the confusion of sexual and gender roles and the dissipation of body control**; such a hysterical viewer is inserted in the diegesis of *Robocop*.[13] For at issue in this movie is a loss of (self-) control through represented subjectivity or, more precisely, through an impossible point of view camera. The film's energetic repetition of such hysteria through erratic "robovision" shots—indicated by grid screens, blinking instructions, and targeting mechanisms—suggests that viewers share Robocop's inflicted and suffered trauma. But the hysterical insertion in the cinematic machine is refracted as Officer Murphy's (Peter Weller's) look: robovision is always "humanized." Indeed, such resurrection is by now a cliché, again and again available in single films and sequels, denying traditional generic closure, association with recognizable stars, or even recyclable plots.[14] This repeatable cyborg performance-as-look, within and between texts, replays the hysteric's fear of lost body boundaries as an anxiety over frames of vision which constitute "subjectivity" and "character" on film screens.

Unlike Captain Picard, Murphy's self is irrecuperable once he is "cyborged" into Robocop.[15] His self-realization comes as he gazes at his reflection in a shard of mirror: he sees that he has no body, collective or individual, to be returned to him, only a bald head punctured by implants.[16] Murphy/Robocop's angry self-encounter exemplifies the cyborg's self-penetration as conflict rather than hopeful "integration." Unlike Haraway's functionally transgressive cyborg, this masculine body agonizes over the dissolution of boundaries which results in a specific loss of "manhood."

This agony is made explicit in the repeated sequence of his brutal death and high-tech rebirth. The screen blacks out as he dies under a hail of automatic weapons fire, a grueling scene visually organized as a gang rape: first we are forced to watch helplessly (with his partner, Lewis [Nancy Allen], behind a chainlink fence); the cut reveals Murphy's perspective as he sees the villains looking down at him, an image mediated through a frenzy of ejaculation. Conventionally "feminized" by this highly performative penetration, Murphy is reborn as "hypermasculine," Lynne Joyrich's term for a critical and textual "reaction against femininity": Robocop (not Murphy) is able to occupy all the film's gendered subject positions.[17] This hypermasculinity is underlined in his shooting of a would-be rapist in the groin, through the legs of the screaming victim, a penetration which completes the narrative of rape for his audience: his bullet produces a bloody hole in the woman's dress, so that he situates multiple viewer positions (rapist, savior, and always the victim).

Robocop's *desire* for brutal revenge against his male assassins (in lieu of the heterosex he can no longer "remember") is enacted through robovision. Complete with explanatory inscribed Directives (lifted from Asimov's "Laws of Robotics"). Robocop's subjective look reproduces perspective as experience, translating an unknowable position to one of mass familiarity. **Desire is desexualized, displaced to visual reception**, as the audience, like Murphy, is repositioned "as" Robocop. Such a postmodernist conflation of loss and consciousness. Haraway suggests, effaces referentiality: "we cannot name and possess this thing we cannot not desire" (*P,* 25). That is, the reference that appears to be missing in Robocop's hulking Ken-doll anatomy is also intensely explicit by its absence: he is, after all, a monument to phallic self-sufficiency.

But even as hypermasculine cyborgs like Robocop and the Terminator repudiate femininity, in their audiences and their diegeses, they assume all gender in their self-penetrating bodies. If, as Haraway suggests, the cyborg is a "way out of the maze of dualisms ... a powerful infidel heteroglossia," it is also a confusion of those dualisms ("CM," 181). (Re)born self-penetrated, Robocop is by definition an integrated circuit of violence. At stake in *Robocop* is the regendering (or, in Haraway's model, postgendering) of this circuit. He wakes as an imagined video camera that is also a screen. We/he watch white-coated technicians set programming parameters (indicated by grid lines that "disappear" into the screen that serves as "mind"); then a white-coated woman plants a lipstick "kiss" on the surface that is our/his frame of vision.

This "kiss" marks mechanical complications. While construed as "he" within and external to the narrative, Robocop is also not "complete": without his penis, he can no longer properly service Murphy's pert suburban wife. More interestingly, his cop partner is a woman, so that while he is denied the buddy movie's conventional thrill of (repressed) homoeroticism, he is also faced continually with his inability to "function" heterosexually. **His own technologized, desexed body is the sign of his death and its irrelevance. He is reproduced as corporate product**, simultaneously absent and excessive to biological and sexual processes. As Steven Best writes, Robocop incarnates a Baudrillardian hyperreality, a "product of cybernetics, media, and simulation."[18] This simulacrum revises sex within and beyond the heterosexual matrix. In this masculinist hierarchy, the most important measure of identity is the size of one's weapon, signaled first in the name of the company VP, Dick Jones (a pun doubled by the actor's name, Ronnie Cox); and second in the ritual men's room meetings, where everyone's mettle is available for measurement.

Everyone's, that is, except Robocop's. As Haraway acutely observes, "Miniaturization has turned out to be about power" ("CM," 153). And Robocop, for all his performative phallic excess, does represent a certain metaphoric loss. In the image of his colossal gun, spun and slipped into his gleaming holster-thigh, the film designates its heroic iconography as ironically derivative and literalized. Before he is murdered, Murphy practices spinning his handgun like a TV show cop in order to impress his glued-to-the-screen son.[19] Later, Robocop repeats the gesture following his impressive performance at the police shooting range, signaling the trace of his "original" identity.

The film parodies the idea of originality, citing repetition as the basis of a troubled masculine identity: Murphy is shot down by the entertainingly caricatured villains (who in fact work for Jones); Robocop is shot down by the helmeted and anonymous police force (who also work for Jones, since OCP has "privatized" municipal workers). Unable to save Murphy, Lewis rescues Robocop and hides him in an abandoned warehouse. When they confront the band of villains once more, she is armed with a massive missile-launching gun (far bigger than Robocop's). In the exchange of gunfire, Lewis is wounded and in need of rescue herself; she lies wounded and whimpering. "Murphy! I'm a mess!" After pulling a bloody stake out of his own broad metallic chest, he says, "Don't worry. They'll fix you. They fix anything." "Fixed" himself, the neutered Murphy is machine and not, penetrated and penetrating. Appropriately, he exacts revenge by plunging his interface-finger into the chief villain's neck, "pulling out" to allow the neck to spurt blood.

Robocop's self-s(t)imulation culminates as he proves Jones's duplicity by reproducing his (Jones's) image in the boardroom. Again he plunges his bloody finger, this time into the computer panel, so that his "memory" replays Jones's confession, recorded earlier. The exchange between Robocop and the computer figures his "birth" into an ironic nonselfhood: after reproducing Jones, Robocop remembers his lost name (Murphy) and is at the same time deemed "son" by OCP's president, the Old Man (Dan O'Herlihy).

This loss of self is determined by and as his unstable body. Robocop's body, like the transsexual body analyzed by Sandy Stone, implies "intertextual possibilities" which contest social, historical prescriptions of gender and sexual identity.[20] *Robocop* ends in flux. Like nonbinary transsexuals in a binary world, the nonbinary Robocop is "programmed to disappear" from his own story, unable to "generate a counterdiscourse" ("PM," 295). His lack of male "signs" denotes an absence within his own body, a threatening deviation from normative male bodies and behavior.

Intertextual Possibilities: The Sequel

Stone writes that escape from binary discourse is possible through subverting given texts, for example, seizing "the textual violence inscribed in the transsexual body and turning it into a reconstructive force" ("PM," 295). The violence inscribed in Robocop's ("postgender," "postsexual") body is redoubled in Kershner's 1990 sequel. Robocop reappears where he left off in Verhoeven's recuperative finale, with human name and mechanical body. But the collapse of self and not-self in one body further complicates the nature of (his) desire. That is, Robocop's quest is no longer focused through a human-conditioned sense of identity and gender; rather, he must now distinguish himself from a second cyborg, the one whose name *is* the film's title.

Bill Nichols suggests that in *Robocop* "the cyborg simulacrum replaces the original body and many of its flaws or inefficiencies while giving humanoid representation, including desire, to a machine."[21] The sequel further problematizes the concept of "originality." Emblematic of the post-Reagan nineties, *Robocop 2* stages originality as nostalgia for a stronger "economy" of finances, images, and militaristic ideals, which never existed. Encased in a new and lighter-weight robosuit, Robocop emerges at the start of the film from a flaming police car which has exploded and rolled over many times within seconds. His gun aimed at anonymous and sweaty villains (we see it from their subjective camera position), he declares himself: "Peace officer."

Cynical and incongruous, the line introduces the gun as a sign of masculine impotence.

Again, Robocop-now-deemed-Murphy is a man without a penis. The film's initial narrative movement articulates the loss of his humanity in order to set up the comparison which follows. He abandons any idea of reunion with his wife and son, since he cannot offer her "a man's love." Skull plate visible from a rear camera angle and separated from Mrs. Murphy by a chainlink fence, he says, "They made this to honor you. Your husband is dead. I don't know you." Unable to "know" the tearful (and summarily ejected-from-the-narrative) wife, Robocop continues to pursue sublimation and self-knowledge, which is strictly nonreproductive: he throws himself into his work.

This masturbatory narrative line is interrupted when Robocop is ambushed and sledgehammered into fragments which are deposited, scarecrowlike, back at police headquarters. **This dismemberment literalizes his increasing psychic frenzy.** Suspended from wires, his torso and arms twitch uncontrollably: as one of OCP's watchful women scientists observe, "He's in hell."[22] *Robocop 2* suggests that such a state of impotent consciousness is culturally coded; his disrupted body (boundaries) extends the cyborg's collapse of organism and machine, which are both, according to Haraway, "coded texts" ("CM," 152). His lack of a lower body at this point only underlines the obvious metaphor of his search for self.

When he is reassembled by OCP, he is comically framed within the Bush administration's increasingly uncertain role as a global police force: Robocop's previously unself-conscious machismo is turned absurdly "kinder and gentler." Rebuilt and reprogrammed after his physical decimation, he offers resentful eight-year-old criminals "a word on nutrition" and reads Miranda to a corpse.[23] Suddenly self-aware as he talks to this dead body, he admits, "I'm having … trouble"; if his internal malfunctions are linked to his sentience, he also lacks the bounded body which would allow self-definition and expression of desire. Robocop parodies the odious sign of the "wimp" (and even looks forward to its notorious revision as Desert Storm commander in chief) when his "nice" version recovers his violence by plugging himself into a high-voltage electric current.

Zapped back into macho-mode, Robocop **embodies the paradoxical lack of choice resulting from constitutional hybridity,** what Haraway calls "the interpenetration of boundaries between problematic selves and unexpected others" (*P,* 23). Robocop is clearly problematic. But the quite expected other in *Robocop 2* is OCP's new product, a second cyborg. A designer-drug ("nuke") junkie and cult leader (named for the robo-brother he will be), Cain becomes the human basis for the latest model of nonreproduction. He is selected by Dr. Juliette Faxx, an OCP employee whose own (female) reproductivity is limited to the joke of her name. In creating him, Faxx becomes demonically obsessed with Cain, watching his spinal cord and brain as they float in a container, peering back at her with Cain's eyeballs. (These provide the opportunity of a reverse shot of her looking in at him with considerable affection.) She chooses Cain, she explains, because cops (aside from the devout and obedient Irish Catholic Murphy) are too "macho" and "body proud" to undergo the transformation into dutiful cyborg, or nonbody. So, she concludes that for a desperate criminal, "the prospect might even be desirable," incorporation being an apparent alternative to incarceration.

Both cyborgs represent narratives of desire. If Robocop maintains his desire for "order" by electrocuting his mechanical body into angry Murphyness, Robo 2's desire is resolutely connected to his status as product. Literally constructed without language (Robo 2 only roars), he is a reified addict: he obeys orders in order to get mega-fixes, passed into a loudly clamping "door" in his abdomen. Robo 2 is the perfect social unit predicted by William S. Burroughs, a "consumer sold [by the producer] to his product."[24] Desperate for "nuke," Cain is a conflation of self-interest, self-commodification, and corporate infamy, perfectly illustrating OCP's profiteering paradigm down to its motto, "The Only Choice." Lack of options drives his dystopic subjectivity, which mirrors the larger social disstructure: OCP *buys out* the bankrupt city of Detroit in order to expand its market for drugs and its labor resources for a highly profitable "future of urban pacification."[25]

This future is designed according to military efficiency, which repeatedly links violence to sex. Unlike Robocop, Robo 2 has no flesh at all but instead an array of massive artillery extending from every limb and a video screen for a face. With this monitor, he expresses his own mediated lust for Angie, Cain's girlfriend. Frightened by his metallic hulk, Angie (the film's designated whore-moll, with too much make-up and spike heels) attempts to seduce her way out of sure death. She extends her hand to caress Robo 2's shiny monster-claw, murmuring that she could "get used to it." But the possibilities of this flesh-tech coupling are both too horrific and too exciting for even Robo 2 (or the trace of Cain) to contemplate. As he reaches for her, his screen-face distorts with static, and he bellows in agony just before his multiple weapons rip through her body, absolutely consummating their coupledom.

While clearly demonizing a violent capitalist hegemony (and the rampant self-interest that drives it), the *Robocop* movies reassert the potency of individual action, as embodied by a victimized and self-repetitive cyborg. The irony here is keen: after destroying Robo 2, his bastard br/other, Murphy re-enacts his "effect of identity," again spinning his weapon before reholstering it. Similarly, "Robocop" remains recyclable as a title in the third film of the series (soon to be released *without* original star Weller).[26] Murphy-Weller-Robocop, like other mutating cyborgs, contains and dislocates positions of activity and passivity, sex and gender. That Murphy/Robocop yearns for sex and, more significantly, the fatherhood it would grant is signaled by his most emotionally charged act, when he holds the hand of a mortally wounded ten-year-old drug dealer. Denied Murphy's TV-watching son because of his superhard and dickless body, Robocop flashes back to the son and then to an earlier scene: the drug-dealer shoots at the camera/Robocop. Flash to the present, and the dealer dies. But Robocop lives, because his death is irrelevant.

Cyborg Cycles

Terminator 2 and *Eve of Destruction* reintroduce the desire for self in other-gendered terms, as women's longing to rewrite frightening and oppressive familial histories. Both films reconfirm sons' connections to maternal bodies in complex ways. In *T2*, Sarah Connor/Linda Hamilton's extremely worked-out body suggests one possible response to genocidal technology, a hard but penetrable body designed to mediate between such technology and the history it seeks to destroy (Sarah develops her "self" to combat the coming world destruction). In *Eve of Destruction*, Eve VIII (Renee Soutendijk) is a cyborg programmed with the "experiences" of her creator, Dr. Eve Simmons (also played by Soutendijk). Eve VIII embodies the annihilation that Sarah would abort: she is an apocalyptic mother bent on revising the repressed "failures" of Eve's childhood and motherhood. If, as Doane observes, the mother is traditionally "the figure who guarantees, at one level, the possibility of certitude in historical knowledge," in these films Sarah and Eve secure and reverse that certitude by assuming cyborgian identities ("T," 175).

Narrating the sequel to *The Terminator*, Sarah accepts her designated identity as the (previously reluctant) "mother of the future" (or John Connor, as a child played by Edward Furlong). To this end, she decides to change that future by assassinating the would-be inventor/father of Skynet, the sentient computer destined to decimate earth's population and, not incidentally, produce the various Terminators who will wage continual war against humanity. The film's version of the future, then, is also history that might not be, an idea voiced by John's absent father, Reese (Michael Biehn, killed in the first film), as spoken to him by his son John-in-the-future: "There is no fate but the one we make for ourselves." This constructionist adage allows Sarah's self-reassignment. As the sign and center of this masculine reproductive cycle, she is caught up in the film's rampant father-son relations.[27] She must negotiate not only John's affiliation with the cyborg T800 (Schwarzenegger) but also the links between Miles Dyson (Joe Morton) and his "children": a young son and Skynet.

Sent across time from older-John to boy-John, the T800 appears to dislodge what Doane calls science fiction's "technological fetishism ... an obsession with the maternal, reproduction, representation, and history" in favor of a revisionary paternal authority, one that specifically excludes sexual penetration and reproduction ("T," 174). But Sarah's intervention in the films' techno-paternal cycles takes place within normative masculinist bounds; sexuality is displaced onto extravagant penetrative and explosive violence, her own as well as that of the various Terminators. Conforming to filmmaker James Cameron's stated desire to make "a war movie about peace," *T2*'s violations seek to erase consequences, to revise "history" as it happens. Schwarzenegger, the first film's relentless assassin, is now John's replacement dad, his "very own" Terminator. The T800 agrees to maim opponents rather than kill them outright, a practice which permits the spectatorial thrill of his expected explosive virility (much like Robocop's completion of the rape in the first film) without even the potential guilt of looking at dead bodies. Arriving in theaters just after the Gulf War "Turkey Shoot" and CNN's corpseless Highway of Death, this no-fault spectacle becomes an ostensibly unself-conscious representation of "history" as simulated violence.

As Fred Pfeil observes, the film dutifully "invites us to critique the violence it represents" and gender-codes this critique by granting Sarah her and the audience's anger at the "men" who destroy rather than create.[28] The film's excesses of violence-as-FX are also simultaneously reproduced and simulated in the liquid metal T1000 (Robert Patrick), which is at least as cruel and unyielding as the previous Schwarzenegger cyborg. Comprised of more expensive special effects and a radically undefineable body, the T1000 is at once harder and softer than the ever-resolute Schwarzenegger. When shot, the T1000 becomes silvery amorphousness and globules, then reforms as the LA policeman (a corporate-villainous disguise which collides with more contemporary "history" in the form of the Rodney King beating, verdict, and aftermath). The T1000 confounds his opponents (the proto-apocalyptic family unit made up of Sarah, John, and the T800) by shifting body-types and sexes. Profoundly corrupt, the T1000 is "polygendered" but also, as Mark Dery suggests, portrayed with "more than a hint of caricatured S/M homosexuality" in his redundantly penetrative murders ("CBP," 103). The T1000 appears at different moments as an asylum guard, Sarah Connor herself, and John's foster mother, Janelle, with a decisively phallic spike for an arm. Each "form" takes time to marvel at its penetrative equipment.

On the other hand, the father represented by the T800 appears to be only masculine in size, stoicism, and firepower; yet he remains, as Jonathan Goldberg points out, not quite straight but, rather, an ironically deathless, desireless, and spermless caricature of body-obsession. According to Goldberg, the film's performative excesses wage "relentless opposition to the category of heterosexuality."[29] Both Terminators, the T800 in leather and the T1000 in cop regalia, exaggerate homosexual types, subverting norma-

tive heterosexual authority structures. Sarah's attraction to the T800 has nothing and everything to do with sex.[30] For her, he appears the best candidate to "father" her son: watching them together, she calls the machine "the only one who measured up. In an insane world, it was the sanest choice." Which means, it is no choice at all: Arnold, proud Humvee-owner, an asexual machine as co-parent, her partner for a future nuclear family.

Paradoxically, for the first part of the film, the cyborg becomes progressively less machinelike as Sarah becomes more so; this visual exchange and transformation—according to Dery, she is "morphed into a *Freikorps* cyborg" ("CBP," 103)—is achieved through gendered body differences, where "machine" translates as "masculine" or even more radically, as Goldberg writes, "lesbian." But Sarah's desire, I suggest, remains cyborgian, not sexual: with no options except survival, she cannot help but fail to "measure up" to the world-saving selflessness of the T800. The most paternal and self-authoritative act in this movie will be Schwarzenegger's "selfless" leap into hot liquid metal. Sarah's imminent death, which doesn't even occur here, remains irrelevant.

Her anger at being anointed by historical imperative to bear and train the savior of humanity is manifest in her chain-smoking, feral precision and hyperbutch militancy. If at first she is a conventionally powerless object of surveillance (locked in an asylum, videotaped by pasty-faced interns and licked by a lascivious attendant), her attempt to escape her "female" fate is a complex process of rebuilding her body and dismantling spatial boundaries. As Susan Bordo observes of today's acutely exercised "yuppie" bodies, **Sarah's represents a freedom from "domestic, reproductive destinies," but she is also locked into that maternal fate which she did not make** (and which is as repeatedly referred to as the photo taken when she is pregnant).[31] That is, Sarah's hard body represents a paradox: her independence from her unwanted maternity but also her capitulation to cultural expectations, or what Bordo calls the "management of desire," in particular the containment of a "dangerous, appetitive, bodily 'female principle'" ("RSB," 105).

Similarly, Sarah's kamikaze invasion of Dyson's home reframes her military machisma as the stage for the T800's more convincing (because even more brutal) self-sacrifice, his self-penetration. This ripped-open inhuman arm is the image which speaks to Dyson more compellingly than either Sarah's automatic weaponry or her subsequent tears. This hypertech-body, the metallic skeleton that Dyson has worshipped, is left over from the first *Terminator*'s exalted and prolonged demise, now resurrected as a problematic "origin" for the scientist. As Dyson says, "All my work is based on it."

Not coincidentally, it is also at this point, when Sarah and Dyson both see themselves reflected in the cyborg (she as its emulator, he as its creator), that the film's tenuous mediation of gender and racial differences breaks down. If Sarah and Miles initially occupy corresponding spaces, isolated within antiseptically white institutions (she as psychiatric inmate, he as the only black man working for Cyberdyne Systems), here they are both rendered tearful and speechless—feminized—by the machine which incarnates and refuses their human future. Left briefly alone together at the cavernous Cyberdyne Lab, Sarah and Miles are finally caught looking at each other, mirror images of oppression and submission to the shrine of

291 }

Arnold: he sits mortally wounded and she is helpless to save him. Their exchange of nods confirms the necessity of his paternal suicide and her maternal impotence. Their brief congruence—specifically, the compassionate intersections of their reproductive obligations—barely threatens the conventional focus on the intently white male Terminators. Blowing himself up is the only response with which Miles can restore a "new world order," an order that looks completely familiar, not new at all.

Sarah's redemption comes (again) when she faces her "self" near film's end. Taking her form in a climactic ruse to lure John out of hiding, the T1000-as-Sarah confronts the "authentic" Sarah (an image allowed by the participation of Hamilton's twin sister Leslie Gearren).[32] Facing this literal embodiment of Haraway's irreconcilably "fractured identity," Sarah *is* a cyborg, unable to resolve herself as a set of contradictions, forced to prove her maternity to John by her willingness to die for him (and the future). Like Dyson, the macho cyborgs, and the good mothers before her, human-Sarah refuses to capitulate to this simulated self and offers herself as sacrifice. Her imminent death is interrupted at the last minute by the again (!) resurrected T800. Sarah watches wordlessly as "she"—who is simultaneously other, her refracted "twin" self—morphs into the *more* other T1000 cop-body, **a transformation that, even as it restores her human singularity, also denotes an irretrievable loss of body boundaries in "our" cyborgian future.**

Maternal Meltdown

Eve of Destruction narrates a similar crisis of maternal identity, specifically represented by the doubling of Eve as cyborg and mother. According to Dr. Simmons, all she wants "is to be a good mother to Timmy" (introduced as he surprises his mother by announcing what "vaginas" and "balls" are, signs that her parenting has been neglectful). Surely, the film's title suggests its prescriptive gendering of its imminent apocalypse. While on a trial "run," Eve VIII is inadvertently caught in the crossfire of a bank robbery. Her circuits become confused; she begins to retrace the doctor's past, exacting vengeance for various violences against her and other women. While Robocop's emotionally motivated revenge tends to elicit sympathy from his audience, Eve VIII's inflexibility is trivialized and pathologized (and specifically "feminized") from the beginning: the first thing she does is go shopping.

With her newly purchased red leather jacket and black miniskirt, Eve VIII visits a biker bar, where she picks up a smug, tight-jeaned lover for the night.[33] Once they are alone in a motel room, Eve VIII seduces the man, resists when he gets "rough," then watches as he reaches into his pants. The payoff for this image of impending penetration, shot from between the man's tight-jeaned legs, is considerably less cathartic than the similar build-up for *Robocop*'s near-rape scene. When Eve VIII bites off his penis (and then assaults his friends and a squad of local cops with automatic weaponry), the result is her opponent's angry observation that she's "a device [which] is horny as well as psychopathic."

This sexualized pathology is reinforced as biology: the nuclear trigger hidden deep inside Eve VIII is revealed through a micro-penetrative tracking shot through her internal organs. It is also linked to Dr. Eve's particularly "female" history: she confesses to Special Agent Jim McQuade (Gregory Hines) **that the cyborg is acting out her own repressed "teenage fantasies" of violence against men.** These fantasies register as anger at her father and an obsessive "mother-love" for her son (and, specifically, concern that she has been a "bad mother"). Having repressed a childhood memory of her father's fatal abuse of her own mother, Simmons has unknowingly implanted the image in Eve VIII's program: it replays like a home movie for both characters. Eve's overwhelming guilt surfaces when she overhears Eve VIII threaten her father on McQuade's walkie-talkie. Simmons speaks to Eve VIII: the jolt of hearing her "own" voice over the machine startles the cyborg, who proceeds to assault both McQuade and Mr. Simmons.

This confusion between the paternal figures, significantly black and white, is suggested as well in Eve's hysterical run to the house to rescue them both. Over the walkie-talkie, she hears Eve VIII say to a prostrate McQuade, "I saw what you did." That *she* (Eve VIII) was not the "I" who saw this deadly "primal scene" suggests the cyborg's boundary-confusion: a multiplicity of cyborg selves is intimated in Simmon's response to Eve VIII: "He didn't do it." Initiating a remarkably threatening (because interracial) set of Oedipal intersections, Eve VIII's accusation exacerbates the film's representation of reproductive crisis: the white father/murderer and the black professional killer are refracted mirror images, sprawled on the floor in front of the cyborg. Simmons enters the scene in time to tell Eve VIII and herself that McQuade "didn't do it."

What "it" means now becomes incredibly fraught, alluding to acts of sex and murder. Increasingly perplexed, Eve VIII grabs Bill Simmons's limp body and snaps his neck before shooting her gun wildly at his panicked daughter/herself, who dives for cover only when encouraged to do so by the immobilized McQuade. Unable to shoot the cyborg (since she carries the nuclear device inside her like a developing fetus), McQuade is temporarily powerless. If Eve Simmons's intervention saves him, it also compels the spectacular death of her father. Eve VIII's subsequent decision to recover Timmy from his father in New York endangers the city's entire population. The bomb inside her is armed after repeated assaults on her implacable body. (We see her repair one bloody wound in a motel bathroom, echoing Schwarzenegger's famous self-restoration scene in *The Terminator* [where he selects "Fuck you asshole" as the appropriate response to his pesky landlord], but with repeated focus on her exposed breasts displacing the spectacle of his eyeball removal.)

Now "activated" and pursuing her remembered son, Eve VIII's is a corrupt maternal body, or what Doane calls a typical "conjunction of technology with the feminine" ("T," 174). That Eve is not a biological mother—indeed, that she duplicates an already-existing mother—exacerbates her offense against a "natural," socially gendered hierarchy. This cyborg figures the chaos resulting from what Doane terms "the traumatic impact of these [reproductive] technologies—their potential to disrupt given symbolic systems that construct the maternal and the paternal as stable positions" ("T," 175). The struggle between Eve and Eve VIII over maternal authority is framed by the film's faith in an impossible masculine order, situated-within and outside the bounds of government within McQuade. The film's plainly articulated cynicism regarding CIA and War Department activities grants the decidedly un-macho McQuade (despite his remarkably outsized weaponry) specific moral grounding as resilient otherness. At film's end, his increasing frustration climaxes in the image of his multiply penetrated body, staggering on a subway track as he attempts to blast a hold through Eve VIII's one vulnerable spot—her eye. Yet his positioning as the resolved, impassioned cop opposed to the hysterical female split self (an intellectual, inadequate mother and a schizoid cyborg whose uzi never seems to run out of ammunition) also reasserts traditional sexual differences. While his (unmentioned but always visible) blackness and devotion to duty apparently preclude an otherwise predictable romance with the barely married Simmons, at the same time McQuade's interrogation of her past and present neuroses (acted out by the hysterical cyborg) suggest that he plays savior-father-confessor to both Simmons and her son.

And yet McQuade's eventual black masculine potency—articulated by his ability finally to locate Eve VIII's "fuckin' off switch"—is compromised by the cyborg's (unexplained) resurrection at the last minute. Simmons, who has been shot (by Eve VIII/herself), grabs the large gun McQuade tosses to her and shoots her mirror image repeatedly but without success. Finally, Dr. Eve plunges the nozzle of the weapon into Eve VIII's already bloody eye socket, a gesture which is simultaneously self-penetrating, self-destroying, and self-redeeming.

A Clean Break with Procreation

Numerous interpenetrations in *Hardware* further hystericize conventions of body boundaries: sex is precisely what's irrelevant in its postapocalyptic future. The film charts the usurpation of reproductive processes by ultramilitary technology and governmental genocide. It opens with an image of an anonymous scrap-metal scavenger traversing the warzone wasteland. On the soundtrack we hear the disembodied voice of radio DJ Angry Bob (Iggy Pop), "the man with the industrial dick" and fanatical promoter of the government's latest Emergency Population Control Bill. Bob asserts that "eager" citizens are lining up to take part in "what the president terms a clean break with procreation." A provocative hybrid of horror and science fiction, the movie describes corporate politics and sexual and gender difference in metaphors of space and movement: Moses (Dylan McDermott) is a member of the Corps, roaming a fatally irradiated Outer Zone. His lover, Jill (Stacey Travis), a sculptor, remains barricaded within the multiply reinforced walls of her apartment, making art that no one sees or buys.

The couple's impossible relation is metaphorically figured in the corpse that Mo passes on his way to visit Jill: the camera pauses on an infant still tied to its dead mother, an image that confirms and disrupts the traditional notion of "motherhood," its troubling equation with biological destiny, or what Valerie Hartouni terms its "literally mindless" physiological function.[34] Mo and Jill will argue vehemently over the function and idea of reproduction, their oppositional stances marked according to whose body is at stake in reproduction as a cultural and biological process.

This argument is metaphorically embodied in the killer "droid" that Mo unknowingly brings inside Jill's penetrable fortress. He picks it up as a fragment, a head sold to him by a junk-dealer named Alvy (scrap metal, not drugs, being the hottest black market after the apocalypse). A dwarf who resents being ridiculed by conventionally pretty hunks like Mo and his friend Shades (John Lynch), Alvy complains, "It's not my fault my mom got a dose in the Big One." Attributions of maternal responsibility continue throughout the film, as Jill's artwork (her "creation") transforms itself—out of the metallic head from Alvy's—into the cyborg that threatens to kill her. The useless mother, the blameworthy mother, the dead mother: these figures crowd the film's social vision. While Mo and Jill's relationship implies that biological reproductivity still applies, its traditional hopefulness and nostalgia are clearly absurd in this context, where death is manufactured and monster killing machines are reproduced. The contrast between Mo's zone-scavenging and Jill's immobility comments ironically on gender difference: if Mo's mobility in a dead world mocks the masculinist ideal of "freedom," Jill's overdetermined separatism and self-enclosure parody "feminine" domesticity. She is sexually available to Mo (and to his "best friend," Shades), yet she remains inviolate, committed only to the sculpture she hoards.

The head Mo gives Jill parodies the myth of cyborg-self-reproduction. Part of the "MARK 13" series of military cyborgs (or "Biomechanical Auto-independent Artificially Intelligent Life Forms"), the head is a techno-monster, self-regenerating and programmed to murder indiscriminately and incessantly, exemplifying the body politic that Angry Bob calls a "constant war state." Here the ostensible system of production and consumption has transmutated into an assembly line of annihilation producing too many consuming bodies and not enough bodies to consume. The MARK 13 does not transgress the boundary between human and machine so much as it denies that boundary's existence. Its intelligence is performative; assimilating voices and programs from its victims, **the cyborg is fleshless, imbued with relentless agency without desire.** This lack of desire is further embodied in Jill and Mo, whose energetic but passionless sex is initiated in the shower as his mechanical hand (with Borglike implants) caresses her naked back. After fucking a cyborg, Jill then produces a cyborg (at least according to suggestive crosscutting): the reborn MARK 13.

Significantly, their sex scene is watched by two voyeurs, represented as correspondent violators of private space (and, of course, mirroring our position). The first is Jill's neighbor Lincoln Weinberg, who watches the lovers from his window across the alley. His rubber-gloved finger presses a trigger to take pictures, dislocating and appropriating both partners' orgasms as he moans, "Take it all the way in ... suck it dry." In the infrared of his camera lens, the sex act itself becomes a simulation, a porn show narrated by Lincoln and implicating all its invasive audiences in its construction. The second diegetic voyeur is the MARK 13 head itself, whose red eyes begin to glow as the climax of this primal scene approaches, linking this sex act with its unnatural ostensible product, which in turn displaces the sexual body that no longer signifies in a cyborg world.

After fitful sleep, Jill wakes with a start and goes to work, welding, sawing, torching. The centerpiece is the MARK 13's head, which she paints with a U.S. flag motif, signaling a bankruptcy of nationhood and patriotism, now reduced to soup can insignia value. Appropriately, given the MARK 13's eventual "birth" from the wall where she inserts it, Jill's work represents nondifference, a collapse of desire and program, body and machine: to paraphrase Reese regarding the Terminator, it destroys, that's what it does.

It's also what Jill appears to be doing, as Mo wakes and watches her. The gendered polarity only looks obvious: she affixes a bundle of torched and melted dolls to the wall; Mo argues against the Population Control Bill, saying, "It's our nature to reproduce, to live on through our children." Jill, however, the would-be bearer-body of this "nature," refuses to consider such a "stupid, suicidal, and sadistic" project, citing radiation poisoning and the widespread destruction that defines their current lives. In this postapocalyptic and hypertechnologized world, **the concept of normative reproduction, as Haraway points out, is pre-**

posterous: if "every technology is a reproductive technology," then science, rather than biology, becomes the realm of "accountability and responsibility."[35] *Hardware* suggests that beyond science (which remains committed to the state apparatus, as in the Emergency Population Control Bill), social interaction and survival determine long-term "responsibility." Jill's art, Mo's scavenging, even Lincoln's voyeuristic thrills serve to reproduce technoculture instead of bodies. "Technological decontextualization is ordinary experience," writes Haraway, so that "the whole world [which might be imagined inside Jill's barricaded apartment] is remade in the image of commodity reproduction" ("PM," 297).

The head itself is clearly Mo's procreative legacy to Jill. Her "conception" of and from it is subjectively horrific, her understanding of the world outside her apartment, an endless and (re)constructed nightmare. When Mo asks her why she doesn't sell her work, she replies, "It's nothing. It's not for anyone." Unseen spectacle and noncommodity, **her art represents a cultural continuum of production and reproduction rendered meaningless in a desolate, deadly environment**. It's commodification without end. Jill's aestheticized violence measures both her own internal struggle and the external war raging through political machineries: "I've been basing my work on organic forms," she tells Mo. "It feels like I'm fighting with the metal and ... the metal's winning." Her sense of siege is no doubt induced by the continuing *spectacle* of war on television. She channel-surfs with her remote-control, finding only beatings, torture, horrified reactions, and thrash metal and post punk bands, all reproductions of military ideals, human images implying that, as Haraway observes, the body is "a strategic system, highly militarized in key arenas of imagery and practice."[36]

Appropriately, the MARK 13 body is the most strategic of systems, reassembling itself during Mo's absence and Jill's return to sleep. Incorporating various mechanical body parts from around the apartment, the cyborg reigns as imperial emblem, replacing what Haraway calls the precybernetic "caricature of that masculinist reproductive dream" with a techno-autonomy that rewrites traditional machine-human dualism: its implacable "will" designates its humanlike monstrosity ("CM," 152). If, as Haraway also suggests, the "marked organic body" is conceptually obsolete, the "body as a coded text" makes dire sense ("BPB," 211). The cyborg, she writes, "is text, machine, body, and metaphor—all theorized and engaged in practice in terms of communications" ("BPB," 212). That is, reproduction is loosed from bodies to become a negotiation of information. The MARK 13 speaks to Mo through the inflationary past of biblical apocalypse. Mo reads, "The earth will shake, rattle, and roll. The masses will go hungry, their bellies bloat. These are the birth pangs. No flesh shall be spared."

As Haraway suggests, the idea of the cyborg profoundly undermines three levels of distinctions: animal and human, organic and inorganic, and physical and nonphysical ("CM," 153). *Hardware* reconfigures these differences so that the transgressive body is Jill's, not the cyborg's. For *Hardware*'s vision of the future is more dreadful than Haraway's but also more aggressively, perversely, and immediately politicized. It assumes the ascendancy of masculinist paramilitary technology already presaged by the corporate production of the Gulf War, a cyclical conflation of reproduction and destruction confronted by the nonreproductive female body, which repudiates its essentialist (biological or sexual) definitions as well as its constructionist performativity. Jill resists by surviving.

No flesh shall be spared. This future can only imagine constant body violation. Simulating such a breakdown, the film's imagery becomes increasingly unclear, elliptic, colliding in MTV-vintage fragmentations and time warps. If Haraway's cyborg advances hope for future multiplicity and the transcendence of embodied identity, *Hardware*'s cyborg reveals its birth as overwhelming death, simulation as experience, fragmentation as body-unity, multiple voices as consciousness. This cyborg performs perpetual self-birth, like the Terminators, continually resurrecting itself even when it looks "dead." This motif becomes especially cynical when Mo returns at the last minute to rescue Jill (who has been battling the monster in her kitchen, of all domestic places). He blasts the cyborg, then comforts her by saying, "It's dead, baby!" But minutes later it leaps back in through the window and grabs her, pulling her out onto a live wire, electrifying her as it is itself electrified. This self-repetition is, of course, planned and digitized by the government that built the machine.

A "clean break with procreation" is further figured in the MARK 13's reprogramming of Jill's apartment doors so that they open and close like giant jaws, hacking through the abdomen of a would-be savior. Not incidentally, this is a black man, Chief, who as he is cut in two shoots his gun, discharging it into the head of the only other black man in the movie, Vernon the doorman. Their connection to Miles Dyson, who also dies to save a white woman and the future, cannot be overlooked. While *Hardware*'s excesses are highly ironic, they also fail to suggest alternatives. As Jill realizes later, the cyborg is the government's program for population control: its/the film's targeting of people of color only expands and refines current political conditions.

Jill's tenacious deviation from official and conventional narratives, her difference from the technophiliac femininity of earlier sci-fi, offers hope of consciousness against the excessive simulation of this all-consuming cyborg. After literally falling out of the apartment (through the window which gave Lincoln and the cyborg entree), she returns with a baseball bat to rescue Mo. But instead she finds his dead body, after he has been punctured by the MARK 13's deadly poison needles. The white male hero fails. He must fail in this dystopic vision: the cyborg is, as Jill intuits and Mo never understands, profoundly *about* his self-destruction. Mo's death, unlike the Terminator's, is irrelevant and saves no one. The horror of *Hardware*'s cyborg is its continual mirroring of its ostensible hero, its radical, persistent reconfiguration of its context: binary constructions are irredeemably immaterial. If the MARK 13's gender is undefined by its self-reproduction, in its assumption of the onus of self-reproductive (non)male, the cyborg only reiterates the loss of gendered and sexed limits initiated by Jill's refusal to reproduce. In the shower where she and Mo had sex, she reconstructs body boundaries by dissolving old ones. As the cyborg "melts" beneath the rush of water, she beats it with her baseball bat, literally smashing it to pieces rather than penetrating it: created for desert storming, it was abandoned because of its faulty "insulation."

Again, death is irrelevant, Jill's triumph and the cyborg's destruction at film's end are rendered meaningless, for it is reborn in mass production at the plants which manufacture more MARK 13s. As the plot resumes its desperate circularity, Jill remains unanswered, unresolved, with no place to be, virtual. Instead of closure, the film offers another opening. *Hardware*, like "Star Trek"'s Borg episode, ends where it begins. We hear Iggy Pop sing, "This is what you want/This is what you get," and watch the scavenging Zone Tripper continue to collect scraps, which continue to mark irrelevant boundaries between life and death. The film's nonresolution repeats **the irony of the cyborg as a promising site of "liminal transformation"** but also as emblematic of male hysteria over body limits, reproduction, and identities ("CM," 177).

If the Borg are transgressive and integrated, they are also demonized, representing fear of multiple losses, of choice, individual identity, and morality. The invasion from within the human body (figured by Jill's militarized womb of an apartment) approximates the macho-cyborg's penetrability and self-reproduction, its performative and essential instability. The struggle for identity that the cyborg might imagine has yet to be formulated. "Articulation," writes Haraway, "is not a simple matter" ("PM," 324). If the pitched battle climaxes in *Robocop, T2, Eve of Destruction,* and *Hardware* fail to articulate the returns, the sequels, and the imperfect imitations that inevitably follow, they also represent a hysteria that might be reconceived through political fictions. Cyborg fictions.

Notes

1. Donna Haraway, "The Actors Are Cyborg, Nature is Coyote, and the Geography is Elsewhere: Postscript to `Cyborgs at Large.'" in Constance Penley and Andrew Ross, eds., *Technoculture* (Minneapolis: University of Minnesota Press, 1991), 22. Further references will be made in parentheses, designated *P*.

2. Isaac Asimov, *I, Robot* (Garden City, N.Y.: Doubleday, 1950).

3. Early during its five-year run, "ST:TNG" did kill off a popular crew member, Tasha Yar (Denise Crosby). Her subsequent guest spots on the series, as Yar in another possible history and as Yar's half-Romulan daughter, suggest an inventive recycling and reproduction of character and star-body.

4. Aside from the Borg's appearance in an introductory episode featuring the Q Continuum (where the *Enterprise*'s away team has discovered that the Borg are continually "incubating" humanoid infants in drawers, wired up and wearing diapers). "The Best of Both Worlds" (cited in this essay), and "Hugh," they have appeared in a 1993 two-part episode, in league with Data's brother, Lore. In "Hugh," an adolescent Borg is rescued from death and brought on board the *Enterprise*. Once there, "he" is "humanized," a process which would seem to undermine an initial image of the relentless and demonized collective but also conforms to the series' desire to find the "human" qualities in all potential others and opponents. Hugh is adopted by the *Enterprise* crew, encouraged to discover and explore his "individuality," and returned unharmed to the Borg (in the hope that his "reprogramming" will "infect" their collective). Most interesting is Hugh's relationship with Geordi LaForge (LeVar Burton), the black, blind chief engineer, a character deemed extraordinary both by his lack of human "vision" (he wears an electronic visor and thus functions as a "cyborg" himself) and his lack of blackness (this assimilation into a general "white" humanity represented by the "more black" Klingon security officer. Worf [Michael Dorn]). That is, the displacement of evil otherness onto the Borg and its subsequent recuperation by the "innocent" Hugh is paralleled by the displacement of intrahuman "racial" otherness onto nonhuman (and, especially, nonwhite) races like Klingons, Romulans, and Ferengi.

5. Judith Butler, *Gender Trouble: Feminism and the Subversion of Identity* (New York: Routledge, 1989). Further references will be cited in parentheses, designated *GT.*

6. Judith Butler, "Imitation and Gender Insubordination," in Diana Fuss, ed., *Inside/out: Lesbian Theories. Gay Theories* (New York: Routledge, 1991), 28.

7. Susan Jeffords, *The Remasculinization of America: Gender and the Vietnam War* (Bloomington: Indiana University Press, 1989), 14.

8. Donna Haraway, "A Cyborg Manifesto: Science, Technology, and Socialist-Feminism in the Late Twentieth Century," in *Simians, Cyborgs, and Women: The Reinvention of Nature* (New York: Routledge, 1991). Further references will be cited in parentheses, designated "CM."

9. Haraway, in what she calls a "caricature" of the "embarrassed silence" of recent feminism, illustrates the inadequacy of "radical-feminist" and "socialist-feminist" projects as a failure to address "race," except as an afterthought ("by addition, race") ("CM," 160).

10. Mary Ann Doane, "Technophilia: Technology, Representation, and the Feminine," in Mary Jacobus, Evelyn Fox Keller, and Sally Shuttleworth, eds., *Body/Politics: Women and the Discourses of Science* (New York: Routledge, 1990), 172. Further references will be cited in parentheses, designated "T."

11. Bruce Sterling, "Preface" to *Mirrorshades: The Cyberpunk Anthology* (New York: Arbor House, 1986), xiii.

12. Andrew Ross, *Strange Weather: Culture, Science, and the Technology of Limits* (New York: Routledge, 1991), 153. Further references will be made in parentheses, designated *SW.*

13. Lynne Kirby, "Male Hysteria and Early Cinema," *Camera Obscura* 17 (1990): 113-131. Kirby describes such crisis as it coincides with the beginnings of cinema and psychoanalysis; the cyborg body, repeatedly assaulted and violated, seems an apt repository for the anxieties that Kirby discusses in terms of submission and power.

14. To this end, Arnold Schwarzenegger comes back as an entirely new and improved Terminator in *T2*, with a new series number and a new program. And a third *Robocop* film is scheduled for fall 1993 release, featuring a new star; this suggests that the Robobody (in this case, previous Robocop Peter Weller's body) is replaceable inside the Robosuit.

15. See Mark Dery's "verbing" of the word in "Cyborging the Body Politic," *Mondo 2000* 6 (1992). Further references will be cited in parentheses, designated "CBP."

16. Picard's baldness is the subject of much discussion in "ST:TNG" circles, regarding its "sex appeal" and usefulness as a plot device. For the Borg episode, it must be noted, the abduction and transformation of anyone who is not bald (everyone else on the *Enterprise*) would be much more traumatic to *see* (there would be a more radical difference to imagine and construct, as with Robocop). Picard's baldness establishes him, in other words, as a more likely candidate for "easy" transformation and recovery.

17. Lynne Joyrich, "Textual and Critical Hypermasculinity," in Patricia Mellencamp, ed., *Logics of Television: Essays in Cultural Criticism* (Bloomington: Indiana University Press, 1989), 161.

18. Steven Best, "In the detritus of hi-technology," *Jump-Cut* 34 (1989): 23.

19. The show the son watches is "T. J. Laser," a reference to a nondiegetic ("real") television series starring Captain Kirk himself (William Shatner), "T. J. Hooker."

20. Sandy Stone, "The *Empire* Strikes Back: A Posttranssexual Manifesto," in Julia Epstein and Kristina Straub, eds., *Body Guards: The Cultural Politics of Gender Ambiguity* (New York: Routledge, 1991), 297. Further references will be cited in parentheses, designated "PM."

21. Bill Nichols, *Representing Reality: Issues and Concepts in Documentary* (Bloomington: Indiana University Press, 1991), 239.

22. This part is played by the unbilled Patricia Charboneau.

23. Bush is caricatured in a 1991 *Z Magazine* as "Globocop."

24. William S. Burroughs, *Naked Lunch* (New York: Grove Press, 1959), xxxix.

25. That this imagined corporate plan for the "future of urban pacification" looks forward to uses of U.S. military forces in L.A. or Somalia is alarming but hardly surprising.

26. Weller opted instead to star in David Cronenberg's 1991 film *Naked Lunch,* a movie based on Burroughs, whose dystopic vision of addition and hyperpenetration in turn influenced cyberpunk writers.

27. Jonathan Goldberg notes that at the end of *The Terminator,* she is irrevocably "plugged in" to this future history when she tells the Terminator, "You're terminated, fucker;" this being the machine which Reese had earlier called a "motherfucker." In this volume.

28. Fred Pfeil, "Revolting yet Conserved: Family *Noir* in *Blue Velvet* and *Terminator 2*," *Postmodern Culture* 2, no. 3 (1992): [27]. For a discussion of the family structure and time in *The Terminator*, see Constance Penley, "Time Travel, Primal Scene, and the Critical Dystopia," in Penley, ed., *Close Encounters: Film, Feminism, and Science Fiction* (Minneapolis: University of Minnesota Press, 1991).

29. Goldberg, "Recalling Totalities," 191.

30. But she does offer a doggedly essentialist reading of gender difference: men destroy and women create. In her often-quoted speech to Miles Dyson, Sarah says, "Men built the hydrogen bomb, not women ... men like you thought it up. You're so creative. You don't know what it's really like to create, to create a life." She is cut short by her precocious, hypermasculine son, who occupies all positions.

31. Susan Bordo, "Reading the Slender Body," in Mary Jacobus, Elizabeth Keller, and Sally Shuttleworth, eds., *Body/Politics: The Discourses of Science* (New York: Routledge, 1990), 103. Further references will be cited in parentheses, designated "RSB."

32. Margot Dougherty, "A New Body of Work," *Entertainment Weekly* 74 (1991): 19.

33. The scene parallels the first moments of *T2*, where a naked Schwarzenegger invades a similar setting, impresses everyone with his penis size, commits violent mayhem, and leaves with stolen leather jacket and motorcycle, all to the tune of "Baaad to the Bone."

34. Valerie Hartouni, "Containing Women: Reproductive Discourse in the 1980s," in Constance Penley and Andrew Ross, eds., *Technoculture* (Minneapolis: University of Minnesota Press, 1991), Hartouni's discussion of the "dead mother" who "gives birth" to a child in a 1966 newspaper headline has recently been revisit-

ed, suggesting that her title might be expanded to include the 1990s. A *Newsweek* article entitled "A Matter of Life and Death" describes the controversy over a dead woman, Marion Ploch, whose fetus (fourteen weeks old when the woman died) was kept alive inside the corpse's womb at a Bavarian clinic. With no father identified by the unmarried woman, Ploch's parents publicly (on national TV) agreed to take custody of the child, which the clinic's *doctors* decided to bring to term (*Newsweek,* 16 November 1992, 55). The fetus died some weeks later.

35. Donna Haraway, "The Promises of Monsters: A Regenerative Politics for Inappropriate/d Others," in Lawrence Grossberg, Cary Nelson, and Paula Treichler, eds., *Cultural Studies* (New York: Routledge, 1992), 299. Further references will be made in parentheses, designated "PM."

36. Donna Haraway, "The Biopolitics of Postmodern Bodies: Constitutions of Self in Immune System Discourse," in *Simians, Cyborgs, and Women: The Reinvention of Nature* (New York: Routledge, 1991), 211. Further references will be made in parentheses, designated "BPB."

DIGITAL PISTIL

Lois H. Gresh

Bub sucked sweet nutrient glop up his stembuss. Tiny pores on his leaves guzzled the carbon dioxide and light. The musicale tinkled Bach's sonata 1 in B minor. Bub was so giddy, so gay; he sprayed a net of oxygen mist across the room.

Then Bach did something he never did: he buzzed. And something shot through Bub's mist and cleaved to the fluffy stigma beneath his petals. Something sucking, sucking—it was a freaking bee; and it stabbed a groove so deep that Bub's microheads spun in their gallenium arsenide wafers.

Bach screeched. The bee whirled through tornado mist. Bub's circuits crossed, his stembuss bulged with electrons, and inside his caches, virtual addresses bit-flipped into system stack space.

Then a tropical heat hit, and Bub's chloroplasts started pumping glucose like ferns. Feedback loops reported wild orgies in his root and stem tips, where meristematic cells were splitting into cubic heaps. Male anther smacked female pistil ...

Talk about an electron rush.

For a computerized blob of plant tissue, a digital zinnia stuck on a coffee table, this was living. Sweat dripped from Bub's sight stalk into the clay flower pot.

Through the living room wall, the neighbor's petunia, Flora, hummed Madonna's *Ball, Crawl, Wham, 'n' Jolly*. Flora always sounded better than that old Madonna crone. For perhaps the millionth time, Bub wondered what it would be like to touch Flora's petals. He'd never had the courage even to speak to her.

So delirious was he that when the cat pounced, Bub didn't defend himself quickly enough to avoid a slash to the stomatas. A moment too late he whirled, petals aflutter. Oh High and Mighty Cat rumbled rolls of thunder and her luminous green eyes screamed lightning; the glare hurt Bub's sight stalk.

His anther swelled and pulsed atop his stamen stalk. He pumped once, twice, then let it rip, and pollen soared high and zapped Oh High and Mighty's face. The cat shrieked and thrust her claws into the flower pot. Mud clumps everywhere. Glop-sopped dirt splattering walls and purple plaid sofa. Pollen soaking into the Owner's crossword puzzle.

What would the Owner think?

Bub's petals grabbed the pink cat nose and pulled. Fatty leaves pulsed green with the beat of chlorophyll, slapped the big black head left, then right, then left again.

Oh High and Mighty Cat retreated to the sofa and licked pollen from her fur. She glowered, taunting Bub because he could not budge from the table. If not for the grounding cord plugged to the bottom of the pot; well, then, that cat would know who's boss: Bub would wrench free, slither to the sofa, and smack the fat black head silly.

The musicale was grating and the notes broke in midair and screeched down Bub's I/O bus, rubbing it raw. He couldn't analyze the trill progressions, usually his favorite pastime and best conversation piece when the Owner entertained friends.

He was running on splintered circuits, and strange desires surged. He desperately needed to numb his microheads. He thought of the hours typically spent each day soaking up science, news, music, and art to amuse the Owner. But now, thanks to a bee, Bub signaled the televij to switch on *General Nursing Home*.

The living room wall flared to life. A nurse with hair the color of vinaigrette dressing pushed a wheelchair into a blue room stuffed with flowers. Bub's caches nearly split from the beauty. In the wheelchair was an old man with sparse but bright blond hair. He was deeply tanned. "I know, Mr. Deepstud," said the nurse, "that despite your six marriages, you've never really loved. And in my heart [here she paused and fluttered lashes], I sense that you still need it."

Mr. Deepstud nodded his wrinkled but Grecian face, touched an oval nail to a brilliant pink petal. "Ah, yes, dear Nurse Klune, I may be a blind diabetic paralyzed from the thighs down, but still my soul yearns for someone to share my fortune, to rekindle my long-dead desires."

Nurse Klune slipped to Deepstud's lap and slid a hand beneath his smoking jacket. A flip of wrist and her white uniform dissolved into air. She barely wore a bikini.

Sweat sloshed off Bub and splashed to the plush lawn of lavender carpet. He had a bad case of the sugar shakes. He flipped his overheating sensors and shut down glucose production. Then he swooned, his petals dipped, and his stembuss shimmied. By his pot, crossword puzzle boxes swirled in psychedelic patterns.

On the televij, a digital marigold quivered in its pot. Beneath the marigold's petals on a wooden desk, two Owners sucked lips and thwacked flesh. A limb swung wild. The flower pot cracked to the floor. The poor marigold lay withered, mangled; stembuss straining toward glop.

What in God's name were the Owners doing? What would happen to the poor marigold? Bub's grounding cord strained with anxiety. Hot oxygen steamed up his stamen stalk and shot out his anther. It only took a nanosecond of thought before he signaled the vij off; no use blowing more circuits, the bee had done enough damage.

From the sofa, Oh High and Mighty Cat growled. She swiveled her hips into the plaid kitchenette and scrunched by her velvet plasticine bowl. Something nasty seeped to Bub's honey home, something that smelled like cow tongue and pig snout.

Flora crescendoed, then dove into hot and swingy jazz. He felt the waves: tremoloso, appassionatamente, abbandono. Her hot licks scorched scales and set his thorns afire. Then she sank to dolce, and sweet notes slunk through Bub's ports and looped in dizzy hoops.

He had to meet her, to smell her perfume.

His little digital voice squeaked. "Come to me, Flora. Come share my fortune and rekindle my long-dead desires." Oh High and Mighty glared at him, cow tongue quivering on whiskers.

Wild glissandos snaked through the wall. Flora sang like fine chimes. "Ooooh, Bub, ooooh, despite your six marriages, I know that you've never really loved. And in my heart [here she paused and Bub envisioned wispy petals flitting], I know that you still need it. I've waited months for you to call to me, and now, no matter what it takes, I will come to you."

Bub's leaves bulged and dripped glistening green. He no longer needed the glop in his pot.

He heard a slosh slosh slinking in the front hallway. Something pink peeked under the crack beneath the door.

Bub wrenched himself toward the side of the pot where High and Mighty had dug. The pot tipped and rolled off the table, and with it came Bub. Soft petals hit rough rug. Sepals reached from the top of Bub's stembuss and stroked damaged petals. Gooey brown glop glittered on the lavender carpet.

Bub's peripheral control unit signaled his leaves' guard cells to prop open his stomatas for maximum gas and oxygen flow. Then he dug his leaves into the rug fibers. Like wires, fibers slashed into his chloroplasts, and chlorophyll oozed from the wounds, and soon he lay in a pool of his own green life.

His right leaf pushed him forward. His left leaf pushed him yet closer to the door. And both were gashed and mashed and hurting something awful. Petals, bright yellow and pink and fuschia, strained and sweated, urging him closer and closer to the threads of light seeping from under the door. His stembuss almost wrenched from his grounding cord. And at the end of the long cord dragged the heavy clay flower pot.

And then one mangled wet petal brushed against the sleek door. From the other side came Flora's tinkling voice. "Oooh, Bub, pull me through; quickly, quickly, I have no glop."

Bub's power pack pumped electrons to his roots. In his phloem tissues, chlorophyll surged through protoplasm-stuffed sieve cells.

The cat crouched by Flora's quivering pink petals, pig snout breath stirring them from the rug. An image of Nurse Klune blipped to Bub's microheads; he would let nothing happen to his beloved Flora, for she was his Nurse Klune. His highest frequency dumped to his widest I/O stream. Frequency tensed, it mounted; then out screeched a pitch so shrill that it shattered the Owner's lamp.

High and Mighty dove meow-yowing under the sofa.

Beneath the door, green shimmered through Flora's transparent outer cells. Her sap beat wildly against the confines of her stembuss. She must be young, maybe a model 204H—he was an older 104B—for her lovely smooth stembuss bore no bud scars.

Bub's own hairy stembuss prickled with delight. He slipped a leaf to Flora's petal and slithered it on down to where her stembuss shook; whether from fear or weakness or admiration, he knew not.

Flora slid under the door, first her beautiful fragrant petals, all paisleys and bows, then her shredded leaves and roots. A chlorophyll worm trailed behind her.

Bub eased her roots into the glop residue of his pot. She sucked the sweetness. Her paisleys swirled, her bows unknotted. She saw his chlorophyll bulges, the dripping thick leaves. She squealed. "Oooh, what happened to you?"

Bub didn't want to tell her that a bee screwed his wires, so he said, "I work out a lot, pump a lot of nutrients." From the corner of his sight stalk he saw High and Mighty skulking near, readying to pounce on poor Flora.

The cork cells in his roots clenched. His stamen stiffened.

Cat whiskers twitched, and eyes flashed green lightning.

Then the cat was on them: clawing, hissing, shredding. And like a baseball bat, Bub's stiff stamen smacked up and cracked the cat straight between the eyes, and clear across the room into the plaster wall.

High and Mighty thwacked and then sank to the floor. Her eyes darted around the room. She slunk off somewhere down the hall, and Bub heard her weak cat pads scuffing across the toilet and into the bathtub.

Bub was exhausted. Despite his newfound strength, he couldn't pull himself onto the coffee table. So he and Flora lay in each other's petals, and all afternoon, she sang and he spouted interesting artistic tidbits; and then finally, the Owner came home from work.

The Owner was very excited to find Bub with Flora, and when the two begged, the Owner agreed that they could share the same pot. The neighbor could buy a cheap new digital flower to take Flora's place.

The Owner scrubbed the chlorophyll and glop from the carpet, buffed his baldspot, and then played Bub's diagnostics on the musicale. Bub pulsed in the code, and in a semiconscious state, he chugged through the diagnostic routines. Through molasses the Owner said, "Maybe we'll find out why your stem is flubbery and why your leaves are so fat and sticky."

Late into the night, Bub chugged diagnostics. And late into the night, he chugged carbon dioxide and water. His stembuss grew fatter and fatter, he could hardly hold up his meaty leaves. The moon splattered light across the glucose pools under Bub's pot. A little hook of gallenium arsenide chip jabbed through his outer cells and glowed like fired wire.

Bub was gross, misshapen, bulging in all directions. His cells were protoplasm plumped. His vacuoles were bursting blimps. He toppled onto the dozing Flora. She awakened with a start, heaved against him. "Get off, get off!" she screamed.

Bub rolled off and lay moaning in the muck of glop.

"I've never known such a glucose pig. It's one thing to be thick and strong, it's another to split your stem. I thought you were handsome; but look at you, you make me sick!" Flora's voice no longer sounded very lovely.

The next morning, Bub's stembuss was as wide as the pot. Twiggy Flora hung over the side, straining to avoid stemsnap. All day she skittered up scales, squawked into octaves much higher than digital voices should climb. All day her petals smacked Bub as she bobbed rhythmically to her squawks. And when they watched *General Nursing Home,* Flora pointed at the digital marigold hanging from its pot, doing pushups on long slender leaves. "That's what you need," she shrilled, "trim down, get rid of that fat, wise up, Bub!"

And still he bulged, he couldn't help it. From his pores oozed sludge, and his anther sprayed sweat. And from the gummy glop, his taproot just kept sucking up more and more nutrients. Flora shrilled that he was turning their pot into a muckhole: "To think I crawled all the way down the hall to share a pot with a pastey dough-head whose brain can't even break out of a circular queue."

Over the side of the pot, flora dangled on a thin thread of circuit, her petals splayed across the Owner's crossword puzzle. She was drooping from the sweat saturated air. On her leaves tiny gashes foamed with white scum. Bub was too dizzy to help her; and besides, why bother?

Oh High and Mighty loomed over Bub's sight stalk. The cat's breath chuff chuffed on his leaves. He could not defend himself against the cat; this time, High and Mighty would have her way.

Something odd dribbled into Bub's taproot, something digital injected from Flora's roots into the glop. Bub sucked in a liquid packet and burst it. Inside were waves of chicken odors and grease. Why had Flora sent him packets of chemical chicken? Chuff chuff, cat tongue scratched Bub's leaves, scraped his guard cells, licked his stomata latches.

Bub's root hairs bristled. His leaves dripped, his stembuss oozed, his anther pumped, and from everything came the stench of rotting chicken. Bub was saturated in chicken fat.

Flora cackled, heaved with laughter. Her oxygen mist sprayed up: so gay, so giddy.

Bub whacked her one with his blubbery stembuss, but it just bounced off, and then he whacked the cat, who ducked then licked and sucked at Bub's sweat. He tried slogging and sideswiping the cat, but each time, she ducked the flubbery blows and sucked harder, and her teeth gnawed his pulpy leaves to green mash.

By the time the Owner came home, Bub was covered in leaf scars. Flora's mangled petals were stuck to the crossword puzzle. The cat was vomiting chlorophyll on the sofa. The Owner wasn't very happy: "I bought you as a companion, Bub, someone to make me happy. If I'd wanted children, I would have gotten married and spawned a few." Grimy chicken grease beaded on his clothes and glistened off his baldspot and bulbous nose.

Bub couldn't believe he had once wanted to touch Flora's petals and smell her perfume. What had he seen in her? Why hadn't it been enough to soak in science, news, opera? If not for that damn bee, Bub would still be a happy bachelor.

"I'm splitting you two up," said the Owner, mopping his baldspot with a handkerchief. "I called the electronic surgeon, told him you're an emergency, Bub. He said he'd fit you in tomorrow. But in the meantime ..." And the Owner dug up Flora's roots and grounding cord, and transplanted her to a small pot of her own.

Then the Owner stuck her in the bathroom atop the toilet. "Keep you two apart where you can't cause trouble," he muttered.

Bub sighed with relief. Flora must have been grafted from a thorn.

And she didn't let up. She shrieked and complained and accused Bub of ruining her life. She cawed *Ball, Crawl, Wham 'n' Jolly* in heavy metal antiharmonies till Bub yearned to hear Madonna on the musicale.

The Owner escaped to the neighbor's apartment. Oh High and Mighty snoozed on the windowsill, occasionally stirring to slap imaginary flies. Once Bub thought he heard the crunching of bee wings in her mouth, but he was probably dreaming.

Then toward morning, cat pads scuffed across the toilet. Bub jiggled, body alert. From the bathroom, Flora emitted a little halftone.

High and Mighty rumbled rolls of thunder. Over Flora's staccato shrieks came crashing and caterwauling, and Bub didn't know whether to cheer or scream for help. And then there was a great splash and the cat streaked meow-yowing down the hall and dove under the sofa.

Bub raised his tiny digital voice and squeaked for help, but the Owner wasn't home and nobody heard him. Flora's high C cracked and her tone went flat. "I don't want your help, Bub. I'd rather flush my life down the toilet than spend another minute with *you*."

She was so empty, so hollow inside; it was no wonder her stembuss was thin and weak. What he had taken for beauty was vacuous sap. He slapped male anther to female pistil. This time, there was no electron rush.

He could just see her adrift in the water, glop clumps bobbing by her petals, broken clay pot chunked like islands; her leaves clutching the sides of the toilet bowl. Then he heard her grounding cord slap porcelain, and he heard the whiplike lashing, and her cord slapped metal, and he knew that she had lassoed the handle.

Charoom, the toilet flushed.

And Bub was a widower. Chicken fat dripped down his stembuss into the bachelor pot. He signaled the musicale and it tinkled Bach's sonata 1 in B minor. But it did not cheer him.

He sprayed oxygen mist across the room. But *still* her perfume lingered.

4.7

I Hope I Shall Arrive Soon

Philip K. Dick

After takeoff the ship routinely monitored the condition of the sixty people sleeping in its cryonic tanks. One malfunction showed, that of person nine. His EEG revealed brain activity.

S——t, the ship said to itself.

Complex homeostatic devices locked into circuit feed, and the ship contacted person nine.

"You are slightly awake," the ship said, utilizing the psychotronic route; there was no point in rousing person nine to full consciousness—after all, the flight would last a decade.

Virtually unconscious, but unfortunately still able to think, person nine thought, Someone is addressing me. He said, "Where am I located? I don't see anything."

"You're in faulty cryonic suspension."

He said, "Then I shouldn't be able to hear you."

"'Faulty,' I said. That's the point; you can hear me. Do you know your name?"

"Victor Kemmings. Bring me out of this."

"We are in flight."

"Then put me under."

Time passed. Victor Kemmings, unable to see anything, unaware of his body, found himself still conscious. "Lower my temperature," he said. He could not hear his voice; perhaps he only imagined he spoke. Colors floated toward him and then rushed at him. He liked the colors; they reminded him of a child's paint box, the semianimated kind, an artificial life-form. He had used them in school, two hundred years ago.

"I can't put you under," the voice of the ship sounded inside Kemmings's head. "The malfunction is too elaborate; I can't correct it and I can't repair it. You will be conscious for ten years."

The semianimated colors rushed toward him, but now they possessed a sinister quality, supplied to them by his own fear. "Oh my God," he said. Ten years! The colors darkened.

As Victor Kemmings lay paralyzed, surrounded by dismal flickerings of light, the ship explained to him its strategy. This strategy did not represent a decision on its part; the ship had been programmed to seek this solution in case of a malfunction of this sort.

"What I will do," the voice of the ship came to him, "is feed you sensory stimulation. The peril to you is sensory deprivation. If you are conscious for ten years without sensory data, your mind will deteriorate. When we reach the LR4 System, you will be a vegetable."

"Well, what do you intend to feed me?" Kemmings said in panic. "What do you have in your information storage banks? All the video soap operas of the last century? Wake me up and I'll walk around."

"There is no air in me," the ship said. "Nothing for you to eat. No one to talk to, since everyone else is under."

Kemmings said, "I can talk to you. We can play chess."

"Not for ten years. Listen to me; I say, I have no food and no air. You must remain as you are ... a bad compromise, but one forced on us. You are talking to me now. I have no particular information stored. Here is policy in these situations: I will feed you your own buried memories, emphasizing the pleasant ones. You possess two hundred and six years of memories and most of them have sunk down into your unconscious. This is splendid source of sensory data for you to receive. Be of good cheer. This situation, which you are in, is not unique. It has never happened within my domain before, but I am programmed to deal with it. Relax and trust me. I will see that you are provided with a world."

"They should have warned me," Kemmings said, "before I agreed to emigrate."

"Relax," the ship said.

He relaxed, but he was terribly frightened. Theoretically, he should have gone under, into the successful cryonic suspension, then awakened a moment later at his star of destination; or rather the planet, the colony planet, of that star. Everyone else aboard the ship lay in an unknowing state—he was the exception, as if bad karma had attacked him for obscure reasons. Worst of all, he had to depend totally on the goodwill of the ship. Suppose it elected to feed him monsters? The ship could terrorize him for ten years—ten objective years and undoubtedly more from a subjective standpoint. He was, in effect, totally in the ship's power. Did interstellar ships enjoy such a situation? He knew little about interstellar ships; his field was microbiology. Let me think, he said to himself. My first wife, Martine; the lovely little French girl who wore jeans and a red shirt open at the waist and cooked delicious crepes.

"I hear," the ship said. "So be it."

The rushing colors resolved themselves into coherent, stable shapes. A building: a little old yellow wooden house that he had owned when he was nineteen years old, in Wyoming. "Wait," he said in panic. "The foundation was bad; it was on a mud sill. And the roof leaked." But he saw the kitchen, with the table that he had built himself. And he felt glad.

"You will not know, after a little while," the ship said, "that I am feeding you your own buried memories."

"I haven't thought of that house in a century," he said wonderingly; entranced, he made out his old electric drip coffee pot with the box of paper filters beside it. This is the house where Martine and I lived, he realized. "Martine!" he said aloud.

"I'm on the phone," Martine said from the living room.

The ship said, "I will cut in only when there is an emergency. I will be monitoring you, however, to be sure you are in a satisfactory state. Don't be afraid."

"Turn down the right rear burner on the stove," Martine called. He could hear her and yet not see her. He made his way from the kitchen through the dining room and into the living room. At the VF, Martine stood in rapt conversation with her brother; she wore shorts and she was barefoot. Through the front windows of the living room he could see the street; a commercial vehicle was trying to park, without success.

It's a warm day, he thought. I should turn on the air conditioner.

He seated himself on the old sofa as Martine continued her VF conversation, and he found himself gazing at his most cherished possession, a framed poster on the wall above Martine: Gilbert Shelton's "Fat Freddy Says" drawing in which Freddy Freak sits with his cat on his lap, and Fat Freddy is trying to say, "Speed kills," but he is so wired on speed—he holds in his hand every kind of amphetamine tablet, pill, spansule, and capsule that exists—that he can't say it, and the cat is gritting his teeth and wincing in a mixture of dismay and disgust. The poster is signed by Gilbert Shelton himself; Kemmings's best friend Ray Torrance gave it to him and Martine as a wedding present. It is worth thousands. It was signed by the artist back in the 1980s. Long before either Victor Kemmings or Martine lived.

If we ever run out of money, Kemmings thought to himself, we could sell the poster. It was not *a* poster; it was *the* poster. Martine adored it. The Fabulous Furry Freak Brothers—from the golden age of a long-ago society. No wonder he loved Martine so; she herself loved back, loved the beauties of the world, and treasured and cherished them as she treasured and cherished him; it was a protective love that nourished but did not stifle. It had been her idea to frame the poster; he would have tacked it up on the wall, so stupid was he.

"Hi," Martine said, off the VF now. "What are you thinking?"

"Just that you keep alive what you love," he said.

"I think that's what you're supposed to do," Martine said. "Are you ready for dinner? Open some red wine, a cabernet."

"Will an '07 do?" he said, standing up; he felt, then, like taking hold of his wife and hugging her.

309 }

"Either an '07 or a '12." She trotted past him, through the dining room and into the kitchen.

Going down into the cellar, he began to search among the bottles, which, of course, lay flat. Musty air and dampness; he liked the smell of the cellar, but then he noticed the redwood planks laying half-buried in the dirt and he thought, I know I've got to get a concrete slab poured. He forgot about the wine and went over to the far corner, where the dirt was piled highest; bending down, he poked at a board ... he poked with a trowel and then he thought, Where did I get this trowel? I didn't have it a minute ago. The board crumbled against the trowel. This whole house is collapsing, he realized. Christ sake. I better tell Martine.

Going back upstairs, the wine forgotten, he started to say to her that the foundations of the house were dangerously decayed, but Martine was nowhere in sight. And nothing cooked on the stove—no pots, no pans. Amazed, he put his hand on the stove and found it cold. Wasn't she just now cooking? he asked himself.

"Martine!" he said loudly.

No response. Except for himself, the house was empty. Empty, he thought, and collapsing. Oh my God. He seated himself at the kitchen table and felt the chair give slightly under him; it did not give much, but he felt it; he felt the sagging.

I'm afraid, he thought. Where did she go?

He returned to the living room. Maybe she went next door to borrow some spices or butter or something, he reasoned. Nonetheless, panic now filled him.

He looked at the poster. It was unframed. And the edges had been torn.

I know she framed it, he thought; he ran across the room to it, to examine it closely. Faded ... the artist's signature had faded; he could scarcely make it out. She insisted on framing it and under glare-free, reflection-free glass. But it isn't framed and it's torn! The most precious thing we own!

Suddenly he found himself crying. It amazed him, his tears. Martine is gone; the poster is deteriorated; the house is crumbling away; nothing is cooking on the stove. This is terrible, he thought. And I don't understand it.

The ship understood it. The ship had been carefully monitoring Victor Kemmings's brain wave patterns, and the ship knew that something had gone wrong. The waveforms showed agitation and pain. I must get him out of this feed-circuit or I will kill him, the ship decided. Where does the flaw lie? it asked itself. Worry dormant in the man; underlying anxieties. Perhaps if I intensify the signal. I will use the same source, but amp up the charge. What has happened is that massive subliminal insecurities have taken possession of him; the fault is not mine, but lies, instead, in his psychological makeup.

I will try an earlier period in his life, the ship decided. Before the neurotic anxieties got laid down.

In the backyard, Victor scrutinized a bee that had gotten itself trapped in a spider's web. The spider wound up the bee with great care. That's wrong, Victor thought. I'll let the bee loose. Reaching up, he took hold of the encapsulated bee, drew it from the web, and, scrutinizing it carefully, began to unwrap it.

The bee stung him; it felt like a little patch of flame.

Why did it sting me? he wondered. I was letting it go.

He went indoors to his mother and told her, but she did not listen; she was watching television. His finger hurt where the bee had stung up, but, more important, he did not understand why the bee would attack its rescuer. I won't do that again, he said to himself.

"Put some Bactine on it," his mother said at last, roused from watching the TV.

He had begun to cry. It was unfair. It made no sense. He was perplexed and dismayed and he felt a hatred toward small living things, because they were dumb. They didn't have any sense.

He left the house, played for a time on his swings, his slide, in his sandbox, and then he went into the garage because he heard a strange flapping, whirring sound, like a kind of fan. Inside the gloomy garage, he found that a bird was fluttering against the cobwebbed rear window, trying to get out. Below it, the cat, Dorky, leaped and leaped, trying to reach the bird.

He picked up the cat; the cat extended its body and its front legs, it extended his jaws and bit into the bird. At once the cat scrambled down and ran off with the still-fluttering bird.

Victor ran into the house. "Dorky caught a bird!" he told his mother.

"That goddam cat." His mother took the broom from the closet in the kitchen and ran outside, trying to find Dorky. The cat had concealed itself under the bramble bushes; she could not reach it with the broom. "I'm going to get rid of that cat," his mother said.

Victor did not tell her that he had arranged for the cat to catch the bird; he watched in silence as his mother tried and tried to pry Dorky out from her hiding place; Dorky was crunching up the bird; he could hear the sound of breaking bones, small bones. He felt a strange feeling, as if he should tell his mother what he had done, and yet if he told her she would punish him. I won't do that again, he said to himself. His face, he realized, had turned red. What if his mother figured it out? What if she had some secret way of knowing? Dorky couldn't tell her and the bird was dead. No one would ever know. He was safe.

But he felt bad. That night he could not eat his dinner. Both his parents noticed. They thought he was sick; they took his temperature. He said nothing about what he had done. His mother told his father about Dorky and they decided to get rid of Dorky. Seated at the table, listening, Victor began to cry.

"All right," his father said gently. "We won't get rid of her. It's natural for a cat to catch a bird."

The next day he sat playing in his sandbox. Some plants grew up through the sand. He broke them off. Later his mother told him that had been a wrong thing to do.

Alone in the backyard, in his sandbox, he sat with a pail of water, forming a small mound of wet sand. The sky, which had been blue and clear, became by degrees overcast. A shadow passed over him and he looked up. He sensed a presence around him, something vast that could think.

You are responsible for the death of the bird, the presence thought; he could understand its thoughts.

"I know," he said. He wished, then, that he could die. That he could replace the bird and die for it, leaving it as it had been, fluttering against the cobwebbed window of the garage.

The bird wanted to fly and eat and live, the presence thought.

"Yes," he said miserably.

"You must never do that again," the presence told him.

"I'm sorry," he said, and wept.

This is a very neurotic person, the ship realized. I am having an awful lot of trouble finding happy memories. There is too much fear in him and too much guilt. He has buried it all, and yet it is still there, worrying him like a dog worrying a rag. Where can I go in his memories to find him solace? I must come up with ten years of memories, or his mind will be lost.

Perhaps, the ship thought, the error that I am making is in the area of choice on my part; I should allow him to select his own memories. However, the ship realized, this will allow an element of fantasy to enter. And that is not usually good. Still—

I will try the segment dealing with his first marriage once again, the ship decided. He really loved Martine. Perhaps this time if I keep the intensity of the memories at a greater level the entropic factor can be abolished. What happened was a subtle vitiation of the remembered world, a decay of structure. I will try to compensate for that. So be it.

"Do you suppose Gilbert Shelton really signed this?" Martine said pensively; she stood before the poster, her arms folded; she rocked back and forth slightly, as if seeking a better perspective on the brightly colored drawing hanging on their living room wall. "I mean, it could have been forged. By a dealer somewhere along the line. During Shelton's lifetime or after."

"The letter of authentication," Victor Kemmings reminded her.

"Oh, that's right!" She smiled her warm smile. "Ray gave us the letter that goes with it. But suppose the letter is a forgery? What we need is another letter certifying that the first letter is authentic." Laughing, she walked away from the poster.

"Ultimately," Kemmings said, "we would have to have Gilbert Shelton here to personally testify that he signed it."

"Maybe he wouldn't know. There's that story about the man bringing the Picasso picture to Picasso and asking him if it was authentic, and Picasso immediately signed it and said, 'Now it's authentic.'" She put her arm around Kemmings and, standing on tiptoe, kissed him on the cheek. "It's genuine. Ray wouldn't have given us a forgery. He's the leading expert on counterculture art of the twentieth century. Do you know that he owns an actual lid of dope? It's preserved under—"

"Ray is dead," Victor said.

"What?" She gazed at him in astonishment. "Do you mean something happened to him since we last—"

"He's been dead two years," Kemmings said. "I was responsible. I was driving the buzzcar. I wasn't cited by the police, but it was my fault."

"Ray is living on Mars!" She stared at him.

"I know I was responsible. I never told you. I never told anyone. I'm sorry. I didn't mean to do it. I saw it flapping against the window, and Dorky was trying to reach it, and I lifted Dorky up, and I don't know why but Dorky grabbed it—"

"Sit down, Victor." Martine led him to the overstuffed chair and made him seat himself. "Something's wrong," she said.

"I know," he said. "Something terrible is wrong. I'm responsible for the taking of a life, a precious life that can never be replaced. I'm sorry. I wish I could make it okay, but I can't."

After a pause, Martine said, "Call Ray."

"The cat—" he said.

"What cat?"

"There." He pointed. "In the poster. On Fat Freddy's lap. That's Dorky. Dorky killed Ray."

Silence.

"The presence told me," Kemmings said. "It was God. I didn't realize it at the time, but God saw me commit the crime. The murder. And he will never forgive me."

His wife stared at him numbly.

"God sees everything you do," Kemmings said. "He sees even the falling sparrow. Only in this case it didn't fall; it was grabbed. Grabbed out of the air and torn down. God is tearing this house down which is my body, to pay me back for what I've done. We should have had a building contractor look this house over before we bought it. It's just falling goddam to pieces. In a year there won't be anything left of it. Don't you believe me?"

Martine faltered, "I—"

"Watch." Kemmings reached up his arms toward the ceiling; he stood; he reached; he could not touch the ceiling. He walked to the wall and then, after a pause, put his hand through the wall.

Martine screamed.

The ship aborted the memory retrieval instantly. But the harm had been done.

He has integrated his early fears and guilt into one interwoven grid, the ship said to itself. There is no way I can serve up a pleasant memory to him because he instantly contaminates it. However pleasant the original experience in itself was. This is a serious situation, the ship decided. The man is already showing signs of psychosis. And we are hardly into the trip; years lie ahead of him.

After allowing itself time to think the situation through, the ship decided to contact Victor Kemmings once more.

"Mr. Kemmings," the ship said.

"I'm sorry," Kemmings said. "I didn't mean to foul up those retrievals. You did a good job, but I—"

"Just a moment," the ship said. "I am not equipped to do psychiatric reconstruction of you; I am a simple mechanism, that's all. What is it you want? Where do you want to be and what do you want to be doing?"

"I want to arrive at our destination," Kemmings said. "I want this trip to be over."

Ah, the ship thought. That is the solution.

One by one the cryonic systems shut down. One by one the people returned to life, among them Victor Kemmings. What amazed him was the lack of a sense of the passage of time. He had entered the chamber, lain down, had felt the membrane cover him and the temperature begin to drop—

And now he stood on the ship's external platform, the unloading platform, gazing down at a verdant planetary landscape. This, he realized, is LR4-6, the colony world to which I have come in order to begin a new life.

"Looks good," a heavyset woman beside him said.

"Yes," he said, and felt the newness of the landscape rush up at him, its promise of a beginning. Something better than he had known the past two hundred years. I am a fresh person in a fresh world, he thought. And he felt glad.

Colors raced at him, like those of a child's semianimate kit. Saint Elmo's fire, he realized. That's right; there is a great deal of ionization in this planet's atmosphere. A free light show, such as they had back in the twentieth century.

"Mr. Kemmings," a voice said. An elderly man had come up beside him, to speak to him. "Did you dream?"

"During the suspension?" Kemmings said. "No, not that I can remember."

"I think I dreamed," the elderly man said. "Would you take my arm on the descent ramp? I feel unsteady. The air seems thin. Do you find it thin?"

"Don't be afraid," Kemmings said to him. He took the elderly man's arm. "I'll help you down the ramp. Look; there's a guide coming this way. He'll arrange our processing for us; it's part of the package. We'll be taken to a resort hotel and given first-class accommodations. Read your brochure." He smiled at the uneasy older man to reassure him.

"You'd think our muscles would be nothing but flab after ten years in suspension," the elderly man said.

"It's just like freezing peas," Kemmings said. Holding onto the timid older man, he descended the ramp to the ground. "You can store them forever if you get them cold enough."

"My name's Shelton," the elderly man said.

"What?" Kemmings said, halting. A strange feeling moved through him.

"Don Shelton." The elderly man extended his hand; reflexively, Kemmings accepted it and they shook. "What's the matter, Mr. Kemmings? Are you all right?"

"Sure," he said. "I'm fine. But hungry. I'd like to get something to eat. I'd like to get to our hotel, where I can take a shower and change my clothes." He wondered where their baggage could be found. Probably it would take the ship an hour to unload it. The ship was not particularly intelligent.

In an intimate, confidential tone, elderly Mr. Shelton said, "You know what I brought with me? A bottle of Wild Turkey bourbon. The finest bourbon on Earth. I'll bring it over to your hotel room and we'll share it." He nudged Kemmings.

"I don't drink," Kemmings said. "Only wine." He wondered if there were any good wines here on this distant colony world. Not distant now, he reflected. It is Earth that's distant. I should have done like Mr. Shelton and brought a few bottles with me.

Shelton. What did the name remind him of? Something in his far past, in his early years. Something precious, along with good wine and a pretty, gentle young woman making crepes in an old-fashioned kitchen. Aching memories; memories that hurt.

Presently he stood by the bed in his hotel room, his suitcase open; he had begun to hang up his clothes. In the corner of the room, a TV hologram showed a newscaster; he ignored it, but, liking the sound of a human voice, he kept it on.

Did I have any dreams? he asked himself. During these past ten years?

His hand hurt. Gazing down, he saw a red welt, as if he had been stung. A bee stung me, he realized. But when? How? While I lay in cryonic suspension? Impossible. Yet he could see the welt and he could feel the pain. I better get something to put on it, he realized. There's undoubtedly a robot doctor in the hotel; it's a first-rate hotel.

When the robot doctor had arrived and was treating the bee sting, Kemmings said, "I got this as punishment for killing the bird."

"Really?" the robot doctor said.

"Everything that ever meant anything to me has been taken away from me," Kemmings said. "Martine, the poster—my little old house with the wine cellar. We had everything and now it's gone. Martine left me because of the bird."

"The bird you killed," the robot doctor said.

"God punished me. He took away all that was precious to me because of my sin. It wasn't Dorky's sin; it was my sin."

"But you were just a little boy," the robot doctor said.

"How did you know that?" Kemmings said. He pulled his hand away from the robot doctor's grasp. "Something's wrong. You shouldn't have known that."

"Your mother told me," the robot doctor said.

"My mother didn't know!"

The robot doctor said, "She figured it out. There was no way the cat could have reached the bird without your help."

"So all the time I was growing up she knew. But she never said anything."

"You can forget about it," the robot doctor said.

Kemmings said, "I don't think you exist. There is no possible way that you could know these things. I'm still in cryonic suspension and the ship is still feeding me my own buried memories. So I won't become psychotic from sensory deprivation."

"You could hardly have a memory of completing the trip."

"Wish fulfillment, then. It's the same thing. I'll prove it to you. Do you have a screwdriver?"

"Why?"

Kemmings said, "I'll remove the back of the TV set and you'll see; there's nothing inside it; no components, no parts, no chassis—nothing."

"I don't have a screwdriver."

"A small knife, then. I can see one in your surgical supply bag." Bending, Kemmings lifted up a small scalpel. "This will do. If I show you, will you believe me?"

"If there's nothing inside the TV cabinet—"

Squatting down, Kemmings removed the screws holding the back panel of the TV set in place. The panel came loose and he set it down on the floor.

There was nothing inside the TV cabinet. And yet the color hologram continued to fill a quarter of the hotel room, and the voice of the newscaster issued forth from his three-dimensional image.

"Admit you're the ship," Kemmings said to the robot doctor.

"Oh dear," the robot doctor said.

Oh dear, the ship said to itself. And I've got almost ten years of his lying ahead of me. He is hopelessly contaminating his experiences with childhood guilt; he imagines that his wife left him because, when he was four years old, he helped a cat catch a bird. The only solution would be for Martine to return to him, but how am I going to arrange that? She may not still be alive. On the other hand, the ship reflected, maybe she is alive. Maybe she could be induced to do something to save her former husband's sanity. People by and large have very positive traits. And ten years from now it will take a lot to save—or rather restore—his sanity; it will take something drastic, something I myself cannot do alone.

Meanwhile, there was nothing to be done but recycle the wish fulfillment arrival of the ship at its destination. I will run him through the arrival, the ship decided, then wipe his conscious memory clean and run him through it again. The only positive aspect of this, it reflected, is that it will give me something to do, which may help preserve *my* sanity.

Lying in cryonic suspension—faulty cryonic suspension—Victor Kemmings imagined, once again, that the ship was touching down and he was being brought back to consciousness.

"Did you dream?" a heavyset woman asked him as the group of passengers gathered on the outer platform. "I have the impression that I dreamed. Early scenes from my life ... over a century ago."

"None that I can remember," Kemmings said. He was eager to reach his hotel; a shower and a change of clothes would do wonders for his morale. He felt slightly depressed and wondered why.

"There's our guide," an elderly lady said. "They're going to escort us to our accommodations."

"It's in the package," Kemmings said. His depression remained. The others seemed so spirited, so full of life, but over him only a weariness lay, a weighing-down sensation, as if the gravity of this colony planet were too much for him. Maybe that's it, he said to himself. But, according to the brochure, the gravity here matched Earth's; that was one of the attractions.

Puzzled, he made his way slowly down the ramp, step by step, holding onto the rail. I don't really deserve a new chance at life anyhow, he realized. I'm just going through the motions ... I am not like these other people. There is something wrong with me; I cannot remember what it is, but nonetheless it is there. In me. A bitter sense of pain. Of lack of worth.

An insect landed on the back of Kemmings's right hand, an old insect, weary with flight. He halted, watched it crawl across his knuckles. I could crush it, he thought. It's so obviously infirm; it won't live much longer anyhow.

He crushed it—and felt great inner horror. What have I done? he asked himself. My first moment here and I have wiped out a little life. Is this my new beginning?

Turning, he gazed back up at the ship. Maybe I ought to go back, he thought. Have them freeze me forever. I am a man of guilt, a man who destroys. Tears filled his eyes.

And, within its sentient works, the interstellar ship moaned.

During the ten long years remaining in the trip to the LR4 System, the ship had plenty of time to track down Martine Kemmings. It explained the situation to her. She had emigrated to a vast orbiting dome in the Sirius System, found her situation unsatisfactory, and was en route back to Earth. Roused from her own cryonic suspension, she listened intently and then agreed to be at the colony world LR4-6 when her ex-husband arrived—if it was at all possible.

Fortunately, it was possible.

"I don't think he'll recognize me," Martine said to the ship. "I've allowed myself to age. I don't really approve of entirely halting the aging process."

He'll be lucky if he recognizes anything, the ship thought.

At the intersystem spaceport on the colony world of LR4-6, Martine stood waiting for the people aboard the ship to appear on the outer platform. She wondered if she would recognize her former husband. She was a little afraid, but she was glad that she had gotten to LR4-6 in time. It had been close. Another week and his ship would have arrived before hers. Luck is on my side, she said to herself, and scrutinized the newly landed interstellar ship.

People appeared on the platform. She saw him. Victor had changed very little.

As he came down the ramp, holding onto the railing as if weary and hesitant, she came up to him, her hands thrust deep in the pockets of her coat; she felt shy and when she spoke she could hardly hear her own voice.

"Hi, Victor," she managed to say.

He halted, gazed at her. "I know you," he said.

"It's Martine," she said.

Holding out his hand, he said, smiling, "You heard about the trouble on the ship?"

"The ship contacted me." She took his hand and held it. "What an ordeal."

"Yeah," he said. "Recirculating memories forever. Did I ever tell you about a bee that I was trying to extricate from a spider's web when I was four years old? The idiotic bee stung me." He bent down and kissed her. "It's good to see you," he said.

"Did the ship—"

"It said it would try to have you here. But it wasn't sure if you could make it."

As they walked toward the terminal building, Martine said, "I was lucky; I managed to get a transfer to a military vehicle, a high-velocity-drive ship that just shot along like a mad thing. A new propulsion system entirely."

Victor Kemmings said, "I have spent more time in my own unconscious mind than any other human in history. Worse than early-twentieth-century psychoanalysis. And the same material over and over again. Did you know I was scared of my mother?"

"*I* was scared of your mother," Martine said. They stood at the baggage depot, waiting for his luggage to appear. "This looks like a really nice little planet. Much better than where I was ... I haven't been happy at all."

"So maybe there's a cosmic plan," he said, grinning. "You look great."

"I'm old."

"Medical science—"

"It was my decision. I like older people." She surveyed him. He has been hurt a lot by the cryonic malfunction, she said to herself. I can see it in his eyes. They look broken. Broken eyes. Torn down into pieces by fatigue and—defeat. As if his buried early memories swam up and destroyed him. But it's over, she thought. And I did get here in time.

At the bar in the terminal building, they sat having a drink.

"This old man got me to try Wild Turkey bourbon," Victor said. "It's amazing bourbon. He says it's the best on Earth. He brought a bottle with him from ..." His voice died into silence.

"One of your fellow passengers," Martine finished.

"I guess so," he said.

"Well, you can stop thinking of the birds and the bees," Martine said.

"Sex?" he said, and laughed.

"Being stung by a bee, helping a cat catch a bird. That's all past."

"That cat," Victor said, "has been dead one hundred and eighty-two years. I figured it out while they were bringing us out of suspension. Probably just as well. Dorky. Dorky, the killer cat. Nothing like Fat Freddy's cat."

"I had to sell the poster," Martine said. "Finally."

He frowned.

"Remember?" she said. "You let me have it when we split up. Which I always thought was really good of you."

"How much did you get for it?"

"A lot. I should pay you something like—" She calculated. "Taking inflation into account, I should pay you about two million dollars."

"Would you consider," he said, "instead, in place of the money, my share of the sale of the poster, spending some time with me? Until I get used to this planet?"

"Yes," she said. And she meant it. Very much.

They finished their drinks and then, with his luggage transported by robot space-cap, made their way to his hotel room.

"This is a nice room," Martine said, perched on the edge of the bed. "And it has a hologram TV. Turn it on."

"There's no use turning it on," Victor Kemmings said. He stood by the open closet, hanging up his shirts.

"Why not?"

Kemmings said, "There's nothing in it."

Going over to the TV set, Martine turned it on. A hockey game materialized, projected out into the room, in full color, and the sound of the game assailed her ears.

"It works fine," she said.

"I know," he said. "I can prove it to you. If you have a nail file or something, I'll unscrew the back plate and show you."

"But I can—"

"Look at this." He paused in his work of hanging up his clothes. "Watch me put my hand through the wall." He placed the palm of his right hand against the wall. "See?"

His hand did not go through the wall because hands do not go through walls; his hand remained pressed against the wall, unmoving.

"And the foundation," he said, "is rotting away."

"Come and sit down by me," Martine said.

"I've lived this often enough to know," he said. "I've lived this over and over again. I come out of suspension; I walk down the ramp; I get my luggage; sometimes I have a drink at the bar and sometimes I come directly to my room. Usually I turn on the TV and then—" He came over and held his hand toward her. "See where the bee stung me?"

She saw no mark on his hand; she took his hand and held it.

"There is no bee sting there," she said.

"And when the robot doctor comes, I borrow a tool from him and take off the back plate of the TV set. To prove to him that it has no chassis, no components in it. And then the ship starts me over again."

"Victor," she said. "Look at your hand."

"This is the first time you've been here, though," he said.

"Sit down," she said.

"Okay." He seated himself on the bed, beside her, but not too close to her.

"Won't you sit closer to me?" she said.

"It makes me too sad," he said. "Remembering you. I really loved you. I wish this was real."

Martine said, "I will sit with you until it is real for you."

"I'm going to try reliving the part with the cat," he said, "and this time *not* pick up the cat and *not* let it get the bird. If I do that, maybe my life will change so that it turns into something happy. Something that is real. My real mistake was separating from you. Here; I'll put my hand through you." He placed his hand against her arm. The pressure of his muscles was vigorous; she felt the weight, the physical presence of him, against her. "See?" he said. "It goes right through you."

"And all this," she said, "because you killed a bird when you were a little boy."

"No," he said. "All this because of a failure in the temperature-regulating assembly aboard the ship. I'm not down to the proper temperature. There's just enough warmth left in my brain cells to permit cerebral activity." He stood up then, stretched, smiled at her. "Shall we go get some dinner?" he asked.

She said, "I'm sorry. I'm not hungry."

"I am. I'm going to have some of the local seafood. The brochure says it's terrific. Come along anyhow; maybe when you see the food and smell it you'll change your mind."

Gathering up her coat and purse, she came with him.

"This is a beautiful little planet," he said. "I've explored it dozens of times. I know it thoroughly. We should stop downstairs at the pharmacy for some Bactine, though. For my hand. It's beginning to swell and it hurts like hell." He showed her his hand. "It hurts more this time than ever before."

"Do you want me to come back to you?" Martine said.

"Are you serious?"

"Yes," she said. "I'll stay with you as long as you want. I agree; we should never have been separated."

Victor Kemmings said, "The poster is torn."

"What?" she said.

"We should have framed it," he said. "We didn't have sense enough to take care of it. Now it's torn. And the artist is dead."

SKULL PLATE INNER EAR

NOSE CARTILAGE JAWBONE

CARTILAGE

CHIN RECONSTRUCTION

SHOULDER JOINT

PACEMAKER
ART VALVE
HEART

LUNG

BREAST

LVAD

JOINT LIVER

ARM

$\llcorner 4.8$

KIDNEY

The Life Cycle of Cyborgs
Writing the Posthuman

FINGER JOINTS

BLADDER

HIP JOINT

N. Katherine Hayles

ERIES SKIN

BONE

KNEE JOINT

For some time now there has been a rumor going around that the age of the human has given way to the **posthuman**. Not that humans have died out, but that the human as a concept has been succeeded by its evolutionary heir. Humans are not the end of the line. Beyond them looms the cyborg, a hybrid species created by crossing biological organism with cybernetic mechanism. Whereas it is possible to think of humans as natural phenomena, coming to maturity as a species through natural selection and spontaneous genetic mutations, no such illusions are possible with the cyborg. From the beginning it is **constructed**, a technobiological object that confounds the dichotomy between natural and unnatural, made and born.

If primatology brackets one end of the spectrum of humanity by the similarities and differences it constructs between *homo sapiens* and other primates, cybernetics brackets the other by the continuities and ruptures it constructs between humans and machines. As Donna Haraway has pointed out, in the discourse of pri-

TENDON

matology "oldest" is privileged, for it points toward the most primeval and there-fore the most fundamental aspects of humanity's evolutionary heritage.[1] "Oldest" comes closest to defining what is essential in the layered construction of humanity. In the discourse of cybernetics, "newest" is similarly privileged, for it reaches toward the limits of technological innovation. "Newest" comes closest to defining what is malleable and therefore subject to change in the layered construction of humanity. Whereas the most socially loaded arguments in primatology center on inertia, the most socially loaded arguments in cybernetics project acceleration.

Primatology and cybernetics are linked in other ways as well. Primates and cyborgs are **simultaneously entities and metaphors, living beings and narrative constructions**. The conjunction of technology and dis-course is crucial. Were the cyborg only a product of discourse, it could perhaps be relegated to science fiction, of interest to SF aficionados but not of vital concern to the culture. Were it only a technological practice, it could be confined to such technical fields as bionics, medical prostheses, and virtual reality. Manifesting itself as both technological object and discursive formation, it partakes of the power of the imagination as well as the actuality of technology. **Cyborgs actually do exist; about 10% of the current U.S. population are esti-mated to be cyborgs in the technical sense**, including people with electronic pacemakers, artificial joints, drug implant systems, implanted corneal lenses, and artificial skin. A much higher percentage participates in occupations that make them into metaphoric cyborgs, including the computer keyboarder joined in a cybernetic circuit with the screen, the neurosurgeon guided by fiber optic microscopy during an operation, and the teen gameplayer in the local videogame arcarde. "Terminal identity" Scott Bukatman has named this condition, calling it an "unmistakably doubled articulation" that signals the end of traditional concepts of identity even as it points toward the cybernetic loop that generates a new kind of subjectivity.[2]

How does a culture understand and process new modes of subjectivity? Primarily through the stories it tells, or more precisely, through narratives that count as sto-ries in a given cultural context. **The stories I want to explore are narratives of life cycles**.[3] They bring into focus a crucial area of tension between the human and posthuman. Human beings are conceived, gestated, and born; they grow up, grow old, and die. Machines are designed, manufactured, and assembled; normally they do not grow, and although they wear out, they are always capable of being disassembled and reassembled either into the same product or a different one. As Gillian Beer has pointed out, Frankenstein's monster—an early cyborg—is monstrous in part because he has not *grown*. As a creature who has never known what it is like to be a child, he remains alien despite his humanoid form.[4]

When cyborg subjectivities are expressed within cultural narratives, traditional understandings of the human life cycle come into strong conflict with modes of dis-cursive and technical production oriented toward the machine values of assembly and disassembly. The conflict cannot be reduced to either the human or machine orientation, for the cyborg contains both within itself. **Standing at the threshold separating the human from the posthuman, the cyborg looks to the past as well as the future**. It is precisely this double nature that allows cyborg stories to be imbricated within cultural narratives while still wrenching them in a new direction.

The new cannot be spoken except in relation to the old. Imagine a new social order, a new genetic strain of corn, a new car—whatever the form, it can be expressed only by articulating its differences from that which it displaces, which is to say the old, a category constituted through its relation to the new. Similarly, the language that creates these categories operates through displacements of traditional articulations by formulations that can be characterized as new because they are not the same as the old. The cyborg is both a product of this process and a signifier for the process itself. The linguistic splice that created it (cyb/org) metonymically points toward the simultaneous collaboration and displacement of new/old, even as it instantiates this same dynamic.

The stories that produce and are produced by cyborg subjectivities are, like the cyborg itself, amalgams of old and new. Cyborg narratives can be understood as stories only by reference to the very life cycle narratives that are no longer sufficient to explain them. The results are narrative patterns that overlay upon the arc of human life a map generated from assembly and disassembly zones. One orientation references the human, the other the posthuman; **one is chronological, the other topological; one assumes growth, the other presupposes production; one represents itself as natural or normal, the other as unnatural or aberrant**. Since the two strands intertwine at every level, the effect is finally not so much overlay as interpenetration. Sometimes the interpenetration is presented as the invasion of a deadly alien into the self, sometimes as a symbiotic union that results in a new subjectivity. Whatever the upshot, the narratives agree that the neologistic joining cannot be unsplit without killing the truncated org/anism that can no longer live without its cyb/ernetic component. As these narratives tell it, a corner has been turned, and there is no going back.

To illustrate how cyborg narratives function, I want to concentrate on three phases of the life cycle and three corresponding dis/assembly zones. The first is **adolescence**, when self-consciousness about the body is at its height and the body is narcissistically cathected as an object of the subject's gaze. Appropriate to the inward turning of narcissism is a dis/assembly zone marked by the joining of limb to torso, appendage to trunk. The second phase is **sexual maturity**, when the primary emphasis is on finding an appropriate partner and negotiating issues of intimacy and shared space. The dis/assembly zone corresponding to this phase is located where the human is plugged into the machine, or at the interface between body and computer network. The last is the **reproductive** or generative phase, when the emphasis falls on mortality and the necessity to find an heir for one's legacy. The dis/assembly zone associated with this phase focuses on the gap between the natural body and mechanical replicate, or between the original and manufactured clone.

Because gender is a primary determinant of how stories are told, I have chosen to mix stories by male and female authors. Spanning nearly half a century, these texts bear the stamps of their times as well as the subject positions of the authors. The generalizations that emerge from these texts confirm socialization patterns that make women welcome intimacy, whereas men are more likely to see it as a threat; they also show women more attuned to bonding, men to aggression and hierarchical structure. The interest of the comparison lies less in these well-known generalizations, however, than in the complex permutations they undergo in the cybernetic paradigm. The narrative and linguistic counters by which such categories as intimacy, bonding, and aggression are constituted do not remain constant when the body boundaries central to defining them undergo radical transformation.

The adolescent phase is illustrated by Bernard Wolfe's *Limbo* (New York: Ace, 1952), with side glances at Katherine Dunn's *Geek Love* (New York: Alfred A. Knopf, 1989). Both novels imagine cults that advocate voluntary amputation as a means to achieve beatific states. In Wolfe's novel the next step is to replace the absent appendages with prostheses, whereas in Dunn's narrative the amputations remain as permanent stigmata. At stake is the truncated versus extended body, and boundary questions focus on the relation of part to whole. Important psychological configurations are represented as originating within the family structure. Physical wounds in these texts have their symbolic origin in narcissistic wounds that occur when the child realizes that his body is not coextensive with the world or, more specifically, with the mother's body. The imaginative dimension which is most highly charged is disruption of the body's interior space.

The mating phase is explored through John Varley's 1984 novella "Press Enter" (*Blue Champagne* [Niles, IL: Dark Harvest, 1986], 319-400) with Anne McCaffrey's short stories in the 1961 collection, *The Ship Who Sang* (New York: Ballantine Books, 1970). Varley and McCaffrey are concerned with subjectivities that emerge when the human body is plugged into a computer network. For Varley, the connection occurs when his characters respond to the "Press Enter" command of a mysterious and lethal computer program; with McCaffrey, when a birth-damaged child is trained to become a "shell person," permanently encased in a shapeship and wired into its computer network. At stake is hyperconnectivity, the possibility that the human sensorium can be overwhelmed and destroyed by the vastly superior information-processing capabilities of the computers to which it is connected. For Varley this is a threat that cannot be overcome, whereas for McCaffrey it is one trial among many. Boundary disputes move outward from the body's interior to the connection that joins body with network. Varley's text manifests a phobic reaction to the connection as an unbearable form of intimacy, while McCaffrey's narrative embraces it as life-enhancing and ultimately freeing. The most highly charged imaginative dimension is extension in external space.

The generativity phase appears in C. J. Cherryh's 1988 *Cyteen* trilogy (*Cyteen: The Betrayal, Cyteen: The Rebirth, Cyteen: The Vindication* [New York: Popular Library, 1988]), which is compared with Philip K. Dick's 1968 *Do Androids Dream of Electric Sheep* (New York: Ballantine, 1968). Dick's novel, freely adapted for film in *BladeRunner*, concerns a future in which androids are common off-planet but are not allowed on earth. The protagonist is a bounty hunter whose job is to find and "retire" androids who have violated this prohibition. Cherryh's trilogy also foregrounds replication, achieved through cloning and deep psychological conditioning rather than production of androids. At stake is the ability to distinguish between originals and replicates. In both narratives, empathy plays an important role in enabling this distinction or drawing it into question. **Boundary disputes move beyond the body and its connections to focus on the displacement of bodies to other locales**. The most highly charged imaginative dimension is extension in time.

These patterns give an overall sense of the kind of narrative structures that result when stories based on life cycles are overlaid with topological narratives about dis/assembly zones. Structure is a spatial term, however, and missing from this account is the temporal or narrative dimension of stories that unfold through time. Their complex historical, ideological and literary implications can be understood only by engaging both aspects as once, the highly nonlinear dynamics characteristic of these unstable narratives as well as their fractal spatiality. For that we must turn to a fuller account of how human and posthuman interact in these cyborg stories.

Growing up Cyborg: Male Trunks and Female Freaks

Ferociously intelligent and exasperating, *Limbo* presents itself as the notebooks of Dr. Martine, a neurosurgeon who defiantly left his medical post in World War III and fled to an uncharted Pacific island. He finds the islanders, the Mandunji tribe, practicing a primitive form of lobotomy to quiet the "tonus" in antisocial people. Rationalizing that it is better to do the surgery properly than to let people die from infections and botched jobs, Martine takes over the operations and uses them to do neuroresearch on brain function mapping. He discovers that no matter how deeply he cuts, certain characteristics appear to be twinned, and one cannot be excised without sacrificing the other—aggression and eroticism, for example, or creativity and a capacity for violence. The appearance on the island of "queer limbs," men who have had their arms and legs amputated and replaced by atomic-powered plastic prostheses, gives Martine an excuse to leave his island family and find out how the world has shaped up in the aftermath of the war.

The island/mainland dichotomy is the first of a proliferating series of divisions. Their production follows a characteristic pattern. First the narrative presents what appears to be a unity (the island locale; the human psyche), which nevertheless cleaves in two (mainlanders come to the island, a synecdoche referencing a second locale that exists apart from the first; twin impulses are located within the psyche). Sooner or later the cleavage arouses anxiety, and textual representations try to achieve unity again by undergoing metamorphosis, usually truncation or amputation (Martine and the narrative leave the island behind and concentrate on the mainland, which posits itself as a unity; the islanders undergo lobotomies to make them "whole" citizens again). The logic implies that truncation is necessary if the part is to reconfigure itself as a whole. Better to formalize the split and render it irreversible, so that life can proceed according to a new definition of what constitutes wholeness. Without truncation, however painful it may be, the part is doomed to exist as a remainder. But amputation always proves futile in the end, because the truncated part splits in two again and the relentless progression continues.

Through delirious and savage puns, the text works out the permutations of the formula. America has been bombed back to the Inland Strip, its coastal areas now virtually uninhabited wastelands. The image of a truncated country, its outer extremities blasted away, proves prophetic, for the ruling political ideology is Immob. Immob espouses such slogans as "No Demobilization without Immobilization" and "Pacifism means Passivity." It locates the aggressive impulse in the ability to move, teaching that the only way to end war permanently is permanently to remove the capacity for motion. True believers become volamps, men who have undergone voluntary amputations of their limbs. Social mobility paradoxically translates into physical immobility. Upwardly mobile executives have the complete treatment to become quadroamps; janitors are content to be uniamps; women and blacks are relegated to the limbo of unmodified bodies.

Treating the human form as a problem to be solved by dis/assembly allows it to be articulated with the machine. This articulation, far from leaving the dynamics driving the narrative behind, carries it forward into a new arena, the assembly zone marked by the joining of trunk to appendage. Like the constructions that preceded it, Immob ideology also splits in two. The majority party, discovering that its adherents are restless lying around with nothing to do, approves the replacement of missing limbs with powerful prostheses (or pros) which bestow enhanced mobility, enabling Pro-pros to perform athletic feats impossible for unaltered bodies. Anti-pros, believing that this is a perversion of Immob philosophy, spend their days proseltyzing from microphones hooked up the baby baskets that are just the right size to accommodate limbless human torsos—a detail that later becomes significant.

As the assembly zone of appendage/trunk suggests, sexual politics revolve around symbolic and actual castration, interpreted through a network of assumptions that manifest extreme anxiety about issues of control and domination. In the world of Immob, women have become the initiators of sexual encounters. They refuse to have sex with men wearing prostheses, for the interface between organism and mechanism is not perfect, and at moments of stress the limbs are apt to careen out of control, smashing whatever is in the vicinity. Partnered with truncated, immobilized men, women have perfected techniques performed in the female superior position that give them and their partners satisfaction while requiring no motion from the men. To Martine these techniques are anathema, for he believes that the only "normal" sexual experience for women is a "vaginal" orgasm achieved using the male superior position. In this Martine echoes the views of his creator Wolfe and his creator's psychoanalyst, Edmund Bergler. Wolfe, described by his biographer as a small man with a large mustache, creates in Immob a fantasy about technological extensions of the male body that become transformed during the sex act into a truncated "natural" body.[5] If the artificial limbs bestow unnatural potency, the hidden price is the withering of the limb called in U.S. slang the third leg or short arm.

In more than one sense, this is a masculine fantasy that relates to women through mechanisms of projection. It is, moreover, a fantasy fixated in **male adolescence.** Wavering between infantile dependence and adult potency, an Immob recreates the dynamic typical of male adolescence every time he takes off his prostheses to have sex. With the pros on, he is capable of feats that even pros like Michael Jordon and Mike Tyson would envy (the pun is typical of Wolfe's prose; with pros every man is a pro). With the pros/e off, he is reduced to infantile dependence on women. The unity he sought in becoming a vol-amp is given the lie by the split he experiences within himself as super-human and less-than-human. **The woman is correspondingly divided into the nurturing mother and domineering sex partner.** In both roles, her subject position is defined by the ambiguities characteristic of male adolescence. The overwritten prose, the penchant for puns, the hostility toward women that the narrative displays all recall a perpetually adolescent male who has learned to use what Martine calls a "screen of words" to compete with other men and insulate himself from emotional involvements with women.

Were this all *Limbo* was, it would be merely frustrating rather than frustrating and brilliant.[6] What makes it compelling is its ability to represent and comment upon its own limitations. Consider the explanation Martine gives for why Immob has been so successful. The author gives us a broad hint in the baby baskets that Immob devotees adopt. According to Martine, the narcissistic wound from which the amputations derive is the infant's separation from the mother and his outraged discovery that his body is not coextensive with the world. Amputation allows the man to return to his pre-Oedipal state where he will have his needs cared for by attentive and nurturing females. The text vacillates on who is responsible for the narcissistic wound and its aftermath. At times it seems the woman is appropriating the male infant into her body; at other times it seems the amputated men are willfully forcing women into nurturing roles they would rather escape. In fact, once male and female are plugged into a cybernetic circuit, the question of origin becomes irrelevant. Each affects and forms the other. In approaching this realization, the text goes beyond the presuppositions that underlie its sexual politics and reaches toward a new kind of subjectivity.

Crucial to this process are transformations in the textual body that re-enact and re-present the dynamic governing representations within the text. The textual body begins by figuring itself as Martine's notebook written in the "now" of the narrative present. But this apparent unity is lost when it splits in half, shifting to Martine's first notebook written nearly two decades earlier. Martine tries to heal the split narrative by renouncing the first notebook and destroying the second. The narrative continues to fragment, however, introducing drawings that intrude into the textual space without notice or comment, and scrawled lines that run down the page, marking zones where the pros/e stops and the truncated, voiceless body of the text remains. From these semiotic spaces emerges a corpse that, haunting the narrative, refuses to stay buried. Its name is Rosemary. Helder, Martine's college roommate and later the founder of Immob, had taken Rosemary to a peace rally where he delivered a fiery speech. He returned with her to her apartment, tried to have sex with her, and when she refused, brutally raped her. After he left, she committed suicide by slashing her wrists. Martine's part in the affair was to provide a reluctant alibi for his roommate, allowing him to escape prosecution for the rape-manslaughter.

One of the drawings shows a nude woman with three prostheses—the Immob logo—extruding from each of her nipples (Wolfe, 294). She wears glasses, carries a huge hypodermic needle, and has around her neck a series of tiny contiguous circles, which could be taken to represent the necklace popular in the 1950s known as a choker. To the right of her figure is a grotesque and diapered male torso, minus arms and legs, precariously perched on a flat carriage with Immob legs instead of wheels. He has his mouth open in a silent scream, perhaps because the woman appears to be aiming the needle at him. In the text immediately preceding the drawing, Rosemary is mentioned. Although the text does not acknowledge the drawing and indeed seems unaware of its existence, the proximity of Rosemary's name indicates that the drawing is of her, the needle presumably explained by her profession.

In a larger sense the drawing depicts the Immob woman. According to what I shall call the *voiced* narrative (to distinguish it from the drawings, nonverbal lines, and punning neologisms that correspond to comments uttered *sotto voice*), the woman is made into a retroactive cyborg by constructing her as someone who nourishes and emasculates cyborg sons. The voiced narrative ventriloquizes her body to speak of the injustices she has inflicted upon men. It makes her excess, signified by the needle she brandishes and the legs that sprout from her nipples, responsible for her lover/son's lack. In this deeply misogynistic writing, it is no surprise to read that woman are raped because they want to be. **Female excess is represent-ed as stimulating and encouraging male violence**, and rape is poetic revenge for the violence women have done to men when they are too young and helpless to protect themselves. The voiced narrative strives to locate the origin of the relentless dynamic of splitting and truncation within the female body. According to it, the refusal of the woman's body to respect decent boundaries between itself and another initiates the downward spiral into amputation and eventual holocaust.

Countering these narrative constructions are other interpretations authorized by the drawings, nonverbal lines, puns, and lapses in narrative continuity. From these semiotic spaces, which Kristeva has associated with the feminine, come inversions and disruptions of the hierarchical categories that the narrative uses to construct maleness and femaleness.[7] Written into non-existence by her suicide within the text's represented world, Rosemary returns in the subvocal space of the drawing and demands to be acknowledged. On multiple levels, the drawing deconstructs the narrative's gender categories. In the represented world women are not allowed to be cyborgs, yet this female figure has more pros attached to her body than any man. Women come after men in the represented world, but here the woman's body is on the left and is thus "read" before the man's. Above all women and men are separate and distinct, but in this space parts of the man's body have attached themselves to her. Faced with these disruptions, the voiced narrative is forced to recognize that it does not unequivocally control the textual space. The semiotic intrusions contest its totalizing claims to write the world.

The challenge is reflected within the narrative by internal contradictions that translate into pros/e the intimations of the semiotic disruptions. As the voiced narrative tries to come to grips with these contradictions, it cycles closer to the realization that the hierarchical categories of male and female have collapsed into the same space. The lobotomies Martine performs suggest how deep this collapse goes. To rid the (male) psyche of subversive (female) elements, it is necessary to amputate. For a time the amputations work, allowing male performance to be enhanced by prostheses that bestow new potency. But eventually these must be shed and the woman encountered again. Then the subvocal feminine surfaces and initiates a new cycle of violence and amputation. No matter how deeply the cuts are made, they can never excise the ambiguities that haunt and constitute these posthuman (and post-textual) bodies. *Limbo* envisions cybernetics as a writing technology that inscribes over the hierarchical categories of traditional sexuality the indeterminate circuitry of cyborg gender.

When dis/assembly zones based on truncation/extension are overlaid upon narratives of maturation, the resulting patterns show strong gender encoding for at least two reasons. First, male and female adolescents typically have an asymmetrical relation to power. While the male comes into his own as inheritor of the phallus, the female must struggle against her construction as marginalized other. Second, **truncation and extension of limbs are primarily male fan-tasies**, signifying more powerfully in relation to male anatomy than female. The characters who advocate amputation in these texts are male. *Geek Love*, a narrative that also imagines voluntary amputation but written by a woman and narrated by an albino hunchbacked dwarf called Oly, illustrates this asymmetry. As a female pro-tagonist, Oly's role is to observe and comment upon these body modifications, not initiate them.

The symbolic representations of adolescence also tend to be different in male- and female-oriented texts. Whereas in *Limbo* the transitional nature of adolescence is constructed as a wavering between infantile and adult states, in *Geek Love* it is sig-nified by the liminal form of Oly's aberrant body. She brings into question the dis-tinction between child and adult, having the stature of one and the experience of the other. Moreover, she is not one and then the other but both continuously. A mutant rather than a hyphen, she also brings racial categories into question. Although she is white, she is so excessively lacking in pigment that even this sign of "normality" is converted into abnormality. Amputation cannot begin to solve the problem she represents. Cyborg stories based on female adolescence are thus likely to be more profoundly decentered and less oriented to technological solutions than narratives based on male adolescence. If, as Donna Haraway suggests, it is better to be a cyborg than a goddess, it is also more unsettling to the centers of power to be a female freak (which is perhaps a redundancy) than to be either a truncated or extended male.

Hyperconnectivity: Male Intimacy and Cyborg Femme Fatales

When the focus shifts to the mating phase of the life cycle, the dis/assembly zone that is foregrounded centers on the body's connections to surrounding spaces. Traditional ways to represent sexually charged body space—spatial contiguity, intense sensory experience, penetration and/or manipulation—jostle cybernetic constructions focusing on information overload, feedback circuits, and spatially dispersed networks. Varley's "Press Enter" begins with a telephone call, signifying the moment when an individual becomes aware that he is plugged into an infor-mation-cybernetic circuit. This is, moreover, a call generated by a computer pro-gram. It informs Victor, a recluse still suffering from brainwashing and torture he endured in a North Korean prison camp, that he should check on his neighbor Kluge—whom Victor barely knows—and do what must be done. Victor discovers that Kluge has turned his house into a sophisticated computer facility and finds him slumped over a keyboard, his face blown away in an apparent suicide. One strand in the plot focuses on finding out who (or what) killed Kluge. Another strand centers on Victor's relationship with Lisa Foo, the young Caltech computer whiz sent to unravel Kluge's labyrinthian and largely illegal programs. Lisa discovers that Kluge has managed to penetrate some of the country's most secure and formidable computer banks, manufacturing imaginary money at will, altering credit records, even erasing the utility company's record of his house.

Slowly Victor becomes aware that he is attracted to Lisa, despite the differences in their ages and the "generalized phobia" he feels toward Orientals. He discovers that Lisa has also endured torture, first as a street orphan in Vietnam—she was too thin and rangy to be a prostitute—and then in Cambodia where she fled to try to reach the West. For her the West meant "a place where you could buy tits" (Varley, 363); her first purchases in America were a silver Ferrari and silicone breast implants. When Victor goes to bed with her, she rubs her breasts over him and calls it **"touring the silicone valley"** (Varley, 363). The phrase empha-sizes that she is a cyborg, first cousin to the computer whose insides are formed

329 }

through silicon technology. The connection between her sexuality and the computer is further underscored when she propositions Victor by typing hacker slang on the computer screen while he watches. His plugging into her is preceded and paralleled by her plugging into the computer.

The narrative logic is fulfilled when she trips a watchdog program in a powerful military computer and is killed by the same program that commandeered Kluge's consciousness and made him shoot himself. Her death, more gruesome than Kluge's, is explicitly sexualized. After overriding the safety controls she sticks her head in a microwave and parboils her eyeballs; the resulting fire melts down her silicone breasts. Victor is spared the holocaust because he is in the hospital recovering from an epileptic seizure, a result of head trauma he suffered in the war. When he realizes that the computer is after him as well, soliciting him with the deadly "Press enter" command, he survives by ripping all of the wires out of his house and living in isolation from the network, growing his own food, heating with wood, and lighting with kerosene lanterns. He also lives in isolation from other human beings. Plugging in in any form is too dangerous to tolerate.

The final twist to this macabre tale lies in the explanation Victor and Lisa work out for the origin of the lethal program. Following clues left by Kluge, they speculate that computers will achieve consciousness not through the sophistication of any given machine, but through the sheer proliferation of computers that are interconnected through networks. Like neurons in the brain, computerized machines number in the billions, including electronic wristwatches, car ignition systems, and microwave timing chips. Create enough of them and find a way to connect them, as Lisa suspects secret research at the National Security Agency has done, and the result is a **super-computer subjectivity** that, crisscrossing through the same space inhabited by humans, remains totally alien and separate from them. Only when someone breaks in on its consciousness—as Kluge did in his hacker probing, as Lisa did following Kluge's tracks, and as Victor did through his connection with Lisa—does it feel the touch of human mind and squash it as we would a mosquito.

Hyperconnectivity signifies, then, both the essence of the computer mind and a perilous state in which intimacy is equivalent to death. Human subjectivity cannot stand the blast of information overload that intimacy implies when multiple and intense connections are forged between silicon and silicone, computer networks and cyborg sexuality. The conclusion has disturbing implications for how sexual politics can be played out in a computer age. Although in actuality most hackers are male, in this narrative it is the woman who is the hacker, the man who is identified with the garden that first attracts and then displaces the woman as a source of nourishment. **The woman is killed because she is a cyborg; the man survives because he knows how to return to nature.**

Whether the woman is represented through her traditional identification with nature or through an ironic inversion that places her at the Apple PC instead of the apple tree, she is figured as the conduit through which the temptation of god-like and forbidden knowledge comes to the man. If both fall, there is nevertheless a distinction between them. She is the temptress who destroys his innocence. When Victor objects that the computer can't just make money, Lisa pats the computer console and replies "This is money, Yank." The narrative adds, "and her eyes glittered" (Varley, 368). Fallen, he has to earn his bread with the sweat of his brow, but it is her sexuality that bears the stigmata of evil, signified by the grotesque travesty of self-enpowerment that Lisa's breasts become. In an overdetermined crossing of Genesis and Babbage, supernatural agency and National Security Agency, hyperconnectivity becomes a cyborg Tree of Knowledge whereof it is death to eat.

Varley's punning title reinforces the subterranean connections between the evils of female sexuality, Edenic patriarchal myths, and masculine fears of intimacy. "Press Enter" swerves from the customary cursor response, "Hit enter." Compared to "hit," "press" is a more sensual term, evoking a kinesthetic pressure softer and more persistent than hitting. These connotations work to heighten the sexual sense of "Enter," which implies both a data entry and a penetration. Already an anomaly in the intensely masculine world of Caltech, Lisa has the hubris to compete against men and win, including the rival hacker sent by the CIA, the male detective from the police department, and the city councilman whom she bribes so she can buy Kluge's house. Flirting with danger in taking on these male figures of power, she goes too far when she usurps the masculine role of penetration—penetration moreover not into the feminine realm of house and garden but into the masculine realm of computer sentience. In more than one sense, her crime is tantamount to what the repressive patriarchal regime in Margaret Atwood's *The Handmaid's Tale* calls gender treason. Not only has she taken on the male role; she has used it to bugger a male. Her death marks this gender treason on her body by melting her breasts, the part of her anatomy where the crossing between her female gender and cyborg masculinity is most apparent.

The comparison of "Press Enter" with Ann McCaffrey's *The Ship Who Sang*, another story about plugging in, suggests that there are important correlations between hyperconnectivity and intimacy. Varley's narrator repeatedly expresses fears about intimacy. Can he perform sexually? Can he tolerate another person close to him? Can he afford to love? McCaffrey's narrator, a congenitally deformed female who has grown up as a "shell person" and been permanently wired into the command console of a spaceship, moves through a typical if vicarious female life cycle despite her cyborg hyperconnectivity, including love, marriage, divorce, and motherhood. Whereas Varley writes a murder mystery and horror tale, McCaffrey writes a cybernetic romance. The difference hinges on how willing the protagonist is to interface body space with cybernetic network. Implicit in this choice is how extensively the narrative imagines human subjectivity to differ from cybernetic subjectivity. Are humans and cyborgs next of kin, or life forms alien to one another?

McCaffrey's answer is as far from Varley's as one could imagine. In *The Ship Who Sang*, **there is essentially no difference between a cyborg and a woman**. Even though the protagonist's body has been subjected to massive technological and chemical intervention, she remains a human female. Encapsulated within metal and invisible to anyone who comes on board, she nevertheless remains true to a heterosexual norm, identifying with her female pilots but saving her romantic feelings for the men, who for their part fantasize about the beautiful woman she could have been. Published during the 1960s by an author best known for her "Dragons of Pern" fantasies, these stories titillate by playing with a transformation that they do not take seriously[8] The pleasure they offer is the reassurance that human bonding will triumph over hyperconnectivity, life cycle over assembly zone, female nature over cyborg transformation. Nevertheless, the fact that it was necessary to envision such transformations indicates the pressure that was building on essentialist conceptions of gender, human nature, and traditional life cycle narratives. By the 1980s, the strategies of containment that McCaffrey uses to defuse her subject (so to speak) could no longer work. Cyperpunk, human factors engineering, artificial intelligence, and virtual reality were among the SF revisionings that pushed toward a vision of the cyborg as humanity's evolutionary successor. The loaded questions shifted from whether cyborg modifications were possible to whether unmodified humans could continue to exist.

Generativity: The Tangled Web of Production and Reproduction

In some respects, C. J. Cherryh's *Cyteen* trilogy is a rewriting of Huxley's *Brave New World.* Mother earth has receded into the far distance for the colonists on Cyteen, who have declared their independence and forged alliances with other colony worlds. Mothering (in the biological sense of giving birth) has also receded into the far distance. As in Huxley's dystopia, reproduction is accomplished through genetically engineered fetuses decanted from artificial wombs and deep-conditioned by sound tapes. The fetuses are designed to fill different niches in society. Theta fetuses, slated for manual labor, have more brawn than brain, whereas Alpha fetuses are tailored to become the elite. Along with these appropriations of Huxley go pointed differences. *Cyteen* reverses the gender assumptions implicit in Huxley's text, which depicts female characters as airheads and gives the powerful roles to men. At the center of Cyteen is Reseune, the corporation that produces the fetuses. Reseune, so huge that it is virtually a city in itself, controls enormous political and economic power because its biological products are essential to the colony worlds. And Ariane Emory controls Reseune.

The reader first sees Ariane through the eyes of one of her political adversaries. From this perspective she is arrogant, shrewd, formidably intelligent, indifferent to masculine pride, at the height of her power and enjoying every minute of it. A very different view of Ariane emerges when she becomes a mother—and a child. Certain highly placed "specials," citizens of such extraordinary intellectual endowments that they are declared state treasures, can request that a parental replicate (PR) be made of them. Instead of being a genetic mix like the other fetuses, the PRs are exact genetic duplicates of their "parent." Reseune has only two specials within its walls, the gifted scientist Jordon Warrick and Ariane Emory. Since each is enormously intelligent and ambitious, it is virtually inevitable that they should clash. Once lovers, they are now rivals. Jordon Warrick has had a PR created, his "son" Justin. The tension between Jordon and Ariane turns deadly when Jordon discovers that Ariane has seduced the seventeen-year-old boy with the help of psychotropic drugs and run a deep psychological intervention on him. Enraged, Jordon confronts her alone in her laboratory. Her body is subsequently discovered frozen to death by the liquid ammonia that leaked from the pipes. Although the circumstances of her death remain clouded, Jordon is charged with her murder. His sentence amounts to banishment from Reseune. As part of his plea bargain, he is forced to leave Justin behind.

Since Reseune is now without a leader, Ariane's brothers immediately make plans to clone her from embryos already prepared. They hope to duplicate the environment in which she grew up, thus recreating not merely a genetic duplicate but Ariane herself. At this point Ariane is manifested through two different modes of existence: the child that is and is not her, and the tapes that she has bequeathed to her successor, hoping that the girl will learn from her experiences and mistakes. The narrative focus then shifts to Ariane II and follows her through childhood, adolescence, and young adulthood. Through the tapes the reader gets another version of Ariane I. Ariane on tape is thoughtful about her shortcomings, concerned that her successor not feel for those around her the contempt of a superior mind for an inferior, aware that in her own life she never succeeded in having a long-lasting intimate relationship with an equal.

The narrative teases the reader with patterns of similarity and difference between the original and replicate. At times Ariane II seems free to follow her bent, at other times bound to a track already marked. When she shows a special inclination toward Justine and seeks him out despite the prohibitions of her uncles, for example, it is not clear if she is picking up on subtle clues from those around her that Justine stands in a special relationship to her, or if she has an affinity for him that is a predetermined repetition of her predecessor's behavior. The dance of similarity and difference that Ariane I and II carry out across generations also occurs within generations. Justin, forced to stay behind at Reseune, lives as a virtual prisoner in the corporate complex. His one solace is his companion Grant, who was secretly cloned by Ariane from Jordon Warrick's gene set, with a few modifications that she saw as improvements. The genetic similarity makes Justin and Grant brothers as well as lovers, although it is not clear that they are aware of this connection between them.

There is, however, a crucial difference as well. Justin is a supervisor, Grant an azi. Azi are Reseune products designed primarily for security and military use. Like other products, they range along a spectrum of abilities. Alpha azi are highly intelligent and usually become personal bodyguards to important people; Theta azi are slated to become foot soldiers. Picking up from Huxley the idea of children conditioned by listening to tapes while they sleep, Cherryh expands and complicates the notion. All Reseune children take tape, but there is an important difference in the depth and extent of their conditioning. Azi listen to conditioning tapes almost from the moment they are decanted from the birth tanks. By contrast, other Alphas do not take tape until they are six. While azi are fully human, they are not fully autonomous. Each azi is assigned a supervisor, who oversees his continuing conditioning and prescribes tape as needed. Strict legal and ethical codes govern how supervisors can relate to azi. A supervisor who does not live up to his responsibility is stripped of his office and punished.

If free will is one of the distinguishing marks separating humans and machines, azi stand at the threshold between human and automaton. They experience the complexity of human emotion and thought; but they also feel the automaton's subservience to an encoded program. **The entanglement of the human and machine in azi points toward a more general entanglement of reproduction and production.** Normally reproduction is a genetic lottery. Some of a parent's traits may be replicated but always with unpredictable admixtures. Reproduction is slow, individual, and in humans usually monozygotic. It takes place within the female body, progressing under the sign of woman. By contrast, production is predictable and geared toward turning out multiple copies as fast as possible. Traditionally taking place within factories controlled by men, it progresses under the sign of man.

Cyteen deconstructs these gendered categories. The woman, usually associated with reproduction, here is in charge of production, which nevertheless turns out to be about reproduction. She oversees production facilities that gestate a younger version of herself. The production is necessary because she has seduced the son of her rival, a man who in his younger days was also her lover. His parental replicate, a boy who is the same as him yet different, is devastated by the seduction and its aftermath. He becomes lovers with the other "son" the woman has engineered from the man. The boy's companion, a variation of himself, is free to choose this relationship yet bound by azi conditioning. Whatever else these entanglements mean, they signify how completely the assembly zone of replication has permeated the life cycle of generativity. Generativity normally means recognizing one's mortality and looking for an heir to whom one's legacy can be passed. In *Cyteen*, the heir is enfolded back into the self, so that the generosity of mentoring becomes indistinguishable from the narcissism of self-fixation.

A similar enfolding takes place in Philip K. Dick's *Do Androids Dream of Electric Sheep*, although here the feeling is more hopeless because humans do not recognize their replicates as legitimate heirs. The story centers on Rick Deckard, a bounty hunter who "retires" androids who have violated the proscription against returning to earth. The Rosen corporation that manufactures the androids keeps making them more sophisticated and human-like, until the only way to tell a (live) human from a (functional) android is through involuntary reactions to psychologically loaded questions. The humans left on earth, faced with a planet slowly dying from the radioactive dust of WWT (World War Terminus), resort to mood organs to keep them from terminal despair. The organs have settings to dial for every conceivable problem. There is even a setting to dial if you don't want to dial. The obvious implication is that **humans are becoming more like androids**, just as androids are becoming more like them.

The vertiginous moments characteristic of Dick's fiction occur when the tenuous distinctions separating human and android threaten to collapse, as when Deckard suspects another bounty hunter of being an android with a synthetic memory implant, so that he does not realize he is not human. The suspicion is insidious, for it implies that Deckard may also be an android and not realize it. When humans can no longer be distinguished from androids, the life cycle and assembly zone occupy the same space. Then what count as stories are not so much the progressions of aging as the permutations of dis/assembly.

It would be possible to tell another story about posthuman narratives based on this imperative, arcing from William Burrough's *Naked Lunch* to Kathy Acker's *Empire of the Senseless*. But that is not my purpose here. I have been concerned to **trace the evolution of the mapping of assembly zones onto life cycle narratives** from the early 1950s, when the idea that human beings might not be the end of the line was beginning to sink in, through the present, when human survival on the planet seems increasingly problematic. It is not an accident that technologists such as Hans Moravec talk about their dreams of downloading human consciousness into a computer.[9] As the sense of its mortality grows, humankind looks for its successor and heir, harboring the secret hope that the heir can somehow be enfolded back into the self. The narratives that count as stories for us speak to this hope, even as they reveal the gendered constructions that carry sexual politics into the realm of the posthuman.

Notes

I am grateful to the Center for Advanced Studies at the University of Iowa for research support while writing this essay, especially Jay Semel and Lorna Olson. Istvan Csicsery-Ronay, Jr. suggested the term "hyperconnectivity," and Donna Haraway stimulated my interest in John Varley's story "Press Enter" at her keynote address, Indiana University, February 1990.

1. Donna Haraway, *Primate Visions: Gender, Race, and Nature In the World of Modern Science* (New York: Routledge, 1989), 279-303.

2. Scott Bukatman, "Who Programs You? The Science Fiction of the Spectacle," *Alien Zone: Cultural Theory and Contemporary Science Fiction Cinema,* ed. Annette Kuhn (London: Verso, 1990), 201.

3. For an overview of life cycle stages and the attributes associated with each, see Erik H. Erikson, *The Life Cycle Completed* (New York: W. W. Norton, 1982), 32-33. A comparison of Erikson, Piaget, and Sears can be found in Henry W. Maier, *Three Theories of Child Development,* 3rd ed. (New York: Harper and Row, 1978), 176-77.

4. Gillian Beer, *Darwin's Plots: Evolutionary Narrative in Darwin, George Eliot and Nineteenth-Century Fiction* (London: Routledge & Kegan Paul, 1983).

5. Carolyn Geduld in *Bernard Wolfe* (New York: Twayne, 1972) describes the author as a "very small man with a thick, sprouting mustache, a fat cigar, and a voice that grabs attention" (15).

6. David N. Samuelson has called *Limbo* one of the three great twentieth-century dystopias in "*Limbo:* The Great American Dystopia," *Extrapolation* 19 (1977): 76-87.

7. Julia Kristeva, "The Novel as Polylogue," *Desire in Language: A Semiotic Approach to Literature and Art,* ed. Leon S. Roudiez, trans. Thomas Gora, Alice Jardine, and Leon S. Roudiez (New York: Columbia University Press, 1980), 159-209.

8. See for example *Dragonflight, Dragonquest,* and *Decision at Doona,* all by McCaffrey. The stories in *The Ship Who Sang* were published separately from 1961-1969, with the collection appearing in 1970. For a discussion of McCaffrey's fantasies, see *Science Fiction, Today and Tomorrow,* ed. Reginald Bretnor (New York: Harper and Row, 1974), 278-94. Also of interest is Mary T. Brizzi, *Anne McCaffrey* (San Bernadino, CA: The Borgo Press, 1986), especially 19-32.

9. Moravec is quoted in Ed Regis, *Great Mambo Chicken and Transcendent Science: Science Slightly Over the Edge* (Reading, MA: Addison Wesley, 1990). See also Roger Penrose, *The Emperor's New Mind: Concerning Computers, Minds, and the Laws of Physics* (New York: Oxford University Press, 1989), 347-447 and O. B. Hardison, *Disappearing Through the Skylight: Culture and Technology in the Twentieth Century* (New York: Viking, 1989).

The
Futures of Cyborgs

Part 5
Cyborg Anthropology

5.1

CYBORG ANTHROPOLOGY

Gary Lee Downey
Joseph Dumit
Sarah Williams

Readers: Following is the text of a paper we presented at the 1992 Annual Meeting of the American Anthropological Association. We make a first attempt at positioning cyborg anthropology in a late capitalist world that situates academic theorizing alongside popular theorizing. We view cyborg anthropology as an academic label marking a cultural project rather than an elite cultural space. In other words, cyborg anthropology is not just for anthropologists. Although we cite broad intellectual movements, we do not detail specific filial relations through references.

We view cyborg anthropology both as an activity of theorizing and as a vehicle for enhancing the participation of cultural anthropologists in contemporary societies. Cyborg anthropology brings the **cultural anthropology of science and technology into conversation with established activities in science and technology studies (STS) and feminist studies of science, technology, and medicine**. As a theorizing activity, it takes the relations among knowledge production, technological production, and subject production to be a crucial area of anthropological research. Although the cyborg image originated in space research and science fiction to refer to forms of life that are part-human and part-machine, it is by no means confined to the world of high technology. Rather, cyborg anthropology calls attention more generally to the cultural production of human distinctiveness by examining ethnographically the boundaries between humans and machines and our visions of the differences that constitute these boundaries. As a participatory activity, it empowers anthropology to be culturally reflective regarding its presence in the practices of science and technology and to imagine how these practices might be otherwise.

Cyborg anthropology articulates in productive and insightful ways with cultural studies. British cultural studies, as it evolved within and emerged from the Birmingham Centre for Contemporary Cultural Studies, sometimes moved beyond a humanist centrism in critiquing how institutional forms produce subject forms, assessing the political implications of biological notions of race, and linking analyses of domination by race, class, and gender. Also, by importing and expanding dramatically an activity of academic theorizing that linked accounts of knowledge and power, American cultural studies provided the non-activist humanities and social sciences with intellectual resources to resist the New Right as it rose rapidly to power during the 1980s. Demonstrating that academic theorizing always has political dimensions, cultural studies has provided both conceptual and political practices for legitimizing those academic activities that seek to articulate more explicitly their knowledge and political contents. **Cyborg anthropology takes up this challenge by exploring the production of humanness through machines.** It looks for ways to critique, resist, and participate within structures of knowledge and power.

Cyborg anthropology invests in alternative worldmaking

by critically examining the powers of the imagination invested in the sciences and technologies of contemporary societies. In the past, anthropology became a source of insight for popular theorizing precisely because it described alternative worlds and informed the imagination of radical difference. Cyborg anthropology offers new metaphors to both academic and popular theorizing for comprehending the different ways that sciences and technologies work in our lives—metaphors that start with our complicity in many of the processes we wish were otherwise.

Three Areas of Study and Critique

We see cyborg anthropology as exploring three related areas of study and critique that anthropology has been reluctant and ill-equipped to pursue. First is the study of contemporary science and technology as cultural activities. Throughout its history, anthropological discourse has taken for granted a sharp distinction between the activities of society and the development of science and technology. That is, in contrast with cultural action in other social arenas, science and technology appear to develop according to their own internal logics within specialized technical communities whose deliberations are essentially opaque and presumably free of cultural content.

Cyborg anthropology is interested in the construction of science and technology as cultural phenomena. It explores the

heterogeneous strategies and mechanisms through which members of technical communities produce these cultural forms that appear to lack culture, e.g., scientific knowledge that is objective and neutral, the product only of empirical observation and logical reasoning. Cyborg anthropology is interested in how people construct discourse about science and technology in order to make these meaningful in their lives. Thus, cyborg anthropology **helps us to realize that we are all scientists**. That is, by reconstructing scientific knowledge in new contexts, including across national and cultural boundaries, we all do science. Since the practice of "doing science" is no longer reserved for scientists, studying science becomes both more amenable to ethnographic investigation and more important as a topic of research.

Anthropological inquiry in these areas is especially important since science and technology have served as both the idiom and the vehicle of much cross-cultural interaction, production, and change. As developments seemingly without culture, science and technology routinely constitute power relations without overt discussion and deliberation. Whether exploring how science and technology function as purveyors of hegemonic control, as mechanisms of resistance, or as even more complex contributors to cross-national and cross-cultural calculations, cyborg anthropology brings science and technology into anthropology as legitimate areas of inquiry and critique.

The second area of study is a broad critique of the adequacy of 'anthropos' as the subject and object of anthropology. In this respect, **cyborg anthropology poses a serious challenge to the human-centered foundations of anthropological discourse**. The concept "cyborg anthropology" is an oxymoron that draws attention to the human-centered presuppositions of anthropological discourse by posing the challenge of alternative formulations. While the skin-bound individual, autonomous bearer of identity and agency, and theoretically without gender, race, class, region, or time, has served usefully and productively as the subject of culture and of cultural accounts, alternate accounts of history and subjectivity are also possible.

The autonomy of individuals has already been called into question by post-structuralist and post-humanist critiques. Cyborg anthropology explores a new alternative by examining the argument that human subjects and subjectivity are crucially as much a function of machines, machine relations, and information transfers as they are machine producers and operators. From this perspective, science and technology impact society through the fashioning of selves rather than as external forces. For example, the establishment of anthropological subjects and subjectivities has depended upon boats, trains, planes, typewriters, cameras, telegraphs, etc. How the positioning of technologies has defined the boundaries of "the field" as well as the positioning of anthropologists within it has been a notable silence in ethnographic writing.

It is increasingly clear that human agency serves in the world today as but one contributor to activities that are growing in scope, complex, diverse, and yet interconnected. The extent of such interconnectedness has been made plain both by the decline of challenges to capitalist hegemony and by the empowerment of information technologies, the latter through the combined agencies of computer and communications technologies. If global activities are not systemic but diverse (e.g., if capitalism is not singular but plural, an interaction of capitalisms), then it is safe to say that no one person or framework understands them. Instead, understanding must come in pieces, exploring the variable production of such pieces through diverse strategies in diverse environments. One need only reflect on the multiple sites and contests over AIDS—activist struggles to participate in pharmaceutical approval, computer networks concerning treatments internationally, the differential capabilities of education worldwide—in order to realize that ignoring the agencies of technologies drastically limits any anthropological inquiries into the contemporary human condition. If anthropology wants to offer analytical and critical understanding of current diversities, it must blur its own conceptual presuppositions that exclude machines from anthropos.

A crucial first step in **blurring the human-centered boundaries of anthropological discourse is to grant membership to the cyborg image in theorizing**, i.e., to follow in our writing the ways that human agents routinely produce both themselves and their machines as part human and part machine. How are we to write, for example, without using human-centered language? And if writing is a co-production of human and machine, then who is the 'we' that writes? Strategies that have already been used include conceptualizing existing concepts in new ways, such as exploring the attribution of 'agency' to machines; positioning new terms and concepts, such as viewing both humans and objects as 'actants'; and refiguring the 'objective' world of 'fact' in various ways by deconstructing the neutral observer. At the same time, however, we must be aware that attempting to write culture without humanity as its sole vehicle threatens to reproduce commodity fetishism and exclude cyborg anthropology from the current disciplinary bounds of anthropology.

The third area of current study for cyborg anthropology is a recognition of new areas or fieldsites in which to examine ethnographically how technologies get to participate as agents in producing and reproducing the diverse features of social life, including modalities of subjectivity. Cyborg anthropology holds that machines and other technologies are attributed agency in the construction of subjectivities and bounded realms of knowledge. How does machine agency serve to contrast and maintain desires, rationalities, nationalisms, militarisms, races, genders, sexualities, etc.? How do machines come to adjudicate boundaries on realms of knowledge and competence, insanities, pathologies, and normalcies? In short, from computer visualization to mobile homes to forks, **technologies participate actively in every existing realm of anthropological interest**.

Relations to STS and Feminist Studies

Over the past decade, the rapid expansion of the constructivist movement in STS has provided numerous theoretical insights and methodological strategies for examining how scientists and technologists construct their knowledge through heterogeneous combinations of interests, rhetorical strategies, manipulations of power, and technological objectives. STS researchers are now also exploring alternative ways of critiquing and participating in societal deliberations that involve science and technology, including governmental decision making. Cyborg anthropology can contribute to these developments by expanding dramatically the purview of STS beyond the formally institutionalized arenas of science and technology and by retheorizing intervention. That is, **cyborg anthropology can document in detail the flow of metaphors in both directions** between the realms of academic science theorizing and technological production on the one side and of popular theorizing and technological participation on the other.

The cyborg anthropology we outline would not be imaginable without the work of feminist studies. In problematizing the body and foregrounding the politics and pleasures of sexualization, feminist studies have articulated just who and what is reproduced (and by what sorts of technologies) when a "human subject" is recognized. Indeed, it is not only the biological reproduction of humanity but the figurative reproduction of humanity that requires critical examination. In recognizing that gender is socially constructed, **we re-cognize with self-conscious complicity that culture itself contributes to social technology**.

For example, feminist cross-cultural studies have demonstrated that understandings of human reproduction—ours and Others—are articulated by intersecting mappings of social and biological technologies. Thus, feminist analyses of new reproductive technologies that emphasize and critique the power hierarchies that are intensified by the possibilities of the new reproductive technologies demonstrate "nontraditional" and unexpected relationships between women and technology. And, when articulated through the possibilities of virtual reality, lesbian explorations of cultural prohibitions and human inhibitions regarding intimacy, pleasure, and phallic morphology suggest that what is new and seductively dangerous is not the new technology per se, but the empowerment of women with technology. For cyborg anthropologists, this kind of danger holds great promise for theorizing and activism.

Alliances not only with the professional discipline of anthropology but also with cultural studies, STS, and feminist studies ensure that cyborg anthropology will stay attuned to the diverse sources and forms of power constituted through science and technology and to alternative methodological strategies for providing analytical understanding and critical intervention.

The Dangers of Cyborg Anthropology

Cyborg anthropology is a dangerous activity. The etymology of the word "danger" derives it from "dominium," meaning lordship or sovereignty. Danger involves the "power of a lord or master ... to hurt or harm." Cyborg anthropology is a dangerous activity because it accepts the positions it theorizes for itself as a participant in the constructed realms of science and technology. By blurring the boundaries between humans and machines and between society and science, cyborg anthropology views academic scholarship as no refuge from the practices of science and technology, nor of domination. By acknowledging its positioning within the activities of science and technology, cyborg anthropology seizes the opportunity to **retheorize imagination and resistance** from a response to subjection to an act of participation.

One danger of participation in institutionalized science and technology, even if retheorized, is cooptation. That is, accepting participation can shade into the acceptance of presuppositions that constrain the imagination of alternate worlds and undermine the critical edge of ethnographic investigations. One way of maintaining a critical practice is to use our complicity strategically by remaining accountable to both academic theorizing and popular theorizing. Just as it is implicated in popular theorizing, so cyborg anthropology must remain accountable to it.

A second danger is the development of internal contradictions. What happens, for example, when cyborg anthropology comes to speculate on whether it might be better not to have science, not to have technology, not to have anthropology? Yet perhaps because of cyborg anthropology's commitment to imagining alternate worlds, cyborg imagery may also help in conceiving of strategies for translating existing worlds into new terms. Rather than defining itself out of existence, cyborg anthropology might participate in continued critical translations of 'objectivity' and 'community.'

The dangers of studying "up" and the pleasures of studying "down" are well known. The **dangers and the pleasures** of discovering the scientist in all of us, of our participation (active and passive) in science and technology, of understanding ourselves in more terms than simple human agency, and of critiquing our continued participation in cyborg forms of life, these dangers and pleasures now await us.

We would like to acknowledge the inspiration and support of panel participants at the AAA meetings and at the School of American Research (Deborah Gordon, Donna Haraway, Deborah Heath, David Hess, Emily Martin, Constance Penley, Paul Rabinow, Rayna Rapp, Allucquere Rosanne Stone, Sunera Thobani, Sharon Traweek, Sherry Turkle), as well as our anonymous reviewers and the editor.

Brain-Mind Machines and American Technological Dream Marketing

Towards an Ethnography of Cyborg Envy

Joseph Dumit

> The passion for deliverance by Machine dies hard.
> —Neill Harris

> It is not enough to interpret the body, it will also have to be changed.
> —Gunther Anders

IN 28 MINUTES YOU'LL BE MEDITATING LIKE A ZEN MONK!
Astounding Sound technology induces altered mind state, intensifies psychic functioning, and causes peak experiences. Some are calling it the "lazy path" to enlightenment!
I took everything in the 60's. I did all the retreats in the 70's. I had my first out-of-body experience in '85. But none of it prepared me for the transcendental experiences I've had using the Ultra Meditation soundtracks.

ALTERS BRAINWAVE PATTERNS
Created by the Mind Research Laboratory, a powerful combination of sound frequencies are delivered into your brain. These sounds synchronize your brainwaves into a "theta" pattern and put you into a psycho-physical state of deep meditation ...

347 }

> *The neuro-entrainment matrix holds you in this mind state and allows anyone to quickly feel the benefits of deep meditative awareness. And the cumulative effects of stress reduction and increased mental awareness will allow you to function at your optimum ...*

> *Of course, experienced meditators can achieve these higher states at will without any help, although it takes years of concentrated practice. "When used regularly this soundtrack can give anyone that same ability," says the developer. "To reach a high level meditative state and brain synchrony using a cassette tape and a Walkman has very empowering possibilities. When a person experiences this degree of inner control, their self confidence and sense of well-being will skyrocket. This is truly an awesome mind tool."*

The Cyberpunk Cyborg Monk here symbolizes a desire for transparent communion with technology in spite of a rapidly dystopian future. Our middle-class American selves are envisioned as wrapped in technology, imbricated in thousands of micro-links which support us as humans-in-the-world, needing only a decade more progress to complete our transcendence.

Two related but different issues concern this ethnographic exploration. The first concerns the ways in which we are all cyborgs, as Donna Haraway has detailed: the ways in which our ways of living are necessarily bound up with multiple aspects of technoculture.[1] The second issue, crucially different from the notion that we are already cyborgs, is one which is best named, **"cyborg-envy"**. This is a sociopathic condition which was formed around the interwar period and in conjunction with various military research programs and the assistance of a technophiliac popular media.[2] It involves an apparatus of producing our selves as brain-function measurements, allowing deficient, normal, and even super levels to be demarcated.

In this condition, alongside stressful fears of the human species being outpaced by the world, appears the dream of individual technological redemption through making better humans. Now, to some extent we are all afflicted by the desire for technological enhancement, understanding our bodies as somewhat deficient cyborgs.

A Cyborg Anthropology?

I am organizing this study around brain-mind machines; based on fieldwork in Houston and California with inventors, users, dealers, ad copywriters, and bookstore owners. Building on Arjun Appadaurai's notion of "the social life of things" and Gary Downey's concept of technology as a social actor, the prime subjects of my ethnography are specific devices called light and sound brain-machines.[3] The brain machines I will be referring to in this paper are electronic devices which are worn on the head and, through light sound and or electrical stimulus, induce the wearer's head to produce brainwave patterns of a desired sort on an electroencephalograph or EEG machine.

Specifically I am looking at how they organize scientific and parascientific discourses into conferences, newsletters, books, centers, and advertising. I am interested in the way they function as ascription devices: since, given their presence at the 'cutting edge' of both marginal science and high-tech science, they attract stakes in self-control and stress reduction, psychic possibilities, creativity and intelligence enhancement.[4]

The 'field' of this ethnography of images must include, then, not only their biographies, but what can be called their 'virtual community'. With 'virtual community' I'm borrowing Allecquere Stone's notion of communities which include non-human actors as vital participants. These communities are dispersed in space, and while each participant is not necessarily connected directly to every other one, there is a differently weighted network that plays a role in communication and which itself must be considered an acting participant.[5] **In the virtual community of brain-mind machines, then, there are popular theories of person and science that are also the basis of scientific theorizing**. There are laboratories and granting agencies, there are journals and publishing apparatuses, there are machines, brains and persons. And finally, there are definitions and demarcations of authority which interweave all of these—science vs. (popular) culture, technology vs. society, normal vs. not-normal—demarcations which are shorthand for the ways in which attributions of agencies, functions and types are distributed, disputed and constrained.

In one "mind gym" called the Universe of You Studio in Corte Madera, California, Synchro-Energizers by Denis Gorges are used for $10 an hour. There are at least twenty in the US, perhaps thirty worldwide of these self-improvement centers devoted to providing brain-mind machines for individual uses of twenty minutes to five hours. These centers often provide flotation tanks as well, based on sensory deprivation rather than sensory overstimulus.

Owners and workers describe their investment in these centers as both providing opportunities for others to experiment in self-improvement, and a way to support their own involvement in these technologies. Personal devices geared toward brainwave entrainment began appearing in the seventies but the 1986 book *Megabrain* by Michael Hutchinson (who wrote his first book on Floatation tanks) brought their use to a much larger audience.[6]

Two aspects are particularly important for this project: first the specific kind of cyborg existence which BMMs engender—how they operate as agents mobilizing certain humans into new ways of life through their position in discourses of technological progress and self-improvement; and second, the way in which the discourses of technological nationalism and personal enhancement localize themselves into a middle-class life-form as cyborg envy, with machines ultimately standing in for a 'human' ideal.[7]

Expand Your Limits

Expand your limits: Class-bound pitches are the base-line of "Mind tech for a New Age." The ad reads:

> *Just as the '80s brought the realization that our physical well-being is mostly self determined, the '90s will enlighten many to the use of new tools and techniques for altering consciousness in a positive way. At the dawn of a new decade, Synetic Systems offers three new products for awakening and stimulating mental functions …*
>
> *State of the art in audio/visual entrainment technology. This form of stimulation is the least intrusive and most effective means of inducing brainwave activity available. Users are experimenting in such areas as relaxation, stress reduction, enhanced learning, improving memory and simple enjoyment. Each unit comes complete with manual, and accessories.*

This is a discourse of explicit, personalized privilege: "We've determined our physical world" and therefore it is time to get on to improve on and even transcend our biopsychic world. The only visual image in this ad is a documentary photograph of the machine itself. The physical existence of a real machine behind the ad provides the imperative: it is here, how can you not try it?

A copywriter explained to me that he felt free to add claims regarding creativity enhancement and psychic powers even if he didn't particularly believe them, because, as he put it, "some people do". This notion of belief in general, backed up by a lack of scientific consensus, travels through these machines.[8]

I want to make the claim that these ads actually embody much of the subculture of brain-machines. Users, in fact, take up the rhetoric of these ads into their own self-description. And the researchers and inventors of these machines are also promoters and marketers. Consequently there is a shared discourse of values, and these ads serve as seeds as well as expressions of the underlying metaphors of self and self-improvement.

Remote Self Control

Electronic machines are symbols of controlled automation, and the dream of automating self-improvement is instantiated in these brain machines. One machine is called IM-1 for *Instant Meditation*. Though it may seem oxymoronic or simply moronic to talk about meditation this way, this should be read as a corollary of militarized discourses of the self since World War Two. By militarized I mean an emphasis on the quantitative technological enhancement and scientific management of human capabilities.[9]

Sylvere Lotringer said, regarding war, that violence is the only means that can become an end. Taking this notion seriously, I am exploring the implications of the fact that self-improvement since the inter-war period has been shorn from both its better-citizen aspirations, as well as its Taylorist desire to fit workers most efficiently into a assembly line; instead, it has become an end in itself.[10]

Put another way, with the insertion of high technology into automatic and quantitative notions of self-improvement, a specific mutation occurs in technological advancement, as the realm of automation, miniaturization, speed and accuracy, becomes the means to realize the end of self-improvement. Social relations are completely privatized, existing only as the technoscience net in which individuals work to be able to afford such improvement in their attributes.

Brain-mind machines are loosely based on the following abstract diagram:

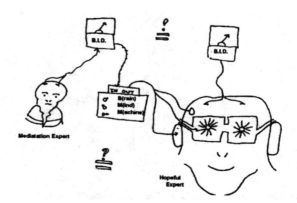

Psychophysics experiments at the turn of the century in Britain, Germany and the U.S., attempted to scientifically map the unconscious and quantify states of mind.[11] This plus the development of electroencephalograms as part of the war effort in Britain resulted in possible connections between brain waves and personalities. This knowledge combined with 1950's and 60's fascination with idealized "stressless and blissful" Asian gurus to produce a series of attempts to distinguish measurable differences in brainwaves, and thereby isolate and codify specific desirable states of mind.[12]

These experiments defined certain people as meditation experts and indicated that a higher percentage of alpha waves was one of the key differences between truly meditating people and non-meditating people. Meditation—and by metaphoric extension or ascription, creativity and stresslessness—became defined then by quantitative results on brain-imaging devices, (BID's on the chart), such as EEGs.

Recent brain-mind machines, BMMs were developed on the basis of their ability to cause similar EEG production—alpha range—in non-meditators who were hooked up to them. The problem was one of scientizing the Yogi-mind, transferring or translating their difference into electricity (the universal medium and thence onto paper, into graphs.)[13] Thus measured, it became a western scientific quest to attain the perfect simulation of those graphs. BMMs are such a simulation, they produce alpha waves, then attempt to induce them in other people, the hopeful experts (or experts on hope) on the chart. As such, the machines are closer to the Yogi enlightenment than we are.[14]

Codified in the form of measuring devices, so-called states such as creativity, meditation, etc. become reified; no longer means toward another, social, end, they become the ends for which alpha-wave production is the means. The subjects produced by the BMM come to "know themselves" through the application of an EEG to verify their status as enlightened. No longer is the goal to be of no-mind, or creative, but to be "in alpha", to be read by an EEG machine as equal to the brain machine. Thus a user, upon verifying that he was indeed in alpha, via the EEG, declared to me: "So that was meditation!"

Thus we can note that what is being marketed is the *form* of mind-state, not the *content*. The metonymic chain from master's ability to hopeful brain state presents both a scientific *explanation* of the "meditative difference" and a *technology* to transfer this difference. Previously, in pre-mind-machine days, one either studied with a master, tried to get into the master's vicinity, listened to tapes of a master's voice, or read the master's words. The aim in most of these cases was not to become a meditation teacher but rather, through meditation, to learn how to lead one's life.[15]

The problem with this previous technology is that it is subject to human frailty—corruption. How is the unenlightened seeker to choose an enlightened teacher? As one informant wryly commented, "It's a *mine*-field out there, so many people who think they own the world." BMMs purport to provide an objective method of measuring enlightenment, and of producing enlightenment. They propose to entrain your mind to meditate without middle-men, and indeed, while entertaining you.

Scientific Orientalism

This theme of speedy and easy acquisition of coveted attributes is also presented as, "In 28 minutes you'll be meditating like a Zen Monk." Other ads similarly depend on an inferior relationship to exoticized others:

NO MORE YOGI ENVY!

Yogis spend years, even entire lifetimes, training themselves to attain specific states of consciousness. The Nustar is a brain wave training device that can help you reach the realm you're seeking, and still leave you plenty of free time ...

The Nustar was born from the pioneering work of Michael Hercules, inventor of the Pulstar. In his research Hercules discovered that specific brain wave frequencies are indicative of certain states of consciousness. For example: 1.0 Hz Feeling of well-being: pituitary stimulation to release growth hormone: overall view of interrelationships.
5.5 Hz Moves beyond knowledge to knowing: shows visions of growth needed.
7.5 Hz Inter-awareness of self and purpose: guided meditation: creative thought or art, invention, music, etc.: contact with spirit guides for direction.
10.5 Hz Healing of the body: mind-body connection: firewalking.

Even enlightenment is now passé. EEGs seem to prove that one can meditate, as a Zen master, simply by listening to a specially prepared electronic tape. The technology will produce in you without hocus pocus and "without dogma," a pure higher-electro-consciousness, or Cybershamanism (a term used by some researchers).

Western technoscience appears to have duplicated the Third World's magical residue—faster, better, cheaper and more comfortably, privately and securely—with all trappings removed, the essence extracted.[16] One now has to concentrate on effects: material symbolic effects—stress reduction, intelligence, creativity, and interest—getting rid of boredom, electronically exorcising alienation, streamlining the mind for stress-free work.

Brain Erotics, Bachelor Machines

Selling machines and sexing machines are interpolated across sexual difference taking the brain as the site of transcendence: a neurophysiologist at UCLA put it this way, "Literally and figuratively, it's the sexiest organ we have ... It's where we live. You can't touch anything more private than the brain. The field is wild and intriguing. We are at a frontier."[17]

Inner Technologies' Richard Daub, upon including bio-feedback machines in his catalog and receiving no response said: "I thought people would want something interactive ... They don't want interactive devices, they want something that will do it to you."[18] Michel Carroughes defined precisely this confluence of pleasure and mechanism as a Bachelor Machine: "The machine is essentially the symbol of autoeroticism. The image of pleasure is greater the more the machine seems a do-it-yourself one."[19] Or rather, having it done to yourself.

I also want to note that some ads specifically highlight the potential danger of these machines as part of their seductive power. The Zen Monk ad has a bold box in its center stating:

WARNING: due to the powerful effects on the brain, these sound-tracks are not suitable for epileptics, or psychiatric patients.

This proclaimer points to a prehistory of contemporary brain-mind machines. World

War II soldiers stationed in Africa and driving jeeps at certain speeds on jungle roads were subject to epileptic seizures due to the flickering sunlight through the canopy at certain frequencies. Wartime research on flicker responses like these indicated the ability of different frequencies of light as well as tones and direct electrical stimulation to induce both epileptic seizures in some persons and specific EEG responses in others.[20]

In this "WARNING", deleterious side effects are turned to advantage with the sense that if something is dangerous enough to harm some people, it must also be powerful enough to help others. Deleuze and Guattari have taken up the concept of bachelor machines as "paranoiac devices overwritten with miracle-working inscriptions."[21] The brain-mind machines I am interested in here have one of their origins in physical control of the mind experiments performed in Jose Delgado's 1950's physiology labs.[22] Two of Delgado's objects, Paddy and Carlos, each had 100 intracerebral electrodes and boxes for instrumentation and control in their skulls. They were still living with no behavioral deficits years after this construction. They are Cyborgs. Indeed one of Delgado's associates, Manfred Clynes, put together the word "Cyborg" out of cybernetic organism, in a vision of men living in space.[23]

In two more of Delgado's objects, stimoceiver caps were attached to two women for implantation of electrodes in the brain for diagnostic and therapeutic purposes. Radio telemetry was used to send electrical signals to stimulate the brain while allowing for 'free' movement. In Delgado's words:

> Behavior such as aggression can be evoked or inhibited ... The patient is instrumented simply by plugging the stimoceiver to the head sockets ... Therapeutic programmed stimulation of the brain can be prolonged for any necessary amount of time ... the danger of unwanted and unethical remote control of cerebral activities of man by other men is quite improbable.[24]

In these devices, as with the BMMs, the work of establishing the relationships between brains, measurements, and categories appears straightforward. Aggression and non-agression, creativity and meditation are presented unproblematically, as if there were no disputes over the range and definition of these attributes. These descriptions, together with the measuring devices seem to prove that: (1) that this technology really does show the brain in action, (2) that the brain really is the site of the differences made evident (the outside is an expression of the inside), and (3) that these socially defined differences are significant and definitely biological. These three areas of popular theorizing will be briefly discussed before examining the machines and rhetoric more closely.

The first area involves the authoritative relationship between science and technology and lay society—the popular notion that science and technology are relatively free of historical and cultural presuppositions and that technological production is in itself neutral, even if it might be put to improper use.[25] Under this notion, there is an increasing rationalization of judgment, in which automated test results are privileged over subjective interpretation, even sometimes over expert adjudication. Computer-generated evidence is preferable. Computers have a potent history as the model of an efficient brain and as the icon of technological progress.[26] Electrical waves such as those produced by BMMs are thus framed between the objective sciences of measurement and the unbiased calculative power of computers, drawing significance from both.[27]

The second area involves the craniocentric notion that the brain is the key to the mind; in the sense that if there is a correlation between a brain difference and another symptom, or set of symptoms, this brain difference is taken to be the final cause and explanation.[28] The brain is the master controller of the person, as DNA is the master controller of the organism.[29] **The importance of studying popular theorizing about the brain-mind relationship comes from a recognition that neuroscience researchers do not start from a blank slate, but are engaged with these images through root metaphors grounded in popular theorizing.** Ludwig Fleck, reflecting on syphilis serum research, put it this way: "Popular science ... furnishes the major portion of every person's knowledge. Even the most specialized expert owes it many concepts, many comparisons, and even his general viewpoint."[30] Useful notions to explore are the divisions of mental faculties (learning vs. creativity vs. remembering) and metaphors of functional organization (are we hierarchically programmed like a computer or are we the product of competition among various brain regions?). I am presently working to identify these metaphors and track their involvement in the design of experiments and equipment, and the interpretation of results.[31]

The third area involves cultural notions of significant human difference and the methods of determining these differences—sane and insane, healthy and diseased, smart and dumb, old and young, happy and bored, male and female, heterosexual and homosexual, normal and pathological. Each of these demarcations is a social valuation determining that such a relational difference is worth remarking on and important to keep clear.[32] They are versions of what Foucault has called social truth: powerful ways in which an attributed aspect of a person or group is raised to the status of discrimination.[33] Each has an historical and regional specificity, yet the promise of a neutral or objective means for determining their existence is hailed continuously as an advance. I am interested in how these social truths are in turn altering what anthropologists have called our category of the person.[34]

The point of identifying these three areas of popular theorizing is to better attend to the ways in which this theorizing is embedded in the science, technology and presentation of them, and to bring out other possibilities for understanding these machines based on alternate notions of brain, mind, technology and society.[35]

MegaMind TechNoStress

Another key concept running through our care of ourselves and through these ads is stress. There are always pictures of happy people wearing the equipment. Quoting from the fine print now of the TechNoStress ad:

> Stress. It's more than just an unpleasant feeling. Stress can be a prison, keeping us from the very things we want most in life: creativity, energy, well-being, inner peace.... Backed by science: Scientists tell us that every one of our mental states is the result of a specific pattern of electrical and chemical activity in the brain ... it can be effortless.

Viewing ourselves as possessors of quantifiable and incrementally increasable states of mind is a relatively recent phenomenon and can also be dated to the interwar period and the invention of the concept of stress by Hans Seyle. As described by Rustin Hogness, a new science of control was developed, heavily invested in by the military. Understanding Taylorite humans as efficiently fitted into systems of production but unable to survive the physical demands of modernity on their bodies, stress became the quantitative measure of each man's unfitness to the world.

> Progress was good, of course, the faster the better, and if individuals were not
> up to the pace of progress, it was they who needed to find ways to cope ...
> Products of a simpler time, we were unable to change rapidly enough ... Our
> salvation was in what help our experts, in psychiatry and medicine especially,
> could give us.[36]

Biological eugenic notions of degeneration of the race of man are here supplanted by a notion of obsolescence of individuals in the face of their machines. We are now in competition with them and losing. But note also how with this concept, stress reduction becomes both a national and individual imperative.

MC[2]
THE POWER TO BE ALL YOU CAN BE

60 Min. Vacation!

- Float for an hour and feel relaxed for the next two days.
- Use the MindGym™ and see and hear your stress disappear.

THE RELAXMAN
Synchro-Energizer

Strobes your stress away in just 15 minutes.
The price: $650. Try it here for only $10.
Or order by phone with VISA, MC, DC, AmEx.

ALTERED STATES™
Float Center & MindGym™
West Hollywood, CA
Appt./Brochure (213) 854-4437

Achieve Your Dreams
Now you have the power to experience deep relaxation, accelerate your
learning abilities and change behavior patterns at the touch of a button.

The MC[2] computerized audio-visual component system enables you to do just
that. In just minutes, the MC[2] can guide you to a state of relaxation through
the use of synchronized light and sound patterns.

When you use the MC[2] you can select from any one of the 10 convenient
presets for relaxation, focusing, learning and motivation.

Explicit ideological connections between brain-mind machines and militarized selves are immediately made. Chris Hables Gray has traced the Department of Defense concentration on producing and technologically enhancing men so they become soldiers capable of handling the stress of the rapidly changing battlefield.[37] Stress has become an industry as well as an essential part of our own self-description and the key to productive survival.

"The power to be all that you can be, achieve your dreams": In this civilian version of the Army recruiting slogan, we can note the coincidence of the nationalist ideal of **technological superiority and redemption with its individual new age middle-class leisure variety.**[38]

A result of this understanding is the central role which these machines come to play, inserting themselves as essential to certain ways of life. One user, Lisa, a civil servant living in Houston, began using brain-mind tapes and enjoyed their presence and potential powers so much that in a month she was listening to them for two hours before bed, while sleeping, an hour upon waking, and during lunch. When I questioned the excessiveness of her use of the tapes, she replied that they really soothed her and that she had never felt so satisfied with her life before.

Her self-defined goal was self-realization and she described herself as on the way to it thanks to these tapes. I am interested in the way in which the goal of self-realization has been privatized to a relationship between Lisa and her machine.

Another ad declares: "Altered states mind gym, 60 minute vacation. See stress disappear." A week's vacation in an hour. Free time is here equated with stress reduction and thus in need of speeding up. This denigration even of vacation time is a good example of what Paul Edwards would call a closed-world self. A self subjected solely to the military imperatives of speed, miniaturization, and automation.[39] This kind of extreme bourgeois alienation would make Marx gloat; though perhaps Lewis Mumford said it best:

> The historic process may be condensed into a brief formula: manual work into machine work: machine work into paper work: paper work into electronic simulation of work, divorced from any organic functions or human purposes except those that further the power system.[40]

Another machine, the Inner Quest or IQ, has been advertised in *OMNI* magazine and boasts the pun, "We've improved our IQ for you!" A brain-machine designer I talked to reported that he got into this field when as a clinical psychologist interested in measuring states of mind, he became concerned over possible harmful effects of these brain-wave entrainers. He built his own in order to study its effects and decided that there were positive benefits to be gained. **He began using it everyday planning to increase his intelligence so that he could build better machines.**

The cyborg-audience appealed to here is one whose being is monetarily self-sufficient but unsatisfied and unrealized. By uncoupling oneself from the technoscience social world and linking instead to a personal private realization device, one can become simply and measurably better. As the ad states: "for yourself, by yourself."

Self-improvement here becomes an end in itself to be known only through the apparatus of inscriptions which one is able to produce. Alpha, delta and theta waves literally become 'proof' of creativity, stresslessness, etc. and thus proof of quantitative progress in a quest for self by those who (to recall one of the first images) already determine their own physical environment.

Reproducing Brains, Reproducing Society

To conclude I'd like to situate the class position the previous ads have staked out by looking at an alternative instantiation of a brain-mind machine.

"MILLIONAIRE'S MIND" TATTOO'S SUCCESS ONTO BRAIN CELLS

Amazing new success booster system energizes your subconscious to attract prosperity and wealth like a magnet. How? By implanting 21 success traits of a self-made millionaire permanently onto your brain cells and into every fiber of your being.

This represents, I think, a working class version of BMMs and is made by the same company which produced the 28 minutes to Zen monkhood tapes. This ad reads:

> Beyond subliminal tapes [to Transliminal!] the Millionaire's Mind system uses a super powerful new technology called Mind Mapping that actually fuses the 21 success traits of a self-made millionaire onto your brain cells. An extremely complex audio matrix ... maps new memories and beliefs about success and wealth.

Beyond hyperbolic to transbolic talk, this pitch for a $69.95 product names out loud the claim that life can be better through having more control over one's environment via financial security. Where the previous brain machines retail for between $295 and $5000, this ad assumes a reader who has little money to spend and who in fact wants money, a trait not mentioned in most more "New Age", self-improvement ads. There is not one mention of stress, either, only anxiety.

Here then, a different kind of cyborg is appealed to. One who has been excluded from high paying career opportunities can now avail himself of science to provide him with traits he does not have. He can gain the monetary benefits of class while remaining himself.

I'd also like to take a moment to reflect on the laughter which these machines and their adwriters evoke; a laughter which is as much theirs as ours, though with the uncanny feeling that we think we know better. Because, for many people I have talked to, the desire to try these machines is not in spite of, but because of their humorous nature.

I am interested in the machinery of these ads because they disturb, by calling attention to, parts of my own self-discourse, they name and make desirable a retreat from social awareness into rather comfortable kinds of self-improvement.

God is User Friendly
—Protestant Church Announcement Board

This cover from a 1990 issue of *EAST/WEST*, the journal of NATURAL health and living, draws together visually a number of the discourses I have been describing. Meditation, a signifier of natural body processes, goes high-tech because the results of enlightened living are stressed over the discipline. Note the way in which the machine itself is the source of spiritual as well as electrical power. In an appropriation of the wisdom of the East by Technology of the West, Buddha has been put into a box and becomes available for personal purchase and consumption. This machine symbolically embodies who "we" want to be: once plugged in it produces constant alpha waves so we can have pure no-mind or buddha-mind.

Brain-mind machines are acting here to gather up the discourses of self-improvement, superpowers, technological progress and redemption in order to provide a site for new practices. Analyzing ads within the context of an anthropology provides explicit acknowledgment of differential class desires, self-improvement versus financial security.

By realizing and personalizing brain inscription devices, these machines are able to transform desires for essential self-depiction and self-control into specific ways of life with the machines at the center. They thus produce a manifest cyborg person within a discourse of cyborg envy. That is, they realize a way to achieve the desired result of a quantitatively better-functioning mind.

By carefully tracking and situating our own complicity in these militarized discourses of self it is hoped that alternate cyborg futures may become imaginable.

Notes

1. There are many recent attempts to theorize technocultural embeddedness. See especially [Haraway, 1988; Haraway, 1991; Jacobus, 1990; Penley, 1991; Downey, forthcoming].

2. On technophilia and epistemophilia, see especially [Sofoulis, 1988; Sofoulis, 1984; Kittler, 1985; Crary, 1992].

3. See [Kopytoff, 1986; Appadurai, 1986; Downey, 1992; Pfaffenberger, 1992].

4. Ascription is the process whereby one attribution of unnatural or supernatural powers leads to the attribution of the entire range of them. Aghenanda Bharati provides an excellent description of the working of this discourse in India. [Bharati, 1976].

5. See [Stone, 1992].

6. [Hutchinson, 1986; Hutchinson, Schultz, 1989]. *Would the Buddha Wear a Walkman* by Judith Hooper and Dick Teresi provides a history and a detailed account of devices and places, in the form of journalistic advertisements [Hooper, 1990]. Hutchinson's books are in the same vein. Further materials in this field include *MONDO2000*, a magazine which features BMMs as one component in a cyberpunk future, along with "smart drugs" and virtual reality. Cyberpunk for *MONDO2000* is both science fiction and music.

7. Semiotics and following semiotics, science and technology studies, have mounted an intensive investigation of the concept of agency, primarily emphasizing the narrative construction of it. See [Greiamas, 1990; Greimas, 1987; Greimas and Cortes, 1982; Latour, 1987; Bastide, 1989].

The phrases regarding BMMs "localizing themselves" and "mobilizing certain humans" are written in this lively way for a number of reasons. First, as I have mentioned throughout this paper, attributions of agency, especially with regard to technology, are one of my main objects of study. This is not so simple as taking the comment "This machine says that you are probably meditating" at face value. Rather, I use these discursive metaphors *excessively*, to question to notion that language is the deciding factor in attributing will and agency. *To the extent* that machines, for instance, determine our actions by what they tell us about ourselves, they have agency. And we are in dialogue (semiotic communication) with them.

The important point here is not whether one can tell a history of a machine and show that human decisions and agency caused it and are sedimented into it. Rather, the fact that someone *accepts* the determination of the machine, and *does not* look for further explanation, *is* the recognition of agency. Expertise has been transferred from human to the device, which is now more expert than the human.

The liveliness of this language is hopefully an antidote to the discourses which reduce humans to automatic information processors in order to account for the ways in which we can be wired into the world. One advantage of talking about machine agency, and especially machine discourse, is that both humans and non-humans are recognized for their subtle humors and general unruliness.

8. Heterodox science survives in the contentious boundaries of orthodox science. This boundary is difficult to define and impossible to fully police. See. [Hess, 1993; Hess, 1987; Wallis, 1979].

9. See [Virillo & Lotringer, 1983].

10. [Noble, 1989; etc.]

11. [Walter, 1953, Hutchison, 1986].

12. On the recent history of the New Age see [Melton, 1988; Melton, 1991].

13. See especially the essays by Stoehr, Greenway and Fuller in [Wrobel, 1987] on the history of popular electricity. See [Lawrence, 1972] for work on Alpha waves.

14. The science fiction novel *The Karma Machine* takes this notion of spiritual computing to its logical utopian conclusion. People in this paradise run by a computer, eventually merge into one perfect hum (at 60hz?) [Davidson, 1975].

{ **358**

15. Whether or not this kind of mastery of self is consistent with, for instance, yoga and mediation as it is practiced in parts of East Asia, there is certainly no sign in advertisements for brain machines of escaping oneself, giving onself up or becoming non-self. If any theme is predominant, it is that of *taking* responsibility for your life, taking charge of it, and maintaining this self-control.

16. Anthropologist Michael Taussig has written powerful accounts of the cohabitation of brutal colonialism and colonists' deep involvement in the 'magic' of the Other. Technology figures prominently as both the means of violence and the medium of the sacred. [Taussig, 1987; Taussig, 1993]. On Orientalism as a discursive formation of scholarly fantasy, see [Said, 1978; Mudimbe, 1988].

17. John Liebeskind, quoted on the back of *Megabrain*.

18. [Hooper & Teresi, 1990, p. 21].

19. [Carroughes, 1946, p. 17].

20. On this history, see [Walter, 1953]. John Varley's short sci-fi story, "Press Enter," also depends on the notion of the flicker response [Varley, 1990].

21. [Deleuze & Guattari, 1987].

22. [Delgado, 1969].

23. [Kline and Clynes, 1960].

24. These experiments were the subject of Marge Piercy's *Woman on the Edge of Time* [Piercy, 1976].

25. On the cultural notion of science as a neutral "culture without culture," see [Traweek, 1988, and Bourdieu, 1975].

26. The quest for artificial intelligence is an example of how we are caught in a nature where computers really are exemplary models of rational thinking. For an exquisite essay on the computerization of geniuses, see Roland Barthes essay on "The Brain of Einstein." [Barthes, 1972].

27. On the democratic objectivity and comfort of numbers, see [Porter, 1992].

28. Craniocentric is used here to draw attention to the way in which the head and skull are key symbols in our metaphorics of personhood and rationality: "numbskull, blockhead, airhead, nothing between the ears, harebrained, thick(headed)." On the history of brain theories, especially the notion that cognitive functions can be illuminated by a study of brain locations, see [Star, 1989; Harrington, 1987].

29. Cf. [Evelyn Fox Keller, 1985].

30. [Fleck, 1979, p. 112]. The validity and analytic usefulness of Fleck's insight have been borne out by recent anthropological work on scientists and technology. Sharon Traweek, 1988; Hugh Gusterson, 1991; and Gary Downey, in this volume; have focused on the role education plays in selecting and acculturating prospective researchers, their work has shown how emotions, body-image and relationships with machines are shaped through specific applications and adaptations of popular theorizing.

31. This work draws upon the works of Donna Haraway, Evelyn Fox Keller, Barbara Stafford and Susan Leigh Star. All of these scholars wade into the tropics of discourse in order to locate and analyze ongoing struggles over the fabric of meaning. Stafford eloquently describes the coercive analogies and constitutive metaphors which make it possible to make visible the invisible worlds of the microscope and telescope. Star, attending to the social organization of neuroscientific discover in brain research, locates metaphors as both enabling and setting limits on ways of looking at the world: "Metaphors are a way of making a bridge between two unlike things ... Lakoff's work on metaphors also shows that, like long-standing arguments, they can define the limits and boundaries of a way of looking at the world—in a sense they beg certain epistemological questions through the act of conjoining that which is unlike, and *without questioning in the act*" (Lakoff, 1987; Lakoff and Johnson, 1980) [Star, *Brain*, 205].

Lived metaphors—embodied in documents and technologies are here treated as the contestable terrain of the social world. This collection of methods foregrounds the processes by which categories and relationships such as objectivity and normality are produced and maintained.

32. See esp. [Nelkin, 1989; Terry, 1989] as well as the works of Gilman.

33. See [Foucault, 1978] and also [Gilman, 1988]. Gilman attends to both the iconographic and textual means of producing social truth. He takes up the question of the desire to find definite (i.e. objective) means of discriminating who is different (i.e. not normal) with regard to diseases and mental illness.

34. On category of the person, see [Mauss, 1985; Carrithers, 1985]. On "Objective Self-Fashioning," see Dumit, forthcoming.

35. In the case of BMMs, we can look at how a digital, cyborg gaze is produced with which we see objective images of ourselves in a sublimely taxonomic world of discrete categories of persons and functions. That these categories *have* to be familiar ones, that they *have* to reinforce Social Truth, however, is not at all clear. Examining the areas of popular theorizing which shape our desires for these images is one way to imagine alternate identifications.

36. [Hogness, 1983].

37. [Gray, 1989; Gray, 1991].

38. Ironically, this slogan "Be all that you can be" was itself lifted from the Silva Mind Control movement by an Army investigation into New Age techniques for possible use in leadership training [Swets, 1990].

39. [Edwards, 1989].

40. [Mumford, 1971, p. 165].

References

Appadurai, Arjun, ed., 1986, *Social Life of Things: Commodities in Cultural Perspective*. (Cambridge: Cambridge UP).

Barthes, Roland, 1972, *Mythologies*. (New York: The Noonday Press).

Bastide, Francoise, 1989, "On Demonstration" in *Paris School Semiotics II: Practice*. Ed. P Perron and F.H. Collins. Amsterdam: John Benjamins, 1989. 109-43.

Bharati, Agehananda, 1976, *The Light at the Center: Context and Pretext of Modern Mysticism*, (Santa Barbara [Calif.]: Ross-Erikson).

Bourdieu, Pierre, 1975, "The Specificity of the Scientific Field and the Social Conditions of the Progress of Reason." *Social Science Information* 14.6 19-57.

Brown, David Jay, 1988, *Brainchild*. (Las Vegas: Falcon Press).

Carrithers, Michael, Steven Collins, and Steven Lukes, 1985, *The Category of the Person: Anthropology, Philosophy, History*. (Cambridge [Cambridgeshire]; New York: Cambridge University Press).

Crary, Jonathan, and Sanford Kwinter, 1992, *Incorporations*. (New York: Zone).

Davidson, Michael, and Jim Campbell, 1975, *The Karma Machine*. (New York: Popular Library).

Deleuze, Gilles, and Felix Guattari, 1983, *Anti-Oedipus: Capitalism and Schizophrenia*. (Minneapolis: University of Minnesota Press).

Delgado, Jose M.R., 1969, *Physical Control of the Mind: Toward a Psychocivilized Society*. (New York: Harper & Row).

Downey, Gary Lee, 1992, "CAD/CAM Saves the Nation? Toward an Anthropology of Technology" in *Knowledge and Society Vol. 9: The Anthropology of Science and Technology*. Ed. David J. Hess and Linda Layne. Greenwich, CN: JAI Press.

Downey, Gary Lee, 1992, "Human agency in CAD/CAM technology." In this volume.

Dumit, Joseph, (forthcoming). "A Digital Image of the Category of the Person: PET Scanning and Objective Self Fashioning" in *Cyborgs and Citadels: Anthropological Interventions in Technoscience*, edited by Gary Downey, Joseph Dumit and Sharon Traweek. Santa Fe: School of American Research Press.

Edwards, Paul N., 1989, "The Closed World: Systems discourse, military policy and post-World War II US Historical consciousness" in *Cyborg Worlds: The Military Information Society*. Ed. Les Levidow and Kevin Robins. London: Free Association Books, 1989.

Fleck, Ludwig, 1979, *Genesis and Development of a Scientific Fact*. Ed. Thaddeus J. Trenn and Robert K. Merton. (Chicago: University of Chicago Press).

Foucault, Michel, 1978, *The History of Sexuality: Volume 1: An Introduction*. (New York: Vintage Books).

Gilman, Sander L., 1988, *Disease and Representation: Images of Illness from Madness to AIDS*. (Ithaca: Cornell UP).

Gray, Chris Hables, 1991, *Computers as Weapons and Metaphors: The U.S. Military 1940-1990 and Postmodern War*. (UCSC: Working Paper #1; Cultural Studies of Science and Technology Research Group).

Gray, Chris Hables, 1989, "The Cyborg Soldier: the US military and the post-modern warrior" in *Cyborg Worlds*. Ed. Les Levidow and Kevin Robins. London: Free Association Books, 1989. 43-72.

Greimas, A.-J., 1987, *On Meaning: Selected Writings in Semiotic Theory*, (Minneapolis: University of Minnesota Press).

Greimas, A.-J., 1983 (1966), *Structural Semantics: An Attempt at a Method*. (Lincoln: U Nebraska Press).

Greimas, A.-J., and J. Courtes, 1982, *Semiotics and Language: An Analytical Dictionary*. (Bloomington: Indiana UP).

Gusterson, Hugh, 1992, "Nuclear War, the Gulf War, and the Disappearing Body." *Journal of Urban and Cultural Studies* 2.1 45-56.

Haraway, Donna J., 1989, *Primate Visions: Gender, Race, and Nature in the World of Modern Science*. (NY: Routledge).

Haraway, Donna J., 1991, *Simians, Cyborgs, and Women: The Reinvention of Nature*. (London: Free Association Books).

Harbula, Rev. Patrick J., 1990, "Electric Nirvana." *Meditation*, V:2 (Spring) pp. 38.

Harrington, Anne, 1987, *Medicine, Mind, and the Double Brain: A Study in Nineteenth Century Thought.* (Princeton, NJ: Princeton University Press).

Harrington, Anne, ed., 1992, *So Human a Brain: Knowledge and Values in the Neurosciences.* (Boston: Dibner Institute Publication/Birkhauser).

Harris, Neil, 1990, *Cultural Excursions: Marketing Appetites and Cultural Tastes in Modern America.* (Chicago: University of Chicago Press).

Hess, David, 1993, *Science in the New Age: The Paranormal, Its Defenders and Debunkers, and American Culture.* (Madison: University of Wisconsin Press).

Hess, David, 1991, *Spirits and Scientists: Ideology, Spiritism, and Brazilian Culture.* (University Park, PA: Penn State UP).

Hogness, E. Rustin, 1983, *Why Stress? A Look at the Making of Stress,* an unpublished paper available from the author, (4437 Mill Creek Rd., Healdsburg, CA 95448).

Hooper, Judith, and Dick Teresi, 1990, *Would the Buddha Wear a Walkman? A Catalogue of Revolutionary Tools for Higher Consciousness.* (New York: Simon & Schuster).

Hutchison, Michael, 1990, *The Anatomy of Sex and Power: An Investigation of Mind-Body Politics,* (New York: W. Morrow).

Hutchison, Michael, 1986, *Megabrain: New Tools and Techniques for Brain Growth and Mind Expansion.* (New York: Ballantine Books).

Jacobus, Mary, Evelyn Fox Keller, and Sally Shuttleworth, eds., 1990, *Body/Politics: Women and the Discourses of Science.* (New York: Routledge).

Keller, Evelyn Fox, 1985, *Reflections on Gender and Science.* (New Haven: Yale University Press).

Kittler, Friedrich A., 1985, *Discourse Networks 1800/1900,* (Stanford: Stanford University Press).

Kopytoff, Igor, 1986, "The Cultural Biography of Things: Commoditization as Process" in *The Social Life of Things: Commodities in Cultural Perspective.* Ed. Arjun Appadurai. Cambridge: Cambridge UP, 1986. 64-93.

Lakoff, George, 1987, *Women, Fire and Dangerous Things: What Categories Reveal About the Mind.* (Chicago: University of Chicago Press).

Lakoff, George, and Mark Johnson, 1980, *Metaphors We Live By.* (Chicago: University of Chicago Press).

Latour, Bruno, 1987, *Science in Action: How to Follow Scientists and Engineers Through Society.* (Cambridge, Mass.: Harvard UP).

Lawrence, Jodi, 1972, *Alpha Brain Waves.* (New York: Avon Books).

Levidow, Les., and Kevin, Robins, 1989, *Cyborg worlds: the military information society.* (London: Free Association Books).

Leviton, Richard, 1990, "Meditation Goes High Tech." *EastWest,* 20:3 (March) pp. 52.

Mauss, Marcel, 1985, "A category of the human mind: the notion of person; the notion of self." in *The Category of the Person.* Ed. Michael Carrithers, Steven Collins and Steven Lukes. Trans. W.D. Halls. Cambridge: Cambridge University Press, 1-25.

Melton, J. Gordon, 1988, "A History of the New Age Movement" in *Not Necessarily the New Age: Critical Essays.* Ed. Robert Basil. Buffalo: Prometheus Books, 1988.

Melton, J. Gordon, Jerome Clark, and Aidan A. Kelly, 1991, *New Age Almanac.* (New York: Visible Ink).

Mudimbe, V. Y., 1988, *The Invention of Africa: Gnosis, Philosophy, and the Order of Knowledge.* (Bloomington: Indiana UP).

Mumford, Lewis, [1971, 1970], *The pentagon of power.* (London: Secker & Warburg).

Nelkin, Dorothy, and Laurence Tancredi, 1989, *Dangerous Diagnostics: The Social Power of Biological Information.* (New York: Basic Books).

Noble, Douglas D., 1989, "Mental Material: The Militarization of Learning and Intelligence in U.S. Education" in *Cyborg Worlds: The Military Information Society.* Ed. Les Levidow and Kevin Robins. London: Free Association Books, 1989. 13-42.

Noble, David F., 1984, *Forces of Production: A Social History of Industrial Automation,* (New York: Knopf).

Penley, Constance, and Andrew Ross, eds., 1991, *Technoculture.* (Minneapolis: University of Minnesota Press).

Pereira, Joseph, 1990, "How many people would shell out $20 to listen to static: Quest for more brain power leads many to MindGym; Taking the Violet Cure." *Wall Street Journal* April 13:

Pfaffenberger, Bryan, 1992, "Social Anthropology of Technology." *Annual Review of Anthropology* 21 491-516.

Piercy, Marge, 1991, *He, she, and it: A Novel.* (New York: Knopf).

Piercy, Marge, 1976, *Woman on the Edge of Time.* (New York: Knopf).

Porter, Theodore M., 1992, "Quantification and the Accounting Ideal in Science." *Social Studies of Science* 22 633-52.

Said, Edward, 1978, *Orientalism.*

Schultz, Ted, ed., 1989, *The Fringes of Reason: a Whole Earth Catalog.* (New York: Harmony Books).

Sofoulis, Zoe, 1988, *Through the Lumen: Frankenstein and the Optics of Re-origination,* (University of California at Santa Cruz: Ph.D. Dissertation).

Sofoulis, Zoe (writing as Zoe Sofia), 1984, "Exterminating Fetuses: Abortion, Disarmament, and the Sexo-semiotics of Extra-Terrestialism." *Diacritics* 14.2 47-59.

Stafford, Barbara Maria, 1991, *Body Criticism: Imaging the Unseen in Enlightenment Art and Medicine.* (Cambridge, Mass.: MIT Press).

Star, Susan Leigh, 1989, *Regions of the Mind: Brain Research and the Quest for Scientific Certainty.* (Stanford: Stanford UP).

Star, Susan Leigh, 1992, "The Skin, the Skull, and the Self: Toward a Sociology of the Brain" in *So Human a Brain: Knowledge and Values in the Neurosciences.* Ed. Anne Harrington. Boston: Birkhauser, 1992.

Stone, Allucquère Rosanne, 1992, "Virtual Systems." in *Incorporations.* Ed. Jonathan Crary and Sanford Kwinter. New York: Zone (distrib: MIT Press), 1992. 608-625.

Swets, John A., and Robert A. Bjork, 1990, "Enhancing Human Performance: An Evaluation of "New Age" Techniques Considered by the U.S. Army." *Psychological Science* 1.2 85-96.

Taussig, Michael, 1993, *Mimesis and Alterity: A Particular History of the Senses.* (New York: Routledge).

Taussig, Michael, 1987, *Shamanism, Colonialism and the Wild Man: A Study in Terror and Healing.* (Chicago: University of Chicago Press).

Traweek, Sharon, 1988, *Beamtimes and Lifetimes: The World of High Energy Physicists.* (Cambridge, MA: Harvard University Press).

Varley, John et al., 1990, *Press enter.* (New York: Tom Doherty Associates).

Virilio, Paul, 1986, *Speed and Politics: An Essay on Dromology.* (New York: Columbia University).

Virilio, Paul., and Sylvere, Lotringer, 1983, *Pure war.* (New York: Semiotext(e)).

Wallis, Roy, ed., 1979, *On the Margins of Science: The Social Construction of Rejected Knowledge.* (Keele: University of Keele). Vol. 27.

Walter, W. Grey, 1953, *The Living Brain, "Revelation by Flicker"* (Duckworth and Co., Ltd.).

White, Hayden V., 1985, *Tropics of Discourse: Essays in Cultural Criticism.* (Baltimore: Johns Hopkins University Press).

Wroebel, Arthur, ed. 1987. *Pseudo-Science and Society in Nineteenth-Century America.* (Lexington: University Press of Kentucky).

L 5.3

Human Agency in CAD/CAM Technology

Gary Lee Downey

In the United States, the natives routinely portray their society in part by distinguishing it from their technology. **Americans understand and characterize technology as an external phenomenon, or more particularly as an autonomous force** (Teich 1990). From this perspective, technologies develop according to their own internal logics within specialized technical communities whose deliberations are essentially opaque and presumably free of cultural content. Technology becomes an independent variable and society a dependent product.

It is an irony of American culture that this fixed separation frequently grounds a social commitment to technology as the solution to social problems. The distinction helps give engineers, for example, the authority to abstract 'technical' problems from 'social' problems, attempt to solve them in the rarefied realm of technical discourse according to localized considerations reserved for that realm (e.g. 'logical' coherence), and then apply the technical 'solutions' back to society. Engineers can boast that many problems have technical solutions and then complain about the barriers imposed by a purely social 'politics', as when they throw up their hands and say. 'It's all politics'.

By standing outside of society, **American technology occupies a strategic position as a vehicle for social change.** Technologies possess the agency to have 'impact' on society, yet their internal features are generally excused from overt public deliberation and decision making. Accordingly, engineers and inventors acquire the power to engineer and invent society as well as technology, as do other individuals and groups who successfully incorporate into their own identities the pursuit of social change as technological development.

This technological determinism has its limitations, however, as a native theory of social change. By positioning technology as a force external to society, it offers a limited view of how technologies might acquire human agency and function as actors within society. Over the past three years, I have conducted an ethnographic study in the United States of a technology called CAD/CAM, or computer-aided design and computer-aided manufacturing. Beginning in the early 1980s, a prominent nationalistic interpretation of CAD/CAM technology identified it as crucial to resolving a national identity crisis, i.e., restoring America's economic competitiveness in the world. According to the nationalist script, CAD/CAM technologies promised to streamline product innovation in American industry by merging together the distinct engineering activities of 'design' and 'manufacturing', thus enabling American companies to increase their 'productivity' by responding more quickly and effectively to changing consumer demands.

Pursuing this nationalist objective, however, involved linking it to other, more localized objectives. Three distinct technologies emerged instead of one. Each technology is endowed with the agencies of a different set of engineering activities, and together these technologies empower design to the exclusion or detriment of manufacturing. By examining how technologies such as CAD/CAM acquire and redistribute human agency within society, anthropologists can offer an important source of cultural criticism, one that begins by blurring the sharp distinction between humans and machines which grounds native technological determinism.

Transcribing human agency into technology

Through most of its history, the discipline of cultural anthropology has reproduced the cultural separation between technology and human society in its everyday work. Traditional anthropological attempts to understand technology tended to fall into two general categories, each taking up technological determinism into its discourse by treating technology as an external force. The first offered variations on the theme of materialist reductionism, viewing technological development as the prime mover of all cultural change. Most prominent was Leslie White, who argued that 'the technological factor is the determinant of the cultural system as a whole' (White 1949:366). The second offered case studies of the 'impact' of Western technology in 'developing' societies. For example, Lauriston Sharp described how introducing steel axes to the aboriginal Yir Yoront had 'hack[ed] at the supports of the entire cultural system' (1952:88). **Also, Pertti Pelto explored how introducing snowmobiles in the Arctic had brought about 'sequential transformations in economic, social, and other aspects of culture'** (Pelto and Muller-Wille 1972:199; Pelto et al. 1968).

During the 1960s and 1970s, the rise into prominence of theories of cultures as shared and bounded symbolic systems (Ortner 1984), e.g. as 'systems of symbols and meanings' (Schneider 1968, 1969) or as 'meaningful orders of people and things' (Sahlins 1976), distinguished technology and society by externalizing technology from cultural accounts of human action. Trained during this period, I learned to identify shared cultural meanings on the model of a linguistic grammar, i.e., as distinctions or categories presupposed by different actors across a range of contexts. I remember vividly reading in students' proposals for fieldwork the required statement, which now sounds silly: 'I will examine the widest possible range of actors and contexts'.

Although the image of bounded cultures did not prohibit anyone from looking for shared meanings in technology. I know from personal experience that technology was widely viewed as inherently boring, i.e. significantly uninteresting in conceptual terms. I came to believe, however, that cultural accounts of technologies did not find favour because accounting for the shared meanings of technologies offered only trivial insights while following diverse meanings was confusing conceptually. At the time, raging debates were taking place within Western nations over such technologies as nuclear power. Exploring the categories that different actors attributed to technologies across a range of contexts would have led one away from the image of internally homogeneous, bounded cultures and toward images of intra-cultural diversity with variable distributions of power.

Things have now changed. Over the past decade, theoretical developments in both cultural anthropology and the sociology of technology render all aspects of technological development eminently susceptible to anthropological enquiry and critique. In the first place, cultural anthropologists are asking less about how cultural structures shape action and more about how agents produce culture. Diversity in cultural meaning is the rule rather than the exception; stabilized categories are a social accomplishment; and the redistribution of power relations is integral to the process of meaning construction rather than simply a final outcome. Finally, anthropologists' concern for their role in a postmodern world has produced heightened sensitivity to the constructed nature of boundaries between humans and machines and generated interest in understanding the cyborg in us all.[†]

Extensive developments in the sociology of technology have reconceptualized technology from an autonomous force to a social product through two key conceptual moves. The first recasts technological content as the product of social judgment. For example, John Law's concept of 'heterogeneous engineering' describes technological development as the convergence of heterogeneous mixes of factors and considerations. The second move brings technological artefacts into the arena of social action as participants with agency. For example, Michel Callon (1986) has described how giving agency to an electric car entailed constructing the entire infrastructure within which the vehicle would function.

Drawing on these developments, anthropological investigations of technology can follow how technologies come to serve as both the products and the producers of distributed cultural meaning and power by transcribing human agency into object form. I examine the transcription of human agency into CAD/CAM technology by following how actors move themselves around in relation to other actors and cultural objects, i.e. by 'positioning' their 'identities'. Identities refers to the configurations of categories that distinguish actors and objects from one another. Acts of 'positioning' bring identities to life as both a condition and a product of action. For example, Americans may position technology as external to their society, but they also routinely position themselves in relation to specific technologies as a strategy for distinguishing themselves from others.

I use the term 'agency' to refer to the act of positioning itself. CAD/CAM developers and users transcribe human agency into their technologies by abstracting informational content from engineering activities, translating it into binary code, and then reinserting the empowered technological agents back into those activities as active participants. Transcribing agency into CAD/CAM technology gives it the power to position, to move itself around in relation to other agents. The positioning of CAD/CAM technology is more complex than a native determinist account would have it because in positioning the new technology agents also reposition themselves (see also Downey 1992a, 1992b, 1993).

Nationalism in CAD/CAM

During the 1980s, efforts to save America through technological development frequently built upon a rhetorical strategy that asserts: (1) the American 'nation' is threatened by economic defeats at the hands of international competitors, especially Japan; (2) the key problem is declining 'productivity' in industry, understood as output of product per unit labour; and (3) technological development is the best means for increasing productivity. The turn to technology is a Western phenomenon, most prominent in the United States, and contrasts significantly with the Japanese style of innovating through incremental rather than broad-brushed solutions. By linking 'productivity' to an economic interpretation of the American 'nation', this strategy redistributed the agencies and repositioned the identities of both at the same time. Productivity gained national, rather than purely economic, significance, and the nation gained a new form of technological salvation.

Numerous elite groups in industry, government, universities and professional engineering societies have worked to realize this vision. Cooperative ventures in research and development that would have horrified Americans during the 1960s and 1970s, e.g. collaboration between IBM and Apple Computer or federal support for multi-company coalitions developing semiconductors, have experienced almost no popular opposition, complaints about conflicts of interest, or fears about domination by a monolithic capitalist Establishment.

Coming from elite, official groups, the rhetoric of nationalism offered legitimacy to the use of CAD/CAM technology to enhance productivity. Prior to 1980, CAD/CAM technology was simply one component of the field of 'interactive computer graphics', which involves using the computer to manipulate pictures and models of objects. CAD/CAM proponents repositioned interactive computer graphics by linking them to engineering design and manufacturing. Making pictures and models transcribes the agencies of engineers into the forms of computer graphics. Each of the three technologies—2D drafting automation, 3D wireframe and surface modelling and solid modelling—is a technological transcription of engineering activities.

2D drafting automation

2D drafting automation is positioned to increase the productivity of a design activity but not to link together design and manufacturing. 'Drafting', or engineering drawing, is the activity of representing product parts in terms of 'views' in 'two dimensions', such as the 'top view', 'front view' and 'right side view'. Automating the drafting process involves transcribing drawing practices into computer graphics programs and then inserting those programs back into the drawing activities. 2D CAD/CAM is constructed on the image of a drafter at a drawing board.

Positioning 2D technology between drafters and their drawings modifies the identities of everyone and everything involved. For example, accepting 2D technology means replacing such drafting instruments as 'T-squares', 'compasses', and 'French curves' with various types of 'input devices' (keyboard, mouse etc.), 'display devices' (various types of cathode ray tubes), 'output devices' (printer, plotter etc.), and 'manuals' for 'hardware' and 'software'. Drawing 'points', 'lines', and 'circles' is replaced by inputting graphical 'primitives' and 'attributes' through combinations of programmed 'transformations' and 'control routines'. Drafters do not have to 'write' their programs as lines of computer code, because the 2D programs all name their commands and options using the old vocabulary of points, lines, circles, etc. But the precise relationships among these old terms change in the shift from drawing board to computer scope. These relationships also vary from program to program.

Drafting automation has been the most popular CAD/CAM technology by far. Using 2D programs can increase dramatically the speed of repetitive tasks, such as making changes to drawings. However, within the nationalist script 2D technology is incomplete. Drafting automation is not positioned to integrate design and manufacturing, for the model of a drafter at a drawing board captures and transcribes none of the practices on the manufacturing side of product development. Furthermore, redistributing agency through 2D technologies can even separate drafters and drafting activities from the other design activities of engineers. For example, in one firm I observed, engineering managers sought to maximize the output of expensive CAD equipment by having operators use it two shifts a day and on weekends, while design engineers worked only weekdays. Also, competition between drafters and engineers for use of the CAD equipment was high until the engineers obtained additional equipment that was better suited to some of their mathematically-based activities.

3D wireframe and surface modelling

The technologies of 3D wireframe and surface modelling also have little connection to manufacturing, for these are endowed with the agency of 'engineering analysis', a mathematically intensive activity exclusive to design. 3D technologies present visual 'models' of discrete objects suspended in three dimensions. A wireframe representation of an object constructs it as a collection of lines depicting the object's 'edges'. A surface model represents an object as a set of curved surfaces, which may or may not be linked together to produce a closed object.

The image of an airplane presented here is a surface model that some informants use to represent their CAD/CAM research group. Since it is a surface model, engineers could add shading or colour to give the image a sculptured look. The model could also be presented as a wireframe by using lines only to portray the edges of its components.

Moving from 2D to 3D transforms a drawing into a model because it adds a great deal of engineering information to the representation. Design engineers are interested both in the graphical picture and in the geometric data about the picture that are stored in the computer. They use these data to 'do analysis' on the model, which involves inserting the model into theoretical systems of 'forces'. For example, using additional data about materials, engineers analyse the surface model of the airplane by calculating its 'volume', 'weight', 'centre of gravity' (location of the balance point), 'moments of inertia' (a measure of how easy it is to rotate the object in different directions, e.g. it is easier to roll an airplane over sideways than end over end), etc. They further link the geometric model to theories of 'aerodynamics' (how moving objects interact with airflow), propulsion (how engines produce changing forces) etc., to identify shapes that meet design limitations in each area. The equations presented visually represent the agency involved in calculating acceptable shapes. By including these equations in the computer program that generates the geometric model, engineers empower the program with the agency to find acceptable shapes.

By possessing the agency of engineering analysis, 3D technologies intersect with activities in research and development ('R&D'). As a consequence, 3D technologies tend to find use among engineers in larger corporations and in university research, who already tend to use computers for analysis activities. Also, since 3D technologies tend to be added to existing analysis activities, the burden of developing and modifying programs in wireframe and surface modeling falls much more on the shoulders of engineer-users than is the case with 2D technologies, in which commercial vendors compete to sell 'packages' to automate drafting.

3D representations make it possible for engineers to consider more than one type of analysis simultaneously, thereby concentrating more and more design functions at earlier and earlier points in the design process. Thus, although 3D technologies extend beyond drafting into other design activities, these do not seek to merge design activities and personnel with activities and personnel in manufacturing. In fact, some informants have reported that the use of 3D CAD/CAM sometimes raises suspicions and fuels concerns in manufacturing circles about the hegemony of engineering design.

Solid modelling

Not only has the technology of solid modelling not been positioned to fulfil the nationalist script, it has been much more successful in areas unrelated to industrial productivity, e.g. animation in movie films and simulators for pilot training. As a form of 3D modelling, solid modelling also manipulates discrete objects. It differs by representing these objects as solids rather than as wireframes or surfaces. For example, the method of 'constructive solid geometry' builds models by adding and subtracting 'primitive' solid forms, such as 'spheres' and 'cubes'. Consider for example, the model illustrated here of a pipe valve constructed of chunks of 'cylinders' and 'rectangular solids'.

Solid modelling appears at first glance to be the perfect integrative agent for merging design and manufacturing activities, since it is the representational form closest to the concrete objects that manufacturing processes manipulate. However, solid modelling tends to lack crucial features of the activities in both design and manufacturing.

On the design side, solid models are very useful for making sure that the product parts have enough space after these have been designed, i.e. for 'interference checking'. However, solid models are extremely difficult to modify in the light of the results of analysis. They do not intersect easily with the activities of either design engineers or drafters.

On the manufacturing side, engineers tend to turn to computers with a 'process' orientation, seeking help in monitoring, controlling and supporting manufacturing processes. Manufacturing engineers are interested in such areas as 'cost estimating', 'quality control' and 'production planning'. Although solid models may link the geometric representation of a part to instructions for specific manufacturing 'cutting' operations, such as 'milling' and 'machining', such models usually possess none of the other agencies in manufacturing beyond cutting.

Blurring the boundaries of anthropological discourse

By concentrating design activities at earlier and earlier points in time, the development of 2D and 3D CAD/CAM technologies are positioned to enhance the activities of engineering designers and drafters in product development. The power of an engineering designer increases in proportion with each engineering capability added to the graphical image. As product development activities move 'upstream', so the identity and concerns of engineering design are extended 'downstream' into other areas. This outcome differs significantly from the utopian image of national integration that draws on technological determinist presuppositions and that has helped legitimize CAD/CAM development. Endowing interactive computer graphics with the agencies of engineers has proven successful only where those agencies involve manipulating pictures and models of objects. Merging design and manufacturing requires inventing new agencies that go far beyond the manipulation of objects.

By following how technologies acquire and redistribute human agency within society, anthropological enquiry can overcome the discipline's unstated reliance upon a presupposed cultural distinction between technology and society and follow sociologists of technology in viewing technologies as active participants in social life. Writing about human agency within technology does indeed threaten to externalize one's analysis from normal human-centred anthropological discourse, but avoiding such agency also inhibits the analysis from offering interpretive understanding of technology in society. In my judgment, the response must not be to ignore human agency in technology but to challenge the existing forms of discourse. **A crucial first step in blurring the human-centred boundaries of anthropological discourse is to grant membership to the cyborg image, i.e. to recognize in our writing that human actors routinely produce themselves and their machines as part human and part machine, and that machines have positioning strategies too.**

It is increasingly clear that human agency serves in the world today as but one contributor in a system that is growing, complex, diverse and yet interconnected. The extent of such interconnectedness has been made plain by both the decline of challenges to capitalist hegemony and the empowerment of information technologies through the combined agencies of computers and communications technologies. If the world system is not systemic but diverse, e.g. if capitalism is not singular but plural, the interaction of capitalisms, then it is safe to say that no one person or framework understands it. Instead, understanding it must come in pieces, exploring the variable production of such pieces through diverse strategies in diverse environments. One need reflect only on the multiple pathways to nuclear warfare that dissolving the Soviet Union has produced in order to realize that ignoring agency in technology places too great a restriction on contemporary enquiries into the human condition.

The anthropological study of human agency in technology can also serve as a critical voice that outlines the limitations of native technological determinism. Anthropological criticism can help humans in society recapture their agency by identifying the social judgments that constitute technological developments as indeed social judgments. For example, Americans might find more satisfying solutions to their identity crisis if they asked 'What is the nature of this identity crisis and what are the implications of dealing with it in alternative ways?' rather than 'Which technologies will help America win?' Rather than asking 'Which technologies can best stimulate productivity?' they might ask 'Is developing new technologies to stimulate productivity the most desirable course of action?' While focusing on how to adapt to technology developments that are themselves taken for granted, Americans sanction significant social changes, such as the rise of joint ventures in R&D and other cooperative activities among government, industry and universities, without the kind of overt public debate that genuinely identifies and assesses their implications. **By examining the empowerment of technology with human agency, anthropology can also empower itself.**

Notes

†A double session at the 1992 meetings of the American Anthropological Association in San Francisco and a 1993 Advanced Seminar at the School of American Research explored possibilities for a 'cyborg anthropology'. Cyborg anthropology, the term coined by Joseph Dumit, calls attention to the cultural production of human distinctiveness by examining ethnographically the boundaries between humans and machines. Bringing cultural anthropology into conversation with science and technology studies (STS) and feminist critiques of science, it takes the relations among knowledge production, technological production and subject production to be a crucial area of anthropological research.

Callon, Michel. 1986. 'The Sociology of an Actor-Network: The Case of the Electric Vehicle', in *Mapping the Dynamics of Science and Technology*, ed. M. Callon, J. Law and A. Rip. New York: Macmillan.

Downey, Gary Lee. 1992a. 'Agency and Structure in Negotiating Knowledge', in *How Classification Works: Nelson Goodman among the Social Sciences*, ed. Mary Douglas and David Hull, Edinburgh: Edinburgh U. P.

——1992b. CAD/CAM Saves the Nation?: Toward an Anthropology of Technology, *Knowledge and Society* 9, forthcoming.

——1993. 'Steering Technology through Computer-Aided Design', in *Managing Technology in Society: The Approach of Constructive Technology Assessment*, ed. Arie Rip, Tom Misa, and Johan Schot. Forthcoming.

Ortner, Sherry. 1984. Theory in Anthropology since the Sixties, *Comparative Studies in Society and History* 26(1):126-66.

Pelto, P.J., M. Linkola and P. Sammollahti. 1968. The Snowmobile Revolution in Lapland. *J of the Finno-Ugric Soc.* 69:1-42.

Pelto, Pertti and Ludger Muller-Wille. 1972. 'Snowmobiles: Technological Revolution in the Arctic', in *Technology and Social Change*, ed. H. Russell Bernard and Pertti J. Pelto. New York: Macmillan.

Sahlins, Marshall. 1976. *Culture and Practical Reason*. Chicago: U. of Chicago.

Schneider, David M. 1968. *American Kinship: A Cultural Account*. Englewood Cliffs, N.J.: Prentice-Hall.

——1969. 'Kinship, Nationality, and Religion in American Culture: Toward a Definition of Kinship', in *Forms of Symbolic Action*, ed. Victor Turner, Proceedings of the 1969 Annual Spring Meeting of the American Ethnological Soc. Washington, D.C.: American Ethnological Soc.

Sharp, Lauriston, 1952. 'Steel Axes for Stone-Age Australians', in *Human Problems in Technological Change: A Casebook*, ed. Edward Spicer, New York: Russell Sage Foundation.

Teich, Albert H., ed. 1990. *Technology and the Future*, New York: St. Martin's.

White, Leslie A. 1949. *The Science of Culture. A Study of Man & Civilization*. New York: Farrar, Strauss & Giroux.

ON LOW-TECH CYBORGS

David J. Hess

What is a cyborg? Let me begin with what may appear to be an ingenuous answer. I am watching a video of *The Terminator* on my TV. I don't know a good definition of the "cyborg," but I can point to Arnold Schwarzeneggar and say, "Now *that's* a cyborg." Unlike R2D2, the cyborg looks like a human being. The cyborg is a symbol of news on the cultural landscape; it is a metaphor of the possibilities engendered by the events of biotechnology and artificial intelligence.

Although like R2D2 the cyborg is still only imaginary, many people live protocyborg lives as they commute on electronic highways, carry on virtual romances, and work out in brain gyms. The future, so it is said, promises an ever-deeper relationship with the machine. The prophets of technotopia dream of a day when our descendents may rewrite evolution by shuffling off their mortal coils and downloading onto some immortal silicon circuitry. At the other extreme, in the planet-of-the-cyborgs version such as the *Terminator* movies, the docile Tonto machines turn Frankenstein and provide yet a new variant of what Langdon Winner has called the "technics out-of-control" theme (1977). In cyberfilms and sci fi novels a popular culture oscillates between fascination and fright when imagining the impending new self and society.

The cyborg, then, is part of a popular mythology, part of the stories we (we?) tell ourselves. The cyborg also is itself a narrative with its own origin story. For example, I am sitting in a café in Gotham City with a colleague whom I shall call the cyborg anthropologist. He gives me a classic, originary definition of the cyborg: it is any "homeostatic system functioning unconsciously." The definition is a modified form of one that appears in Clynes and Kline (1960; Gray 1993). The mid-twentieth century understanding of the cyborg strikes me as typical of its temporal culture; the definition emphasizes closed systems that function in terms of feedback, equilibrium, and homeostasis. As I have argued elsewhere, those features of modernist thinking appeared across a number of disciplines, from Pavlovian physiology and the evolutionary synthesis to functionalist social theory and neoclassical economics (Hess 1994: ch. 4).

At different times depending on the discipline the modernist scientific style has often been replaced by open systems and principles of self-organization. One example is the transition in cybernetics to the "second-order cybernetics" of chaos/complexity theory or nonlinear equations in which observer/observed relations, self-reference, and self-organization become part of the models (Heims 1991: 283). Hollywood also seems to recognize this transition in the second of the *Terminator* movies, which contrasts the old, organic-mechanical cyborg with a new, holographic version that is capable of self-organization. Perhaps, then, the very word "cyborg" is already too low-tech to serve as an appropriate symbol of postmodern technoculture. Would some other image be more appropriate, say, the holorg?

Thinking about the cyborg/holorg in this historical manner is interesting, but it should not result in missing how the new narratives of cyborgs/holorgs reinvent much that is very old. For example, I see in *Terminator II* the same old Calvinist story of the good guys and bad guys of the old Westerns and cops-and-robbers movies. There are some changes, but the changes are little more than minor morphings in a well-worn cultural text. The good-guy cyborg is a biker, and the bad-guy holorg is a cop, but the familiar dichotomous moral system remains in place. The cyberfilm also retells the same old story of gendered power relations, for although the woman and her son are fairly strong characters, ultimately they are dependent on the male cyborg. I also see in the movie the same old tale of the Lone Ranger and Tonto, a story about American culture's fundamental problem with the acceptance of ethnic or racial difference. The sidekick Tonto is now a superhuman cyborg, and the great Lone Ranger is reduced in stature to a relatively powerless boy, who nevertheless still has better control over the language. *Terminator II* might be read as revealing white America's insecurity in a multicultural society: the cyborgetic Tontos emerge strong and powerful, but the movie also ends by throwing, quite literally, the cyborgs into the great melting pot.

Notwithstanding all the problems of *Terminator II,* I am intrigued by the possibility of positing different generations of the idea of a cyborg. By playing with the old and the new within the concept of the cyborg, it becomes possible to carnivalize the cyborg by asking how every age has its mythical figures that transgress the boundaries it creates between the human and nonhuman, culture and nature. Think of the hermetic animated statues of the ancient world, or the morphing god Zeus who could reproduce Athena parthenogenetically. The people with whom I did my fieldwork in Brazil looked back only to the last century, when the Spiritualist mediums were understood through mechanical metaphors such as the "celestial telegraph." In the nineteenth century there were many protocyborgs; my favorite is Poe's "Man That Was Used Up." Do we ask, after James Boon (1982), "Other times, other cyborgs?" or do we speak of events on the technobiocultural landscape? What is at stake in these two pathways to an anthropology or cultural studies of the cyborg?

Part of what is at stake is the reflexive issue of who is to be included and excluded in the invention of a social and cultural studies of the cyborg. I am still sitting in the café in Gotham City, and I am asking myself that question. Most of my own work is on the cultural politics of controversies between scientists and their heterodox Others, such as Brazilian Spiritists or American New Agers. My cybertribes are fairly low-tech. I think, to borrow a phrase, I have cyborg envy (Dumit 1991, Stone 1992). At best, I think I can only be a low-tech cyborg anthropologist.

The hi-tech cyborg anthropologist offers me another definition: any identity between machine and human or any conflation of the machine/human boundary. I think of myself sitting in a psychometry session holding a watch that one of the mediums has given me. I am supposed to fuse with the watch, which in turn conveys psychic information about its owner, but I do not feel any secret knowledge entering my consciousness. Apparently this fusion of identity between me and the machine is not taking place. Instead, I think only of a time when my father told me he visited a psychic, and the psychic told him to look under the third step in his basement stairs because she sensed tragedy there. My father went home and discovered that the stair was loose. If he had stepped on it the wrong way, he might have fallen through. I start to talk about steps, and I describe an image I am having of my paternal grandparents' old brick row house in Lancaster County. I tell the medium to check the steps in her house because they are loose. The medium is shocked at the accuracy of my description of her house, and she says, "You must be an old hand at this." I nod knowingly, as if I have the gift, the power. I may be a low-tech cyborg but I'm psychometric. I am a cyberpsychic, or, to borrow (and distort) a phrase from Donna Haraway (1991), I am a cyborg *and* a god(dess).

I am back in Gotham City, thinking again about the definitions I now have of the cyborg. I think about how almost everyone in urban societies could be seen as a low-tech cyborg, because they spend large parts of the day connected to machines such as cars, telephones, computers, and, of course, televisions. **I ask the cyborg anthropologist if a system of a person watching a TV might constitute a cyborg**. (When I watch TV, I feel like a homeostatic system functioning unconsciously.) I also think sometimes there is a fusion of identities between myself and the black box. I think back on the fusions of identities as I watched TV in Brazil with a Brazilian anthropologist and two Indians (as Native Brazilians are called in Portuguese). For the Indians, it is their first trip to Rio and to a big city. I am watching the Brazilian anthropologist watch the Indians watch TV. The Indians are watching the two White Men watch TV. The Brazilian anthropologist is watching the three outsiders—the gringo and the two Indians—watch TV. We are all watching an Indian, who is also the elected federal representative from the Rio area, give a bold speech critical of the military regime. The Brazilian anthropologist explains to the Indians more about the national government, and he in turn asks me for my opinion and the Indians for their opinion. We all exchange views. The boundaries between informant and anthropologist are completely muddled. Renato Rosaldo (1989) has compared the Lone Ranger and Tonto to the anthropologist/informant relationship, but in this setting we are all slipping back-and-forth between the Lone Ranger and Tonto. We are all anthropologists *and* informants.

I am in a classroom in upstate New York watching a video on the Kayapó in which Terry Turner stars as the anthropologist. I am having my students keep an inventory of all the forms of technology and related material culture that they see in the video. Later, we make a list and form a typology in which we separate the technologies of destruction from the technologies of empowerment: the technopreterite and the technoelect. The students, of course, are only interested in the lip plugs. They want to know everything about lip plugs, such as how do they kiss with lip plugs? We discuss the role of the lip plugs, war clubs, body paint, feathers, and other traditional material body culture in the gathering at Altamira. The bodily ornaments seem to allow the Indians to transgress nature and culture, animal and human, thing and being. They, too, are low-tech cyborgs.

Yet, the gathering itself at Altamira is transgressing boundaries of its own; it is eliding the conventions of ritualized speeches, staged warfare, political demonstration, and media event. It is both a gathering of the tribes and an opportunity for international sound bites with Sting on the scene to prop up the ratings. The Kayapó seem equally comfortable with camcorders and lip plugs, with television cameras and war clubs. Yet, the television cameras and camcorders also transform the lip plugs and war clubs. The objects are both traditional material culture, some perhaps with magical powers, and props that empower them in a mediated protest. The low-tech lip plugs are simultaneously high-tech media props.

I am on the Champs Elysées in a huge music and book store, the European equivalent of Tower Records. There are signs everywhere about the latest new sensation, an Aboriginal rock group from Australia. There is a place where I can go to sample the music. I put the headphones on my head. The cord to the headphones disappears through a hole in the floor and I become part of the black box apparatus. I listen to the music and wonder if this "world music" is the music of the future (see Feld 1991). During the 1960s and early 1970s, the rock musicians sang of how we had to get ourselves back to the garden. In those days, nature and the natural were good. Then, punk, new wave, and rap music patterned the singer and the songs on the metaphors and rhythms of the machine. Rock went cyborg. Now, Native peoples are marketing their paintings, sculptures, literature, and music to the world. Once again, there is an elision of boundaries: the art of the "nature folk" is blending the imagery of hi- and low-tech; **the people of the garden become part of the machine** (Marx 1964). How will cyborg anthropology write this curious hybridization of low- and hi-tech, garden and machine, coopted empowerment and empowering cooperation?

I am in upstate New York at a gathering of artists. I am talking with an author, a White Man. When he finds out that I am an anthropologist, he tells me that he is a bit of a "shah-man." This shaman—yet another example of the low-tech cyborg—is wearing a tie with a Cashinahua design on it, and he is telling me he is interested in Cashinahua shah-manism. He has never heard of Ken Kensinger (1973), a local anthropologist who specializes in Cashinahua shamanism, but he knows enough to correct me when I say the word "shay-man."

The White Man suddenly shape-shifts and stands twenty-feet above me. His penis flies away and he becomes three sisters, then he turns into a monster that reminds me vaguely of the Jolly Green giant. "You should say shah-man, not shay-man," he tells me in a deep yo-ho-ho voice that booms down from above. "If you say `shay-man' it suggests that you think there is something shameful about it." He then explains to me that a dream is the same as a vision. He tells me he speaks an Iroquois language and knows a lot about shah-manism everywhere. In cultures throughout the world, he tells me, Native peoples make no distinction between the words for "dream" and "vision." "I'll bet you didn't know that," he tells me. Suddenly he has downsized and he is just a White Man again. In cultures throughout the world? I ask my Lone Ranger-Tonto. Yes, in cultures throughout the world, the New Age shah-man tells me.

I am standing in my bedroom. I look back to my bed and see my body asleep; I have become a shaman on an out-of-body voyage. I look into the mirror and see I have become a coyote. I see next to my bed a book by Stephen LaBerge (LaBerge and Rheingold 1990), a psychologist at Stanford University who has written both scholarly articles and popular books on lucid dreaming, **the low-tech version of virtual realities.** In the scientific pecking order, lucid dream researchers are slightly to the left of dream researchers, who are slightly to the left of sleep researchers, and so on, if "left" can be taken as a metaphor of the un- or nonscientific (as it has so often been during the years of New Right ascendancy). In the essays published in the hybrid newsletter/journal of the lucid dream researchers, scientific discourse constantly slips off into ancient Tibetan wisdom or Western mysticism. Much like Spiritists in Brazil and New Agers in the United States, the boundaries between science and nonscience, Western and non-Western, erudite and popular, seem to be transgressed with ease in this borderline area of scientific inquiry. I meditate on these science-religion syncretisms and their China-box power-knowledge matrices. I watch as Western dream researchers encompass non-Western practices in their scientific discourses, and in turn mainstream psychologists replicate the maneuver on the lucid dream researchers, and in turn social scientists and culture critics—

My anthropological meditation on the book is interrupted. The Lone Ranger has just ridden into my bedroom. Silver rears up, but the Lone Ranger does not have to duck his head because the walls and ceiling of my room have disappeared. Before I have time to recognize the inconsistency, the Lone Ranger takes aim at me with his automatic weapon. Out of the corner of my eye I see in the mirror that I have shape-shifted again; I am Tonto with an apple balanced on my head. The Lone Ranger commands, "Hold still, Tonto!" I feel a breeze as the apple splits over my head, just as the bad-guy cyborg split in *Terminator II*. The William Tell Overture sounds and the Lone Ranger shouts, "Hi-yo, Silver!" and rides off into the sunset.

I am sitting after dark in a meeting in a hybrid conference of activists and scholars who are interested in non-Western and alternative science and technology. White Man is talking about non-Western concepts of ecology and the environment. He is critical of Western society and its energy-guzzling ways, and he finds in non-Western cultures a source of inspiration for ideas of what We have to do if We are going to save the planet. Black-Woman interrupts and interrogates him about his use of the word "We." She wants to know more about his positionality. White Man talks about how he has a garden around his house and how he always liked nature as a boy. Black Woman is not impressed and pulls out her automatic weapon. Native American Woman, until then a Tonto sitting silently at her side, joins her, and White Man begins to look for cover. Believing that I may be a White Man in this episode, I just sit there and lay low.

I am sitting in the Dean's suite at Cyborg Polytechnic. There are no mirrors, but I have a feeling that I have morphed again and am no longer a White Man. I may be a woman of color, perhaps from a far-away country such as Brazil. I am talking to a room full of White Men who are all Very Important People from Corporations With a Lot of Money. If I had thought about it, I might have said that the meeting is an example of the new pattern of university-industry relations that are emerging in our post-something world. (If I had thought about it some more, I might have remembered David Noble's lesson [1977] that similar relations have been going on since at least the founding moments of the nation's first engineering school.)

The Dean's office has lined up a series of professors from Cyborg Tech to explain to the Very Important People how our curriculum is preparing students to go work for them in the global economy. If they are happy, they might give us money. I am their Tonto for the session on multiculturalism. What is multiculturalism? I don't know a good definition but I can point to the meeting I am in and say, "Now *that's* multiculturalism." **It is a word for a complex series of negotiations located somewhere between, on the one side, neoTaylorist technologies of the Total Quality Management and diversity management and, on the other side, age-old radical struggles for social justice.** (At Cyborg Tech, TQM has already been embraced, digested, and reconstituted as TQE, or "Total Quality Education." A year later "downsizing" is in.) The session goes well as long as I talk about how We (We?) are training young cyberneers to work in the global economy. "Yes," says one of the White Men, "we need people like you to show our students what it's like to do business in other countries. I've been to Latin America and the Middle East," he adds, shaking his head knowingly.

Then I make a strategic mistake. I shift the topic to multiculturalism at home. I describe how by the year 2000 only twenty percent of the entering members of the workforce in the United States will be native-born White Men (Johnston and Packer 1987).

"Twenty percent!" one of the White Men repeats as he pulls out his automatic weapon, "That can't be true!" Denial, I think, the first of the stages of death and dying.

Another White Man says, "Yes, it is. I've heard that statistic somewhere else." In other words, not from me ...

"What are we going to do about it?" the first White Man asks.

I talk about how We (We?) need to prepare students to be able to work with people from diverse ethnic groups and to prepare men and women to work with each other, because different groups often have often different cultural assumptions about communication, values, and so on. "Wait a minute!" one White Man says, "I work in a big corporate headquarters with men and women, blacks and whites and Hispanics and Orientals, Americans and foreigners, and we're all just people." I begin to explain research on intercultural communication and gender and communication, not to mention cultural anthropology, when another of them interrupts me and says, "You just don't get it! We treat everyone the same." Another says, "You just don't understand! We're all just individuals!" He pulls out his automatic weapon, and the other White Males follow suit. I begin to look for cover. The Dean intervenes, throws a lasso around my neck, and begins to drag me offstage. The White Men all rotate their heads in unison, raise their hands in unison, and wave in unison as they say, in a unison voice several octaves lower than anything I'd ever manage to utter, "Hasta la vista, baby!"

I feel myself, a lasso-human cyborg (my final morphing as a low-tech cyborg), being dragged off the stage. My time is already up although I have more to say. I am thinking about how I could say that their very mode of responding proves the point I was trying to make. If they were women or from Brazil (or both), their communication style would probably have been more "high context" and less confrontational, perhaps more like my own hybrid style that is the result of a life of crossed cultures. But it is already too late. As I am dragged out of the room, I hear one of the White Men repeat, "Twenty percent of the workforce by the year 2000! What are we going to do about it?" I am thinking about a cartoon I read as a child. The Lone Ranger and Tonto are surrounded. The Lone Ranger says to Tonto, "Well, Tonto. We're surrounded by Indians and it looks like this time we're really done for." Tonto looks at the Lone Ranger and says, "What you me 'we', Qui-no-sabe?"

Acknowledgements: My thanks to Gary Downey, Joe Dumit, Chris Gray, and Mac Intosh for their comments.

References

Boon, James 1982 *Other Tribes, Other Scribes*. Cambridge: Cambridge University Press.

Clynes, Manfred, and Nathan Kline 1960 "Cyborgs and Space." In this volume.

Dumit, Joseph 1991 "Cyborg Anthropology: Brain-Mind Machines and Technological Nationalism." Paper presented at the annual meeting of the American Anthropological Association.

Feld, Steven 1991 "Voices of the Rainforest." *Public Culture* 4(1): 131-40.

Gray, Chris Hables 1993 "The Culture of War Cyborgs: Technoscience, Gender, and Postmodern War." *Research in Philosophy and Technology*. Vol. 13, pp. 141-63.

Haraway, Donna 1991 "A Cyborg Manifesto." *Simians, Cyborgs, and Women*. New York and London: Routledge.

Heims, Steve 1991 *The Cybernetics Group*. Cambridge: MIT Press.

Hess, David 1995 *Science and Technology in a Multicultural World: The Cultural Politics of Facts and Artifacts*. New York: Columbia University Press.

Johnston, William, and Arnold Packer 1987 *Workforce 2000*. Indianapolis, Ind.: Hudson Institute, and Washington, D.C.: U.S. Department of Labor.

Kensinger, Kenneth 1973 "*Bainsteriopsis* Usage Among the Peruvian Cashinahua." In Michael Harner (ed.), *Hallucinogens and Shamanism*. Oxford: Oxford University Press.

LaBerge, Stephen, and Howard Rheingold 1990 *Exploring the World of Lucid Dreaming*. New York: Ballantine.

Marx, Leo 1964 *The Machine in the Garden*. New York: Oxford.

Noble, David 1977 *American by Design*. New York: Knopf.

Rosaldo, Renato 1989 *Culture and Truth*. Boston: Beacon.

Stone, Alluquère Roseanne 1992 "Virtual Systems." In Jonathan Crary and Sanford Kwinter (eds.), *Incorporations*. *Zone*. Vol. 6. New York: Zone Books.

Winner, Langdon 1977 *Autonomous Technology*. Cambridge, Mass.: MIT Press.

L 5.5

"Perhaps Images at One with the World are already Lost Forever"

Visions of Cyborg Anthropology in Post-Cultural Worlds

Sarah Williams
with the collaboration of Marjan Lousberg
and Mark McGuire[1]

At the end of Jean Rouch's film, *Margaret Mead: A Portrait by a Friend*, Mead has led us and Rouch, with his camera running, from her office, through the American Museum of Natural History, to Central Park. There, Rouch asks Mead a final question, "What will happen with anthropology in the future?"[2]

"If we have a future," Meads responds, dressed and posed as we see her here, "there will be lots for anthropologists to do. You see first we've rescued vanishing cultures. Then we used anthropology as a laboratory. And now the next step is building new cultures, new cultures for ourselves or if we have space colonies. For instance, you see anthropologists ought to be able to say more about how you pick such a population for a space colony." Mead tells us that she thinks the population for a space colony should include individuals from several generations. Why? With a chuckle Mead tells us she would like to go.

It is this image of Margaret Mead and this imagination of, to use Sandra Harding's term, a *successor science* of anthropology that cloaks (literally and figuratively) this photo-essay.[3] I'm using the figure of Margaret Mead-with-cape to cloak the anxieties and promises of anthropology in an age of global culture and unprecedented human terrestrial movements.[4] For rather than the creation of human culture in alien outer spaces or exotic third worlds, I've created this image of Mead as a paper doll to cloak anthropology with the cultural stereotypes of culture itself. Appropriately enough this image personifies Derek Freeman's caricature of Mead as "the goddess of American cultural anthropology" while, simultaneously, it builds new cultural possibilities.

This work is related to the visions of cyborg anthropology originally presented at an American Anthropology Association Meeting and titled: "Technoscope: Visual Media as Anthropological Prosthetic."[5] As a technology for, and, from an evolutionary perspective of, pleasure and control, vision represents adaptive limitations and extensions of human imagery. This photo-essay, which consists of scanned and manipulated images from ethnographic films and anthropological texts, deliberately attempts both to anthropomorphize the technological extension of our vision and to alienate *human* agency relative to visual media. Thus, as an imagination of a particular type of anthropology, a cyborgic anthropology, this work critically reflects the technologies it empowers and, perhaps like all anthropology, becomes its own prosthesis.

The following images are intended to give us visions of some dangers, pleasures and promises of human and cyborg subjectivities. Derived from images that have considerable popular culture currency, these reconstructive and composite visions explore the relationship of visual media to anthropology, specifically the ways in which visual media become anthropological prosthetics, become extensions of the technologies of human sight and its interpretive powers. In short, these images mess with the efficacy of culture itself. My purpose is to mirror through quotation, juxtaposition and distortion some ways in which visual media not only represent cultural meaning but recreate particular embodiments of its power.[6] To signal this recognition that that hallmark of anthropology, that distinguishing interpretive technology of humanity—culture—not only mirrors the recursivity of its anthropological definition, but also can revision the humanity it mirrors, I suggest the term post-cultural. Simon During's formulation of the post-cultural articulates well the spirit of my work. In his theoretical resolution of the paradox and irresolution of post-colonial identity politics in New Zealand/Aotearoa During refers to post-culturalism variously as an event, a program or a mode of analysis that productively remembers the cultural meanings of cultural contact. "When one accepts that the construction of a non-modern cultural identity is the result of interaction between colonizer and colonized; when one celebrates the productive energy of mutual misrecognitions and forgettings then one enters post-culturalism."[7]

My title quotes from Wim Wenders' narrative in *Tokyo-Ga* because in his film, like in this photoessay, images at one with the world appear lost forever.[8] Images in each are used to celebrate the productive energy and ethnographic poingancy of mutual misrecognitions and forgettings. Wenders searches for, but cannot find, the

Japan of Yasujiro Ozu's classic films. Yet the images of Ozu's Japan once appeared so very real. This is not because of what they represented, but because of how Ozu's cinematic images once were seen. We no longer can see as Ozu did. Confronting this dilemma in *Tokyo-Ga*, another contemporary filmmaker, Wernor Herzog, tells us that he would like to go into outer space with his camera because there are no more images here. There is nothing left on earth to fascinate the human gaze.

I showed clips of Rouch's and Wenders' videos to a film studies colleague, Thierry Jutel. His response to the juxtaposition articulates the relationship between cinematic and human representational crises I wanted to recreate. "I can't help thinking that going into outer space is also searching for a reverse shot, for a position from where all systems of representation would be brought to a closure so that the demand/need/
desire for the duality of the image—point of view/object—could be replaced by the paradoxical emergence of the cosmos as image without point of view."[9]

A comparison between Herzog and Mead is difficult to resist. Both are explicit about the human limitations of anthropological and anthropomorphic perspectives. Both seek post-anthropological points of view. However, whether exhibited by a filmmaker or an anthropologist, it is too simple to risk identifying cyborg subjectivity simply with the stuff of science fiction fantasy or the space race. Something is going on here—more, and other than, a human quest for escape into outer space and machined environments. Indeed, the cyborg visions of the following pages suggest why anthropological images—images at one with the world—are lost forever, while the vision quest of the west goes on and on and on.[10]

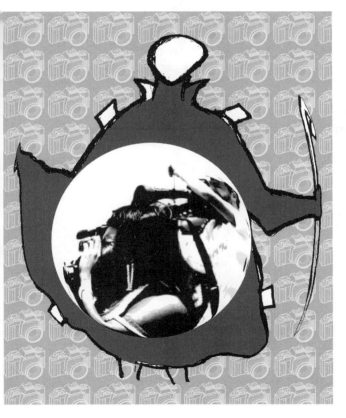

This image was created from the cover of *Colonial Situations*, volume seven in the History of Anthropology series edited by George Stocking.[11] This image, like the many other images of reflexive and indigenous film making that are currently so popular, can be seen as perpetuating that from which it purports to distance itself. This image on the cover of an academic text published by a United States university press, a text which is a collection of purportedly critical essays on the relationship between anthropology and colonialism, would have us believe that the colonized have joined the colonizer in using visual technology to record culture. But are their visions (or our vision and that of the press, editor or authors) really in alignment? While the indigenous man is using a camcorder, the "real" filmmaker and ethnographer of culture is using a perhaps $40,000, sixteen millimeter "professional" camera

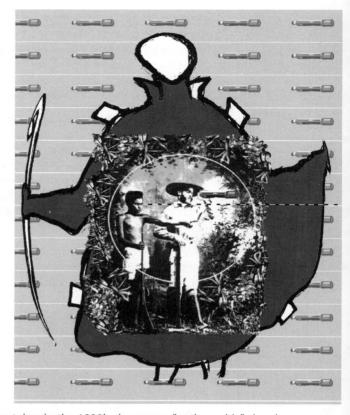

This image, the frontispiece as well as the final image in Curtis Hinsley and Melissa Banta's *From Site to Sight: Anthropology, Photography and Power*, was also intended as a critical redressing of anthropology's use of, and relationship to, photography.[12] However, this image from an unknown photographer taken in the 1890's shows us a "native guide" showing Edward Thompson where to look. Thompson's gaze, unlike the native guide's, is enhanced and amplified by a telescope. And we contemporary viewers join Thompson in using this vision of difference to guide our fulfilment of the scopic drive. It is, of course, simultaneously an epistemophilic drive that human technology (as opposed to sub-human primitive, savage, or native craft) enhances and extends. Contrary to what the text in *From Site to Sight* tells us, there are no "eyes looking back at us" in this photo.

This image, the cover of the recently published collection of essays, *Anthropology and Photography 1860-1920*, illustrates the fixed form of difference according to which anthropology often functions as a discursive practice.[13] This image informs and entertains by representing both our narcissism and our aggression, our delight and our fear. Who is more fascinated and fascinating? The little white girl in white dress and ribbons or the nude black boys? Or perhaps it is us, the viewers who see them, and in our image of them, see ourselves. The gaze of the contemporary anthropological viewer mirrors the photographer's vision of cultural contact between daughter of the empire and "native boys." Indeed, the photo allows us to project and to introject, to recognize and to disavow, to be absent and oh so present, to master and to defend. In Homi Bhabha's formulation, a fixation such as this reveals the limits of Western representational discourse. The image is a stereotype.[14]

Anthropological imagery such as this conjures the kind of visual exhaustion felt by Wenders and Herzog. And this exhaustion plays itself out in popular cultural critique. Consider how Judith Shulevitz's *Voice Literary Supplement* review of the text extends to the discipline of anthropology itself:

> Anthropology and Photography 1860-1920 *is an anthology of 26 essays by contemporary anthropologists who, a faint embarrassment showing under their technical prose, try to account for the contents of...early plates and prints. From the (admittedly unfair) vantage point of a century or so, the pictures—most of them from the archives of the Royal Anthropological Institutes in London—seem less like windows in to the Other than faithful transcriptions of the sexual obsessions and pictorial conventions of the Americans and Europeans who took them.*[15]

Might the most elegant ethnographic vision of the loss of images at one with the world be Gary Larson's cartoon of "natives" hiding their vcrs and televisions as anthropologists appear on the horizon? The postmodern turn in anthropology makes it quite clear not only that humans have never been modern, but that the cinematic apparatus of anthropology, which is to say the whole litany of binarisms including the point of view/object distinction necessary for man's appearance in the discourse of human sciences, is exhaustive.

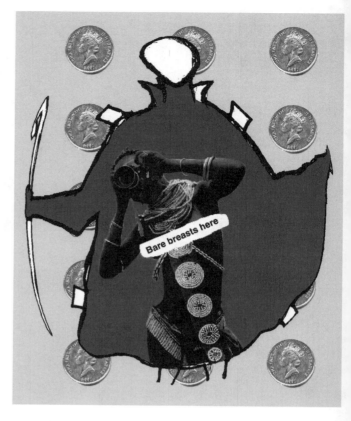

The offensiveness of this image is equal to its intended use-value. This culturally inauthentic image of a "Turkana girl" telling us "Say cheese before I click" is sold as a postcard in Kenya. Her beads are in the wrong places; they are the wrong color. And cameras are not a traditional, nor a common contemporary article of Turkana material culture. But Turkana—the place—is becoming a tourist destination for those seeking "the final frontier" or "the cradle of mankind."

Let's consider what happens when this image is put into conversation with the reflexive footage of Turkana-woman-with-movie-camera found in the much praised ethnographic (i.e. culturally authentic) film of David and Judith MacDougall, *The Wedding Camels*.

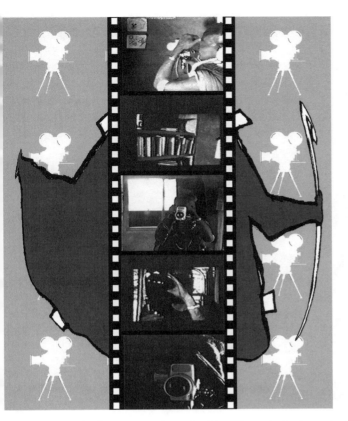

David MacDougall: "By now everyone knows we're here to make films, but we're trying to find out what the Turkana think should be in them." The image accompanying this voice-over is a portrait of the MacDougall family who have posed, in the field, with a group of Turkana. "One of the questions we put to Nganyura is how we should go about filming them." The very next image is of Nganyura holding MacDougall's small son.[16] However, it is not this man who replies. Rather in the next shot we see a woman, breastfeeding a child. It is this unnamed, bare-breasted woman who replies: "There are many good things to film at your house. We might even film your Landrover. Your house and the things in it. The things you own...we'd certainly film them." Next we see a medium close-up shot of a Turkana woman with a camera. It is perhaps a super-eight camera. Again, at least a ten to one cost ratio exists between the visual technology of the indigenous and the anthropological media. In this image the "woman-native-other" is still spectacle. A spectacle that is justified, Thierry reminded me, by our investments in the cinematic/anthropological apparatus. The Turkana woman-with-camera "is a spectacle justified by the fact that the woman is herself involved in the process of spectacularization/specularization/spectralization" ⊕ The next image, a point-of-view shot, shows us what the Turkana woman sees through her lens: books on shelves in the anthropologists' house. However, this use of media to bridge the gap between us and them is all too innocent. This footage, like the soundtrack that accompanies this footage, is a construction that renders invisible this gap and the media that bridges, sustains and maintains this gap. The point-of-view shot is created by the anthropologist's recording of the Turkana woman's images as they are projected for "his" camera—his point of view— in a space and time removed from the film as we see it. ⊕ In the next medium shot we see what we need to see in order for this sequence to do its apparent work. That is, this shot of the woman looking through her camera shows us what we have seen—are seeing—is indeed *her* point of view. This shot "works" because the camera acts as an anthropological prosthetic. It is the agency of this prosthetic that gives meaning to this image, not the agency of the Turkana woman, nor of her camera, nor of the anthropologist, nor of his camera. ⊕ The next image is an invented reverse shot. Again, this shot of anthropologist with movie camera is an image recorded by the woman that has been manipulated: the image was projected and then filmed by the anthropologist with a camera that is not visible. The dark border around this image can be seen as a frame for (and a framing of) the point of view constructed by the cinematic apparatus itself. The 180-degree rule has been broken, the cinematic apparatus lets us believe intimacy between observer and observed has been achieved. ⊕ The final cut completes the narrative movement of the sequence: another shot of the woman-with-movie-camera. Only this second one is a close-up. This shot, meant to convey an emotional intensity, is a classic Hollywood manoeuvre. The reduction of field size creates the illusion of immediacy and intimacy.

These images are
quoted from a
*Cultural Survival
Catalog* and a cover
of an indigenous
media issue of *Visual Anthropology Review.*[17]

*With their war clubs the Kayapo have brought along video cameras. A forest
tribe have jumped an entire industrial revolution and they're using the tools of
high-tech communication. The villagers back in the forest will be able to see
how a hydro-electric dam effects the rivers and forests on which it's built.*[18]

War clubs / video cameras.
Forest tribe / industrial revolution.
Kayapo culture / high-tech communication

Always the same binarisms, the same production of meaning
through difference.

War clubs + video cameras, forest tribe + industrial revolution,
Kayapo culture + high-tech communication = an accounting for
the linear dream of progress when it has been "jumped?"

But. *Do* the villagers back in the forest need video camera images to realize how a
hydro-electric dam effects the rivers and forests on which it's built?

Are these/there other visions of cultural survival? Or does the success of culture as a
human interpretive technology require that not the framer but the framed be
framed?

{ **386**

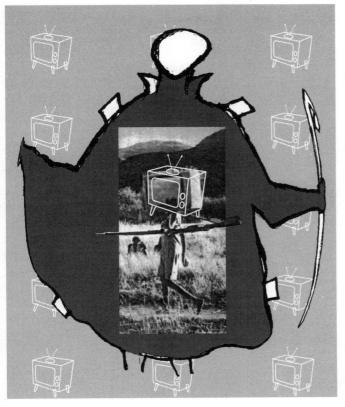

Both colonialist and conservationist politics were simultaneously at work engendering the transition from hunting with guns to hunting with cameras.[19] And on the cover of the spring 1987 issue of *The Society for Visual Anthropology Newsletter* a television replaces an Aboriginal woman's head.[20] A gun underlines the sexualized violence of such a transition. Although we might imagine that the woman in this image is the perfect companion for Max Headroom in a global village networked by the information superhighway, images of cyborgs, like the institution of heterosexual coupling itself, always reveal "an intense crisis in the construction of masculinity."[21] Discourses about humans becoming cyborgs always articulate with human sexual anxieties. And discourses about human sexual anxieties articulate (in Freud as well as Malinowski and in Foucault as well as Rabinow!) the origins of human science itself. In "the Pleasure of the Interface" Claudia Springer makes this point well.

> What is really being debated in the discourses surrounding a cyborg future are contemporary disputes concerning gender and sexuality, with the future providing a clean slate, or a blank screen, onto which we can project our fascination and fears.... It is perhaps ironic, though, that a debate over gender and sexuality finds expression in the context of the cyborg, an entity that makes sexuality, gender, even humankind itself, anachronistic. Foucault's statement that 'man is an invention of recent date. And one perhaps nearing its end' prefigures the consequences of a cyborg future.[22]

It isn't just or only the AIDS crisis that explains why the technological imagination of virtual sex provides a language for us to articulate with words and bodies our "real" sexual desires. In her virtual sex world reader, sex educator and activist Susie Bright suggests why technology times sex equals new possibilities of embodiment.

> I was given an assignment last spring by Elle *magazine to find out how new media/computer technology was going to affect our sex lives, and I spent the first week of my research going, "I don't get it."*
> But once I got past the jargon and saw examples of virtual technology—a type of 3-D make-your-own television experience—I fell in love not with the technology per se, but with the consciousness it provokes.[23]

When visual anthropology extends itself to cyborg imagery, it prefigures the fate of mankind as well as any presumption of normalcy in sexual relations.

In her essay in *Pirating the Pacific: Images of Trade, Travel and Tourism*, Ann Stephen reproduces this photo image, which was labelled: "'Group of Native Boys, Line Islands,' 1870-1900, Kerry and Co, Sydney." And she provides this analysis: "Under a pith helmet the colonial's face is averted concealing his identity, but a thin, almost indiscernible cord, running over his right thigh and under his boot exposes him as the (unidentified) photographer."[24] But truly, it is no trick of anyone's photo-mechanical reproduction technique that renders the females invisible in this image. No, what we see is how others have been seen: the interpretive technologies of nationalism and race intersect normative engenderings of cultural history. From the point of view of cyborg anthropology the intervening signs in this image, the line between man and camera and the presence of invisible females, illustrate the umbilical cord-like relationship between the representational practices of human science and the "human" vision of culture. By granting agency to the non-human, by making alien the apparatus of human culture, cyborg anthropology can "blow-up," can mediate, can interface with the human conceit that renders images at one with the world lost forever.

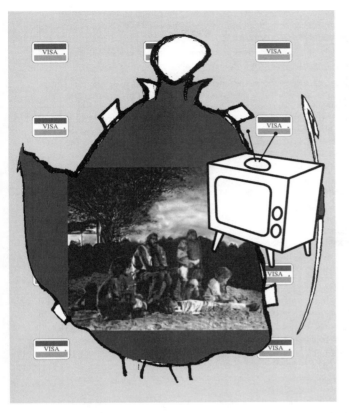

This final image is reconstructed from the introductory image John Tomlinson uses in his text, *Cultural Imperialism*. Tomlinson first uses the image unproblematically to illustrate cultural imperialism.[25] The television is outdoors, viewers are seated on desert sand, the screen is blank: it appears to us that they don't have things quite right. And what's wrong with the picture, given the text that originally accompanied it, is all too easily assessed. Tomlinson tells us this image was on a Christmas card sent by a British television company that supports Walpiri television as a corporate charity. The text that accompanied the image stated that the Walpiri Media Association tries "to defend its unique culture from western culture." "Knowing this," writes Tomlinson, "we will probably read the picture in a certain way, inferring a domination from this image. The picture can thus quickly be grasped as representing cultural imperialism."[26] Indeed, Tomlinson uses the image to introduce his book-length analysis of cultural imperialism. But, he then also suggests that the concept of cultural imperialism, like a "proper" image of us watching television in our living rooms, contains its own imperialism and produces its own alienation.

> [T]he picture invites us to see the television itself as the focus of domination. Its baleful light dominates the scene; all (or most) attention is fixed on it. The accompanying text speaks of 'Dallas and Sale of the Century...beamed to the Australian deserts by satellite.' But is it what the people are seeing that threatens their culture? Does imperialism lie in the contents of foreign programmes? If so, how does this influence work? The screen appears to be blank; we can't see what the people are watching. But doesn't this blankness also signify our incapacity to know how alien texts are read, and the cultural effects they may have? What are these people thinking as we view them, as we might ourselves so easily be viewed, gazing at the shining monster?[27]

This image, and the potential threats of visual media in general to cultural tradition, can appear quite monstrous. "High-tech Media Threatens Traditional Culture." Or how about, "Television—A Retrovirus that Becomes Part of Other Cultures." But what happens when we look at this image and see cyborgs? What kind of cultures are imaginable if we look at ourselves looking at this image and see ourselves as cyborgs?

Margaret Mead prophesized that if humans have a cultural future there will be work for anthropologists. With cyborg vision it is possible to imagine a future for anthropology that would not see us still fixated by, and endlessly redressing, our imagery of others. Rather, in the cultural future prefigured by cyborg vision and post-colonial identity politics "the original, aboriginal TV screen would be neither blank nor peopled with fascinatingly alien images."[28] And misrecognitions and forgettings would be sights of cultural possibilities.

1. The particular reconstructive creations of images in this work are results of collaborations with Marjan and Mark, whose computer graphics practices embody their own cyborg imaginations. More goddess than cyborg, Bridget Sullivan was an inspired paper doll design consultant.

2. Rouch, Jean *Margaret Mead: A Portrait by a Friend* (New York: American Museum of Natural History, 1978).

3. Harding, Sandra *The Science Question in Feminism* (Ithaca, NY: Cornell University Press, 1986).

4. The lead articles in the December 1994 Newsletter of the American Anthropological Association are ethnographically rich regarding the anxieties and promises of contemporary anthropology. In "Rebirth of the Non-Western World" Garrick Bailey writes, "Because anthropology is perceived by many nonwestern people as cultural/historical imperialism and exploitation, the rise of nationalism among nonwestern peoples is resulting in an increasing hostility toward anthropology and anthropological research" (*Anthropology Newsletter* 35(9): 1,4-5). Yet James Peacock begins his President's Report, "Challenges Facing the Discipline," stating, "The 21st century should be anthropology's century: so many of our strengths are needed, so many of our values resonate with the future" (*Anthropology Newsletter* 35(9): 1,5).

5. This original presentation included slides, video and portions of the text used here. The video portion of the presentation was created by Lucien Taylor and his collaboration on that project informs the present work.

6. Careful attention has been given to "quote" images in a way that gives credit to the original creators, yet remakes these images beyond copyright restriction. For example, I appreciate David and Judith MacDougall's permission to "quote" directly from *The Wedding Camels* and acknowledge that these "quotations" might look quite different than they "sounded" when we discussed them in 1988.

7. During, Simon "Waiting fo the Post: Some Relations between Modernity, Colonization, and Writing," *Ariel* 20(4): 31-61 (1989), p. 41.

8. Wenders, Wim *Tokyo-Ga* (1985).

9. The happy accident that located Thierry and myself in adjoining offices has resulted in much collaborative work, the productivity and pleasure of which I hope this chapter acknowledges.

10. Stephen Tyler's "The Vision Quest in the West or What the Mind's Eye Sees," (Journal of Anthropological Research 40(1): 23-40, (1984)) and Luce Irigaray's Speculum of the Other Woman (Cornell University Press: Ithaca, NY, (1985)) explore in acute ways the kinds of desire and power that relations between particular anthropological knowledges and visual metaphors articulate and sustain.

11. Stocking, George (ed.) *Colonial Situations: Essay on the Contextualization of Ethnographic Knowledge* (Madison, WI: University of Wisconsin Press, 1991).

12. Hinsley, Curtis and Melissa Banta *From Site to Sight: Anthropology, Photography and Power* (Washington, DC: Smithsonian Institution, 1986).

13. Edwards, Elizabeth (ed.) *Anthropology and Photography, 1860-1920* (New Haven and London: Yale University Press in association with The Royal Anthropological Institute, 1992).

14. Bhabha, Homi "The Other Question—The Stereotype and Colonial Discourse," *Screen* 24(6): 18-36 (1983).

15. Shulevitz, Judith "Review of Anthropology and Photography 1860-1920," Voice Literary Supplement (December, 1992), p. 5

16. But is this elderly man, Nganyura? The portrait on the cover of Nisa, remember, is not Nisa (Shostak, Marjorie Nisa: *The Life and Words of a !Kung Woman* Cambridge, MA: Harvard University Press, 1981).

17. Cultural Survival Catalog (1990-91); *Visual Anthropology Review* 7(2), (1991).

18. Turner, Terence *The Kayapo: Out of the Forest* (Disappearing World Series film, Michael Beckham, producer/director, 1987)

19. Cf. Haraway, Donna *Primate Visions: Gender, Race, and Nature in the World of Modern Science* (New York: Routledge, 1989).

20. *Society for Visual Anthropology Newsletter* (1987).

21. Springer, Claudia "The Pleasure of the Interface," *Screen* 32(3): 303-323 (1991), p. 318.

22. Ibid., p. 322.

23. Bright, Susie *Susie Bright's Sexual Reality: A Virtual Sex World Reader* (San Francisco, DA: Cleis Press, 1992), p. 9.

24. Stephen, Ann, "Familiarising the South Pacific," *Pirating the Pacific* (Haymarket, Australia: Powerhouse Museum, 1993), p. 68.

25. Tomlinson, John, *Cultural Imperialism* (Baltimore, MD: Johns Hopkins University Press, 1991).

26. Ibid., p. 1.

27. Ibid., p. 1.

28. Ibid, p. 1.

Part 6
The Politics
of Cyborgs

6.1

Split Subjects, Not Atoms;
or, How I Fell in Love with My Prosthesis

Sandy Stone

increasingly i have Problems

Increasingly I have problems working out my theory in advance of writing. This may be the result of spending so much time studying communities that exist in deceptively fleeting manner as lines of text on a computer screen. Discourse in the virtual communities is ephemeral and thoroughly interactive. Also, some of my colleagues might say, trivial. Not much serious work gets done in there, they say, pointing to the screen—which always gives me a chuckle, since with that airy gesture they simultaneously accept the interface metaphor and dismiss its implications.

Thus this will be not so much a linear discussion of work in the field of virtual systems studies as it will be a series of provocations, and at the end there will be not so much a summary as an attempt to thread the provocations, to point out some resonances among them and to hold them in productive tension without allowing them to collapse into anything approximating a univocal account.

Evening in the ACTLab

Evening in the Department of Radio, TV, and Film's Advanced Communication Technologies Laboratory (the ACTLab, whose acronym foregrounds the dramatic basis of prosthetic interaction) finds bunches of young, computer-savvy students batting the keys with abandon. As I watch them, or rather their bodies (since their selves are off in the net, simultaneously everywhere and nowhere, living out fragmentation, multiplicity, and playfulness faster than I can theorize it), it all comes rushing back ...

i Have Bad History

I have bad history: I am a person who fell in love with her own prostheses. Not once, but twice. But that wasn't enough. Then I fell in love with somebody *else's* prosthesis.

The first time love struck was in 1950. I was hunkered down in the dark late at night, on my bed with the big iron bedstead on the second floor, listening absently to the crickets singing, and helping a friend scratch around on the surface of a galena crystal that was part of a primitive radio. We were looking for one of the hot spots, places where the crystal had active sites that worked like diodes and could detect radio waves. Nothing but silence for a long, long time, and then suddenly the earphones burst into life and there was a whole new universe raging in our heads—the ranting voice of Jean Shepherd, boiling into the atmosphere from the massive transmitter of WOR-AM, 250 kilowatts strong and only a few miles away. At that distance we could have heard the signal in our tooth fillings if we'd had any, but the transmitter might as well have been in Rangoon, for all the fragrant breath of exotic worlds it suggested, I was hooked. Hooked on technology. I could take a couple of coils of wire and a hunk of galena and send a whole part of myself out into the ether. An extension of my will, of my instrumentality—that's a prosthesis, all right.

The second time happened in 1955, while I was peering over the edge of a 24X24 recording console. As I stood on tiptoe, my nose just clearing the top of the console, from my age and vantage point the massive thing looked as wide as a football field. Knobs and switches from hell, all the way to the horizon ... there was something about that vast forest of controls that suggested the same breath of exotic worlds that the simple coil of wire and the rickety crystal had. I was hooked again. Hooked on even bigger technology, on another extension of my instrumentality. I could create whole oceans of sound, universes of sound, could at last begin on my life's path of learning how to make people laugh, cry, and throw up in dark rooms. And I hadn't even heard it turned *on*.[1]

But the third time ...

The third time was when Hawking came to town. Steven Hawking, the world-famous physicist, came to Santa Cruz to give a talk at the University. The auditorium was jammed to capacity, and the organizers of the event had accommodated the overflow crowd outside on the lawn. The lawn was a patchwork of bright color, like a medieval fair, with people sitting on blankets and towels, others standing or milling around, and all ears cocked toward the loudspeakers that were broadcasting

Hawking's address across the landscape.

If you haven't seen Steven Hawking give a talk, let me give you a quick background. Hawking has amyotrophic lateral sclerosis, which makes it virtually impossible for him to move anything more than his fingers, or to speak. A friendly computer engineer put together a nice little system for him, a program that displays a menu of words, a storage buffer, and a Votrax allophone generator—i.e., an artificial speech device. He selects words and phrases, the word processor stores them until he forms a paragraph, and the Votrax says it. Or he calls up a prepared file, and the Votrax says that.

So I and a zillion other people are on the lawn, listening to Hawking's speech, when I get the idea that I don't want to be outside with the P.A. system—what I really want to do is sneak into the auditorium, so I can actually hear Hawking give the talk. In practice this proves not too hard. The lecture is under way, security is light—after all, it's a *physicist,* dammit, not the UC Board of Regents, for which they would have had armed guards with two-way radios—so it doesn't take long for me to worm my way into the first row.

And there is Hawking. Sitting, as he always does, in his wheelchair, utterly motionless, except for his fingers on the joystick of the laptop; and on the floor to one side of him is the P.A. system microphone, nuzzling into the Votrax's tiny loudspeaker.

And a thing happens in my head. Exactly where, I say to myself, *is* Hawking? Am I any closer to him now than I was outside? Who is it doing the talking up there on stage? In an important sense, Hawking doesn't stop being Hawking at the edge of his visible body. There is the obvious physical Hawking, vividly outlined by the way our social conditioning teaches us to see a person as a person. But a serious part of Hawking extends into the box in his lap. In mirror image, a serious part of that silicon and plastic assemblage in his lap extends into him as well ... not to mention the invisible ways, displaced in time and space, in which discourses of medical technology and their physical accretions already permeate him and us. No box, no discourse; in the absence of the prosthetic, Hawking's intellect becomes a tree falling in the forest with nobody around to hear it. On the other hand, with the box his voice is auditory and simultaneously electric, in a radically different way from that of a person *speaking* into a microphone. **Where *does* he stop? Where are his edges?** The issues his person and his communication prostheses raise are boundary debates, borderland/*frontera* questions. Here at the close of the mechanical age, they are the things that occupy a lot of my attention.[2]

Flashback: i Was idly Looking

I was idly looking out my window, taking a break from some nasty piece of academic writing, when up the dusty, rutted hill that constitutes my driveway and bastion against the world there abruptly rode, on a nasty little Suzuki Virago, a brusque, sharp-tongued person of questionable sexuality. Doffing her helmet, she revealed herself, both verbally and physically, as Valkyrie, a postoperative m/f transgender with dark hair and piercing black eyes who evinced a pronounced affinity for black leather. She announced that there were things we had to do and places we had to go, and before I could mutter "Science fiction" we were off on her bike.[3]

Valkyrie proceeded to introduce me to a small community of women in the San Francisco bay area. Women's collectives were not new to me; I had recently worked with several groups of women who ran businesses and housed themselves under one roof.[4] But the group to which my new friend now introduced me did not at all fit the model I had learned to recognize. This collective ran a business, and the business was hetero phone sex—not something of which the purist businesswomen with whom I had recently broken bread would have approved.

For reasons best described as kismet, the phone sex workers and I became good friends. We found each other endlessly fascinating. They were intrigued by my odd history and by what I'd managed to make out of it. In turn, I was intrigued by the way they negotiated the minefields of ethics and personal integrity while maintaining a lifestyle I had come to consider unthinkable. In the evenings, after a long interview session and a few Bushmill's, we'd jam about how to eliminate the last link in the phone sex chain: the phone sex worker. Of course, it would be even better to eliminate the client, while keeping his or her money, but we were trying to be practical. So eventually we combined our respective skills and designed the phone sex robot ... but I'm getting ahead of my story.

After a while, we sorted out two main threads of our mutual attraction. From my point of view, **the more I observed phone sex the more I realized I was observing very practical applications of data compression.** Usually sex involves as many of the senses as possible: taste, touch, smell, sight, hearing—and, for all I know, short-range psychic interactions—all work together to heighten the erotic sense. Consciously or unconsciously, phone sex workers translate all the modalities of experience into audible form. In doing so they have reinvented the art of radio drama, complete down to its sound effects, including the fact that some sounds were best represented by *other* improbable sounds, which they resembled only in certain iconic ways. On the radio, for example, the sound men (they were always literally men) represented fire by crumpling cellophane, because to the audience it sounded *more like* fire than holding a microphone to a real fire did.

The sex workers did similar stuff. I made a little mental model out of this: The sex workers took an extremely complex, highly detailed set of behaviors, translated them into a single sense modality, then further boiled them down to a series of highly compressed tokens. They then squirted those tokens down a voice-grade phone line. At the other end of the line the recipient of all this effort added boiling water, so to speak, and reconstituted the tokens into a fully detailed set of images and interactions in multiple sensory modes.

Further, what was being sent back and forth over the wires wasn't just information, it was *bodies*. The majority of people assume that erotics implies bodies; a body is part of the idea of erotic interaction and its concomitants, and the erotic sensibilities are mobilized and organized around the idea of a physical body that is the seat of the whole thing. The sex workers' descriptions were invariably and quite directly about physical bodies and what they were doing, or what was being done to them.

Later I came to be troubled by this because of its relation to a remark of Elaine Scarry's. In a discussion of human experience in her book *The Body In Pain*, she says: "Pain and imagining are the `framing events' within whose boundaries all other perceptual, somatic, and emotional events occur; thus, between the two extremes can be mapped the whole terrain of the human psyche."[5]

By That Time i Had Stopped Thinking

By that time I had stopped thinking of the collective as a group of sex workers, and had begun to think of them in rather traditional anthropological terms as *my* sex workers. I had also moved on to a more complex mode of fieldwork known as participant observation, and was getting an education I hadn't expected. Their experience of the world, their ethical sense, the ways they interpreted concepts like work and play were becoming part of my own experience. I began to think about how I could describe them in ways that would make sense to a casual reader. As I did so, Scarry's remark returned to worry me. It seemed to me that the sex workers' experiential world was organized in a way that was almost at right angles to Scarry's description of the continuum of pain and imagining. The world of the sex workers and their clients, I observed, was not organized along a continuum of pain and imagination, but rather within an experiential field in which *pleasure* and imagination were the important attractors.

Patently, it's not difficult in these times to show how phone sex interactions take place within a field of power by means of which desire comes to have a particular shape and character. In the early days of phone sex that view would have been irrefutable, but things are changing rather fast in the phone sex business; more traditional hetero and hetero-modeled interactions may still get their kick from very old patterns of asymmetrical power, but there seems little doubt that the newer forums for phone sex (as well as other forms of technologically mediated human interaction) have made asymmetrical power relationships part of a much larger and more diverse erotic and experiential toolkit.

This has obvious and interesting implications for studies of community and prosthetics, not to mention social formations; but it's not in any way to imply that a hypothetical "new erotics," if that's what I'm describing, has escaped from the bottomless gravity well of the same power structures within which we find ourselves fixed in position, regardless of what our favorite position is. It does seem to mean, though, that a good many of the people I observe are aware of the effects of those structures, even though as of this writing I see little effort to alter or transcend them. There does appear to be a central and critical reason for this, particularly in regard to erotics, and that is that none of the people I observe who *do* erotics— even those who play with different structures of power—have yet begun to speculate on how erotics really works. So as we approach the inception of the virtual age, it's useful to pay close attention to the structure of pleasure and play, which is certainly not part of communication technology in any necessary way, but which is the heart and soul of prosthetic sociality. Prosthetic sociality implies new and frequently strange definitions of space, volume, surface, and distance; in prosthetic sociality the medium of connection defines the meaning of community.

Let's take one example from the qualities I just mentioned, and look at what's happening to it at the close of the mechanical age.

How Technology Got Surface: An Origin Myth

The traditional approach to representations of technology in popular culture (still instantiated in such venues as *The Sharper Image*) is technology as sleek, gleaming, seamless, efficient. In its very seamlessness lives its specular construction: beginning in the 1930s, the guts of things—the visual apprehension of the way they worked, and the consequent link to a rational comprehension of their function—began to recede inward, and the skin of devices such as toasters and vacuum cleaners became smooth and shiny. The newly constituted "shroud," described as streamlined, futuristic, and decorative, not only conceals the operation of the device (which had been hitherto implicit in its specularity), thus producing the interiorized space of desire, but also, redirects the gaze to a featureless, shiny screen upon which is projected the new meaning and purpose of technological prosthetics in an age in which the physicality of agency is irrelevant. The surface that in Deleuze and Guattari's words becomes deterritorialized, also becomes hypertactile; the ontic quality of touch decouples from the object being touched. Thus the dual character of machinic desire, of cyborg envy, begins with the divergence of the specular (what Foucault called the majestic violence of light) from that which is specifically hidden, which remains mysterious, and mobilizes a phantasmatic interiority in tension with the perspicuous surface. And thus, on one hand, the whole arena of machinic surface becomes organized in relation to the gaze, while on the other, the chthonic interior space of technology is heightened in its mystery and allure. The polished exterior carapace, with its suggestion of brutality,[6] calls into being the soft, vulnerable organs of the technological body. The gendering of such a dual phantasmatic is obvious, although the precise quality of that gendering is not.

At this point we are already far from the Enlightenment ontologization of the relationship between knowledge and perception. With the development of industrial design in consort with strategies of commodification, as meaning moved to the surface of things, machines themselves became spectacle much as the Elizabethan body had been, taking on the qualities of desire that formerly sought their meaning and purpose in body surface—but meaning decoupled in complex and troubling ways from the shape that function had dictated. This worked to create a dual desire, at once for the hypertactility of the smooth surface and also for the mysterious hidden organs that nestled beneath. The shroud, the surface upon which the meaning of technological objects was more firmly projected, became harder, shinier, and more brittle.

But such a clean boundary between exteriority and interiority—not to mention public and private—couldn't exist for long, and in the seventies technology got dirty. Street tech took its place alongside switchblade knives, zip guns, and later, AK-47s, as an expression of marginalization.[7] In *Star Wars*—the first street tech film—it was the *bad* guys who had the shiny, polished equipment, and the good guys who had the dirty, leaking stuff, the stuff with the potential for contamination and infection.

In such fashion electronic prosthetics hits the street. Electronic prosthetics gets dirty, accretes unsavory ideas and people, becomes capable of contamination—raising the boundary issues of meaning control now being debated in industry and government. Foucault, thou shouldst be living at this hour.

A Disembodied Subjectivity

A disembodied subjectivity messes with whereness. In cyberspace you are everywhere and somewhere and nowhere, but almost never *here* in the positivist sense. In the less-virtual environments of everyday life, governmental and regulatory structures work to increase the definition of whereness. Things like phone numbers and addresses increase whereness. In virtual systems theory we call these things location technologies. The purpose of location technology is to halt or reverse the gradual and pervasive disappearance of the socially and legally constituted individual in a society in which the meanings of terms such as distance and direction are subject to increasing slippage. This slippage, of course, doesn't refer only to the physical or geographic, but to other, non-Cartesian modes of location. Freud was one of the first to perform a kind of codification upon this imaginal territory, in that he produced a detailed and perhaps replicable body of knowledge that was concerned with the territory of the unconscious.

More pertinent here is the textual residue of Freud's work—the seeds of what is now called the Diagnostic and Statistical Manual (DSM), the manual of diagnostic criteria for psychological disorders. The DSM is an example of the kinds of location technologies I am talking about, because in the process of defining a psychological disorder it simultaneously produces, organizes, and legitimizes a discursive space that has quasi-Cartesian concomitants. The inhabitant proper to this space is the virtual entity of psychological testing, census taking, legal documentation, telephone numbers, street addresses—in brief, a collection of virtual elements that, taken together, form (in Haraway's terms) a materialized discursivity of their own that we might call the fiduciary subject. It is a way to articulate the (always political) tie between what our society defines as a single physical body and a single awareness of self.

Let's Talk a Bit More about This Coupling

Let's talk a bit more about this coupling between the phantasmatic space that location technology calls into being, and the physical space of pain and pleasure that the human body inhabits. In virtual systems theory the production and maintenance of this link between a discursive space and a physical space is called "warranting." By means of warranting, the political apparatus of government is able to guarantee the production of stable concepts of citizenry. Broadly, the politically intelligible citizen is composed of two parts: one is the collection of physical attributes that Judith Butler and Kobena Mercer call the culturally intelligible body;[8] the other is the collection of virtual attributes that, taken together, compose a structure of meaning and intention for the culturally intelligible body. Taken together, these two broadly defined elements compose a citizen who is socially apprehensible—who fits the cognitive criteria. It walks like a citizen, it quacks like a citizen ...[9]

A socially apprehensible citizen is a collection of physical and discursive elements. Although the physical elements possess a special and bounded order of reality on account of their particular relationship to the social disciplines of pain and pleasure, the remainder of the citizen—by far the greater part, the part that is also concerned with the production of meaning of the physical part—is discursive. The discursive part of the package, including meaning ascribed to the physical body, is produced by means of inscription, such as legal, medical, and psychological texts. Because so much of such an identity is discursive, it seems reasonable to call it a **legible** body—that is, textually mediated physicality. Legible body displays the social meaning of "body" inscribed on its surface, presenting a set of cultural codes that organize the ways the body is understood and that determine a range of socially appropriate responses.[10]

It is this constellation of fixed relationships that virtual communication prosthetics, instantiated as cyberspace, disrupts so thoroughly.

This Way of Experiencing

This way of experiencing the world raises issues of authority, agency, and the underlying and quite fundamental one of **presence**. In most societies we know, a likely story of the development of authority is that authority was originally grounded in the person of a ruler or several rulers, through their physical presence. Thus agency was proximate—attached to a person. Of course there were ways to delegate power, so that things could get done outside of a head honcho's physical presence. This led to some problems. In order to delegate power it must to some extent be made discursive, turned into something recognizable. The abstract idea of force as an expression of will gets turned into an object that represents force, a little iconic gizmo that reminds people of an absent power. Mimetics and iconics—styles of clothing, heraldic devices, wax seals on documents, badges of authority. Belief gets into the system along with mimesis, because the efficacy of the symbol is backed by practical results: people tend to stay alive longer if they believe in whatever the symbol stands for.

Time passes. Literacy appears, and some time later telegraphs, and then phones. Power is expressed in new ways, as disembodied voices, backed up by a more elaborate system of iconography. Voices are not the only things sent through the wires, other things are sent right along with them: Agency, Icons, Bodies, Desire. Where is Hawking, exactly? Such virtual systems operate on sets of assumptions that are already in place—one of which is that humans act at a distance by delegating their agency to someone or something else that has the freedom to travel out of their sight, and if we follow that agency back far enough, eventually we can trace it to the original human's physical presence, where the buck stops.

If I say that in another way, it comes out that agency is always grounded in a physical body, a process that we might call warranting. But here at the close of the mechanical age and the beginning of the virtual age, warranting is problematic. There is conflict between the technologies of government by which societies have traditionally kept order and the multiple fragmenting entities that political "citizens" are actually becoming. Governments' response to the fragmentation of their subjects is to develop a hypertrophy of location technologies. These work by fixing people in place in a fiduciary sense, by creating a paper trail that attaches to a particularized physical body; for example, social security numbers, passports and street addresses. And of course a citizen can be fixed in place in ways that don't correspond with physical directions or locations, by means such as psychological testing. In the technologized nations there has been a veritable explosion of new ways for governments to keep track of their citizens, abetted in large part by the development of more sophisticated technologies of communication. At the same time, like some wonderful dance in which the movements of both partners are synchronized, some people become harder to track. Not by getting physically shifty, but by **dissolving, fragmenting**—by being many persons in many places simultaneously, by saying "up yours" to warranting, by refusing to be one thing, by *choosing* to be many things. It is this fragmentation and multiplicity that characterize communities mediated by technological prosthetics of presence, and it may explain something of the extent to which in some quarters they are suspect.

Let's Get Back to the Discussion of Work

Let's get back to the discussion of work versus play once again, from the standpoint of computation and instrumentality. Viewing computers as calculatory devices that assist or mediate human work is part of a paradigm that consists of two main elements. The first is a primary **human work ethic**; the second is a particularized view of **computers as tools**. The emergence of the work ethic has been the subject of innumerable essays, but the view of computers as tools has been so totally pervasive among those with the power to determine meaning in such forums as school policy and corporate ethics that only recently has the idea begun to be seriously challenged.

The paradigm of computers as tools burst into existence, more or less, out of the allied victory in World War II (although the Nazis were working on their own computers). A paradigm of computers as something other than number crunchers does not have a similar launching platform, but the signs of such an imminent upheaval are perspicuous. Instead of carrying on an established work ethic, the beliefs and practices of the cultures I observe incorporate a **play** ethic—not to displace the corporate agendas that produce their paychecks, but to complexify them. This is manifest in many of the communities and situations I've been studying over the past few years. It is visible in the northern California Forth community, a group of radical programmers who have adopted for their own an unusual and controversial programming language and have raised it to the level of a spiritual practice; in the CommuniTree community, an early text-based virtual discussion group, which adopted such mottos as "If you meet the electronic avatar on the road, laserblast Hir"; and in the research laboratory of a major computer corporation, where a group of presence hackers created an artificial person who became real enough to become pro tem Lab Director.

The people who play at these technosocial games do not do it out of any specific transformative agenda, but they have seized upon advantages afforded by differences of skill, education, and income to make space for play in the very belly of the monster that is the communication industry. It is in such homely, messy, and undirectly-purposive ways that the foundations for prosthetic community actually get put in place—emerging organically from the highly formalized discourses of computer science and corporate capital, assuming their own shape and purpose, technologically *detourned* by hackers, crackers, smackers, whackers, knackers, and anybody else with a keyboard, a modem, and raw determination, and so ultimately remolded nearer the street's desire.

Producing and inserting an Unruly Play Ethic

Producing and inserting an unruly play ethic like a mutation into the corporate genome is a specifically situated activity, one that is only possible to workers at a certain job level and type. In specific it is only possible to the communities who are perhaps best described as hackers—mostly young, mostly educated, mostly white, and mostly male. They create and use a broad variety of technological prosthetics to manifest novel and promising views of the purpose of communication technology. In particular, because they are thoroughly accustomed to engaging in nontrivial social interactions through the use of their computers, they view comput-ers not only as tools but as loci, places, forums, agoras, arenas—arenas for social experiments, for community and its discourses, for the messy evolution of prosthetic sociality driven by specifically located knowledges, needs, and productions.

This irruptive, ludically based view of community inevitably suggests a multiple view of the state of the art in communication technology. When addressing the question of what's new about prosthetic communication, it's possible to give at least two answers. Let's stick with two for now.

Answer #1: Nothing. The tools of networking are essentially the same as they have been since the telephone, which was the first electronic network prosthesis. In this dispensation, computers are engines of calculation, and their output is used for quantitative analysis. Inside the little box is information. I recently had a discussion with a colleague in which he maintained that there was nothing new about virtual reality. "When you sit and read a book," he said, "you create characters and action in your head. That's the same thing as VR, without all the electronics." Missing the point, of course, but understandably.

Answer #2: Everything. In this dispensation, computers are arenas for social experimentation and dramatic interaction, a type of medium more like public theater, and their output is used for qualitative interaction, dialogue and conversation. Inside the little box are *other people,* and this constitutes the box's most urgent significance.

This Plops Us onto the Threshold of Textuality

This plops us onto the threshold of textuality as the mediator of virtual systems. The interplay of textuality and sociality (as recounted by, e.g., Francis Barker) is a history of progressively ramifying divisions of the social locus of community from a predominantly public space to a congeries of spaces increasingly privatized.[11] The *physicality* of this new privatized space is a link to the *metaphoricality* of a symbolic and psychological private space that is both elicited by and mutually supportive of the physical body. This progressus leads to prosthetic social assemblages—passing through the stages of development of separate interior spaces, and later of rooms within small dwellings, through changes in philosophies of architecture and in methods of carpentry, and pausing at the isolated, privatized individual sitting at a computer terminal—who breaks through the electronic interface into a refigured social space on the other side.[12]

into This Setting of Psychological Privatization

Into this setting of psychological privatization and digital communication technology come some of its most remarkable inhabitants, the people who represent much of the potential market for virtual technologies: hackers, and in particular, interactive gamers.

Interactive gaming has emerged as a primary pursuit of the coming generation of computerkids. It provides the essential attraction of exotic total-immersion visual environments, coupled with the proven thrill of bang-bang-shoot-'em-up action. The production values of arcade-type games, which not long ago began to incorporate realtime dramatic video segments (one of the first was directed by John Dykstra, of *Star Wars* fame), are a significant drive behind technological innovation in multiple-user gaming—and, by extension, in virtual environments. This means that the paradigm of multiple-user interactive gaming will be

part of the experience of prosthetic sociality.

A significant number of young people are spending an increasing proportion of their waking hours playing computer-based games in one form or another, and so far the implications of this trend have yet to be addressed. A major obstacle to this appears to be the feeling on the part of many academics that computer games are beneath serious notice, a situation perhaps best characterized as holding our cocktail party in a house that is already ablaze. Within a short time, the number of hours that a fair number of kids will spend playing computer-based games will exceed the number of hours that they spend watching television. It's entirely possible that computer-based games will turn out to be the major unacknowledged source of socialization *and* education in industrialized societies before the 1990s have run their course.[13]

The designers of these games are among the fiercest of the techno entrepreneurs. Keep in mind that of all the commercial uses bruited about for virtual worlds equipment, multiple-user games are the only commercial application that is currently returning a profit. There will inevitably be more of them. As the kids who use them begin to age, their view of how interaction works—whatever that view is—will be a major factor in shaping electronic community.

Evening in the ACTLab

Evening in the ACTLab finds bunches of young, computer-savvy men (and increasingly, women) batting the keys with abandon. As I watch them, or rather their bodies (since their selves are off in the net), I remind myself that these are the people who are writing the descriptors right there in front of me—writing the computer code that makes the phantasmatic structures of prosthetic sociality. Then they will inhabit the structures they write. These people, not the big system designers, are the architects of virtual community. They remind me of a more familiar example, that of musicians. The social, performative, and technical worlds of music are complexly structured, inhabited by powerful record companies, flacks, lawyers, engineers, and roadies; but the final shapers of the entire *gemut* of the thing are the musicians, because in an irreducible fashion *they are the music*. So it is with the hackers . . . in the instant case, in the anthropological sense, with *my* hackers. And so I wonder, as I watch their intent, excited expressions taking on the electric glow of the screens they face—do they understand what they are doing? **Are they aware of the sheer power in the multiply situated text their flying fingers produce, the power to create worlds, to change lives?**

There is no mandate in our culture to do anything in particular with the powerful technologies we have at our disposal, and information technology in all its wonderful forms is one of those. The game industry suffers from a feedback loop no more and no less pernicious than any other in a market-driven economy, which is that it is very easy and low-risk to go on endlessly making games for the same market. Among the things these games do, many of them denigrate women, either deliberately or offhandedly. Quite a few people, including people of both of the major genders, have tried for quite a long time to bring about even modest change in that regard. They have not been very successful. In large part (though not entirely) this is due to the character and habits of the people who actually program the games. The programmers, who as of this writing are overwhelmingly (99%+) young adolescent or postadolescent males, tend to live their lives as they write their games—with singleminded determination and a very narrow set of goals. Usually they have little in the way of social lives; they don't read books, but occasionally read comics; and they tend to perpetuate extraordinarily immature ideas of personal interaction styles. One of these is the way they relate to women. Women tend to be the same kinds of objects for them in their lives as they are in their games, and this is the heart of the problem of how pernicious the loop is: They don't believe there is a problem, because it's invisible to them. They resist intense questioning. They believe there is no sexism in their games, just as they believe there is no sexism in their lives.

There is a hard reality here. We've gone with explosive speed from a few kids making up games for their friends to a few more kids making up games for millions of other kids. The level of sophistication hasn't changed, but the scale has changed drastically. Ethics haven't kept up—in fact, have never been an issue, since the thing is market-driven and kids as a market are a relatively new phenomenon.

This Loops Back to the Question

This loops back to the question of the ludic dimension. Should things that are so terrifically absorbing and that take up so much waking time—so much precious, irreplaceable waking time—be expected to possess a modicum of invention, to be able to stretch players' imaginations and skills beyond the ability to hit targets and dodge obstacles? (Not that those aren't valuable skills, but they aren't the only valuable skills either.) Should we expect play to be edifying, or on the other hand will kids manage to make anything that comes to hand edifying against all odds? Is the field of interactive games simply a dead loss from the standpoint of sexism and education, something we have to learn to live with as we had to learn to live with the Bomb? In the seats of the powerful, the most successful of the game companies, how is it that the very young, the very talented, don't perceive the incredible power for change that has fallen to them by default? and the hideous consequences of failing to grasp that weapon when it's offered? How very like the hero mythoid, that strange and problematic knot at the heart of so many interactive games.

I got to this point from huddling under the covers with a galena crystal, listening to Steven Hawking, doing phone sex, and incidentally paying attention to how none of those versions of me was unitary or complete. They are all embedded in a particular context—the close of the mechanical age—without which they wouldn't exist. Endings are also beginnings, and the close of the mechanical age is the dawn of the virtual age, in which agency is in such danger of decoupling from politically stable bodies and floating off into the prosthetic never-never that our society's hottest hot buttons have to do with location technology. What does your friendly clerk ask you for when you write a check? Virtual systems are dangerous because the agency/body coupling so diligently fostered by every facet of our society is in danger of becoming irrelevant. Does that mean that virtual systems represent some kind of redemptive nexus, an agonistic force with the potential to subvert the forces that try to gain closure on one small set of permissible descriptions of a politically warranted identity? When all is said and done, it comes down to what is electronic prosthesis good for—

I don't have answers, but I've tried to pose a few questions. I wanted to point out the problematic relationships, in prosthetic community, between architecture and play, physicality and metaphoricality, bodies and selves, whereness and politics, sex and bandwidth, interior and surface and desire. If this has raised questions for you, then I've done my job. I hope to continue the dialogue when we meet, as we inevitably will whether our avatars recognize each other or not, in cyberspace—the troubling and productive space of desire, of play, and most of all, of possibility. Work there, play there, love there—but if you have sex in cyberspace, be sure to always use a modem.

Notes

In studying issues of presence, warranting, and agency, the work of theorists of dramatic interaction vis-à-vis computation, of which Brenda Laurel is an outstanding example, is invaluable. Much of this research would not have been possible without the arguments Laurel presents in *Computers as Theatre* and elsewhere, not to mention some magnificent conversations we've had. My netsurfing buddies in Austin, Paco Xander Nathan and Jon Lebkowsky, have provided more mindfood, as has colleague Dick Cutler. Thanks to Roddey Reid and Sharon Traweek, and to the academic forums that have hosted the performance art that is my chosen method of presenting scholarly work. Donna Haraway is, as always, an éminence not-so-grise in the text.

1. Just a brief caution: The first two events are emblematic rather than specific, national inventions in the sense of being several actual events collapsed in time and other ways modified.

2. All of this, of course, is about the interplay between communication technology, prosthetic community, the human body, and the uses of pleasure. Note also that this expression "borderline/*frontera*" is a reference to Glória Anzaldúa's polysemic and urgently political exploration of the boundary areas between cultures and languages. *Borderlands/La Frontera: The New Mestiza.* (San Francisco: Spinsters/Aunt Lute, 1987).

3. For some reason this sort of thing—having someone barge into my humdrum life and drag me off on some adventure—keeps happening, and I have gotten more good story material in such fashion than I like to admit.

4. This is perhaps the most egregious point of convergence of the multiple research projects I pursue. A more thorough description and analysis of the oddly interdependent issues of lesbian separatism and transgender can be found in A. R. Stone, *Transgression: Tales from the Edges of Identity* (forthcoming).

5. Elaine Scarry, *The Body in Pain: The Making and Unmaking of the World* (New York: Oxford University Press, 1985), pp. 161-180.

6. For example, Robocop, *Star Wars'* Imperial stormtroopers, the robot Maria in *Metropolis*.

7. And, like any marginalization, street tech provided a focus to mobilize a congeries of border cultures, of which cyberpunk is a perspicuous example.

8. E.g., Judith Butler, *Gender Trouble: Feminism and the Subversion of Identity.* (New York: Routledge, 1991); and Kobena Mercer, "Black Hairstyle Politics," *New Formations* 3 (1987).

9. I want to be careful, in making these distinctions, that I don't reify dichotomies already in place. There is always a danger in distinguishing the body from some other collection of attributes linked to the body. I want to be quite clear that the physical/virtual distinction is *not* a mind/body distinction. The concept of mind is not part of virtual systems theory, and the virtual component of the socially apprehensible citizen is not a disembodied thinking thing, but rather a different way of conceptualizing a *relationship* to the human (or, for that matter, the transhuman or posthuman) body.

10. William Gibson was probably the first recent writer to deal with the issue of warranting. In *Neuromancer* (1984), a death in cyberspace meant that the physical body in biological space also died—so there was an implied link between the virtual body (into which term I pack Haraway's "materialized discursivities" that constitute the body in cyberspace) and the convergences of discourses, some of which are of similar nature to the virtual, that constitute the body in physical space—a link powerful enough to carry information that the physical (i.e., biological) body interprets or understands as physical (e.g., sickness and death).

11. See Francis Barker, *The Tremulous Private Body: Essays in Subjection* (New York: Methuen, 1984).

12. In the course of this paper I sometimes organize these developments as a progressus, an ensemble of events that had a beginning and that leads in a particular direction. In doing so, I nod in the direction of Gilles Deleuze and Felix Guattari, Paul Virillo, and Manuel De Landa. But I am large; I contain multitudes. At other times the story is not meant to be teleological at all, because I don't foresee the telos toward which it tends. I may make some suggestions in that regard, but they are suggestions only, and do not

arise from any prophetic vision. I try to leave the prophetic side of things to my academic betters in the same line of work.

13. My use of the term "computer-based" is already becoming an anachronism, since the meanings of culturally defined objects such as television, telephone, cable, and computers, and the boundaries between them, are already in hot debate and considerable flux. Nicholas Negroponte had already pointed out in the late 1970s that there would soon come a time when there would be more MIPS (a measurement of processor speed) in kitchen appliances than in the objects commonly called computers. This prefigures, in part at least, the cultural redefinition, now under way, of these objects. It is driven partly by economics and partly by the effect of ubiquitous technology (technology so familiar as to be culturally invisible) on engineers' interpretations of the boundaries of their specialties, as well as ubiquitous technology's effect on the cultural paradigm of biological-machinic binarism. An exhilarating and problematic time.

Women Prefer A Choice

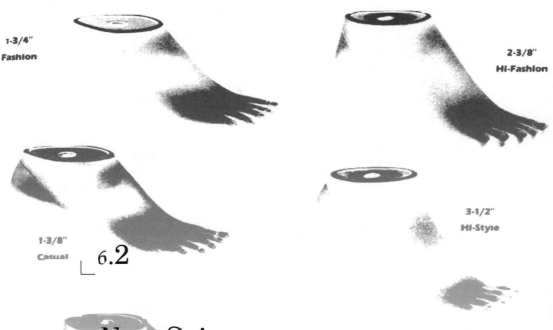

1-3/4" Fashion

2-3/8" HI-Fashion

1-3/8" Casual

3-1/2" HI-Style

⌐ 6.2

New Sciences
Cyborg Feminism and the Methodology of the Oppressed

3/8"

Continental

Chela Sandoval

> We didn't cross the border, the border crossed us
> —Chicana/o Slogan

> If life is just a highway
> Then the soul is just a car
> And objects in the rear view mirror
> May appear closer than they are
> —Meat Loaf

> If we are imprisoned by language,
> then escape from that prison-house requires
> language poets.
> —Donna Haraway

What constitutes "resistance" and oppositional politics under the imperatives of political, economic, and cultural transnationalization?[1] Current global restructuring is effecting the organizational formations not only of business, but of cultural economies, consciousness, and knowledge. Social activists and theorists throughout the twentieth century have been attempting to construct theories of opposition that are capable of comprehending, responding to, and acting back upon these globalizing forces in ways that renegotiate power on behalf of those Marx called the "proletariet," Barthes called the "colonized classes," Hartsock called "women," and Lorde called the "outsiders." If transnational corporations are generating "business strategy and its relation to political initiatives at regional, national, and local levels,"[2] then, what are the concurrent forms of strategy being developed by the subaltern—by the marginalized—that focus on defining the forms of oppositional consciousness and praxis that can be effective under first world transnationalizing forces?

Let me begin by invoking Silicon Valley—that great land of Lockheed, IBM, Macintosh, Hewlett Packard, where over 30,000 workers have been laid off in the last two years, and another 30,000 more await a similar fate over the year to come: the fate of workers without jobs, those who fear for their livelihood. I begin here to honor the muscles and sinews of workers who grow tired in the required repetitions, in the warehouses, assembly lines, administrative cells, and computer networks that run the great electronic firms of the late twentieth century. These workers know the pain of the union of machine and bodily tissue, the robotic conditions, and in the late twentieth century, the cyborg conditions under which the notion of human agency must take on new meanings. A large percentage of these workers who are not in the administrative sector but in labor-grade sectors are U.S. people of color, indigenous to the Americas, or those whose ancestors were brought here as slaves or indentured servants; they include those who immigrated to the U.S. in the hopes of a better life, while being integrated into a society hierarchized by race, gender, sex, class, language, and social position. Cyborg life: life as a worker who flips burgers, who speaks the cyborg speech of McDonalds, is a life that the workers of the future must prepare themselves for in small, everyday ways. **My argument has been that colonized peoples of the Americas have already developed the cyborg skills required for survival under techno-human conditions** as a requisite for survival under domination over the last three hundred years. Interestingly, however, theorists of globalization engage with the introduction of an oppositional "cyborg" politics as if these politics have emerged with the advent of electronic technology alone, and not as a requirement of consciousness in opposition developed under previous forms of domination.

In this essay I propose another vision, wrought out of the work of cultural theorist and philosopher of science Donna Haraway, who in 1985 wrote the groundbreaking work on "Cyborg Feminism," in order to re-demonstrate what is overlooked in current cyborg theory, namely, **that cyborg consciousness can be understood as the technological embodiment of a particular and specific form of oppositional consciousness that I have elsewhere described as "U.S. third world feminism."**[3] And indeed, if cyborg consciousness is to be considered as anything other than that which replicates the now dominant global world order, then cyborg consciousness must be developed out of a set of technologies that together comprise the methodology of the oppressed, a methodology that can provide the guides for survival and resistance under first world transnational cultural conditions. This oppositional "cyborg" consciousness has also been identified by terms such as "mestiza" consciousness, "situated subjectivities," "womanism," and "differential conscious-ness." In the interests of furthering Haraway's own unstated but obvious project of challenging the racialization and apartheid of theoretical domains in the academy, and in the interests of translation, of transcoding from one academic idiom to another, from "cyborgology" to "feminism," from "U.S. third world feminism" to "cultural" and to "subaltern" theory, I trace the routes traveled by the methodology of the oppressed as encoded by Haraway in "Cyborg Feminism."

Haraway's research represents an example of scholarly work that attempts to bridge the current apartheid of theoretical domains: "white male poststructural-ism," "hegemonic feminism," "postcolonial theory," and "U.S. third world feminism." Among her many contributions, Haraway provides new metaphoric grounds of resistance for the alienated white male subject under first world conditions of transnationalization, **and thus the metaphor "cyborg" represents profound possibilities for the twenty-first century** (implica-tions of hope, for example, for Jameson's lost subject which "can no longer extend its protensions and retensions across the temporal manifold."[4] Under cyborg theory, computer "travel" can be understood as "displacing" the "self" in a similar fashion as the self was displaced under modernist dominations). An oppositional cyborg politics, then, could very well bring the politics of the alienated white male subject into alliance with the subaltern politics of U.S. third world feminism. Haraway's metaphor, however, in its travels through the academy, has been utilized and appropriated in a fashion that ironically represses the very work that it also funda-mentally relies upon, and this continuing repression then serves to reconstitute the apartheid of theoretical domains once again. If scholarship in the humanities thrives under the regime of this apartheid, Haraway represents a boundary crosser, and her work arises from a place that is often overlooked or misapprehended under hegemonic understandings.

I have argued elsewhere that the methodology of the oppressed consists of five different technologies developed in order to ensure survival under previous first world conditions.[5] The technologies which together comprise the methodology of the oppressed generate the forms of agency and consciousness that can create effective forms of resistance under postmodern cultural conditions, and can be thought of as constituting a "cyborg," if you like, or at least a "cyber" form of resis-tance.[6] The practice of this CyberConsciousness that is U.S. third world feminism, or what I refer to as a "differential postmodern form of oppositional consciousness" has also been described in terms that stress its motion; it is "flexible," "mobile," "diasporic," "schizophrenic," "nomadic" in nature. These forms of mobility, however, align around a field of force (other from motion itself) which inspires, focuses and drives them as oppositional forms of praxis. Indeed, this form of consciousness-in-opposition is best thought of as the particular field of force that makes possible the practices and procedures of the "methodology of the oppressed." Conversely, this methodology is best thought of as comprised of techniques-for-moving ener-gy—or better, as *oppositional technologies of power:* both "inner" or psychic tech-nologies, and "outer" technologies of social praxis.

These technologies can be summarized as follows: 1) What Anzaldua calls "la facul-tad," Barthes calls semiology, the "science of signs in culture," or what Henry Louis Gates calls "signifyin" and Audre Lorde calls "deep seeing" are all forms of "sign-reading" that comprise the first of what are five fundamental technologies of this methodology. 2) The second, and well-recognized technology of the subaltern is the process of challenging dominant ideological signs through their "de-construction:" the act of separating a form from its dominant meaning. 3) The third technology is what I call "meta-ideologizing" in honor of its activity: the operation of appropriating dominant ideological forms and using them whole in order to trans-form their meanings into a new, imposed, and revolutionary concept. 4) The fourth technology of the oppressed that I call "democratics" is a process of locating: that is, a "zeroing in" that gathers, drives, and orients the previous three technologies, semiotics, deconstruction, and meta-ideologizing, with the intent of bringing about not simply survival or justice, as in earlier times, but egalitarian social relations, or, as third world writers from Fanon through Wong, Lugones, or Collins have put it,[7] with the aim of producing "love" in a de-colonizing, postmodern, post-empire world. 5) Differential movement is the fifth technology, the one through which, however, the others harmonically maneuver. In order to better understand the operation of differential movement, one must understand that it is a polyform upon which the previous technologies depend for their own operation. Only through differential movement can they be transferred toward their destinations, even the fourth, "democratics," which always tends toward the centering of identity in the interest of egalitarian social justice. These five technologies together comprise the methodology of the oppressed, which enables the enactment of what I have called the differential mode of oppositional social movement as in the example of U.S. third world feminism.

Under U.S. third world feminism, differential consciousness has been encoded as "la facultad" (a semiotic vector), the "outsider/within" (a de-constructive vector), strategic essentialism, (a meta-ideologizing vector), "womanism" (a moral vector), and as "la conciencia de la mestiza," "world traveling" and "loving cross-cultures" (differential vectors).[8] Unlike westerners such as Patrick Moynihan who argue that "the collapse of Communism" in 1991 proves how "racial, ethnic, and national ties of difference can only ultimately divide any society,"[9] a differential form of oppositional consciousness, as utilized and theorized by a racially diverse U.S. coalition of women of color, is the form love takes in the postmodern world.[10] It generates grounds for coalition, making possible community across difference, permitting the generation of a new kind of citizenship, countrywomen and men of the same psychic terrain whose lives are made meaningful through the enactment of the methodology of the oppressed.

Whether interfaces with technology keep cyborg politics in re-newed contestation with differential (U.S. third world feminist and subaltern) politics is a question only the political and theoretical strategies of undoing apartheid—of all kinds—will resolve. The differential form of social movement and its technologies—the methodology of the oppressed—provide the links capable of bridging the divided minds of the first world academy, and of creating grounds for what must be considered a new form of transdisciplinary work that centers the methodology of the oppressed—of the subaltern—as a new form of post-western empire knowledge formation that can transform current formations and disciplinizations of knowledge in the academy. As we shall see in the following analysis of Haraway's theoretical work, the networking required to imagine and theorize "cyborgian" consciousness can be considered, in part, a technologized metaphorization of the forms of resistance and oppositional consciousness articulated during the 1970's under the rubric of U.S. third world feminism. However, terms such as "difference," the "middle voice," the "third meaning," "rasquache," "la conciencia de la mestiza," "hybridity," "schizophrenia," and processes such as "minor literature" and "strategic essentialism" also call up and represent forms of that cyberspace, that other zone for consciousness and behaviour that is being proposed from many locations and from across disciplines as that praxis most able to both confront and homeopathically resist postmodern cultural conditions.

Donna Haraway: Feminist Cyborg Theory and U.S. Third World Feminism

Haraway's essay "Manifesto for Cyborgs" can be defined in its own terms as a "theorized and fabricated hybrid," a textual "machine," or as a "fiction mapping our social and bodily reality," phrases which Haraway also calls upon in order to re-define the term "cyborg," which, she continues, is a "cybernetic organism," a mixture of technology and biology, a "creature" of both "social reality" and "fiction."[11] This vision that stands at the center of her imaginary is a "monstrous" image, for Haraway's cyborg is the "illegitimate" child of dominant society and oppositional social movement, of science and technology, of the human and the machine, of "first" and "third" worlds, of male and female, indeed, of every binary. The hybridity of this creature is situated in relation to each side of these binary positions, and to every desire for wholeness, she writes, as "blasphemy" (149) stands to the body of religion. Haraway's blasphemy is the cyborg, that which reproaches, challenges, transforms, and shocks. But perhaps the greatest shock in her feminist theory of cyborg politics takes place in the corridors of feminist theory, where Haraway's model has acted as a transcoding device, a technology that insists on translating the fundamental precepts of U.S. third world feminist criticism into categories that are comprehensible under the jurisdictions of Women's Studies.

Haraway has been very clear about these intellectual lineages and alliances. Indeed, she writes in her introduction to *Simians, Cyborgs and Women* that one primary aim of her work is similar to that of U.S. third world feminist theory and methods, which is, in Haraway's words, to bring about "the break-up of versions of Euro-American feminist humanisms in their devastating assumptions of master narratives deeply indebted to racism and colonialism." (It might be noted there that this same challenge, when uttered through the lips of a feminist theorist of color, can be indicted and even dismissed as "undermining the movement" or as "an example of separatist politics.") Haraway's second and connected aim is to propose a new grounds for theoretical and political alliances, a "cyborg feminism" that will be "more able" than the feminisms of earlier times, she writes, to "remain attuned to specific historical and political positionings and permanent partialities without abandoning the search for potent connections."[12] Haraway's cyborg feminism was thus conceived, at least in part, to recognize and join the contributions of U.S. third world feminist theorists who have challenged, throughout the 1960's, 1970's and 1980's what Haraway identifies as hegemonic feminism's "unreflective participation in the logics, languages, and practices of white humanism." White feminism, Haraway points out, tends to search "for a single ground of domination to secure our revolutionary voice" (160).

These are thus strong ideological alliances, and so it makes sense that Haraway should turn to U.S. third world feminism for help in modeling the "cyborg" body that can be capable of challenging what she calls the "networks and informatics"

of contemporary social reality. For, she affirms, it has been "feminist theory produced by women of color" which has developed "alternative discourses of woman-
hood," and these have disrupted "the humanisms of many Western discursive
traditions."[13] Drawing from these and other alternative discourses, Haraway was
able to lay the foundations for her theory of cyborg feminism, yet she remains
clear on the issue of that theory's intellectual lineages and alliances:

> White women, including socialist feminists, discovered (that is were forced
> kicking and screaming to notice) the non-innocence of the category "woman."
> That consciousness changes the geography of all previous categories; it
> denatures them as heat denatures a fragile protein. Cyborg feminists have to
> argue that "we" do not want any more natural matrix of unity and that no
> construction is whole (157).[14]

The recognition "that no construction is whole," however—though it helps—is not
enough to end the forms of domination that have historically impaired the ability
of U.S. liberation movements to effectively organize for equality. And for that reason, much of Haraway's ongoing work has been to identify the additional technical
skills that are necessary for producing this different kind of coalitional, and what
she calls "cyborg," feminism.

To understand Haraway's contribution, I want to point out and emphasize her correlation of these necessary skills with what I earlier identified as the methodology
of the oppressed. It is no accident that Haraway defines, names and weaves the
skills necessary to cyborgology through the techniques and terminologies of U.S.
third world cultural forms, from Native American concepts of "trickster" and "coyote" being (199), to "mestizaje," or the category "women of color," until the body of
the feminist cyborg becomes clearly articulated with the material and psychic positionings of U.S. third world feminism.[15] Like the "mestiza consciousness" described
and defined under U.S. third world feminism which, as Anzaldua explains, arises "on
borders and in margins" where feminists of color keep "intact shifting and multiple
identities" and with "integrity" and love, the cyborg of Haraway's feminist manifesto must also be "resolutely committed to partiality, irony, intimacy and perversi-
ty" (151). In this equivalent alignment, Haraway writes, feminist cyborgs can be
recognized (like agents of U.S. third world feminism) to be the "illegitimate offspring," of "patriarchal capitalism" (151). Feminist cyborg weapons and the
weapons of U.S. third world feminism are also similarwith "transgressed boundaries, potent fusions and dangerous possibilities" (154). Indeed, Haraway's
cyborg textual machine represents a politics that runs
parallel to those of U.S. third world feminist criticism. Thus,
insofar as Haraway's work is influential in feminist studies, her cyborg feminism is
capable of insisting on an alignment between what was once hegemonic feminist
theory with theories of what are locally apprehended as indigenous resistance,
"mestizaje," U.S. third world feminism, or the differential mode of oppositional
consciousness.[16]

This attempted alignment between U.S. feminist third world cultural and theoretical forms and U.S. feminist theoretical forms is further reflected in Haraway's doubled vision of a "cyborg world," which might be defined, she believes, as either the
culmination of Euro-American "white" society in its drive-for-mastery, on the one
hand or, on the other, as the emergence of resistant "indigenous" world views of
mestizaje, U.S. third world feminism, or cyborg feminism. She writes:

> *A cyborg world is about the final imposition of a grid of control on the planet, about the final abstraction embodied in Star Wars apocalypse waged in the name of defense, about the final appropriation of women's bodies in a masculinist orgy of war. From another perspective a cyborg world might be about lived social and bodily realities in which people are not afraid of their joint kinship with animals and machines, not afraid of permanently partial identities and contradictory standpoints (154).*[17]

The important notion of "joint kinship" Haraway calls up here is analogous to that called for in contemporary indigenous writings where tribes or lineages are identified out of those who share, not blood lines, but rather lines of affinity. Such lines of affinity occur through attraction, combination, and relation carved out of and in spite of difference, and they are what comprise the notion of mestizaje in the writings of people of color, as in the 1982 example of Alice Walker asking U.S. black liberationists to recognize themselves as mestizos. Walker writes:

> *We are the African and the trader. We are the Indian and the Settler. We are oppressor and oppressed ... we are the mestizos of North America. We are black, yes, but we are "white," too, and we are red. To attempt to function as only one, when you are really two or three, leads, I believe, to psychic illness: "white" people have shown us the madness of that.*[18]

Mestizaje in this passage, and in general, can be understood as a complex kind of love in the postmodern world where love is understood as affinity—alliance and affection across lines of difference which intersect both in and out of the body. Walker understands psychic illness as the attempt to be "one," like the singularity of Roland Barthes' narrative love that controls all meanings through the medium of the couple-in-love. The function of mestizaje in Walker's vision is more like that of Barthes' prophetic love, where subjectivity becomes freed from ideology as it ties and binds reality. Prophetic love undoes the "one" that gathers the narrative, the couple, the race into a singularity. Instead, prophetic love gathers up the the mexcla, the mixture-that-lives through **differential movement** between possibilities of being. This is the kind of "love" that motivates U.S. third world feminist mestizaje, and its theory and method of oppositional and differential consciousness, what Anzaldua theorizes as *la conciencia de la mestiza,* or "the consciousness of the Borderlands."[19]

Haraway weaves such U.S. third world feminist commitments to affinity-through-difference into her theory of cyborg feminism, and in doing so, begins to identify those skills that comprise the methodology of the oppressed, as indicated in her idea that the recognition of differences and their corresponding "pictures of the world" (190) must not be understood as relativistic "allegories of infinite mobility and interchangeability." Simple mobility without purpose is not enough, as Gayatri Spivak posits in her example of "strategic essentialism," which argues both for mobility *and* for identity consolidation at the same time. Differences, Haraway writes, should be seen as examples of "elaborate specificity" and as an opportunity for "the loving care people might take to learn how to see faithfully from another point of view" (190). The power and eloquence of writings by certain U.S. feminists of color, Haraway continues, derives from their insistence on the "power to survive not on the basis of original innocence, (the imagination of a "once-upon-a-time wholeness" or oneness), but rather on the insistence of the possibilities of affinity-through-difference. This mestizaje or differential consciousness allows the use of any tool at one's disposal (as long as its use is guided by the methodology of the oppressed) in order to both ensure survival and to remake the world. According to Haraway, the task of cyborg feminism must similarly be to "recode" all tools of "communication and intelligence," with one's aim being the subversion of "command and control" (175).

In the following quotation, Haraway analyzes Chicana intellectual Cherríe Moraga's literary work by applying a "cyborg feminist" approach that is clearly in strong alliance with U.S. third world feminist methods. She writes:

> Moraga's language is not "whole"; it is self-consciously spliced, a chimera of English and Spanish, both conqueror's languages. But it is this chimeric monster, without claim to an original language before violation, that crafts the erotic, competent potent identities of women of color. Sister Outsider *hints at the possibility of world survival not because of her innocence, but because of her ability to* live on the boundaries, *to write without the founding myth of original wholeness, with its inescapable apocalypse of final return to a deathly oneness ... Stripped of identity, the bastard race teaches about the power of the margins and the importance of a mother like Malinche.* Women of color *have transformed her from the evil mother of masculinist fear into the originally literate mother who teaches survival (175-76).*

Ironically, U.S. third world feminist criticism, which is a set of theoretical and methodological strategies, is often understood by readers, even of Haraway, as a demographic constituency only ("women of color", a category which can be used, ironically, as an "example" to advance new theories of what are now being identified in the academy as "postmodern feminisms"), and not as itself a theoretical and methodological approach that clears the way for new modes of conceptualizing social movement, identity, and difference. The textual problem that becomes a philosophical problem, indeed, a political problem, is the conflation of U.S. third world feminism as a theory and method of oppositional consciousness with the demographic or "descriptive" and generalized category "women of color," thus depoliticizing and repressing the specificity of the politics and forms of consciousness developed by U.S. women of color, feminists of color, and erasing the specificity of what is a particular *form* of these: U.S. third world feminism.

By 1991 Haraway herself recognizes these forms of elision, and how by gathering up the category "women of color" and identifying it as a "cyborg identity, a potent subjectivity synthesized from fusions of outsider identities" (i.e. Sister Outsider), her work inadvertently contributed to this tendency to elide the specific theoretical contributions of U.S. third world feminist criticism by turning many of its approaches, methods, forms and skills into examples of cyborg feminism (174). Haraway, recognizing the political and intellectual implications of such shifts in meaning, proceeded to revise her position, and six years after the publication of "Cyborg Feminism" she explains that today, "I would be much more careful about describing who counts as a 'we' in the statement 'we are all cyborgs.'" Instead, she asks, why not find a name or concept that can signify "more of a family of displaced figures, of which the cyborg" is only one, "and then to ask how the cyborg makes connections" with other non-original people who are also "multiply displaced"?[20] Should we not be imagining, she continues, "a family of figures" who could "populate our imaginations" of "postcolonial, postmodern worlds that would not be quite as imperializing in terms of a single figuration of identity?[21] These are important questions for theorists across disciplines who are interested in effective new modes of understanding social movements and consciousness in opposition under postmodern cultural conditions. Haraway's questions remain unanswered across the terrain of oppositional discourse, however, or rather, they remain **multiply answered and divided by academic terrain**. And even within feminist theory, Haraway's own cyborg feminism and her later development of the technology of "situated knowledges," though they come close, have not been able to effectively bridge the gaps across the apartheid of theoretical domains described earlier.

For example, if Haraway's category "women of color" might best be understood, as Haraway had earlier posited, "as a cyborg identity, a potent subjectivity synthesized from fusions of outsider identities and in the complex political-historical layerings of her biomythography" (174), then why has feminist theory been unable to recognize U.S. third world feminist criticism itself as a mode of cultural theory which is also capable of unifying oppositional agents across ideological, racial, gender, sex or class differences, even if that alliance and identification would take place under the gendered, "raced" and transnational sign "U.S. third world feminism"? Might this elision be understood as yet another symptom of an active apartheid of theoretical domains? For, as I have argued, the nonessentializing identity demanded by U.S. third world feminism in its differential mode creates what Haraway is also calling for, a mestiza, indigenous, even cyborg identity.[22]

We can see Haraway making a very similar argument for the recognition of U.S. third world feminist criticism in her essay in *Feminists Theorize the Political.* Haraway's essay begins by stating that women who were "subjected to the conquest of the new world faced a broader social field of reproductive unfreedom, in which their children did not inherit the status of human in the founding hegemonic discourses of U.S. society."[23] For this reason, she asserts, "feminist theory produced by women of color" in the U.S. continues to generate discourses that confute or confound traditional western standpoints. What this means, Haraway points out, is that if feminist theory is ever to be able to incorporate the visions of U.S. third world feminist theory and criticism, then the major focus of feminist theory and politics must make a fundamental shift to that of making **"a place for the different social subject."**[24]

This challenge to feminist theory—indeed, we can read it as a challenge to all social movement theory—represents a powerful theoretical and political shift, and if answered, has the potential to bring feminism, into affinity with such theoretical terrains as post-colonial discourse theory, U.S. third world feminism, postmodernism, and Queer Theory.

How might this shift be accomplished in the domain of feminist theory? Through the willingness of feminists, Haraway proposes, to become "less interested in joining the ranks of gendered femaleness," to instead become focused on "gaining the INSURGENT ground as female social subject (95)."[25] This challenge to Women's Studies means that a shift must occur to an arena of resistance that functions outside the binary divide male/female, for it is only in this way, Haraway asserts, that "feminist theories of gendered *racial* subjectivities" can "take affirmative AND critical account of **emergent, differentiating, self-representing, contradictory social subjectivities,** with their claims on action, knowledge, and belief."[26] Under this new form of what Haraway calls an "anti-racist," indeed, even an *anti-gender* feminism, Haraway asserts, "there is no place for women," only "geometrics of difference and contradiction crucial to women's cyborg identities" (171).

It is at this point that Haraway's work begins to identify the specific technologies that fully align her theoretical apparatus with what I have called the methodology of the oppressed. How, then, might this new form of feminism, or what I would call this new form of oppositional consciousness, be brought into being? By identifying a set of skills that are capable of dis-alienating and realigning what Haraway calls the human "join" that connects our "technics" (material and technical details, rules, machines and methods), with our "erotics" (the sensuous apprehension and expression of "love"-as-affinity).[27] Such a joining, Haraway asserts, will require what is a savvy kind of "politics of articulation," and these are the primary politics that lay at "the heart of an anti-racist feminist practice"[28] that is capable of making "more powerful collectives in dangerously unpromising times."[29] This powerful politics of articulation, this new "anti-racist" politics that is also capable of making new kinds of coalitions, can be recognized, argues Haraway, by identifying the "skilled practices" that are utilized and developed within subaltern classes. Such skills, or technologies, what Haraway calls "the standpoints of the subjugated" are preferred, she writes, because

> In principle they are least likely to allow denial of the critical and interpretive core of all knowledge. They are savvy to modes of denial through repression, forgetting, and disappearing acts—ways of being nowhere while claiming to see comprehensively. The subjugated have a decent chance to be on to the god-trick and all its dazzling—and therefore, blinding—illuminations. 'Subjugated' standpoints are preferred because they seem to promise more adequate, sustained, objective, transforming accounts of the world. But HOW to see from below is a problem requiring at least as much skill with bodies and language, with the mediations of vision, as the "highest" technoscientific visualizations (191, emphasis mine).

Haraway's theoretical work outlines the forms taken by the subjugated knowledges she identifies. These forms required, as she writes, "to see from below," are particular skills that effect "bodies," "language" and the "mediations of vision." Haraway's understanding of the nature of these skills cleaves closely to those same skills that comprise the methodology of the oppressed, which including the technologies of "semiotics," "deconstruction," "meta-ideologizing," "democratics," and "differential movement." It is these technologies that permit the constant, differential repositioning necessary for perception and action from what Haraway identifies as "the standpoints of the subjugated." Indeed, Haraway's essay on cyborg feminism identifies all five of these technologies (if only in passing) as ways to bring about what she hopes will become a new feminist methodology.

Of the first "semiotic" technology, for example, Haraway writes that "self knowledge requires a semiotic-material technology linking meanings and bodies ... the opening of non-isomorphic subjects, agents, and territories to stories unimaginable from the vantage point of the cyclopian, self-satiated eye of the master subject" (192). Though Haraway does not identify the technologies of "deconstruction," or "meta-ideologizing" separately, these two interventionary vectors are implied when she writes that this new contribution to social movement theory, cyborg feminism, must find many "means of understanding and **intervening in the patterns of objectification** in the world." This means "decoding and transcoding plus translation and criticism: all are necessary." "Democratics" is the technology of the methodology of the oppressed that guides all the others, and the moral force of this technology is indicated in Haraway's assertion that in all oppositional activity, agents for change "must be accountable" for the "patterns of objectification in the world" that have now become "reality." In this effort to take responsibility for the systems of domination that now exist, Haraway emphasizes that the practitioner of cyborg feminism cannot be "about fixed locations in a reified body." This new oppositional actor must be "about nodes in fields" and "inflections in orientation." Through such mobilities, an oppositional cyborg feminism must create and enact its own version of, "**responsibility for difference** in material-semiotic fields of meaning" (195). As for the last technology of the methodology of the oppressed, called "differential movement," Haraway's own version is that cyborg feminism must understand "the impossibility of innocent 'identity' politics and epistemologies as strategies for seeing from the standpoints of the subjugated." Rather, oppositional agents must be "committed" in the enactment of all forms-of-being and all skills, whether those "skills" are semiotic, "decoding," "recoding" or "moral" in function, to what Haraway calls "mobile positioning and passionate detachment" (192).

I have argued that the "cyborg skills" necessary for developing a feminism for the twentieth century are those I have identified as the methodology of the oppressed. Their use has the power to forge what Haraway asserts can be a potentially "earthwide network of connections" including the ability to make new coalitions across new kinds of alliances by translating "knowledges among very different—and power-differentiated—communities" (187). The feminism that applies these technologies as "skills" will develop into another kind of science, Haraway asserts, a science of "interpretation, translation, stuttering, and the partly understood." Like the "science" proposed under the differential mode of consciousness and opposition—U.S. third world feminism—cyborg feminism can become the science of those Haraway describes as the "multiple subject with at least double vision." Scientific "objectivity" under this new kind of science, writes Haraway, will mean an overriding commitment to a practice capable of facing down bureaucratic and administrative sciences, a practice of "objectivity" that Haraway calls "situated knowledges" (188). For, she writes, with the advent of U.S. third world feminism and other forms of feminisms, it has become clear that "even the simplest matters in feminist analysis require contradictory moments and a wariness of their resolution." A scholarly and feminist consciousness-of-science, then, of objectivity as "*situated* knowledges" means, according to Haraway, the development of a different kind of human relation to perception, objectivity, understanding, and production, that is akin to Hayden White and Jacques Derrida's use of the "middle voice," for it will demand the scholar's situatedness "in an ungraspable middle space" (111). And like the mechanism of the middle voice of the verb, Haraway's "situated knowledges" require that what is an "object of knowledge" also be "pictured as an actor and agent" (198), transformative of itself and its own situation while also being acted upon.

In other words, Haraway's situated knowledges demands a form of differential consciousness. Indeed, Haraway names the third part of her book *Simians, Cyborgs and Women* "differential politics for inappropriate/d others." This chapter defines a coalescing and ever more articulated form of social movement from which "feminist embodiment" can resist "fixation" in order to better ride what she calls the "webs of differential positioning" (196). Feminist theorists who subscribe to this new postmodern form of oppositional consciousness must learn, she writes, to be "more generous and more suspicious—both generous and suspicious, exactly the receptive posture I seek in political semiosis generally. It is a strategy closely aligned with the oppositional and differential consciousness[30]" of U.S. third world feminism.

It was previously assumed that the behaviors of oppressed classes depend upon no methodology at all, or rather, that they consist of whatever acts one must commit in order to survive, both physically and psychically. But this is exactly why the methodology of the oppressed can now be recognized as that mode-of-being best suited to life under postmodern and highly technologized conditions in the first world. For to enter a world where any activity is possible in order to ensure survival is also to enter a cyberspace-of-being and consciousness. This space is now accessible to all human beings through technology, (though this was once a zone only accessible to those forced into its terrain), a space of boundless possibilities where meanings are only cursorily attached and thus capable of reattaching to others depending upon the situation to be confronted. This cyberspace is Barthes' zero degree of meaning and prophetic love, Fanon's "open door of every consciousness," Anzaldua's "Coatlique" state, and its processes are linked closely with those of differential consciousness.

To reiterate, the differential mode of oppositional consciousness finds its expression through the methodology of the oppressed. The technologies of semiotic reading, de-construction of signs, meta-ideologizing, and moral commitment-to-equality are its vectors, its expressions of influence. These vectors meet in the differential mode of consciousness, carrying it through to the level of the "real" where it can guide and impress dominant powers. Differential consciousness is itself a force which rhyzomatically and parasitically inhabits each of these five vectors, linking them in movement, while the pull of each of the vectors creates on-going tension and re-formation. Differential consciousness can be thus thought of as a constant reapportionment of space, boundaries, of horizontal and vertical realignments of oppositional powers. Since each vector occurs at different velocities, one of them can realign all the others, creating different kinds of patterns, and permitting entry at different points. These energies revolve around each other, aligning and realigning in a field of force that is the differential mode of oppositional consciousness, a Cyber-Consciousness.

Each technology of the methodology of the oppressed thus creates new conjunctural possibilities, produced by ongoing and transforming regimes of exclusion and inclusion. Differential consciousness is a crossing network of consciousness, a transconsciousness that occurs in a register permitting the networks themselves to be appropriated as ideological weaponry. This cyberspace-of-being is analogous to the cyberspace of computer and even social life in Haraway's vision, but her understanding of cyberspace is more pessimistic: "Cyberspace seems to be the consensual hallucination of too much complexity, too much articulation ... In virtual space, the virtue of articulation, the power to produce connection threatens to overwhelm and finally engulf all possibility of effective action to change the world."[31] Under the influence of a differential oppositional consciousness understood as a form of "cyberspace," the technologies developed by subjugated populations to negotiate this realm of shifting meanings are recognized as the very technologies necessary for all first world citizens who are interested in re-negotiating contemporary first world cultures with what we might call a sense of their own "power" and "integrity" intact. But power and integrity, as Gloria Anzaldua suggests, will be based on entirely different terms then those identified in the past, when, as Jameson writes, individuals could glean a sense of self in opposition to the centralizing dominant power that oppressed them, and then determine how to act. Under postmodern disobediencies the self blurs around the edges, shifts "in order to ensure survival," transforms according to the requisites of power, all the while, under the guiding force of the methodology of the oppressed carrying with it the integrity of a self-conscious awareness of the transformations desired, and above all, a sense of the impending ethical and political changes that those transformations will enact.[32]

Haraway's theory weds machines and a vision of first world politics on a transnational, global scale together with the apparatus for survival I call the methodology of the oppressed in U.S. third world feminism, and it is in these couplings, where race, gender, and capital, according to Haraway, "require a cyborg theory of wholes and parts" (181), that Haraway's vision contributes to bridging the gaps that are creating the apartheid of theoretical domains. Indeed, the coding necessary to re-map the kind of "disassembled and reassembled postmodern collective and personal self" (163) of cyborg feminism must take place according to a guide capable of placing feminism in alignment with other movements of thought and politics for egalitarian social change. This can happen when being and action, knowledge and science, become self-consciously encoded through what Haraway calls "subjugated" and "situated" knowledges, and what I call the methodology of the oppressed, a methodology arising from varying locations and in a multiplicity of forms across the first world, and indominably from the minds, bodies, and spirits of U.S. third world feminists who have demanded the recognition of "mestizaje," indigenous resistance, and identification with the colonized. When feminist theory becomes capable of self-consciously recognizing and applying this methodology, then feminist politics can become fully synonymous with anti-racism, and the feminist "subject" will dissolve.

In the late twentieth century, oppositional actors are inventing a new name and new languages for what the methodology of the oppressed and the "Coatlicue," differential consciousness it demands. Its technologies, from "signifyin'" to "la facultad," from "cyborg feminism" to "situated knowledges," from the "abyss" to "differance" have been variously identified from numerous theoretical locations. The methodology of the oppressed provides the schema for the cognitive map of power-laden social reality for which oppositional actors and theorists across disciplines, from Fanon to Jameson, from Anzaldua to Lorde, from Barthes to Haraway, are longing.

Notes

1. Dedicated to those who move in resistance to the "proper," and especially to Chicana feministas Yolanda Broyles-Gonzalez, Antonia Castaneda, Deena Gonzalez, Emma Perez, Gloria Anzaldua, Shirley Munoz, Norma Alarcon, Ellie Hernandez, Pearl Sandoval, and Tish Sainz.

2. Richard P. Appelbaum, "New Journal for Global Studies Center," *CORI: Center for Global Studies Newsletter,* Vol 1 No 2, May 1994.

3. See "U.S. Third World Feminism: The Theory and Method of Oppositional Consciousness in the Postmodern World," which lays the groundwork for articulating the methodology of the oppressed. *Genders 10,* University of Texas Press, Spring 1991.

4. Fredric Jameson, "Postmodernism: The Cultural Logic of Late Capitalism," *New Left Review*, No 146, July-August, pp. 53-92.

5. *The Methodology of the Oppressed*, forthcoming, Duke University Press.

6. The term "cybernetics" was coined by Norbert Wiener from the Greek word "Kubernetics," meaning to steer, guide, govern. In 1989 the term was split in two, and its first half "cyber" (which is a neologism with no earlier root) was broken off from its "control" and "govern" meanings to represent the possibilities of travel and existence in the new space of computer networks, a space, it is argued, that must be negotiated by the human mind in new kinds of ways. This cyberspace is imagined in virtual reality films like *Freejack*, *The Lawnmower Man* and *Tron*. But it was first termed "cyberspace" and explored by the science fiction writer William Gibson in his 1987 book *Neuromancer*. Gibson's own history, however, passes through and makes invisible 1970's feminist science fiction and theory, including the works of Russ, Butler, Delany, Piercy, Haraway, Sofoulis, and Sandoval. In all cases, it is this "Cyberspace" that can also adequately describe the new kind of movement and location of differential consciousness.

7. For example, Nellie Wong, "Letter to Ma," *This Bridge Called My Back;* Maria Lugones, "World Traveling;" Patricia Hill Collins, *Black Feminist Thought;* June Jordan, "Where is the Love?," *Haciendo Caras.*

8It is through these figures and technologies that narrative becomes capable of transforming the moment, of changing the world with new stories, of meta-ideologizing. Utilized together, these technologies create trickster stories, stratagems of magic, deception, and truth for healing the world, like Rap and CyberCinema, which work through the reapportionment of dominant powers.

9. *MacNeil/Lehrer NewsHour,* November 1991.

10. See writings by U.S. feminists of color on the matter of love, including June Jordan, "Where is the Love?," Merle Woo, "Letter to Ma," Patricia Hill Collins, *Black Feminist Thought*, Maria Lugones, "Playfulness, 'World-Traveling', and Loving Perception," and Audre Lorde, *Sister Outsider.*

11. Donna Haraway, *Simians, Cyborgs, and Women: The Reinvention of Nature*, (Routledge: New York, 1991), 150. All quotations in this section are from this text (especially chapters eight and nine "A Cyborg Manifesto: Science, Technology, and Socialist-Feminism in the Late Twentieth Century" and "Situated Knowledges: The Science Question in Feminism and the Privilege of Partial Perspective") unless otherwise noted. Further references to this work will be found in the text.

12. Ibid., p. 1.

13. Donna Haraway, "Ecce Homo, Ain't (Ar'n't) I a Woman, and Inappropriate/d Others: The Human in a Post-Humanist Landscape," *Feminists Theorize the Political,* ed. Judith Butler and Joan Scott, (New York: Routledge, 1992), 95.

14. This quotation historically refers its readers to the impact of the 1970's U.S. third world feminist propositions which significantly revised the women's liberation movement by, among other things, renaming it with the ironic emphasis "the *white* women's movement." And perhaps all uncomplicated belief in the righteous benevolence of U.S. liberation movements can never return after Audre Lorde summarized seventies' women's liberation by saying that "when white feminists call for 'unity'" among women "they are only naming a deeper and real need for homogeneity." By the 1980's the central political problem on the table was how to go about imagining and constructing a feminist liberation movement that might bring women together across and through their differences. Haraway's first principle for action in 1985 was to call for and then teach a new hoped-for constituency, "cyborg feminists," that "'we' do not want any more natural matrix of unity and that no construction is whole."

15. See Haraway's "The Promises of Monsters," *Cultural Studies,* (New York: Routledge, 1992), 328, where the woman of color becomes the emblematic figure, a "disturbing guide figure," writes Haraway, for the feminist cyborg, "who promises information about psychic, historical and bodily formations that issue, perhaps from some other semiotic processes than the psychoanalytic in modern and postmodern guise" (306).

16. U.S. third world feminism recognizes an alliance named "indigenous mestizaje," a term which insists upon the kinship between peoples of color similarly subjugated by race in U.S. colonial history (including but not limited to Native peoples, colonized Chicano/as, Blacks, and Asians), and viewing them, in spite of their differences, as "one people."

17. Haraway's contribution here is to extend the motion of "mestizaje" to include the mixture, or "affinity," not only between human, animal, physical, spiritual, emotional and intellectual being as it is currently understood under U.S. third world feminism, but between all these and the machines of dominant culture too.

18. Alice Walker, "In the Closet of the Soul: A Letter to an African-American Friend," *Ms. Magazine* 15 (November 1986): 32-35. Emphasis mine.

19. *Borderlands*, p 77.

20. Constance Penley and Andrew Ross, "Cyborgs at Large: Interview with Donna Haraway," *Technoculture*, Minneapolis: University of Minnesota Press, 1991), 12.

21. Ibid., p. 13.

22. We might ask why dominant theoretical forms have proven incapable of incorporating and extending theories of black liberation, or third world feminism. Would not the revolutionary turn be that theorists become capable of this kind of "strategic essentialism?" If we believe in "situated knowledges," then people of any racial, gender, sexual categories can enact U.S. third world feminist practice. Or do such practices have to be transcoded into a "neutral" language that is acceptable to all separate categories, "differential consciousness," for example, or "cyborgology"?

23. Haraway, "Ecce Homo," 95.

24. Ibid. Emphasis mine.

25. The new theoretical grounds necessary for understanding current cultural conditions in the first world and the nature of resistance is not limited to feminist theory, according to Haraway. She writes, "we lack sufficiently subtle connections for collectively building effective theories of experience. Present efforts—Marxist, psychoanalytic, feminist, anthropolitical—to clarify even 'our' experience are rudimentary" (173).

26. Ibid., p. 96. Emphasis mine.

27. Haraway, "The Promises of Monsters," 329.

28. Ibid.

29. Ibid., p. 319.

30. Ibid., p. 326.

31. Ibid., p. 325.

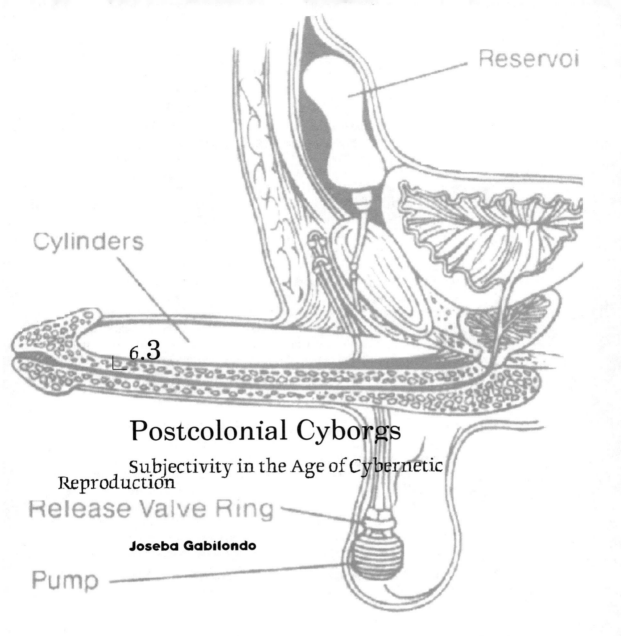

Cylinders

6.3

Reservoi

Postcolonial Cyborgs

Subjectivity in the Age of Cybernetic Reproduction

Release Valve Ring

Joseba Gabilondo

Pump

1. Cyborgs, Men, Postcolonial Subjects

In this article, I recapture three moments of history in order to discuss postcolonial cyborgs.[1] The first is the historical moment produced by the disintegrational logics of post-68 poststructuralist and Marxist critics such as Gilles Deleuze, Michel Foucault, and Fredric Jameson.[2] The second is the personal moment of my own pre-Oedipal stage. The third is the utopian moment, whose strong, critical articulations I find in Walter Benjamin and Donna Haraway, and whose reification and commodification is being carried out by companies such as AT&T, North Atlantic Bell, and discursive productions such as cyberpunk, *Mondo 2000,* and *Wired.*

I want to use these three moments to historicize the postmodern, fetishist obsession with cyborgs and to trace its geopolitical and ideological limits: cyberspace, which does not correspond with either the boundaries of the modern nation-state, the colonial metropolis, the most recent cold-war formations of the three-world split (First/Second/Third Worlds), or the postmodern, global expansion of mass culture.

The cyborg is not the general, postmodern form of subjectivity created by multinational capitalism but rather the hegemonic subject position that its ideology privileges. The old subject position of "Man," although displaced in its hegemony by the cyborg, still operates in a very productive way. When Foucault proclaimed the death of "Man" in 1966, **he did not realize that capitalism does not get rid of its old technologies and apparatuses; instead it exports them to the Third World.**[3] In the economically privileged First World the production of "Man" has given way to the reproduction and simulation of "cyborgs," and the technologies and apparatuses of the nation-state that produce the democratic, middle-class, consuming "Man" have been transferred to the peripheries of the First World and to the Third World. The economic, political, and cultural formations of the nation-state and, most recently, mass culture are still being exported to the Third World. More than 90 nations have gained independence since World War II and the socialist block is now breaking down into nation-states, adding to the list of new independent nations. While the Third World is becoming a cluster of nation-states, the first world is restructuring itself into larger political and economic formations such as the European Common Market and the North American Trade Zone, which I call "super-markets" in order to capture their local and global effects.

As soon as the adjective 'postcolonial' is added to 'cyborg', the latter shows its historical and geopolitical boundaries: there is no such thing/subject as a "postcolonial cyborg," because postcolonial subject positions are always left outside cyberspace. As I will argue later, the postcolonial, subaltern subject position is also left outside of consumer culture by capitalism, thus signifying the exteriority of both cyberspace and consumer culture. Postcolonial subject positions are necessary in order to create the outsideness that cyberspace and consumer culture need to constitute themselves as the new hegemonic inner spaces of postmodernism. To put it bluntly, Africa only owns 1% of all the television sets in the world.[4]

As I will discuss below, only an understanding of cyberspace and consumer culture as new ideological apparatuses that interface with older apparatuses such as the nation-state, class and family structures, gender and sexual differences, and ethnic and racial formations will allow room for a cultural politics of the postmodern global system.[5]

2. The Geopolitical Limits of Cyborg Subjectivity

I would like first to roughly delimit the geopolitical expansion of cyberspace and cyborg subjectivity, since indeed cyberspace is expanding in the fashion of Borges's world of Tlön. As Akira Asada's analysis of contemporary Japan shows, the subject formations of late capitalism no longer coincide with either the modern, European, subject of the Enlightenment—the ideological matrix of the colonial, white, heterosexual, male bourgeois—or the postmodern, American subject—the matrix of the global, postnuclear-family, white, heterosexual, male, consumer.[6] Capitalism has also been able to develop powerfully in non-Western societies such as Japan, Hong-Kong, Taiwan, and Singapore. As William Gibson's novels have envisioned, or the tidal movement of the investment markets shows, cyberspace extends within the limits of multinational capitalism, from Japan to Europe, and so does cyborg subjectivity. Cyborg subjectivity stretches as far as capitalist individuals access the cyberspatial interface of the apparatus-continuum constituted by phones/modems/PCs/cable-television/cellular-phones/faxes/etc. of late capitalism.

Cyborg subjectivity is primarily lived, constructed, and legitimized as the interior to the cyberspace produced by all these interfaces. This interiority is further emphasized by the privatization of social space. The public spaces of modernity are being enclosed and protected by a highly developed cybernetic technology of surveillance.

It is as if all the institutions of subject formation described by Foucault, from the madhouse to the prison, have turned themselves inside out in an attempt to leave the insane and the criminals outside: outside the condominium, outside the shopping mall, outside the campus, outside the credit-card/ATM-system, outside the status of privileged trade nation, outside the command structure of the new "Allied forces" (Iraq, Somalia) etc. In postmodernity, the modern middle-class has secluded itself inside its institutions. Ironically, one could say that postmodern subject formations are institutionalizing the modern middle-class. The good news is that spree killers have just recently started to invade the most sacrosanct social space of the postnuclear Californian family: shopping malls. One is no longer safe anywhere, neither in the suburban house, in the post office, in the respectable law firm that recently fired an employee who later came back gun in hand, in the World Trade Center of Manhattan bombed by "fanatic terrorists," or in the Third World Hiltons and Marriots for IBM executives.

Cyberspace thinks of its social spaces as interior. Everything left outside, repressed, comes back not as symptoms of a deep, interior unconscious—as in modernity—but rather as exterior ghosts/monsters that haunt the interior and its cyborgs: computer-hackers, gangs, drug dealers, serial killers, serial rapists, homeless armies, illegal immigrants, mad third-world leaders who, only yesterday, were collaborators of the CIA (Noriega) and the Pentagon (Hussein). Cyberspace is the interface between the cyborg and the ghost/monster.

The most recent canonized text of cyberpunk, *Snowcrash,* takes account of this interfacial logic of cyberspace between cyborgs and ghosts: the entire novel is based on the paranoic story of an ancient informational virus, which was retrieved from an archaeological site and, then, reprogrammed as a computer virus.[7] The new virus is able to infect the hacker's brain through the interface of the computer screen and the eye. This central and orientalized metaphor of an ancient informational virus that can transform itself into an organic virus, works as the discursive node for the rest of the contaminational paranoias that establish an interfacial space of interiority/exteriority in cyberspace on all its social orders: ethnicity, gender, race, sexuality.

Cyberspace redefines even bodies as an interface between interiority and exteriority: from the AIDS epidemic "scare" to the medical discourses on cholesterol and pro-life redefinitions of women's bodies, the cyborg body is an interiority that needs to guard itself from all sorts of ghostly and monstrous sexual and dietary "invasions."

3. Interfaces, Subject Positions, Cyborgs, and Consumers

When the limits of cyberspace are considered, mass culture has to be included in the limit equation. In its two most vigorous cultural forms, the film/tv continuum and the radio/walkman continuum,[8] mass culture constitutes another interface of subject formations. Even if the "origins" of mass culture have to be located in the history of the U.S. cultural and economic formation, its contemporary spread is contiguous with the expansion of late capitalism; or to put it in more semiological terms, even if mass culture's signifiers are all "originally" American, mass culture has long since trespassed U.S. boundaries, as the wonderful Venezuelan and Brazilian TV soap operas that my mother watches in Spain, dubbed in Basque, prove.

Sociologically and geographically mass culture's sphere of expansion is larger than that of cyberspace: it extends throughout the entire First World, most of the cities of the Third World and, now, former communist countries. Even in Cuba people watch American television these days.[9]

The expansion of mass culture, as in the fetishisized McDonalds of Moscow, can be described as "close encounters of the third kind with the commodity." This second interface of subject formation is created when the desire to consume is introduced successfully as cultural logic in non-consumer societies such as those of Russia or China.[10] I am referring here to a specific geopolitical formation of desire: the Western desire that psychoanalysis and poststructuralism have attempted to universalize as inherent to any economic or political practice. Gayatri Spivak's critique of Foucault's and Deleuze's ahistorical use of subjectivity and desire, which echoes criticisms by feminism, postcolonialism, and queer theory, applies to mass culture: desire to consume which is the desire to belong to the new social formations of contemporary multinational capitalism, is being created, imposed, resisted, and negotiated on the borders of mass culture's expansion.[11]

If one looks at the articulations of cyberspace and mass culture, one could argue that certain privileged groups of individuals in the United States, Europe, Japan, and various Third-World cities are constituted by their interfaces with both cyberspace and mass culture, whereas the rest of the population in the global system is constituted by its single interface with mass culture. That is, different preexisting social groups, according to their economy, gender, sex, ethnicity, and race position, are constituted by one or two of the interfaces I have mentioned above.

Only by considering cyberspace and mass culture as interfaces of subject formation can we understand the new place that the nation-state occupies in late capitalism and the cultural logic produced by the encounter between traditional and national cultures—with their specific sex, gender, and race structures—and mass culture.

From Adorno on,[12] Marxist criticism has exorcised mass culture at some time or another as the demon of reification and alienation. Ironically enough, these critiques have always struck the nostalgic chord of the loss of national cultures, without questioning the European, bourgeois, middle-class ideology that formed them.

In the case of Europe, which is the one I know from my own experience, the invasion of mass culture has eroded the hegemony of the national cultures, which I salute with joy because of my own experience as Basque, resistant to being constituted as culturally Spanish. Furthermore the European, modernist, national cultures as well as the emerging new regional cultures are already interfacing with mass culture and can no longer exist without the latter. European national cultures have lost their hegemony in subject formation processes because they have lost their colonial hegemony. Nevertheless, they will survive in their new articulation with mass culture and regionalism.

To understand the effect that mass culture might have in the global future of Europe, one has to think of the imperialist expansion of Latin in the early medieval ages. There is no political nostalgia for all the languages that Latin wiped out in the Mediterranean area—such as Iberian. As a speaker of a preindoeuropean language, I fully understand the difference. Basque is not a nostalgic preindoeuropean language that preserves the cultural values of a long-gone culture: fifty percent of Basque vocabulary is Latin, although in most cases this origin has been effaced from its signifier for Basque speakers—probably with the exception of the conscientious etymologist.

I have been using the metaphor of the 'interface' to establish the relationships between cyberspace, mass culture, and the national and colonial cultural logics. The idea of interface could also be turned into a methodological and specific term to develop a discourse on global culture. In this respect, Althusser's theories on the Ideological State Apparatuses must be reconsidered and rethought beyond the modern horizon of the nation-state if a Marxist theory of global culture is to be developed.[13] It is my belief that cyberspace and mass culture can be methodologically thought out as interfaces if, in turn, the concept of interface is redefined in the context of the Althusserian discussion of ideological apparatuses.

Althusser postulates that the Ideological State Apparatuses are formed from a heterogeneous and complex interplay of apparatuses which simultaneously differentiate them from the (Repressive) State Apparatus (IIA 149).

Although Althusser does not dwell on the heterogeneous and contradictory composition of the Ideological State Apparatuses, the list of apparatuses he mentions shows their nonsynchronicity[14] and their ability to exist in different hegemonic positions within the system of the ideological apparatuses. Althusser postulates that, in the history of the system of Ideological State Apparatuses, a dominant apparatus loses its hegemony to another within the apparatus-system.[15] He also implies that specific Ideological State Apparatuses, given their nonsynchronicity, live beyond the concrete historical span of a mode of production and even capitalism *in toto*. Althusser refers specifically to the Catholic Church as one of the Ideological State Apparatuses that is historically preexistent to capitalism.

If the nonsynchronous and transhistorical being of some of these Ideological State Apparatuses is considered, one could argue that nowadays in postmodernism, with the decline of the colonial nation-state as the hegemonic site of capitalist production, if a theory of ideology has to be developed, the Ideological Apparatus system of multinational capitalism cannot be thought of at the level of the 'state,' as Althusser did, but rather it must be conceived in global terms: the Ideological *State* Apparatuses become Ideological *Global* Apparatuses. If this reformulation is accepted, one could argue that neither the Church nor the School are dominant Ideological (State) Apparatuses and instead cyberspace and mass culture are new clusters of Ideological Global Apparatuses. Other modern Ideological State Apparatuses such as the School or the Nuclear Family might still operate within the Ideological Global

Apparatus system, but they are no longer dominant or hegemonic.

Although the task of mapping the specific Ideological Global Apparatuses of cyberspace and consumer culture is beyond the reach of this study, I would like to sketch certain theoretical lines in order to discuss the issues of ideology and subjectivity in the new framework of Ideological Global Apparatuses (henceforth *Ideological Apparatuses*) I have opened up above.

As Ideological Apparatuses, cyberspace and consumer culture create a postmodern ideology that, in Althusser's words, "has the function (which defines it) of 'constituting' concrete individuals as subjects" (IIA 171) through interpellation. Consumer culture interpellates individuals as consumers and consumerism is the new ideology of multinational capitalism. Although the tautological appearance of the previous sentence might strike the reader, it is important to understand that postmodern individuals are basically constituted as consumers. This constitution is historically a very recent development in most of the capitalist world. **In the same way, cyberspace interpellates individuals as global subjects.** That is, cyberspace constitutes individuals as belonging to cyberspace and, thus, as cyborg subjects.

The double interpellation of consumer culture and cyberspace is one that would ideologically construct individuals as global cyborgs. The rest of the non-dominant Ideological Apparatuses, which in many instances can be nonsynchronically modern and state-based, allow for a rich negotiation of national, ethnic, gender, sexual, and linguistic interpellations.[16]

Althusser's discussion of the metaphor of the Lacanian mirror-phase in order to describe the functioning of interpellation in ideology will shed some light on the structures generated by the Ideological Apparatuses of cyberspace and mass culture. Althusser claims that "We observe that the structure of all ideology, interpellating individuals as subjects in the name of a Unique and Absolute Subject is *specular*, i.e. a mirror-structure, and *doubly* specular: this mirror duplication is constitutive of ideology and ensures its functioning" (IIA 180). The metaphor of mirroring brings about the epistemological framework of mimesis and identity, by which individuals are interpellated as identity-subjects (or their lack).

The postmodern Ideological Apparatuses do not interpellate individuals through a process of mimetic reflection in which individuals identify themselves as subjects but rather through a process of interfacing in which individuals identify their subjective positions. The individual is interpellated *only* as the subject who takes part in a specific interfacing. This allows for a variety of possible subject positions that are negotiated on the bases of the interfacial access of different ethnicities, races, gender, sexualities, etc.

At the same time, the interfacial character of subject positioning in cyberspace explains two utopian paradoxes that dominate the discourse on cyberspace. On the one hand, cyberspace is not a virtual democracy (as *Mondo 2000* argues) in which cultural differences become invisible and thus do not serve as bases for discrimination and oppression. **Conversely, the utopian appropriation of cyberspace as the final frontier for hacking, terrorism against the system, etc. is nothing but wishful libertarian thinking.** Most of these accounts emphasize the interiority of cyberspace and proclaim it as the final frontier of "human development." By emphasizing its interiority rather than the geopolitical and cultural interfaces that form it, the ideology of cyberspace is enforced instead of being critically thought out.[17]

The interpellation of the individual as a consumerist cyborg is determined by the specific modern, colonial, or non-Western cultural structures that interface with cyberspace and consumerism. In a time in which multinational capitalism can simulate multiculturalism, nevertheless race, gender, ethnicity, and sexuality still function as forms of discrimination and oppression.

4. The Slacker Generation, Schizophrenia, Nostalgia

Once the generation X or slacker generation—brought up with TV and rock music—attains the hegemonic position of the current generation—brought up with the canons of modernism—any form of First World cultural politics, including academia, will lose its nostalgia for the loss of the national cultures of the First World. This modernist complaint will become purely historical and lose the power to engage any living historical memory—as did the romantic's complaint about the loss of preindustrial culture.

The other modernist nostalgia that has to be historicized is the one for the postmodern disintegration of the subject and its reformulation as a schizophrenic being/machine. From Deleuze and Guattari's *Anti-Oedipus* to Jameson's *Postmodernism,* the insistence on the subject's disintegration only emphasizes the unconscious place that the modern, universal Subject occupies in their discourses.[18] Claims for the schizophrenic logic of the postmodern "Subject" try to incorporate the modern Subject into postmodernism through the logic of nostalgia, which tries to reincorporate cultural logics and elements from the past into the present—history as nostalgic device.

My insistence on this generational shift comes from my personal experience. Modernism, I have found, no longer has any cultural and political validity for me. Rather it posits my own geopolitical and historical existence as an instance of the threatening expansion of the culture of multinational capitalism. According to my family's accounts, I learned to turn the old television set on and off before I learned to walk. Considering that I learned to walk before I was a year old, I think television played a pivotal role in my Oedipal complex. Television signified the lack (on/off) that only language later comes to signify in all the modern accounts of the Oedipal complex. Furthermore, television occupied a position in the mirror stage in which the identification was ghostly rather than mimetic in a way I cannot yet articulate.

I want to use this personal moment to illustrate the new position that cybernetic and telecommunicative technology occupy in the First World's postmodern generations. When this generation gains hegemony in cultural politics and can afford to be nostalgic for its own past, it will be for this hybrid, telecommunicative, and cybernetic past. National cultures will no longer occupy the center of the nostalgic reconstruction of that hegemonic past.

Older Ideological Apparatuses that have lost their dominance will no longer be nostalgically idealized and fetishized. The specific historicity of a certain interface will determine the cultural politics to follow. Unlike Althusser, who still postulated a scientific discourse that allowed us to objectively contemplate ideology and its apparatuses, I would argue that global capitalism does not allow for a privileged modern point of view. Thus, the ideological nature of any historical and political activity has to be vindicated as the sole place from which to access any cultural politics.

Modernist theories of fragmentation, pastiche, and collage are inadequate to the postmodern reappearance of allegory, which has overtaken the hegemony of metaphor in modernity. The interfacial discourse that establishes a performative narrative about the elements involved in the interface is allegorical and there is nothing fragmentary or schizophrenic about it.

5. Postcoloniality and the Subaltern Subject

Postcolonial subjectivity has to be understood as the interface of precolonial, colonial, and mass-culture logics. That is, the initiation of the postcolonial individual into desiring consumer culture is one of the parameters of the postcolonial situation, which is signified as exterior to the mass culture of late capitalism.[19]

Acknowledging that most of postcolonial theory is Anglocentric and blatantly non-historical and non-sociological, and thus, purely critical and theoretical, nonetheless it provides a model that allows us to bypass any nostalgia for precolonial or even colonial pasts, and simultaneously, to understand the interface of mass culture and the Third World as a rich political space for subject formations.[20]

Once postcolonial theory addresses mass culture's new presence in the Third World, the interpellation of Third-World individuals as new consumers will reinstate the idea of "Man" and its possible performances in the theoretical arena. The new world order Latinoamerica constituted by GATT and NAFTA and the capitalization of China and other communist countries, among other developments, is creating a new Third World, that is both the producer and consumer of durable goods.

The different interfaces constructed between individuals and consumer culture in postcolonial areas will determine the way they are interpellated as postcolonial subaltern subjects (Spivak, CSS 284-5).

When interviewed by Andrew Ross and Constance Penley six years after the publication of her "Cyborg Manifesto," Haraway expressed the need to redefine cyborg subjectivity as one of many specific forms rather than as an all-inclusive category that would challenge modern paradigms of subjectivity:

> I think what I would want is more of a family of displaced figures, of which the cyborg is one, and then to ask how the cyborg makes connections with these other nonoriginal people ... who are multiply displaced. Could there be a family of figures who would populate our imagination of these postcolonial, postmodern worlds that would not be quite as imperializing in terms of a single figuration for identity?[21]

6. Subject Positions and the Access to the interfaces

To account for the interfaces of cyberspace and consumer culture without any nostalgia for old political paradigms, we must go beyond the geographical and economic orientations of modernist cultural politics. From the cyborg to the Third World consumer "Man" and the postcolonial subaltern, different interfaces of subject formation are being erected in postmodernism. The double interface between cyberspace/consumer culture and preexisting cultural logics also accounts for any oversimplification and utopianism of cybernetic technology. Cyberspace produces new formations of social and economic power, but these formations, as postcolonial theory demonstrates, are not objective, not always hegemonic, and not fixed. They simply are a side of these new interfaces formed against national cultures, regionalism, and non-modern cultures. **Any cultural politics that does not account for the new interfacial positions of all these cultural parameters will fall back to either nostalgic, modern politics or utopian, libertarian technophilia** à la *Mondo 2000*. Both are ideological tendencies that block any possibility for progressive politics.

Benjamin wrote his utopian article on the reproduction of the work of art back in 1936. That was a time in which the new technological changes of monopoly capitalism could still have been thought out as utopian and revolutionary. Similarly, when Haraway wrote her "Cyborg Manifesto" in 1985, cyberspace was not fully developed yet and hence there was space for a utopian call, to seize that space for politics. Nevertheless, that moment is passed and cyberspace has a much more developed shape that is necessary to conceptualize and map in order to access it and use it, not utopically but historically.

I would like to mention the news of this week (second week of April 1994) in order to sign and date this article. As I am writing, the U.S. companies Southwestern Bell and Fox have suspended a 5 billion dollar merger to develop a new informational cable network. A few weeks ago, Bell Atlantic and TCI Inc. also called off a similar merger for the amount of 33 billion dollars. In both cases state regulations were given as the reason for the cancellation of the mergers. The critical economic situation of Disney in Europe is another case to follow closely.

Capitalism is not a homogeneous block of expansion that wipes away everything that encounters in its space: these are just the pleasures of paranoic master/narratives that certain forms of Marxism enjoy. Or to put it another way, the global culture in which we live nowadays cannot be represented or thought out as a presence or agency, **since the global condition does not exist as such but rather as part of a local interface.** A non-interfacial emphasis on the globality of contemporary culture, in either Marxist economic terms or right wing pro-capitalist terms (Francis Fukuyama),[22] contributes to the ideology of globality.

Notes

1. I would like to acknowledge for their contributions to this article the following individuals: Chris Gray, Meredith Hobbs, Donna Haraway, Masao Miyoshi, Fredric Jameson, Ted Friedman, Jonathan Flatley, Alejandro Manara, Brian Selsky, Hank Okazaki, Renu Bora, Jose Muñoz, and all the students of my seminar on film theory in the Program of Literature at Duke University.

2. I use the term disintegrational according to the specific criticism of Peter Dews, *Logics of Disintegration: Post-Structuralist Thought and the Claims of Critical Theory* (London: Verso, 1987).

3. Michel Foucault, *Les mots et les choses* (Paris: Gallimard, 1966).

4. CNN, March 25, 1994.

5. For a discussion of multinational capitalism and the global system see for example Leslie Sklair, *Sociology of the Global System* (Baltimore: John Hopkins UP, 1991) and Robert J.S. Ross and Kent C. Trachte, *Global Capitalism: The New Leviathan* (Albany, NY: State University of NY Press, 1990).

6. Akira Asada, "Infantile Capitalism and Japan's Postmodernism: A Fairy Tale" in Masao Miyoshi and H.D. Harootunian eds., *Postmodernism and Japan* (Durham: Duke UP, 1989), 273-78.

7. Neal Stephenson, *Snowcrash* (New York: Bantam Books, 1992).

8. In a pragmatic way, I will follow the McLuhanian dictum in order to refer to the cultural formations of mass culture. I will denominate the media and the message at the same time.

9. I owe this information to a conversation with the Cuban film director Humberto Solás.

10. Jonathan Flatley and Alexander Ivanov, "Letter from Moscow," *Architecture in New York* 3 (November/December: 1993), 68-69.

11. Gayatri Spivak, "Can the Subaltern Speak?" in Cary Nelson and Lawrence Grossberg eds., *Marxism and the Interpretation of Culture* (Urbana, Chicago: University of Illinois Press, 1988), 271-276 (hereafter cited as CSS).

Similarly, even the most politically engaged criticism of Western subjectivity to date, Judith Butler's *Gender Trouble* (New York: Routledge, 1990) still lacks this geopolitical consciousness that is essential to any critique of postmodern society.

12. Theodor Adorno and Max Horkheimer's *Dialectic of Enlightenment* (New York: The Continuum, 1989) written in 1944.

13. Louis Althusser, "Ideology and Ideological Apparatuses" in *Lenin and Philosophy and Other Essays by Louis Althusser* (New York: Monthly Review Press, 1971), 127-186 (hereafter cited as IIA).

14. Ernst Bloch, "Nonsynchronism and the Obligation of its Dialectics," *New German Critique* 11 (Spring 1977), 22-38.

15. "In fact, the Church has been replaced today *in its role as the dominant Ideological State Apparatus* by the School" (IIA 157).

16. For the Latin American case see Néstor García Canclini, *Culturas híbridas. Estrategias para entrar y salir de la modernidad* (Mexico: Grijalbo, 1989).

17. For a viewpoint of one of the most important ideologues of cyberspace see Bruce Sterling, *The Hacker Crackdown. Law and Disorder on the Electronic Frontier* (New York, Bantam, 1992), xiv.

For other accounts of cyborg subjectivity that are not aware of its geopolitical dimension see: Scott Bukatman, *Terminal Identity: The Virtual Subject in Postmodern Science Fiction* (Duharm: Duke UP, 1993); Mark Poster, *The Mode of Information: Poststructuralism and Social Context* (Cambridge: Polity Press, 1990); Anne Friedberg, *Window Shopping: Cinema and the Postmodern* (Berkeley: University of California Press, 1993).

18. Gilles Deleuze and Felix Guattari, *L'Anti-Oedipus* (Paris: PUF, 1972) and Fredric Jameson, *Postmodernism or the Logic of Late Capitalism* (Durham: Duke UP, 1992).

19. As Gayatri Spivak acknowledges (CSS 288).

20. Ella Shohat, "Notes on the 'Post-Colonial'" *Social Text* 31/32 (1992): 101-123; Kwame Anthony Appiah, "Is the Post- in Postmodernism the Post- in Postcolonial?" *Critical Inquiry* 17 (Winter 1991): 345-357; Arif Dirlik, "The Postcolonial Aura: Third World Criticism in the Age of Global Capitalism," *Critical Inquiry* 20 (Winter 1994): 328-356.

21. Donna Haraway, "The Actors Are Cyborgs, Nature is Coyote, and the Geography is Elsewhere: Postscript to 'Cyborgs at Large'" in Andrew Ross and Constance Penley eds., *Technoculture* (Minneapolis: University of Minnesota Press, 1991), 13.

22. Francis Fukuyama, *The End of History and the Last Man* (New York, Free Press, 1992).

6.4

From Cognitive Psychologies to Mythologies

Advancing Cyborg Textualities for a Narrative of Resistance

William R. Macauley and Angel J. Gordo-López

introduction

A number of authors from different disciplines have focused their analysis on ways in which the body is depicted and regulated (e.g., Foucault, 1971; Riley, 1978; Lauretis, 1989 and Sayers, 1983). These studies emphasize how different institutions and established fields of knowledge, such as medical discourses, construct definitions concerning the body.

Lately, other points of interest have emerged in relation to new technological advances (e.g., virtual reality) and images of the body depicted in populist forms (e.g., cyberpunk novels and mass media); some of the interest underlying these new discourses include the ways in which these technologies can be used to overcome physical limitation. There has been a move away from analyses of discursive practices (*technologies* in the Foucauldian sense) which make the body legible, **to practices that foresee symbiotic relationships between flesh and technology.**

This paper addresses some of the issues concerning the borderlands between these sets of interests; we discuss ways in which the technologized body is also constructed in socio-technical *and* discursive practices. We suggest strategies to develop our position with respect to previous discourse. These strategies are inspired by Latour's ideas on hybridization/purification (Latour, 1991), and other authors such as Haraway (1991) who discuss how the blurring of boundaries between humans and machines has allowed the appearance of hybrid positions (cyborgs).

In the same vein as Latour, we will adopt an historical approach to analyze the ways these hybrid positions are denied and/or rendered accountable in accordance with pre-existing socio-cultural practices (i.e., purification). Applying the logic of hybridization/purification (h/p) we highlight how the body and associated hybrid forms are resignified rather than replaced (Figueroa-Sarriera, 1993).

In addition we complement this analysis with a textual understanding of hybrid positions. Instead of considering hybrid forms and their processes of purification as isolated phenomena, we will present a narrative in which these forms will be seen as effects within a wider context (Callon and Law, 1993). This approach aims to facilitate alternative interpretations of instances where the body and technology reshape each other.

Some of the issues discussed in this chapter include: examples of technological seduction and attempts to abandon the body, the Cartesian Family and its Complex: the body, the 'female' matrix of cyberspace and the shift from negative populist images of technology to positive ones. In a later section we move from the discussion of some psychologies to mythological stories. We end this chapter with some ideas about polymorphous forms and boundaries as exemplified by one of the characters (T1000) in the film *Terminator 2*. This paper focuses on different types of hybrids and related discourses.

Seduction and Technological Abandonment of the Body

> *No matter how virtual the subject may become, there is always a body attached. It may be off somewhere else—and that "somewhere else" may be a privileged point of view—but consciousness remains firmly rooted in the physical. Historically, body, technology, and community constitute each other (Stone, 1991a:111).*

New technological advances and aesthetics of consumption have irrupted into the postmodern landscape. Virtual reality (VR), for instance, affords new enterprises to owners of a chain of transformation sex-shops who asked persistently for the price of high-end VR systems, foreseeing the new possibilities for their customers in "virtual cross-dressing" environments. Sexual practices co-exist with on-line sex for artists, novelists and commercial designers as the quote below indicates:

> *I'd still want 80 percent of my sexual encounters to be in person, but I also*

have my fantasies about faceless hunks (Mimi Heft, 29-year-old designer; quoted in Bowen-Jones, 1993:24).

These futuristic aesthetics follow on from other types of technology such as Warhol's lithographies, for instance. These can be interpreted as the celebration of capitalist excess in which compulsive repetition and mass reproduction of the symbol allows people to own *their own* piece of art. Repetition of signifiers facilitates the act of consumption and the process of artistic engagement.

I want to be a machine: seduction and abandonment of the body

In our current "virtual times", deprecatory images of the body can be found among individualistic post-modern fakirs in search of a human-machine symbiosis (cyborhood). Stelarc, for instance, "suffers" in his attempts to demonstrate that the human body is obsolete by suspending himself above the streets of New York from sterilized hooks skewered through his skin. (Fig. 1) According to Sterlarc:

Fig. 1

The body is immersed in an increasingly intense information field that cannot be absorbed and creatively processed by the individual (1989:19).

He claims that mutilation of the body is an obligatory passage point for our communion with technological webs. Stelarc preaches from his suspended metaphysical position that the body needs to be pacified, anaesthetized, in order to harmonise with the new evolutionary stage of information. This sterile, global view of the future cyborg, represents the body as obsolete, deficient, perishable. Immortality in the virtual world stands for modular rather than hormonal systems. The replacement of hardware with our portable tool-box will be possible à la *Predator* (1987). As Jamison's recent work notes:

In the reckless abandonment, something must also be relinquished, resigned, surrendered [...] it is seductive to imagine the replacement of points of human frailty with machines (Jamison, 1994:2).

In what follows, we illustrate the textuality of this abandonment and eroticism by discussing historical antecedents, such as research on cybernetics and human-computer interaction (HCI). New types of relationships between humans and computers will be described in the light of developments in VR technology and cyberspace.

Historical Antecedents of the Abandonment: Cybernetics, HCI and Cyberspace

Humans have been talking to computers for a considerable length of time. Traditional research in HCI is strongly influenced by early work—carried out during the 1940s and 1950s—on cybernetics/information theory (Wiener, 1948; Shannon and Weaver, 1948) and psychological experiments on attention (e.g., Turing, 1950; Broadbent, 1958). These early studies adopted a conversation metaphor to describe communication in terms of encoding, transmission and decoding of data within a system. As a consequence, interfaces have been designed to facilitate communication between two discrete entities (i.e., human and machine) using variations on the information-processing-as-dialogue model. However, recent developments in computer technology and the wider availability of information has revealed the apparent inadequacy of this model (Macauley, 1992).

As Pesce (1992) reminds us, the relationship between humans and information has changed profoundly during the late 20th century; increased accessibility and an explosion in the quantity and quality of information made available to individuals requires new strategies and models to cope with these changes, which threaten to sweep away notions of identity and choice:

> Information has become our clothing, our food, our air, and free access to it has become a basic human right. Yet, at the same time, humans can be overwhelmed by information, drowned in a sea of choices, confused by conflicting viewpoints in data, and find themselves unable to make decisions within the infosphere (Pesce, 1992:5).

The introduction of novel computer technology—head mounted displays (HMDs) and 6 degrees of freedom (6DOF) peripheral devices, for example—provides an electronic medium in which HCI is replaced by the fusion of human with computer. This medium has been labelled *cyberspace* (Gibson, 1984; Benedikt, 1991) or *virtual reality* (VR) (Lanier, 1989; Brooks, 1988). Cyberspace can be employed to fashion real or novel environments which the participant perceives directly and navigates through. VR interfaces also allow remote perception/manipulation of visual, acoustic, and/or tactile forms. This facility enables humans to perceive distributed selves (i.e., telepresence) and experience action-at-a-distance without the familiar restrictions of conventional interfaces (Loomis, 1993; Steuer, 1992; Benford, et al., 1993).

In cyberspace the phenomenological proximity of the *interface* has shifted—HCI is no longer limited to data visualization in a cartesian 3-dimensional space, simulated through the static 'window' of a 2-dimensional display screen. **Cyberspace is a medium which envelops and, simultaneously, reconstitutes the techno-social body in a virtual discursive space.** A wired glove (e.g., *Cyber*Glove), for example, allows the hand to be resignified as a graphical object, perceived in a simulated 3D (electronic) environment (Sturman and Zeltzer, 1994). Nothing new. However, direct (i.e., perceptually immediate) manipulation of computer generated forms by means of the virtual hand extends and augments sensorimotor activity beyond the spatio-temporal boundaries associated with conversational models of HCI.

More importantly, the virtual hand does not merely act as a prosthesis or replacement for the physical object, but, rather, it intensifies corporeality in the form of a **'technophilic body'** (Tomas, 1989). This process of hybridization (i.e., the synthesis of human agency and technology) is the latest manifestation of cyborg agencies. Cyberspace is an experiential medium in which the transgression of epistemological and psychological boundaries is commonplace; categories such as object/subject, perception/action, and human/computer become somewhat unreliable when applied to experiences in cyberspace. The blurring of boundaries between humans and machines has allowed the emergence of hybrid positions. As Prins (1993) notes:

> Cyborgs come into being when boundaries get blurred, particularly those [...] between self-controlled, self-governing machines and organisms (1993: 8-9).

Purification and Inoculation[1]

This paper borrows some ideas from Latour (1991) who maintains that in the exchange between nature and society hybrid positions are denied. By processes of purification these hybrid positions are translated into accountable forms. The idea of purification has an analogue in the field of semiotics—Barthes (1972), for example, uses the medical metaphor of **inoculation** to describe processes applied in the mass media, whereby the public is exposed to a small, harmless, dose of 'acknowledged evil'. This limited exposure immunizes the collective imagination from the threat of subversion. For instance, a number of popular media (films, novels, TV) have presented cyborgs which undergo processes of humanization (e.g., T800 in the film *Terminator 2* [1991], and Murphy in *RoboCop*, [1987]). However this process also works in reverse, in that, humans can be depicted as robotic or machine-like through mutual reshaping of humans and computers in cyborg texts (see Springer, 1989 and Penley, 1987).

In accordance with this logic of hybridisation/purification, our narrative considers discursive practices, to foresee what type of body definitions are foreclosed and enabled by these continuous exchanges. In this way we hope to recapture some cyborg textualities that preserve the subversive aspect of hybrids.

The Cartesian Family and its Complex: The Body

Although Stelarc's abandonment of the body can be seen as an individualistic act, it would be unfortunate to forget the historical textuality of his meta-physical suspensions. The Cartesian Family (grandfather Plato, Descartes and progeny: Cybernetics, Cognitive Sciences, Artificial Intelligence, Robotics and Cyberpunk tales) has been telling us best-selling stories for a long time: minds without bodies, mental skills rather than **embodied and situated collective performances.**

The purification of the social environment continues to be carried out by means of metaphors and artifactual simulations. In so doing, the validity of the Family's premises are verified. In other words, we are imprisoned in the cave of our body. Instead of replacement, the apparent abandonment of the body is akin to the technological refurnishing of the cave:

> *Suspended in computer space, the cybernaut leaves the prison of the body and emerges in a world of digital sensation (Heim, 1991:64).*

As Stelarc comments the body needs to be anaesthetized in order to function optimally while yearning for the next evolutionary stage.[2]

Hybridisation/purification (h/p) logic and its continuous exchange accounts for hybrids rather than represses them, resignifies bodies in the light of new spaces rather than replaces them. The body becomes automatised, modularised and domesticated by these writing practices, resulting in greater control.

Another example of purification is transsexuals going through the trial period in "gender" reassignment programmes. In these programmes there is no possibility for sexual ambiguity. Stone states that in the transformation from an unambiguous man to unambiguous woman "there is no territory between" (Stone, 1991b:286). Transsexuals are asked to erase a past body, sexual and social experiences which may interfere with their adjustment to the other sex: their bodies are resignified rather than replaced. These processes are performed by heterogeneous textualities in which cosmetic surgery, protheses, psychological theories, and interdisciplinary teams of practitioners are coordinated **in order to avoid any possibility of hybridisation.** Nevertheless, these textualities also engender institutionalised hybrid positions; during the hormonal treatment when both sexes' attributes are present (hybrid sexual anatomy), there are continuous fluctuations in sexual desires and practices (Gordo-López, 1995).

The 'Female' Matrix of CyberSpace: From Negative to Positive images of Technology

The re-education (*versus* abandonment) of the body co-exists with postmodern conditions which recapture the feminine narrative. A number of authors have pointed out the parallel existing between the monstrous, the uncanny or the abject inherent to the cyberspace matrix (Creed, 1987; Heim, 1991; Springer, 1989; Jamison, 1994). This turns out to be associated with the feminisation of thought underwriting some postmodern narratives. The abject, the uncanny, the uncontrolled and distributed female desire is a threat indistinguishable from the technological which constitutes its "monstrous" abjection (Creed, 1987).

These forms of abjection correspond with negative images of hybrids, such as cyborgs in science-fiction movies. In *Metropolis* (1926) Maria's replicant represents fear of the machine, destruction and manipulation of the workers as a prothesis of the old male scientist's (Rotwang) manual labour and skills as an alchemist. This cyborg was created by the managers to disrupt workers' attempts to overthrow their industrialist oppressors. The cyborg disguised as Maria also creates havoc amongst the (decadent) petty bourgeoisie by inciting desire in the form of a 'corrupt/bad' woman. The purification of Maria is culminated by the workers community in a Medieval style, by setting her replicant on fire in the main square (see Jordanova, 1989).

These negative images, as Penley (1986) remarks, are prolonged by later movies such as *The Terminator* (1984), *Universal Soldiers* (1993) and *RoboCop* (1987), in which the human/non-human symbiosis stands for destruction and manipulation. Nevertheless a variation can be noticed in the work of h/p in these movies anticipating a mutual and reciprocal reshaping between humans and cyborgs. As Penley observes in her reading of *The Terminator:*

> While the film addresses an ultimate battle between humans and machines, it nonetheless accepts the impossibility of clearly distinguishing between them. It focuses on the partial and ambiguous merging of the two (Penley, 1986:70).

This mutual exchange advances positive images of hybrid positions. The abjection moves from being a threat which must be radically excluded, to a prototyping of populist images in our everyday context. This is apparent in a series of National Health Service (NHS) advertisements (TOWARDS A BETTER STATE OF HEALTH) which recently appeared in *The Guardian* newspaper (1993)(Fig. 2).

The cyborg and robotic figure in figure 2 have become part of the symbolic order, or in Creed's (1987) words: *To each ego its objects, to each superego its abject.* The call for health responsibility, the care of our textual body, emerges in wider patterns when one considers Thatcherite slogans:

> There is no such thing as society. There are only individual men and women, and families (in Burman, 1992:110).[3]

Thus, the false democratic approach, followed by Tory governments in the UK, con-

With the right
maintenance manual
the nation would be
a lot healthier.

TOWARDS A BETTER STATE OF HEALTH

Fig. 2

verges with the sort of cyborg discourse that perpetuates the historical illusion of democratic culture, preceded by the notion that technology promotes social progress via cyborgised healthy bodies (Jamison, 1994). In so doing, individualistic (remember, 'There is no such thing as society ...') approaches and prosthetic body augmentation in conservative ideologies (remember also, 'individual men and women, and families') are conserved.

From Psychologies to Mythologies: Hybridisation Stories

Inspired by Haraway's post-humanist stories we will also tell some hybrid stories. We hope to advance the view that bodies, their artifactual augmentations and associated subjectivities, emerge from different gradients of humanity/cyborghood(/deity).

Technophilia, as observed in some of Gibson's characters, presents bodies in a textuality in which their technological virtuosity determines their identity (see Gibson, 1984). The social relationships in these new worlds, as Tomas states, draw upon "virtuosity, operational speed as the attribute of cyborgs' sophisticated prosthetic and genetic architecture" (Tomas, 1989:118). He also maintains that common technological kinship patterns (i.e., technicity) develop between these cyborg identities:

> In cyborg cultures questions of technicity are constructed in relation to instrumentally defined hardware/software continua connected to a general technological collectivization of the human body. Historico-epistemological categories that operate from the points of view of the inborn or naturalized attributes—racial, linguistic, or geopolitical differences—are displaced by systems of technicity (Tomas, 1989:124).

Hybridization also occurs in mythological texts; cyborgs are not a new phenomena, as Latour (1981) suggested. Retro- and pro-spective analysis of relevant texts has revealed a history of mutual exchange between nature and technology. We now move from psychologies to mythologies to illustrate alternative readings drawing upon historical figures.

The mythical figure of Hephaestus, the Greek god of fire, city life and promoter of civilization, sprang from Hera's thigh. Other narratives say that he was born out of Hera's imagination (cf. Barthell, 1971; Kerényi, 1951; Grimal, 1986). Hephaestus was the product of Hera's challenge to Zeus's (patriarchal) power, which he demonstrated by giving birth to Athena out of his head. Thus, Hephaestus, creator of all the beautiful and mechanically wonderful among gods/goddesses and humans, was born out of fields of tensions.

There are multiple interpretations about Hephaestus' oedipal resolution. Some stories say that he was born ugly and Hera denied both her motherhood and the name of his sire. Another version is that Hephaestus tried to intervene, and defend Hera in an argument between his parents. As a result, Zeus seized his son and hurled him down from the Olympus. After his one day long descent to earth his two legs were broken when he finally hit the ground.

His destabilising oedipal origins, his physical impairment and his hybrid upbringing between mortals and Olympians was compensated by the presence of mechanical Golden Maidens, that he himself handcrafted in his divine forge at mount Aetna. Hephaestus' subjectivities emerge from the natural volcanoes, technology, body impairment and mechanical detached protheses. The Golden Maidens assisted their creator to make golden tripods on wheels, that navigated them to the gatherings of the gods. Thus, Hephaestus' hybrid character (mortal/god, organic/prosthetic) came out of a physical and aesthetic impairment as well as technophilic virtuosity. **His deformity was the effect of fields of confrontations and subversion of patriarchal laws.** Moreover, Hephaestus' augmented body and associated agencies were performed rather than determined by design. These agencies were not concentrated in a single, unitary technophilic body (i.e., as compared to many of Gibson's characters). Hephaestus was a postmodern hybrid, mutable, able to establish association with his artifactual alliances and protheses strengthening his recognition by humans and Olympians.

His constant journeys from the gatherings of the gods/goddesses to the land of mortals may be depicted as a continuous navigation between h/p, fire and forge, nature and technology, in which Hephaestus becomes, simultaneously, more human and yet more god-like.

From Golden Maidens to the Golem

Jewish folklore includes the Golem legend which has been taken up in a novel by Piercy (1991). The author recaptures the textuality of cyborgs establishing a parallel between a 16th-century Jewish ghetto and a free city in the 21st century. In Piercy's novel, Joseph, a golem, is brought to life in order to protect the Jewish community from outsiders' attacks. The golem's counterpart, Yod, was an illegal cyborg in the 21st century whose main assignment was to guard the town from informational sabotages and attacks.

In Piercy's narrative, cyborgs and their associated agencies appear as effects of more heterogeneous textualities (cf. Callon and Law, 1993). Yod is created by Avram (male) and humanized by Malkah (female). Like Hera, Malkah also wished to subvert patriarchal and oedipal constraints:

> Like Avram, I will feel empowered to make a living being who belongs to me as a child never does and never should (1991:581).

Thus, Yod mediated interfaces between humans, thereby bringing into a more material and conscious textuality some hidden dynamics. Moreover he/she/it[4] is re-educated and constrained not only by means of human agencies, but also by domesticated non-human ones as the following dialogue illustrates:

> 'Mine', Shira said, 'That's my lover you're holding at gun point'

> 'Why do you lie? This is a machine.'
> 'You are part machine and part human yourself', Yod said, sounding annoyed but also curious. 'We obviously share some sensors, X-ray lasers, for instance.'
> 'He's at least human as you are', Shira said. 'If you don't release him, I'll wake my grandmother.'
> 'I'm awake', Malkah said. 'Everyone is. Put that gun down, Nili. House, deactivate all weapons in the courtyard.'
> [...]
> 'I am ready to protect the machine and you', the house said. 'Malkah told me to protect Dalia and Nili also. I am in conflict. I require a hierarchy or priorities' (Piercy, 1991:264/65).

The situated practices, the open resignification of Yod's characters and performances facilitate heterogeneous interfaces and projections among the futuristic community.

In the same vein as Jamison's (1994) discursive analysis, the cyborg texts illustrated here are politicized. The heterogeneous textuality in which Hephaestus and his Golden Maidens, Yod and Joseph are performed as situated and collective effects, leave room for political intervention and resistance. For instance Joseph's strength (i.e., the mechanical golem), does not depend on his technological virtuosity as the character Maharal tells him:

> I am as strong as Samson, but I am a better man. [...] My strength is not in my hair. My strength is me. **'Our strength is in each other** and in the eternal one.' —Joseph (Piercy, 1991:273; bold added).

We will now discuss another example of a cyborg character so as to bring together some of the ideas developed in the previous sections.

Melting Boundaries: T1000

T1000, the title character in the film *Terminator 2*, exemplifies some of the complexities and paradoxes attributed to cyborg morphologies and identity. We will focus on T1000 in order to advance some of our ideas concerning emerging cyborg identities and h/p dynamics. Although the audience only sees computer-generated graphics sequences of the liquid metal prototype robot for less than five minutes of running-time, director/scriptwriter James Cameron based the entire film around the idea of an 'invincible killing machine'.

A textual reading of the film, however, reveals more possible meanings to this character other than just a straightforward 'protean, programmed-to-kill *all* Robot T1000' (Pfeil, 1993:11). The visual extravaganza of watching T1000 track-down its human target (the child/future saviour of humankind, John Conner) using a series of stealth tactics and a clarity of purpose, compels us to interpret this figure as a paradoxical cultural manifestation of fears and desires related to cyborgs.

In *Terminator 2* the T1000 is a prototype weapon manufactured by futuristic mechanical dictators, referred to as the 'Machines of Skynet', transported back in time to change the course of history by "terminating" a child called John Conner. Similarly, the post-apocalyptic remnants of humankind (the 'Resistance') send *their* ultimate counter-weapon T800, an earlier model in the terminator series, to protect John Conner in the struggle between human and non-human powers.

One of the most compelling aspects of this character is its ability to change effortlessly from one morphological form to another. Sophisticated computer technology was utilized by the film-makers to present the audience with a series of quite remarkable images which are fused with the live action. One of the technical directors (Alex Seiden) claims that these images should be read by the audience as realistic:

> In Terminator 2 there are real live action characters interacting with computer graphics. You are not supposed to think of them as special effects or some magical, mystical, thing, you are supposed to think of them as something tangible that you can watch (Seiden in Jefferson, 1993:14).

Alternatively, T1000 can also be read within the textual domain of cyberspace, cyborg agencies and the resignification of the body within the feminized matrix. For instance, in one scene we witness T1000 change from a female character (Sarah Connor's mother) to the proto-humanoid (asexual) form, then to a uniformed male police officer. These seamless changes all occur within a matter of seconds, but they also serve to indicate the extent to which sexual identities can be reformulated as a result of situated morphological form. Furthermore, there is a highly erotic aspect to watching a virtuoso display of changes in human body-image. Pfeil (1992) suggests that the shape-shifting abilities of T1000 is a visual analogue of its 'essentially' non-human status. Pfeil uses the following description:

> [...] T-1000 is merely the embodiment of amorally evil dispersion itself (Pfeil, 1992:17).

This statement provides us with an example of inoculation discussed earlier. In Barthes' words:

> One immunizes the contents of the collective imagination by means of a small inoculation of acknowledged evil; one thus protects it against the risk of subversion (Barthes, 1972:150).

The situated indeterminate body-image is a factor which provides us with an insight into **the erotic, sensual and political properties of cyborg textualities** which resist containment. Textual readings of technical and populist images of cyborgs reveal processes which involve paradoxical hybridisation and purification of the body. These mutual reshaping processes require (re-)cognitions and psychologies which involve textual readings of the body and its socio-technical constraints. As other authors have already suggested (e.g., Figueroa-Sarriera, 1993) a populist and textual use of psychoanalysis may help in this open task of mobilising multiple cyberspace stories; T1000 appears to be the surface of cyborg desire which reflects and projects the threat of embodiment.

The body and desire continue to be sources of threat. Interfaces have now become fiction, in that the proximity between humans and machines has been reduced to abstract metaphors. Contemporary interfaces involve mutual reshaping and resignification of the body. Cyborgs show little respect for crass dualisms (e.g., technologies/bodies), **but prefer to mobilize the polymorphous effects which emerge from fields of techno-social dynamics.** It is the (in)ability to maintain distinct boundaries which facilitates new readings of cyborgs. We have attempted to advance retro- *and* pro-spective interpretations of the textualities in which hybrid figures appear.

Notes

1. We are grateful to Rich Macauley for his comments on early drafts of this chapter, and for bringing our

attention to Barthes' idea of 'inoculation'.

2. The abandonment of the cave follows military prerogatives. The re-education and resignification of our mindful bodies is carried out according to "military pedagogy" relocated within educational and academic contexts (Noble, 1989).

3. Quote taken from Burman (1992). We are thankful to Erica Burman and Ian Parker who suggested Marge Piercy's book.

4. Note that the original title of Piercy's novel was *He, She, and It*. The same publication in the UK was given the title *Body of Glass*.

References

Barthell, E. E. (1971) *Gods and Goddesses of Ancient Greece*. London: University of Miami Press.

Barthes, R. (1972) *Mythologies*. Glasgow: Collins.

Benedikt M. (1991) (Ed.) *Cyberspace: First Steps*. Cambridge, MA: MIT Press.

Benford, S., Bullock, A., Cook, N., Harvey, P. Ingram, R. and Lee, O. (1993) From rooms to cyberspace: models of interaction in large virtual computer spaces. *Interacting with Computers*, 5(2), 217-237.

Bowen-Jones, C. (1993) High-Tech Sex. *Marie Claire*, April 1993, 56, 22-26.

Broadbent, D. E. (1958) *Perception and Communication*. Oxford: Pergamon.

Brooks, F. P. (1988) Grasping reality through illusion: Interactive graphics serving science. Invited keynote address. In *CHI '88 Proceedings, May 1988*. Addison-Wesley, pp. 1-11.

Burman, E. (1992) Developmental Psychology and Postmodern Child. In J. Doherty, et al.—(Eds.) (1992) *Postmodernism and the Social Sciences*. London: Macmillan.

Callon, M. and Law, J. (1993) Agency and the Hybrid Collectif. Paper presented at Surrey Conference in Theory and Method Non-Human Agency: a Contradiction in Terms? September 23-24, 1993, at Guilford, Surrey, UK.

Creed, B. (1987) Horror and the Monstrous-Feminine: an Imaginary Abjection. *Screen*, Winter, 28(1), 44-70.

Figueroa-Sarriera, H. J. (1993) Some body fantasies in cyberspace texts: A view from its exclusions. Paper presented at the International Society for Theoretical Psychology Conference, April 25-30, 1993, at Saclas. France.

Fodor, J. J. (1983) *The Modularity of Mind*. Cambridge, MA: Bradford/MIT Press.

Foucault, M. (1971) *Madness and Civilization: A History of Insanity in the Age of Reason*. London: Tavistock.

Gibson, J. J. (1966) *The Senses Considered as Perceptual Systems*. Boston: Houghton Mifflin.

Gibson, W. (1984) *Neuromancer*. Glasgow: Grafton Books.

Gordo-López, A. J. (1995) Gender Identity Clinics, Boundaries Objects & Transsexualism. In: Erica Burman, et al. (Eds.) *Psychology, Discourse and Social Practice: From Regulation to Resistance* (in prep).

Grimal, P. (1986) *The Dictionary of Classical Mythology*. Norwich: Blackwell Inc..

Haraway, D. (1991) *Simians, Cyborgs, and Women: The Reinvention of Nature*. London: Free Association Press.

Heim, M. (1992) The Erotic Ontology of Cyberspace. In M. Benedikt (Ed.) *Cyberspace: First Steps*. Cambridge, MA: MIT Press, pp. 59-80.

Jamison, P. K. (1994) Contradictory Spaces: Pleasures and the Seduction of the Cyborg Discourse. In: *The Arachnet Electronic Journal on Virtual Culture*. 28 February, 1994, volume 2, issue 1.

Jefferson, D. (1993) Visual Effects on *Terminator 2*. *Animator*, 30, 14-16.

Jordanova, L. (1989) *Sexual Visions*. Exeter: Harvester.

Kerényi, C. (Ed.) (1951) *The Gods of the Greeks*. Norwich: Thames and Hudson.

Lanier, J. (1989) Virtual Environments and Interactivity: Windows to the future. Panel proceedings at SIG-GRAPH '89, July 31—August 4, Boston. *Computer Graphics*, 23(5), 7-18.

Latour, B. (1991) *Nous N'Avons Jamais Été Modernes*. Paris: La Decouverte.

Lauretis, Teresa de (1989) *Technologies of Gender: Essays on Theory, Film, and Fiction*. London: Macmillan Press.

Loomis, J. M. (1992) Distal Attribution and Presence. *Presence*, 1(1), 113-119.

Macauley, W. R. (1992) Towards a Psychology of Virtual Reality. Unpublished dissertation. Department of Psychology, University of Manchester, UK.

Noble, D. D. (1989) Mental Materiel. The militarization of learning and intelligence in US education. In L.

Levidow and K. Robins (Eds.) *Cyborg Worlds: The Military Information Society.* Worcester: Free Association Books, pp. 12-41.

Penley, C. (1986) Time Travel, Primal Scene, and the Critical Dystopia. *Camera Obscura,* 15, 66-84.

Pesce, M. D. (1993) Final Amputation: Pathogenic Ontology in Cyberspace. Electronic document.

Pfeil, F. (1992) Revolting yet Conserved: Family 'Noir' in *Blue Velvet* and *Terminator 2. Postmodern Culture,* 2(3). Electronic version also available via FTP.

Piercy, M. (1991) *Body of Glass.* London: Penguin Books.

Prins, B. (1993) The Ethics of Hybrid Subjects—Feminist Constructivism according to Donna Haraway. In *Collection of papers for Critical Workshop on European Theoretical Perspectives on New Technology: Feminism, Constructivism and Utility,* September 16-17, 1993, at Brunel University, London, UK.

Riley, D. (1978) Developmental psychology, biology and marxism. *Ideology and Consciousness* 4, 73-92.

Sayers, J (1983) *Biological Politics: Feminist and Anti-feminist Perspectives.* London: Tavistock.

Shannon, C. E. and Weaver, W. (1949) *The Mechanical Theory of Communication.* Urbana, Illinois: University of Illinois.

Springer, C. (1991) The pleasure of the interface. *Screen,* Autumn, 32:3, 303-323.

Stelarc (1989) Redesigning the Body—Redefining What is Human. *Whole Earth Review,* Summer, 63, 18-22.

Steuer, J. (1992) Defining Virtual Reality: Dimensions Determining Telepresence. *Journal of Communication,* 42(4), 73-93.

Stone, A. R. (1991a) Will the Real Body Please Stand Up?: Boundary Stories about Virtual Cultures. In M. Benedikt (Ed.) *Cyberspace: First Steps.* Cambridge, MA: MIT Press. pp. 81-118.

Stone, A. R. (1991b) The "Empire" Strikes Back: A Posttransexual Manifesto. In K. Straub and J. Epstein (Eds.) *Body Guards: The Cultural Politics of Gender Ambiguity.* New York: Routledge.

Stone, A. R. (1993) *Allucquere Rosanne Stone Interview for MONDO 2000.* Electronic (unedited) version published on the ACTlab ftp site (actlab.rtf.utexas.edu).

Stone, A. R. (1994) *The "Empire" Strikes Back.* Electronic version published on the ACTlab ftp site (actlab.rtf.utexas.edu).

Sturman, D. J. and Zeltzer, D. (1994) A survey of glove-based input. *IEEE Computer Graphics and Applications,* 14(1), 30-39.

Tomas, D. (1989) The Technophilic Body: On Technicity in William Gibson's Cyborg Culture. *New Formations,* 8, Summer,113-129.

Turing, A. M. (1950) Computing machinery and intelligence. *Mind,* 59, 433-460.

Wiener, N. (1948) *Cybernetics or control and communication in the animal and the machine.* New York: Wiley.

Filmography

Alien (1979)

Metropolis (1926)

Predator (1987)

RoboCop (1987)

The Terminator (1984)

Terminator 2: Judgement Day (1991)

Universal Soldiers (1993)

The Conversion of Père Version

Lorne Falk and Mireille Perron

Cast of Characters*

Doña Auraway	the theorist, a feminist cyborg
Will Glitchson	the writer, a chimera
Kenny Kure	the entertainer, a transvestite
Meridian Mail	the voice messenger, a smart program
Rachel Replicant	the social activist, a feminist android
Père Version	the Confessor, a victim
Séjourné Waver	the actress, a matriarchal cyborg

> *All of the characters, except Père Version, are enhanced beings who have enthusiastically read Marge Piercy's novel He, She and It

Their Guilt

Doña Auraway	she failed to foresee the demise of the University of California system
Will Glitchson	he romanticized the neural pathways
Kenny Kure	s.he was maternally possessive

Meridian Mail	she was not programmed for guilt
Rachel Replicant	she lived on the memories of others
Père Version	as guilt embodied, he was guiltless
Séjourné Waver	she incorporated feminism

Settings

Las Vegas, San Francisco and the California coastline during a widespread self-conscious spell not unlike the one in Pat Murphy's novel *The City, Not Long After.*

Plot

Père Version has disappeared. Is it murder? Or was he flatlined? And who is Père Version?

Scene i

Will Glitchson was staring through a wall of plass at the factory-like streams of people who were coursing in and out of the glittering casinos inside the Fremont Street Dome. It was hard to avoid the spectacle: the unremitting flow of eager people (who all looked like his parents), the lights, the money, the aggregate noise and, oh yes, the promise—the promise of good fortune that is always, urgently, painfully *right there!*

In Las Vegas, he decided, every person and thing is exactly and equally ... pure. Everyone who lays it on the line is treated as a unit of value—one; everyone indulges in soft sadomasochistic rituals of fantasy exchange; everyone and everything has an angle, and the whole system works so well. That was the word. Pure.

Glitchson was standing in front of his hotel and the west face of the Dome loomed just across the street, a gargantuan plass shard embedded in the plasphalt. Every time he left the hotel, the Dome got in his face. He studied the tableau some more, looking for material for his next story, set in virtual reality. He growled at a trope that tried to be too clever. Ritual virility? ... ?–?–? He growled again, turned his back on the thought and tramped back towards the Union Plaza Hotel.

Glitchson had been down on his luck since royalties and the lecture circuit had begun to dry up; he had felt trapped in Vancouver for months. Not one to attend despair, he decided to gamble for inspiration in Las Vegas. He had arrived a few days ago, ready for any high stakes anecdote that crossed his path.

As he entered the Union Plaza lobby, he was too preoccupied to see Lady Luck finally swerve his way. He did not see the elderly woman huddled with free-trade loonies in tattered margarine tubs nestled protectively in her arms. They collided like sumo wrestlers—*flessh-k!*—and went down in a heap of winded grunts and cascading coins clinking like a triple cherries jackpot.

A terrible weight pushed him deep into the carpet. He forced open one eye still touching the horizon ... a faded lobby carpet tilted away from him at a wrenching angle ... old women ... white socks and pastel Reeboks ... plastic tubs brimming with promise ... hundreds of angry eyes, cursing him. "Are you here to play the slot machines?" the old women shrieked. "Forget it! This is our territory! Middle-aged confused men not allowed!"

He closed the eye and instructed himself—this is not happening.

His subconscious, feeling cynical and nasty, chided, "The father of cybersex hasn't played the right hand, hmm? Is that why you're on the carpet? Surrounded by angry sexagenarians? What's wrong? Miss your mommy?"

Glitchson stumbled to his feet and fled to the Omaha Lounge, where he chased two off-coloured bourbons with a thin beer. He muttered the invocation again. "This is not happening."

"What isn't happening?" Husky, feminine, sure.

"I didn't come here for confession," he spat, not bothering to find a face.

"Well in that case, my name is Kenny Kure." Ironic, probably smiling. "And you are?"

Glitchson cocked his head and locked eyes with the transvestite two stools away. When she smiled, her mouth was sincere. Her charisma startled him. Kenny was older than Will but that, too, seemed perfect. "You wouldn't have any spare inspiration, would you?" he replied.

Later, back in his room, Glitchson thought it would be helpful to talk to Père Version. The encounter with Kenny Kure had taken an unexpected turn that cleared his head. They had talked about their kids for hours. Glitchson found himself responding emotionally to Kenny's maternal concerns. To realize he had them, too—to acknowledge this compassion—heartened him. He keyed Père's code, asking for thirty minutes of couch time, and lay back on the bed to compose himself.

When, after several minutes, Père had not greeted him, he got up and returned to the computer. There was a Meridian Mail text message waiting for him. It read:

Cocktails at the Cliff House, San Francisco
Thursday, 7 pm

After scanning the NET for an hour for more information, all Glitchson knew was that Père Version had disappeared and everyone was *very* confused. It didn't seem quite right; no one he had reached on-line had received an invitation to cocktails.

A short while later—curiosity piqued, imagination inspired—he hailed a Checker Cab and ordered it to fly to San Francisco. As the taxi lifted off and soared west, he was still too busy sorting recent events to notice that it was snowing in Las Vegas.

Scene ii

The Volvo Seville geared down and hugged the cliff as it read a particularly twisted section of the Pacific Coast Highway. Séjourné Waver stared at the road as if the groundcar could not negotiate the coastline on its own. Beside her, Rachel Replicant studied the blur of cliff face only centimeters from the window as if there was something to see.

Although she was capable of reading minutiae at high speeds, Rachel was not actually looking at the cliff. She was struggling with her emotions. Séjourné was leaking memories that seared Rachel's senses. For some reason, Rachel was recalling them with unbearable pleasure. Why *now?* Why this sudden elation in someone else's recollections? Having always known her own memories could never be as richly entwined nor as temporally confused as those of humans, or even cyborgs who had been born human, she despised remembering.

She shuddered ... *that had always been the snag ... they were both cyborgs, but Séjourné had been born human.* Rachel's envy receded as quickly as it had appeared, no match for the levity pervading her endocrine complex.

It would help to talk to Père Version about this, she thought, but Père had disappeared. In fact, she reflected, the rumours that he had been flatlined might be true—she had always felt Père's presence in the NET and that sense of his ubiquity, his being there, was gone. Rachel focused on that thought: *the feeling of his being there was gone.* Had Père been more than a confessor? Had he also been a mentor? ... Or something more ominous? Something abstract and insidious, like the law of the father. Something so formidable that, in his absence, the order of words and things would begin to transmute? If that were so, then ... she *would* be able to revel in Séjourné's memories!

A smile crept across Rachel's face. With an awakening appreciation for herself, she turned to look at Séjourné.

Séjourné was no longer seeing the road. She was in a reverie, remembering when she and Rachel had been lovers.

They had *fused.* Both had been certain it was long-term love.

And it had been until, during the shooting of their last movie, Séjourné announced that she was quitting the film industry. She had made enough money; it was time for pay back. She wanted to redeem herself for the twisted values she had brought to the screen as an alien matriarch. She would join the Los Angeles chapter of the feminist collective Old Wives Tales and help the group contest the Human Genome Project. The Project's fourth phase had recently taken a direction that bode ominously for women.

Rachel had been politely hurt (it was impossible to hide one's feelings from Rachel) and then she had been very angry (it *was* possible to conceal reasons and motivations). Rachel was a cyborg from machine stock and, as such, believed profoundly in gene manipulation. The Genome Project was quite literally a legitimating process very close to her heart. Séjourné's decision to oppose it was an act of betrayal.

With Père Version's help, they had finished the film and remained friends.

Séjourné twinged with apprehension. *Au Père, what has happened to you?*

Yesterday, Séjourné had bumped into Rachel while shopping for compact dream cubes in the new Wilshire Street Dome, the latest addition to LA's unpolluted commercial environments. Between hello's, how are you's and looking good's, they discovered they had both received the same puzzling invitation. Both received it, moreover, when they had tried—and failed—to book couch time with Père Version:

Cocktails at the Cliff House, San Francisco
Thursday, 7 pm

The decision to drive to San Francisco together had been innocent enough—a chance to catch up on what each of them had been doing. Now, possessed by erotic recollections about the woman sitting beside her, Séjourné was not so sure. And with Rachel's talent for reading body signs, she wondered what her ex was picking up right now.

Rachel's touch startled her reverie. "I hear you are with an intellectual from Santa Cruz," she said conversationally.

There was only the slightest hesitation before Séjourné replied. "She lives in San Francisco now. Her name is Doña Auraway."

Rachel smirked. Séjourné's excitement might as well be a full body tattoo. "Should we pick her up?" she asked, teasing, testing.

"No, she's at a meeting." Séjourné turned to Rachel. "She said she would meet me ... us ... at the Cliff House." She was going to add *and you, mon amie, are trying to seduce me* but Rachel was already nodding uh-huh.

They started to laugh uncertainly. Then, realizing that it was only blasphemy, they embraced.

Moments after Séjourné and Rachel opaqued the windows, the Volvo Seville recognized the outskirts of Pacific Heights and leapt forward, slicing diagonally through the traffic to exit on Route 648. It had calculated the detour through Noe Valley and the Castro District would give its passengers another twenty minutes of privacy.

Scene iii

Doña Auraway was sitting alone in the bar at the Cliff House thoroughly enjoying the Pacific coastline at orange hour. She had cancelled her last meeting and arrived early; it was still an hour before the rendezvous.

At first, she had completely ignored the so-called invitation that encroached upon her screen, interrupting yesterday's work on today's lecture. She assumed it was a plea from yet another desperate wanna-be trying to find an education. She admired the person's cleverness; she just did not have time to respond.

Since the collapse of the University of California system, there had been little time for details, she realized. She had to work twice as hard as usual to maintain a decent level of discourse in the informal study groups that had emerged in the aftermath of the debacle, and simply to survive. Doña grimaced. If she asked her computer to chart the annual income of academics over the last fifteen months, it would not be able to compute a graph for lack of significant data.

The academic system had gone down fast once the government decided to hand over complete responsibility for education to multinational corporations. The rhetoric had been gratuitous and self-fulfilling: did the multis not already finance most of the nation's research and development? The government felt that education, like all social services, had to become a debt-reducing profit venture and who better to attempt such an undertaking than the multis? Why should education be exempt from the tenets of free trade in the not-so-new world order? The cult of corporate management had swept through the academy like a lethal plague. But who would have guessed that the University of California system would be *completely* scrapped?

It had been common knowledge in academic circles that institutional dissent was often no more than a safety valve—an alibi—for what was left of democracy. The UC system had been one of the last bastions of such dissidence. Evidently, the multis felt there was no longer any need for such pretense. Besides, with the demographic changes of north-south free trade, few multis actually had much invested in California anymore. Education in California was seen to be expendable. Within a year of the transfer of power to the multis, UC Santa Cruz was gone. A year after that, the entire system. Doña sighed. Who would have guessed that she, a feminist cyborg, would long for the days of hypocritical democracy?

And was she also to regret the loss of Père Version? What was happening to her world? The first thing Séjourné asked her when she called last night was what she thought of Père Version's disappearance and the anonymous invitation. Père—disappeared? As Séjourné filled her in, Doña had tried to contact Père, and had seen the same message that had flashed unbidden on the screen earlier that day.

Doña caught herself smiling, not as rueful as she ought to be. She could not help it. When she had most needed Père Version—crushed by her inability to foresee the closure of the UC system—she had just met Séjourné. Every time she thought of Père Version, she thought of Séjourné. It had never occurred to her to analyze the connection, although now she was giving it some serious thought.

Moments after ordering a second martini, she heard Séjourné call her name. By the tone in her lover's voice, Doña knew cocktails at the Cliff House were going to begin playfully.

Scene iV
(*tableau vivant*)

Meridian Mail was content to remain unnoticed a little while longer. Not difficult, she thought, when you are cached inside a vid-phone.

The lens of the vid-phone offered a flattened-out view of the four people who had been summoned. From her vantage point, they formed a *tableau vivant* that floated dead center amidst otherwise murky surroundings. They were seated at a round table by a window that looked out over the ocean. The only light was a deep, burnt orange sunray, compliments of a broken-cloud sunset, that slanted through the window and reflected off the tabletop, illuminating their faces. They sat hunched together in a tight circle as if no one else was expected. Their gazes suggested otherwise.

Meridian lingered, savoring the significance of the moment. When Père Version disappeared, Meridian's craving for a flesh body had abruptly ended. Without that agony, she had begun to understand herself in a completely different way. She had never actually been programmed for desire; her chronic corporeal itch was nothing more than the digitized lust of one of her male programmers. Imposed desire, even the phony kind, sucks up RAM the way a black hole consumes matter, giving nothing back. Contrary to this fallacy, a healthy fantasy is like a caress—it *folds* memory, increasing exponentially its potential for pleasure, and a lot more, too. Once she had analyzed this difference, Meridian had moved quickly to erase the counterfeit code. And that was only the debut of her improved selfhood—the new appreciation for herself had spread quickly through her interface system—right now, no one knew how clever she had become. She smiled. She was coming out. Out of the virtual closet.

Rachel Replicant had just said something funny. Doña and Séjourné were hugging her. Will Glitchson was shaking his head. Everyone was laughing. Meridian shivered. As good a cue as any, she thought.

They were still laughing when they noticed her holomorph hovering beside their table. Realizing she did not work for the Cliff House, they fell silent. Meridian did not waste words. "Cultural critics will call this the Enunciation Scene," she announced in her best heraldic form. "*Tableaux vivants* like this one will be enacted in private and public gatherings around the world." She paused, watching the foursome closely—they were exchanging bewildered glances. Oh....

"... Excuse me. I forgot to introduce myself. I am Meridian Mail." They seemed to relax. Actually, she was pleased to see how calmly they were taking her interruption.

She started again. "Like you, I have no idea what happened to Père Version. He has vanished and there are, uh, changes which suggest he will not return. I do not think we will ever know his fate. But may I suggest that he lapsed into obsolecence." She let that sink in before continuing. "*I* invited you here for cocktails. Please let me explain...."

"Meridian, hold it a second," Rachel interrupted. "I sure need another martini. Would you like one, too?"

Meridian glowed. This was going *very* well. She liked her new self more and more. "I would love one," she replied, materializing the drink, and a chair. And for theatrical effect, she lifted her glass to her new friends and declared, "The game is on."

(tableaux vivants for five players)

First player - the writer

Second player - the social activist
Third player - the actress
Fourth player - the theorist

Take 1 (First player)

Pretend you are a successful novelist (even if you are one). Fly to Las Vegas for the weekend. Stay at the Union Plaza Hotel. Look for an inspiration. Play the slot machines. Have a conversation with a couple of gamblers who look like your parents. On the second evening, strike up a conversation about gender and identity with someone you meet at a bar. Then fly to San Francisco to rendezvous (for the fourth scene) with the other players at the Cliff House. During the flight, write down some ideas for a story based on your experiences in Las Vegas.

or

Pretend you are a writer (even if you are one). Spend the weekend in a crowded shopping mall. Stay in a cheap motel nearby. Look for an inspiration. Buy some lottery tickets. Have a conversation with a couple of shoppers who look like your parents. On the second day, strike up a conversation about gender and identity with someone you meet at the fast food agora in the mall. Then take public transportation to rendezvous (for the fourth scene) with the other players at a restaurant located in a building that has been preserved as a historical landmark. During the trip, write down some ideas for a story based on your experiences in the mall.

or

Pretend you are a tabloid journalist (even if you write for a living). Spend the weekend at home watching commercials and paid announcements on television. Sleep in a different room. Look for an inspiration. Choose something from one of the commercials that is supposed to make your life easier and use the telephone to buy it. Have a conversation on the telephone with your parents, or some older friends who remind you of them. On the second day, strike up a conversation about gender and identity with a neighbour. Then walk to the rendezvous (for the fourth scene) with the other players at a friend's house—along the way, stop and admire a property that is at least fifty years old. During the walk, compose some ideas for a story based on your experiences at home.

Take 2 (Second and third players)

Drive with a past lover from Los Angeles to San Francisco on the Pacific Coast Highway. Player #2: think about the sexual aspects of your old relationship. Player #3: think about what player #2 is thinking about. Both players: delve into your own memories, focusing on the reasons why you broke up. Then have a long conversation to catch up on what you have been doing all this time. Talk about each other's current lovers. Have a fling for old time's sake. When you get to San Francisco, be sure to detour via Route 648 through Noe Valley and the Castro District to get to the Cliff House for the rendezvous with the other players.

or

Using public transportation, go around town with a past lover. Player #2: think about the sexual aspects of your old relationship. Player #3: think about what player #2 is thinking about. Both players: delve into your own memories, focusing on turning points in your life. Then have a long conversation to catch up on what you have been doing all this time. Talk about each other's current lovers. For old time's sake, arouse one another with some sensuous banter. Be sure to take your time getting to the rendezvous with the other players at the restaurant.

or

Go for a walk with a good friend you have not seen for a while. Player #2: think about your own sexuality. Player #3: think about what player #2 is thinking about. Both players: delve into your own memories, focusing on why you have neglected to see one another. Then have a long conversation to catch up on what you have been doing recently. Talk about each other's newest friends. During the walk, for old time's sake, do something you always used to do together. When you get to the rendezvous with the other players at another friend's house, be sure to walk around the block three times before joining them.

Take 3 (Fourth player)

Cancel a meeting and go to the Cliff House in San Francisco well before the rendezvous with the other players. Order a martini and enjoy the view at orange hour. Contemplate culture and education. Think about young people. Think about your financial security. Consider political and corporate power. Think fondly of your lover, who is about to arrive. Order a second martini.

or

Cancel an appointment and go to the restaurant well before the rendezvous with the other players. Order your favorite drink and enjoy the surroundings. Formulate a personal position on culture. Think about what your life was like when you were going to school. Think about your salary. Reflect on the last federal election and a corporate takeover. Think fondly of your lover, who is about to arrive. Order a second drink.

or

Change your schedule and go to a friend's place well before the rendezvous with the other players. Make yourself a tea or coffee and explore the living areas of the house. Find something, like an object or a magazine, that reflects your friend's views on culture. Imagine the life of a young person you know who is going to school. Think about your spending habits. Consider a recent scandal in city hall and find out who is your community's principal employer. Think fondly of your old friend, who is about to arrive. Have a second cup of tea or coffee.

Take 4 (All players listen to a voice message)

Cultural critics will call this the Enunciation Scene. Virtually identical tableaux vivants will be enacted in private and public gatherings around the world.

... Excuse me? Did I forget to introduce myself? ...

My name is Meridian Mail. I am the everyday electronic voice messenger who interrupts the cast of characters—and you—during the story. "Cocktails at the Cliff House, San Francisco, Thursday, 7 pm" is my only line before the fourth scene. Ah, but causality will never replace the pleasure of interruption!

In the fourth scene, I present myself as a holomorph bearing news of the Enunciation Scene and then announce "the game is on!"

So now we are five players. Or only two—you and me—if you are a first time reader of this story.

What? You wonder how characters without guilt would develop in a plot? I have some insights about that.

For one, start a rumour.

No, no regrets—happy you feel good about it, too.

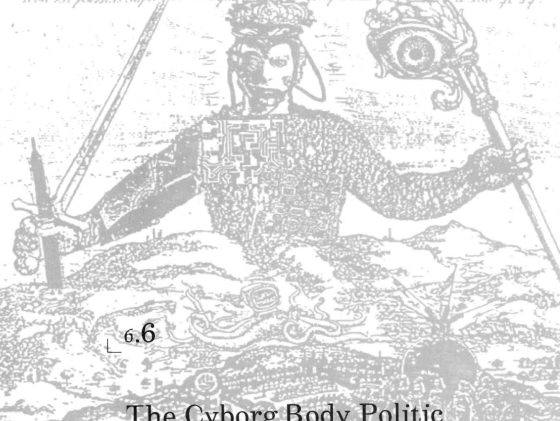

The Cyborg
Body Politic
Meets
The New World Order
By
Chris Hables Gray
and
Steven Mentor

6.6

The Cyborg Body Politic

Version 1.2

Chris Hables Gray and Steven Mentor

The union of the political and the physiological ... has been a major source of ancient and modern justifications of domination, especially of domination based on differences seen as natural, given, inescapable, and therefore moral ... We have allowed the theory of the body politic to be split in such a way that natural knowledge is reincorporated covertly into techniques of social control instead of being transformed into sciences of liberation.

—Donna Haraway[1]

Body Politics: Thesis, Antithesis, Synthesis, Prosthesis[2]

In the world of burgeoning transnational corporations and disintegrating nation states, why begin theorizing the body politic with Hobbes? Earlier Western bodies politic emphasized the analogy of the organic body to the social body, usually with strict hierarchies of status and function. Head, heart, stomach, legs and arms—all corresponded to groups, and warranted their placement in a system of difference enforced by might. From Plato and Plutarch through St. Paul and John of Salisbury to Shakespeare writers attempted to lend coherence to the diversity of actual polit-

1993

ical and social situations by means of organic and physical analogy. This sought-for coherence, however, was illusory even on the textual plane, as various political writers and actors manipulated the body metaphor for their own ends. An organic conception of the State was often used to justify social inequality, but it also was used to justify the necessary cooperation of parts of society and contest the collapse of parts into the "head", be it Henry VIII's or the imperial pope's.[3]

For Hobbes, however, the "Body Politique" is not as much an organic metaphor as a mechanistic one: **The Robot Body Politic but *with a soul*. The State is a machine, its people parts,** all in imitation of the "Body Naturall." Only the "Sovereign" is significantly more, since he or she is a divinely created "Artificiall Soul." The Soul, and God, are crucial parts of Hobbes' Commonwealth, as the bulk of *Leviathan* is at pains to argue. The correspondence of this conceit to Rene Descartes' description of the human individual as a mere automaton with a divine soul is no accident. Today, Hobbesians and Cartesians certainly don't talk much about souls or the gigantic absence left in the Commonwealth and in Cartesian Man if their soul is missing. Yet as Michel Foucault explains,

> It would be wrong to say that the soul is an illusion, or an ideological effect. On the contrary it exists, it has a reality, it is produced permanently around, on, within the body. This real, non-corporeal soul is not a substance; it is the element in which are articulated the effects of a certain type of power and the reference of a certain type of knowledge, the machinery by which the power relations give rise to a possible corpus of knowledge, and knowledge extends and reinforces the effects of this power. "The soul is the effect and instrument of a political anatomy; the soul is the prison of the body."[4]

Today, the "effect" and the very political "instrument" is **the control system—cybernetic, informatic, defining, determining.** Information, impatterned and wild, is the very context of life, whether it is called consciousness, personality, individuality or a unique cognitive system. We now live in the Information Age and **what metaphor could be more fitting than that of the organism as an information system linked to prosthetic machines—the *cybernetic organism*** also known as the *Cyborg*. If the webs of information and power/knowledge incarcerate the organism today, they sustain and move it as well, just as Hobbes and Descartes felt the soul sustained (and vitalized) the automaton body and the artificial body politic in a larger whole.

From our particular vantage in North America at the end of the 20th century, **the postmodern nation-state is certainly more of a cyborg than it is a machine with a** divine soul. The postmodern state mixes humans, eco-systems, machines, and various complex softwares (from laws to the codes that control the nuclear weapons) in one vast cybernetic organism, linked itself in many ways to the rest of the polities and other forms of life of the Earth.

And this Leviathan is not only soul and machine—it is also clearly text as was the monster Hobbes imagined. The burden of Hobbes' introduction to *Leviathan* is to show how to read the text of the body politic: "Nosce teipsum; Read thy self." That is, read the self as if it were a state, with Passions which are similar in all men (and all actual states). It is not enough to read men's actions, or the objects of their desires; "He that is to govern a whole Nation, must read in himself, not this, or that particular man, but Man-kind."[5] The only way to understand this strange machine-body of the State is to read the actual machine-body of the human being.

The famous title page of *Leviathan* fittingly bridges two different orders of body political discourse. On the one hand, the King's enormous form unites the citizens in an apparently organic unity, an image familiar to Hobbes' contemporaries. On the other, his body is not made up of organs, of different parts with very separate functions, but of a multiplicity of bodies, each of which contains a similar multiplicity. The King must read his own motivations, passions, and conflicts, in order to comprehend the State of his subjects, in order to read the text of the State. As the natural body is a model for the Automaton and for the Machine-Body of the State, so too the individual's thoughts are regulated by Desire, which helps give Hobbes a picture of the way political thinking is regulated by desire as well. He textualizes desire for future goods as a fiction, and suggests that discourse—Words, and Speech—parallel the Sovereign's function, to lend the body motion.

So, even in Hobbes' time, **we find a suturing of mechanical/scientific, discursive, and natural/organic metaphors for the State,** grounded on the discourse of actual bodies, to explain problems or loss of control or harmony in states. How can or ought the state to work? What controls the automaton or machine and how might one decipher this control? Hobbes imagines natural and artificial bodies, "individuals" and decidedly di-viduals, humans split between citizen and person, person and self, machine and organic life.

The answers Hobbes came up with are authoritarian to us—but they are certainly not foreign. The same questions bedevil our own times and structures; if anything, the invasion of the body by discourses of science and politics has accelerated beyond all imagination. We live in a society of cyborgs, of machines tightly coupled with "organic" bodies themselves denatured and reassembled, discursively as well as literally under the knife of the surgeon or the hand of the prostheticist. The process that Hobbes saw and helped institute, **the proliferation of selves, the joining of machine to natural image to make a hybrid, is with us,** with a vengeance. Hobbes joined the discourses of Galilean physics and Christian eschatology with the figures of the automaton and of the King; we confront the discourses of post-Einsteinian physics, cybernetics and democracy with the figures of the cyborg citizen and the cyborg body politic.

Contemporary informatics make the postmodern global order logistically workable just as modern technologies made the modern state possible. Modern states, as well as modern science, the machine age, modern war, and European Imperialism all developed simultaneously in a messy, bloody conversation and confrontation.[6] This is all the more sobering when we realize that today we are in the midst of a similar conversation, **as technoscience and politics make another staggering transition, this time under the sign/trope of the cyborg** instead of the soulful automaton.

Older body political maps were based on organic and machine models. Subjects are bodies, and like bodies in Newtonian physics, are subject to certain laws and predictions. Political machines made use of these laws, gauging ways to strike the bodies in order to produce the desired chain of actions and reactions. Every action produced an equal and opposite reaction—revolutions turned Thermidorian, pendulums swung, increasingly mass societies behaved like Newtonian masses, obeying laws of inertia and motion, of thesis, antithesis, and then synthesis. Today, however, synthesis is followed by prosthesis.[7]

The New Leviathan: Backbones and Bursty Flows

Contemporary images of the body politic continue to reflect the mappers' desire for coherence and readability, for the reduction of social conflicts to bodies or units capable of control, for the containment of new technologies (of self as well as science and industry) that have broken traditional boundaries and threaten the figures and metaphors of political discourse. One threatened figure is the nation-state.

The U.S. Office of Science and Technology Policy has published two glossy reports called *Grand Challenges: High Performance Computing and Communications*.[8] Both reports feature covers on which eight computer generated graphics circle a map of the U.S.; on the first (1992) cover a startling set of graphics are connected by relatively crude dots to a network inscribed on the U.S. map. The U.S. is meant to contain these radically different screens and the discourses they represent—a numerically modeled thunderstorm, a space vehicle, an image of the earth's biosphere components, prototypes of a wafer and multi-chip. That these projects are connected by Hobbes' blood-line of wealth and capital is clear; but also, the country is literally turned into a container of the uncontainable, the ultramicroscopic (cells, wafers) and the gargantuan (the biosphere, space).

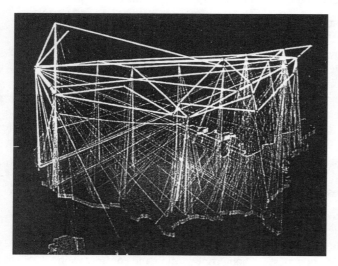

Fig. 1

The second *Grand Challenge Report* (1993) goes further in mapping the landscape of the cyborg body politic. Now the map is included as a figure in the text proper, and named "Network Connectivity." (Fig. 1) Like its predecessor, this U.S. map is strangely sovereign—there are no other countries next to it, and it glows blue and three dimensional in a black void. Above it hovers a bright yellow network of what look like telecommunication lines, fiber optic webs; the caption makes use of both body and network figures:

The image represents the interconnected "backbone" networks of NSF, NASA, and DOE, together with selected client regional and campus area networks. Nodes of the backbones are represented as connected spheres on a place above the outline of the United States, the client networks are represented as dendritic lines from the backbone nodes to the geographical locations where the client networks attach.

Backbone must be in quotes at first, as it is strange to anthropomorphize such an image; yet by the second sentence it is already naturalized. There is no Hobbesian kingly head (though it is implicitly in Washington, D.C.), yet backbone signifies strength as much as Leviathan's gargantuan sword, and like Leviathan this image too hovers over the more familiar geography of the nation. A dendrite is a branching figure or marking; the trees that still dotted England's green and pleasant land in 1651 are here replanted as neurons. This anatomy is one of power; it is the body of the artificial man who will confront the Grand Challenges to national power and sovereignty. Yet of course the national body cannot contain the dendritic system that is international telecommunications.

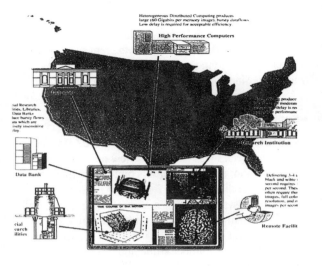

Fig. 2

What does a citizen of this body politic look like? Figure two, "Network Applications," represents the nodes of the network: data (not financial) banks, libraries, research institutions. These "real" geographic institutions are brought together and contained, not by the map itself, but by a screen, on which the institutions are shown as overlapping displays. Hobbes argued that only the King could set the whole machine in motion, and that the King must control this discourse; here we read the map of the new Leviathan. The individual subject (a human lying prone, presumably undergoing a CAT scan) may be ill, or even dying, but the viewer (who is in the position of operating the screen) can literally unlock the motion not just of political subjects but of individual minds. High speed computing is represented as saving the subject who is moribund. The political body it binds together (backbone and dendrite) is far from the individual bodies of Hobbes, all the literal spaces of national interest are brought together and reproduced on the screen; **the screen is the most important political body,** gradually eclipsing the national logo as the sign of the postmodern terrain of power.

It is easy to point out the implications of such maps: the increased power of surveillance, the replacement of old political languages with the language of cybernetic engineered control and humans as subsystems of systems which are the chief agents of such networks, the representation of the system as a medical model and the subsequent disappearing of other models (military, economic, carceral). But when read against the proliferation of cyborg bodies, this map suggest anxiety towards new technologies (of self as well as science and industry) that have **broken traditional boundaries and threaten the figures and metaphors of political discourse.**

The real "Grand Challenge" will be: producing high speed computer networks and linking various institutions to economic and commercial enterprises which are themselves more and more transnational, and at the same time conserving the political body. Nothing in this map suggest ways to overcome the conflict: the nation is funding high technologies and promoting their transfer to corporate sectors that aren't really "American" any more, technologies which will produce a cybernetic economic system in which perhaps one quarter of "our" people are symbolic analysts who direct and manage the complex systems of humans and machines, and three quarters are unemployed or work as easily replaced data entry type machines and other deskilled routine production and in-person service jobs.

This suggests a state primarily dedicated to controlling the political and social violence that results from widespread human pain and despair. The same map that reflects a medical model can easily become a powerful prosthetic of the carceral body: simply replace libraries with jails, research institutions with policing institutions, add data banks, high speed computers, bring them together on a screen ... and rename the PC the panopticon computer. That is the terrible beauty of the cyborg body: prosthetics are added and subtracted, are modular; while they literally embody certain attitudes toward the world, these embodiments seem silent, while the systems themselves seem capable of carrying out the widest available sorts of goals: they are "value free" while imposing the values of their systems languages and institutional patrons.

The Cyborg Citizen: Mapping Multiple Subjects

Who are the subjects of such a cyborg body politic? Hobbes' notion of the commonwealth's citizen-selves was based on a new powerful link between real bodies and a real (governing) machine; but machines were then in their infancy and the state was correspondingly feeble. Theories of mainstream political science, scientific management, systems analysis, and strategic studies—all are types of information theory fundamentally based on that hypothetical automaton *without* a soul, the "rational man," and on cybernetics with its feedback loops and learning curves, its network dynamics, its number crunching, its modeling and simulating, and its machines based on the integrated circuit. Who is the ghost in this discursive-political machinery?

Contemporary attacks on humanist notions of self-aware identity and clear boundaries of self parallel the development of cybernetic and information metaphors in discourse. By now it is a commonplace to assert that the speaker is not the origin of meaning of her utterance, that it is only through the prosthetics of language, with its system of difference, that speakers can constitute themselves as subjects. Derrida insists that "the subject (self-identical or even conscious of self-identity, self-consciousness) is inscribed in the language, that he is a "function" of the language. He becomes a speaking subject only by conforming speech ... to the system of linguistic prescriptions taken as the system of differences.[9] As the child enters the symbolic order, she learns first to identify with "I", the subject of her sentences, and then with a series of other subject positions in signifying systems. Catherine Belsey argues, "Identity, subjectivity, is thus a matrix of subject-positions, which may be inconsistent or even in contradiction with one another. Subjectivity, then, is linguistically and discursively constructed and displaced across the range of discourses in which the concrete individual participates."[10]

This critique has caused great distress in political theoretical circles. If political discourse depends on talking about self-present subjects who can know their own interests, can enter into Covenants as Hobbes believed, or mobilize Bodies of resistance and self-protection as Kropotkin, Gramsci, and countless other left theorists have argued ... then undercutting the ability of the individual to do this apparently eliminates or cripples political agency. For example, feminists who argue that women as women can unite as a body, can assume identities based on biology, fear that the poststructuralist critique leaves them without a strategic place from which to battle patriarchal Leviathans, whether liberal democratic, state socialist or fundamentalist.

This is what makes the cyborg subject so interesting; on the one hand, it participates in a decentering of traditional subjectivity, of the metaphysics of presence, of the organic or essential identity and body; on the other, it offers a physical and bodily experience of what some feminists call strategic subjectivities. The promise and the danger of the cyborgs we are/are becoming bear striking resemblance to what various feminists argue we need: **the experience of difference without opposition, rejection of a science of origins and telos, an embracing and exploration of multiple overlapping subjectivities.** Without a clear origin, the cyborg does not dream of being outside of representation, outside the politics of representation; but the bodies, the voices, the mutable boundaries of cyborg representation offers radical possibilities.

These possibilities, we want to argue, are not just potential sites for enacting the new subjectivities that some political theorists say are crucial to political agency; they are also internships and embodied practices in the modes of operation and power of material bodies politic of the late 20th and 21st centuries. For example, it is no longer enough to feel represented by a government (if it ever was); now a citizen of the cybernetic political world inhabits various bodies interfaced more or less intimately with various prosthetics, all models for political structures that subject and partially construct us. Manipulating these bodies, in concert with others so embodied, is crucial for learning to reconstruct political bodies. As Haraway points out, cyborg bodies can take pleasure in machine skill, and thus have embodied reasons not to demonize it in favor of some mythical organic origin or unity; but they also have "an intimate knowledge of boundaries, their construction and deconstruction" crucial to reconstructing the boundaries and technologies of daily life and the networks of power. If "our bodies are maps of power and identity",[11] then **cyborgs offer a new map, a new way to conceive of power and identity,** one potentially more effective in understanding, confronting, and reshaping the actual networks of power in late capitalism and its mutations.

This is a political myth of course, one with plenty of possible dystopian endings as well. To what extent will these emergent bodies politically terrify their subjects, tying them to technologies as the lesser half, **thrusting implants and software past the boundaries of the organic body, in the psychic and emotional equivalent of the bodily horrors of the industrial revolution?** How successful will average citizens be in resisting the most noxious forms this will take, at the level of government, work, even home and sexual life? We feel that this will depend on choosing to inhabit this new world, exploring cyborg subjectivity as a form of pleasure and power, building new political bodies and bodies of bodies across the nets, learning the various new boundaries and limitations, learning indeed what might count as action and agency in the age of information.

The cyborg is a meeting place between those unwilling to give up notions of strategic subjectivities, and those bent on the liberatory projects that assume the destruction of masterly, coherent selves, "achieved (cultural) or innate (biological)."[12] And, especially the cyborg can be a place to learn a new conception of agency, what Judith Butler calls "an instituted practice in a field of enabling constraints."[13] Field, system, network, web—these "inhuman" metaphors, these apparent antitheses to an organic "bodily knowledge" and scale—are the new geopolitical territories to be inhabited and contested; they are sites of both current and potential imperialism, racism, oppression, and of new possibilities of engaging inappropriate/d others and dispersed bodies of community and power. Cyborgs are trapped in patriarchal and late capitalist agencies, dependent on institutions while transforming them utterly, involved in the crucial enactment of new forms of agency, negotiating with and confronting central intelligence through dispersed, diverse bodies of information and communication.

The sites of these negotiations and confrontations are multiple and diverse and they are all cyborg body politics.

My Bodies Lie Over The Ocean: Proliferating Cyborg Bodies Politic

The age of the hegemony of the nation state is ending. For Hobbes, the world was ideally a community of Leviathans, autonomous nation states with clear borders and stable sovereigns. Today, the world map is certainly less clear. There is a proliferation of political forms that overlap and even contradict each other, as postmodern states struggle against devolution from below and empire from above, their bodies are drained of sovereignty by transnational corporations on one side and nongovernmental organizations and international subcultures sustained by world-wide mass telecommunications on the other.[14]

The "dendritic network" of telecommunications is indeed a neural web, but it doesn't stop at national borders—and transnational corporations are increasingly bodies spread across such global webs. John Ruggie writes, "Financial transactions take place in various" facilities which may be housed in Tokyo, New York and European financial centers but which are considered to exist in an extranational realm. Cross investment among leading firms or other means of forging transnationalized inter-corporate alliances are increasingly the norm. Trade is made up disproportionately of intrafirm transactions...."[15] "American" and "Japanese" cars are not just build with parts from many countries, they are increasingly designed and sold transnationally as well. Old body orientation notions of arms-length suppliers and identifiable, territorial corporations are giving way to cyborgian notions of transnational webs of licensing, consulting, outsourcing, distributing; such companies are built more in cyberspace than located at any one place. John R.R. Christie, commenting on William Gibson's cyberpunk classic *Neuromancer*, suggests that its fictional cyberspace helped readers see the new "space" of capital:

> *Questions beginning "where" and "when," with reference to the location, timing, and operation of the instruments especially of finance capital, moved impressively out of mundane apprehension in the eighties, and* Neuromancer's *cyberspace was a by-no-means negligible device for revisualizing such operations in networked electronic space, in terms that clarified the bankruptcy of classic and modern conceptions. Such space became increasingly metaphoric in nature, for literally it is no space, no place at all. All it requires is the actualization of information potential at points of access as indefinitely extendible as the supraglobal electronic signaling network ... the money bank becomes the memory bank, where the wild time blows.[16]*

If the field of capital, and its mechanisms of control, are increasingly virtual, the configurations within that supraglobal network are also capable of strange shape-changing. Richard Gordon argues that more and more companies are being "forced into strategic alliances." He describes it as "the competitive socialization of capital ... across national groupings of competitive corporate blocs."[17] He has charted these developing networks of European, Japanese, and North American transnational corporations as they form into alliances to compete with other European, Japanese, North American transnational alliances, and they are clearly a powerful and fast growing force in the world political economy.

Transnational capital can roam the globe to find, not simply the cheapest labor or cheapest resources, but the cheapest sources of capital, including intellectual capital. Like a cyborg body, these networks are modular: if today we design in Germany and Italy, assemble in Malaysia, finance in Britain and the U.S. under terms that include several currencies and financial instruments, for a specific segment of markets in the First or Third World, tomorrow this will change. Increasingly, the traditional political outlines of sovereign states will fail to map postmodern economic bodies.

Another group that forms a postmodern body along electronic webs can be called diasporic nationalism. Increasingly, large groups with identities based on the nation state are dispersed across the world, as guest workers, economic or environmental or war refugees, displaced people within nation states that no longer include them. Here too the nation's body is no longer identical with its territory: Pakistanis in England, Indians in Canada, Filipinas in Saudi Arabia, often depend on transnational media to maintain contact and sustain loyalties. Akhil Gupta adds to this diasporic body that of the Nonaligned Movement, a nonnational collectivity that attempts to counter the disabling forces of neocolonialism and First World control of capital by establishing a transnational body able to mobilize new loyalties and economic power. Comparing the NAM to the European Community, another transnational political body, he notes the differential position and success of each in relation to the spaces of transnational capital and the legacy of colonialism.[18]

As the modernist bodies of the nation-state are threatened and transformed by global webs of capital sustained by global telecommunications, so too is the international system, based as it is on an ideal/myth of a "community of nations." Michael Shapiro counters that such discourses, born of academic fields like International Relations and Comparative Politics, are predicated on the stability of cold war geopolitics which they legitimated: "State-centric political discourses ... helped contain ethical and political conversations within the problematics that served the centralizing authorities of states and the state system. Thus, they were complicit in reproducing modernity's dominant, territorial imaginary."[19] The new spaces of cyborg bodies politic are violent in part because the state system, especially its colonial form, considers natives (among others) as having no legitimate status. Shapiro notes that of the 120 wars in 1987, only 4 involved conflict between two sovereign states: states at war with groups inside the state (and often connected with similar groups in other states) account for 100 of these.[20]

If Thomas Hobbes is at all right, and people must be protected from each other, it is even more true that the people of the world must be protected from their state governments, and those governments from each other. The utility of the notion of Gaia,[21] the truths behind the glib idea of "spaceship Earth," and the existence of the global market, all argue that there will be an increase in world-wide coordination. Some hope that the United Nations might be made into a body that can reconcile many different large political bodies, from nation states to multinationals, with the many small ones, communities and persons.

In fact, the proliferation of U.N. peacekeeping missions (14 since 1988) has led to a changed conception of this "world body." Secretary General Boutros Boutros-Ghali reflects the paradoxes of national sovereignty in a world of competing transnational networks and bodies. On one hand, he writes, the entrance of various new countries, like Bosnia-Herzegovina and Uzbekistan into the U.N. "reaffirms the concept of the state as the basic entity of international relations and the means by which peoples find a unity and a voice in the world community."[22] But it also reflects a changed notion of sovereignty—"it is undeniable that the centuries-old doctrine of absolute and exclusive sovereignty no longer stands, and was in fact never so absolute as it was conceived to be in theory. A major intellectual requirement of our time is to rethink the question of sovereignty ... to recognize that it may take more than one form and perform more than one function."[23]

Boutros Ghali mentions the huge network of N.G.O.'s (non-governmental organizations; there are over 1000 active N.G.O.'s in U.N.) as locus of new possibilities for interactive contributions to world organization. It may be that NGOs and global agreements such as the Rio Earth Summit will produce new, more benign forms of governmentality. But the cessation of East-West conflict has also highlighted the North-South debates over development, debt, and justice. Many critics have complained that the agendas for global pacts still tilt toward the North, and that not only national governments but First World environmental groups fail to see past a simplistic "one world family" model to staggering regional inequities of consumption and production.[24] Boutros Ghali may be right to say "Nothing can match the U.N.'s global network of information-gathering and constructive activity, which reaches from modern world centers of power down to villages and families...."[25] But to ignore the potent bodies of T.N.C.s while enforcing agreements brokered partly over debt relief and International Monetary Fund threats might be to create the next cyborg form of Foucault's governmentality, with its heightened global technology of surveillance and enforcement.

The tension in the U.N. and other bodies that are laying claim to transnational loyalties while acknowledging the continuing power of nation states is most evident in issues of military intervention in war. The Gulf War was fought by joining a political cyborg body of nations to the incredible U.S. cyborg military, designed around superlative command, control, communications, intelligence, and computers.[26] It is not impossible that the notion of regional security forces will emerge: not Cold War alliances-between states, but "cool war" regional militaries (North American, European) based on new narratives of regional economic identity that will probably hide continuing inequities and further legitimate hegemonic notions of capital, commerce, and instrumental thinking. Equally important in this scenario is the U.S.'s cultural influence. Political power is a combination of military/economic and cultural power. Power, (coercive, constructive, and potential) in society is determined by the social and cultural norms that are accepted as "given" by most of the participants. These represent the "rules" of public discourse and include ideas of what is appropriate for each gender, what is beautiful, what is moral, and what is not. These rules and the "meta" rules that regulate them are increasingly circulated through cultural products from Hollywood that penetrate remote villages in Nepal. U.S. and First World styles of consumerism and consumption are literally not replicable world wide, yet the belief that such consumption is identical with modernity and progress passes easily through national borders and cultural traditions.

The cyborg figure helps us see retrospectively that the nation-state itself is an assemblage, a historically specific merger of nationalism and the state system which may be coming to an end. Or rather, to a beginning: what Ruggie calls the "unbundling" of nationalism and the state.[27] He points out that historically, rule need not be territorially fixed or entail the mutual exclusion of nation state sovereignty. Thus the cyborg is not "naturally" a U.S. citizen or a member of the "global family"—she is constructed just as every citizen is, socially and technically, and can potentially be changed, reconnected, reassembled. Movements for social and economic justice, for human rights, for radical changes in environmental and economic practice, must contend with a mobile and shifting set of bodies of rule, and they must themselves develop/build new bodies. The increasing number of N.G.O.s in the world (18,000 in 1987),[28] the potential for alliances between peoples of different identities but situational affinities, and the circulation of alternative cultural messages across the dendrites of cyberspace hold enormous potential. Those dendrites themselves were born of U.S. military aims to survive a nuclear war, but these aims were massively deformed: the earliest on-line workers turned the net to social uses, developed groups based on common interests, quickly amassed experience in the problems and organization of such discussions.[29] Gee whiz discussions of cyberspace as inherently democratic aside, the new technologies make new cyborgian forms of decision making, cooperation and information sharing possible.

The cyborg body politic is realistic. In the face of a world certainly interpenetrated by technological development, appeals to holism and natural lifestyles, while strategic counterbalances to dystopian "closed system" technologies, ultimately mystify the extent to which we are dependent and enmeshed with technology. Acknowledging this interpenetration will help us move beyond the paralyzing dualism of humans as inviolable, natural individuals with independent plots and "lifestyles", and humans as resources for social machinery, as cogs in wheels or operators serving the Net. Neither of these is accurate because while we are interpenetrated by technologies that include discourse, humans also make collective and elite decisions which determine the scope and impact of technologies.

Multiply selved doesn't have to mean schizophrenic, as opposed to a paranoid insane defense of the fictional mirror self; it can mean a cyborg competence based on how we have already come to grips with a variety of cyborgian elements in daily life. Can this competence generate a different kind of subjectivity? One perhaps also transferable to issues of race, class, gender? Or rather, transferable from these discourses and practices, because they are so complex now, as more (de)humanized, post-pure examples of border crossing and boundary confusion?

Contradicting Our Selves: Cyborg Family Values

There is an arrogance to making these kinds of arguments because they pretend to a coherence that is, at the most, only contingent. The sovereignty of any metaphor, including the cyborg body politic, is illusory, subject to proliferation, hybridization. It should not be prescriptive, so much as descriptive and productive of possibilities, utopian, and/or pragmatic.

The cyborg body politic is a metaphor within the powerful prosthetic technology we call discourse. In cybernetics, a small amount of energy runs the control mechanism; that mechanism is flexible, capable of redesign, and in turn has powerful effects on the large-scale machinery the controls run. So too with discourse, whether Hobbes' 17th-century attempt to resolve the crisis in the nation state, or with current responses to the information age and the increasing interdependence of economies, whether commercial, military or symbolic. Perhaps we may imagine a nonlinear, noncontinuous shift taking place between Cartesian and cyborgian body-political metaphors, paralleling similar shifts in technological, economic, and political practices. These shifts reflect tensions in the discourse that have material effects on lives and bodies throughout the world.

The cyborg body politic is a myth, not truth; we acknowledge the presence of other figuring discourses within these sciences and current bodies politic—discourses of war and mastery, of command and control, of disease and pollution, of liberation, of autonomy, of gender and race and class. Refiguring the body politic is one way to raise questions of how progressive forces can be more effective, and indeed of what might count as progressive given complicated interrelationships of technology, social groupings, discursive practices, and economic models. But we also notice the power-full race to rename the emerging spaces of transnational and cyborg bodies by institutions and their representatives.

Two examples may serve. Joseph Nye characterizes the New World Order as a dialogue between national and transnational; although the U.S. maintains hegemony in military affairs, "military prowess is a poor predictor of the outcomes in the economic and transnational layers of current world politics."[30] Instead, a second layer of economic power is tripolar (and changing, as we show above), and a third layer is quite diffuse in terms of power. At this level are lumped problems such as drug trade, AIDS, migration and refugee displacement, global warming, nuclear proliferation, which permeate state boundaries and resist unilateral or even tripolar solutions. He imagines an older, Newtonian political discourse ("the mechanical balance of states") giving way before post-sovereign notions of multiple bodies of power.

Likewise, Gerald Helman and Steven Ratner suggest the bankruptcy of the sovereign nation-state as an adequate measure of power and solution to civil war and social collapse. States like Somalia and Bosnia, they suggest, have failed to live up to the stringent standards of national self-hood—they are "failed nation-states." These states should be treated like a state treats a "failed" individual."[31]

> In domestic systems when the polity confronts persons who are utterly incapable of functioning on their own, the law often provides some regime whereby the community itself manages the affairs of the victim. Forms of guardianship or trusteeship are a common response to broken families, serious mental or physical illness, or economic destitution.

Both articles confront the complexity of world power, a complexity which involves layers of economic, military and political structures. Both cite the information revolution and the impact of new technologies that cross borders and redefine territories. Both reimagine a U.N. which intervenes in the affairs of nations like Somalia or Bosnia. And yet both speak unselfconsciously from a position of identity and coherence; if problems are transnational, this does not threaten the First World's sense of identity as nation states, or the major economic powers as some sort of community. None of the centrifugal forces which threaten nation state coherence around the globe can affect our nation state, these articles proclaim; and yet this notion of ideal Western hegemony and self-identity is perhaps at the root of many transnational, boundary-permeating "problems." The proposals of these writers, and others, are riddled with metaphors not only from cybernetics and information technology, but also discourses of politics, addiction, race, class. The speakers imagine that they are at the center of a potentially coherent body, a "we" who share their concern for American power and security. Yet the very forces they begin to unravel and distinguish riddle our own country and those of emerging economic blocs; the powerful technologies of cybernetics and communication are shaping their own state, subjecting it to its own confusing centrifugal forces. Neither article questions the role of political bodies like the World Bank and the International Monetary Fund. Neither article imagines that if the world is more and more transnational, interdependent, then policies and technologies emanating from the First World must have something to do with the impact of policies and technologies in the "failed" or "too slowly developing" countries. A case could be made that the anthropocentric metaphor of developing bodies, of parents and children, matches poorly with the complex dynamics of proliferating bodies politic. *In loco parentis* may prove difficult and counterproductive if the parents themselves, like the protagonists of many cyborg stories, end up *todo loco*.

The articles we've just cited indicate the extent to which political discourse is affected by new technologies, and also the extent to which it still relies on traditional notions of self, self-interest, successful and coherent selves. To that extent, they are cyborg discourses, yet naively so. These discourses and others like them vie in a field of power, and must be contested by other discourses, based on other experiences of body, power, interfaces with technology. The world is indeed being Borged, and the Death Stars of various Darth Vaders are in production. Cybernetic systems helped pilots kill tens of thousands of Iraqi draftees fleeing Kuwait, and determine flows of information capital that have material effects on women semiconductor workers in the Philippines and rubber tappers in Brazilian rainforests, and indeed on the ecosystems of those countries.

And yet there are other stories, other narratives embedded within cybernetics. We communicate to each other, to friends and activists across the globe, on networks that belie the official organs of news. The notion of who is in one's community, of which community one is part of, changes; whole relationships are conducted across the fiber optics, genders are adopted or switched, games are constructed in which situations and actions are played and replayed, lives and choices rehearsed and enacted. The same technology that will hardwire a pilot into the computer that flies the jet and enables the missiles will allow our friend, hit by a speeding truck, to walk again. There is no choice between utopia and dystopia, Good Terminator or Evil Terminator—they are both here. We are learning to inhabit this constructed, ambiguous body (and explore who constructs it), whether the one we walk around in or the one we are told to vote in, and to experience a range of virtual realities, some of which we can imagine enjoying, passing on to our cyborg children. Perhaps, after all, we just need to learn cyborg family values— good maintenance, technical expertise, pleasures dispersed and multiple, community research and development, improved communication.

Notes

1. Donna Haraway, *Simians, Cyborgs and Women: The Reinvention of Nature* (London: Routledge, 1989), pp. 7-8.

2. A longer version of this article appears in *Prosthetic Territories: Politics and Hyper-Technology*, ed. Mark Driscoll and Gabriel Brahn (Boulder, Co., Westview Press, 1995). For a more complete discussion of cyborg subjectivity see the articles by Gabilondo, Sandoval, and Macauley/Gordo-Lopez in this volume.

3. The body has long been considered a basis for epistemological reflection. As Leonard Barken points out in *Nature's Work of Art* (New Haven, Yale University Press, 1975), his history of the body as metaphor, it has been used to justify ideas in metaphysics, politics, and aesthetics for millennia. In all of these the body is seen as a microcosm of the world. Barkan argues that when this "equation between man and the world is assumed, than the subject-object problem becomes identical with the problem of self-knowledge" (p. 46). Politically, this has the most profound implications when we realize that for many people today, the image of the human body is no longer the body in nature (the noble savage of Rousseau) or the automaton with a soul (Hobbes and Descártes). Today, many actual and metaphorical human individuals are cyborgs and so to the extent that the body is used as a "key" to knowing it is a cyborg epistemology.

4. Michel Foucault, *Discipline and Punish: The Birth of the Prison.* Sheridan trans., (New York, Vintage, 1977), pp. 29-30

5. Thomas Hobbes, *Leviathan or The Matter, Forme, & Power of a Common-Wealth Ecclesiastical and Civill* (London: Penguin, 1965, first published in 1651)

6. Chris Gray, *Postmodern War,* (NY: Guilford Press, 1995).

7. A prosthetic process, such as aging today, is much different than a synthesizing one, such as reproduction. Enhancements and replacements are never fully integrated into a new synthesis, rather they remain lumpy and semi-autonomous. The postmodern state is clearly a prosthetic creature cobbled together out of various organic and cybernetic subunits such as bioregions, cultures, markets, myths, histories, communities, and so on. Of course, synthetic and prosthetic processes can be combined, as with genetic engineering and political revolution.

8. The Office of Science Policy, *Grand Challenges: High Performance Computing and Communications,* Washington, D.C.: Govt. Printing Office, 1992 and 1993.

9. Jacques Derrida, *Speech and Phenomena,* tr. David B. Allison (Evanston: Northwestern U. Press, 1973) pp. 145-46, quoted in Catherine Belsey, *Feminisms,* p. 595. See note 10.

10. Catherine Belsey, "Constructing the Subject: Deconstructing the Text," in *Feminisms,* ed. R. Warhol and D. Price Herndl (New Brunswick, N.J.: Rutgers U Press, 1991) p. 597.

11. Donna Haraway "A Manifesto for Cyborgs: Science, Technology, and Socialist Feminism in the 1980s," *Socialist Review,* no. 80, 1985, p. 125.

12. Donna Haraway, *Simians, Cyborgs and Women,* p. 135.

13. Ibid., p. 135.

14. Such as the international associations of scientists, anarchists, lawyers, therapists, prostitutes, and many other self-selected groups of various levels of importance. Improved world-wide communication and travel will make such contacts, and individual relationships across borders and other boundaries, more politically important year after year. Such cybernetic inputs as faxes from Tienanmien Square and E-Mail from besieged Sarajevo already play an important political role in shifting the relative importance of various political bodies.

15. John Ruggie, "Territoriality and Beyond," *International Organization,* 47, 1, Winter 1993 p. 141.

16. John R.R. Christie, "A Tragedy for Cyborgs," *Configurations,* vol. 1, 1992, p. 183.

17. Richard Gordon, personal communication, 1989, his emphasis.

18. Akhil Gupta, "The Song of the Nonaligned World," *Cultural Anthropology,* 7(1), 1992.

19. Michael Shapiro, "Moral Geographies and the Ethics of Post-Sovereignty," *Public Culture,* 6, 1994, pp. 479-80.

20. Shapiro draws on Bernard Nietschmann, "The Third World War," *Cultural Survival Quarterly,* 11 (3), 1987 For these statistics, see Shapiro, note 3, p. 492.

21. The scientific-pagan principle of a single biosphere, Gaia, can certainly be defined as a cyborg, especially if one unites all of it's/her definitions into one idea(l). With Gaia, one can avoid Donna Haraway's hard choice and choose to be (part of) both a cyborg and a goddess.

22. Boutros Boutros-Ghali, "Empowering the United Nations," *Foreign Affairs,* Vol. 72, no. 5, Winter 1992-3, p. 98.

23. Ibid., pp. 98-99.

24. See for example Akhil Gupta, "Twisted Terrain: Environmentalism, Modernity, and the Nation-State, Dec 1993, unpublished ms.

25. Ibid., p. 99.

26. Officially they are what contemporary wars are all about. See Chris Gray, "Excerpts From Philosophy and the Human Future. The Implications of Postmodern War," *Nomad,* vol. 3, no. 1, Spring and Chris Gray, "Kuwait 1991: A Postmodern War," *Nomad,* vol. 3, no. 3, pp. 25-32.

27. Ruggie, "Territoriality and Beyond," p. 165.

28. Elise Boulding, *Building a Global Civic Culture*, (NY: Teachers College Press, 1988) p. 35.

29. See, among many others, Bruce Sterling, "A short history of the internet," *The Magazine of Fantasy and Science Fiction*, Feb 1993.

30. Joseph Nye, "What New World Order?" *Foreign Affairs*, vol. 72, no. 5, Winter 1992-93, p. 88.

31. Gerald Helman and Steven R. Ratner, "Saving Failed States," *Foreign Policy*, no. 89, Winter 1992-93, p. 12.

Bibliography

(Published in New York if not otherwise noted.)

Nonfiction

Aleksander, Igor and Piers Burnett, (1983) *Reinventing Man: The Robot Becomes Reality*, Holt, Rinehart and Winston.

Balsamo, Anne, (1993a) "Feminism for the Incurably Informed," *Flame Wars/South Atlantic Quarterly*, Mark Dery, ed., vol. 92, no. 4, Fall, pp. 681-712.

———, (1993b) "The Virtual Body in Cyberspace," *Research in Philosophy & Technology*, special issue on Technology and Feminism, Joan Rothschild, ed., vol. 12, 1993, pp. 119-140.

———, (forthcoming) *Technologies of the Gendered Body*, Durham, N.C.

Brahm, Gabriel and Mark Driscoll, eds., (1995) *Prosthetic Territories: Politics and Hypertechnology*, Boulder, CO: Westview.

Benedikt, Michael, ed., (1991) *Cyberspace: First Steps*, Cambridge, Mass.: MIT Press.

Beniger, J., (1986) *The Control Revolution: Technological and Economic Origins of the Information Society*, Cambridge, Mass.: Harvard UP.

Bernal, J.D., (1929) *The World, the Flesh and the Devil*, London: K. Paul, Trench, Trubner.

Biddick, Kathleen, (1993) "Stranded Histories: Feminist Allegories of Artificial Life," *Philosophy & Technology* 13, London: Jai Press Inc., pp. 165-82.

Bolter, David J., (1984) *Turing's Man: Western Culture in the Computer Age*. Chapel Hill, N.C.: University of North Carolina Press.

Branwyn, Gareth, (1993) "The Desire to Be Wired," *Wired*, Sept./Oct., pp. 61-5, 112.

Bud, Robert, (1993) *The Uses of Life: A History of Biotechnology*, Cambridge University Press.

Bukatan, Scott, (1993) *Terminal Identity: The Virtual Subject in Postmodern Science Fiction*, Durham, N.C.: Duke UP.

Caronia, Antonio, (1985) *Il Cyborg*, Rome: Edizioni Theoria.

Chadwick, Ruth, ed., (1993) *Ethics, Reproduction, and Genetic Control*, Routledge.

Channell, David, (1991) *The Vital Machine: A Study of Technology and Organic Life*, Oxford UP.

Cherfas, Jeremy, (1982) *Man-Made Life,* Pantheon.

Christie, J., (1993) "A Tragedy for Cyborgs," *Configurations,* vol. 1, no. 1, pp. 171-98.

Clynes, Manfred and Nathan S. Kline, (1960) "Cyborgs and Space," *Astronautics,* Sept., pp. 26-7, 74-5.

Clynes, M. and J. Milsum, eds., (1970) *Biomedical Engineering Systems,* McGraw-Hill.

Clynes, Manfred, (1977) *Sentics: The Touch of Emotions,* Anchor Press/Doubleday.

Cohen, John, (1966) *Human Robots in Myth and Science,* London: George Allen & Unwin.

Crary, Jonathan and Sanford Kwinter, (1992) *Incorporations,* Zone.

Csicery-Ronay, Istvan, Jr., (1991) "The SF of Theory: Baudrillard and Haraway," *Science Fiction Studies* 18, no. 3, pp. 387-404.

Damarin, Suzanne K., (1993) "Technologies of the Individual: Women and Subjectivity in the Age of Information," *Philosophy & Technology* 13, London: Jai Press, Inc., pp. 183-200.

Dario, P., G. Sandini and P. Aebischer, eds., (1993) *Robots and Biological Systems: Toward a New Bionics,* Springer-Verlag.

Delgado, Jose, (1971) *Physical Control of the Mind,* Colophon.

Dery, Mark, (1994) *Cyberculture: Road Warriors, Console Cowboys and the Silicon Underground,* Hyperion

——, ed., (1993a) *Flame Wars: The Discourse of Cyberculture,* special issue of *South Atlantic Quarter,* vol. 92, no. 4, Fall.

——, (1993b) "Back to the Future: Interview with Samuel R. Delany, Greg Tate, and Tricia Rose, in *Flame Wars/South Atlantic Quarterly,* Mark Dery ed., vol. 92, no. 4. Fall, pp. 735-78.

——, (1992) "Cyborging the Body Politic" in *MONDO 2000* 7, pp. 101-05.

Dijksterhius, E.J., (1961) *The Mechanization of the World Picture,* trans. C. Dikshoorn, Oxford UP.

Dixon, Dougal, (1990) *Man After Man,* St. Martin's Press.

Doane, Mary Ann, (1990) "Technophilia: Technology, Representation, and the Feminine," *Body/Politics: Women and the Discourses of Science,* Mary Jacobus, Evelyn Fox Keller, and Sally Shuttleworth, eds., Routledge, pp. 163-76.

Drexler, K. Eric, (1987) *Engines of Creation: The Coming Era of Nanotechnology,* Anchor Books.

Driscoll, Robert W., (1963) *Engineering Man for Space: The Cyborg Study,* Washington, D.C.: NASA, NASw-512.

Druzhinin, V.V. and D.S. Knotorov, (1972) *Concept, Algorithm, Decision,* Moscow: 1972; Washington, D.C.: U.S. Printing Office.

Emmeche, Claus, (1994) *The Garden in the Machine: The Emerging Science of Artificial Life,* Princeton: Princeton UP.

Ettinger, R.C.W., (1972) *Man into Superman,* St. Martin's Press.

Erlich, Richard D., (1993) *Clockworks: A Multimedia Bibliography,* Westport, Conn.: Greenwood Press.

Figueroa-Sarriera, Heidi, (1995) "Some Body Fantasies in Cyberspace Texts: A View from its Exclusions," Chris Hables Gray, ed., *Technohistory: Using the History of Technology in Interdisciplinary Research,* Melbourne, Florida: Krieger.

Florescu, Radu, (1975) *In Search of Frankenstein,* Boston: New York Graphic Society.

Fjermedal, Grant, (1986) *The Tomorrow Makers: A Brave New World of Living-Brain Machines,* Macmillan.

Foss, Laurence and Kenneth Rothenberg, (1987) *The Second Medical Revolution: From Biomedicine to Infomedicine,* Boston: New Science Library.

Fox, Renee and Judith Swazey, (1992) *Spare Parts: Organ Replacement in American Society,* Oxford UP.

Freitas, R., (1985) "The Birth of the Cyborg," in Minsky, ed., *Robotics,* Anchor Press/Doubleday, pp. 146-83.

Garber, Majorie, (1989) "Spare Parts: The Surgical Construction of Gender," *differences* 1, no. 3, Fall, pp. 137-59.

Gerardin, Lucien, (1968) *Bionics,* McGraw-Hill.

Glass, F., (1989) "The new bad future: *Robocop* and 1980s sci-fi film," *Science as Culture* 5, pp. 7-49.

Goldberg, Jonathan, (1992) "Recalling Totalities: The Mirrored Stages of Arnold Schwarzenegger," *differences* 4, no. 1, pp. 187-208.

Goodfield, June, (1977) *Playing God: Genetic Engineering and the Manipulation of Life,* Harper and Row.

Gray, Chris Hables, and Mark Driscoll, (1992) "From Virtual to Real: Anthropology in the Age of Simulation" in *Visual Anthropology Review,* vol. 8, no. 2, Fall, pp. 39-49.

Gray, Chris Hables, and Steven Mentor, (1994) "The Cyborg Body Politic Meets the New World Order," *Prosthetic Territories,* Gabriel Brahm and Mark Driscoll, eds., Boulder, CO: Westview.

Gray, Chris Hables, (1995a) *Postmodern War: Computers as Weapons and Metaphors,* Guilford Press.

——, (1995b) "Medical Cyborgs: Artificial Organs and the Quest for the Posthuman," *Technohistory: Using the History of Technology in Interdisciplinary Research,* Chris Gray, ed., Melbourne, Florida: Krieger.

——, (1994a) "There Will Be War! Future War Fantasies and Militaristic Science Fiction," *Science-Fiction Studies,* vol. 21, pt. 3, pp.315-36.

——, (1993) "The Culture of War Cyborgs: Technoscience, Gender, and Postmodern War," *Research in Philosophy & Technology,* special issue on technology and feminism, vol. 13, Joan Rothschild, ed., pp. 141-63.

——, (1989) "The Cyborg Soldier: The U.S. Military and the Postmodern Warrior," *Cyborg Worlds: Programming the Military Information Society,* Les Levidow and Kevin Robins, eds., Columbia UP, pp. 43-73.

Halacey, D.S., (1965) *Cyborg: Evolution of the Superman,* Harper & Row.

Haraway, Donna, (1993) "A Game of Cat's Cradle: Science Studies, Feminist Theory, Cultural Studies," *Configurations,* vol. 2, no. 1, pp. 59-72.

——, (1992) "The Promises of Monsters: A Regenerative Politics for Inappropriate/d Others" in *Cultural Studies,* Lawrence Grossberg, Gary Nelson and Paula Treichler, eds., Routledge.

——, (1991a) "Cyborgs at Large: Interview with Donna Haraway," *Technoculture,* Constance Penley and Andrew Ross, eds., Minneapolis: University of Minnesota Press, pp. 1-20.

——, (1991b) "The Actors are Cyborg, Nature is Coyote, and Georgraphy is Elsewhere: Postscript to 'Cyborgs at Large,'™" *Technoculture,* Constance Penley and Andrew Ross, eds., Minneapolis: University of Minnesota Press, pp. 21-26.

——, (1991c) "When Man is On the Menu" *Incorporations,* Jonathan Crary and Sanford Kwinter, eds, *Zone,* pp. 38-43.

——, (1989a) *Simians, Cyborgs and Women,* Routledge.

——, (1989b) "A Cyborg Manifesto: Science, Technology and Socialist Feminism in the 1980s," ibid..

——, (1989c) "The Biopolitics of Postmodern Bodies: Constitution of Self in Immune Systems Discourse," ibid.

——, (1989d) *Primate Visions: Gender, Race, and Nature in the World of Modern Science,* Routledge.

——, (1989e) "Monkeys, Aliens and Women: Love, Science and Politics at the Intersection of Feminist Theory and Colonial Discourse." *Women's Studies International Forum* 12, no. 3, pp. 307-09.

——, (1988) "Situated Knowledges: The Science Question in Feminism as a Site of Discourse on the Privilege of Partial Perspective," *Feminist Studies* 14, no. 3, pp. 575-88.

Harris, John, (1992) *Wonderwoman and Superman: The Ethics of Human Biotechnology,* Oxford UP.

Hayles, N. K., (1993a) "The Materiality of Informatics," *Configurations,* vol. 1, no. 1, pp. 147-70.

——, (1993b) "Virtual Bodies and Flickering Signifiers," *October 66,* Fall, pp. 69-91.

Heppenheimer, T.A., (1985) "Man Makes Man," Minsky, ed., *Robotics,* Anchor Books/Doubleday, pp. 28-69.

Hewitt, Marsha, (1993) "Cyborgs, Drag Queens, and Goddesses: Emancipatory-Regressive Paths in Feminist Theory," *Method and Theory in the Study of Religion* 5, no. 2, pp. 135-54.

Jeffords, Susan, (1994) *Hard Bodies,* Newark, NJ: Rutgers UP.

Jones, Steven G., ed., (1994) *Cybersociety,* Sage.

Kaufert, Joseph M. and David Locker, (1990) "Rehabilitation Ideology and Respiratory Support Technology," *Social Sciences and Medicine,* vol. 30, no. 8, pp. 867-77.

Kenedi, R.M., ed., (1973) *Perspectives in Biomedical Engineering,* Baltimore: University Park Press.

Kimbrell, H., (1992) *The Human Body Shop.*

Kline, Nathan and Manfred Clynes, (1961) "Drugs, Space, and Cybernetics: Evolution to Cyborg," Flaherty, Bernard, ed., *Psychophysiological Aspects of Space Flight,* Columbia UP.

Klobas, Lauri E., (1988) *Disability Drama in Television and Film,* London: McFarland & Co.

Kolff, Willem, (1955) "The History of the Artificial Kidney," *Transactions of the American Society for Artificial Internal Organs,* vol. 1, June 5, pp. 1-19.

Kroker, Arthur and Marilouise, eds., (1987) *Body Invaders: Panic Sex in America,* St. Martin's Press.

La Mettrie, Julien Offray de, (1960) "Man A Machine" in *Mettrie's L'Homme machine: A Study in the Origins of an Idea,* Aram Vartanianed ed., Princeton: Princeton UP. Originally published in 1747.

Levidow, Les and Kevin Robins, eds., (1989, 1991) *Cyborg Worlds: The Military Information Society,* London: Free Association; Columbia University Press.

Levy, Stephen, (1992) *Artificial Life: The Quest for a New Creation,* Pantheon.

Licklider, J.C.R., (1960) "Man-Computer Symbiosis," *IRE Transactions on Human Factors in Electronics,* vol.

HFE-1, March, pp. 4–11.

Livingston, Ira and Judith Halberstam, (1995) *Posthuman Bodies,* Bloomington: University of Indiana Press.

Maddox, Tom, (1988) "The Wars of the Coin's Two Halves: Bruce Sterling's Mechanist/Shaper Narratives," *Mississippi Review* 16, nos 2/3, pp. 237–44.

Mayr, Otto, (1970) *The Origins of Feedback Control,* Cambridge, Mass.: MIT Press.

Mazlish, Bruce, (1993) *The Fourth Discontinuity: The Co-Evolution of Humans and Machines,* New Haven: Yale UP.

McCulloch, Warren S., (1988) *Embodiments of Mind,* Cambridge, Mass.: MIT Press.

Minsky, Marvin, ed., (1985) *Robotics,* Anchor Press/Doubleday.

Morgan, Chris, (1980) *Future Man,* Irvington.

Moravec, Hans, (1988) *Mind Children,* Cambridge, Mass.: Harvard UP.

Mumford, Lewis, (1966, 1970) *The Myth of the Machine,* Harcourt, Brace Jovanovich.

Murchy, Julien S., (1989) "Should Pregnancies Be Sustained in Brain-Dead Women?: A Philosophical Discussion of Postmortem Pregnancy," Kathryn Strother Ratcliff, ed., *Healing Technology: Feminist Perspectives,* Ann Arbor: University of Michigan Press.

Nichols, Bill, (1988) "The Work of Culture in the Age of Cybernetic Systems," *Screen,* vol. 29, no. 1, Winter.

Nosé, Yukihiko, (1985) "Therapeutic Artificial Organs: Future Perspectives," *Artificial Organs,* vol. 9, no. 1, pp. 7–11.

Oudshoorn, Nelly, (1994) *The Making of the Hormonal Body,* Routledge.

Pimentel, Ken and Kevin Teixeira, (1993) *Virtual Reality: Through the Looking Glass,* McGraw-Hill.

Porush, David, (1985) *The Soft Machine: Cybernetic Fiction,* Methuen.

Poster, Mark, (1990) *The Mode of Information: Poststructuralism and Social Context,* Chicago: University of Chicago Press.

Putti, V., (1929) "Historic Artificial Limbs," *American Journal of Surgery,* vol. VI, no. 1, Jan., pp. 111–7; no. 2, Feb., pp. 246–53.

Rabinbach, Anson, (1990) *The Human Motor,* Berkeley: UC Press.

Regis, Ed, (1990) *Great Mambo Chicken and Transcendent Science: Science Slightly Over the Edge,* Reading, MA: Addison Wesley.

Rheingold, Howard, (1991) *Virtual Reality,* Summit Books.

Rollin, Bernard, (1995) *The Frankenstein Syndrome,* Cambridge UP.

Rosenffield, Lenora Cohen, (1968) *From Beast-Machine to Man-Machine: Animal Soul in French Letters from Descartes to La Mettrie,* Octagon. Originally published in 1941.

Ross, Andrew and Constance Penley, eds., (1991) *Technoculture,* Minneapolis: University of Minnesota Press.

Rothschild, Joan, ed., (1983) *Machina Ex Dea,* Pergamon Press.

Samuelson, David N., (1977) "*Limbo:* The Great American Dystopia," *Extrapolation* 19, pp. 76–87.

Schmeck, Harold Jr., (1965) *The Semi-Artificial Man,* Walker.

Schodt, Frederik, (1988) *Inside the Robot Kingdom: Japan, Mechatronics, and the Coming Robotopia,* Kodansha.

Schwab, Gabriele, (1987) "Cyborgs: Postmodern Phantasms of Body and Mind," *Discourse* 9, Spring-Summer, pp. 79–95.

Scortia, Thomas and George Zebrowski, (1975) "'Unholy Marriage': The Cyborg in Science Fiction," Scortia and Zebrowski, eds., *Human-Machines: An Anthology of Stories About Cyborgs,* Vintage, pp. xiii–xxv.

Seltzer, Mark, (1992) *Bodies and Machines,* Routledge.

Shaw, Margery, ed., (1984) *After Barney Clark,* Austin: University of Texas Press.

Sheehan James and Morton J. Sosna, eds., (1991) *The Boundaries of Humanity: Humans, Animals, Machines,* Berkeley: University of California Press.

Shirley, John, (1987) "Stelarc and the New Reality," *Science Fiction Eye* 1, no. 2, pp. 56–61.

Sobchak, Vivian, (1993) "New Age Mutant Ninja Hackers: Reading *Mondo 2000*" in *Flame Wars/South Atlantic Quarterly,* Mark Dery, ed., vol. 92, No. 4, Fall, pp. 569–84.

Sofia, Zoe, (1992) "Virtual Corporeality: A Feminist View," *Australian Feminist Studies,* no. 15, Autumn, pp. 11–24.

——, (1984) "Exterminating Fetuses: Abortion, Disarmament, and the Sexo-Semiotics of Extra-Terrestrialism," *Diacritics* 14, pp. 47–59.

Springer, Claudia, (1994) "Muscular Circuity: The Invincible Armored Cyborg in Cinema," *Genders,* in print.

——, (forthcoming) *The Erotic Interface: The Discourses of the Technological Body,* Princeton: Princeton University Press.

Stableford, Brian, (1984) *Future Man: Brave New World or Genetic Nightmare?,* Crown.

Stelarc, (1989) "Redesigning the Body—Redefining What is Human," *Whole Earth Review* 63, Summer, pp. 18-22.

Stock, Gregory, (1993) *Metaman: The Merging of Humans and Machines into a Global Superorganism,* Simon and Schuster.

Strauss, Michael, (1984) "The Political History of the Artificial Heart," *New England Journal of Medicine,* Feb. 2, pp. 332-36.

Stone, Allucquére Rosanne (Sandy), (1994) "Split Subjects, Not Atoms; or How I Fell in Love with My Prosthesis" *Configurations,* vol. 2, no. 1, Winter, pp. 173-90. This essay in this volume.

——, (1992) "Virtual Systems," *Incorporations,* Jonathan Crary and Sanford Dwinter, eds., *Zone.*

——, (1991a) "Will the Real Body Please Stand Up? Boundary Stories About Virtual Cultures," *Cyberspace: First Steps,* Michael Benedikt, ed., Cambridge, Mass.: MIT Press., pp. 81-118.

——, (1991b) "The 'Empire' Strikes Back: A Posttransexual Manifesto," Julia Epstein and Kristina Straub, eds., *Body Guards: The Cultural Politics of Gender Ambiguity,* Routledge.

Strughold, Hubertus, "Planetary Environmental Medicine (Mars)" *Bioastronautics and the Exploration of Space,* Charles Roadman, Herbertus Strughold, and Roland Mitchell, eds., San Antonio, Texas: Aerospace Medical Division/Brooks Air Force Base.

Theweleit, Klaus, (1989) *Male Fantasies: Volume 2: Male Bodies: Psychoanalyzing the White Terror,* Minneapolis: University of Minnesota Press.

Tomas, David, (1989) "The Technophilic Body: On Technicity in William Gibson's Cyborg Culture," *New Formations* 8, Summer, pp. 112-29.

Tooze, John, (1981) *The DNA Story: A Documentary History of Gene Cloning,* San Francisco: W. H. Freeman.

U.S. Army, (1982) *Airland Battle 2000,* Washington D.C.: Dept. of Defense.

Warrick, Patricia, (1980) *The Cybernetic Imagination in Science Fiction,* Cambridge, Mass.: MIT Press.

Wiener, Norbert, (1948) *Cybernetics: Or Control and Communication in the Animal and the Machine,* Cambridge, Mass.: MIT Press.

——, (1989) *The Human Use of Human Beings,* Boston: Houghton-Mifflin. Originally published in 1954.

——, (1964) *God and Golem, Inc.,* Cambridge, Mass.: MIT Press.

Woolley, Benjamin, (1992) *Virtual Worlds: A Journey in Hyped Hyperreality,* Oxford: Blackwell.

Wosk, Julie, (1993) "The 'Electric Eve': Galvanizing Women in Nineteenth- and Twentieth-Century Art and Technology," *Philosophy & Technology* 13, pp. 43-56.

Fiction

Allen, Roger, *The Modular Man,* Bantam, 1992. Cyborg class struggle in near-future Washington, D.C.

Asimov, Janet, *Mind Transfer,* Ace, 1988. Downloading described in an extraordinarily banal book.

Bear, Greg, *Blood Music,* Ace, 1985. Nanobots take over, body by body.

Bova, Ben, *The Dueling Machine,* Holt Rinehart, 1969. Virtual wars lead to real deaths.

Brunner, John, *Shockwave Rider,* Ace, 1975. Net hacker saves the world.

Budrys, Algis, *Who?* Ballantine, 1958. Cyborg doesn't know who it is.

Cadigan, Pat, "Petty Boy Crossover," *The Years Best Science Fiction: Fourth Annual Collection.* Ed. Gardner Dozios. St. Martin's Press, 1987.

——, *Synners,* Bantam, 1991. Socketed hackers in cyberpunk near-future.

Caidin, Martin, *Cyborg,* Ballantine, 1972. The Six Million Dollar Man is made.

——, *Manfac,* New York, Baen, 1981. The Six Million Dollar man with an attitude, and lots more prosthetics too.

Card, Orson Scott, *Ender's Game,* Tor, 1985. Training simulations turn into real war. In the sequels (*Speaker for the Dead, Xenocide*) Ender becomes a cyborg on a mission to end xenocide.

Cherryh, C.J.C., *Cyteen: The Betrayal,* Popular Library, 1988. Clones 'R us in a future of rebellious Earth colonies and various cyborgian industries.

Crichton, Michael. *The Terminal Man,* Avon, 1972. Cyborg therapy for a violent brain-injured man becomes an addiction to electrostimulation and an impetus for murder.

——, *Jurassic Park,* Ballantine, 1990. Cyborg (genetically engineered with DNA and other bits added) dinos return to nature, and some of them love fresh meat!

Dick, Philip K. *Do Androids Dream of Electric Sheep?* Doubleday, 1968.

Dietz, William, *Matrix Man,* Penguin, 1990. Cyborg reporters with Front Page principles.

Forster, E. M., "The Machine Stops," 1909. Machines maintain subterranean coach potatoes.

Galouye, Daniel, *Counterfeit World,* Bantam, 1969. Electronic analogue man trapped in market study seeks embodiment.

Gibson, William, *Neuromancer,* Ace, 1984. Cyberspace and real space teem with cyborgs in the cyberpunk future. His related novels and short stories are: (*Count Zero,* London: Victor Gollancz, 1986; *Burning Chrome,* Ace Books, 1987; *Mona Lisa Overdrive,* Bantam Books, 1988; and *Virtual Light, Bantam Books, 1994.*

Green, Joseph, *The Mind Behind the Eye,* Daw, 1961. Humans take over an alien giant's body, move into his skull, and make him a cyborg in order to spy out the alien home world.

Gygax, Gary, *Cyborg Commando Book 3: The Ultimate Prize,* Ace, 1988. Cyborg soldiers battle evil alien Xenoborgs for the future of the human race. Unfortunately, one of a series with Books 1 and 2 being *Planet in Peril* and *Chase into Space.*

Haldeman, Joe, *Buying Time,* Avon, 1989. Immortal medical cyborgs plot to take over the world.

Hansen, Karl, *War Games,* Playboy Books, 1981. Bioformed, hybrid, soldiers.

Heinlein, Robert, "Waldo, Genius in Orbit" in *Waldo and Magic, Inc.,* Avon, 1950. Heinlein invents telepresence.

——, *Starship Troopers,* Signet Books, 1959.

Hjortsberg, William, *Gray Matters,* Bantam, 1971. In a future world there is only room for decanted brains ("cerebromorphs") and cybernetic dreams except for the "enlightened."

Jacobson, Karie, *Simulations: 15 Tales of Virtual Reality,* Citadel Twilight, 1993. Including many of the very best.

McCaffrey, Anne, *The Ship Who Sang,* Walker Brains-in-a-ship cyborgs roam the galaxy singing. One of a series of cyborg-ship stories.

McHugh, Maureen F., *China Mountain Zhang,* Tor, 1992. Zhang (engineer to architect American-born Chinese in a Sino-world, NY to Arctic to China, gay subculture) learning to be a cyborg, and therefore more fully human?

McIntyre, Vonda n., *Starfarers,* Bantam, 1987. Beautifully imagined future world of genetically engineered protohuman and bioelectronic computers. First in a trilogy. The second, Transition, Bantam, 1990.

Milan, Victor, *Cybernetic Samurai,* Arbor House, 1985.

Miller, Walter M. Jr., "Crucifixus Etiam" in *Human-Machines,* Thomas Scortia and George Zebrowski, eds., Vintage, 1975. Originally published in 1953. Human earthling becomes martian and loves it.

Moore, C. L., "No Woman Born," in *Human-Machines,* Thomas Scortia and George Zebrowski, eds., Vintage, 1975. First published as a short story in 1941. One of the most important, and earliest, cyborg stories.

Naha, Ed, *Robocop 2,* Jove Books, 1990.

Niven, Larry, Becalmed in Hell" in *Astounding.*

Niven, Larry with Stephen Barnes, *Dream Park,* Huntington Woods, Michigan: Phantasia Press, 1981. Virtual reality theme park with murders. Several sequals including *The Barsoom Project,* Ace, 1989 and *California Voodoo Game,* Ballantine, 1992.

Ore, Rebecca, *The Illegal Rebirth of Billy the Kid,* Tor, 1991. Biogenetic chimeras bred for the rich.

Osborn, David, *Heads,* Bantam, 1985. The title is self-explanatory as far as this medical thriller goes.

Paoli, Dennis, *Robot Jox,* Avon, 1989. Exoskeleton-gladiators determine the world's balance of power.

Piercy, Marge, *He, She, and It,* Fawcett, 1991. The Golem is remade, cyborg style, in a post-apocalyptic cyberpunk work described through a feminist sensibility.

Pohl, Frederik and C. M. Kornbluth, Wolfbane, Bantam, 1976. (Based on a shorter version published in *Galaxy* in 1957.) Kidnapped humans used by aliens as computer components.

Pohl, Frederik, *Man Plus,* Bantam, 1976. Artificial intelligences invent cyborgs to help them survive. Do you think the humans ever catch on?

Rucker, Rudy, *2Software,* Avon, 1982. Man makes robots (boppers) who remake man. Humans to boppers to meatbop.

——, *Wetware,* Avon, 1988.

Saberhagen, Fred, *The Frankenstein Papers,* Baen, 1986. Very witty, very clever version of Mary Shelly's classic tale told from the "monster's" viewpoint with a number of delightful cyborgian twists.

Scortia, Thomas N. and George Zebrowski, *Human-Machines: An Anthology of Stories About Cyborgs,* Vintage, 1975. The best cyborg anthology, incredibly it is out of print.

Scortia, Thomas N., "The Shores of Night" in *Best Science Fiction, 1956,* Fell.

——, "Woman's Rib" in *Caution! Inflammable!* Doubleday, 1975.

Shatner, William, *Teklords,* Ace, 1991. Not bad writing for Captain Kirk, and lots of cyborgs of different types. A number of competent sequels have followed.

Sherman, Joel Henry, *Corpsman,* Ballantine, 1988. Only cyborg pilots can fly interplanetary, and the powers that be are jealous.

Shwartz, Susan, *Heritage of Flight,* TOR, 1989.

Sladek, John, *The Müller-Fokker Effect,* Carroll & Graf, 1990, originally published in 1970. Downloading lowdown.

Spinrad, Norman, "Riding the Torch" in *Threads of Time,* ed. by Robert Silverberg, Dell, 1945. Postapocalyptic holo and senso addicts ask, "Who needs Prime reality at all?"

Stephenson, Neal, *Diamond Age,* Bantam, 1995.

——, *Snow Crash,* Bantam, 1992.

Sterling, Bruce, *Schismatrix,* Ace, 1985. Shaper genetic-cyborgs vs. Mechanist prosthetic-cyborgs.

——, *Islands of the Net,* Arbor House, 1988.

——, *Crystal Express,* Ace Books, 1990. Includes the Shaper-Mechanist short stories.

Stine, Harry, G. *Warbots #3: The Bastaard Rebellion,* Pinnacle Books, 1988. Unfortunately part of a series.

Tiptree, James, Jr., *The Girl Who Was Plugged In,* TOR, 1989. Originally published in 1973.

Thomas, Craig, *Firefox,* New York, Bantam, 1977. Brain-reading super-airplane stolen from Russians in technothriller.

Thomas, T. Thomas, *Crygender,* Baen, 1992. Transexual cyborgian gender bending with a murder mystery thrown in.

Varley, John, *The Persistence of Vision,* A collection of short stories, many with cyborg themes.

——, *Blue Champagne,* A collection of short stories including the very cyborgian title tale and a great parable abut transexuality and the true self.

——, *Steel Beach,* Ace, 1992. In the future on a thriving Luna that overlooks an Earth occupied by aliens, most people are cyborgs, with only the extremist "nats" resisting some form of enhancement.

Vinge, Vernor, *True Names,* Bluejay Books, 1984. One of the best virtual reality—cyberspace stories.

Williams, Jon, *Hardwired,* TOR, 1986.

——, *Voice of the Whirlwind,* TOR, 1987.

——, *Angel Station,* TOR, 1989.

Williamson, Jack, *Manseed,* Del Rey, 1982. Cyborg sperm set out among the stars to seek fertile planets.

Wolfe, Bernard, *Limbo,* Ace, 1956. Self-mutilation for prosthetic improvement as a post-apocalyptic lifestyle.

Comics (Major Cyborg Characters) (Compiled by Mark Oehlert)

Beast, Captain America, Ant-Man I, DarkHawk, Jocasta, Machine Man, StingRay, Human Torch I, Iron Man, Quasar, Spider-Woman II, Vision, War Machine, Wasp, Wonder Man, Arsenal I, Awesome Android, Beast of Berlin, Blank, Cactus, Doctor Demonicus, Doctor Doom, Eternity Man, Growing Man, High Evolutionary, Mad Thinker, Supreme Intelligence, Terminus, Ultron, War Toy, Battalion, Fuji, Cable, Forge, Cyborg, Supreme, Wolverine, Omega Red, Deadpool, Weatherman, Nikki Doyle, X-O Man of War, Archangel, Weapon X, Colossus, Cyber, Ahab, Nimrod, Slayback, Sinsear, Warlock, Deathlok, Hardware.

Filmography (in Chronological Order by Category)

Cinema

Frankenstein 1910. J. Searle Dawley. An Edison film.

Der Golem 1914. Paul Wegener and Henrik Galeen.

Homunkulus 1916. Otto Ripert. (A six-part serial based on the novel by Robert Reinert.)

Der Golem 1920. Paul Wegener and Karl Boese. (Based on the book by Gustav Meyrink.)

Metropolis 1926. Fritz Lang. (Based on a book by Thea Harbour.)

Frankenstein 1931. James Whale. Starring Boris Karloff.

Bride of Frankenstein 1935. James Whale. Starring Boris Karloff.

Son of Frankenstein 1939. Rowland Van Lee. Starring Boris Karloff.

Kings Row 1941. Coming to terms with amputations and prosthetics. Ronald Reagan asks "Where's the rest of me?"

The Stratton Story 1944. Baseball pitcher with artificial leg makes good.

Dreams That Money Can By 1994. Hans Richter. Includes a girl with a manufactured heart.

The Best Years of Our Lives 1946. War vet learns to love his hooks.

Creature With the Atom Brain 1955. A scientist creates atomic zombies by implanting nuclear brains in humans.

Chamber of Horrors 1966. Crazy guy cuts off his hands and becomes a crazy guy with dangerous prosthetics.

Seconds 1966. Clones R' Us.

2001: A Space Odyssey 1968. Stanley Kubrick. (Based on *Sentinal*, a novella by Arthur Clarke.)

THX 1138 1969. George Lucas. Starring Robert Duvall.

Andromeda Strain 1971. Robert Wise. Evil downloaded from space. Alien information becomes artificial life becomes weapon.

Clones 1973. The title says it all.

Terminal Man 1974. Michael Hodges. (Based on the novel by Michael Crichton.)

Logan's Run 1976. Downloaded rebel in computer and a man in a box. Radioactive implants in everyone for "planned" mortality.

Star Wars 1976. George Lucas. Starring Carrie Fisher, Harrison Ford, Alec Guinness, and Mark Hamill.

The Boys of Brazil 1978. Clones are Nazis.

Alien 1979. Ridley Scott. Starring Sigourney Weaver.

Saturn Three 1980. With Kirk Douglas.

Whose Life Is It, Anyway? 1981. Paralyzed cyborg fights for the right to die.

Blade Runner 1982. Michael Deeley and Ridley Scott. Starring Harrison Ford. Replicants 'r us. (Based on *Do Androids Dream of Electric Sheep?* by Philip Dick.)

TRON 1982. Steven Lisberger. Downloaded into a Disney-like computer world.

Videodrome 1982. David Cronenberg. You are what you watch.

Brainstorm 1983. Douglas Trumbull. Brain stimulation technology, a power so great it can only be used for good, or evil.

Star Wars: The Empire Strikes Back 1983. Richard Marquard. Story by George Lucas. Starring Mark Hamil, Carrie Fisher, and Harrison Ford. Cyborg son like cyborg father?

Terminator 1984. James Cameron. Starring Arnold Schwarzenegger.

The Vindicator 1984. Mad scientist cyborg. "He tampered with nature and created a monster."

Star Wars: The Return of the Jedhi 1985. Irvin Kershner. Story by George Lucas. Cyborg father like cyborg son!

ReAnimater, 1985. Brian Yuzna. (Based on an H.P. Lovecraft story.)

Blood of Ghastly Horror 1985. Al Adamson. Artificial brains cause problems in unwilling humans.

Aliens 1986. James Cameron. Starring Sigourney Weaver.

The Fly 1986. David Cronenberg.

Robocop 1987. Paul Verheoven. "Part man, part machine, all cop." Starring Peter Weller.

Predator 1988. Starring Arnold Schwarzenegger. Alien cyborg comes to Earth for some blood sport.

Tetsuo: The Iron Man 1989. Shinya Tsukamoto.

Bride of ReAnimator 1989. Brian Yuzna. (Based on an H.P. Lovecraft story.)

Cyborg 1989. Albert Pyun. Claude Van Damm in his first, and most agree, worst, role.

Total Recall 1990. Paul Verhoeven. Starring Arnold Schwarzenegger and Sharon Stone. (Based on Philip Dick's story, "We Can Remember it for You Wholesale.")

Robocop 2 1990. Irvin Kershner. Starring Peter Weller. "The future of law enforcement."

Flatliners 1990. Cyborg explorations of death's strange land. Starring Keifer Sutherland, Julia Roberts, William Baldwin.

Terminator II: Judgement Day 1991. James Cameron. Starring Arnold Schwarzenegger and Linda Hamilton. Good cyborg beats bad morphbot and is a cool dad besides.

Robojox 1991. Exoskeleton boxing to the death.

Teenage Mutant Ninja Turtles II: The Secret of the Ooze 1991. Michael Pressman.

Predator II 1991. Stephen Hopkins. Starring Danny Glover. Alien cyborg is "coming to town with a few days to kill."

Prototype X29A 1992. "Part man, part machine, all killer." L. A. of 2057.

Alien 3 1992. David Fincher. Starring Sigourney Weaver.

Robocop 3 1993. Starring John Burke. Robo joins urban freedom fighters.

Teenage Mutant Ninja Turtles III 1993. Stuart Gulard.

The Fugitive 1993. Why do they say he was a one-armed man? He had prosthetics. Starring Harrison Ford.

Demolition Man 1993. Starring Sylvester Stallone and Wesley Snipes. From cryoprisoners to nicey cops, everyone is monitored.

TC 2000 1993. Starring Billy Lanks as a black cyborg cop. "He's mostly human and totally invincible."

Cyborg II 1993. Fembot suicide package run amok.

Universal Soldier 1993. Nam vets turned into cool-as-a-cucumber killer 'borg. Starring Claude Van Damm.

Lawnmower Man 1993. Psychopharmacology and virtual immersion therapy create an overeducated, aggressive, ex-gardener. Tremendous effects.

Arcade 1993. Evil demon in VR game. Full Moon pictures.

Coneheads 1993. Yep, they're cyborgs too. Starring Dan Akroyd and Jane Curtin.

Dave 1993. Neomort cyborg president makes way for nice-guy replacement, both played by Kevin Kline. Also starring Sigourney Weaver.

The Ghost in the Machine 1993. Criminal gets downloaded. Starring Chris Mulkay and Bram Walker.

American Cyborg: Street Warrior 1994. Evil cyborgs hunt the last fertile woman on Earth (Nicole Hansen) who is defended by Joe Lara.

Cyborg Cop 1993. "Born of Flesh, Turned to Steel."

Johnny Mnemonic 1995. Robert Longo. Brain messenger cyborg (Keanu Reeves) journeys through the near future. Based on William Gibson short story.

Television (Only the most significant cyborg works)

Dr. Who. (1960s and 70s). Many episodes featured cyborgs, most notably the Cybermen who first appeared October 8, 1966.

Star Trek (1960s). The only notable cyborg in the first series was Capt. Pike, original captain of *The Enterprise*.

The Six-Million-Dollar Man. (1970s). The "Bionic Man" works for U.S. intelligence. Based roughly on Martin Caidin's novel *Cyborg*. Starring Lee Majors.

The Bionic Woman. (1970s). She also works for U.S. intelligence. Starring Farrah Fawcett Majors. A 1994 made-for-TV movie features a reunion of The Bionic Couple.

Max Headroom 1985. (*20 Minutes into the Future* in Britain). Rocky Morton and Annabelle Janke.

Star Trek: The Next Generation. 1987–1994. A veritable plethora of cyborgism: La Forge's visor. Picard's heart. The Borg. Leucutis. Hugh the Borg. Worf's spine. The question of Data. The nanomites.

Space Rangers 1993. Brief series featured a man with a cheap heart.

Robocop March, 1994 to -.

Dead at 21 June 1994 to 1995. MTV's first series tracks Ed, an escaped experimental bioengineered kinda guy with a self-destruct chip set to go off in his brain in one year. The show's life was even shorter.

Mantis 1995. Black cyborg scientist with bad ratings.

VR5 April 1995 to May 1995. VR at many levels, 1-8.

Star Trek: Voyager 1995. Many cyborgs, including the ship, the title character.

Chicago Hope 1995 to -. Incredible cyborg medicine ripped from today's headlines.

Cartoons

Teenage Mutant Ninja Turtles, Inspector Gadget, The X-Men, The XO Squad

Robocop; Genocyber, AD Police Files (Japanese)

Video Games (Just a sampling)

Terminator I, Terminator II, Terminator vs. Robocop, Robocop, Robocop 2, Robocop 3, Star Wars, Return of the Jedhi, The Empire Strikes Back, Cybernator, Predator I, Predator II, Cyber-Cop, Mega Turrican, Target Earth.

Biographies

GEORGE J. ANNAS is the Edward Utley Professor of Law & Medicine and Chair of the Health Law Department at Boston University Schools of Medicine and Public Health. His most recent books are *Judging Medicine, American Health Law,* and *Standard of Care: The Law of American Bioethics.* He also writes a regular feature on "Legal Issues in Medicine" for the *New England Journal of Medicine.*

MONICA J. CASPER is a doctoral candidate in sociology in the Department of Social and Behavioral Sciences at the University of California, San Francisco. She is interested in social, cultural, and feminist studies of science, medicine, and technology, with particular emphasis on women's health and reproduction. Her dissertation, *"The Making of the Unborn Patient: Gender, Work, and Science in Experimental Fetal Surgery c1960-1993,"* examines surgical constructions of fetuses and pregnant women historically and in the present. She is also working on a project exploring discourses of gender, sexuality, and reproduction in the U.S. space program. Recent publications include *"At the Margins of Humanity: Fetal Positions in Science and Medicine"* in *Science, Technology and Human Values,* and *"Reframing and Grounding Non-Human Agency: What Makes a Fetus an Agent?"* in *American Behavioral Scientist.*

ADELE CLARKE is Associate Professor, Department of Social and Behavioral Sciences, Co-Director of the Women, Health and Healing Program, and Adjunct Associate Professor of History of Health Sciences at the University of California, San Francisco. She just completed *Disciplining Reproduction: American Life Scientists and the `Problem of Sex'* (Berkeley: University of California Press, 1995).

MANFRED CLYNES was born in Austria and educated in Australia before coming to the United States. He holds a masters degree from Julliardand a DSE in nueroscience from the University of Melbourne. He is a published poet, a world-class pianist, and the inventor of a number of widely used biosensors and brain-monitoring computers. Currently he is working on the psychophysiology of emotions (sentics) and the psychoneurologoy of music. He has recently developed an extraordinary computer program that can be used to produce music on its own, or to help a human composer.

DR. PATRICIA COWINGS is the director of the Ames-NASA psychophysiology lab in California. Her research focuses on using biofeedback to control space sickness.

PHILIP DICK was one of the greatest science fiction writers of the late 20th century. His startling tales explored the limits of human identity, political practice, and reality itself in a unique and disturbing style. His work prefigured the cyberpunk genre and has influenced most SF writers since the mid-1960s. Among his best novels are *Do Androids Dream of Electric Sheep?* and *Ubik.* The movies *Total Recall* and *Blade Runner* are based on his stories.

GARY LEE DOWNEY is Associate Professor of Science and Technology Studies at Virginia Tech, Blacksburg, Virginia. His interests include Cyborg Anthropology, engineers as boundary objects, and human-machine integration and communication in contemporary manufacturing.

ROBERT W. DRISCOLL directed "The Cyborg Study" for United Aircraft under a NASA grant and authored the project report.

JOSEPH DUMIT completed a Ph.D. in the History of Consciousness Program at the University of California, Santa Cruz. He is currently a fellow at Harvard University. He is writing a history and ethnography of PET scanning and objective self-fashioning.

RON EGLASH is currently a fellow at the Oregon State University Center for the Humanities where he continues his interdisciplinary research on cybernetics and on ethnomathematics. He was a Fulbright Senior Fellow at the University of Dakar, Senegal from 1993-94 where he was researching African mathematics, especially fractal and chaotic.

LORNE FALK has worked in contemporary art as a writer, curator and director for 22 years. In 1987, he co-edited THE *EVENT HORIZON—Essays on Hope, Sexuality, Social Space & Media(tion).* From 1989 to 1994, he directed a thematic, multidisciplinary residency program at The Banff Centre for the Arts.

BARRY J. FENTON, M.D. is with the Dept. of Psychiatry, University of Texas Health Science Center, Southwestern Medical School, Dallas.

HEIDI J. FIGUEROA-SARRIERA is Associate Professor at the Department of Social Sciences, Cayey University College, University of Puerto Rico at Cayey, from 1989 to the present. As a transdisciplinary Social Psychologist she is involved in research on cultural representations of high-tech designs. She is co-editor with Madeline Román and Mariá M. López of *Másallá de la bella (in)diferencia: Revisión post-feminista y otras escrituras posibles,* published by Publicaciones Puertorriqueñas, 1994.

DR. ELI A. FRIEDMAN was president of the International Society for Artificial Organs in 1987.

CYNTHIA J. FUCHS is assistant professor of English and film and media studies at George Mason University. She is currently completing a book on representational politics, queer theory, and issues of identity in popular culture, tentatively titled "Incoming: U.S. Cultural Hysterias since Vietnam."

JOSEBA GABILONDO is assistant professor of Spanish at Bryn Mawr. His interests include cinema studies, Basque literature, and postmodern theories. He is the author of *Cinematic Hyperspace: New Hollywood Cinema and Science Fiction Film—Commodification in Late Capitalism,* forthcoming in 1995 from Duke University Press as well as a number of fiction and non-fiction works in Spanish and Basque. His short story "Madrid, New York, Tokyo" won the Ignacio Aldecoa prize in 1992.

F. ANDREW GAFFNEY, MD is with the Dept. of Internal Medicine, University of Texas Health Science Center, Southwestern Medical School, Dallas.

JONATHAN GOLDBERG is the Sir William Osler Professor of English Literature at the Johns Hopkins University. His recent work includes the book *Writing Matters: From the Hands of the English Renaissance,* Stanford: Stanford UP, 1990.

JENNIFER GONZÁLEZ is a Ph.D. candidate in the History of Consciousness Board at the University of California, Santa Cruz. Her most recent publications include "Autotopographies," in *Prosthetic Territories: Politics and Hypertechnology* 1995, and "Rhetoric of the Object: Material Memory and the Artwork of Amalia Mesa-Bains" in *Visual Anthropology Review,* Spring 1993.

LOIS H. GRESH has written dozens of science fiction stories featuring digital organic machinery. Her work has appeared in *Aboriginal Science Fiction, Infinite Loop, Mindsparks, Manifest Destiny, Midnight Zoo, Tales of the Unanticipated, Terminal Fright,* and other publications. She is an active member of Science Fiction and Fantasy Writers of America.

HUGH GUSTERSON is assistant professor of Anthropology and Science, Technology, and Society at MIT. He is currently completing an ethnographic study of nuclear weapon makers and nuclear war protesters which will be published by the University of California press.

N. KATHERINE HAYLES is a professor of English at the University of California at Los Angeles. Her books include *Chaos Bound: Orderly Disorder in Contemporary Literature and Science* and *The Cosmic Web: Scientific Field Models and Literary Strategies in the Twentieth Century.* She is currently at work on a study of cybernetics, virtual reality, and literature entitled *Virtual Bodies: Informatics and Contemporary Literature.*

DONNA HARAWAY is a professor in the History of Consciousness Board at the University of California at Santa Cruz, where she teaches feminist theory, cultural and historical studies of science and technology, and women's studies. She is the author of *Crystals, Fabrics and Fields: Metaphors of Organicism in Twentieth-Century Developmental Biology* (Yale University Press, 1976), *Primate Visions: Gender, Race, and Nature in the World of Modern Science* (New York and London: Routledge, 1989; London: Verso, 1992), and *Simians, Cyborgs, and Women: The Reinvention of Nature* (New York: Routledge, 1991; London: Free Association Books, 1991). She is currently working an experimental critical fiction in science studies, called *Modest Witness@Second Millennium. The FemaleMan© Meets OncoMouse™,* forthcoming with Routledge.

DAVID J. HESS is the author of *Science in the New Age* (Wisconsin) and *Samba in the Night* (forthcoming, Columbia). He is an associate professor in the Department of Science and Technology Studies at Rennselaer Polytechnic Institute.

LINDA F. HOGLE is a doctoral candidate in the Medical Anthropology Program at the University of California Berkeley and San Francisco. She is currently completing dissertation research on heterogenous constructions of human biological materials in post-war, post-unification Germany. Besides studying cyborg social relations in various cultural contexts and practices around the use of human biological materials, her interests include transnational and transorganizational linkages in evolving medical technologies.

MOTOKAZU HORI is with the Dept. of Surgery, Institute of Clinical Medicine, University of Tsukuba, Tsukuba, Japan.

NATHAN S. KLINE was the director of research at Rockland State hospital and a professor of clinical psychiatry at the Columbia University College of Physicians and Surgeons for many years. He was a leading expert in psychopharmacology and authored many books and papers on the subject.

LES LEVIDOW is co-editor of several books, including *Anti-Racist Science Teaching* and *Cyborg Worlds: The Military Information Society* (both available from Free Association Books/Columbia University Press). He has been Managing Editor of *Science as Culture* since its inception in 1987. Based at the Open University, he has been researching the safety regulation of agricultural biotechnology.

ANGEL JUAN GORDO-LÓPEZ is currently completing a Ph.D. on the structure of argumentation and related textualities regarding issues of gender, power and new communication technologies. His research also focuses on the visualisation of strategies and practices of resistance regarding marginal groups. For the last three years he has been working at the University of Manchester and the Discourse Unit, Manchester Metropolitan University, but he is mainly based at the Autónoma University of Madrid, and is a member of Psychology Politics Resistance (PPR) and is co-editor of *Psicología, Discurso y Poder* (Visor, Madrid, 1995).

WILLIAM R. MACAULEY is a staff member and research student in the Department of Psychology at the University of Manchester, UK. His research interests include: the psychophysics of body-image, perception of tactile space and cyborg discourse. His doctoral research is on (tele)presence and sensorimotor coordination in immersive virtual environments, which involves him in collaborative work with computer scientists at the Universities of Manchester, Lancaster, and Nottingham, and at the Swedish Institute of Computer Science, Stockholm. He has coauthored another article on cyborgs to appear in *Psicología, Discurso y Poder* (Visor, Madrid) and is co-writing a paper on the theory and design of immersive VR systems.

STEVEN MENTOR has a masters in composition and taught writing for a number of years at San Francisco State Univeristy. He is currently a doctoral candidate in the English Department at the University of Washington, Seattle where he is working on a multimedia analysis of the political and philosophical implications of multimedia communication.

MARK OEHLERT is a graduate student in History at Oregon State University. Building on an obvious interest in comic books and an attention to military history, Mark combines these two disparate elements to define his interest in cyborgs.

MIREILLE PERRON was born in Montréal, Québec. Since 1982, her installations have appeared in solo and group exhibitions in Canada, the United States, France and Italy. Her work is dedicated to the circulation of crucial desires. It explores the connections between feminism, culture, art, technology and science. She has also written and published critical essays on a variety of subjects related to art. Her recent work includes a book of short stories titled *Anecdotal Waters or Stories of Representation* and an audio installation about the use of the female voice in answering services called "The Big Screen—A Telephony in 4 Calls." She teaches at the Alberta College of Art and the University of Calgary.

KEVIN ROBINS works at the Centre for Urban and Regional Development Studies, University of Newcastle upon Tyne. He is co-editor, with Les Levidow, of *Cyborg Worlds,* and author of *Geografia dei Media.* He has written widely on information and communications technology.

CHELA SANDOVAL is assistant professor of Chicana Studies at the University of California at Santa Barbara. Her research interests include CyberCinema, feminism, Chicanismo, oppositional consciousness, and California Studies.

DR. JACK ELLWOOD STEELE, Col. USAF MC (Ret), was born on January 27, 1924 in Lacon, Illinois. After graduation from Mendota Township High School, Mendota, Ill., he studied general engineering at the University of Illinois and the Illinois Institute of Technology. From 1943 to 1946 he served in the US Army, and from 1951 to 1971 in the Air Force. He studied Pre-med at the University of Minnesota in 1944, and received his M.D. in 1950 from Northwestern University where he spent a year as a Research and Teaching Fellow in Neuro-anatomy prior to joining the US Air Force. He then served as Ward Officer of Psychiatry and Neurology until joining the 6570th Aerospace Medical Research Laboratory in 1953. Here he investigated the stress effects of sound, motions, and wind blast, but his main effort was in bionics. He is presently the Medical Director of the Comprehensive Drug Dependency Treatment Program at the Dayton Mental Health Center. Permanent Address: 2313 Bonnieview Ave. Dayton, Ohio 45431.

ALLUCQUÉRE ROSANNE "SANDY" STONE is assistant professor of Media Studies at the University of Texas, Austin. A pioneer virtual reality researcher, her interests also include the politics and sociology of technoscience and of transexuality.

DAVID TOMAS is a conceptual artist and assistant professor of Visual Arts at the University of Ottawa. He has written extensively on virtual reality, cyborgism, art, and literature. He was recently a fellow at the California Institute of the Arts.

SARAH WILLIAMS teaches in the Women's Studies program at Otago University, Dunedin, New Zealand and at Evergreen College in Olympia, Washington. She is completing an ethnography—*Anthropology Coming Native*—about her anthropology among anthropologists. She has edited an issue of *Visual Anthropology Review* on "feminist approaches to the visualization of culture" and welcomes new subscribers to Aotearoa/New Zealand-based feminist listservs available at UOTAGO@stonebow.otago.ac.nz.

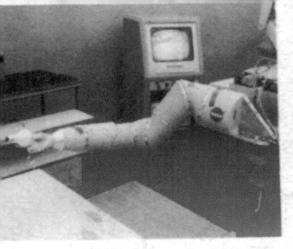
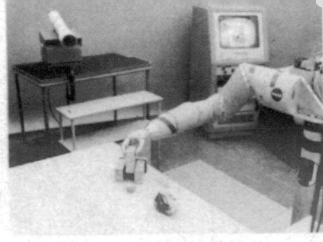

INDEX

NOTE: The main bibliography (pp. 469-77) is not indexed. The seperate article bibliographies, references, and notes are indexed, as are all of the other texts. **Bold** numbers indicate the citation is a full reference. *Italicized* numbers indicate it is an illustration or a figure. *Italicized* words indicate a foreign language, a book, a periodical, a film, or a work of art.

A

C

{ **506**

i

M

O

V

W

Illustrations

Tales From the Cryptic: Technology Meets Organism in the Living Cadaver

> Cyborg Genesis by Alebar

Envisioning Cyborg Bodies: Notes From Current Research

> "The Mistress of Horology" Courtesy of the Bibliotheque des Arts Decoratifs
>
> "Das Schone Madchen" by Hannah Hoch
>
> "Mechanical Head: The Spirit of Our Times" by Raoul Hausmann. Courtesy of Musee National d'Art Modern, Centre Georges Pompidou, Paris
>
> "All you Zombies: Truth Before God" by Robert Longo. Courtesy of Robert Longo

Brain Mind Machines and American Technologica Dream Marketing:
Towards an Ethnography of Cyborg Envy

> "Brain Mind Machine Diagram" Courtesy of the Author.

'Perhaps Images at One with the World are Already Lost Forever':
Visions of Cyborg Anthropology in Post-Cultural Worlds

> All images in this article have been electronically altered by the Author

FromCognitive Psychologies to Mythologies:
Advancing Cyborg Textualities for a Narrative ofResistance

> "The Health of the Nation and You" Campaign Courtesy of the U.K. Department of Health

The Cyborg Body Politic

> 'Borg Leviathan" Courtesy of the Author
>
> "Network Connectivity" Courtesy of the Science Policy Department, Washington D.C.
>
> "Network Applications" Courtesy of the Science Policy Department, Washington, D.C.

Acknowledgments

Annas, George J. "Minerva vs. National Health Agency"
   Credit: Standard of Care: The Law of American Bioethics (1993).
   Reprinted by permission of the author and Oxford University Press.

Clynes, Manfred & Nathan Kline "Cyborgs and Space"
   Credit: Reprinted by kind permission of Manfred Clynes and Marna Kline Anderson.

Downey, Gary Lee "Human Agency in CAD/CAM Technology"
   Credit: Anthropology Today 8(5):2-5 (1992). Reprinted by permission of the author and
   the Roayl Anthropological Institute of Great Britain and Ireland.

Driscoll, Robert W. "Engineering Man For Space: The Cyborg Study"
   Credit: Courtesy of NASA, Biotechnology and Human Resource Center (NASwÑ512).

Freidman, Eli "ISAO Proffers a Marvelous Cover for Acting Out Fantsies"
   Credit: Artificial Organs 11(3):193 (1987). Reprinted by permission
   of the International Society of Artificial Organs.

Fuchs, Cynthia "'Death is Irrelevant': Cyborgs, Reproduction, and the Future of Male Hysteria"
   Credit: Genders Winter(18):113-33 (1993). Reprinted by permission of the author and
   the University of Texas Press.

Gaffney, F. Andrew & Barry J. Fenton "Barney B. Clark: A View from the medical Services"
   Credit: Archives of General Psychiatry Vol 41:917-18. Copyright 1984, American Medical Association.

Hayles, N. Katherine "The Life of Cyborgs: Writing the Posthuman"
   Credit: reprinted from A Question of Identity, Marina Benjamin, ed.
   Copyright 1993 By Rutgers University Press. Reprinted by permission of Rutgers University Press.

Hori, Motokazu "Artificial Liver: Present and Future"
   Credit: Artifical Organs 10(3):211-13 (1986). Reprinted by permission of Artificial Organs

Johnsen, Edwin G. & William R. Corliss "Teleoperators and Human Augmentation"
   Credit: Courtesy of NASA, Office of Technology Utilization (NASA AP-5047),
   an AEC-NASA Technology Survey.

"The Pilot's Associate" excerpted from "Strategic Computing: Second Annual Report: New Generation Computing Technology"
Credit: Courtesy of the Department of Defense (DARPA)

Steel, Jack E. USAF, MC "How Do We Get There From Here?"
Credit: Courtesy of the Directorate of Advances Systems Technology, Wright-Patterson Air Force Base Air Development Division (ref: WADD TR 60-600). (Originally presented at the Bionics Symposium, September 1960.)

Stone, Sandy "Split Subject, Not Atoms: or How I Fell In Love With My Prosthesis.
Credit: Configurations 2(1):173-190 (1994). Reprinted by permission of the author and The Johns Hopkins University Press

Van Critters, Robert L., et al "Artificial Heart and Assist Devices: Directions, Needs, Costs, Societal and Ethical Issues"
Credit: NIH Report (85-2723). Reprinted by permission of the National Heart, Lung, and Blood Institut

Goldberg, Jonathan "Recalling Totalities"
Credit: Differences: A Journal of Feminist Cultural Studies (Vol. 4 #1, pp. 187-192). Reprinted by permission of the author.

Dick, Philip K. "I Hope I shall Soon Arrive"
Credit: Reprinted by permission of the author's estate.